STATE							PAGE
NV	Nevada				...nia		36-37
NH	New Ham...				...ington		114-115
NJ	New Jerse...				...Virginia		36-37
NM	New Mexico	96-99	SC	South Carolina	40-41	WI	Wisconsin	58-59
NY	New York	32-33	SD	South Dakota	82-83	WY	Wyoming	92-93
NC	North Carolina	38-39	TN	Tennessee	38-51	DC	Dist. of Columbia	36-37
ND	North Dakota	84-85	TX	Texas	70-77	PR	Puerto Rico	124
OH	Ohio	52-53	UT	Utah	102-103	VI	Virgin Islands	124
OK	Oklahoma	76-77	VT	Vermont	30-31	WD	World	6-9

UNITED STATES

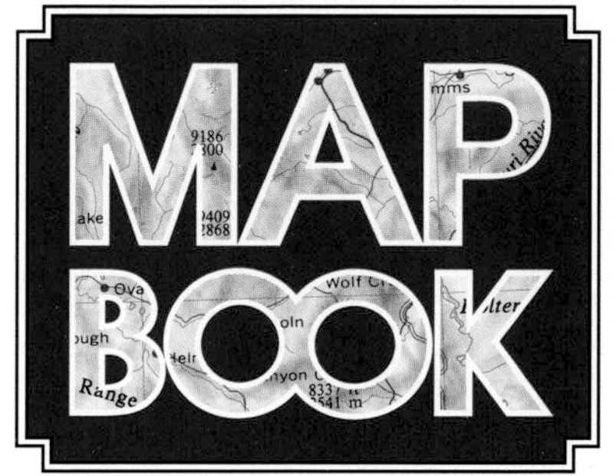

MAP BOOK

Environmental
Atlas

Interarts, Ltd

United States **MAP**BOOK

Published in the United States of America by
Interarts, Ltd   Cambridge, Massachusetts

Environmental maps designed, edited, drawn
and reproduced by the cartographers, geographers,
artists and technicians at :

ESSELTE MAP SERVICE AB	Stockholm, Sweden
MAPS INTERNATIONAL AB	Stockholm, Sweden
INTERARTS, LTD.	Cambridge, MA USA

Design : Turnbull : Design Counsel
Cambridge, MA USA

Introduction : Brian Rosborough
EARTHWATCH
Watertown, MA USA

ISBN No : 1-879856-01-8

Printed in Sweden

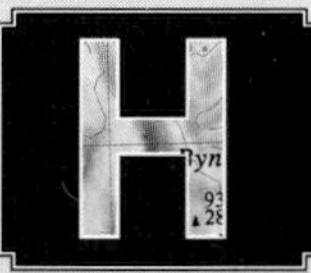

ow many of us call the
United States home, yet reach
for a map if we are asked to locate
a place more than 50 miles from our house?

Dozens of times each day you hear the names of places in
neighboring states never visited. A barrage of media fills
our senses; radio, television, newspapers, magazines and
the bewildering questions brought home by our children
make knowing where we are more of a necessity than an
occasional reference search.

Our abilities to understand the intimate relationships
between our land, climate, topography, politics and
environment are essential to our success as stewards of
this unique place. If we are to practice sustainable living
in the United States we must be comfortable with the
terrain, as familiar as an athlete is with the playing field.

This United States **MAP**BOOK is designed to be your
companion, not hidden away in your library. Its handy
size and unique connections between fact and place say
something about the importance of our sense of where
we are and where we are going.

Just as we move through the years to attain our
aspirations, navigating through life requires that we take
our bearings more than once a week. The United States
MAPBOOK is the best place to start.

Brian A. Rosborough, President
EARTHWATCH
Watertown, Massachusetts

STATISTICS

Environmental World	6-7	North American Landforms	16-17
Political World	8-9	Unique America	18-19
New Worlds	10-11	Environmental United States	20-21
North America	12-13	Political United States	22-23
North American Weather	14-15	States and their Statistics	24-27

NORTHEAST

Maine	28-29	Connecticut, Rhode Island	30-31
Vermont, New Hampshire, Massachusetts	30-31	New York	32-33

EAST

Pennsylvania, New Jersey, New York City	34-35	West Virginia, Virginia, Delaware, Maryland, D. of C.	36-37
		North Carolina	38-39

SOUTHEAST

South Carolina	40-41	Alabama	46-47
Georgia	42-43	Mississippi	48-49
Florida	44-47	Kentucky, Tennessee	50-51

MIDWEST

Indiana, Ohio	52-53	Wisconsin	58-59
Michigan	54-59	Minnesota	60-61
Illinois	56-57		

CENTRAL

Iowa	62-63	Arkansas	66-67
Missouri	64-65		

SOUTH CENTRAL

Louisiana 68-69
Texas 70-77
Oklahoma 76-77

GREAT PLAINS

Kansas 78-79
Nebraska 80-81
South Dakota 82-83
North Dakota 84-85

MOUNTAIN

Montana 86-89
Idaho 88-91
Wyoming 92-93
Colorado 94-95

SOUTHWEST

New Mexico 96-99
Arizona 100-103
Utah 102-103
Nevada 104-109

PACIFIC

California 106-111
Oregon 112-113
Washington 114-115
Alaska 116-121
Hawaiian Islands 122-123

POSSESSIONS

Puerto Rico 124
U.S. Virgin Islands 124

INDEX

Index 125-184

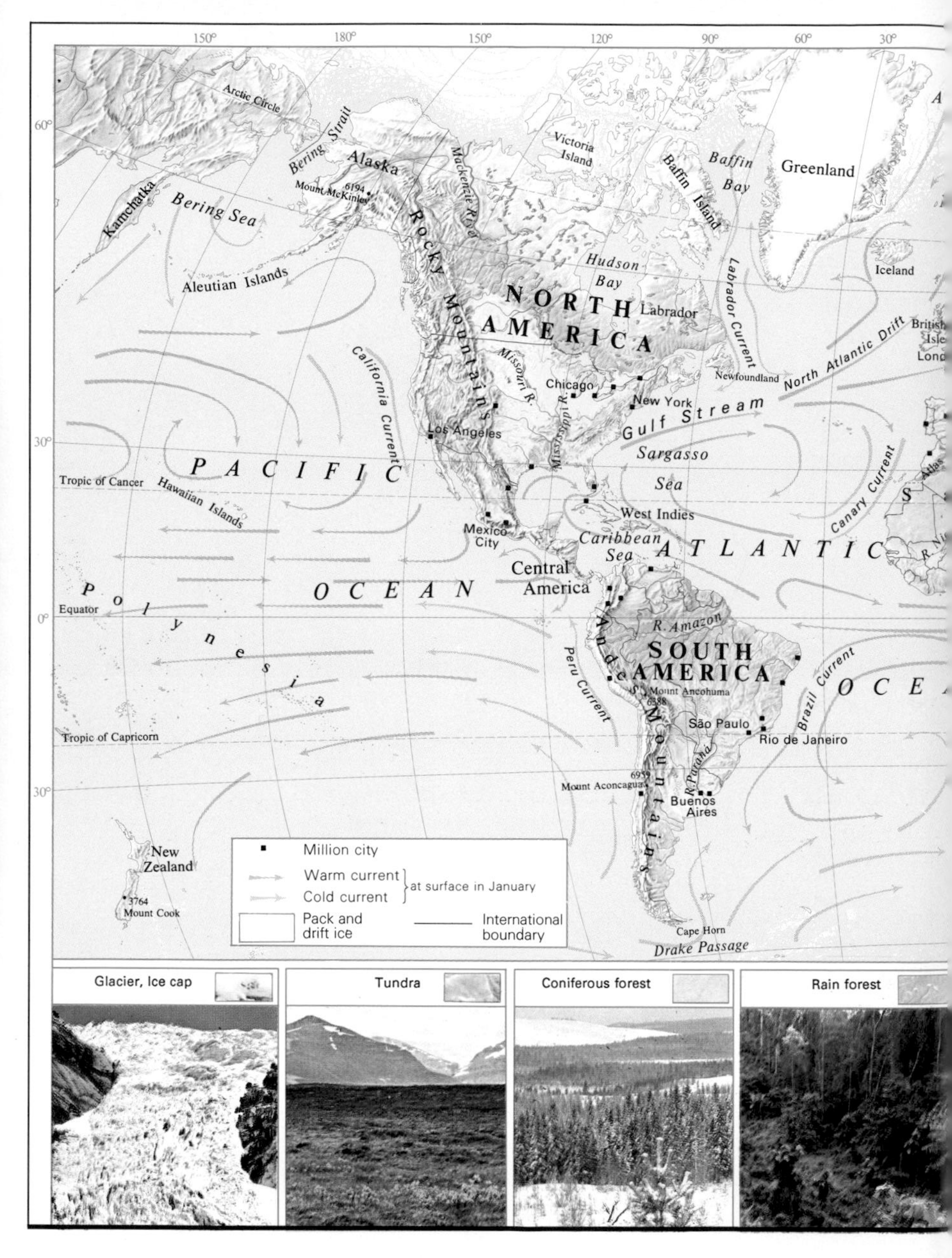

150° 180° 150° 120° 90° 60° 30°

Arctic Circle

60°

Bering Strait
Alaska
Mount McKinley 6194
Kamchatka
Bering Sea
Aleutian Islands

Victoria
Island
Mackenzie R.

Baffin
Bay
Baffin Island

Greenland

A

Iceland

British
Isle
Long

NORTH
AMERICA
Hudson
Bay
Labrador
Newfoundland
Labrador Current
North Atlantic Drift

Rocky Mountains
Missouri R.
Chicago
New York
Gulf Stream
Canary Current
S

California Current
Los Angeles
Mississippi R.

Tropic of Cancer

Sargasso
Sea

R

Atlas

PACIFIC
Hawaiian Islands

Mexico
City
West Indies
Caribbean
Sea
ATLANTIC

30°

P
o
l
y
n
e
s
i
a
OCEAN
Central
America

Equator
0°

R. Amazon
SOUTH
AMERICA
São Paulo
Rio de Janeiro
Brazil Current
OCE

Peru Current
Andes Mountains
Mount Ancohuma

Tropic of Capricorn

R. Plata

Mount Aconcagua 6959
Buenos
Aires

30°

New
Zealand

3764
Mount Cook

Cape Horn
Drake Passage

■ Million city

→ Warm current } at surface in January
→ Cold current

Pack and
drift ice

International
boundary

| Glacier, Ice cap | Tundra | Coniferous forest | Rain forest |

6   ENVIRONMENTAL WORLD

1 foot = 0,30 m
1 meter = 3,28 feet

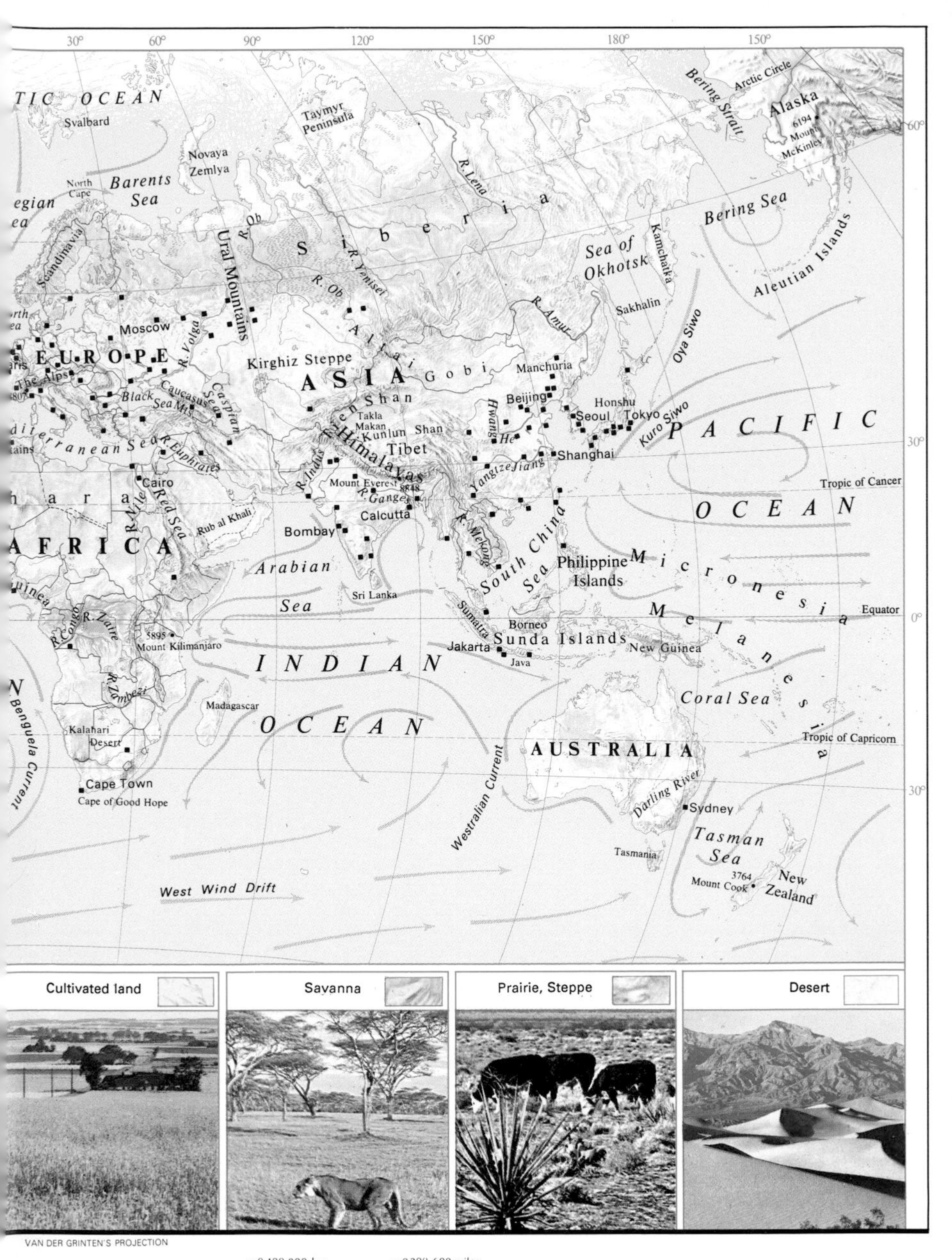

TIC OCEAN
Svalbard
North Cape
Novaya Zemlya
Barents Sea
Taymyr Peninsula
R. Lena
Arctic Circle
Bering Strait
Alaska
6194 Mount McKinley
60°

egian ea
rth ea
Scandinavia
S i b e r i a
Bering Sea
Aleutian Islands
Sea of Okhotsk
Kamchatka

EUROPE
The Alps
Moscow
Ural Mountains
R. Ob
R. Yenisei
R. Ob
Altai
Sakhalin
R. Amur
Oya Siwo
P A C I F I C

Black Sea
Caucasus Mts.
Caspian Sea
Kirghiz Steppe
A S I A
Tien Shan
Gobi
Manchuria
Beijing
Honshu
Seoul
Tokyo
Kuro Siwo
30°

diterranean Sea
ains
R. Volta
R. Euphrates
Takla Makan
Kunlun Shan
Himalayas
Tibet
Hwang He
Shanghai
Yangtze Jiang
O C E A N

Cairo
R. Nile
Red Sea
Rub al Khali
Mount Everest 8848
R. Ganges
Bombay
Calcutta
R. Mekong
South China Sea
Philippine Islands
M i c r o n e s i a
Tropic of Cancer

ara
A F R I C A
Arabian Sea
Sri Lanka
Sunda Str.
Borneo
New Guinea
M e l a n e s i a
Equator 0°

pinca
R. Congo
R. Zaire
8898 Mount Kilimanjaro
R. Zambezi
I N D I A N
Jakarta
Java
Sunda Islands
Coral Sea

N Benguela Current
Kalahari Desert
Madagascar
O C E A N
A U S T R A L I A
Tropic of Capricorn
30°

Cape Town
Cape of Good Hope
Western Australian Current
Darling River
Sydney
Tasman Sea
Tasmania
3764 Mount Cook
New Zealand

West Wind Drift

Cultivated land	Savanna	Prairie, Steppe	Desert

VAN DER GRINTEN'S PROJECTION

Scale 1:180 000 000
at the equator

0° 0 400 800 km
30°
60° 200 600 1000 km

0° 0 200 600 miles
30°
60° 100 300 500 miles

7

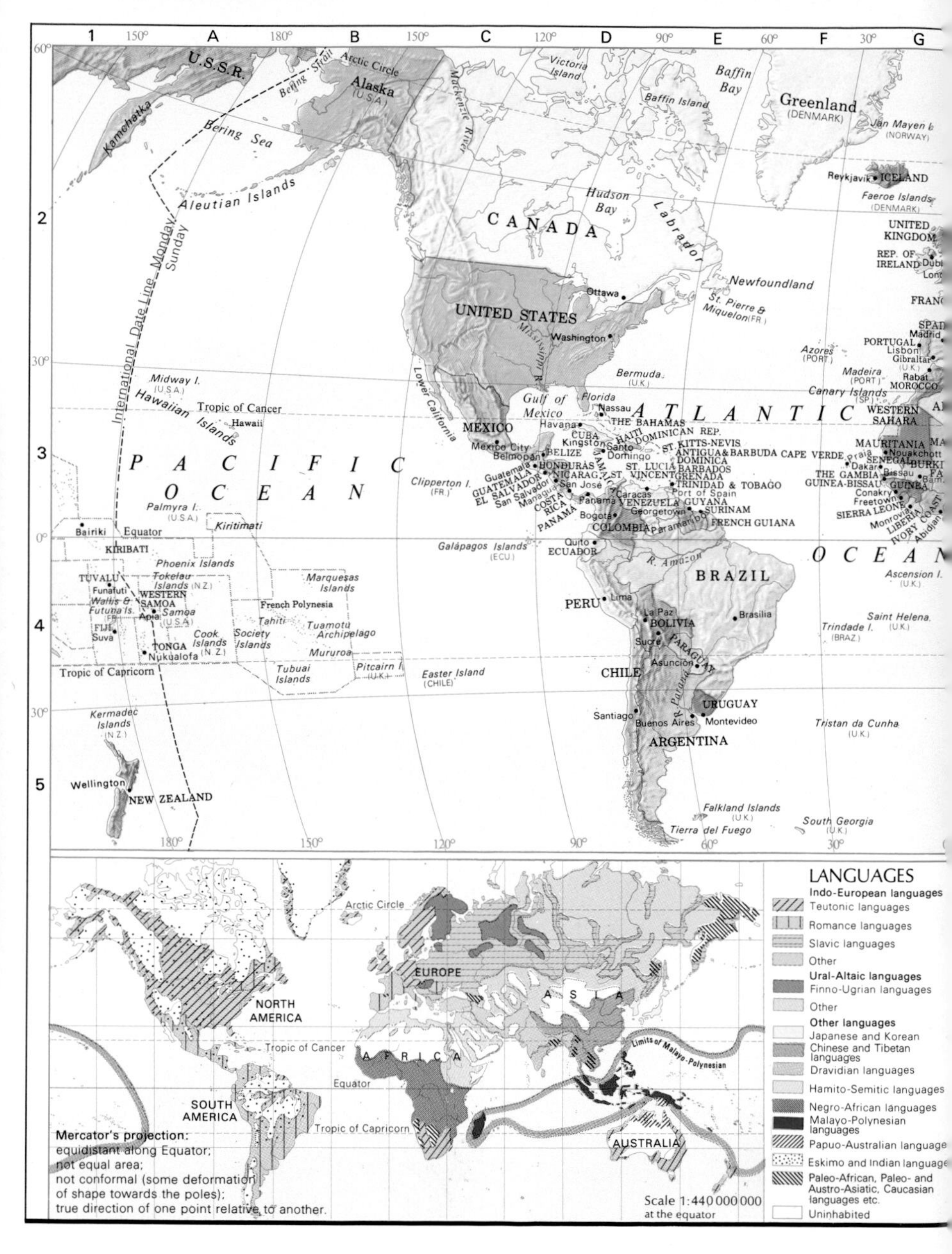

POLITICAL WORLD

8

U.S.S.R.
Kamchatka
Bering Strait
Bering Sea
Alaska (U.S.A.)
Arctic Circle
Aleutian Islands
Mackenzie River
Victoria Island
Baffin Island
Baffin Bay
Greenland (DENMARK)
Jan Mayen I. (NORWAY)
Reykjavík ICELAND
Faeroe Islands (DENMARK)
International Date Line – Monday – Sunday
CANADA
Hudson Bay
Labrador
Newfoundland
St. Pierre & Miquelon (FR.)
Ottawa
UNITED KINGDOM
REP. OF IRELAND Dublin
London
FRANCE
UNITED STATES
Washington
Mississippi
Lower California
Midway I. (U.S.A.)
Hawaiian Islands
Tropic of Cancer
Hawaii
Bermuda (U.K.)
Florida
Azores (PORT.)
Madeira (PORT.)
Canary Islands
SPAIN
Madrid
PORTUGAL Lisbon
Gibraltar (U.K.)
Rabat MOROCCO
WESTERN SAHARA
A T L A N T I C
Gulf of Mexico
Havana
THE BAHAMAS
Nassau
MEXICO
Mexico City
CUBA
Kingston Santo Domingo
DOMINICAN REP.
ST. KITTS-NEVIS
ANTIGUA & BARBUDA
CAPE VERDE
MAURITANIA MALI
Nouakchott
Dakar SENEGAL BURKINA
THE GAMBIA
GUINEA-BISSAU GUINEA
Bissau Conakry
SIERRA LEONE Freetown
LIBERIA
IVORY COAST
Monrovia Abidjan
P A C I F I C   O C E A N
Clipperton I. (FR.)
Guatemala BELIZE Belmopan
GUATEMALA HONDURAS Tegucigalpa
EL SALVADOR San Salvador
San José NICARAGUA Managua
COSTA RICA PANAMA Panama
DOMINICA
ST. LUCIA BARBADOS
ST. VINCENT
GRENADA
TRINIDAD & TOBAGO
Port of Spain
Caracas
Bogotá GUYANA Georgetown
VENEZUELA SURINAM
COLOMBIA Paramaribo
FRENCH GUIANA
Palmyra I. (U.S.A.)
Kiritimati
Bairiki Equator
KIRIBATI
Phoenix Islands
TUVALU Funafuti
Tokelau Islands (N.Z.)
WESTERN SAMOA Apia
Wallis & Futuna Is. (FR.)
American Samoa (U.S.A.)
FIJI Suva
TONGA Nukualofa
Cook Islands (N.Z.)
Society Islands
Tahiti
French Polynesia
Marquesas Islands
Tuamotu Archipelago
Mururoa
Galápagos Islands (ECU.)
Quito ECUADOR
R. Amazon
PERU Lima
BRAZIL
Brasília
Ascension I. (U.K.)
La Paz BOLIVIA
Sucre
PARAGUAY Asunción
Saint Helena (U.K.)
Trindade I. (BRAZ.)
Tropic of Capricorn
Tubuai Islands
Easter Island (CHILE)
Pitcairn I. (U.K.)
CHILE
URUGUAY
ARGENTINA
Santiago
Buenos Aires
Montevideo
Tristan da Cunha (U.K.)
Kermadec Islands (N.Z.)
Wellington
NEW ZEALAND
Falkland Islands (U.K.)
Tierra del Fuego
South Georgia (U.K.)

LANGUAGES (legend, bottom map):

Indo-European languages
Teutonic languages
Romance languages
Slavic languages
Other

Ural-Altaic languages
Finno-Ugrian languages
Other

Other languages
Japanese and Korean
Chinese and Tibetan languages
Dravidian languages
Hamito-Semitic languages
Negro-African languages
Malayo-Polynesian languages
Papuo-Australian language
Eskimo and Indian language
Paleo-African, Paleo- and Austro-Asiatic, Caucasian languages etc.
Uninhabited

NORTH AMERICA
SOUTH AMERICA
EUROPE
ASIA
AFRICA
AUSTRALIA
Arctic Circle
Tropic of Cancer
Equator
Tropic of Capricorn
Limits of Malayo-Polynesian

Mercator's projection:
equidistant along Equator;
not equal area;
not conformal (some deformation
of shape towards the poles);
true direction of one point relative to another.

Scale 1:440 000 000
at the equator

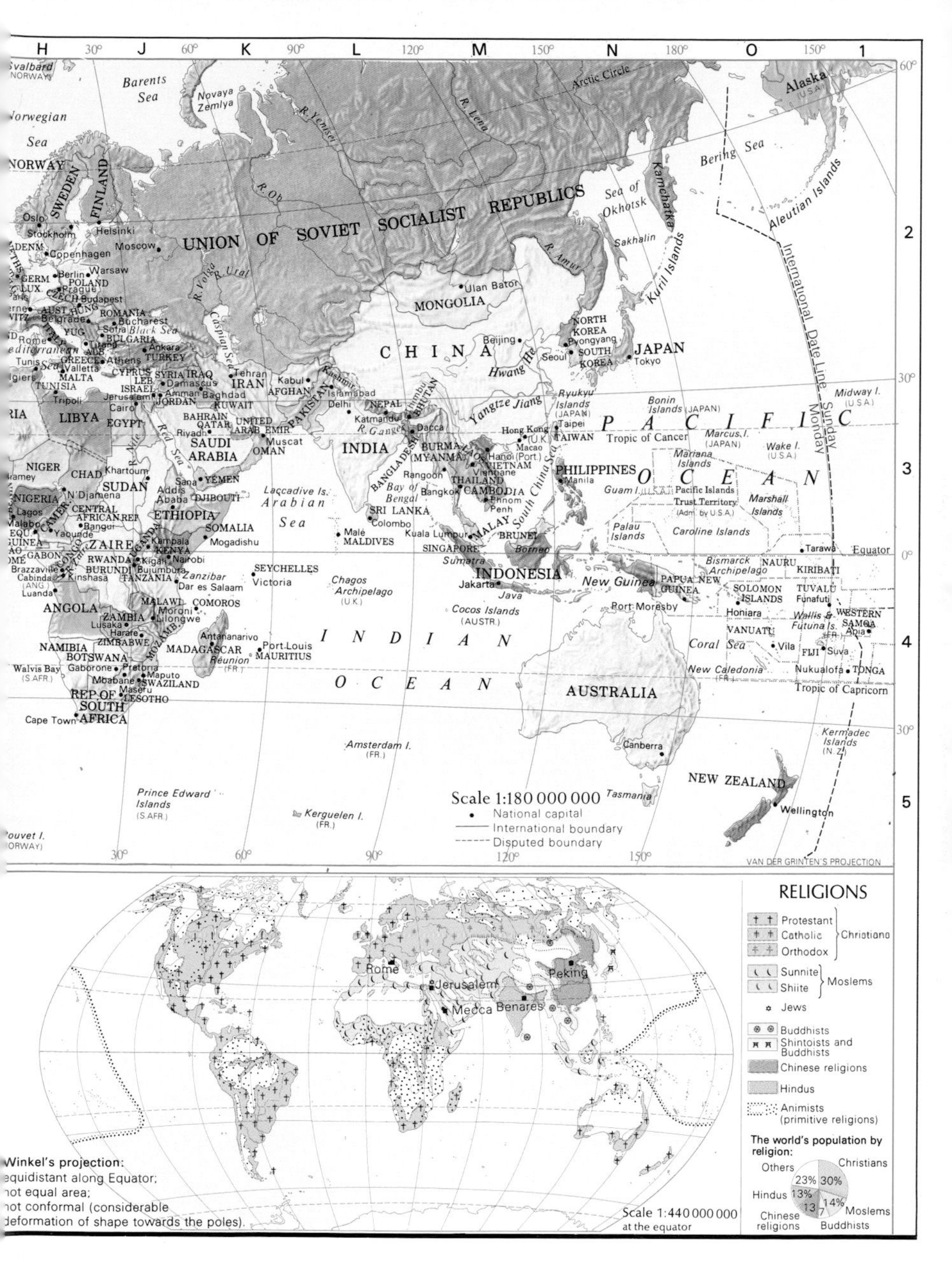

Scale 1:180 000 000
• National capital
— International boundary
- - - Disputed boundary

VAN DER GRINTEN'S PROJECTION

Winkel's projection:
equidistant along Equator;
not equal area;
not conformal (considerable
deformation of shape towards the poles).

Scale 1:440 000 000
at the equator

RELIGIONS

† †	Protestant	⎫
✝ ✝	Catholic	⎬ Christians
✠ ✠	Orthodox	⎭
⌣ ⌣	Sunnite	⎫ Moslems
⌣ ⌣	Shiite	⎭
✡	Jews	
⊛ ⊛	Buddhists	
卐 卐	Shintoists and Buddhists	
	Chinese religions	
	Hindus	
	Animists (primitive religions)	

The world's population by religion:

Others 23%   Christians 30%
Hindus 13%   14% Moslems
Chinese religions 13%   Buddhists

9

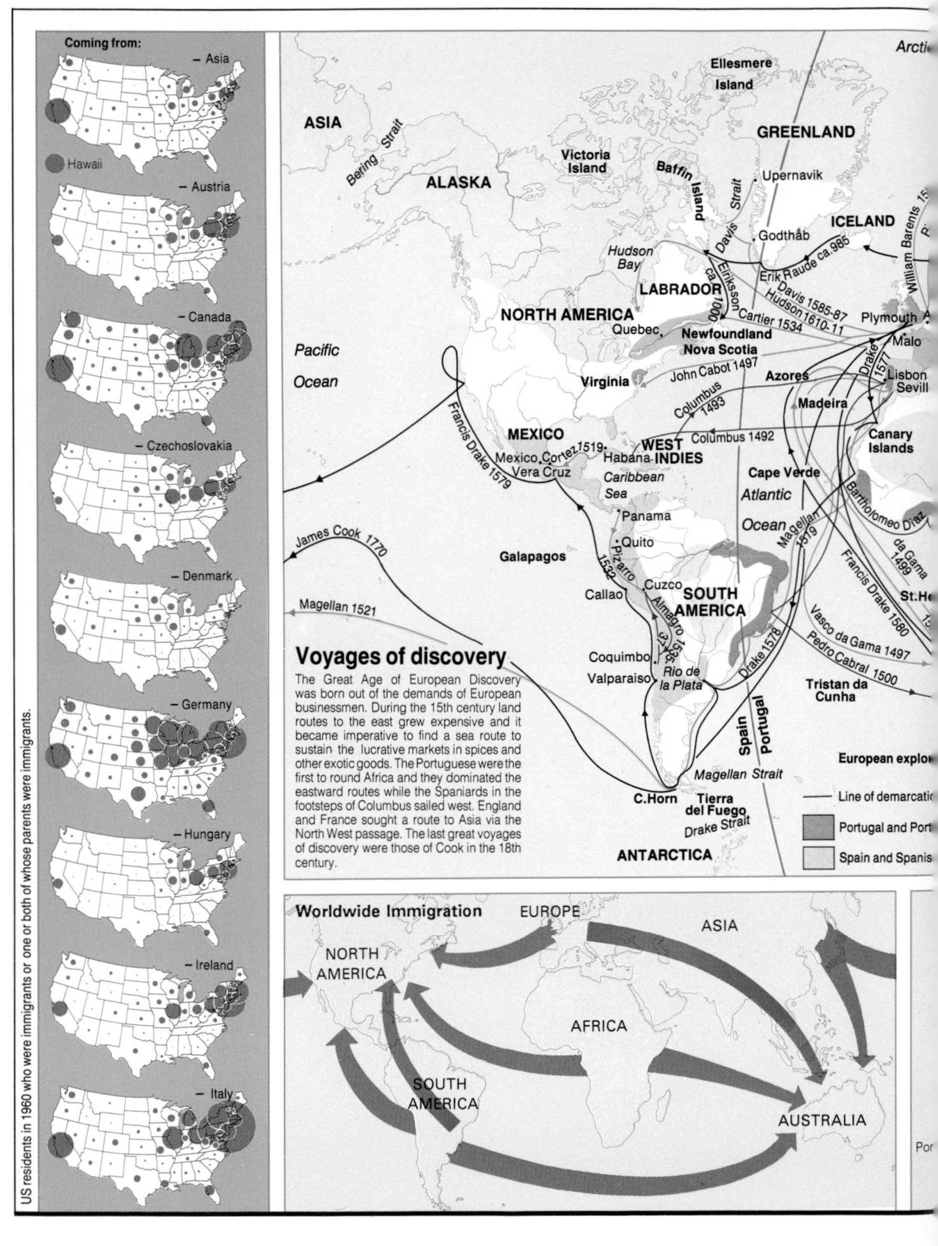

Coming from:

- Asia
- Hawaii
- Austria
- Canada
- Czechoslovakia
- Denmark
- Germany
- Hungary
- Ireland
- Italy

US residents in 1960 who were immigrants or one or both of whose parents were immigrants.

ASIA

Bering Strait

ALASKA

Victoria Island

Ellesmere Island

Baffin Island

GREENLAND

Davis Strait

Upernavik

Godthåb

ICELAND

William Barents 15...

Hudson Bay

Erik Raude ca.985

Eriksson ca.1000

Davis 1585-87

Hudson 1610-11

LABRADOR

NORTH AMERICA

Quebec

Newfoundland

Cartier 1534

Plymouth

Pacific Ocean

Virginia

Nova Scotia

John Cabot 1497

Columbus 1493

Drake 1577

Malo

Azores

Lisbon

Sevill

MEXICO

Francis Drake 1579

Mexico, Cortez 1519

Vera Cruz

Columbus 1492

WEST INDIES

Habana

Caribbean Sea

Madeira

Cape Verde

Bartholomeo Diaz

da Gama

Canary Islands

James Cook 1770

Panama

Atlantic Ocean

Magellan 1519

Francis Drake 1580

St.He...

Magellan 1521

Galapagos

Quito

Pizarro 1532

Cuzco

Almagro 1535-38

SOUTH AMERICA

Callao

Coquimbo

Valparaiso

Rio de la Plata

Drake 1578

Vasco da Gama 1497

Pedro Cabral 1500

Tristan da Cunha

Voyages of discovery

The Great Age of European Discovery was born out of the demands of European businessmen. During the 15th century land routes to the east grew expensive and it became imperative to find a sea route to sustain the lucrative markets in spices and other exotic goods. The Portuguese were the first to round Africa and they dominated the eastward routes while the Spaniards in the footsteps of Columbus sailed west. England and France sought a route to Asia via the North West passage. The last great voyages of discovery were those of Cook in the 18th century.

Spain

Portugal

Magellan Strait

C.Horn

Tierra del Fuego

Drake Strait

ANTARCTICA

European explo...

Line of demarcation

Portugal and Port...

Spain and Spanish...

Worldwide Immigration

EUROPE

ASIA

NORTH AMERICA

AFRICA

SOUTH AMERICA

AUSTRALIA

Por...

10   NEW WORLDS

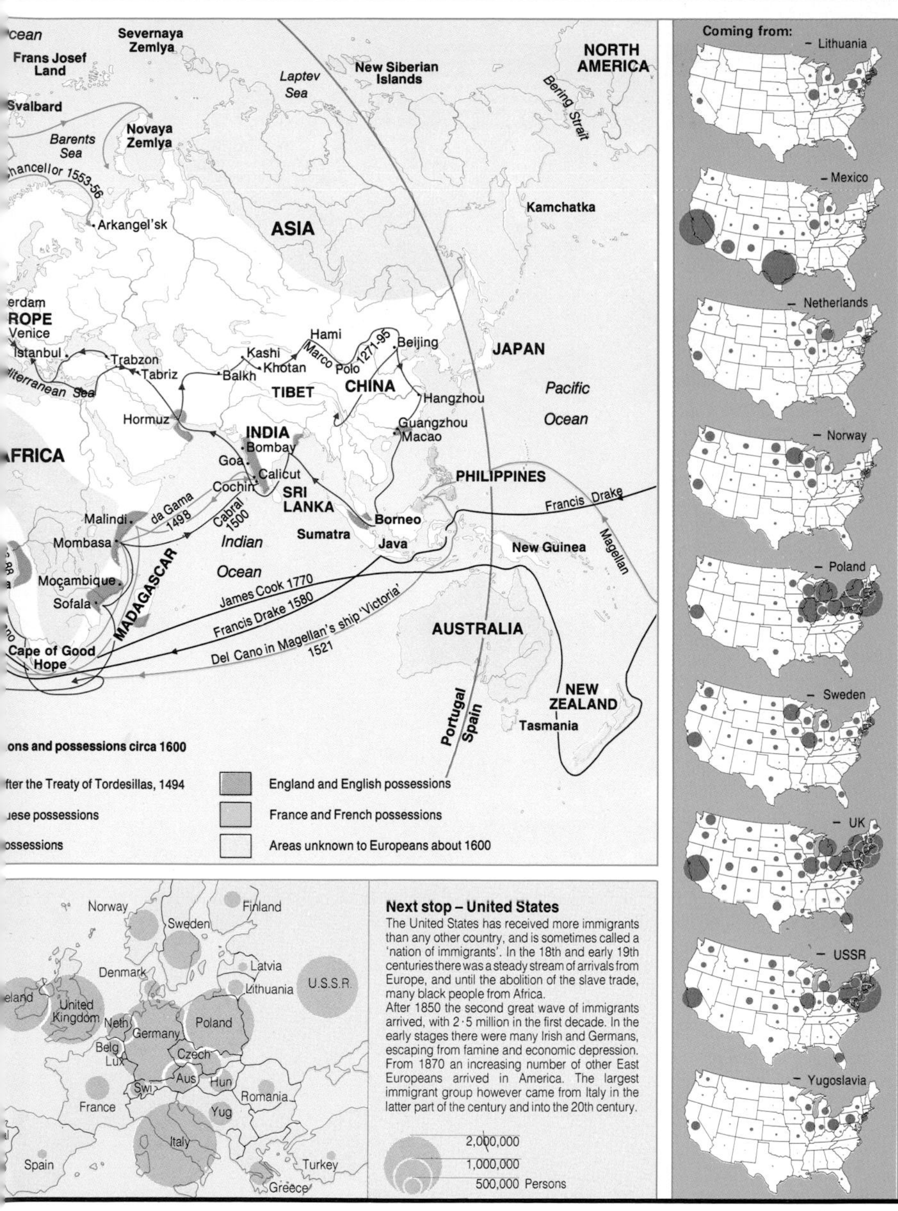

Coming from:
- Lithuania
- Mexico
- Netherlands
- Norway
- Poland
- Sweden
- UK
- USSR
- Yugoslavia

US residents in 1960 who were immigrants or one or both of whose parents were immigrants.

ROPE
Venice
Istanbul
Trabzon
Tabriz
Hormuz
Arkangel'sk
Chancellor 1553-56
Barents Sea
Svalbard
Frans Josef Land
Severnaya Zemlya
Novaya Zemlya
Laptev Sea
New Siberian Islands
NORTH AMERICA
Bering Strait
Kamchatka
ASIA
Hami
Kashi
Khotan
Balkh
Marco Polo 1271-95
Beijing
JAPAN
TIBET
CHINA
Hangzhou
Pacific Ocean
Guangzhou
Macao
INDIA
Bombay
Goa
Calicut
Cochin
da Gama 1498
Cabral 1500
SRI LANKA
PHILIPPINES
Francis Drake
Sumatra
Borneo
Java
New Guinea
Magellan
AFRICA
Malindi
Mombasa
Moçambique
Sofala
MADAGASCAR
Indian Ocean
James Cook 1770
Francis Drake 1580
Del Cano in Magellan's ship 'Victoria' 1521
AUSTRALIA
Cape of Good Hope
Portugal
Spain
NEW ZEALAND
Tasmania

ons and possessions circa 1600
fter the Treaty of Tordesillas, 1494

England and English possessions
France and French possessions
Areas unknown to Europeans about 1600

Norway
Sweden
Finland
Denmark
Latvia
Lithuania
U.S.S.R.
eland
United Kingdom
Neth
Belg
Lux
Germany
Poland
Czech
Aus
Hun
Romania
Swi
France
Yug
Italy
Turkey
Spain
Greece

Next stop – United States

The United States has received more immigrants than any other country, and is sometimes called a 'nation of immigrants'. In the 18th and early 19th centuries there was a steady stream of arrivals from Europe, and until the abolition of the slave trade, many black people from Africa.

After 1850 the second great wave of immigrants arrived, with 2·5 million in the first decade. In the early stages there were many Irish and Germans, escaping from famine and economic depression. From 1870 an increasing number of other East Europeans arrived in America. The largest immigrant group however came from Italy in the latter part of the century and into the 20th century.

2,000,000
1,000,000
500,000 Persons

11

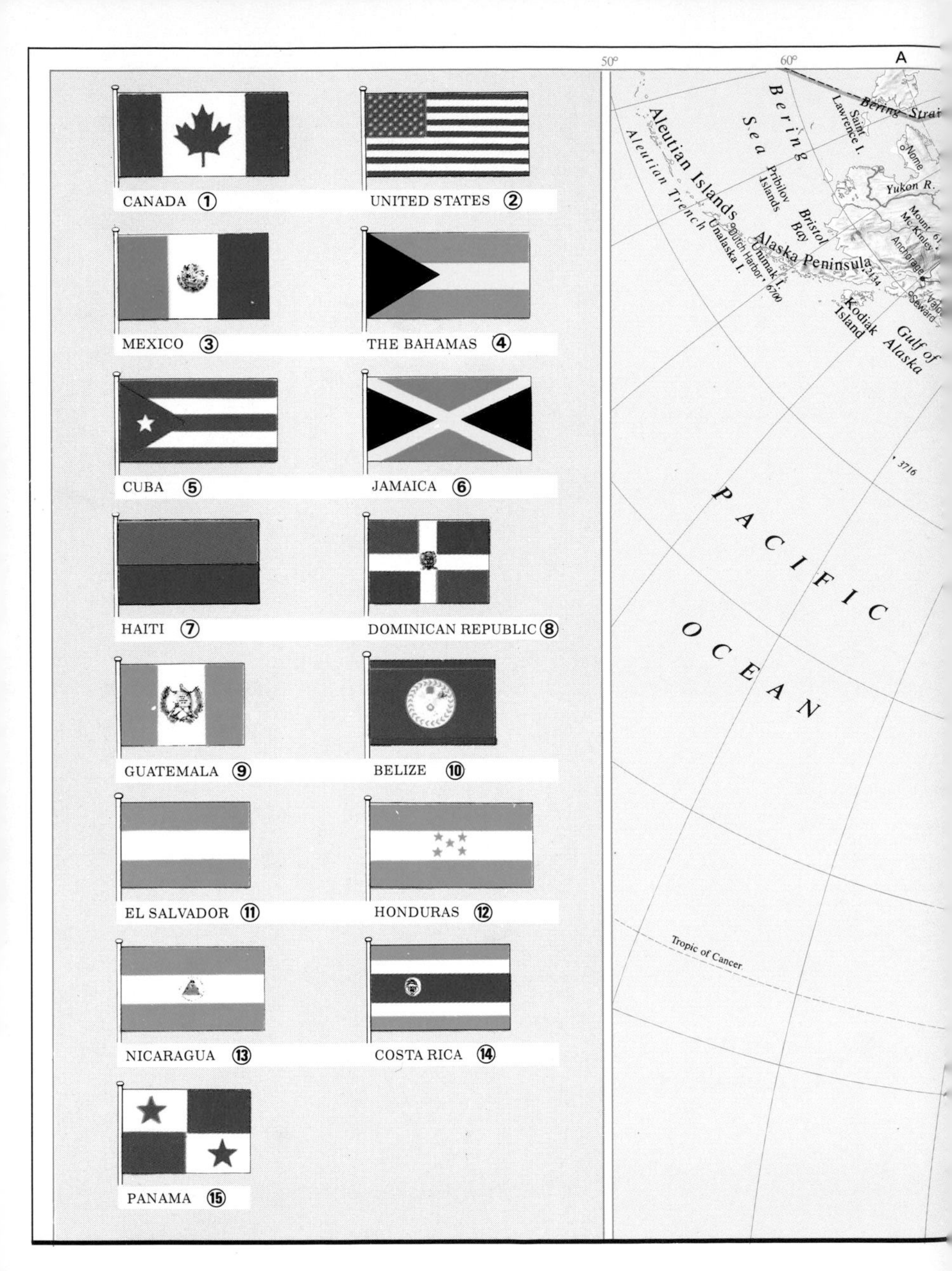

CANADA ①

UNITED STATES ②

MEXICO ③

THE BAHAMAS ④

CUBA ⑤

JAMAICA ⑥

HAITI ⑦

DOMINICAN REPUBLIC ⑧

GUATEMALA ⑨

BELIZE ⑩

EL SALVADOR ⑪

HONDURAS ⑫

NICARAGUA ⑬

COSTA RICA ⑭

PANAMA ⑮

Bering Strait
Saint Lawrence I.
Nome
Bering Sea
Aleutian Islands
Aleutian Trench
Pribilof Islands
Bristol Bay
Unalaska I.
Unimak I.
Alaska Peninsula
Yukon R.
Mount Elias
McKinley
Anchorage
Valdez
Seward
Kodiak Island
Gulf of Alaska

PACIFIC OCEAN

· 3716

Tropic of Cancer

NORTH AMERICA

1 foot = 0,30 m
1 meter = 3,28 feet

Scale 1:50 000 000

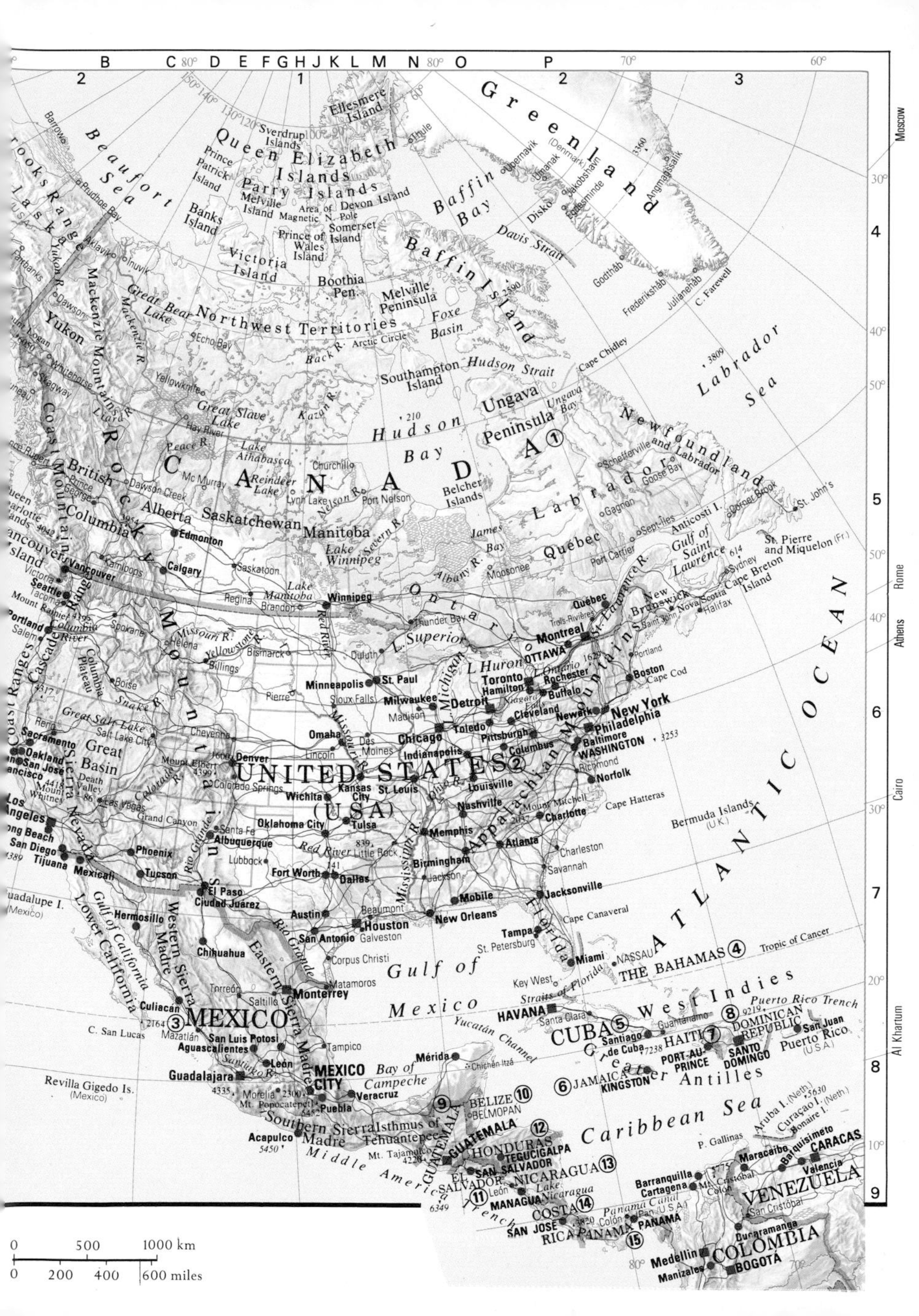

Greenland
(Denmark)
Ellesmere Island
Sverdrup Islands
Queen Elizabeth Islands
Parry Islands
Prince Patrick Island
Melville Island
Devon Island
Area of Magnetic N. Pole
Banks Island
Prince of Wales Island
Somerset Island
Victoria Island
Boothia Pen.
Melville Peninsula
Baffin Bay
Baffin Island
Davis Strait
Thule
Upernavik
Umanak
Jakobshavn
Disko
Egedesminde
Godthåb
Frederikshåb
Julianehåb
C. Farewell
Angmagssalik
Beaufort Sea
Prudhoe Bay
Barrow
Brooks Range
Alaska
Aklavik
Inuvik
Fairbanks
Dawson
Yukon R.
Yukon
Mackenzie Mountains
Mackenzie R.
Great Bear Lake
Northwest Territories
Echo Bay
Back R.
Arctic Circle
Foxe Basin
Southampton Island
Hudson Strait
Cape Chidley
Labrador Sea
Ungava Peninsula
Ungava Bay
Hudson Bay
Whitehorse
Skagway
Yellowknife
Great Slave Lake
Hay River
Liard R.
Kazan R.
Lake Athabasca
Peace R.
Churchill
CANADA
Mc Murray
Reindeer Lake
Lynn Lake
Nelson R.
Port Nelson
Belcher Islands
Newfoundland and Labrador
Schefferville
Goose Bay
Labrador
Gagnon
Corner Brook
St. John's
Dawson Creek
Prince George
Prince Rupert
British Columbia
Alberta
Saskatchewan
Manitoba
Edmonton
Calgary
Saskatoon
Kamloops
Vancouver
Victoria
Vancouver Island
Queen Charlotte Islands
Coast Mountains
Rocky Mountains
Lake Winnipeg
Severn R.
James Bay
Moosonee
Albany R.
Québec
Sept-Îles
Port Cartier
Anticosti I.
Gulf of Saint Lawrence
St. Pierre and Miquelon (Fr.)
Sydney
Cape Breton Island
Nova Scotia
Halifax
New Brunswick
Saint John
Regina
Brandon
Lake Manitoba
Winnipeg
Ontario
Thunder Bay
L. Superior
Duluth
Red River
Québec
Trois-Rivières
Montreal
OTTAWA
St. Lawrence R.
Portland
Seattle
Tacoma
Mount Rainier
Portland
Salem
Columbia River
Spokane
Helena
Missouri R.
Yellowstone R.
Bismarck
Billings
Columbia Plateau
Boise
Snake R.
Cascade Range
Coast Ranges
Great Salt Lake
Salt Lake City
Reno
Sacramento
Oakland
San José
San Francisco
Great Basin
Sierra Nevada
Death Valley
Mount Whitney
Las Vegas
Cheyenne
Denver
Mount Elbert
Colorado Springs
Colorado R.
Grand Canyon
Los Angeles
Long Beach
San Diego
Tijuana
Mexicali
Phoenix
Tucson
Santa Fe
Albuquerque
Rio Grande
El Paso
Ciudad Juárez
Lubbock
Minneapolis
St. Paul
Pierre
Sioux Falls
Milwaukee
Madison
L. Michigan
L. Huron
Detroit
Toronto
Hamilton
L. Ontario
Niagara Falls
Rochester
Buffalo
Boston
Cape Cod
Cleveland
Newark
New York
Philadelphia
Baltimore
WASHINGTON
Richmond
Norfolk
Omaha
Lincoln
Des Moines
Chicago
Toledo
Pittsburgh
Columbus
Indianapolis
UNITED STATES (USA)
Kansas City
St. Louis
Louisville
Ohio R.
Wichita
Nashville
Mount Mitchell
Charlotte
Cape Hatteras
Appalachian Mountains
Oklahoma City
Tulsa
Memphis
Atlanta
Little Rock
Red River
Birmingham
Charleston
Savannah
Fort Worth
Dallas
Jackson
Mississippi R.
Mobile
Jacksonville
Austin
Beaumont
Houston
New Orleans
San Antonio
Galveston
Corpus Christi
Cape Canaveral
Tampa
St. Petersburg
Florida
Miami
Key West
Straits of Florida
NASSAU
THE BAHAMAS
Tropic of Cancer
Bermuda Islands (U.K.)
ATLANTIC OCEAN
Gulf of Mexico
Guadalupe I. (Mexico)
Lower California
Gulf of California
Hermosillo
Western Sierra Madre
Chihuahua
Eastern Sierra Madre
Rio Grande
Matamoros
Monterrey
Torreón
Saltillo
Culiacán
Mazatlán
C. San Lucas
MEXICO
San Luis Potosí
Aguascalientes
Tampico
Guadalajara
León
Santiago R.
MEXICO CITY
Morelia
Mt. Popocatepetl
Puebla
Veracruz
Bay of Campeche
Revilla Gigedo Is. (Mexico)
Acapulco
Southern Sierra Madre
Isthmus of Tehuantepec
Mt. Tajamulco
Middle America Trench
Mérida
Chichén Itzá
Yucatán Channel
HAVANA
Santa Clara
CUBA
Santiago de Cuba
Guantánamo
West Indies
Greater Antilles
JAMAICA
KINGSTON
HAITI
PORT-AU-PRINCE
DOMINICAN REPUBLIC
SANTO DOMINGO
San Juan
Puerto Rico (U.S.A.)
Puerto Rico Trench
BELIZE
BELMOPAN
GUATEMALA
HONDURAS
TEGUCIGALPA
EL SALVADOR
SAN SALVADOR
NICARAGUA
León
MANAGUA
Lake Nicaragua
COSTA RICA
SAN JOSÉ
PANAMA
Panama Canal
Colón
Caribbean Sea
Aruba I. (Neth.)
Curaçao I. (Neth.)
Bonaire I.
P. Gallinas
Barranquilla
Cartagena
Maracaibo
Barquisimeto
CARACAS
Valencia
VENEZUELA
San Cristóbal
Bucaramanga
COLOMBIA
Medellín
Manizales
BOGOTÁ
Moscow
Rome
Athens
Cairo
Al Khartum
0 500 1000 km
0 200 400 600 miles

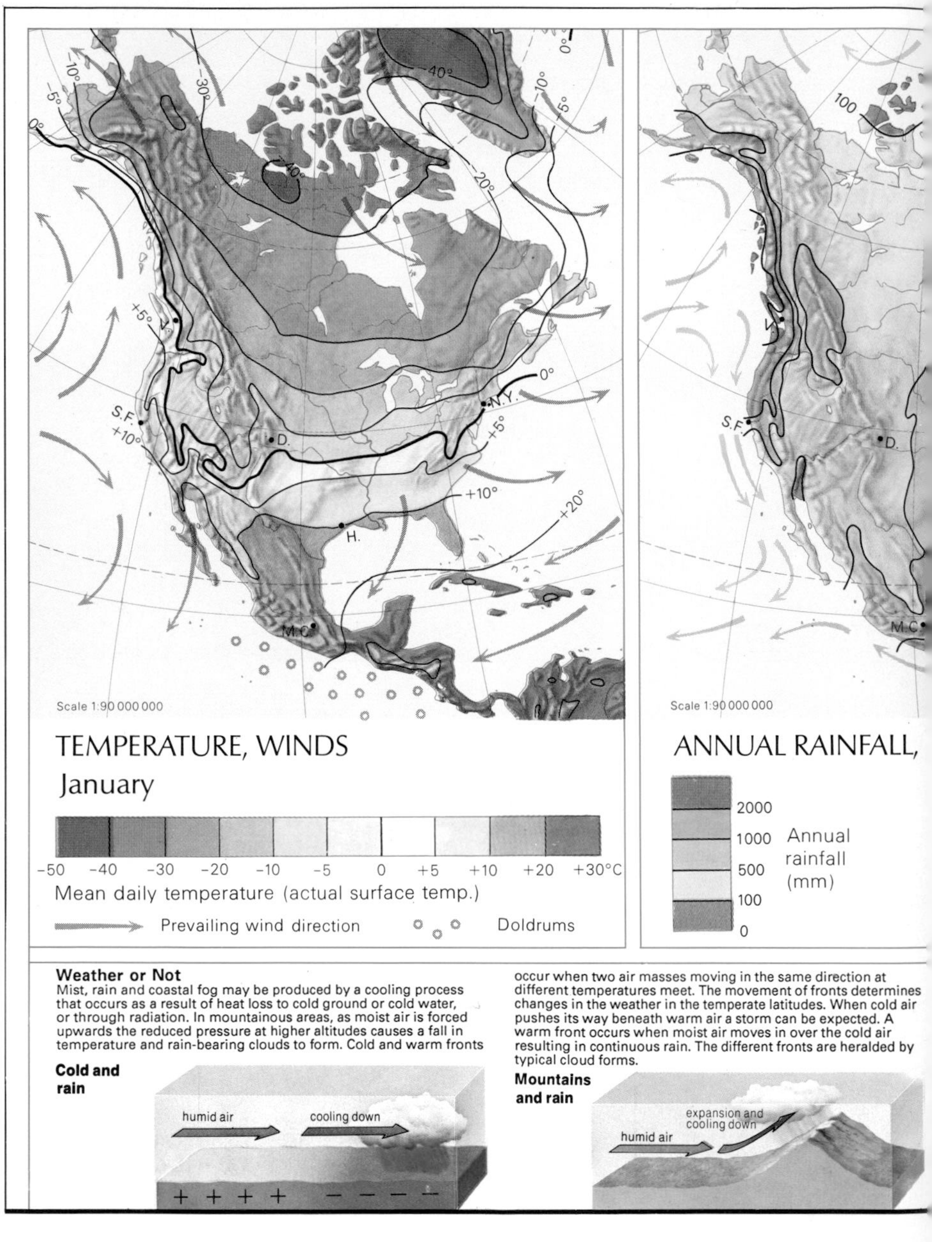

TEMPERATURE, WINDS

January

-50 -40 -30 -20 -10 -5 0 +5 +10 +20 +30°C

Mean daily temperature (actual surface temp.)

→ Prevailing wind direction ○ ○ ○ Doldrums

Scale 1:90 000 000

ANNUAL RAINFALL,

2000
1000 Annual
500 rainfall
100 (mm)
0

Scale 1:90 000 000

Weather or Not

Mist, rain and coastal fog may be produced by a cooling process that occurs as a result of heat loss to cold ground or cold water, or through radiation. In mountainous areas, as moist air is forced upwards the reduced pressure at higher altitudes causes a fall in temperature and rain-bearing clouds to form. Cold and warm fronts occur when two air masses moving in the same direction at different temperatures meet. The movement of fronts determines changes in the weather in the temperate latitudes. When cold air pushes its way beneath warm air a storm can be expected. A warm front occurs when moist air moves in over the cold air resulting in continuous rain. The different fronts are heralded by typical cloud forms.

Cold and rain

humid air   cooling down

+ + + +   − − − −

Mountains and rain

humid air   expansion and cooling down

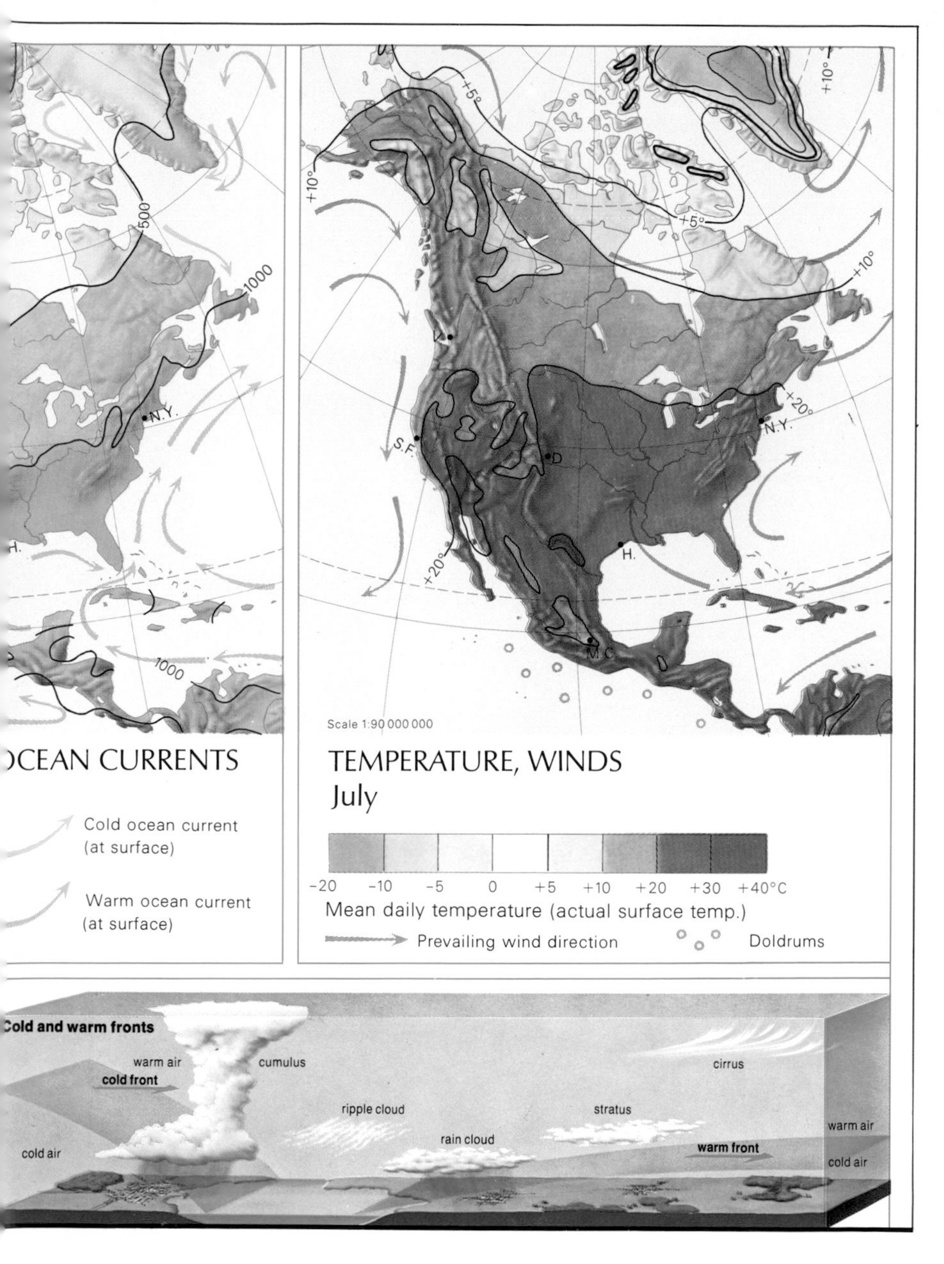

OCEAN CURRENTS

Cold ocean current
(at surface)

Warm ocean current
(at surface)

TEMPERATURE, WINDS
July

Scale 1:90 000 000

−20   −10   −5   0   +5   +10   +20   +30   +40°C
Mean daily temperature (actual surface temp.)

Prevailing wind direction   Doldrums

Cold and warm fronts

warm air   cumulus   cirrus
cold front

                    ripple cloud   stratus

                            rain cloud   warm air
cold air   **warm front**   cold air

15

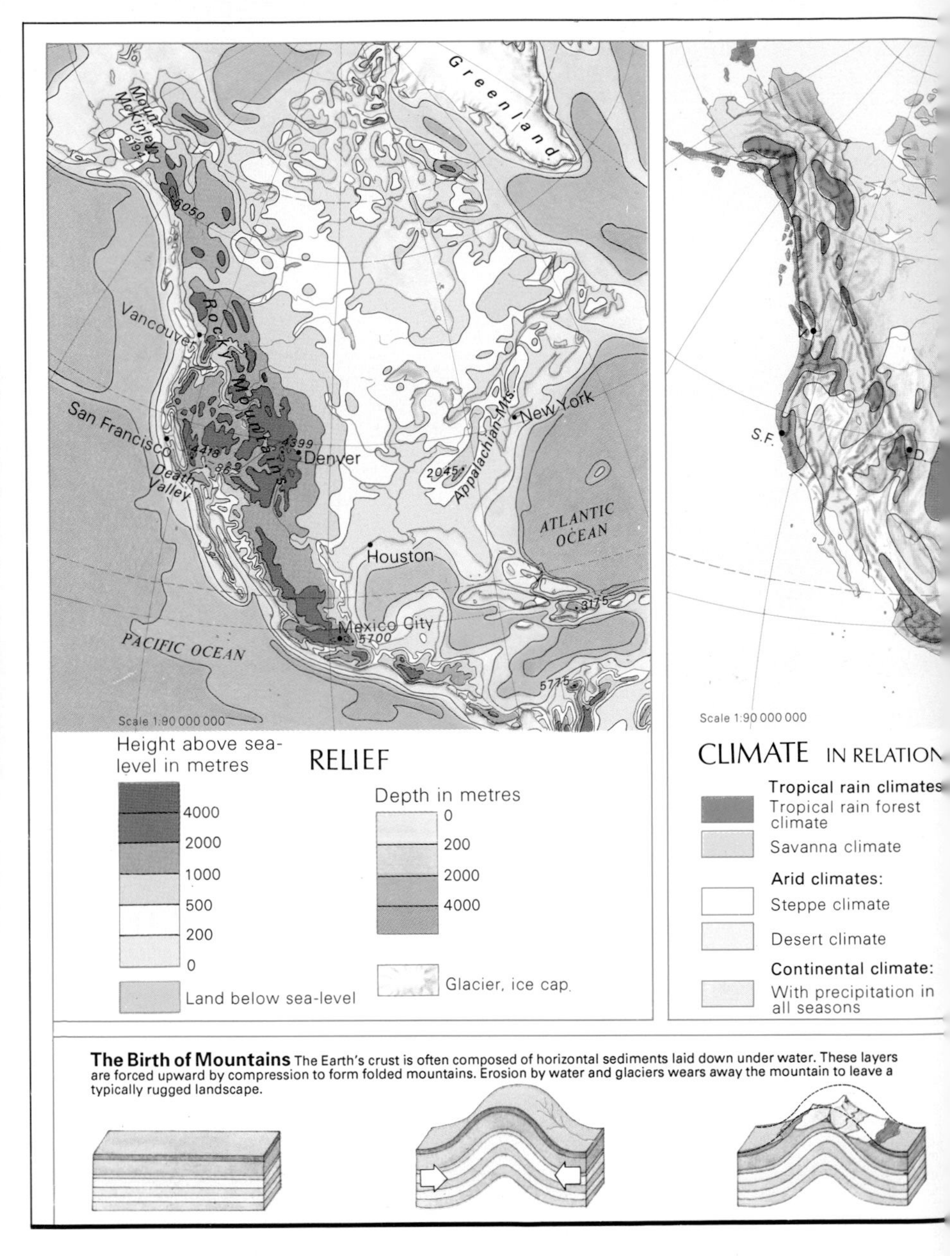

RELIEF

Height above sea-level in metres

- 4000
- 2000
- 1000
- 500
- 200
- 0

Land below sea-level

Depth in metres

- 0
- 200
- 2000
- 4000

Glacier, ice cap.

Scale 1:90 000 000

CLIMATE IN RELATION

Tropical rain climates:
Tropical rain forest climate
Savanna climate

Arid climates:
Steppe climate
Desert climate

Continental climate:
With precipitation in all seasons

Scale 1:90 000 000

The Birth of Mountains The Earth's crust is often composed of horizontal sediments laid down under water. These layers are forced upward by compression to form folded mountains. Erosion by water and glaciers wears away the mountain to leave a typically rugged landscape.

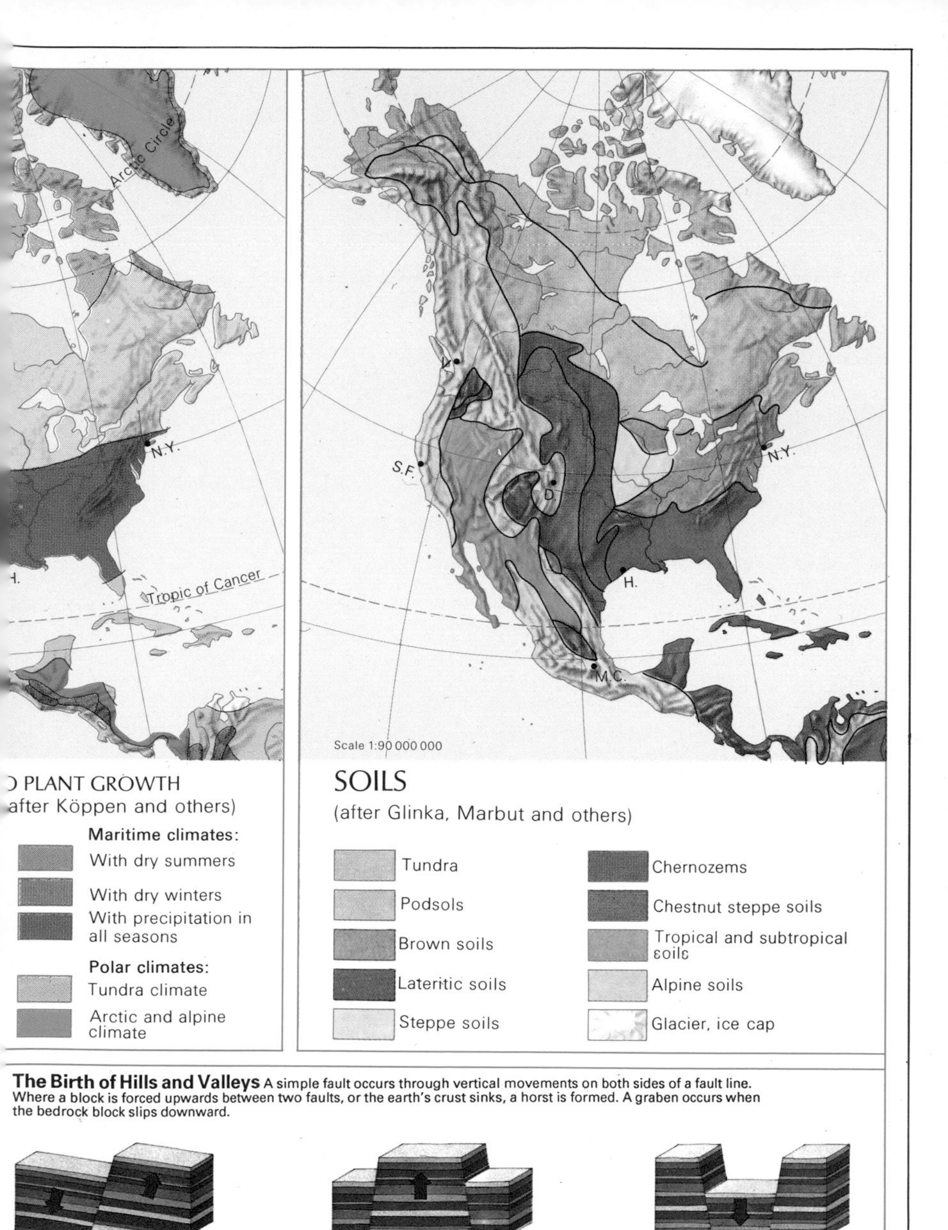

Scale 1:90 000 000

PLANT GROWTH
after Köppen and others)

Maritime climates:
   With dry summers

   With dry winters
   With precipitation in
   all seasons

Polar climates:
   Tundra climate

   Arctic and alpine
   climate

SOILS
(after Glinka, Marbut and others)

   Tundra

   Podsols

   Brown soils

   Lateritic soils

   Steppe soils

   Chernozems

   Chestnut steppe soils

   Tropical and subtropical
   soils

   Alpine soils

   Glacier, ice cap

The Birth of Hills and Valleys A simple fault occurs through vertical movements on both sides of a fault line.
Where a block is forced upwards between two faults, or the earth's crust sinks, a horst is formed. A graben occurs when
the bedrock block slips downward.

UNITED STATES

AREA: 3,615,120 square miles (9,363,123 sq. km)

POPULATION: 248,709,873 (1990)

POPULATION GROWTH PER ANNUM: 0.9%

POPULATION CHANGE 1980-1990: 9.8%

POPULATION GROWTH 1980-1990: 22,167,670 persons

MOST POPULATED COUNTY: New York, NY
(area: 2.2 sq. miles with 68,077 persons per sq. mi.)

BIRTHS: 4.02 million babies born during 1989

LIFE EXPECTANCY: males 69 years, females 77 years

LITERACY: 99%

CAPITAL, POPULATION: Washington D.C. (606,900 persons)

RELIGION: Protestant (33%), Roman Catholic (23%),
Judaism (3%)

CURRENCY: U.S. Dollar = 100 cents

HIGHEST POINT: Mount McKinley, Alaska (20,320 feet)

LOWEST POINT: Death Valley, California (-282 feet)

LONGEST RIVER: Mississippi River (2,348 miles from
Minneapolis, MN, to the Gulf of Mexico)

LARGEST HAILSTONES: 17 inches circumference
(reported in Nebraska, 1928)

OLDEST CONTINUOUSLY INHABITED TOWN: Oraibi,
Arizona (Hopi Village)

NATIONAL PARK SYSTEM: Covers 76 million acres
(3% of total U.S. area)

LARGEST INDIAN RESERVATION: Navaho Laguna Pueblo,
AZ, NM, UT (104,978 persons)

Flag Photo: Steve Proehl, San Francisco

50°   60°

Bering Sea

Cape Prince of Wales
168° 4' W. longitude i
the North American
mainland's most weste
point.

Mount McKinley is North
America's highest peak,
6,194 m. (20,322 ft.).

The Malaspina Glacier
covering an area of 3,84
km² (2,385 mi²), is the
largest on the North
American mainland.

The United States bough
Alaska from Russia in
1867 for $ 7,200,000.

Snake River Canyon
(Hell's Canyon) on the
boundary between Idahc
and Oregon is the world
deepest ravine 2,400 m.
(7,874 ft.) in depth.

The world's loftiest trees
– up to 111 m. (364 ft.) tall –
grow in the redwood forests
of California.

Death Valley is the con
nent's deepest depres-
sion, 86 m. (282 ft.) belc
sea level and also its
hottest place (highest
recorded temperature o
56.7°C. (134°F.)).

Tropic of Cancer

PACIFIC

OCEAN

1 foot = 0,30 m
1 meter = 3,28 feet

Scale 1:50 000 000

Cape Murchison on the Boothia Peninsula at 71° 59' N. latitude is the northernmost point on the continent's mainland.

North America's lowest temperature –78°C. (–172.4°F.) was recorded in the valley of the MacKenzie River.

Four of the world's ten largest lakes are found in North America.

Greenland, with an area of 2,131,000 km² (822,780 mi²) is the world's largest island. Only 341,700 km² (131,931 mi²) is ice-free land. Measurement of the icecap has revealed that Greenland is in fact a number of separate islands covered by ice that in places is up to 4,000 m. (13,123 ft.) thick.

Chubb Crater on the Ungava Peninsula is the world's largest meteorite crater, 3.5 km. (2.2 mi.) in diameter and more than 400 m. (1,312 ft.) deep.

Baffin Bay

Labrador Sea

Cape Charles at 55° 39' W. longitude is the North American mainland's easternmost point.

Hudson Bay

CANADA

Lake Superior, with an area of 82,260 km² (31,760 mi²) is the world's largest fresh water lake and ranks as the world's second largest lake after the Caspian Sea.

Yellowstone is the world's oldest national park, founded 1872. The park is well known for its teeming animal life and for more than a hundred splendid geysers including The Giant, the biggest in the world.

The tidal range in the Bay of Fundy is the largest in the world, 64 ft. between ebb and flow.

The strongest wind ever to be recorded at the earth's surface, 103 m./sec. (230 mi./h.), was measured in New Hampshire in 1934.

North America's highest waterfall and third highest in the world is Yosemite Falls 739 m. (2,425 ft.).

UNITED STATES

ATLANTIC

The Mississippi – Missouri is North America's longest river and with a length of 6,020 km. (3,738 mi.) is the third longest in the world.

Mammouth Cave in Kentucky is the world's longest with 240 km. (149 mi.) of passages on five levels, two lakes, three rivers and eight waterfalls below ground.

The world's mightiest flow of water is the Gulf Stream, 30–40 km. (19–25 mi.) wide with a flow of 55 million m³ (1,950 ft³) per second at a rate of 3–5 knots.

Only the gorge of the Blue Nile is bigger than the Grand Canyon on the Colorado River which is 350 km. (217 mi.) long, up to 21 km. (13 mi.) wide and reaches a depth of 1,800 m. (5,906 ft.).

OCEAN

Gulf of Mexico

THE BAHAMAS

MEXICO

CUBA

HAITI

DOMINICAN REPUBLIC

JAMAICA

Between June and November the Gulf of Mexico and Caribbean Sea are hit by destructive tropical storms, hurricanes, with torrential rain and wind forces up to 100 m./second (225 mi./h.).

BELIZE

HONDURAS

GUATEMALA

EL SALVADOR

NICARAGUA

The Isthmus of Panama is generally considered to be the boundary between North and South America. The southernmost point on the North American mainland is Punta Naranjas at 8° 13' N. latitude.

COSTA RICA

PANAMA

0   500   1000 km

0   200   400   600 miles

1 hour

19

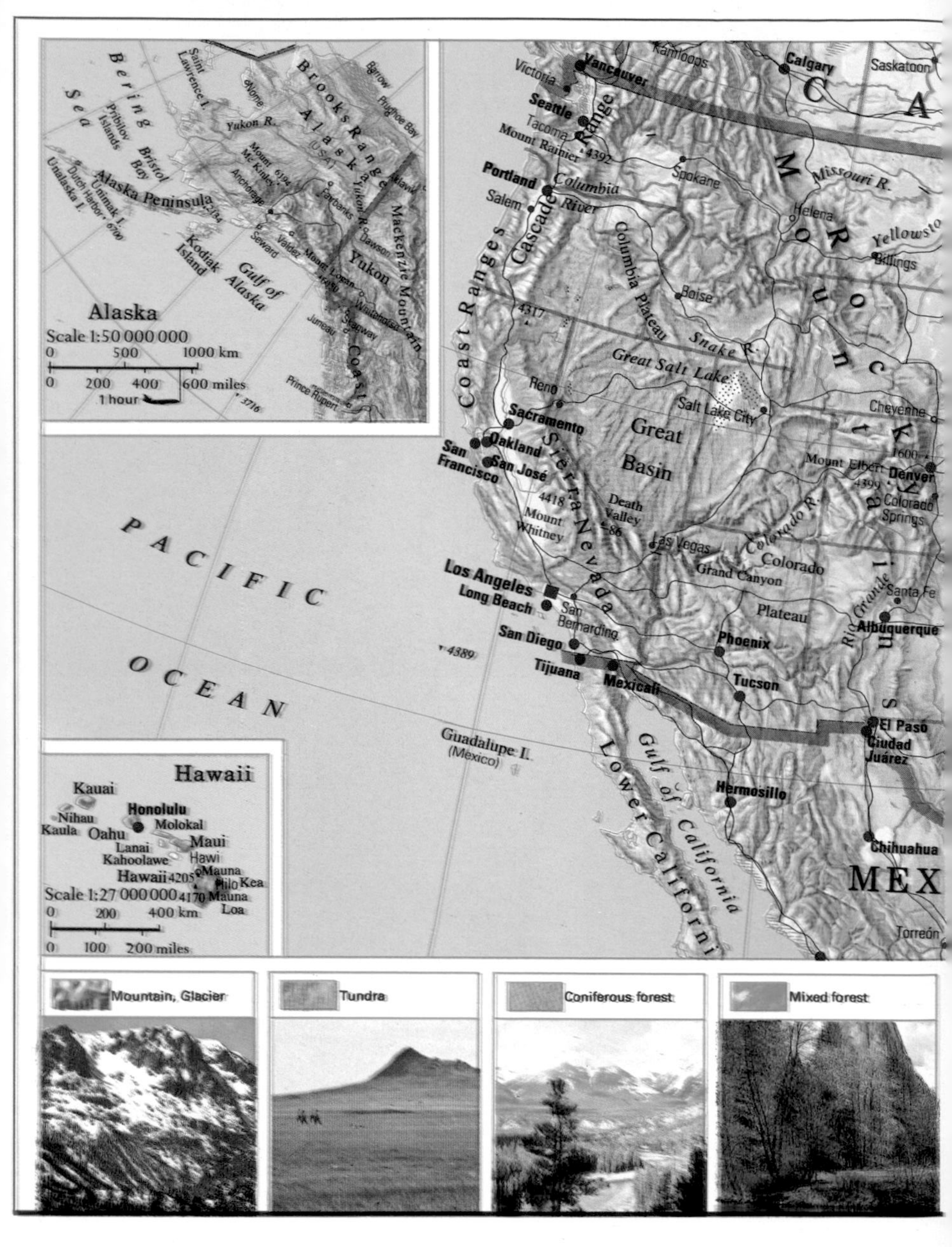

Alaska
Scale 1:50 000 000

0   500   1000 km
0   200   400   600 miles
1 hour

Bering Sea
St. Lawrence I.
Pribilof Islands
Bristol Bay
Alaska Peninsula
Unalaska I. Dutch Harbor
Kodiak Island
Gulf of Alaska
Brooks Range
Barrow
Prudhoe Bay
Point Hope
Nome
Yukon R.
Alaska Range
Mount McKinley 6194
Anchorage
Seward
Valdez
Yukon R.
Yukon–Charley R.
Mackenzie Mountains
Yukon
Prince Rupert
Juneau
5716

Hawaii
Scale 1:27 000 000
0   200   400 km
0   100   200 miles

Kauai
Nihau
Kaula
Oahu
Honolulu
Molokai
Lanai
Kahoolawe
Maui
Hawi
Mauna Kea 4205
Mauna Loa 4170
Hawaii

Victoria
Vancouver
Calgary
Saskatoon
Seattle
Tacoma
Mount Rainier 4392
Kamloops
CA
Portland
Salem
Columbia River
Cascade Range
Spokane
Missouri R.
Helena
Yellowsto
Billings
4417
Columbia Plateau
Snake R.
Boise
Cheyenne
Reno
Great Salt Lake
Salt Lake City
Mount Elbert 4399
Denver
1600
Colorado Springs
Sacramento
Oakland
San Francisco
San José
Great Basin
Sierra Nevada
4418
Mount Whitney
Death Valley -86
Las Vegas
Colorado R.
Grand Canyon
Colorado
Santa Fe
Los Angeles
Long Beach
San Bernardino
San Diego
Tijuana
Mexicali
4389
Phoenix
Tucson
Plateau
Albuquerque
Rio Grande
El Paso
Ciudad Juárez
Coast Ranges
PACIFIC OCEAN
Guadalupe I. (Mexico)
Gulf of California
Lower California
Hermosillo
Chihuahua
MEX
Torreón

Mountain, Glacier
Tundra
Coniferous forest
Mixed forest

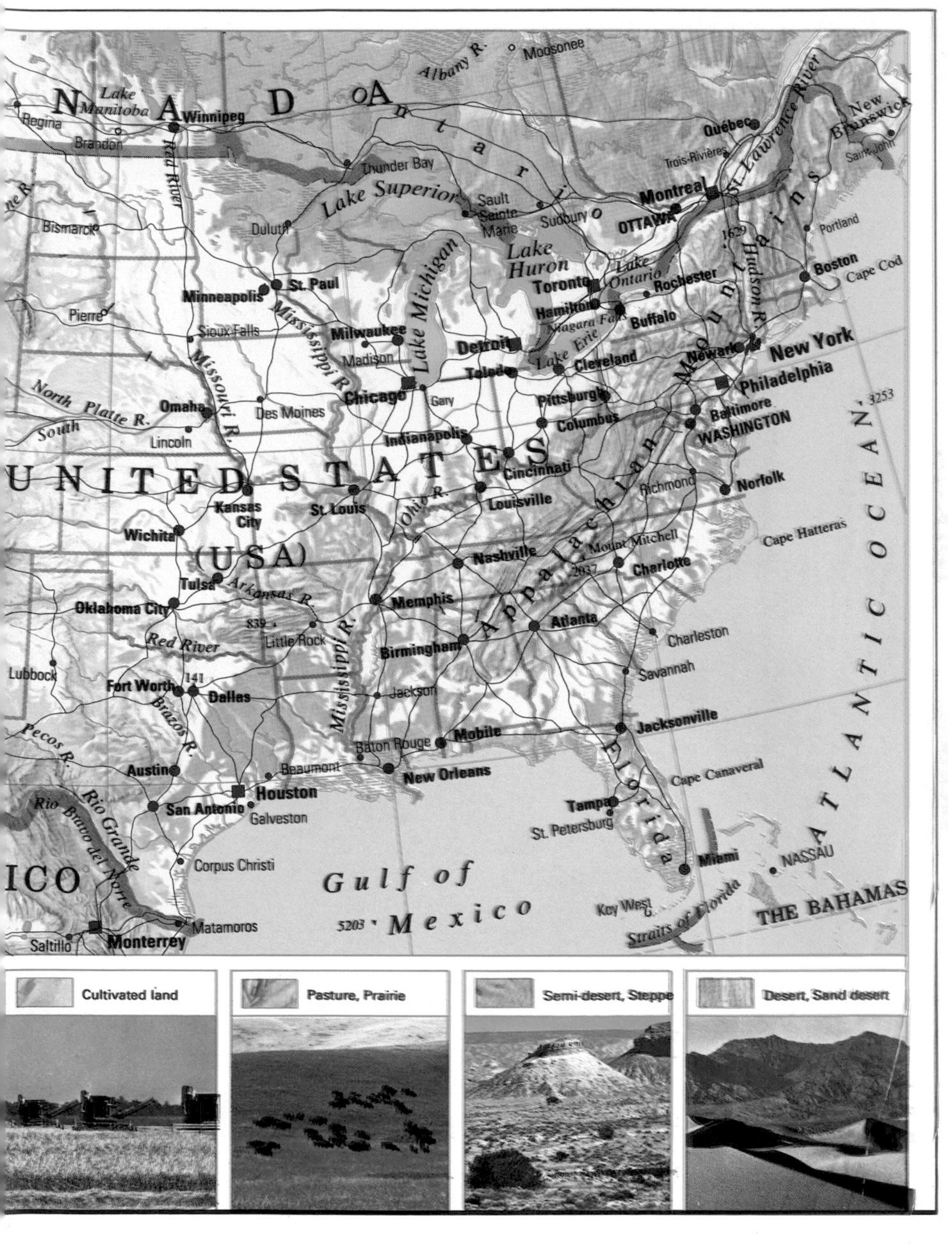

C A N A D A

Regina
Lake Manitoba
Brandon
Winnipeg
Red River
Albany R.
Moosonee

Bismarck
Duluth
Thunder Bay
Lake Superior
Sault Sainte Marie
Sudbury
St. Lawrence River
Québec
Trois-Rivières
New Brunswick
Saint John

Pierre
Minneapolis
St. Paul
Milwaukee
Madison
Lake Michigan
Lake Huron
Toronto
Lake Ontario
Rochester
Hamilton
Niagara Falls
Buffalo
Montreal
OTTAWA
1629
Portland
Boston
Cape Cod

Sioux Falls
Missouri R.
Mississippi R.
North Platte R.
South
Omaha
Des Moines
Lincoln
Chicago
Gary
Detroit
Toledo
Lake Erie
Cleveland
Pittsburgh
Columbus
Cincinnati
Newark
New York
Philadelphia
Baltimore
WASHINGTON
Hudson R.
3253

U N I T E D   S T A T E S

(USA)

Kansas City
Wichita
St. Louis
Ohio R.
Louisville
Richmond
Norfolk
Cape Hatteras

Tulsa
Arkansas R.
Nashville
Mount Mitchell
2037
Charlotte

Oklahoma City
Red River
839
Little Rock
Memphis
Birmingham
Atlanta
Charleston
Savannah
Appalachian Mountains

Lubbock
Fort Worth
141
Dallas
Brazos R.
Jackson
Mississippi R.

Pecos R.
Austin
Beaumont
Baton Rouge
Mobile
New Orleans
Jacksonville
Florida
Cape Canaveral

Rio Grande
Rio Bravo del Norte
San Antonio
Houston
Galveston
Corpus Christi
Tampa
St. Petersburg
Miami
NASSAU

MEXICO
Saltillo
Monterrey
Matamoros
Gulf of
5203
Mexico
Key West
Straits of Florida
THE BAHAMAS

A T L A N T I C   O C E A N

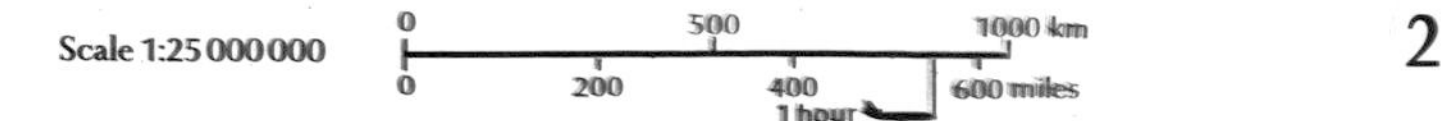

| Cultivated land | Pasture, Prairie | Semi-desert, Steppe | Desert, Sand desert |

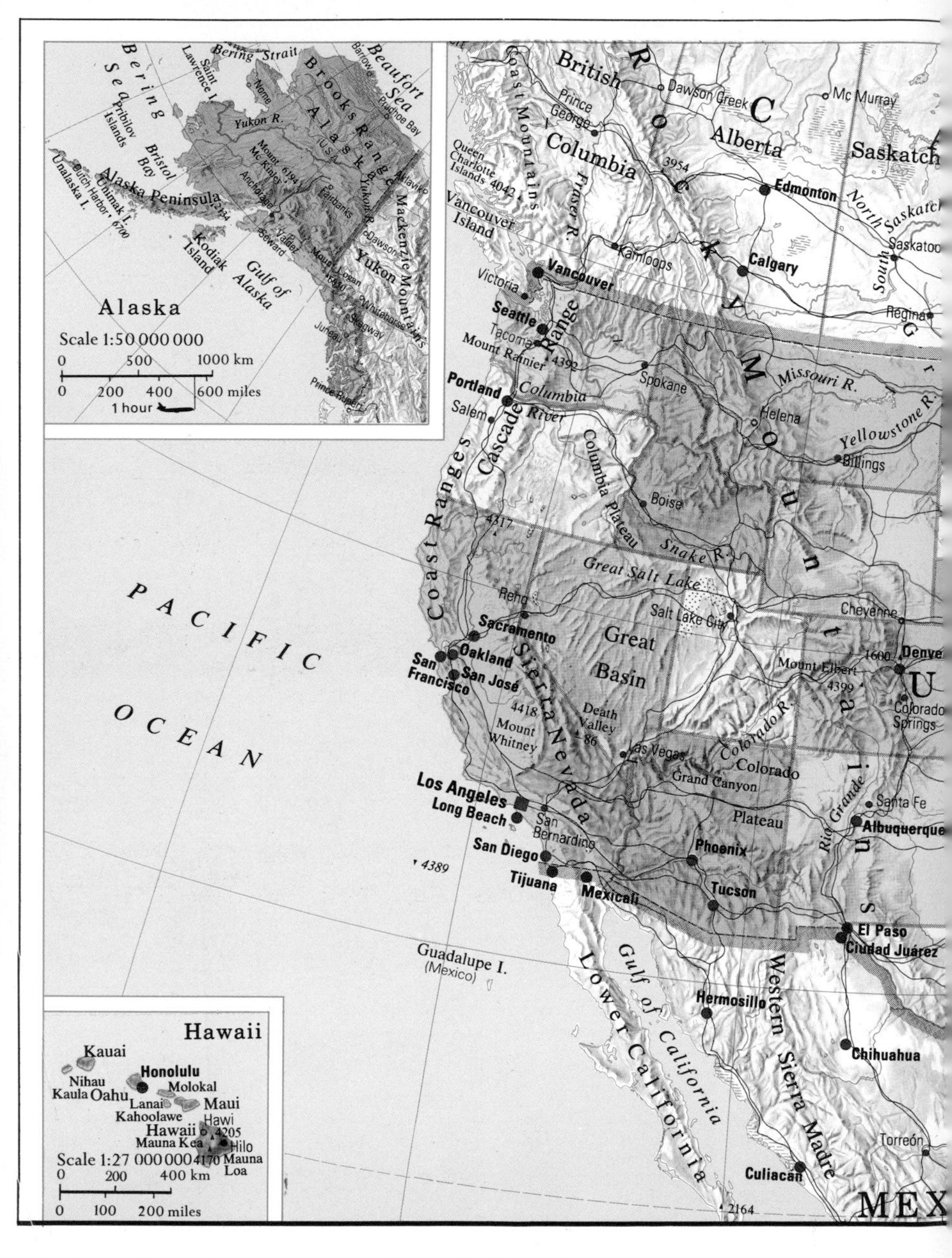
Alaska
Scale 1:50 000 000
Hawaii
Scale 1:27 000 000
PACIFIC OCEAN
Great Basin
Colorado Plateau
Rocky Mountains
Coast Ranges
Cascade Range
Sierra Nevada
Gulf of California
Lower California
Western Sierra Madre
Seattle
Portland
Vancouver
San Francisco
Oakland
Sacramento
San José
Los Angeles
Long Beach
San Diego
Tijuana
Mexicali
Phoenix
Tucson
El Paso
Ciudad Juárez
Albuquerque
Hermosillo
Chihuahua
Culiacán
Edmonton
Calgary
Honolulu

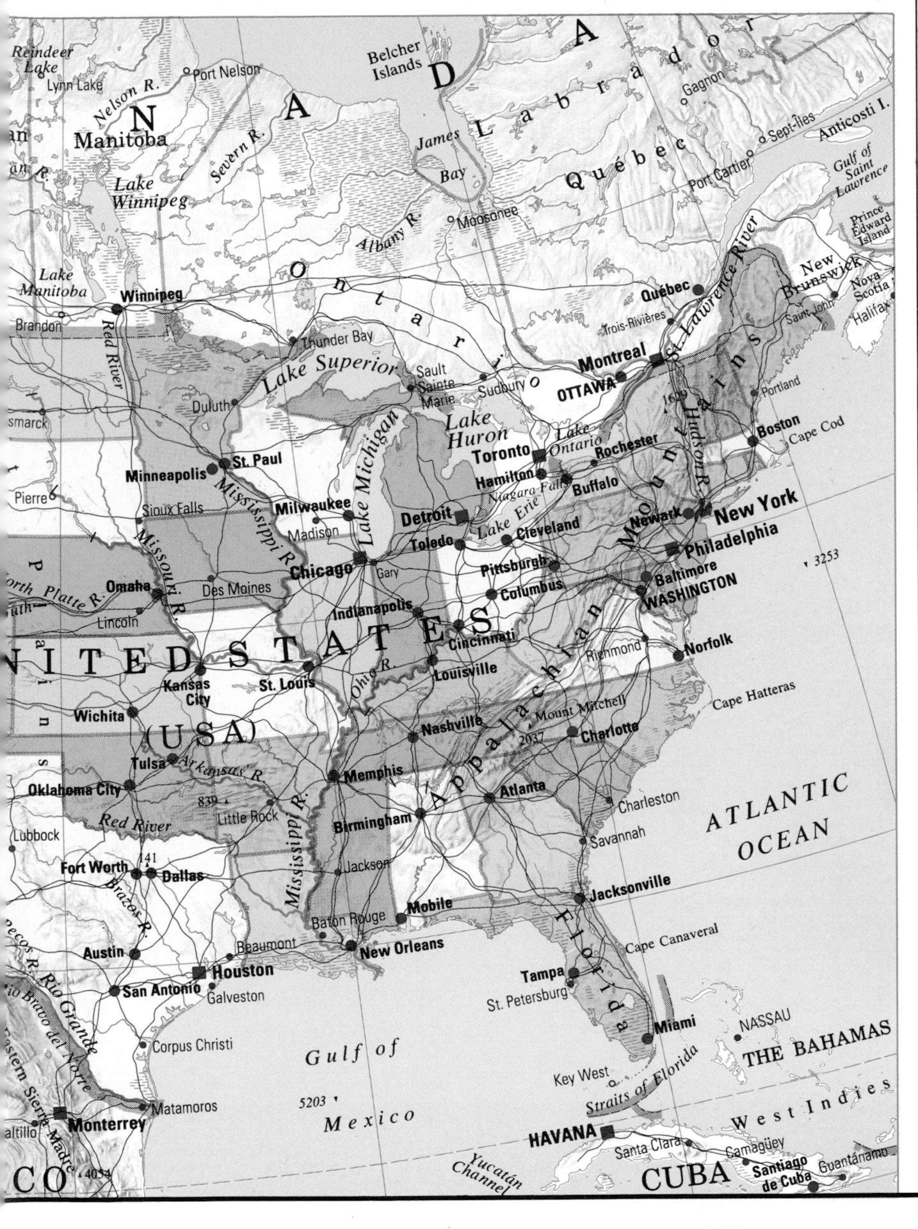

Scale 1:25 000 000

| 0 | 500 | 1000 km |
| 0 | 200 | 400 | 600 miles |

1 hour

23

MAP PAGE	STATE NAME	STATE CAPITAL	STATEHOOD YEAR	1990 POPULATION (rank, % change)	AREA sq.mi. (rank)
NORTHEAST					
30-31	CT Connecticut	Hartford	1788 (5th)	3,287,115 (27/5.8)	5,020 (48)
28-29	ME Maine	Augusta	1820 (23)	1,227,930 (38/9.1)	33,265 (39)
30-31	MA Massachusetts	Boston	1788 (6)	6,016,425 (13/4.9)	8,285 (45)
30-31	NH New Hampshire	Concord	1788 (9)	1,109,250 (40/20.5)	9,280 (44)
32-33	NY New York	Albany	1788 (11)	17,990,455 (2/2.5)	49,110 (30)
30-31	RI Rhode Island	Providence	1790 (13)	1,003,465 (43/5.9)	1,210 (50)
30-31	VT Vermont	Montpelier	1791 (14)	562,760 (49/10)	9,615 (43)
EAST					
36-37	DE Delaware	Dover	1787 (1)	666,170 (46/12.1)	2,045 (49)
36-37	DC Dis. of Columbia	Washington	1800 (-)	606,900 (48/-4.9)	70 (-)
36-37	MD Maryland	Annapolis	1788 (7)	4,781,470 (19/13.4)	10,460 (42)
34-35	NJ New Jersey	Trenton	1787 (3)	7,730,190 (9/5.0)	7,785 (46)
38-39	NC North Carolina	Raleigh	1789 (12)	6,628,635 (10/12.7)	52,670 (28)
34-35	PA Pennsylvania	Harrisburg	1787 (2)	11,881,645 (5/0.1)	45,310 (33)
36-37	VA Virginia	Richmond	1788 (10)	6,187,360 (12/15.7)	40,765 (36)
36-37	WV West Virginia	Charleston	1863 (35)	1,793,475 (34/-8.0)	24,230 (41)
SOUTHEAST					
46-47	AL Alabama	Montgomery	1819 (22)	4,040,585 (22/3.8)	51,705 (29)
44-45	FL Florida	Tallahassee	1845 (27)	12,937,925 (4/32.7)	58,665 (22)
42-43	GA Georgia	Atlanta	1788 (4)	6,478,215 (11/18.6)	58,910 (21)
50-51	KY Kentucky	Frankfort	1792 (15)	3,685,295 (23/0.7)	40,410 (37)
48-49	MS Mississippi	Jackson	1817 (20)	2,573,215 (31/2.1)	47,690 (32)
40-41	SC South Carolina	Columbia	1788 (8)	3,486,705 (25/11.7)	31,110 (40)
50-51	TN Tennessee	Nashville	1796 (16)	4,877,185 (17/6.2)	42,145 (34)
MIDWEST					
56-57	IL Illinois	Springfield	1818 (21)	11,430,600 (6/0.0)	56,345 (24)
52-53	IN Indiana	Indianapolis	1816 (19)	5,544,160 (14/1.0)	36,185 (38)
54-55	MI Michigan	Lansing	1837 (26)	9,295,295 (8/0.4)	58,525 (23)
60-61	MN Minnesota	St. Paul	1858 (32)	4,375,100 (20/7.3)	84,400 (12)
52-53	OH Ohio	Columbus	1803 (17)	10,847,115 (7/0.5)	41,330 (35)
58-59	WI Wisconsin	Madison	1848 (30)	4,891,770 (16/4.0)	56,155 (26)

WATER sq.mi.	STATE BIRD	STATE FLOWER	UNIQUE ENVIRONMENT	STATE NICKNAME	TOURIST INFO
145	Robin	Mtn. Laurel	L.I. Sound	Constitution State	203-258-4290
2270	Chickadee	Wht. Pine Cone	Coastline	Pine Tree State	800-533-9595
460	Chickadee	Mayflower	Cape Cod	Bay State	617-536-4100
285	Purple Finch	Purple Lilac	White Mts.	Granite State	603-271-2666
1730	Bluebird	Rose	Niagara Falls	Empire State	800-255-5697
155	R.I. Red	Violet	Narragansett Bay	Ocean State	800-556-2484
340	Hermit Thrush	Red Clover	Green Mts.	Green Mt. State	802-828-3236
110	Blue Hen Chicken	Peach Blossom	Chesapeake Bay	First State	800-441-8846
5	Wood Thrush	Am. Beauty Rose	Potomac River	Nation's Capital	202-789-7000
625	Balt. Oriole	Black-eyed Susan	Chesapeake Bay	Old Line State	301-263-7940
320	E. Goldfinch	Violet	Palisades	Garden State	800-537-7397
3,825	Cardinal	Dogwood	Great Smoky Mts.	Tarheel State	800-847-4862
420	Ruffled Grouse	Mt. Laurel	Allegheny Mts.	Keystone State	800-847-4872
1065	Cardinal	Dogwood	Blue Ridge Mts.	Old Dominion	800-847-4882
110	Cardinal	Rhododendron	Blue Ridge Mts.	Mountain State	800-225-5982
940	Yellowhammer	Camellia	Cumberland Mts.	Heart of Dixie	800-282-2262
4,510	Mockingbird	Orange Blossom	Everglades	Sunshine State	904-487-1462
855	Brown Thrasher	Cherokee Rose	Coastline	Peach State	800-847-4842
740	Cardinal	Goldenrod	Tennessee Valley	Bluegrass State	800-225-8747
455	Mockingbird	Magnolia	Gulf Coast	Magnolia State	800-647-2290
910	Carolina Wren	Yellow Jessamine	Blue Ridge Mts.	Palmetto State	803-734-0122
990	Mockingbird	Iris	Great Smoky Mts.	Volunteer State	615-741-2158
700	Cardinal	Violet	Lake Michigan	Prairie State	800-223-0121
255	Cardinal	Peony	Indiana Dunes	Hoosier State	800-289-6646
1,575	Robin	Apple Blossom	Lake Michigan	Wolverine State	800-543-2937
4,855	Common Loon	Lady's Slipper	Inland Lakes	North Star State	800-657-3700
325	Cardinal	Scarlet Carnation	Allegheny Mts.	Buckeye State	800-282-5393
1725	Robin	Wood Violet	Green Bay	Badger State	800-372-2737

MAP PAGE	STATE NAME	STATE CAPITAL	STATEHOOD YEAR	1990 POPULATION (rank, % change)	AREA sq.mi. (rank)
CENTRAL					
62-63	IA Iowa	Des Moines	1846 (29)	2,776,755 (30/-4.7)	56,275 (25)
64-65	MO Missouri	Jefferson City	1821 (24)	5,117,075 (15/4.1)	69,695 (19)
66-67	AR Arkansas	Little Rock	1836 (25)	2,350,725 (33/2.8)	53,185 (27)
SOUTH CENTRAL					
68-69	LA Louisiana	Baton Rouge	1812 (18)	4,219,975 (21/0.3)	47,750 (31)
76-77	OK Oklahoma	Oklahoma City	1907 (46)	3,145,585 (28/4.0)	69,955 (18)
70-77	TX Texas	Austin	1845 (28)	16,986,510 (3/19.4)	266,805 (2)
GREAT PLAINS					
78-79	KS Kansas	Topeka	1861 (34)	2,477,575 (32/4.8)	82,275 (14)
80-81	NE Nebraska	Lincoln	1867 (37)	1,578,385 (36/0.5)	77,355 (15)
84-85	ND North Dakota	Bismarck	1889 (39)	639,800 (47/-2.1)	70,700 (17)
82-83	SD South Dakota	Pierre	1889 (40)	696,005 (45/0.8)	77,115 (16)
MOUNTAIN					
94-95	CO Colorado	Denver	1876 (38)	3,294,395 (26/14.0)	104,090 (8)
88-91	ID Idaho	Boise	1890 (43)	1,006,750 (42/6.6)	83,565 (13)
86-89	MT Montana	Helena	1889 (41)	799,065 (44/1.6)	147,045 (4)
92-93	WY Wyoming	Cheyenne	1890 (44)	453,590 (51/-3.4)	97,810 (9)
SOUTHWEST					
100-103	AZ Arizona	Phoenix	1912 (48)	3,665,230 (24/34.9)	114,000 (6)
104-109	NV Nevada	Carson City	1864 (36)	1,201,835 (39/50.1)	110,560 (7)
102-103	UT Utah	Salt Lake City	1896 (45)	1,722,850 (35/17.9)	84,900 (11)
96-99	NM New Mexico	Santa Fe	1912 (47)	1,515,070 (37/16.2)	121,595 (5)
PACIFIC					
116-121	AK Alaska	Juneau	1959 (49)	550,045 (50/36.9)	591,005 (1)
106-111	CA California	Sacramento	1850 (31)	29,760,020 (1/25.7)	158,705 (3)
122-123	HI Hawaii	Honolulu	1959 (50)	1,108,230 (41/14.9)	6,470 (47)
112-113	OR Oregon	Salem	1859 (33)	2,842,320 (29/7.9)	97,075 (10)
114-115	WA Washington	Olympia	1889 (42)	4,866,690 (18/17.8)	68,140 (20)
UNITED STATES					
6-124	USA UNITED STATES	WASHINGTON DC	1776 (1)	248,709,875 (+9.8%)	3,615,120

WATER sq.mi.	STATE BIRD	STATE FLOWER	UNIQUE ENVIRONMENT	STATE NICKNAME	TOURIST INFO
310	E. Goldfinch	Wild Rose	Cornfields	Hawkeye State	800-345-4692
750	Bluebird	Hawthorne	Ozark Mts.	Show Me State	800-647-2290
1,110	Mockingbird	Apple Blossom	Ozark Mts.	Land of Opportunity	800-643-8383
3,230	E. Brown Pelican	Magnolia	Mississippi Delta	Pelican State	800-334-8626
1,300	Flycatcher	Mistletoe	Prairie	Sooner State	800-652-6552
4,790	Mockingbird	Bluebonnet	Gulf Coast	Lone State State	800-888-8839
500	W. Meadowlark	Sunflower	Wheatfields	Sunflower State	800-252-6727
710	W. Meadowlark	Goldenrod	Sand Hills	Cornhusker State	800-228-4307
1,405	W. Meadowlark	Wild Prairie Rose	Red River Valley	Sioux State	800-437-2077
1,165	Ch.Rgnk Pheasant	Pasque Flower	Black Hills	Coyote State	800-843-1930
495	Lark Bunting	Rky.Mt.Columbine	Rocky Mts.	Centennial State	800-433-2656
1,150	Mt. Bluebird	Syringa	Hell's Canyon	Gem State	800-635-7820
1,660	W. Meadowlark	Bitterroot	Sky	Treasure State	800-541-1447
820	Meadowlark	Indian Paintbrush	Tetons	Equality State	800-225-5996
490	Cactus Wren	Saguaro Blossom	Grand Canyon	Grand Canyon State	602-542-8687
665	Mt. Bluebird	Sagebrush	Death Valley	Sagebrush State	800-638-2328
2,825	Seagull	Sego Lily	Monument Valley	Beehive State	801-538-1030
260	Roadrunner	Yucca	Carlsbad Caverns	Land of Enchantment	800-545-2040
20,170	Willow Ptarmigan	Forget-me-not	Aleutian Islands	The Last Frontier	907-465-2010
2,405	Ca. Valley Quail	Golden Poppy	San Andreas Fault	Golden State	800-862-2543
45	Nene	Hibiscus	Kilauea Volcano	Aloha State	808-923-1811
890	W. Meadowlark	Oregon Grape	Columbia River	Beaver State	800-547-7842
1,625	Willow Goldfinch	W. Rhododendron	Oylmpic Nat. Park	Evergreen State	800-544-1800
78,470	AMERICAN EAGLE	AM. BEAUTY ROSE	PEOPLE	MELTING POT	202-208-6843

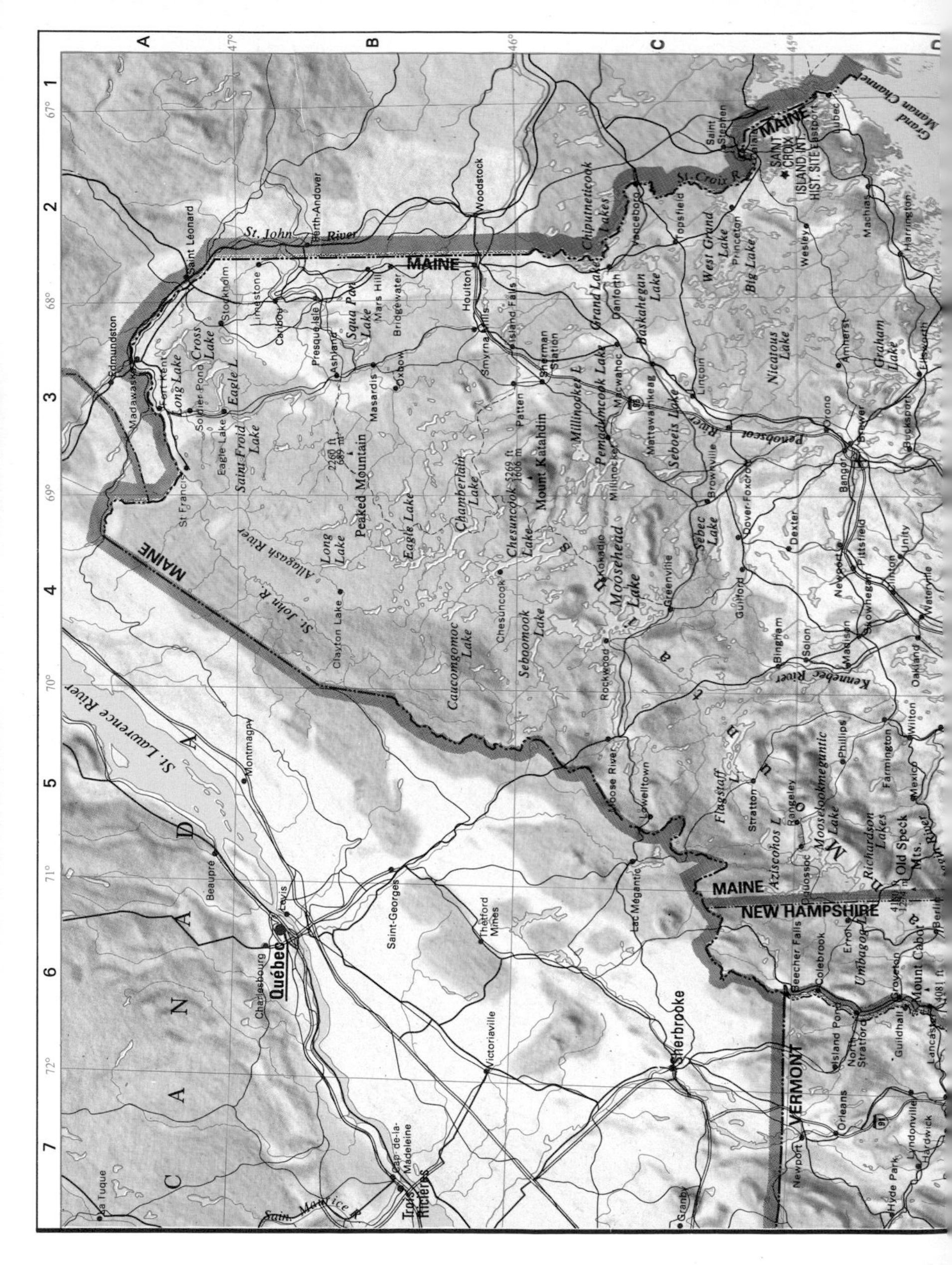

C A N A D A
MAINE
NEW HAMPSHIRE
VERMONT
Québec
Lévis
Charlesbourg
Beaupré
Montmagny
Saint-Georges
Thetford Mines
Victoriaville
Lac Mégantic
Sherbrooke
Granby
Trois Rivières
Cap-de-la-Madeleine
La Tuque
St. Lawrence River
St. John River
St. John R.
Allagash River
Penobscot River
Kennebec River
St. Croix R.
Grand Manan Channel
Edmundston
Saint Léonard
Madawaska
Fort Kent
Perth-Andover
Woodstock
Houlton
Presque Isle
Caribou
Limestone
Stockholm
Mars Hill
Bridgewater
Ashland
Masardis
Oxbow
Smyrna Mills
Island Falls
Sherman Station
Patten
Mattawamkeag
Lincoln
Danforth
Vanceboro
Topsfield
Princeton
Saint Stephen
Calais
Eastport
Lubec
SAINT CROIX ISLAND INT. HIST. SITE
Wesley
Machias
Harrington
Ellsworth
Bucksport
Brewer
Bangor
Orono
Amherst
Millinocket
Brownville
Dover-Foxcroft
Dexter
Guilford
Greenville
Kokadjo
Rockwood
Chesuncook
Clayton Lake
St Francis
Eagle Lake
Soldier Pond
Newport
Pittsfield
Unity
Clinton
Waterville
Oakland
Skowhegan
Madison
Solon
Bingham
Moose River
Jackman
Lowelltown
Stratton
Rangeley
Phillips
Farmington
Wilton
Mexico
Oquossoc
Errol
Berlin
Colebrook
Beecher Falls
Groveton
Guildhall
Lancaster
North Stratford
Island Pond
Orleans
Newport
Lyndonville
Hardwick
Hyde Park
Moosehead Lake
Mount Katahdin 5269 ft 1606 m
Peaked Mountain 2260 ft 689 m
Chamberlain Lake
Chesuncook Lake
Caucomgomoc Lake
Seboomook Lake
Eagle Lake
Long Lake
Millinocket L.
Pemadumcook Lake
Sebec Lake
Seboeis Lake
Baskahegan Lake
Grand Lake
Chiputneticook Lakes
West Grand Lake
Big Lake
Nicatous Lake
Graham Lake
Squa Pan Lake
Cross Lake
Saint Froid Lake
Eagle L.
Long Lake
Flagstaff L.
Aziscohos L.
Mooselookmeguntic Lake
Richardson Lakes
Umbagog L.
Old Speck Mts.
Mount Cabot 4081 ft
67°
68°
69°
70°
71°
72°
45°
46°
47°
A
B
C
D
1
2
3
4
5
6
7

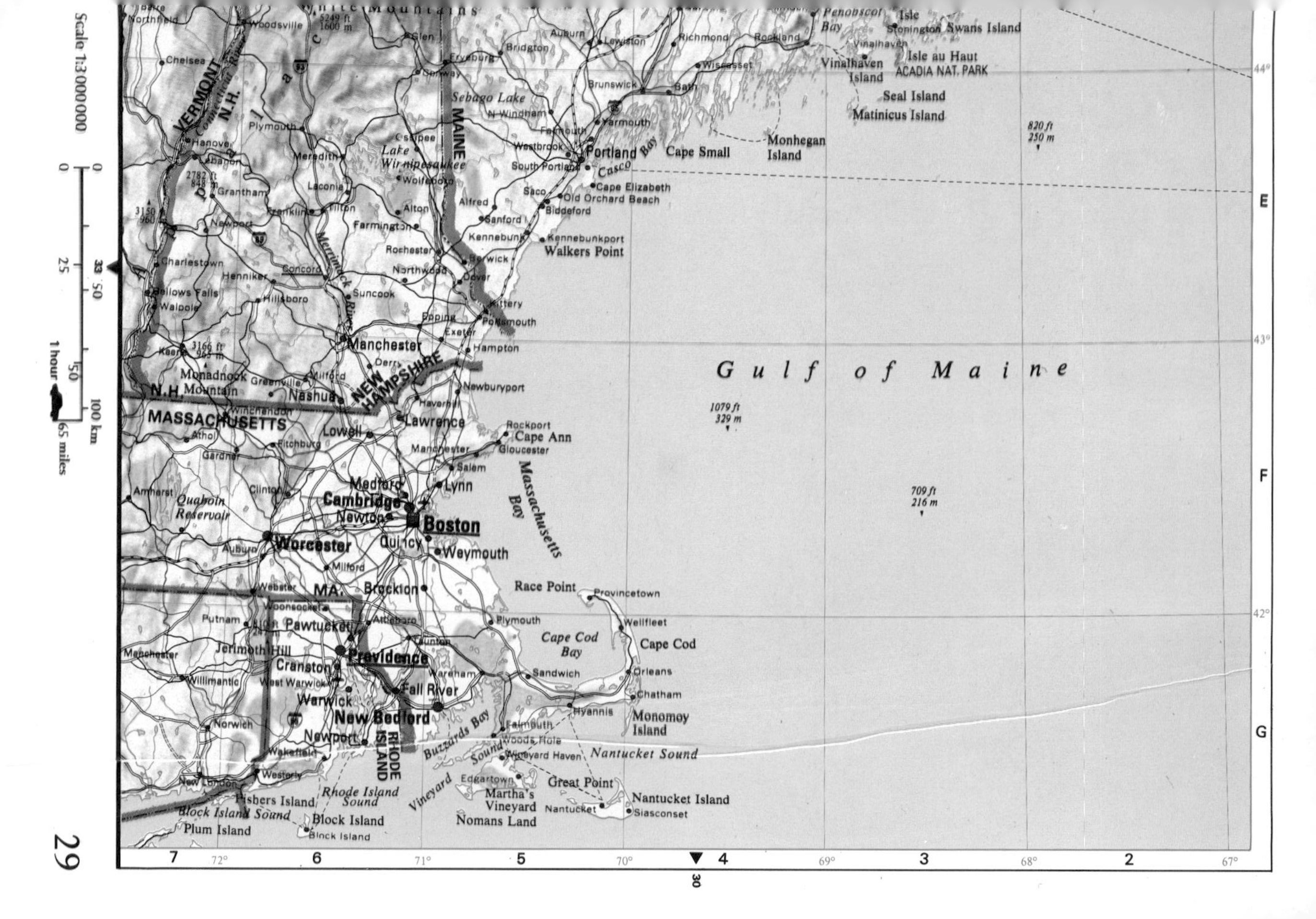

Gulf of Maine

MAINE

MASSACHUSETTS

NEW HAMPSHIRE

VERMONT

N.H.

RHODE ISLAND

Boston
Cambridge
Worcester
Providence
New Bedford
Fall River
Manchester
Lawrence
Lowell
Nashua
Portland
Newport
Pawtucket
Cranston
Warwick
Brockton
Quincy
Weymouth
Lynn
Salem
Gloucester
Cape Ann
Rockport
Newburyport
Plymouth
Provincetown
Race Point
Cape Cod Bay
Cape Cod
Wellfleet
Orleans
Chatham
Monomoy Island
Nantucket Sound
Nantucket Island
Siasconset
Nantucket
Great Point
Martha's Vineyard
Nomans Land
Vineyard Haven
Edgartown
Buzzards Bay
Block Island Sound
Rhode Island Sound
Block Island
Hyannis
Sandwich

Monhegan Island
Cape Small
Cape Elizabeth
Old Orchard Beach
Kennebunkport
Walkers Point
Casco
Saco
Biddeford
Kennebunk
Yarmouth
Brunswick
Bath
Richmond
Rockland
Penobscot Bay
Vinalhaven
Vinalhaven Island
Matinicus Island
Seal Island
Isle au Haut
ACADIA NAT. PARK
Stonington
Swans Island
Isle
Isle au Haut
Winterport

Sebago Lake
Lake Winnipesaukee
Merrimack River
Connecticut River

820 ft
250 m

709 ft
216 m

1079 ft
329 m

30

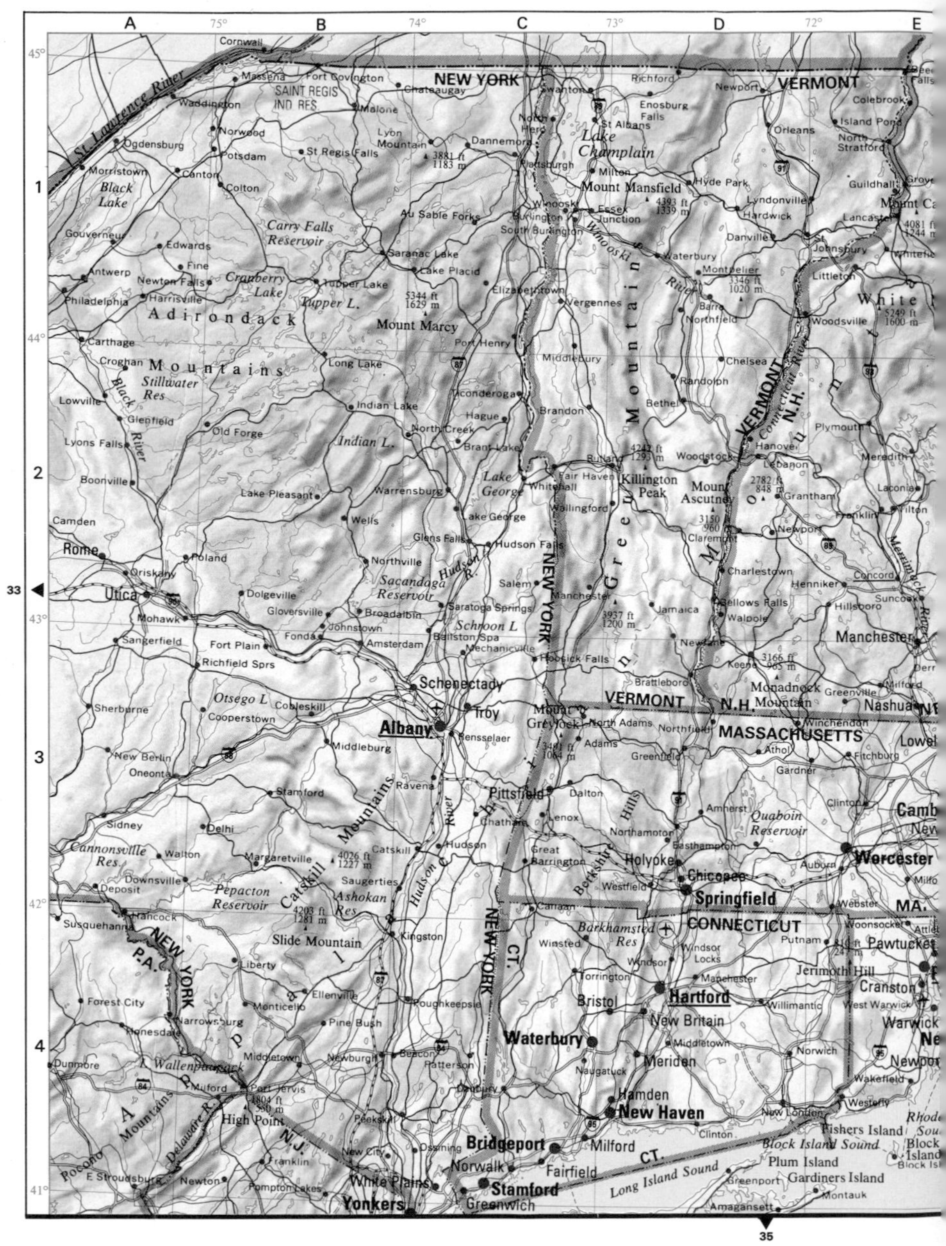

30 VERMONT, NEW HAMPSHIRE, MASSACHUSETTS,

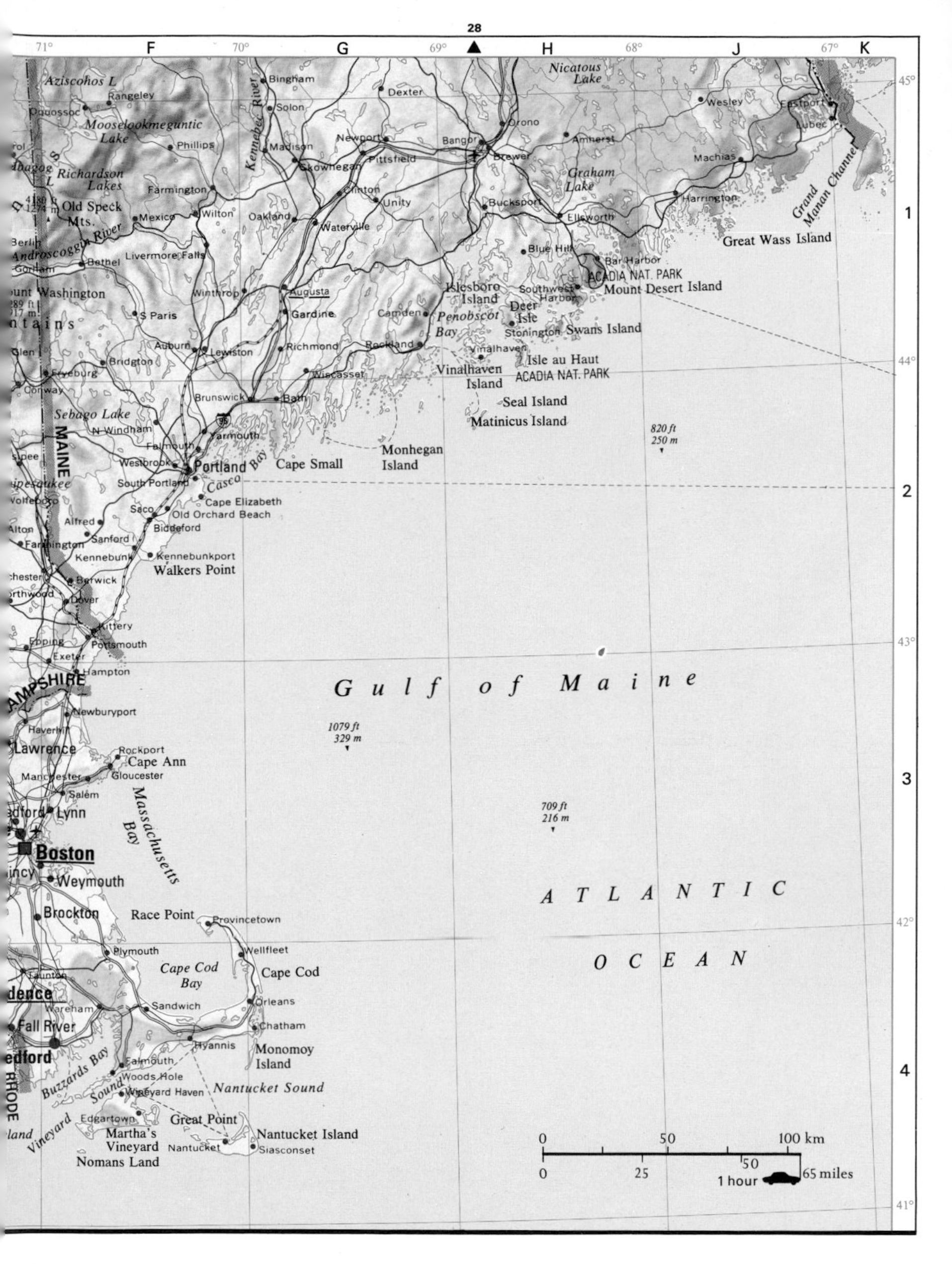

CONNECTICUT, RHODE ISLAND   Scale 1:3 000 000

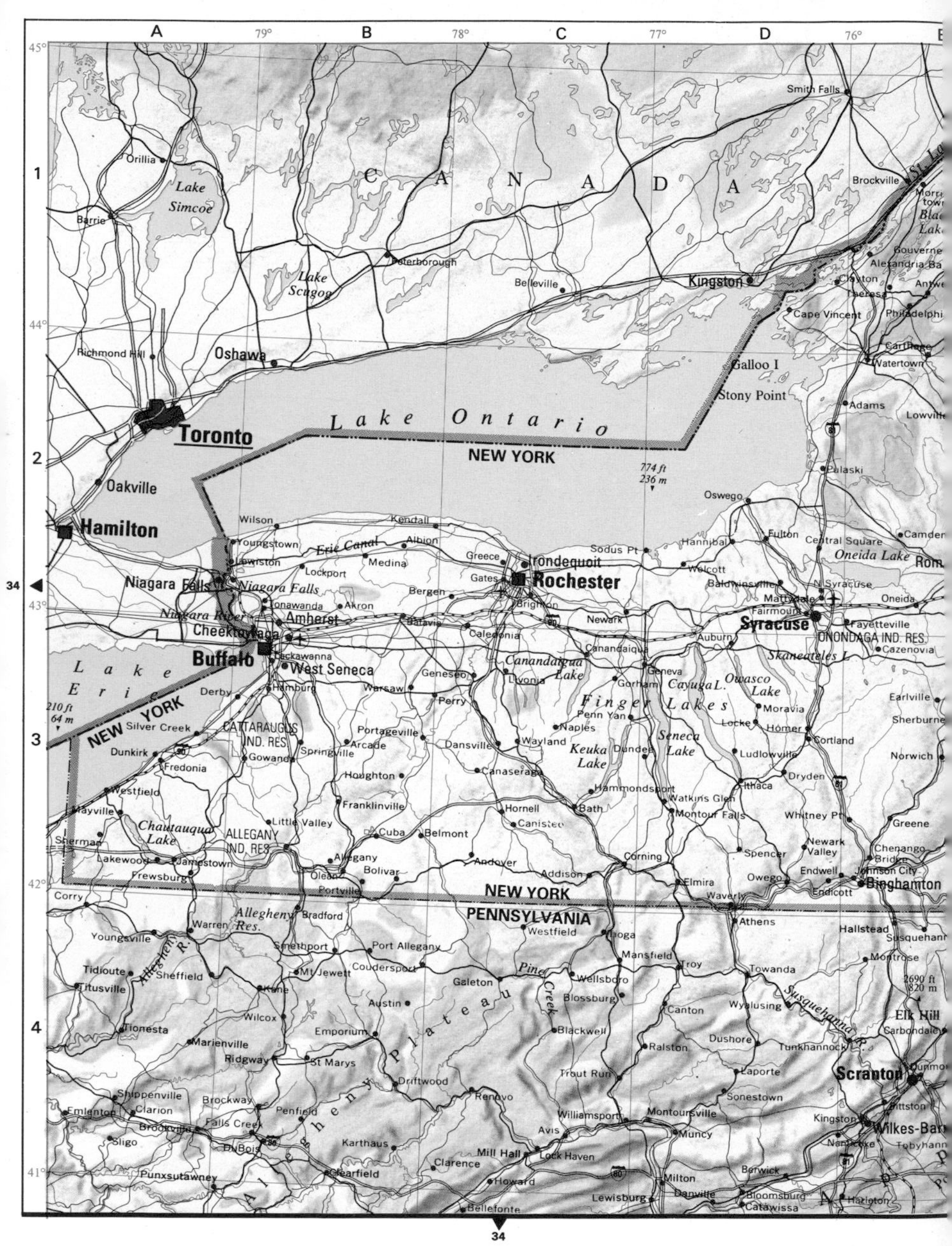
A
79°
B
78°
C
77°
D
76°
45°
44°
43°
42°
41°
1
2
3
4
34
CANADA
Smith Falls
Orillia
Lake Simcoe
Barrie
Brockville
Peterborough
Lake Scugog
Belleville
Kingston
Clayton
Theresa
Alexandria Bay
Cape Vincent
Philadelphia
Carthage
Watertown
Richmond Hill
Oshawa
Galloo I
Stony Point
Adams
Toronto
Lake Ontario
NEW YORK
774 ft
236 m
Pulaski
Oakville
Hamilton
Oswego
Wilson
Kendall
Youngstown
Erie Canal
Albion
Greece
Irondequoit
Sodus Pt
Hannibal
Fulton
Central Square
Oneida Lake
Lewiston
Lockport
Medina
Wolcott
Niagara Falls
Gates
Rochester
Baldwinsville
N. Syracuse
Bergen
Mattydale
Oneida
Tonawanda
Akron
Brighton
Fairmount
Niagara River
Amherst
Batavia
Newark
Syracuse
Fayetteville
Cheektowaga
Caledonia
Auburn
ONONDAGA IND. RES.
Buffalo
Lackawanna
Canandaigua
Cazenovia
West Seneca
Canandaigua Lake
Geneva
Skaneateles L.
Lake Erie
Geneseo
Livonia
Gorham
Cayuga L.
Owasco Lake
Derby
Hamburg
Warsaw
Perry
Earlville
210 ft
64 m
Finger Lakes
Penn Yan
Moravia
Sherburne
Silver Creek
CATTARAUGUS IND. RES
Portageville
Naples
Locke
Homer
Dunkirk
Arcade
Dansville
Wayland
Keuka Lake
Dundee
Seneca Lake
Ludlowville
Cortland
Fredonia
Gowanda
Springville
Norwich
Houghton
Canaseraga
Ithaca
Dryden
Westfield
Hammondsport
Franklinville
Watkins Glen
Mayville
Hornell
Bath
Montour Falls
Whitney Pt
Greene
Chautauqua Lake
Little Valley
Canisteo
Sherman
ALLEGANY IND. RES
Cuba
Belmont
Newark Valley
Spencer
Chenango Bridge
Lakewood
Jamestown
Allegany
Andover
Corning
Johnson City
Frewsburg
Olean
Bolivar
Addison
Endwell
Owego
Binghamton
Corry
Portville
Elmira
Endicott
Waverly
PENNSYLVANIA
Allegheny Res.
Bradford
Athens
Youngsville
Warren
Westfield
Tioga
Hallstead
Susquehanna
Smethport
Port Allegany
Mansfield
Montrose
Tidioute
Sheffield
Allegheny R.
Mt Jewett
Coudersport
Troy
Towanda
Titusville
Kane
Galeton
Pine Creek
Wellsboro
2690 ft
820 m
Austin
Blossburg
Wyalusing
Susquehanna R.
Wilcox
Canton
Elk Hill
Tionesta
Emporium
Blackwell
Dushore
Carbondale
Marienville
Ralston
Tunkhannock
Ridgway
St Marys
Allegheny Plateau
Trout Run
Laporte
Scranton
Driftwood
Shippenville
Renovo
Sonestown
Pittston
Emlenton
Brockway
Clarion
Penfield
Williamsport
Montoursville
Kingston
Wilkes-Barre
Brookville
Falls Creek
Avis
Muncy
Nanticoke
Tobyhanna
Sligo
DuBois
Karthaus
Mill Hall
Lock Haven
Clarence
Berwick
Clearfield
Punxsutawney
Howard
Milton
Lewisburg
Danville
Bloomsburg
Catawissa
Hazleton
Bellefonte

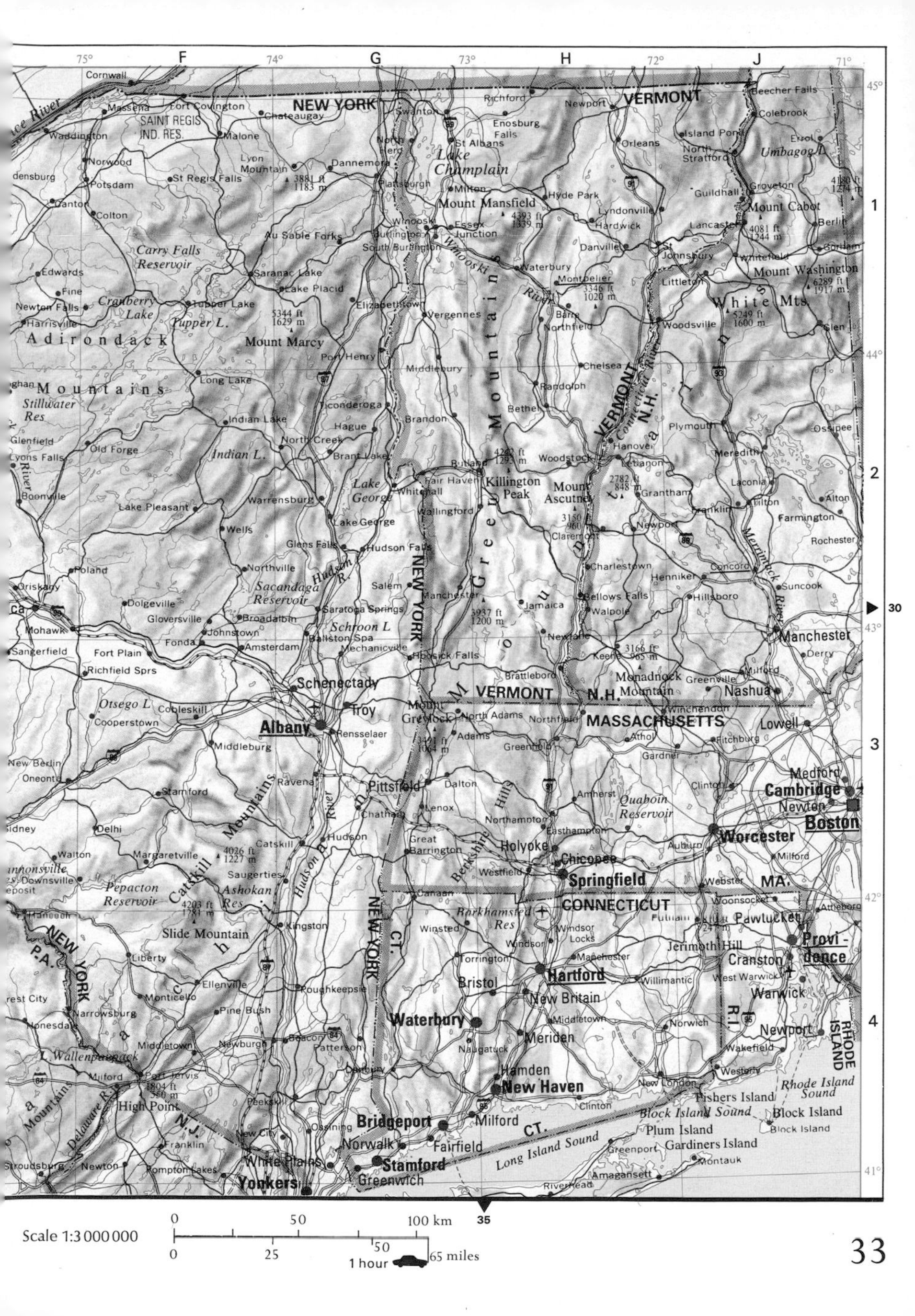

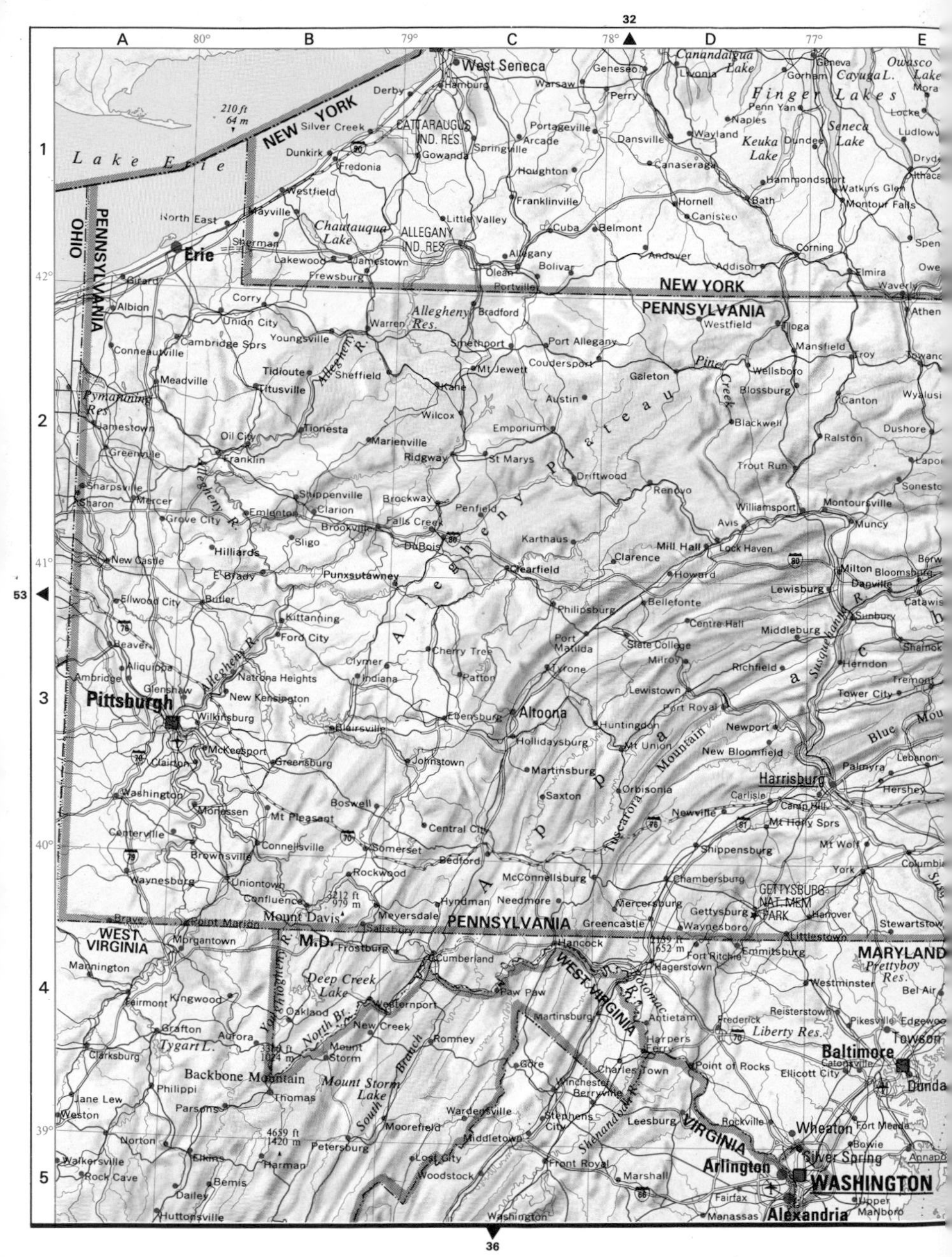
32
A
80°
B
79°
C
78°
D
77°
E
1
2
3
4
5
42°
41°
40°
39°
53
36
Lake Erie
210 ft
64 m
NEW YORK
OHIO
PENNSYLVANIA
West Seneca
Hamburg
Derby
Silver Creek
CATTARAUGUS IND. RES.
Dunkirk
Fredonia
Gowanda
Springville
Arcade
Portageville
Geneseo
Warsaw
Perry
Dansville
Wayland
Canandaigua Lake
Livonia
Geneva
Gorham
Cayuga L.
Owasco Lake
Finger Lakes
Penn Yan
Naples
Seneca Lake
Keuka Lake
Dundee
Canaseraga
Hammondsport
Watkins Glen
Montour Falls
Houghton
Westfield
Mayville
North East
Chautauqua Lake
Little Valley
ALLEGANY IND. RES.
Franklinville
Cuba
Belmont
Hornell
Canisteo
Bath
Erie
Sherman
Lakewood
Jamestown
Frewsburg
Allegany
Olean
Bolivar
Portville
Andover
Addison
Corning
Elmira
Girard
NEW YORK
PENNSYLVANIA
Albion
Corry
Union City
Bradford
Allegheny Res.
Warren
Westfield
Tioga
Mansfield
Troy
Conneautville
Cambridge Sprs
Youngsville
Allegheny R.
Smethport
Port Allegany
Coudersport
Pine Creek
Wellsboro
Meadville
Tidioute
Sheffield
Mt Jewett
Galeton
Blossburg
Titusville
Kane
Austin
Canton
Pymatuning Res.
Jamestown
Tionesta
Wilcox
Emporium
Blackwell
Dushore
Allegheny Plateau
Oil City
Marienville
Ralston
Greenville
Franklin
Ridgway
St Marys
Trout Run
Driftwood
Sharpsville
Sharon
Mercer
Shippenville
Clarion
Brockway
Renovo
Penfield
Williamsport
Montoursville
Grove City
Emlenton
Falls Creek
Avis
Muncy
Brookville
Sligo
Hilliards
DuBois
Karthaus
Mill Hall
Lock Haven
New Castle
E Brady
Punxsutawney
Clarence
Clearfield
Howard
Milton
Bloomsburg
Danville
Lewisburg
Ellwood City
Butler
Philipsburg
Bellefonte
Kittanning
Centre Hall
Middleburg
Sunbury
Beaver
Ford City
Port Matilda
State College
Aliquippa
Clymer
Cherry Tree
Milroy
Richfield
Herndon
Ambridge
Natrona Heights
Indiana
Patton
Tyrone
Susquehanna R.
Glenshaw
Lewistown
Tower City
Pittsburgh
New Kensington
Port Royal
Wilkinsburg
Ebensburg
Altoona
Huntingdon
Newport
Blue Mountain
Blairsville
Hollidaysburg
McKeesport
Mt Union
New Bloomfield
Clairton
Greensburg
Johnstown
Martinsburg
Tuscarora Mountain
Harrisburg
Palmyra
Lebanon
Hershey
Washington
Monessen
Saxton
Orbisonia
Carlisle
Camp Hill
Boswell
Mt Pleasant
Newville
Mt Holly Sprs
Centerville
Central City
Connellsville
Somerset
Shippensburg
Mt Wolf
Brownsville
Bedford
Appalachian
Waynesburg
Rockwood
McConnellsburg
Chambersburg
York
Uniontown
Confluence
3212 ft
979 m
Mount Davis
Hyndman
Needmore
Mercersburg
GETTYSBURG NAT. MEM PARK
Gettysburg
Hanover
Meyersdale
Salisbury
PENNSYLVANIA
Greencastle
Waynesboro
Stewartstown
Point Marion
WEST VIRGINIA
Morgantown
M.D.
Frostburg
Hancock
2139 ft
652 m
Fort Ritchie
Emmitsburg
Littlestown
MARYLAND
Prettyboy Res.
Mannington
Youghiogheny R.
Cumberland
WEST VIRGINIA
Hagerstown
Westminster
Bel Air
Deep Creek Lake
Paw Paw
Potomac R.
Fairmont
Kingwood
Oakland
Westernport
Martinsburg
Antietam
Reisterstown
Pikesville
Grafton
Aurora
North Br.
New Creek
Frederick
Liberty Res.
Towson
Tygart L.
3360 ft
1024 m
Mount Storm
Romney
Harpers Ferry
Clarksburg
Baltimore
Catonsville
Backbone Mountain
Mount Storm Lake
South Branch
Gore
Charles Town
Point of Rocks
Ellicott City
Thomas
Philippi
Winchester
Berryville
Jane Lew
Parsons
Wardensville
Stephens City
Shenandoah R.
Leesburg
Rockville
Wheaton
Fort Meade
Weston
Moorefield
VIRGINIA
Bowie
Norton
4659 ft
1420 m
Petersburg
Middletown
Silver Spring
Walkersville
Elkins
Lost City
Front Royal
Arlington
WASHINGTON
Rock Cave
Harman
Woodstock
Marshall
Bemis
Dailey
Fairfax
Upper Marlboro
Huttonsville
Washington
Manassas
Alexandria

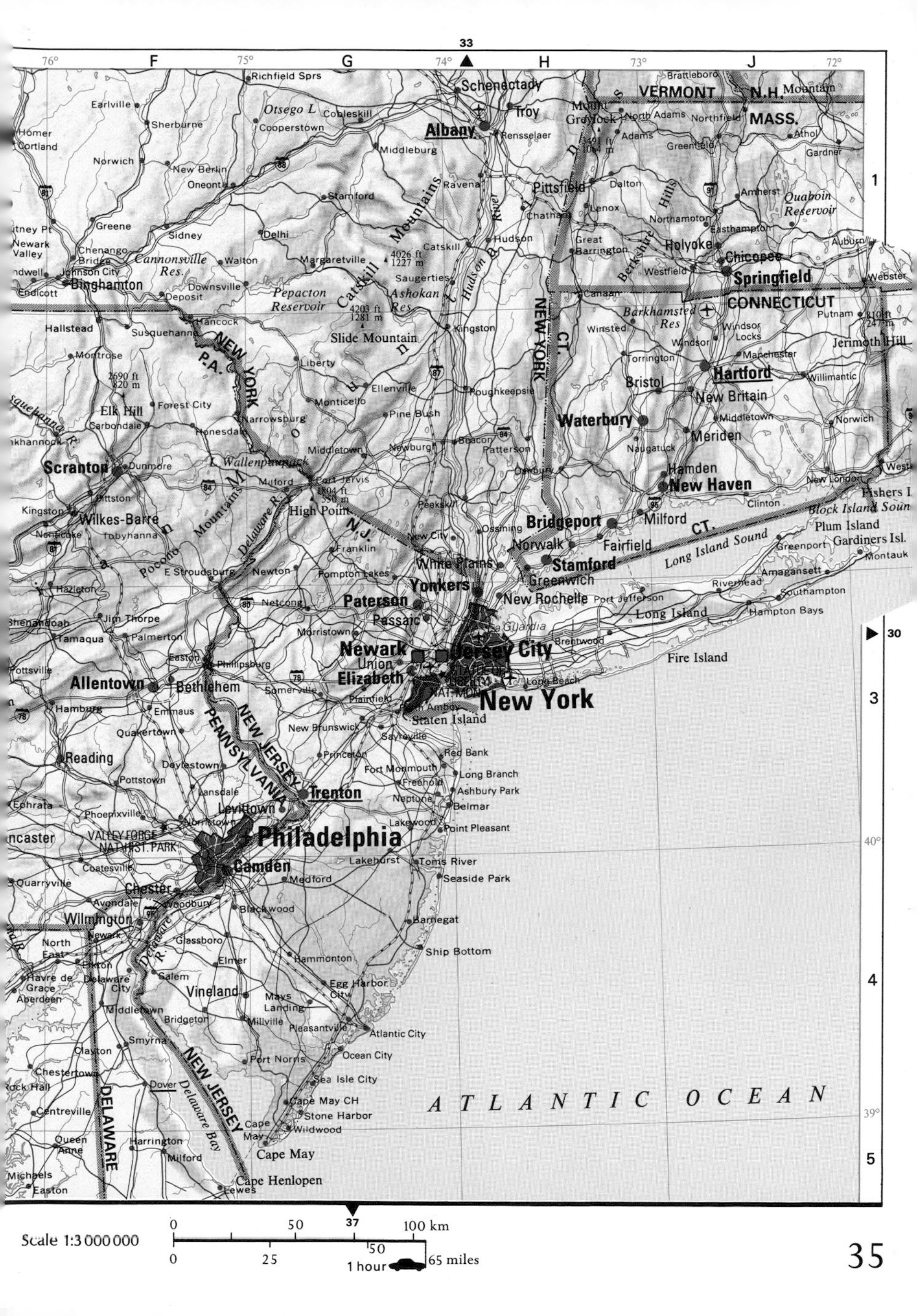

33
76°
F
75°
G
74°
H
73°
J
72°
1
3
4
5
30
40°
39°
Richfield Sprs
Schenectady
VERMONT
N.H.
MASS.
Earlville
Otsego L
Cobleskill
Troy
Albany
Rensselaer
Sherburne
Cooperstown
Homer
Cortland
Norwich
Middleburg
New Berlin
Oneonta
Ravena
Pittsfield
Dalton
Amherst
Quabbin Reservoir
Stamford
Lenox
Chatham
Northampton
Greene
Sidney
Delhi
Hudson
Easthampton
Great Barrington
Holyoke
Chicopee
Springfield
Westfield
Newark Valley
Chenango Bridge
Cannonsville Res.
Walton
Margaretville
Catskill
Johnson City
Binghamton
Endicott
Downsville
Deposit
Saugerties
Ashokan Res.
Pepacton Reservoir
Catskill Mountains
4026 ft 1227 m
4203 ft 1281 m
Hudson R.
Hancock
Hallstead
Susquehanna
Slide Mountain
Kingston
NEW YORK
CT.
CONNECTICUT
Barkhamsted Res
Winsted
Windsor
Windsor Locks
Putnam
Jerimoth Hill
Torrington
Manchester
Montrose
Liberty
P.A.
2690 ft 820 m
Bristol
Hartford
Willimantic
Forest City
Elk Hill
Ellenville
Poughkeepsie
New Britain
Middletown
Carbondale
Narrowsburg
Monticello
Pine Bush
Waterbury
Norwich
Honesdale
Naugatuck
Meriden
Middletown
Newburgh
Beacon
Patterson
Scranton
Dunmore
L. Wallenpaupack
Danbury
Hamden
New Haven
New London
Milford
Port Jervis
1804 ft 550 m
Pittston
High Point
Peekskill
Fishers I
Kingston
Wilkes-Barre
Clinton
Block Island Sound
Tobyhanna
Pocono Mountains
Delaware R.
N.J.
Ossining
Bridgeport
Milford
Plum Island
New City
Norwalk
Fairfield
Long Island Sound
Greenport
Gardiners Isl.
Franklin
Montauk
White Plains
Stamford
E Stroudsburg
Newton
Pompton Lakes
Yonkers
Greenwich
Amagansett
Hazleton
Riverhead
Southampton
Netcong
Paterson
New Rochelle
Port Jefferson
Long Island
Hampton Bays
Jim Thorpe
Passaic
La Guardia
Tamaqua
Palmerton
Morristown
Brentwood
Newark
Jersey City
Fire Island
Easton
Phillipsburg
Union
Pottsville
Allentown
Bethlehem
Elizabeth
Long Beach
Somerville
New York
Hamburg
Emmaus
Plainfield
Staten Island
PENNSYLVANIA
NEW JERSEY
Quakertown
New Brunswick
Sayreville
Red Bank
Princeton
Reading
Doylestown
Fort Monmouth
Long Branch
Freehold
Pottstown
Lansdale
Trenton
Ashbury Park
Neptune
Ephrata
Levittown
Belmar
Phoenixville
Norristown
Lakewood
VALLEY FORGE NAT HIST. PARK
Philadelphia
Point Pleasant
Lakehurst
Toms River
Coatesville
Camden
Medford
Seaside Park
Quarryville
Chester
Avondale
Woodbury
Blackwood
Wilmington
Barnegat
Newark
Glassboro
North East
Elkton
Hammonton
Ship Bottom
Elmer
Havre de Grace
Delaware City
Salem
Egg Harbor City
Aberdeen
Vineland
Middletown
Mays Landing
Bridgeton
Millville
Pleasantville
Atlantic City
Smyrna
Clayton
NEW JERSEY
Ocean City
Port Norris
Chestertown
Sea Isle City
Dover
Delaware Bay
Rock Hall
DELAWARE
Cape May CH
Centreville
Stone Harbor
ATLANTIC OCEAN
Cape May
Wildwood
Queen Anne
Harrington
Cape May
Milford
Michaels
Easton
Cape Henlopen
Lewes
37
Scale 1:3 000 000
0
50
100 km
0
25
50
1 hour
65 miles

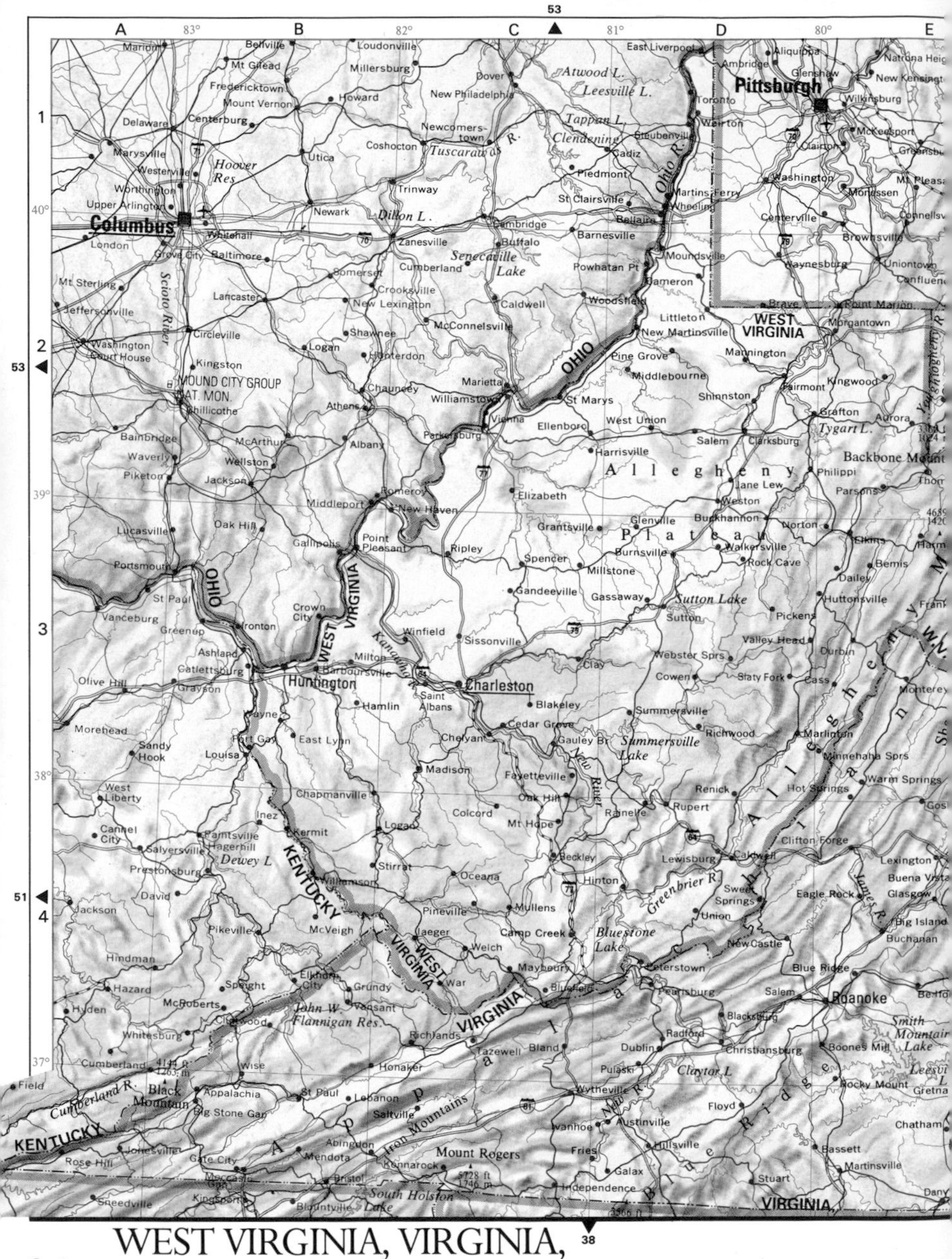

WEST VIRGINIA, VIRGINIA,
DELAWARE, MARYLAND

36

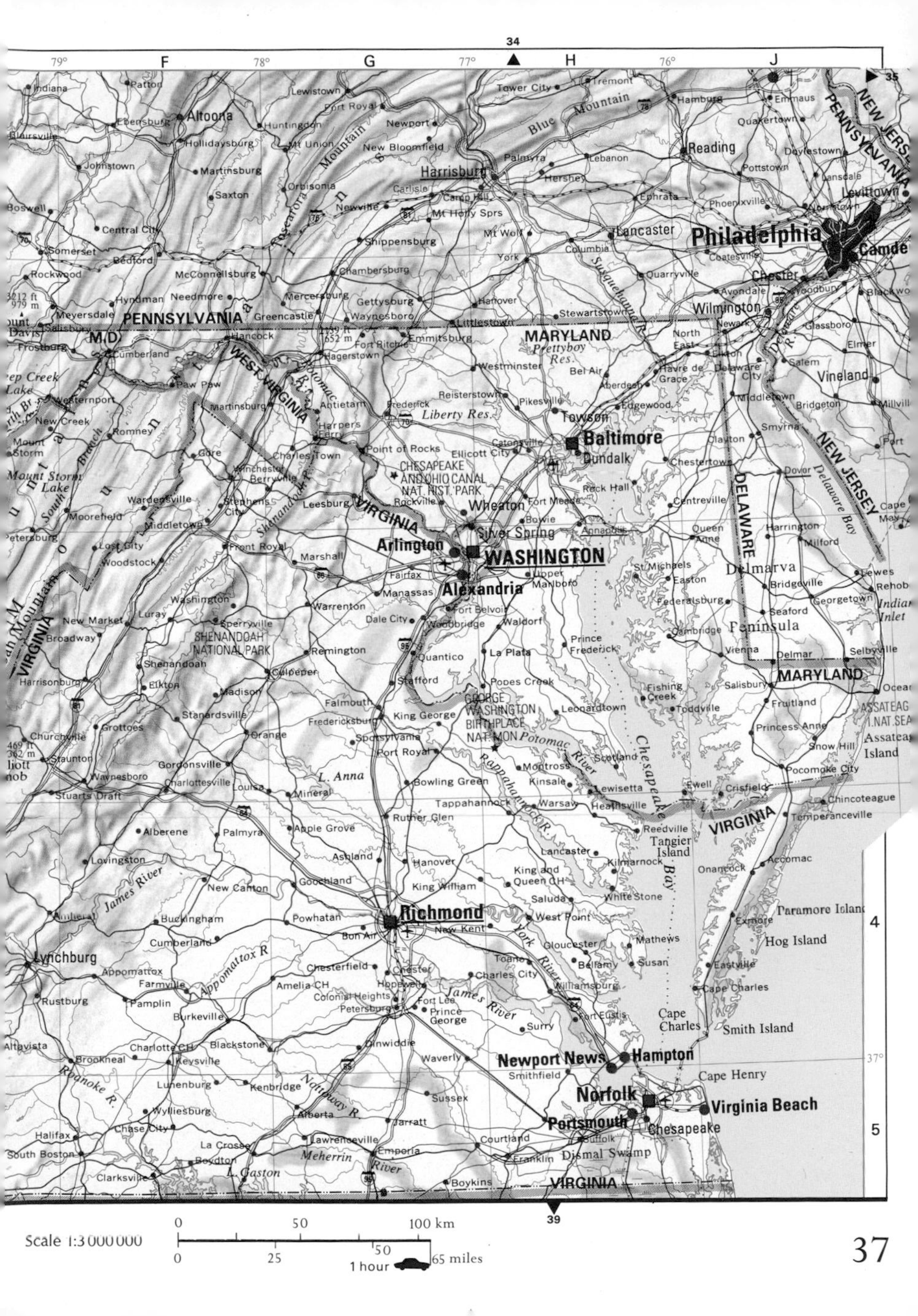
34
79°
F
78°
G
77°
H
76°
J
35
PENNSYLVANIA
NEW JERSEY
Altoona
Harrisburg
Reading
Philadelphia
Camden
Lancaster
York
Chester
Wilmington
Levittown
Allentown
Hamburg
Emmaus
Quakertown
Doylestown
Pottstown
Lansdale
Phoenixville
Norristown
Coatesville
Quarryville
Avondale
Woodbury
Blackwood
Glassboro
Elmer
Salem
Vineland
Bridgeton
Millville
Port
Cape May
Tower City
Tremont
Blue Mountain
Palmyra
Lebanon
Hershey
Ephrata
Columbia
Mt Wolf
Hanover
Stewartstown
Littlestown
Gettysburg
Waynesboro
Chambersburg
Mercersburg
Greencastle
Shippensburg
Newville
Carlisle
Camp Hill
Mt Holly Sprs
New Bloomfield
Newport
Fort Royal
Lewistown
Huntingdon
Mt Union
Orbisonia
Saxton
Martinsburg
Hollidaysburg
Ebensburg
Patton
Indiana
Blairsville
Johnstown
Boswell
Central City
Somerset
Bedford
Rockwood
McConnellsburg
Hyndman
Needmore
Meyersdale
Salisbury
Tuscarora Mountain
3212 ft
979 m
MARYLAND
MD
Frostburg
Cumberland
Hancock
Paw Paw
Emmitsburg
Fort Ritchie
Hagerstown
Westminster
Prettyboy Res.
Bel Air
Aberdeen
Havre de Grace
North East
Elkton
Newark
Delaware City
Middletown
Smyrna
Clayton
Dover
Reisterstown
Pikesville
Towson
Edgewood
Baltimore
Dundalk
Catonsville
Ellicott City
Frederick
Liberty Res.
Antietam
Harpers Ferry
Point of Rocks
Charles Town
CHESAPEAKE AND OHIO CANAL NAT. HIST. PARK
Rockville
Wheaton
Fort Meade
Bowie
Silver Spring
Annapolis
Rock Hall
Chestertown
Centreville
Queen Anne
St Michaels
Easton
Federalsburg
Cambridge
Vienna
Delmar
Salisbury
Fishing Creek
Toddville
Fruitland
Princess Anne
Snow Hill
Pocomoke City
Crisfield
Ewell
Selbyville
Ocean
ASSATEAGUE I. NAT. SEA.
Assateague Island
DELAWARE
Delmarva Peninsula
Harrington
Milford
Bridgeville
Seaford
Georgetown
Lewes
Rehoboth
Indian Inlet
Delaware Bay
WEST VIRGINIA
Potomac R.
Martinsburg
Westernport
New Creek
Romney
Mount Storm
Mount Storm Lake
Gore
Winchester
Berryville
Wardensville
Stephens City
Moorefield
Middletown
Petersburg
Lost City
Woodstock
Front Royal
Shenandoah R.
South Branch
VIRGINIA
Leesburg
Arlington
WASHINGTON
Alexandria
Fairfax
Marshall
Manassas
Upper Marlboro
Fort Belvoir
Warrenton
Dale City
Woodbridge
Waldorf
Prince Frederick
La Plata
Quantico
Remington
Washington
Luray
New Market
Sperryville
Broadway
SHENANDOAH NATIONAL PARK
Shenandoah
Harrisonburg
Elkton
Culpeper
Madison
Stafford
Popes Creek
GEORGE WASHINGTON BIRTHPLACE NAT. MON.
Falmouth
Fredericksburg
King George
Leonardtown
Stanardsville
Grottoes
Churchville
Orange
Spotsylvania
Port Royal
Potomac River
Rappahannock R.
Montross
Scotland
Staunton
Waynesboro
Gordonsville
Charlottesville
Stuarts Draft
Louisa
Mineral
L. Anna
Bowling Green
Kinsale
Lewisetta
Warsaw
Heathsville
Tappahannock
Chesapeake Bay
Reedville
Tangier Island
Chincoteague
Temperanceville
Ruther Glen
Apple Grove
Palmyra
Alberene
Lovingston
Ashland
Hanover
Lancaster
Kilmarnock
King and Queen CH
Onancock
Accomac
New Canton
Goochland
King William
Saluda
White Stone
James River
Buckingham
Powhatan
Richmond
Bon Air
New Kent
West Point
Paramore Island
Exmore
Hog Island
Cumberland
Lynchburg
Appomattox
Appomattox R
Chesterfield
Chester
Toano
Gloucester
Mathews
Bellamy
Susan
Charles City
Eastville
Cape Charles
Farmville
Amelia CH
Hopewell
Colonial Heights
Petersburg
Fort Lee
Prince George
Williamsburg
Rustburg
Pamplin
Burkeville
Surry
Fort Eustis
Smith Island
Altavista
Brookneal
Charlotte CH
Blackstone
Keysville
Dinwiddie
Waverly
Newport News
Hampton
Smithfield
Cape Henry
37°
Roanoke R.
Lunenburg
Kenbridge
Nottoway R.
Sussex
Norfolk
Virginia Beach
Wylliesburg
Alberta
Jarratt
Portsmouth
Chesapeake
Suffolk
Chase City
Halifax
South Boston
La Crosse
Lawrenceville
Emporia
Courtland
Franklin
Dismal Swamp
Boydton
Meherrin River
L. Gaston
Clarksville
Boykins
4
5
39
Scale 1:3 000 000
0
50
100 km
25
65 miles
1 hour

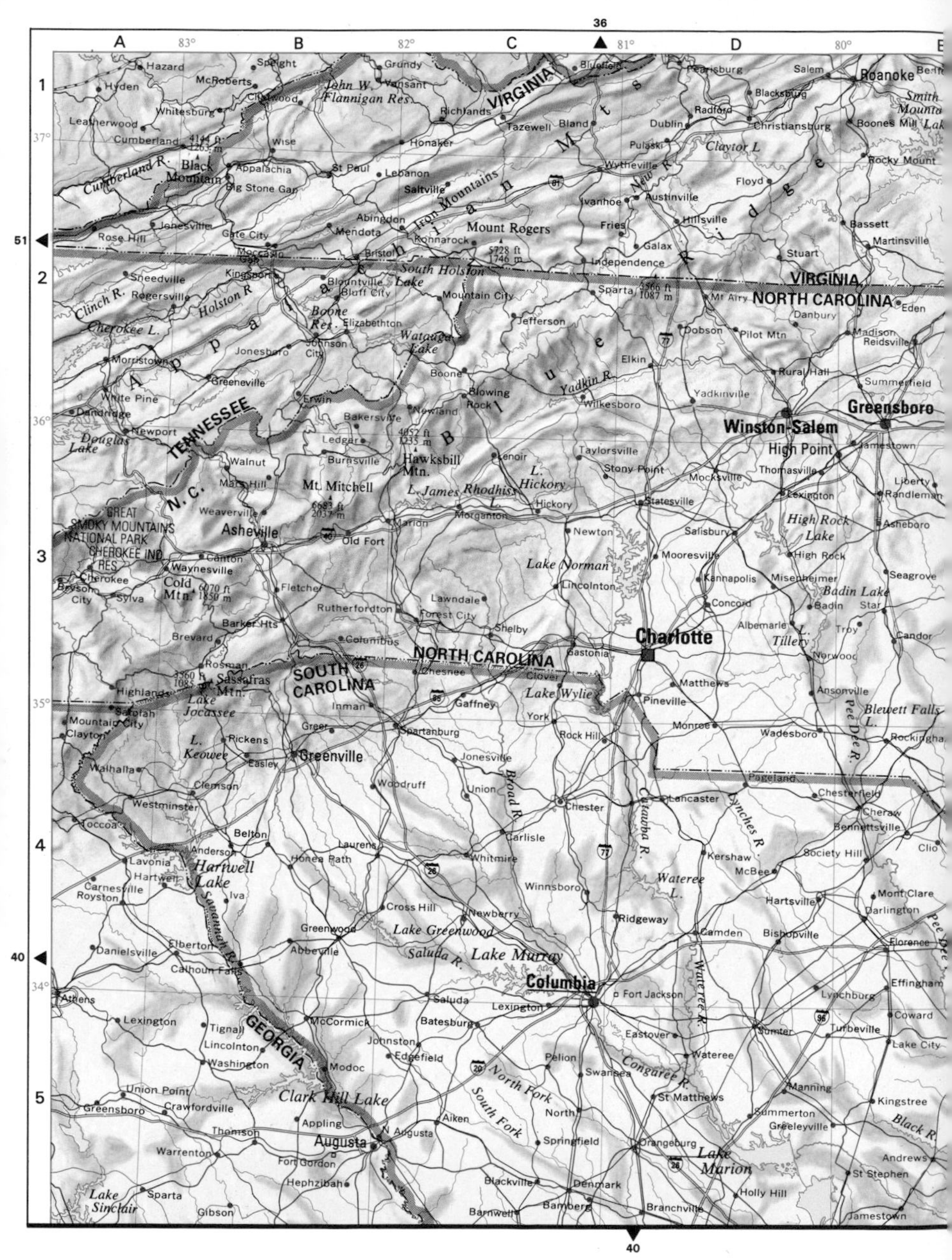

36
A
83°
B
82°
C
81°
D
80°
1
2
3
4
5
51
40
Hazard
Hyden
McRoberts
Speight
Grundy
John W. Flannigan Res.
Vansant
Whitesburg
Richlands
VIRGINIA
Tazewell
Bland
Bluefield
Pearisburg
Salem
Roanoke
Blacksburg
Radford
Christiansburg
Smith Mountain Lake
Boones Mill
Dublin
Pulaski
Claytor L
Leatherwood
Cumberland
Wise
Honaker
Cumberland R.
Black Mountain
4145 ft
1263 m
Appalachia
St Paul
Lebanon
Big Stone Gap
Saltville
Iron Mountains
Wytheville
New R.
Floyd
Rocky Mount
Ivanhoe
Austinville
Jonesville
Rose Hill
Abingdon
Mendota
Mount Rogers
Konnarock
Fries
Hillsville
Bassett
Martinsville
Gate City
Galax
Moccasin Gap
Bristol
5728 ft
1746 m
Independence
Stuart
Kingsport
Sneedville
South Holston Lake
Blountville
Bluff City
Rogersville
Clinch R.
Holston R
Mountain City
Sparta
5566 ft
1087 m
Mt Airy
NORTH CAROLINA
Eden
Danbury
Cherokee L.
Boone Res.
Elizabethton
Jefferson
Dobson
Pilot Mtn
Madison
Reidsville
Watauga Lake
Johnson City
Jonesboro
Morristown
Elkin
Boone
Rural Hall
Greeneville
Yadkin R.
Summerfield
Blowing Rock
Yadkinville
White Pine
Erwin
Wilkesboro
Dandridge
Newland
Winston-Salem
Greensboro
TENNESSEE
Bakersville
Newport
Douglas Lake
Ledger
4052 ft
1235 m
Jamestown
High Point
Burnsville
Hawksbill Mtn.
Lenoir
Taylorsville
Walnut
Stony Point
Thomasville
Liberty
Mars Hill
Mt. Mitchell
L. Hickory
Mocksville
Randleman
L. James
Rhodhiss L.
Lexington
N. C.
6683 ft
2037 m
Hickory
Statesville
Weaverville
GREAT SMOKY MOUNTAINS NATIONAL PARK
Morganton
High Rock Lake
Asheboro
Marion
Newton
Salisbury
Asheville
Old Fort
CHEROKEE IND. RES.
Canton
Mooresville
High Rock
Waynesville
Lake Norman
Cherokee
Kannapolis
Misenheimer
Seagrove
Bryson City
Sylva
Cold Mtn.
6070 ft
1850 m
Fletcher
Lincolnton
Badin Lake
Lawndale
Concord
Badin
Star
Rutherfordton
Forest City
Albemarle
Troy
Barker Hts
Shelby
L. Tillery
Brevard
Columbus
Charlotte
Candor
Rosman
NORTH CAROLINA
Gastonia
Norwood
3560 ft
1085 m
Sassafras Mtn.
SOUTH CAROLINA
Chesnee
Clover
Matthews
Highlands
Lake Wylie
Ansonville
Lake Jocassee
Inman
Gaffney
Pineville
Salem
Mountain City
York
Blewett Falls L.
Clayton
Greer
Spartanburg
Rock Hill
Monroe
Wadesboro
Rockingham
Rickens
L. Keowee
Greenville
Jonesville
Easley
Walhalla
Broad R.
Pee Dee R.
Pageland
Clemson
Woodruff
Union
Chesterfield
Westminster
Chester
Lancaster
Cheraw
Toccoa
Bennettsville
Belton
Carlisle
Catawba R.
Lynches R.
Anderson
Laurens
Society Hill
Clio
Lavonia
Honea Path
Whitmire
Kershaw
Hartwell
Hartwell Lake
McBee
Carnesville
Royston
Iva
Wateree L.
Winnsboro
Mont Clare
Hartsville
Darlington
Cross Hill
Newberry
Ridgeway
Greenwood
Lake Greenwood
Camden
Bishopville
Elberton
Abbeville
Danielsville
Saluda R.
Lake Murray
Florence
Calhoun Falls
Savannah R.
Wateree R.
Columbia
Athens
Fort Jackson
Effingham
Saluda
Lexington
Lynchburg
Lexington
Tignall
McCormick
Batesburg
Coward
GEORGIA
Eastover
Sumter
Turbeville
Lincolnton
Johnston
Edgefield
Lake City
Washington
Modoc
Pelion
Swansea
Wateree
Congaree R.
North Fork
Union Point
Manning
Greensboro
Crawfordville
Clark Hill Lake
South Fork
St Matthews
Kingstree
North
Summerton
Appling
Aiken
Greeleyville
Black R.
Thomson
N Augusta
Augusta
Springfield
Orangeburg
Warrenton
Lake Marion
Andrews
Fort Gordon
St Stephen
Hephzibah
Blackville
Denmark
Holly Hill
Lake Sinclair
Sparta
Gibson
Barnwell
Bamberg
Branchville
Jamestown

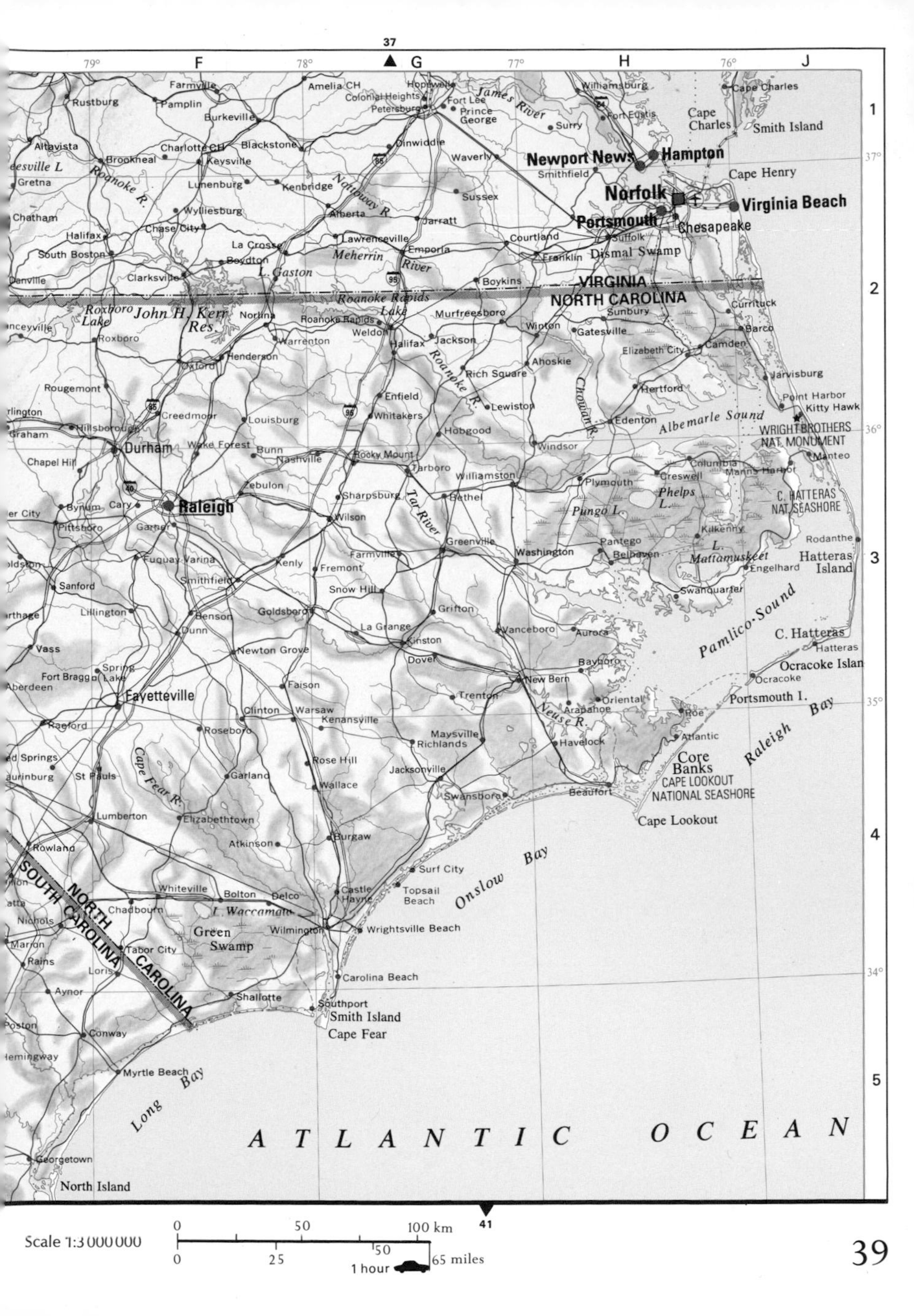

79° F 78° G 77° H 76° J

| | |
|1
|2
|3
|4
|5

Rustburg
Farmville
Pamplin
Amelia CH
Hopewell
Williamsburg
Cape Charles
Altavista
Burkeville
Colonial Heights
Fort Lee
Cape Charles
Smith Island
esville L
Brookheal
Charlotte C.H.
Blackstone
Petersburg
Prince
George
Surry
Fort Eustis
Gretna
Keysville
Dinwiddie
Waverly
Smithfield
Newport News Hampton
Chatham
Lunenburg
Wyliesburg
Alberta
Sussex
Norfolk
Cape Henry
Halifax
Chase City
La Crosse
Jarratt
Courtland
Portsmouth
Virginia Beach
South Boston
Boydton
Lawrenceville
Emporia
Franklin
Suffolk
Chesapeake
Danville
Clarksville
L. Gaston
Meherrin
River
Boykins
Dismal Swamp
Roxboro
John H. Kerr
Norlina
Roanoke Rapids
Murfreesboro
Winton
Sunbury
VIRGINIA
nceville
Lake
Res.
Weldon
Gatesville
Currituck
NORTH CAROLINA
Roxboro
Warrenton
Halifax
Jackson
Ahoskie
Elizabeth City
Camden
Barco
rlington
Oxford
Henderson
Rich Square
Hertford
Jarvisburg
Graham
Creedmoor
Louisburg
Enfield
Lewiston
Edenton
Point Harbor
Kitty Hawk
Chapel Hill
Wake Forest
Whitakers
Hobgood
Albemarle Sound
WRIGHT BROTHERS
NAT MONUMENT
Durham
Bunn
Nashville
Rocky Mount
Tarboro
Williamston
Plymouth
Columbia
Manns Harbor
Manteo
er City
Bynum
Cary
Zebulon
Sharpsburg
Bethel
Creswell
Phelps L.
C. HATTERAS
NAT.SEASHORE
Pittsboro
Raleigh
Garner
Wilson
Greenville
Washington
Pungo L.
Kilkenny
Rodanthe
oldston
Fuquay-Varina
Kenly
Farmville
Pantego
Belhaven
L.
Mattamuskeet
Hatteras
Island
Sanford
Smithfield
Fremont
Snow Hill
Grifton
Vanceboro
Aurora
Engelhard
arthage
Lillington
Benson
Goldsboro
Kinston
New Bern
Bayboro
Swanquarter
Pamlico Sound
C. Hatteras
Vass
Dunn
Newton Grove
La Grange
Dover
Trenton
Oriental
Arapahoe
Hatteras
Fort Bragg
Spring
Faison
Clinton
Warsaw
Kenansville
New Bern
Havelock
Roe
Atlantic
Portsmouth I.
Ocracoke Island
Aberdeen
Fayetteville
Roseboro
Maysville
Richlands
Arapahoe
Raleigh Bay
d Springs
Raeford
St Pauls
Garland
Rose Hill
Wallace
Jacksonville
Beaufort
Core
Banks
CAPE LOOKOUT
NATIONAL SEASHORE
Rowland
Lumberton
Elizabethtown
Atkinson
Burgaw
Swansboro
Cape Lookout
Whiteville
Bolton
Delco
Castle
Hayne
Surf City
Topsail
Beach
Onslow Bay
atta
NORTH
Chadbourn
Green
Swamp
L. Waccamaw
Wilmington
Wrightsville Beach
Nichols
SOUTH
CAROLINA
Tabor City
Marion
CAROLINA
Rains
Shallotte
Carolina Beach
Loris
Aynor
Conway
Southport
Smith Island
Cape Fear
ston
emingway
Myrtle Beach
Long Bay
Georgetown
North Island

A T L A N T I C   O C E A N

Scale 1:3 000 000

0   50   100 km
0   25   50
1 hour   65 miles

39

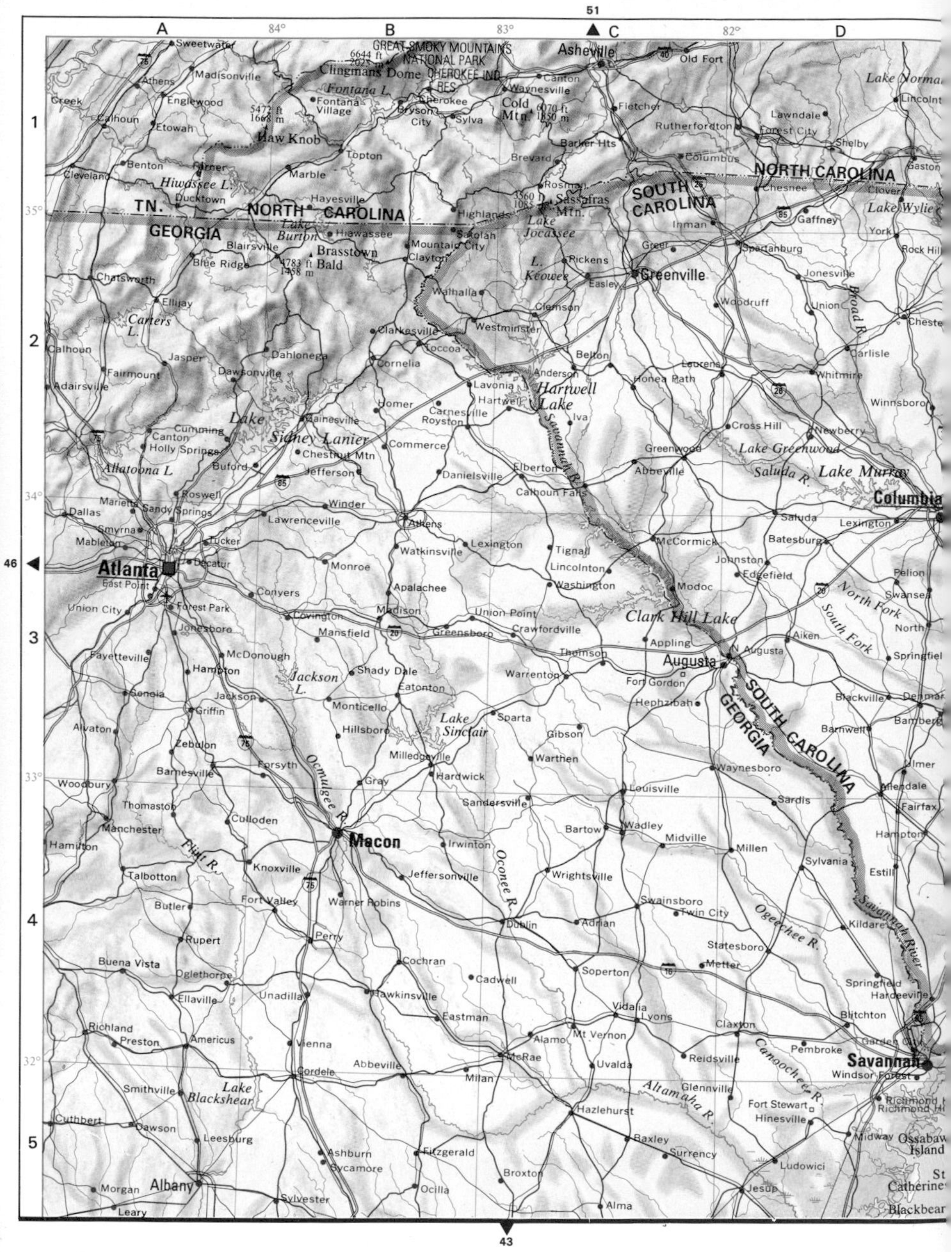

51
A
B
C
D
84°
83°
82°
35°
34°
33°
32°
1
2
3
4
5
46
43
GREAT SMOKY MOUNTAINS NATIONAL PARK
Clingmans Dome
6644 ft
2025 m
CHEROKEE IND. RES.
Fontana L.
Sweetwater
Madisonville
Athens
Englewood
Calhoun
Etowah
Fontana Village
Bryson City
Cherokee
Sylva
Waynesville
Canton
Cold Mtn.
6070 ft
1850 m
5472 ft
1668 m
Haw Knob
Asheville
Old Fort
Fletcher
Lake Norman
Lincolnton
Lawndale
Rutherfordton
Forest City
Shelby
Barker Hts
Columbus
Gastonia
Brevard
Topton
Marble
Benton
Cleveland
Turner
Hiwassee L.
Ducktown
Hayesville
Highlands
Rosman
3560 ft
1085 m
Sassafras Mtn.
SOUTH CAROLINA
NORTH CAROLINA
Chesnee
Clover
Lake Wylie
Gaffney
York
Rock Hill
TN.
GEORGIA
Lake Burton
Hiawassee
Satolah
Lake Jocassee
Inman
Spartanburg
Blairsville
Brasstown Bald
4783 ft
1458 m
Mountain City
Clayton
Blue Ridge
L. Keowee
Pickens
Greer
Greenville
Easley
Chatsworth
Walhalla
Ellijay
Clemson
Woodruff
Union
Jonesville
Broad R.
Chester
Carters L.
Westminster
Clarkesville
Toccoa
Calhoun
Dahlonega
Jasper
Cornelia
Belton
Laurens
Carlisle
Fairmount
Dawsonville
Anderson
Hartwell Lake
Honea Path
Whitmire
Adairsville
Lavonia
Hartwell
Homer
Carnesville
Royston
Iva
Winnsboro
Gainesville
Lake Sidney Lanier
Cross Hill
Newberry
Cumming
Canton
Holly Springs
Commerce
Greenwood
Lake Greenwood
Chestnut Mtn
Buford
Allatoona L.
Jefferson
Danielsville
Elberton
Abbeville
Saluda R.
Lake Murray
Calhoun Falls
Roswell
Marietta
Sandy Springs
Winder
Columbia
Dallas
Lawrenceville
Athens
Saluda
Lexington
Smyrna
Tucker
Mableton
Watkinsville
Lexington
Tignall
McCormick
Batesburg
Atlanta
Decatur
East Point
Monroe
Lincolnton
Johnston
Edgefield
Pelion
Washington
Modoc
North Fork
Swansea
Apalachee
Conyers
Union City
Forest Park
Madison
Union Point
Clark Hill Lake
South Fork
Covington
Jonesboro
Mansfield
Greensboro
Crawfordville
Aiken
North
Appling
N. Augusta
Augusta
Thomson
Springfield
McDonough
Fayetteville
Hampton
Shady Dale
Jackson L.
Eatonton
Warrenton
Fort Gordon
Senoia
Jackson
Hephzibah
Blackville
Denmark
Monticello
Griffin
Lake Sinclair
Sparta
Bamberg
Alvaton
Hillsboro
Gibson
Barnwell
Zebulon
Milledgeville
Warthen
Forsyth
Ocmulgee R.
Barnesville
Hardwick
Waynesboro
Ulmer
Woodbury
Gray
Louisville
Allendale
Sandersville
Sardis
Thomaston
Fairfax
Culloden
Wadley
Manchester
Bartow
Hampton
Macon
Midville
Hamilton
Irwinton
Millen
Flint R.
Oconee R.
Sylvania
Knoxville
Estill
Talbotton
Jeffersonville
Wrightsville
Warner Robins
Savannah River
Fort Valley
Butler
Swainsboro
Twin City
Ogeechee R.
Dublin
Adrian
Kildare
Rupert
Perry
Statesboro
Cochran
Buena Vista
Metter
Soperton
Cadwell
Springfield
Oglethorpe
Hardeeville
Unadilla
Hawkinsville
Ellaville
Eastman
Vidalia
Lyons
Blitchton
Richland
Claxton
Americus
Mt Vernon
Alamo
Preston
Vienna
Pembroke
Garden City
McRae
Savannah
Reidsville
Uvalda
Abbeville
Cordele
Milan
Windsor Forest
Canoochee R.
Smithville
Lake Blackshear
Glennville
Altamaha R.
Fort Stewart
Richmond Hill
Hazlehurst
Hinesville
Cuthbert
Dawson
Leesburg
Baxley
Midway
Ossabaw Island
Surrency
Ashburn
Fitzgerald
Sycamore
Ludowici
St. Catherines
Broxton
Morgan
Albany
Ocilla
Jesup
Sylvester
Alma
Leary
Blackbeard

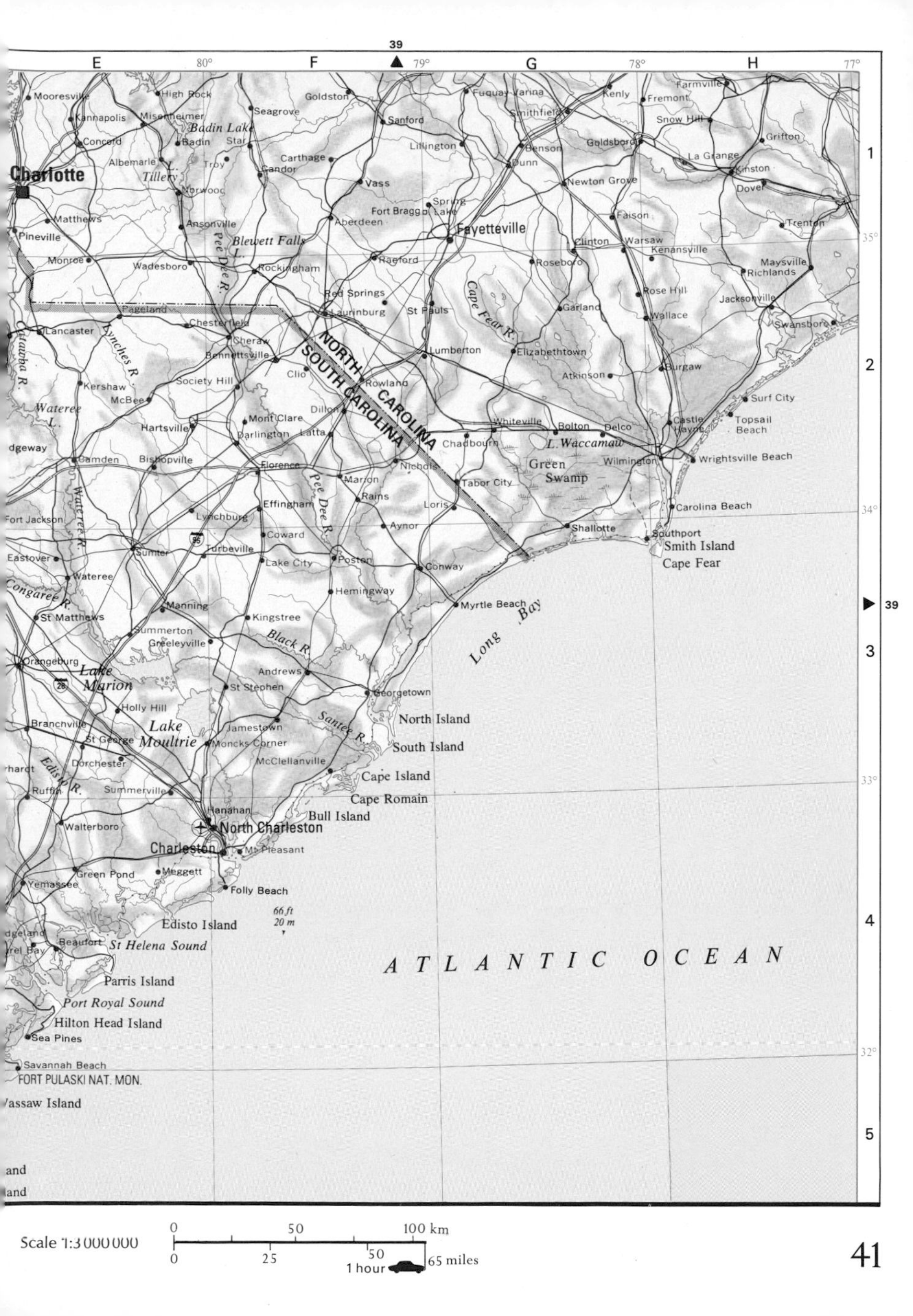

E 80° F 79° G 78° H 77°

Mooresville
Kannapolis
High Rock
Misenheimer
Concord
Badin Lake
Albemarle
Badin
Tillery
Star
Charlotte
Norwood
Matthews
Pineville
Ansonville
Monroe
Wadesboro
Blewett Falls
Lancaster
Pageland
Chesterfield
Society Hill
Kershaw
McBee
Hartsville
Wateree
L.
Camden
Bishopville
dgeway
Ridgeway
Lynchburg
Fort Jackson
Sumter
Eastover
Turbeville
Wateree
Manning
St Matthews
Summerton
Greeleyville
Kingstree
Orangeburg
Lake
Marion
Branchville
Holly Hill
Lake
Moultrie
St George
Jamestown
Dorchester
Moncks Corner
Summerville
McClellanville
Ruffin
North Charleston
Hanahan
Walterboro
Charleston
Mt Pleasant
Green Pond
Meggett
Yemassee
Folly Beach
Edisto Island
66 ft
20 m
St Helena Sound
Beaufort
Parris Island
Port Royal Sound
Hilton Head Island
Sea Pines
Savannah Beach
FORT PULASKI NAT. MON.
Wassaw Island

Goldston
Seagrove
Carthage
Candor
Sanford
Lillington
Vass
Fort Bragg
Aberdeen
Fayetteville
Rockingham
Raeford
Red Springs
Laurinburg
St Pauls
Sheraw
Bennettsville
Clio
Dillon
Rowland
Mont Clare
Latta
Darlington
Florence
Marion
Nichols
Effingham
Rains
Lake City
Poston
Coward
Hemingway
Andrews
St Stephen
Georgetown
North Island
South Island
Cape Island
Cape Romain
Bull Island

NORTH CAROLINA
SOUTH CAROLINA

Pee Dee R.
Pee Dee R.

Fuquay-Varina
Smithfield
Benson
Dunn
Spring Lake
Clinton
Roseboro
Lumberton
Elizabethtown
Atkinson
Whiteville
Bolton
Chadbourn
Tabor City
Loris
Aynor
Conway
Myrtle Beach

Cape Fear R.
Green Swamp
L. Waccamaw
Delco
Wilmington
Castle Hayne
Carolina Beach
Shallotte
Southport
Smith Island
Cape Fear

Kenly
Fremont
Farmville
Snow Hill
Goldsboro
Newton Grove
Faison
Warsaw
Kenansville
Rose Hill
Garland
Wallace
Jacksonville

Grifton
La Grange
Kinston
Dover
Trenton
Maysville
Richlands
Swansboro
Surf City
Topsail Beach
Wrightsville Beach

Long Bay

A T L A N T I C   O C E A N

1
35°
2
34°
3
33°
4
32°
5

Catawba R.
Lynches R.
Wateree R.
Congaree R.
Edisto R.
Santee R.
Black R.

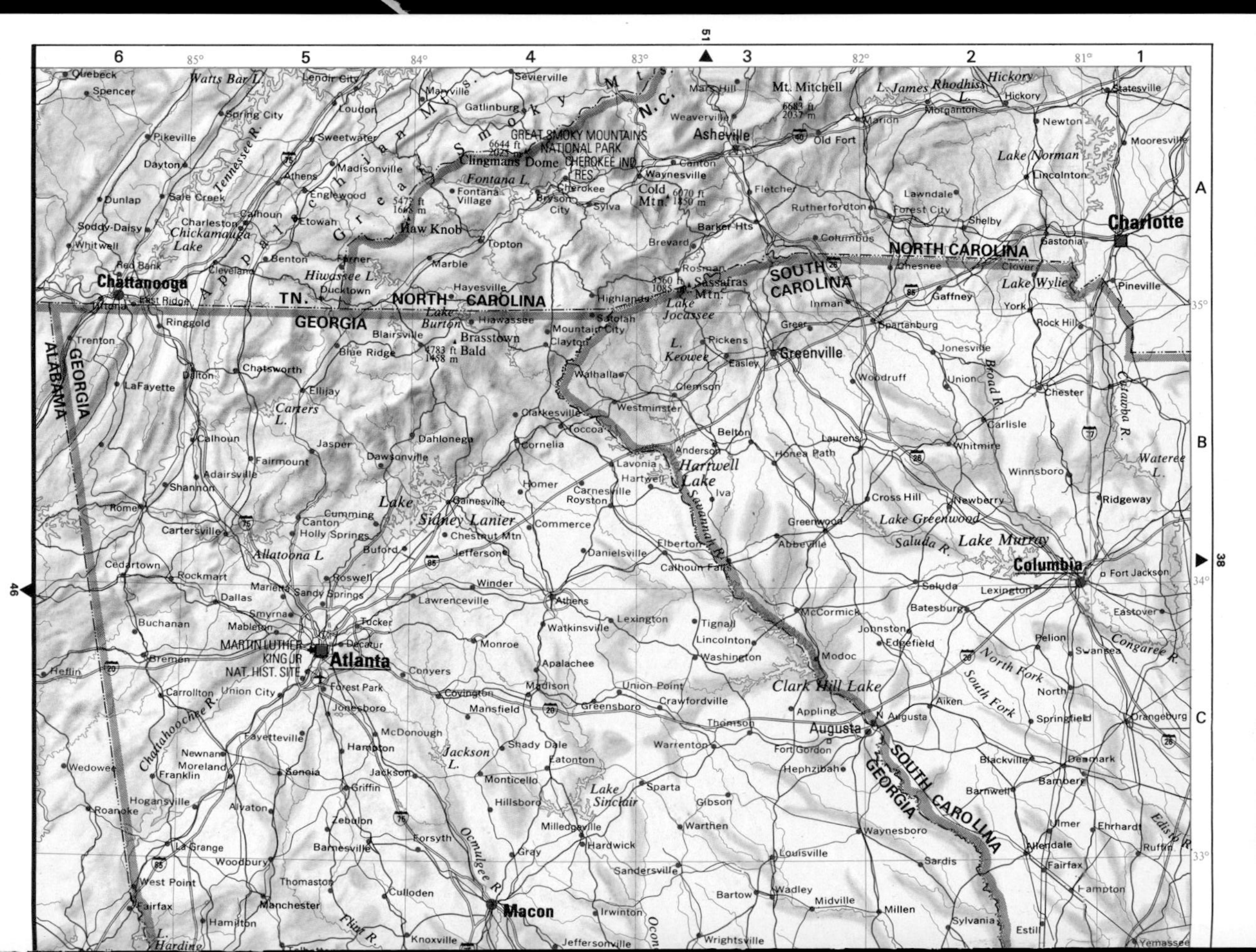

1
2
3
4
5
6
A
B
C
51
38
46
35°
34°
33°
81°
82°
83°
84°
85°
Charlotte
Columbia
Augusta
Macon
Atlanta
Greenville
Asheville
Chattanooga
Spartanburg
Athens
NORTH CAROLINA
SOUTH CAROLINA
GEORGIA
ALABAMA
TN.
N.C.
Lake Murray
Lake Greenwood
Lake Wylie
Lake Norman
Clark Hill Lake
Hartwell Lake
Lake Sidney Lanier
Allatoona L.
Lake Sinclair
Jackson L.
Carters L.
Chickamauga Lake
Watts Bar L.
Fontana L.
L. Keowee
Lake Jocassee
Hiwassee L.
Lake Burton
Savannah R.
Saluda R.
Broad R.
Catawba R.
Congaree R.
Ocmulgee R.
Chattahoochee R.
Tennessee R.
North Fork
South Fork
Flint R.
Edisto R.
Wateree L.
GREAT SMOKY MOUNTAINS NATIONAL PARK
CHEROKEE IND. RES.
Clingmans Dome
Mt. Mitchell
Sassafras Mtn.
Cold Mtn.
Brasstown Bald
Haw Knob
MARTIN LUTHER KING JR. NAT. HIST. SITE

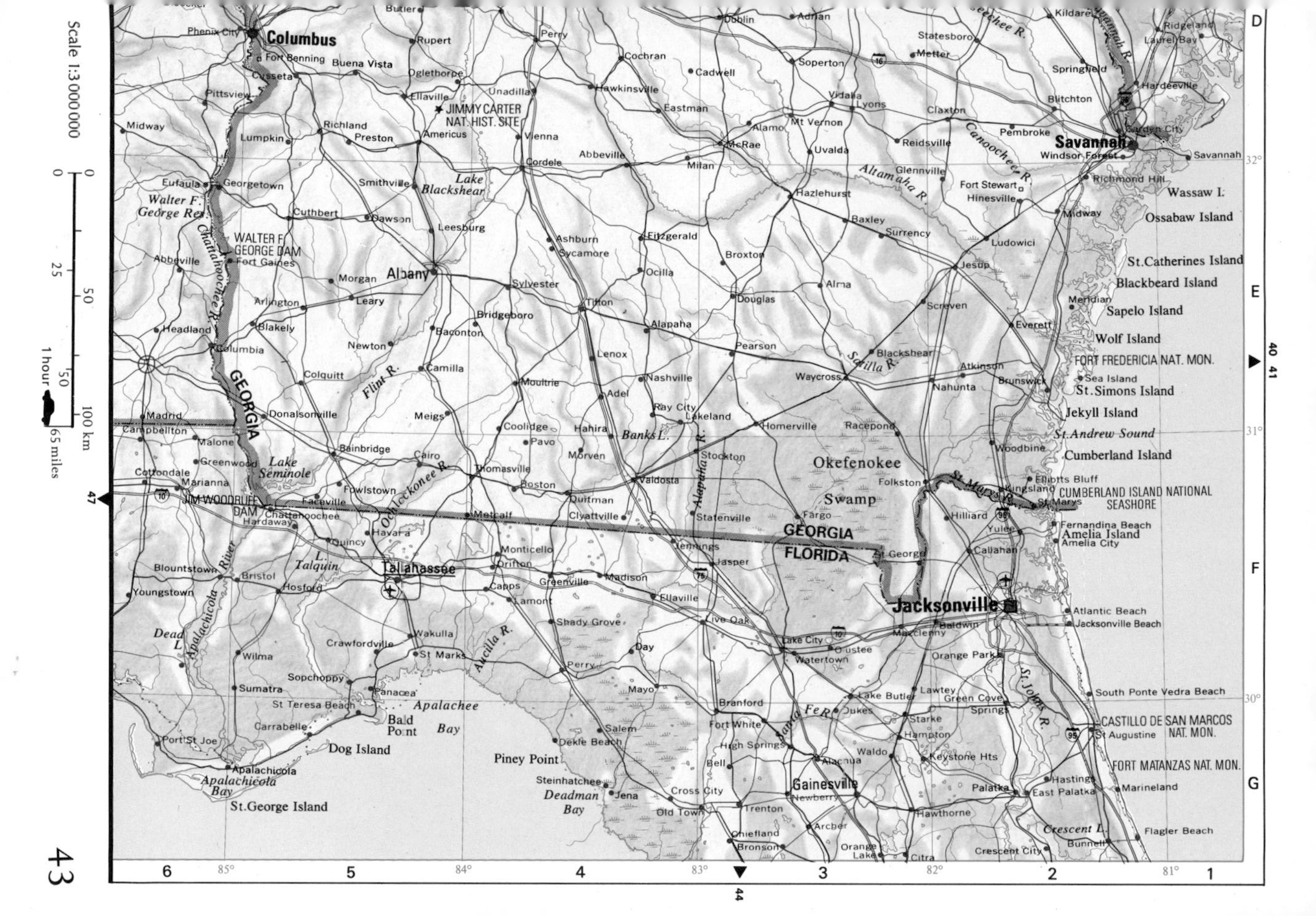

Scale 1:3 000 000

0   50   100 km
0   25   50   65 miles
1 hour

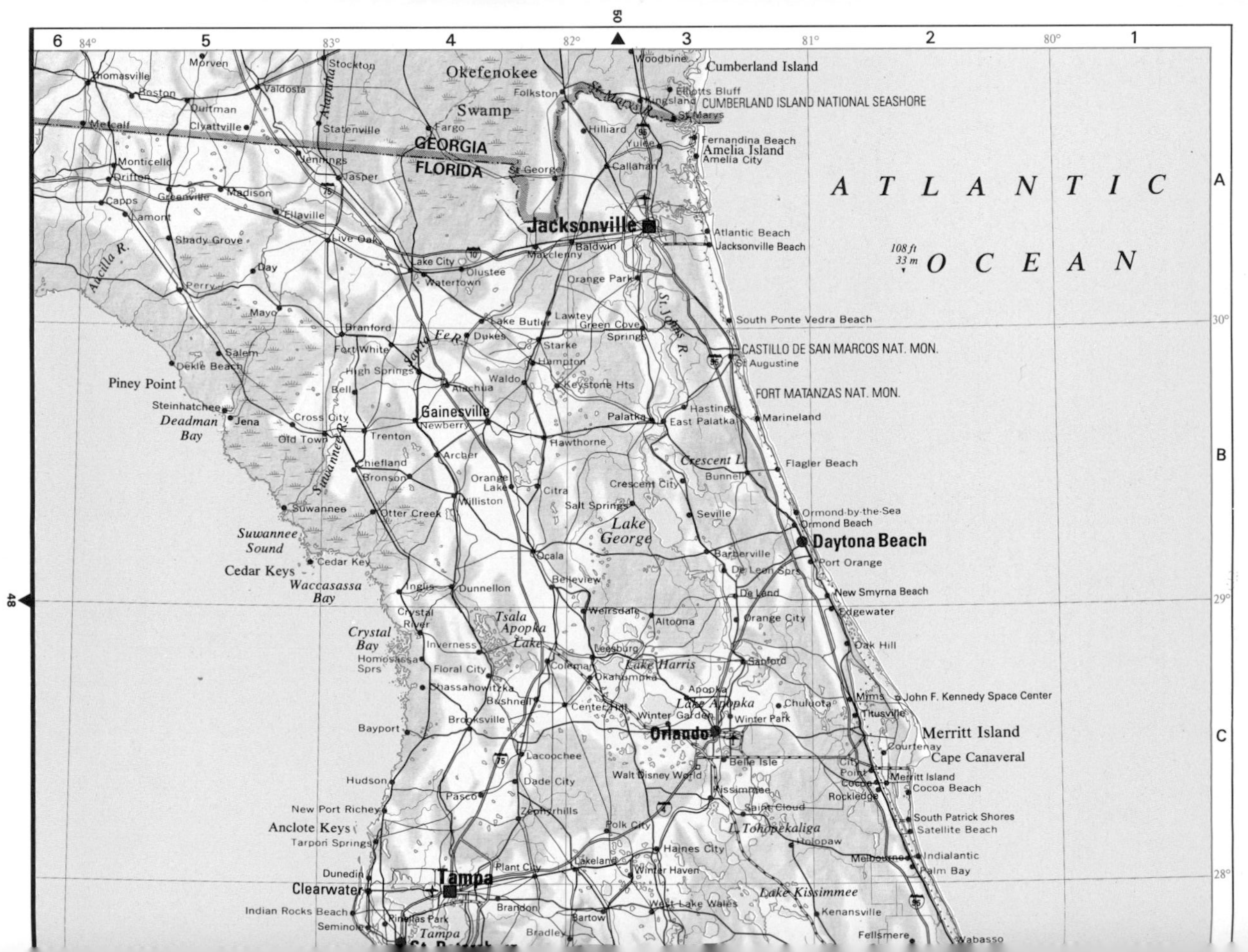

ATLANTIC OCEAN
GEORGIA
FLORIDA
Jacksonville
Daytona Beach
Orlando
Tampa
Gainesville
Clearwater
Merritt Island
Cape Canaveral
Okefenokee Swamp
Cumberland Island
CUMBERLAND ISLAND NATIONAL SEASHORE
CASTILLO DE SAN MARCOS NAT. MON.
FORT MATANZAS NAT. MON.
John F. Kennedy Space Center
Lake George
Lake Harris
Lake Apopka
Tsala Apopka Lake
Crescent L.
L. Tohopekaliga
Lake Kissimmee
St. Johns R.
Suwannee R.
Aucilla R.
Crystal Bay
Waccasassa Bay
Deadman Bay
Suwannee Sound
Cedar Keys
Anclote Keys
Piney Point
108 ft
33 m

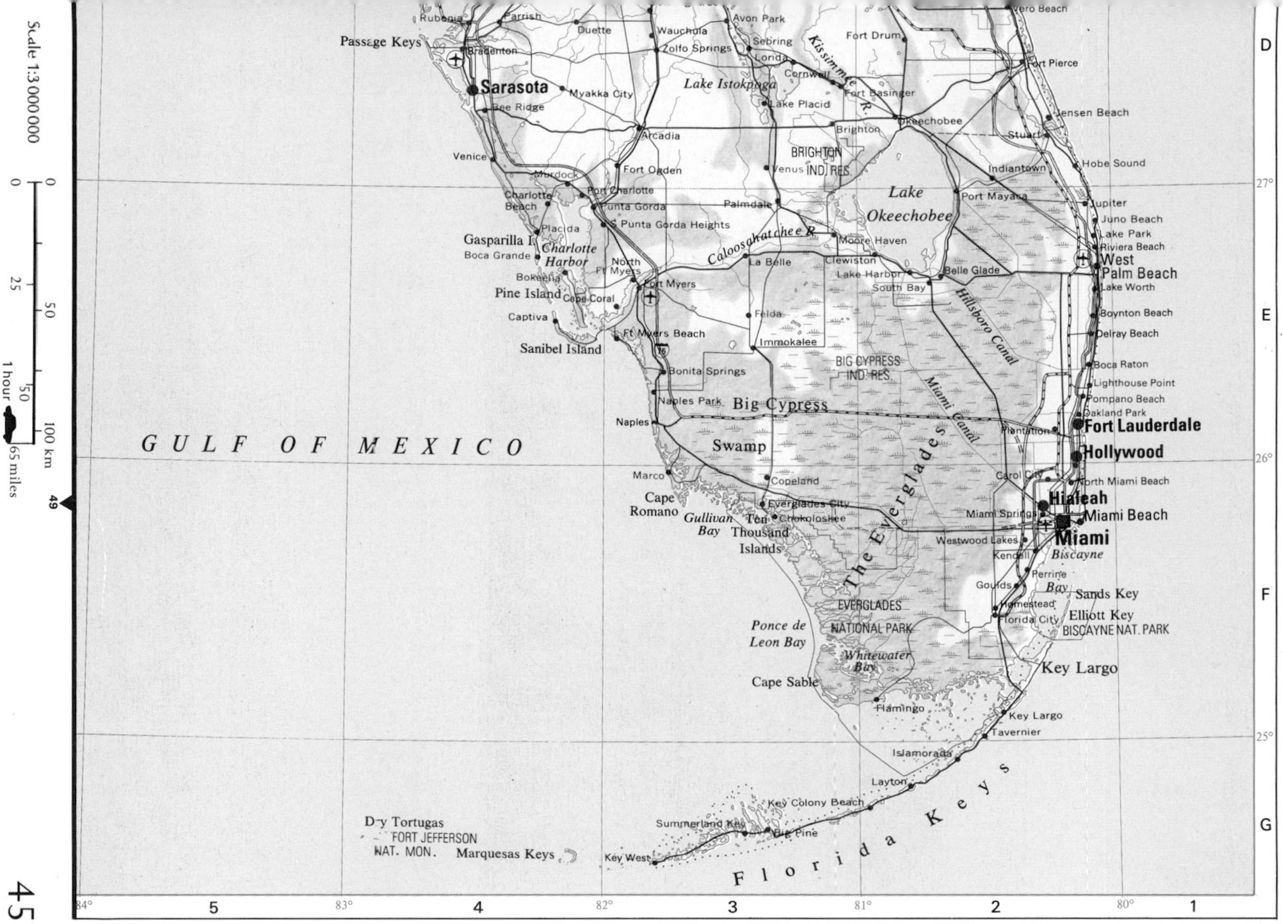

D   27°   E   26°   F   25°   G

1

2

3

4

5

Fort Lauderdale
Hollywood
Hialeah
Miami Beach
Miami

Vero Beach
Fort Pierce
Jensen Beach
Hobe Sound
Jupiter
Juno Beach
Lake Park
Riviera Beach
West
Palm Beach
Lake Worth
Boynton Beach
Delray Beach
Boca Raton
Lighthouse Point
Pompano Beach
Oakland Park
North Miami Beach
North Miami
Biscayne
Key Biscayne
Sands Key
Elliott Key
BISCAYNE NAT. PARK
Florida City
Homestead
Perrine
Kendall
Goulds
Key Largo
Key Largo
Tavernier
Islamorada
Layton
Long Key
Key Colony Beach
Marathon
Summerland Key
Big Pine Key
Key West

Stuart
Indiantown
Fort Mayaca
Belle Glade
South Bay
Lake Harbor
Clewiston
Moore Haven
Okeechobee
BRIGHTON
Venus IND. RES.
Immokalee
Felda
Labelle
SEMINOLE IND. RES.
Ochopee
Copeland
Everglades
Ochopee
Chokoloskee
Flamingo
Cape Sable
Whitewater Bay
Ponce de Leon Bay

Lake Okeechobee

Fort Drum
Okeechobee
Kissimmee R.
Brighton
Lake Placid
Lorida
Venus
Cornwell
Palmdale
Ortona
Caloosahatchee R.

Hillsboro Canal

Miami Canal

The Everglades

EVERGLADES NATIONAL PARK

BIG CYPRESS IND. RES.

Big Cypress Swamp

Naples Park
Bonita Springs
North Naples
Naples
Marco
Cape Romano
Ten Thousand Islands
Gullivan Bay

Fort Myers
Ft. Myers Beach

Sarasota

Avon Park
Sebring
Lake Istokpoga
Wauchula
Zolfo Springs
Arcadia
Fort Ogden
Nocatee
Charlotte Harbor
Punta Gorda
Punta Gorda Heights
Port Charlotte
Gasparilla R.
Boca Grande
Placida
Bonefish
Captiva
Pine Island
Cape Coral
Sanibel Island
Venice
Englewood
Charlotte Beach
Englewood
Myakka City
Oak Ridge
Lake Ridge
Duette
Parrish
Bradenton
Rubonia
Passage Keys

GULF OF MEXICO

Florida Keys

Dry Tortugas
FORT JEFFERSON NAT. MON.
Marquesas Keys

80°
81°
82°
83°
84°

49

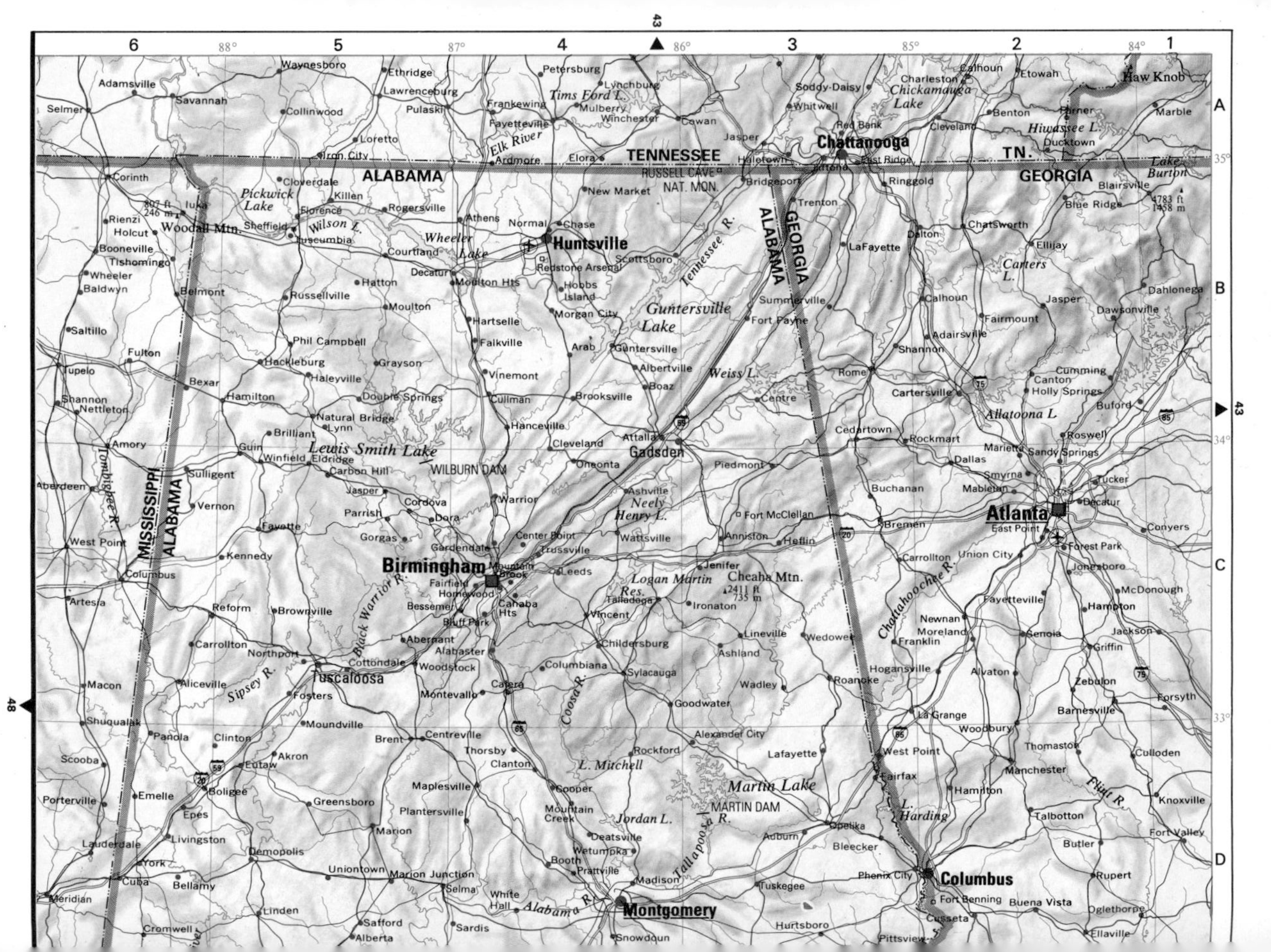
43
A
B
C
D
1
2
3
4
5
6
43
48
84°
85°
86°
87°
88°
35°
34°
33°
TENNESSEE
TN.
GEORGIA
ALABAMA
MISSISSIPPI
Atlanta
Chattanooga
Huntsville
Birmingham
Gadsden
Tuscaloosa
Montgomery
Columbus
Marietta
Rome
Dalton
Decatur
Florence
Tuscumbia
Sheffield
Cullman
Anniston
Talladega
Auburn
Opelika
Selma
Meridian
Tupelo
Corinth
Guntersville Lake
Weiss L.
Martin Lake
Wheeler Lake
Pickwick Lake
Wilson L.
Lewis Smith Lake
Allatoona L.
Carters L.
Chickamauga Lake
Tims Ford L.
Hiwassee L.
Logan Martin Res.
Neely Henry L.
Jordan L.
L. Mitchell
L. Harding
Tennessee R.
Coosa R.
Tallapoosa R.
Chattahoochee R.
Black Warrior R.
Sipsey R.
Tombigbee R.
Alabama R.
Flint R.
Elk River
Cheaha Mtn. 2411 ft 735 m
Woodall Mtn. 807 ft 246 m
Haw Knob
RUSSELL CAVE NAT. MON.
WILBURN DAM
MARTIN DAM

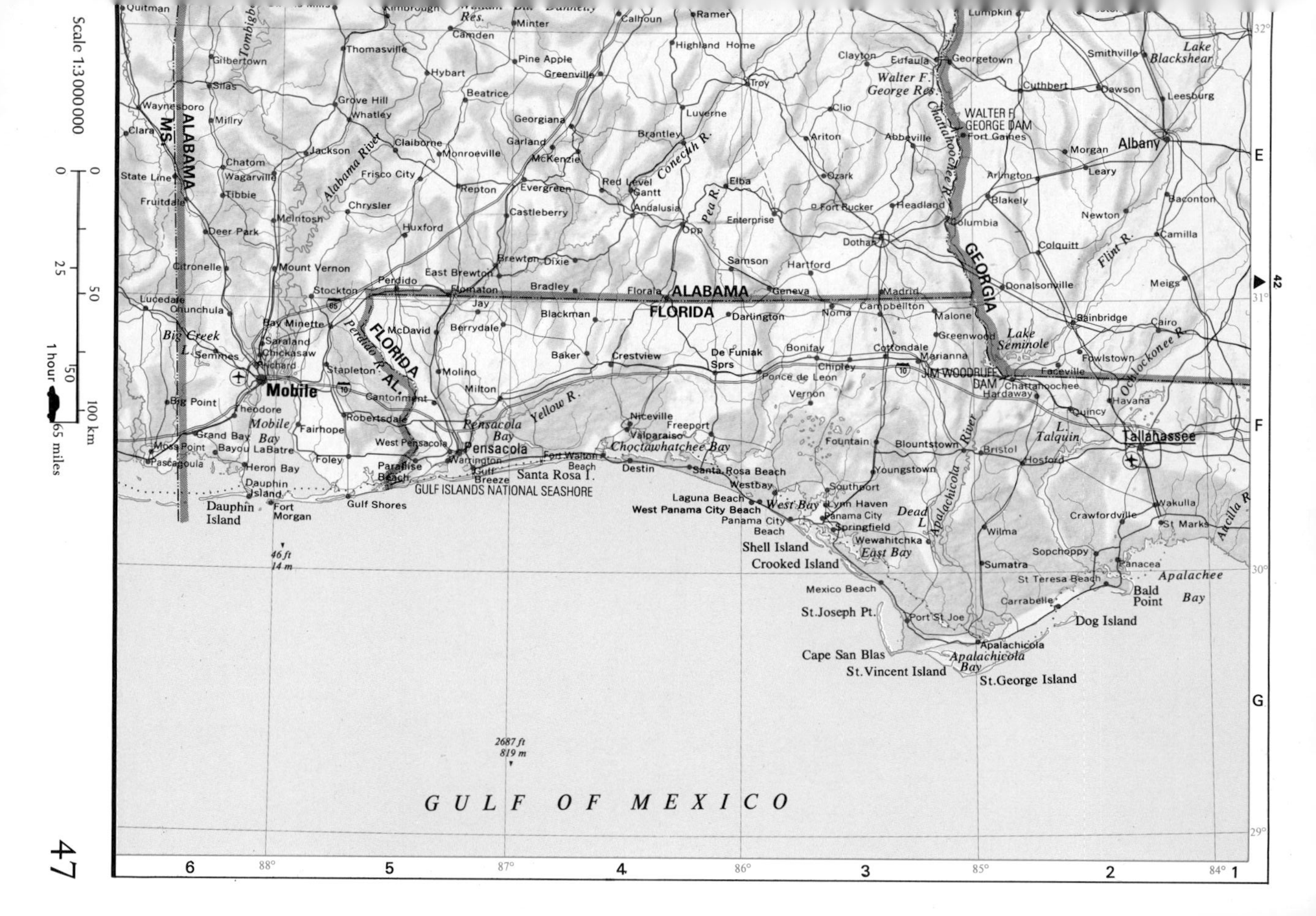

GULF OF MEXICO

GEORGIA

ALABAMA

FLORIDA

FLORIDA

AL

ALABAMA

MS

Mobile

Tallahassee

Albany

Pensacola

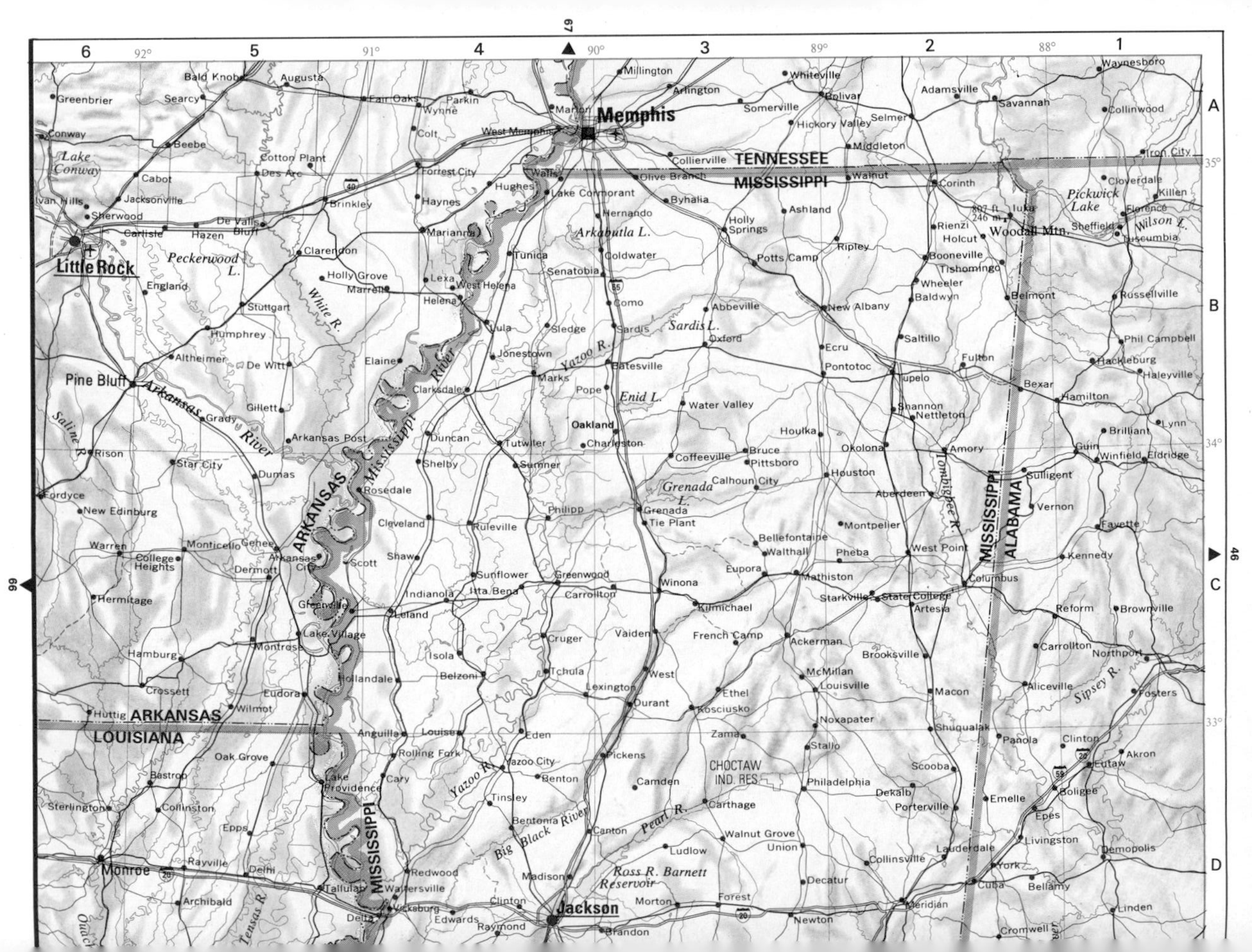

A
B
C
D
1
2
3
4
5
6
46
66
67
35°
34°
33°
88°
89°
90°
91°
92°
TENNESSEE
MISSISSIPPI
ALABAMA
ARKANSAS
LOUISIANA
Memphis
Jackson
Little Rock
Pine Bluff
Monroe
Corinth
Tupelo
Columbus
Starkville
State College
Oxford
Greenwood
Greenville
Vicksburg
Meridian
Clarksdale
Grenada
Holly Springs
Yazoo City
Canton
Philadelphia
Kosciusko
Winona
Cleveland
Indianola
Helena
West Helena
Demopolis
Sheffield
Tuscumbia
Florence
Mississippi River
Arkansas River
White R.
Yazoo R.
Tombigbee R.
Pearl R.
Big Black River
Sipsey R.
Tensas R.
Saline R.
Sardis L.
Enid L.
Grenada L.
Arkabutla L.
Pickwick Lake
Wilson L.
Lake Conway
Peckerwood L.
Ross R. Barnett Reservoir
Woodall Mtn.
807 ft 246 m
CHOCTAW IND. RES.

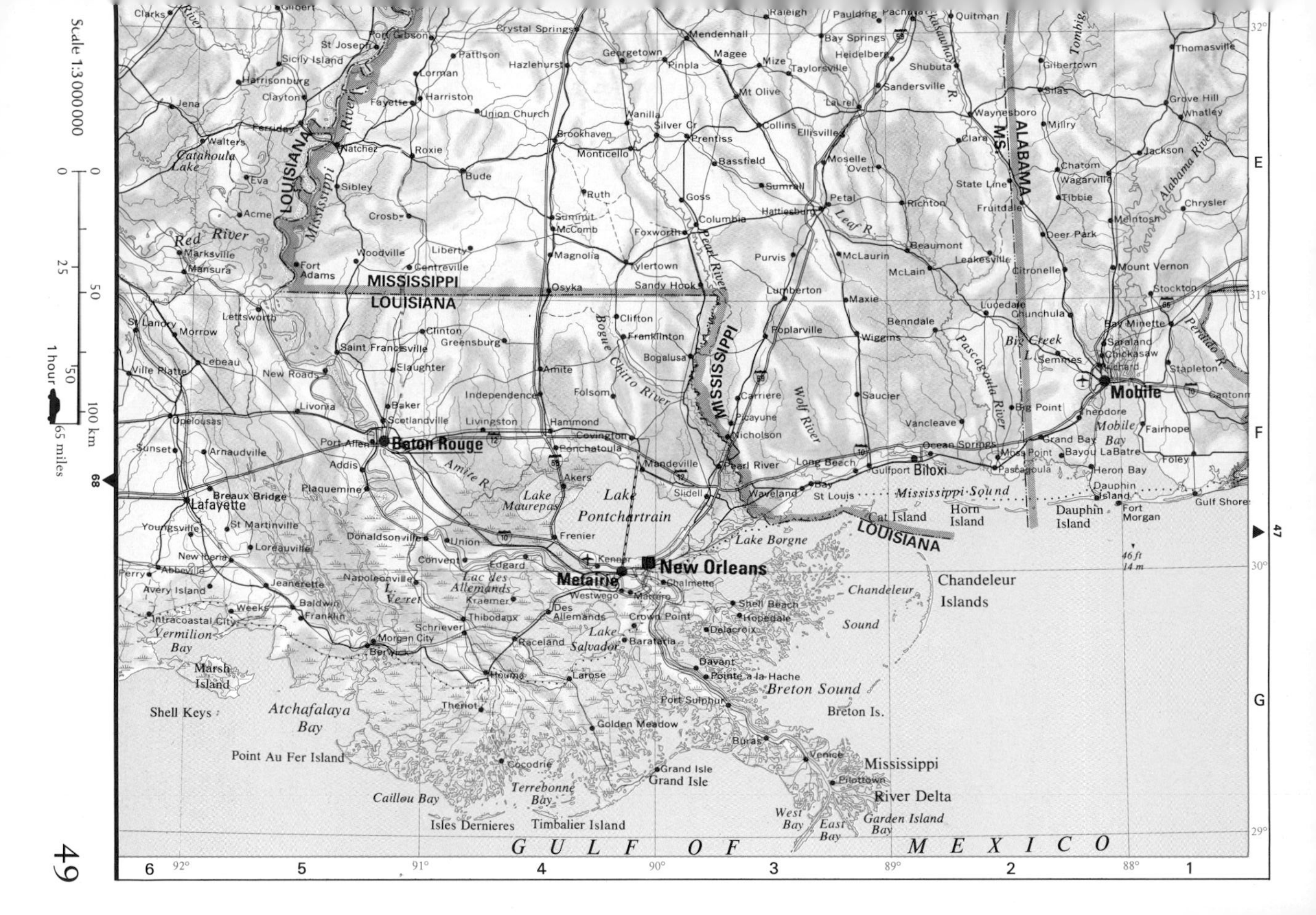

47
68
ALABAMA
MS.
MISSISSIPPI
LOUISIANA
GULF OF MEXICO
Mobile
Mobile Bay
Biloxi
Gulfport
Pascagoula
New Orleans
Metairie
Baton Rouge
Lafayette
Hattiesburg
Lake Pontchartrain
Lake Maurepas
Lake Borgne
Mississippi Sound
Chandeleur Sound
Chandeleur Islands
Breton Sound
Breton Is.
Mississippi River Delta
Dauphin Island
Horn Island
Cat Island
Grand Isle
Timbalier Island
Isles Dernieres
Atchafalaya Bay
Point Au Fer Island
Marsh Island
Vermilion Bay
Shell Keys
Terrebonne Bay
Caillou Bay
Lake Salvador
Pearl River
Pascagoula River
Wolf River
Leaf R.
Bogue Chitto River
Alabama River
Red River
Mississippi River
Catahoula Lake
Amite R.
Scale 1:3 000 000
0
50
100 km
0
25
50
65 miles
1 hour

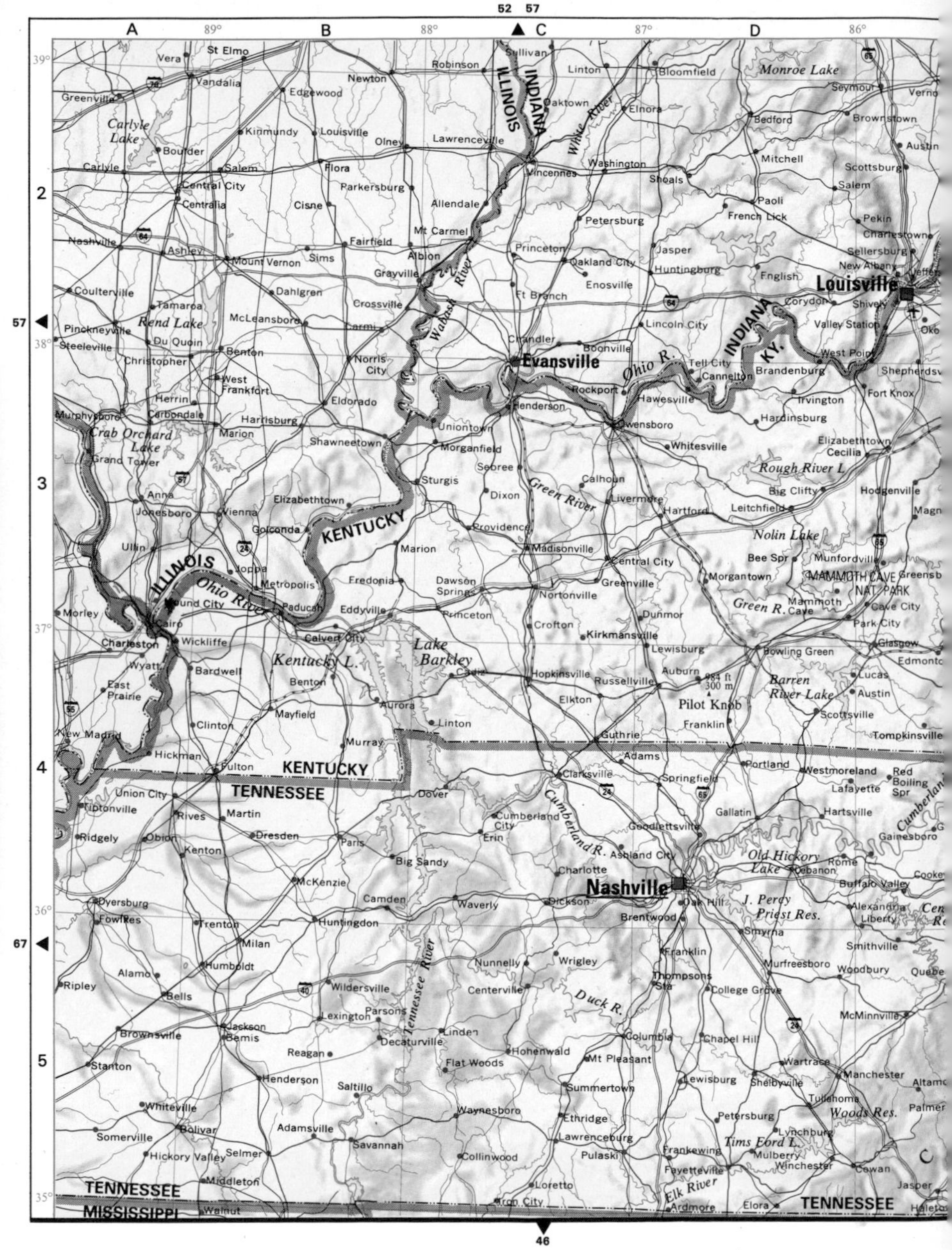
52 57
A
B
C
D
89°
88°
87°
86°
39°
38°
37°
36°
35°
2
3
4
5
57
67
46
ILLINOIS
INDIANA
KENTUCKY
TENNESSEE
MISSISSIPPI
INDIANA KY.
St Elmo
Vera
Vandalia
Greenville
Carlyle Lake
Boulder
Carlyle
Kinmundy
Louisville
Edgewood
Newton
Robinson
Sullivan
Linton
Bloomfield
Monroe Lake
Seymour
Bedford
Brownstown
Oaktown
Elnora
White River
Olney
Lawrenceville
Salem
Flora
Vincennes
Washington
Shoals
Mitchell
Scottsburg
Austin
Central City
Centralia
Parkersburg
Cisne
Allendale
Paoli
French Lick
Petersburg
Pekin
Charlestown
Nashville
Ashley
Mount Vernon
Sims
Fairfield
Mt Carmel
Albion
Grayville
Princeton
Oakland City
Jasper
Huntingburg
Sellersburg
New Albany
English
Louisville
Coulterville
Tamaroa
Dahlgren
Crossville
Wabash River
Ft Branch
Enosville
Corydon
Shively
Rend Lake
McLeansboro
Carmi
Lincoln City
Valley Station
Pinckneyville
Steeleville
Du Quoin
Benton
Chandler
Boonville
Christopher
Norris City
Evansville
Ohio R.
Tell City
Cannelton
Brandenburg
West Point
Shepherdsville
West Frankfort
Rockport
Hawesville
Irvington
Fort Knox
Herrin
Carbondale
Eldorado
Henderson
Murphysboro
Crab Orchard Lake
Marion
Harrisburg
Uniontown
Owensboro
Hardinsburg
Shawneetown
Morganfield
Whitesville
Elizabethtown
Cecilia
Grand Tower
Sebree
Rough River L.
Sturgis
Calhoun
Anna
Dixon
Green River
Livermore
Big Clifty
Hodgenville
Jonesboro
Vienna
Elizabethtown
Hartford
Leitchfield
Golconda
Providence
Nolin Lake
Ullin
Marion
Madisonville
ILLINOIS
Joppa
Metropolis
Ohio River
Central City
Bee Spr
Munfordville
Fredonia
Dawson Springs
Greenville
Morgantown
MAMMOTH CAVE NAT. PARK
Mound City
Paducah
Eddyville
Nortonville
Mammoth Cave
Green R.
Cave City
Morley
Cairo
Princeton
Dunmor
Park City
Wickliffe
Calvert City
Crofton
Kirkmansville
Charleston
Lake Barkley
Lewisburg
Bowling Green
Glasgow
Wyatt
Kentucky L.
Cadiz
Hopkinsville
Russellville
Auburn
984 ft 300 m
Bardwell
Edmonton
East Prairie
Benton
Elkton
Barren River Lake
Lucas
Austin
Pilot Knob
Aurora
Mayfield
Scottsville
New Madrid
Clinton
Linton
Franklin
Guthrie
Tompkinsville
Murray
Hickman
Adams
Fulton
Portland
Westmoreland
Clarksville
Springfield
Red Boiling Spr
Union City
Dover
Lafayette
Tiptonville
Rives
Martin
Cumberland City
Cumberland R.
Gallatin
Hartsville
Ridgely
Obion
Dresden
Erin
Goodlettsville
Gainesboro
Kenton
Paris
Ashland City
Big Sandy
Charlotte
Old Hickory Lake
Lebanon
Rome
Cookeville
McKenzie
Nashville
Buffalo Valley
Dyersburg
Camden
Waverly
Dickson
Oak Hill
J. Percy Priest Res.
Alexandria
Liberty
Fowlkes
Trenton
Huntingdon
Brentwood
Smyrna
Milan
Smithville
Tennessee River
Franklin
Humboldt
Nunnelly
Wrigley
Murfreesboro
Woodbury
Alamo
Ripley
Wildersville
Thompsons Sta
Bells
Centerville
Duck R.
College Grove
Parsons
Lexington
McMinnville
Jackson
Bemis
Brownsville
Decaturville
Linden
Columbia
Chapel Hill
Reagan
Hohenwald
Stanton
Flat Woods
Mt Pleasant
Wartrace
Manchester
Henderson
Lewisburg
Shelbyville
Saltillo
Summertown
Tullahoma
Whiteville
Waynesboro
Ethridge
Petersburg
Woods Res.
Palmer
Bolivar
Adamsville
Lynchburg
Somerville
Savannah
Lawrenceburg
Tims Ford L.
Hickory Valley
Selmer
Collinwood
Pulaski
Frankewing
Mulberry
Fayetteville
Winchester
Cowan
Middleton
Loretto
Elk River
Jasper
Iron City
Walnut
Ardmore
Elora
64
70
57
24
55
65
40

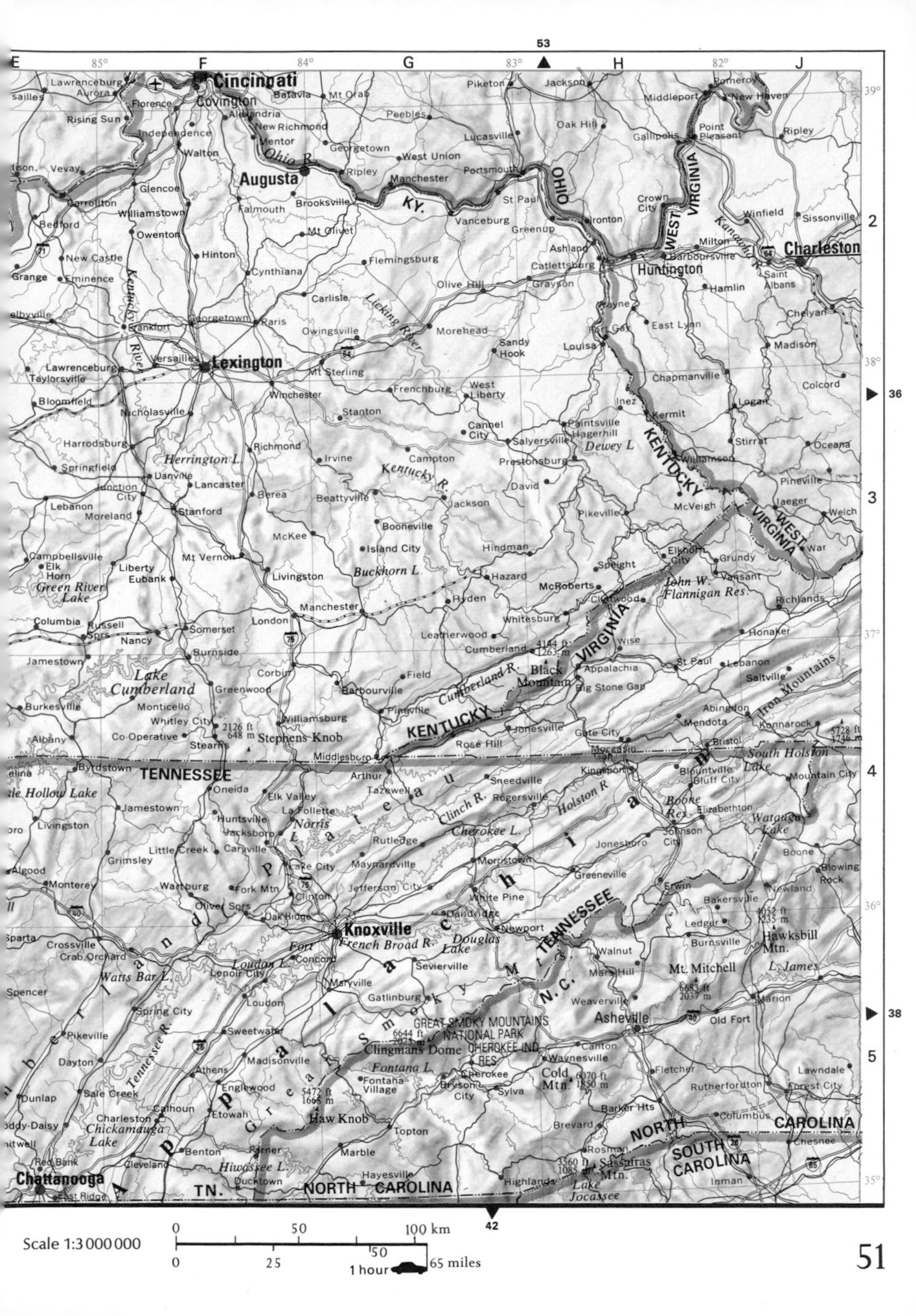

E 85° **F** 84° **G** 83° ▲ **H** 82° **J**

Lawrenceburg Aurora **Cincinnati** Batavia Mt Orab Piketon Jackson Pomeroy 39°
sailles Florence Covington New Haven
Rising Sun Independence Alexandria New Richmond Peebles Middleport
Vevay Walton Mentor Georgetown West Union Oak Hill Gallipolis Point Ripley
Glencoe **Augusta** Brooksville Manchester Portsmouth Pleasant
Borrollton Williamstown Kalmouth St Paul Ironton Crown Winfield Sissonville 2
Bedford Owenton Mt Olivet Vanceburg Greenup City Barboursville **Charleston**
New Castle Hinton Flemingsburg Ashland Milton Saint
Grange Eminence Cynthiana Olive Hill Catlettsburg **Huntington** Albans Chelyan
elbyville Frankfort Carlisle Grayson Hamlin Madison
Lawrenceburg Georgetown Paris Morehead Sandy Louisa Payne East Lynn 38°
Taylorsville Versailles **Lexington** Owingsville Hook Inez Chapmanville Logan Colcord 36
Bloomfield Nicholasville Winchester Mt Sterling Frenchburg West Salyersville Kermit Stirrat Oceana
Harrodsburg Richmond Stanton Liberty Cannel Paintsville Williamson
Springfield Danville Irvine Campton City Hagerhill Dewey L Pineville
Lebanon Junction Lancaster Berea Jackson Prestonsburg McVeigh Jaeger Weich 3
Moreland City Stanford Beattyville Booneville David Elkhorn Grundy War
Campbellsville Mt Vernon Island City Hindman City Vansant
Elk Liberty Buckhorn L Hazard McRoberts John W. Richlands
Green River Eubank Livingston Speight Clingwoods Flannigan Res Honaker
Lake Somerset Manchester Hyden Whitesburg Wise 37°
Columbia Spgs London Leatherwood 4144 m Appalachia St Paul Lebanon
Jamestown Nancy Burnside Cumberland 1263 Black Big Stone Gap Saltville
Lake Corbin Barbourville Mountain Gate City Abingdon Mendota Damascus
Burkesville Monticello Greenwood Pineville Jonesville Bristol South Holston
Albany Whitley City 2126 ft Rose Hill Morristown Kingsport Lake
Co-Operative 648 m Williamsburg Middlesboro Bluff City Mountain City 4
Byrdstown **TENNESSEE** Stephens Knob Arthur Tazewell Blountville Watauga
Hollow Lake Oneida Elk Valley Sneedville Rogersville Johnson Lake
Livingston Jamestown La Follette Holston R City Boone Boone
Algood Huntsville Norris Cherokee L Jonesboro Blowing
Grimsley Little Creek Caryville Maynardville Greeneville Erwin Rock
Monterey Wartburg Lake City Jefferson City White Pine Bakersville Newland
Sparta Oliver Spgs Clinton Dandridge Ledger Burnsville Hawksbill
Crossville Oak Ridge Newport Walnut Mt Mitchell Mtn.
Crab Orchard **Knoxville** Douglas Mars Hill 6683 ft L James
Watts Bar L. Concord French Broad R. Lake 2037 m 38
Spencer Fort Sevierville Marion
Spring City Lenoir City Maryville Gatlinburg Asheville Old Fort
Pikeville Loudon GREAT SMOKY MOUNTAINS Weaverville
Dayton Sweetwater NATIONAL PARK Canton Fletcher Lawndale 5
Athens Madisonville 6644 ft Waynesville Cold Forest City
Sale Creek Englewood Clingmans Dome CHEROKEE IND. Mtn. Rutherfordton
Charleston Etowah 5472 ft RES. 6010 ft Columbus **CAROLINA**
Chickamauga 1666 m Fontana L Cherokee 1830 m Barker Hts Chester
Lake Benton Fontana Bryson Sylva Brevard **NORTH**
Chattanooga Ducktown Village City Rosman **SOUTH**
East Ridge Hiwassee L Marble Topton Haw Knob 5360 ft **CAROLINA** Inman
TN. **NORTH CAROLINA** Hayesville 1085 m Sassafras 35°
Highlands Mtn.
Lake Jocassee

Scale 1:3 000 000

0   50   100 km
0   25   50
1 hour ⊂⊃ 65 miles

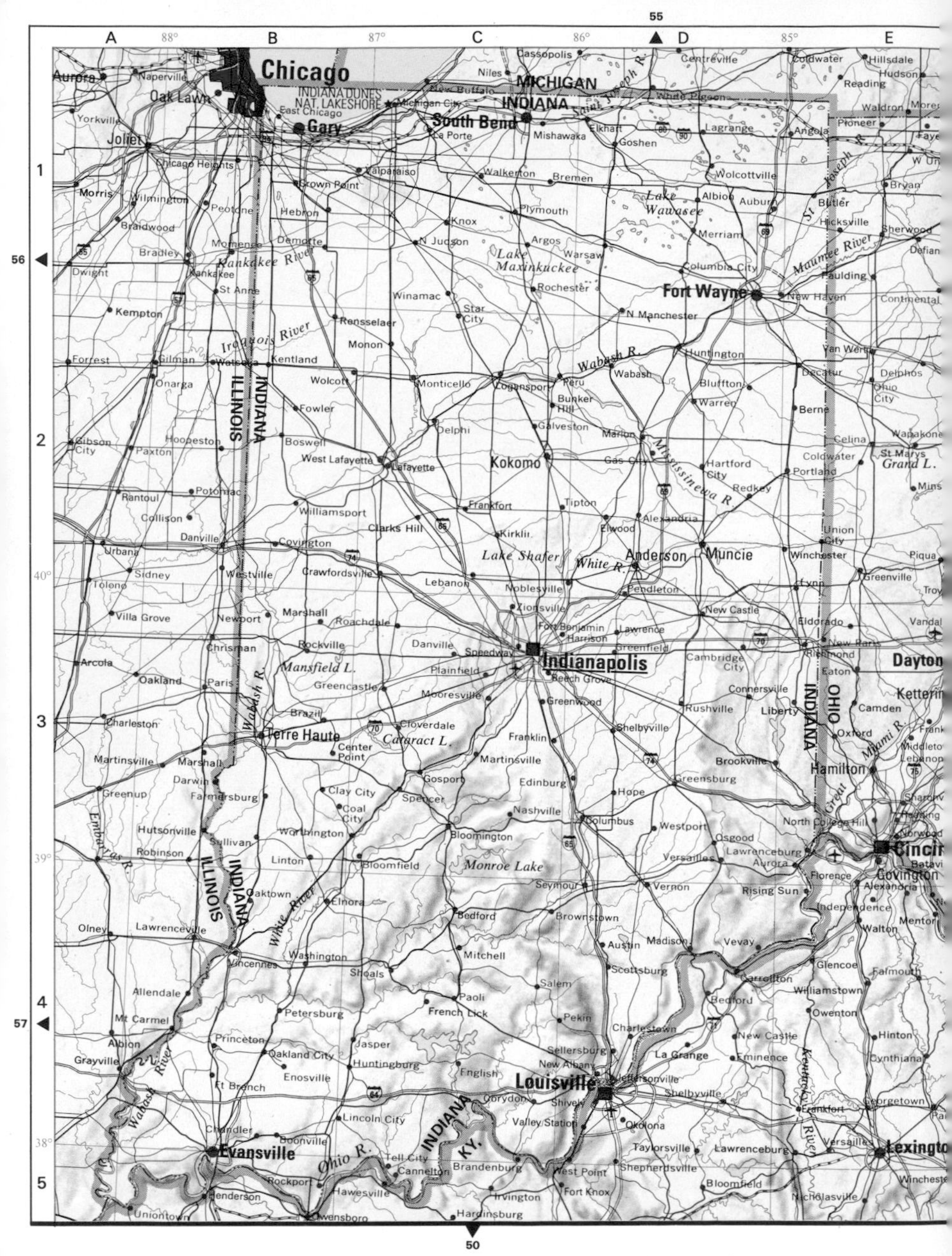
Chicago
MICHIGAN
INDIANA
ILLINOIS
OHIO
Gary
South Bend
Fort Wayne
Kokomo
Indianapolis
Anderson
Muncie
Terre Haute
Evansville
Louisville
Lexington
Dayton
Lafayette
West Lafayette
Joliet
Aurora
Oak Lawn
Kankakee
Danville
Urbana
Vincennes
Bloomington
Columbus
Richmond
Hamilton
Covington
Frankfort
Logansport
Peru
Marion
Elkhart
Goshen
Michigan City
La Porte
Valparaiso
Crown Point
Plymouth
Warsaw
Rochester
Huntington
Wabash
Bluffton
Decatur
Portland
New Castle
Greenfield
Shelbyville
Franklin
Martinsville
Seymour
Madison
Jasper
Bedford
Brazil
Crawfordsville
Lebanon
Noblesville
New Albany
Jeffersonville
Lake Wawasee
Lake Maxinkuckee
Lake Shafer
Monroe Lake
Mansfield L.
Cataract L.
Grand L.
Kankakee River
Iroquois River
Wabash R.
White R.
White River
Mississinewa R.
Maumee River
St. Joseph R.
Great Miami R.
Kentucky River
Ohio R.
INDIANA DUNES NAT. LAKESHORE
KY.
A
B
C
D
E
1
2
3
4
5
55
56
57
50
88°
87°
86°
85°
40°
39°
38°

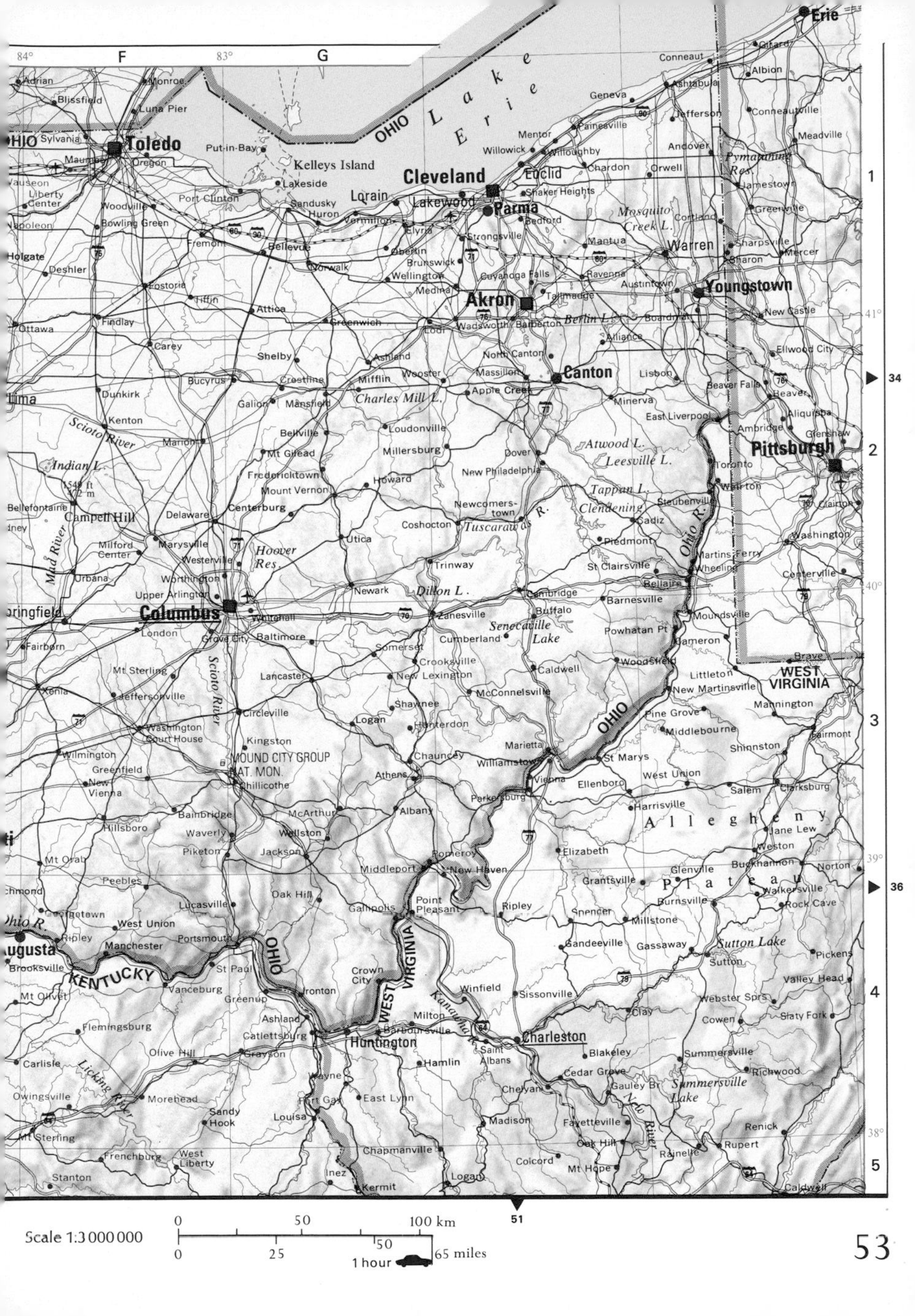

84°
F
83°
G
OHIO Lake Erie
Erie
Girard
Conneaut
Albion
Ashtabula
Geneva
Jefferson
Conneautville
Painesville
Mentor
Willowick
Willoughby
Andover
Meadville
Pymatuning Res.
Adrian
Monroe
Blissfield
Luna Pier
OHIO
Sylvania
Toledo
Put-in-Bay
Kelleys Island
Maumee
Oregon
Lakeside
Cleveland
Euclid
Chardon
Orwell
Jamestown
Wauseon
Liberty Center
Port Clinton
Sandusky
Huron
Lorain
Lakewood
Parma
Shaker Heights
Mosquito Creek L.
Cortland
Greenville
Woodville
Napoleon
Bowling Green
Vermilion
Elyria
Bedford
Fremont
Bellevue
Strongsville
Mantua
Warren
Sharpsville
Mercer
Holgate
Deshler
Norwalk
Oberlin
Brunswick
Wellington
Cuyahoga Falls
Ravenna
Sharon
Fostoria
Tiffin
Medina
Akron
Tallmadge
Austintown
Youngstown
Attica
Findlay
Ottawa
Greenwich
Lodi
Wadsworth
Barberton
Berlin L.
Boardman
New Castle
Carey
Alliance
Shelby
Ashland
North Canton
Ellwood City
Bucyrus
Crestline
Mifflin
Wooster
Massillon
Canton
Lisbon
Beaver Falls
Beaver
Lima
Dunkirk
Galion
Mansfield
Charles Mill L.
Apple Creek
Minerva
East Liverpool
Aliquippa
Kenton
Ambridge
Glenshaw
Scioto River
Bellville
Loudonville
Marion
Atwood L.
Pittsburgh
Mt Gilead
Millersburg
Dover
Leesville L.
Indian L.
Fredericktown
Howard
New Philadelphia
Toronto
1549 ft
472 m
Mount Vernon
Tappan L.
Weirton
Bellefontaine
Centerburg
Newcomerstown
Steubenville
Clendening
Clairton
Campbell Hill
Delaware
Coshocton
Tuscarawas R.
Cadiz
Piedmont
Washington
Mad River
Milford Center
Marysville
Utica
Ohio R.
Westerville
Hoover Res.
Trinway
Martins Ferry
Wheeling
Urbana
St Clairsville
Centerville
Worthington
Bellaire
Upper Arlington
Newark
Dillon L.
Cambridge
Barnesville
Columbus
Buffalo
Springfield
Whitehall
Zanesville
Moundsville
Senecaville Lake
London
Grove City
Baltimore
Cumberland
Powhatan Pt
Cameron
Fairborn
Somerset
Crooksville
Woodsfield
Brave
Mt Sterling
Caldwell
Lancaster
New Lexington
Littleton
WEST VIRGINIA
Xenia
New Martinsville
Jeffersonville
McConnelsville
Mannington
Shawnee
Circleville
Pine Grove
Logan
Hemlock
Middlebourne
Fairmont
Washington Court House
Kingston
Marietta
Shinnston
Wilmington
MOUND CITY GROUP NAT. MON.
Chauncey
Williamstown
St Marys
Greenfield
Chillicothe
Athens
Vienna
Ellenboro
West Union
New Vienna
Parkersburg
Salem
Clarksburg
Harrisville
Bainbridge
McArthur
Albany
Allegheny
Hillsboro
Waverly
Wellston
Jane Lew
Piketon
Jackson
Pomeroy
Elizabeth
Weston
Mt Orab
Middleport
New Haven
Buckhannon
Norton
Peebles
Glenville
Grantsville
Plateau
Walkersville
Oak Hill
Point Pleasant
Ripley
Burnsville
Rock Cave
Lucasville
Gallipolis
Spencer
Millstone
Georgetown
West Union
Ripley
Ohio R.
Manchester
Portsmouth
Sandeeville
Gassaway
Sutton Lake
Pickens
Augusta
Sutton
Brooksville
St Paul
Crown City
Valley Head
KENTUCKY
OHIO
VIRGINIA
WEST
Vanceburg
Mt Olivet
Greenup
Ironton
Winfield
Sissonville
Webster Sprs
Kanawha R.
Clay
Ashland
Milton
Cowen
Slaty Fork
Flemingsburg
Catlettsburg
Barboursville
Huntington
Charleston
Olive Hill
Grayson
Saint Albans
Blakeley
Summersville
Carlisle
Hamlin
Licking River
Cedar Grove
Richwood
Wayne
Gauley Br
Summersville Lake
Owingsville
Morehead
Fort Gay
East Lynn
New River
Sandy Hook
Louisa
Madison
Fayetteville
Mt Sterling
Renick
Oak Hill
Frenchburg
West Liberty
Chapmanville
Rainelle
Rupert
Colcord
Mt Hope
Stanton
Inez
Logan
Kermit
Caldwell
41°
40°
39°
38°
1
2
3
4
5
34
36
51
Scale 1:3 000 000
0
50
100 km
0
25
50
65 miles
1 hour

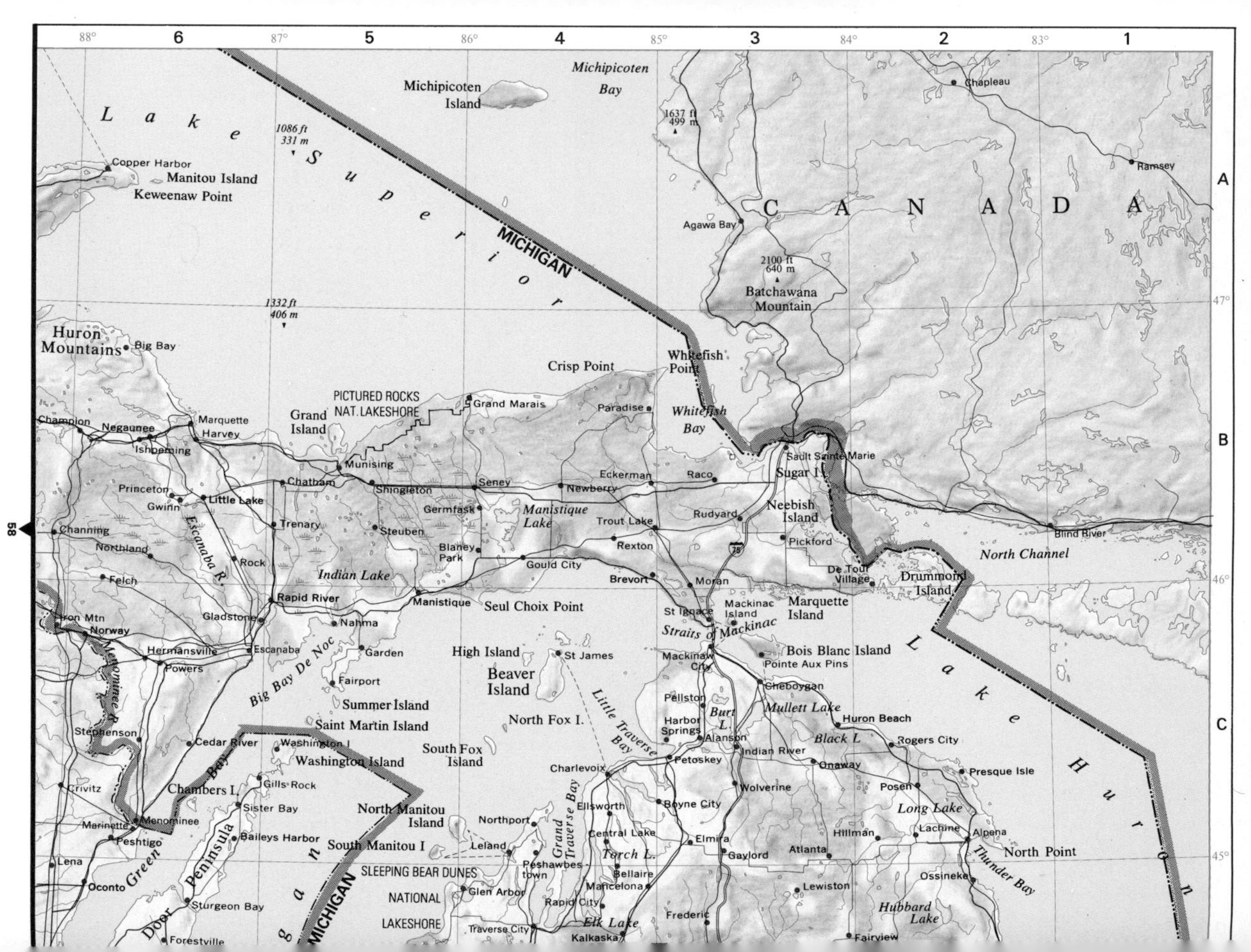
CANADA
MICHIGAN
Lake Superior
Lake Huron
Michipicoten Island
Michipicoten Bay
Batchawana Mountain
2100 ft 640 m
North Channel
Drummond Island
Sault Sainte Marie
Sugar I.
Neebish Island
Whitefish Point
Whitefish Bay
Crisp Point
Grand Marais
PICTURED ROCKS NAT. LAKESHORE
Grand Island
Munising
Marquette
Huron Mountains
Big Bay
Keweenaw Point
Manitou Island
Copper Harbor
Manistique Lake
Indian Lake
Seul Choix Point
Straits of Mackinac
Mackinac Island
Marquette Island
Bois Blanc Island
Beaver Island
High Island
North Fox I.
South Fox Island
Little Traverse Bay
Grand Traverse Bay
SLEEPING BEAR DUNES NATIONAL LAKESHORE
North Manitou Island
South Manitou I
Washington Island
Summer Island
Saint Martin Island
Chambers I.
Big Bay De Noc
Door Peninsula
Green Bay
Escanaba R.
Menominee R.
Mullett Lake
Burt L.
Black L
Long Lake
Torch L.
Elk Lake
Hubbard Lake
Thunder Bay
North Point
Presque Isle
Alpena
Cheboygan
Petoskey
Charlevoix
Traverse City
Escanaba
Menominee
Manistique
Rapid River
58

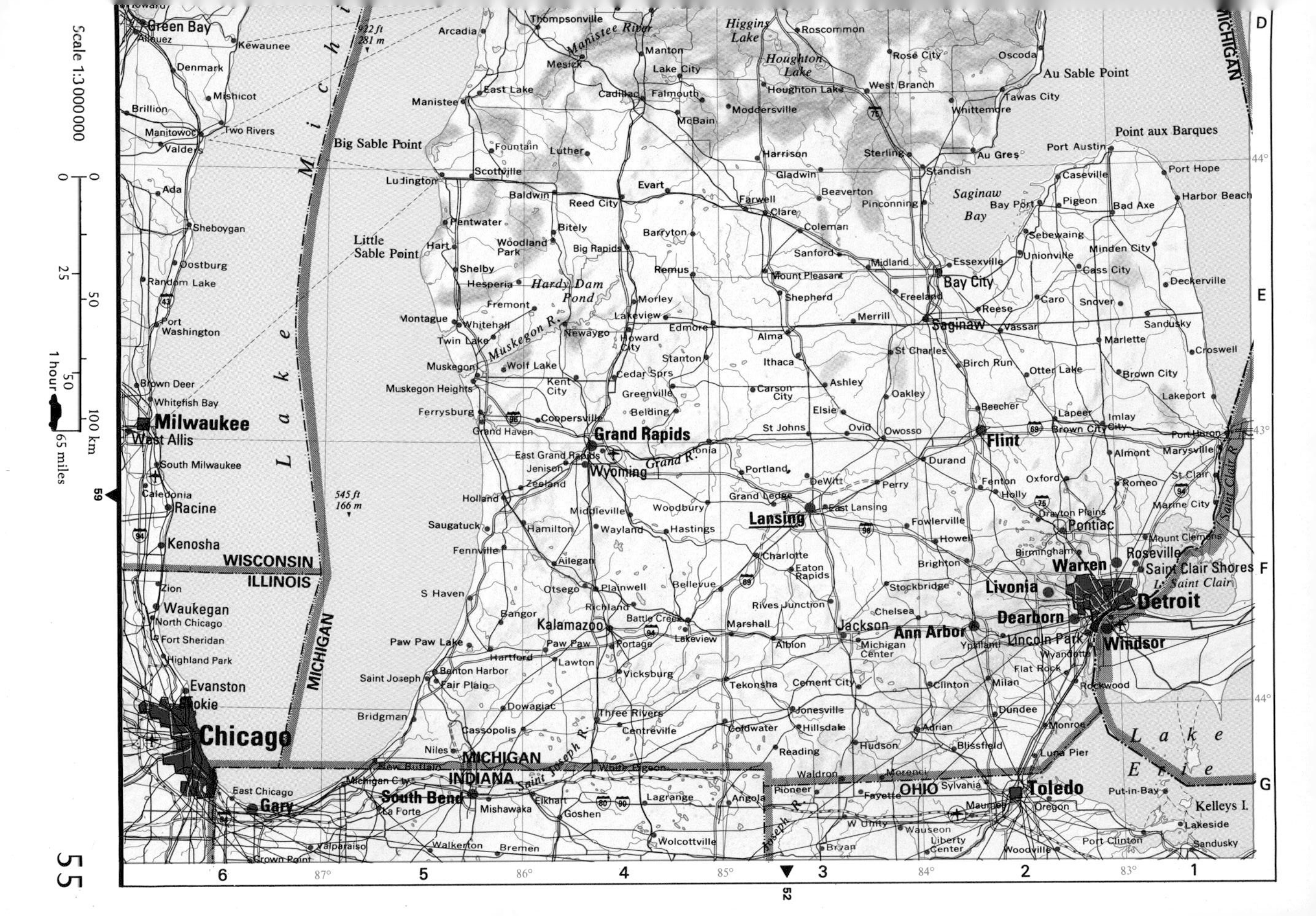
MICHIGAN
Lake Michigan
Lake Erie
L. Saint Clair
Saginaw Bay
Higgins Lake
Houghton Lake
Hardy Dam Pond
Manistee River
Muskegon R.
Grand R.
Saint Joseph R.
Saint Clair R.
Point aux Barques
Au Sable Point
Big Sable Point
Little Sable Point
922 ft 281 m
545 ft 166 m
WISCONSIN
ILLINOIS
INDIANA
OHIO
Green Bay
Kewaunee
Denmark
Mishicot
Brillion
Manitowoc
Two Rivers
Valders
Ada
Sheboygan
Oostburg
Random Lake
Port Washington
Brown Deer
Whitefish Bay
Milwaukee
West Allis
South Milwaukee
Caledonia
Racine
Kenosha
Zion
Waukegan
North Chicago
Fort Sheridan
Highland Park
Evanston
Skokie
Chicago
East Chicago
Gary
Valparaiso
Crown Point
Arcadia
Thompsonville
Mesick
Manistee
East Lake
Manton
Lake City
Cadillac
Falmouth
McBain
Roscommon
Rose City
Oscoda
Tawas City
West Branch
Houghton Lake
Moddersville
Whittemore
Fountain
Luther
Scottville
Ludington
Baldwin
Reed City
Evart
Harrison
Gladwin
Sterling
Standish
Au Gres
Port Austin
Caseville
Port Hope
Harbor Beach
Pentwater
Bitely
Woodland Park
Hart
Big Rapids
Barryton
Farwell
Clare
Beaverton
Pinconning
Bay Port
Pigeon
Bad Axe
Coleman
Sebewaing
Unionville
Minden City
Shelby
Hesperia
Fremont
Remus
Sanford
Midland
Essexville
Bay City
Cass City
Deckerville
Mount Pleasant
Shepherd
Freeland
Caro
Snover
Montague
Whitehall
Twin Lake
Morley
Lakeview
Newaygo
Edmore
Merrill
Reese
Saginaw
Vassar
Sandusky
Marlette
Croswell
Howard City
Alma
St Charles
Birch Run
Muskegon
Wolf Lake
Stanton
Ithaca
Otter Lake
Brown City
Muskegon Heights
Kent City
Cedar Sprs
Greenville
Carson City
Ashley
Oakley
Lakeport
Ferrysburg
Coopersville
Belding
Elsie
Beecher
Lapeer
Imlay City
Grand Haven
Grand Rapids
St Johns
Ovid
Owosso
Flint
Port Huron
Almont
Marysville
East Grand Rapids
Ionia
Durand
Jenison
Wyoming
Portland
DeWitt
Perry
Fenton
Oxford
Romeo
St Clair
Zeeland
Holly
Holland
Middleville
Grand Ledge
Woodbury
Lansing
East Lansing
Drayton Plains
Pontiac
Marine City
Saugatuck
Hamilton
Wayland
Hastings
Fowlerville
Howell
Mount Clemens
Fennville
Allegan
Charlotte
Birmingham
Roseville
Brighton
Warren
Saint Clair Shores
Eaton Rapids
S Haven
Otsego
Plainwell
Bellevue
Stockbridge
Livonia
Detroit
Richland
Rives Junction
Chelsea
Bangor
Kalamazoo
Battle Creek
Marshall
Jackson
Dearborn
Ann Arbor
Paw Paw Lake
Paw Paw
Portage
Lakeview
Albion
Michigan Center
Ypsilanti
Lincoln Park
Windsor
Hartford
Wyandotte
Lawton
Vicksburg
Flat Rock
Saint Joseph
Benton Harbor
Fair Plain
Tekonsha
Cement City
Clinton
Milan
Rockwood
Dowagiac
Jonesville
Dundee
Bridgman
Three Rivers
Cassopolis
Centreville
Coldwater
Hillsdale
Adrian
Monroe
Niles
Reading
Hudson
Blissfield
Luna Pier
New Buffalo
White Pigeon
Michigan City
Waldron
Morenci
Sylvania
Toledo
Put-in-Bay
South Bend
Mishawaka
La Porte
Elkhart
Goshen
Lagrange
Angola
Pioneer
Fayette
Maumee
Oregon
Kelleys I.
Lakeside
W Unity
Wauseon
Liberty Center
Woodville
Port Clinton
Sandusky
Walkerton
Bremen
Wolcottville
Bryan
D
E
F
G
1
2
3
4
5
6
44°
43°
83°
84°
85°
86°
87°
52
59
Scale 1:3 000 000
0 50 100 km
0 25 50 65 miles
1 hour

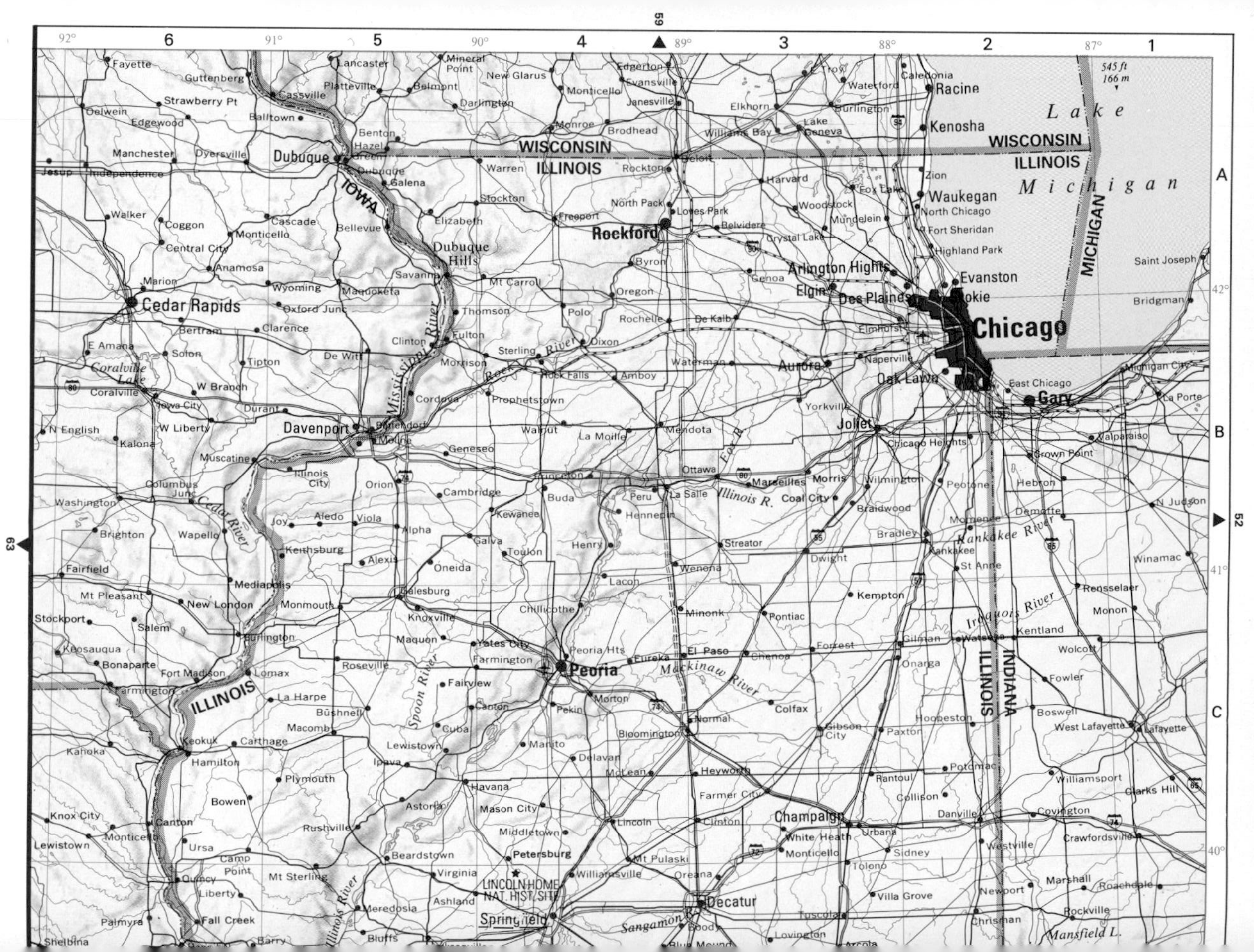
52
59
63
A
B
C
1
2
3
4
5
6
Lake Michigan
545 ft
166 m
MICHIGAN
WISCONSIN
ILLINOIS
INDIANA
IOWA
Chicago
Gary
Evanston
Waukegan
Kenosha
Racine
Arlington Hights
Des Plaines
Elgin
Aurora
Joliet
Rockford
Peoria
Champaign
Decatur
Springfield
Davenport
Dubuque
Cedar Rapids
Kankakee River
Iroquois River
Illinois R.
Mackinaw River
Spoon River
Mississippi River
Cedar River
Sangamon
Illinois River
LINCOLN HOME NAT. HIST. SITE

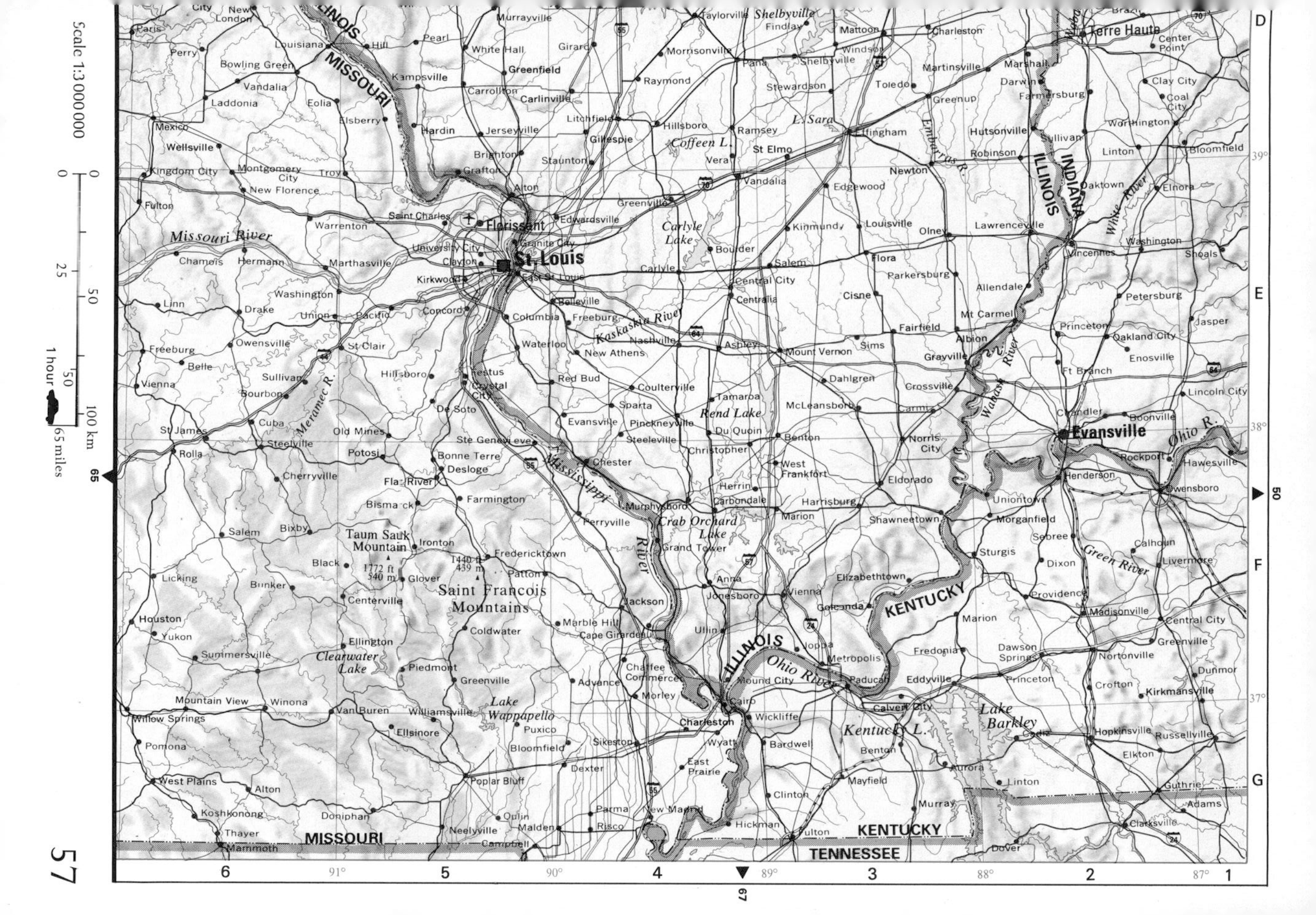

54

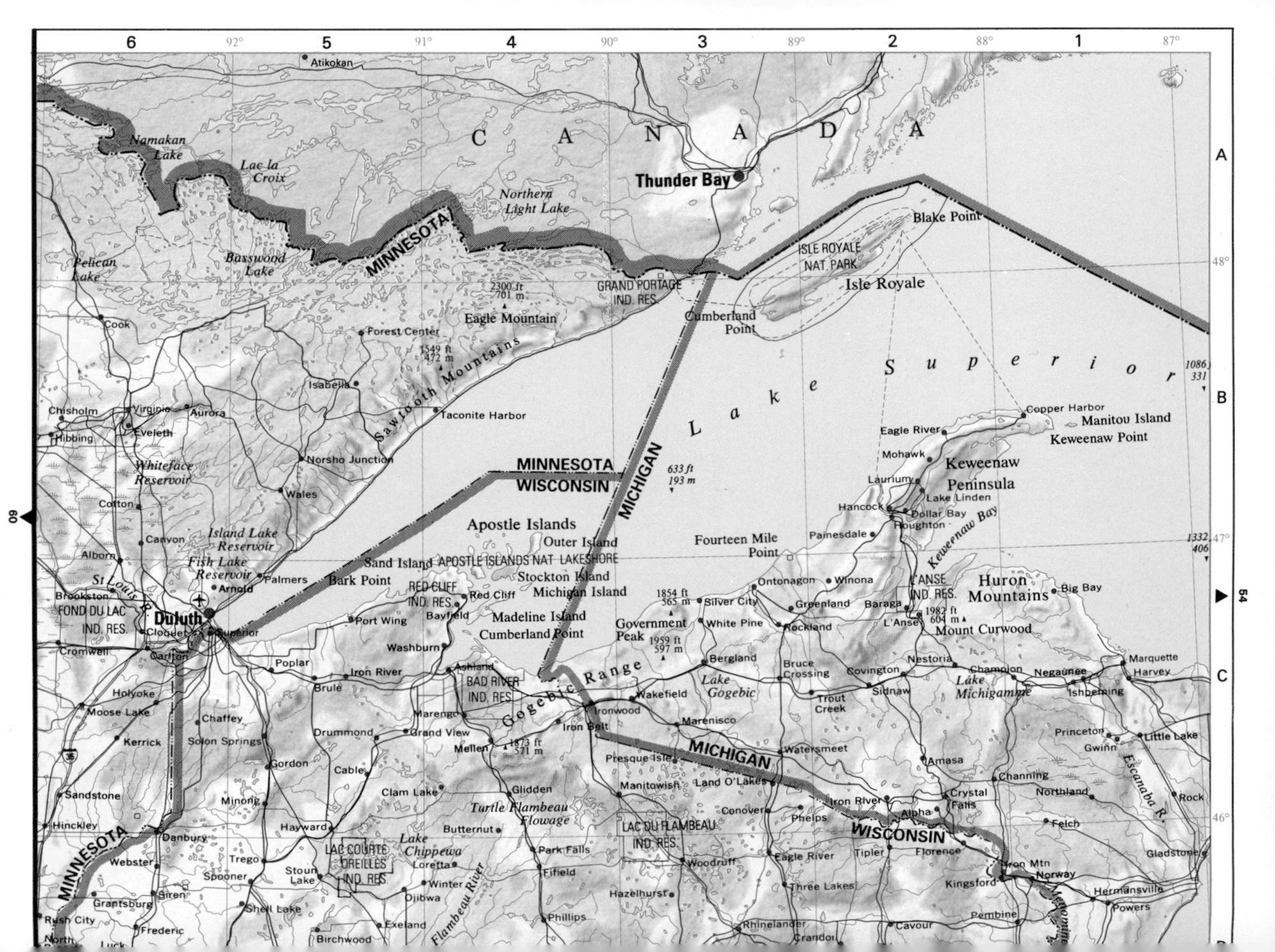

C A N A D A
Thunder Bay
Atikokan
Lake Superior
Isle Royale
ISLE ROYALE NAT. PARK
Blake Point
Cumberland Point
Copper Harbor
Manitou Island
Keweenaw Point
Keweenaw Peninsula
Keweenaw Bay
Eagle River
Mohawk
Laurium
Lake Linden
Dollar Bay
Hancock
Houghton
Painesdale
Huron Mountains
Big Bay
Mount Curwood
L'ANSE IND. RES.
L'Anse
Baraga
Winona
Greenland
Rockland
Ontonagon
Fourteen Mile Point
Silver City
White Pine
Bergland
Lake Gogebic
Government Peak
Gogebic Range
Marenisco
Wakefield
Ironwood
Iron Belt
Marquette
Harvey
Negaunee
Ishpeming
Lake Michigamme
Champion
Nestoria
Covington
Sidnaw
Trout Creek
Bruce Crossing
Watersmeet
Amasa
Crystal Falls
Iron River
Alpha
Florence
Kingsford
Iron Mtn
Norway
Channing
Northland
Felch
Princeton
Gwinn
Little Lake
Escanaba R.
Rock
Gladstone
Hermansville
Powers
Pembine
Cavour
Tipler
Eagle River
Three Lakes
Rhinelander
Phelps
Conover
Land O'Lakes
Presque Isle
Manitowish
Woodruff
LAC DU FLAMBEAU IND. RES.
Hazelhurst
Park Falls
Fifield
Phillips
Turtle Flambeau Flowage
Glidden
Butternut
Flambeau River
Mellen
Marengo
Grand View
Clam Lake
Lake Chippewa
Loretta
Winter
Ojibwa
Exeland
LAC COURTE OREILLES IND. RES.
Cable
Drummond
Hayward
Stone Lake
Birchwood
Shell Lake
Trego
Spooner
Minong
Gordon
Solon Springs
Chaffey
Poplar
Brule
Iron River
Port Wing
Washburn
Bayfield
Ashland
BAD RIVER IND. RES.
RED CLIFF IND. RES.
Red Cliff
Apostle Islands
APOSTLE ISLANDS NAT. LAKESHORE
Outer Island
Stockton Island
Michigan Island
Madeline Island
Cumberland Point
Sand Island
Bark Point
MINNESOTA
WISCONSIN
MICHIGAN
GRAND PORTAGE IND. RES.
Northern Light Lake
Eagle Mountain
Sawtooth Mountains
Taconite Harbor
Forest Center
Isabella
Norsho Junction
Wales
Lac la Croix
Basswood Lake
Namakan Lake
Pelican Lake
Island Lake Reservoir
Fish Lake Reservoir
Whiteface Reservoir
Palmers
Arnold
Duluth
Superior
Cloquet
Carlton
Canyon
Aurora
Virginia
Eveleth
Cotton
Cook
Chisholm
Hibbing
Alborn
Brookston
FOND DU LAC IND. RES.
St Louis R.
Cromwell
Holyoke
Moose Lake
Kerrick
Sandstone
Hinckley
Danbury
Siren
Webster
Grantsburg
Frederic
Rush City

60

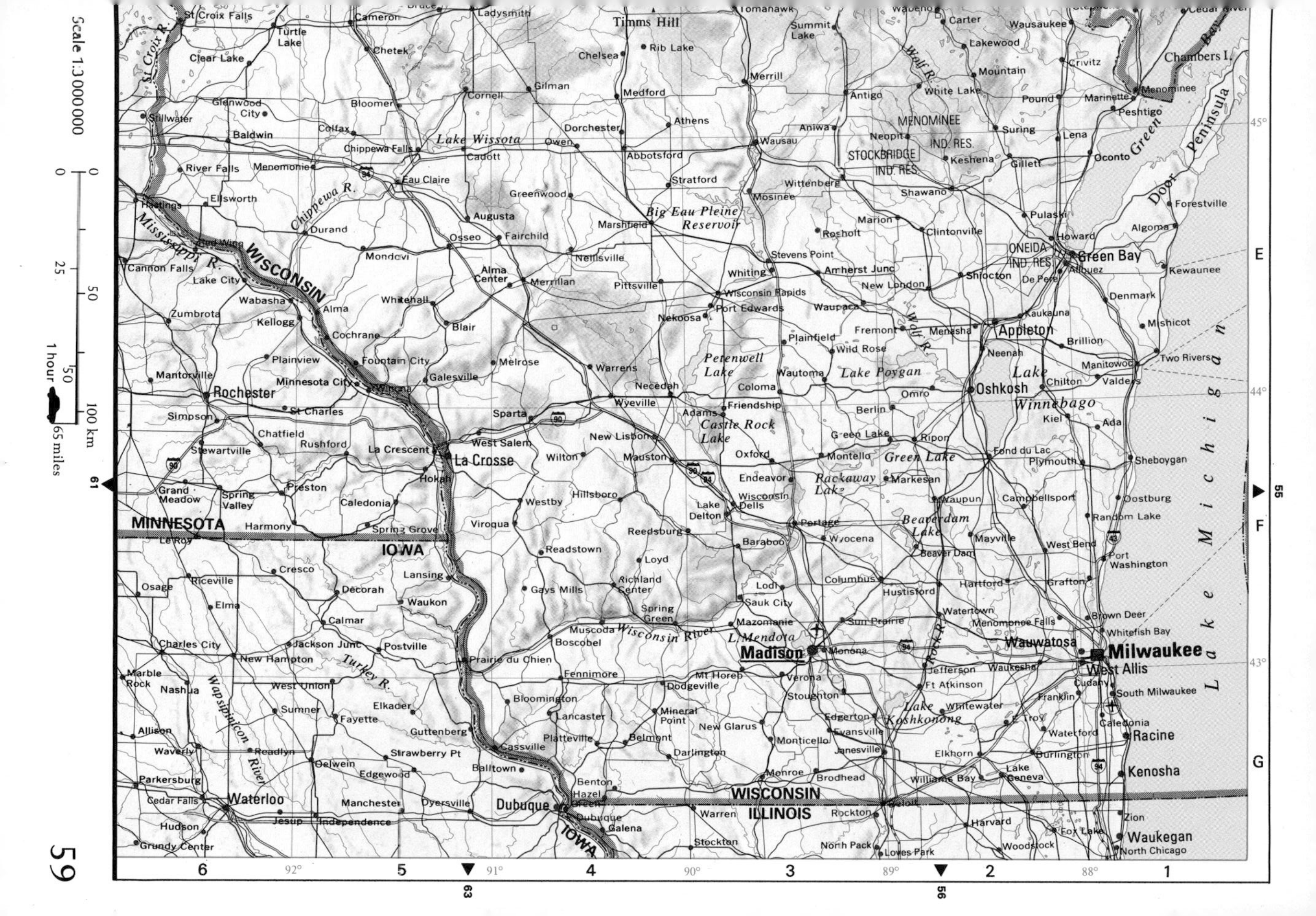

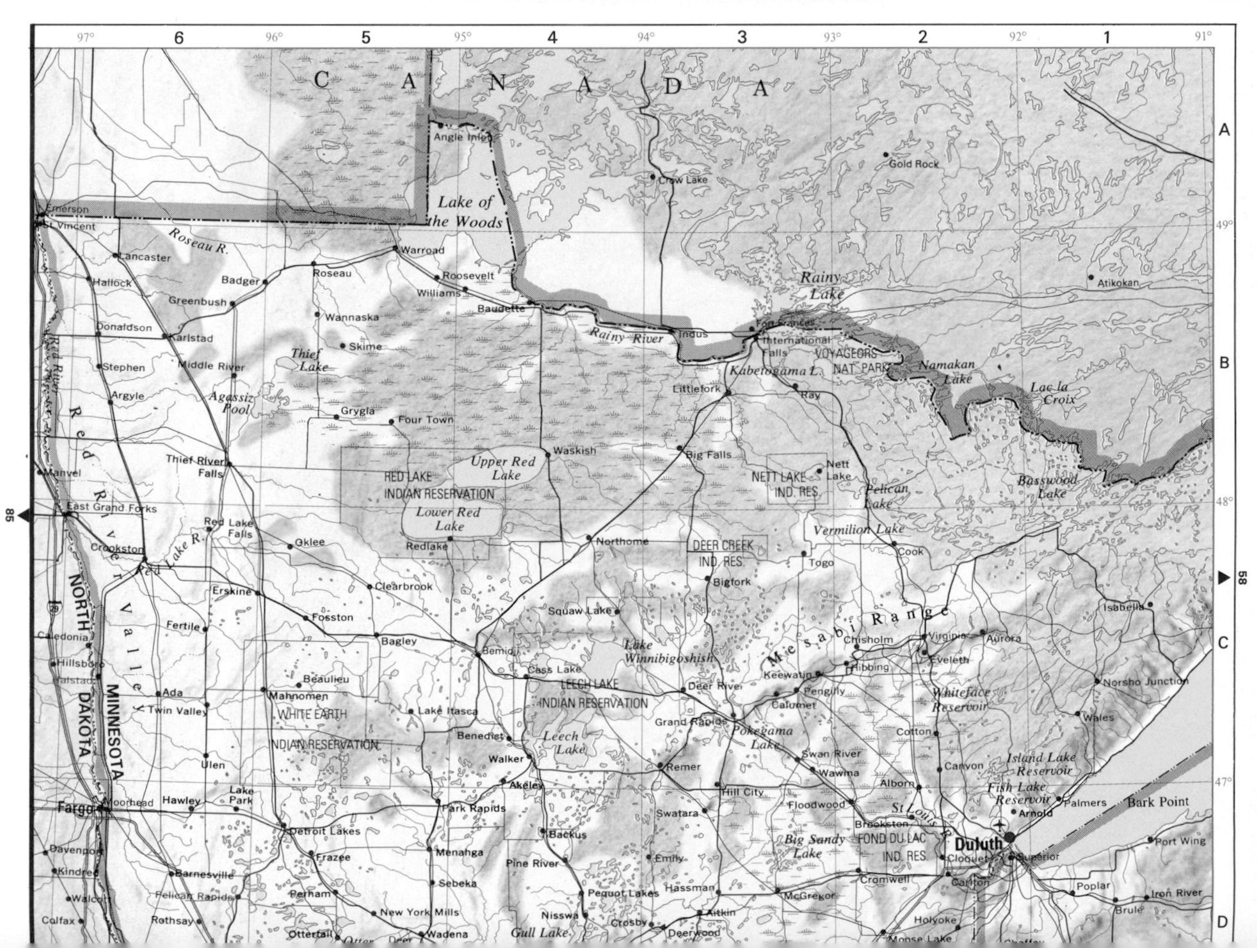

58
85
CANADA
NORTH DAKOTA
MINNESOTA
Lake of the Woods
Rainy Lake
Rainy River
Namakan Lake
Lac la Croix
Basswood Lake
Kabetogama L.
VOYAGEURS NAT. PARK
Upper Red Lake
Lower Red Lake
RED LAKE INDIAN RESERVATION
NETT LAKE IND. RES.
DEER CREEK IND. RES.
LEECH LAKE INDIAN RESERVATION
WHITE EARTH INDIAN RESERVATION
FOND DU LAC IND. RES.
Vermilion Lake
Pelican Lake
Lake Winnibigoshish
Leech Lake
Mesabi Range
Red River Valley
Red River
Roseau R.
Red Lake R.
Thief Lake
Agassiz Pool
Big Sandy Lake
Pokegama Lake
Whiteface Reservoir
Island Lake Reservoir
Fish Lake Reservoir
St. Louis R.
Gull Lake
Bark Point
Duluth
Superior
Fargo
Moorhead
International Falls
Bemidji
Grand Rapids
Hibbing
Virginia
Eveleth
Chisholm
Aurora
Cook
Togo
Isabella
Norsho Junction
Wales
Bigfork
Big Falls
Littlefork
Ray
Nett Lake
Indus
Baudette
Williams
Roosevelt
Warroad
Roseau
Badger
Greenbush
Karlstad
Wannaska
Skime
Grygla
Four Town
Waskish
Northome
Squaw Lake
Deer River
Thief River Falls
Crookston
East Grand Forks
Red Lake Falls
Oklee
Redlake
Clearbrook
Erskine
Fosston
Bagley
Fertile
Ada
Twin Valley
Mahnomen
Beaulieu
Lake Itasca
Cass Lake
Benedict
Walker
Akeley
Ulen
Hawley
Lake Park
Detroit Lakes
Park Rapids
Frazee
Menahga
Sebeka
Backus
Pine River
Pequot Lakes
Nisswa
Crosby
Deerwood
Aitkin
Emily
Hassman
Swatara
Remer
Hill City
McGregor
Cromwell
Floodwood
Swan River
Wawina
Keewatin
Pengilly
Calumet
Cotton
Canyon
Alborn
Brookston
Cloquet
Carlton
Arnold
Palmers
Port Wing
Poplar
Iron River
Brule
Holyoke
Moose Lake
Barnesville
Pelican Rapids
Perham
New York Mills
Wadena
Ottertail
Rothsay
Hallock
Lancaster
Donaldson
Stephen
Argyle
Middle River
Manvel
Angle Inlet
Atikokan
Gold Rock
Crow Lake
Emerson
St. Vincent
Caledonia
Hillsboro
Halstad
Davenport
Kindred
Walcott
Colfax

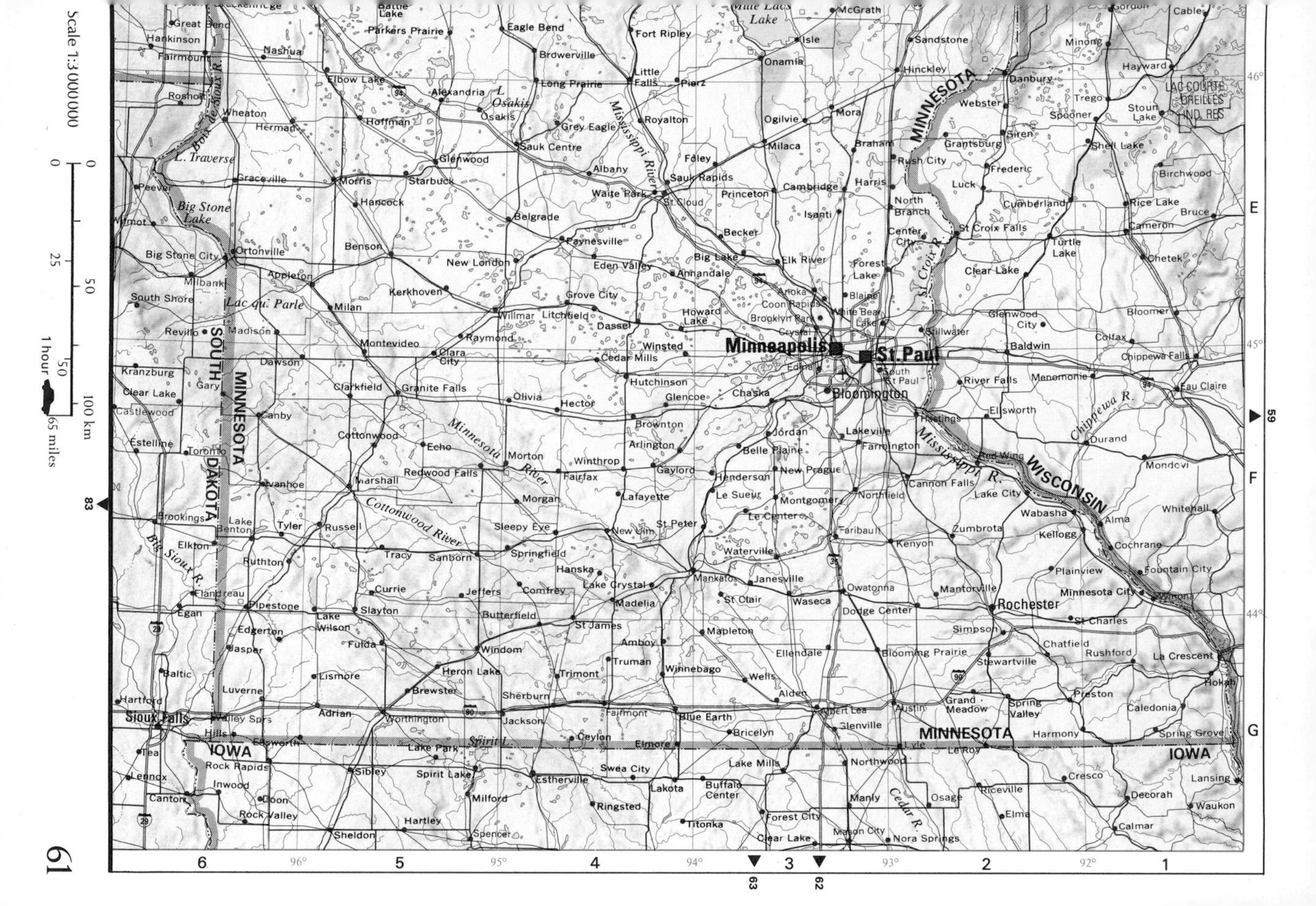
59
62
63
83
E
F
G
1
2
3
4
5
6
46°
45°
44°
92°
93°
94°
95°
96°
MINNESOTA
WISCONSIN
IOWA
SOUTH DAKOTA
Minneapolis
St Paul
Bloomington
Rochester
Mankato
St Cloud
Sioux Falls
Eau Claire
Mississippi River
Mississippi R.
Minnesota River
Cottonwood River
St Croix R.
Chippewa R.
Cedar R.
Big Sioux R.
Bois de Sioux R.
Big Stone Lake
Lac qui Parle
L. Traverse
L. Osakis
Spirit L.
Mille Lacs Lake
LAC COURTE OREILLES IND. RES.
Scale 1:3 000 000
0
50
100 km
0
25
50
65 miles
1 hour

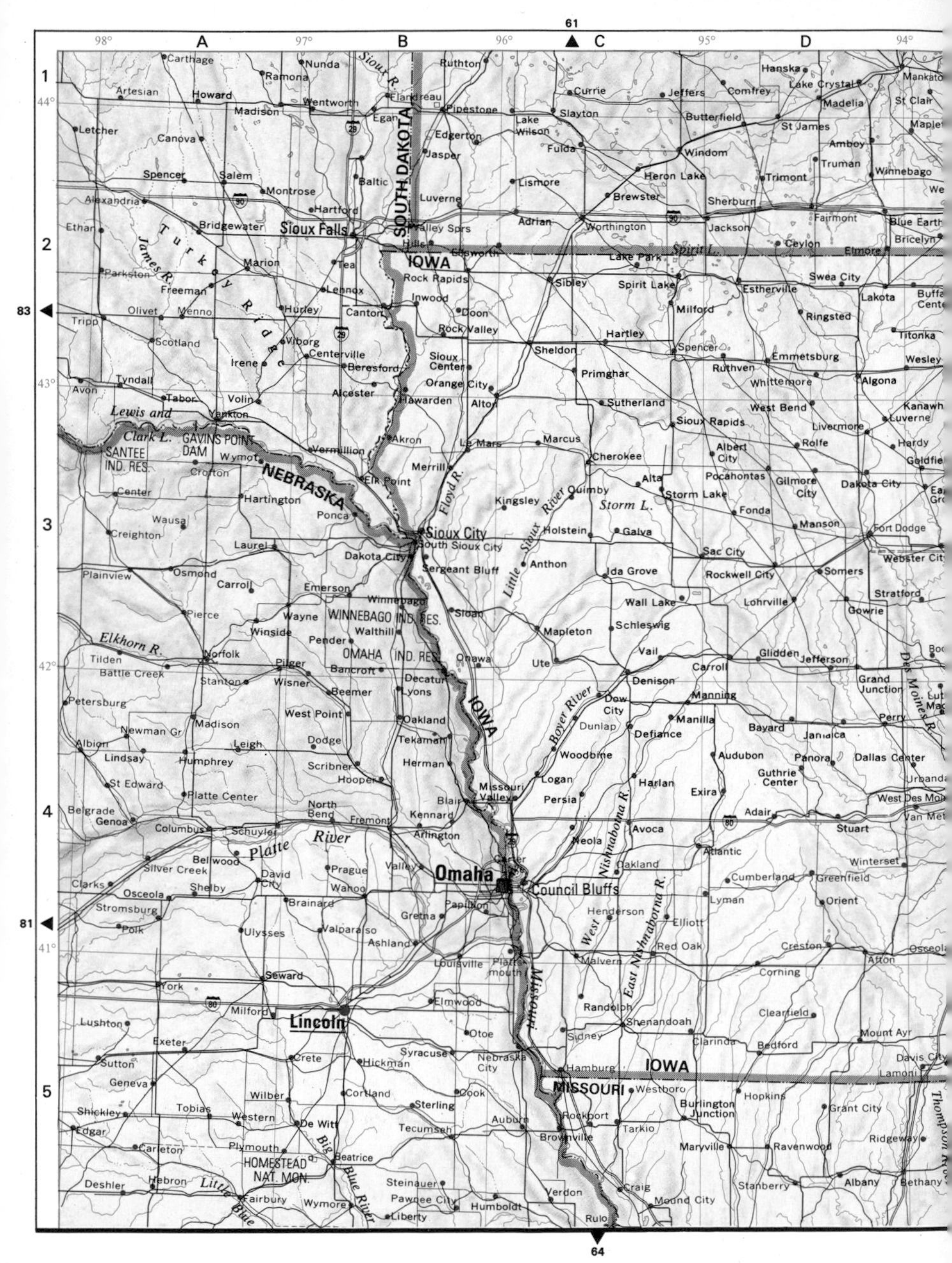

62 IOWA

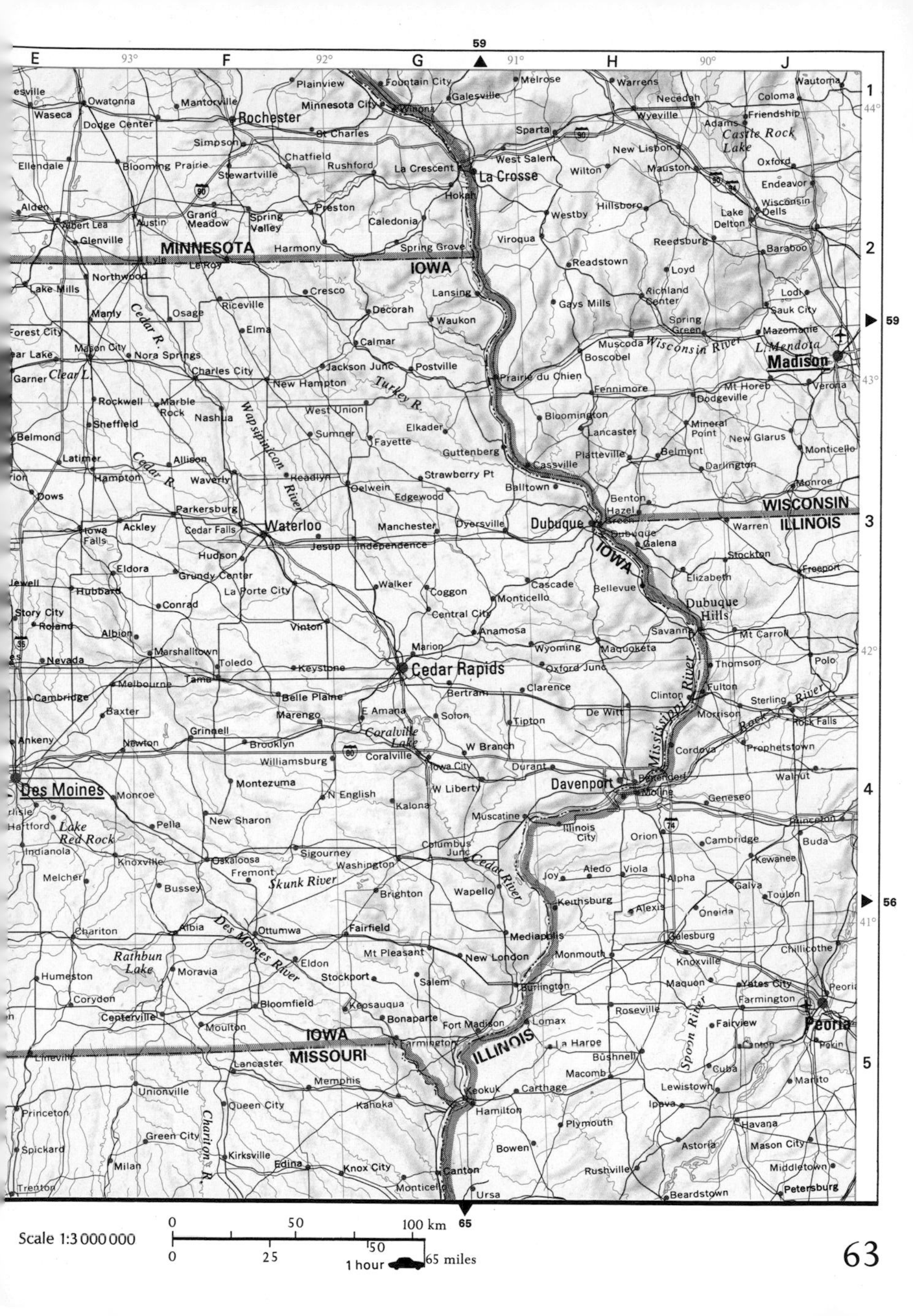

59
E
93°
F
92°
G
91°
H
90°
J
1
2
3
4
5
44°
43°
42°
41°
59
56
65
Waseca
Owatonna
Mantorville
Rochester
Plainview
Minnesota City
Fountain City
Winona
Galesville
Melrose
Warrens
Necedah
Coloma
Wautoma
Friendship
Wyeville
Adams
Castle Rock Lake
Dodge Center
St Charles
Simpson
Sparta
West Salem
New Lisbon
Ellendale
Blooming Prairie
Stewartville
Chatfield
Rushford
La Crescent
La Crosse
Wilton
Mauston
Oxford
Endeavor
Wisconsin Dells
Lake Delton
Alden
Albert Lea
Austin
Grand Meadow
Spring Valley
Preston
Caledonia
Hokah
Hillsboro
Westby
Glenville
MINNESOTA
Harmony
Spring Grove
Viroqua
Reedsburg
Baraboo
IOWA
Le Roy
Lyle
Northwood
Readstown
Loyd
Lake Mills
Cresco
Lansing
Richland Center
Lodi
Manly
Cedar R.
Osage
Riceville
Decorah
Waukon
Gays Mills
Sauk City
Forest City
Elma
Spring Green
Mazomanie
Mason City
Nora Springs
Calmar
Muscoda
Wisconsin River
L. Mendota
Clear Lake
Charles City
Jackson Junc
Postville
Boscobel
Madison
Garner
Clear L.
New Hampton
Turkey R.
Prairie du Chien
Fennimore
Mt Horeb
Verona
Dodgeville
Rockwell
Marble Rock
Nashua
Wapsipinicon
West Union
Bloomington
Sheffield
Elkader
Mineral Point
Belmond
Sumner
Fayette
Lancaster
New Glarus
Monticello
Latimer
Allison
Guttenberg
Platteville
Belmont
Darlington
Hampton
Waverly
Headlyn
Cedar R.
Strawberry Pt
Cassville
Dows
Oelwein
Edgewood
Balltown
Monroe
River
Parkersburg
Benton
Hazel Green
WISCONSIN
ILLINOIS
Iowa Falls
Ackley
Cedar Falls
Waterloo
Manchester
Dyersville
Dubuque
Warren
Jesup
Independence
Galena
Hudson
Stockton
Eldora
Grundy Center
Elizabeth
Freeport
Hubbard
La Porte City
Walker
Coggon
Cascade
Bellevue
Conrad
Monticello
Dubuque Hills
Story City
Roland
Central City
Vinton
Albion
Anamosa
Savanna
Mt Carroll
Marshalltown
Marion
Wyoming
Maquoketa
Nevada
Toledo
Keystone
Cedar Rapids
Oxford Junc
Thomson
Polo
Melbourne
Tama
Clarence
Fulton
Cambridge
Belle Plaine
Bertram
Clinton
Sterling
Rock River
Baxter
Marengo
E Amana
Solon
Tipton
De Witt
Morrison
Rock Falls
Ankeny
Grinnell
Coralville Lake
Newton
Brooklyn
W Branch
Cordova
Prophetstown
Williamsburg
Coralville
Iowa City
Durant
Mississippi River
Montezuma
W Liberty
Davenport
Bettendorf
Moline
Walnut
Des Moines
Monroe
N English
Kalona
Geneseo
Carlisle
Muscatine
Illinois City
Princeton
Hartford
Lake Red Rock
Pella
New Sharon
Orion
Indianola
Columbus Junc
Cambridge
Buda
Sigourney
Kewanee
Knoxville
Oskaloosa
Washington
Cedar River
Aledo
Viola
Fremont
Joy
Alpha
Melcher
Skunk River
Galva
Bussey
Brighton
Wapello
Toulon
Keithsburg
Alexis
Oneida
Chariton
Albia
Ottumwa
Fairfield
Mediapolis
Galesburg
Des Moines River
Rathbun Lake
Mt Pleasant
New London
Monmouth
Chillicothe
Eldon
Knoxville
Humeston
Moravia
Stockport
Salem
Burlington
Maquon
Yates City
Peoria
Corydon
Bloomfield
Keosauqua
Farmington
Centerville
Bonaparte
Roseville
Spoon River
Moulton
Fort Madison
Lomax
Fairview
IOWA
MISSOURI
Farmington
ILLINOIS
La Harpe
Canton
Pekin
Lineville
Lancaster
Bushnell
Cuba
Macomb
Memphis
Carthage
Lewistown
Manito
Unionville
Keokuk
Kahoka
Hamilton
Ipava
Princeton
Queen City
Chariton R.
Plymouth
Havana
Green City
Bowen
Astoria
Mason City
Spickard
Kirksville
Milan
Edina
Knox City
Rushville
Middletown
Canton
Trenton
Monticello
Ursa
Beardstown
Petersburg
Scale 1:3 000 000
0
50
100 km
0
25
50
65 miles
1 hour

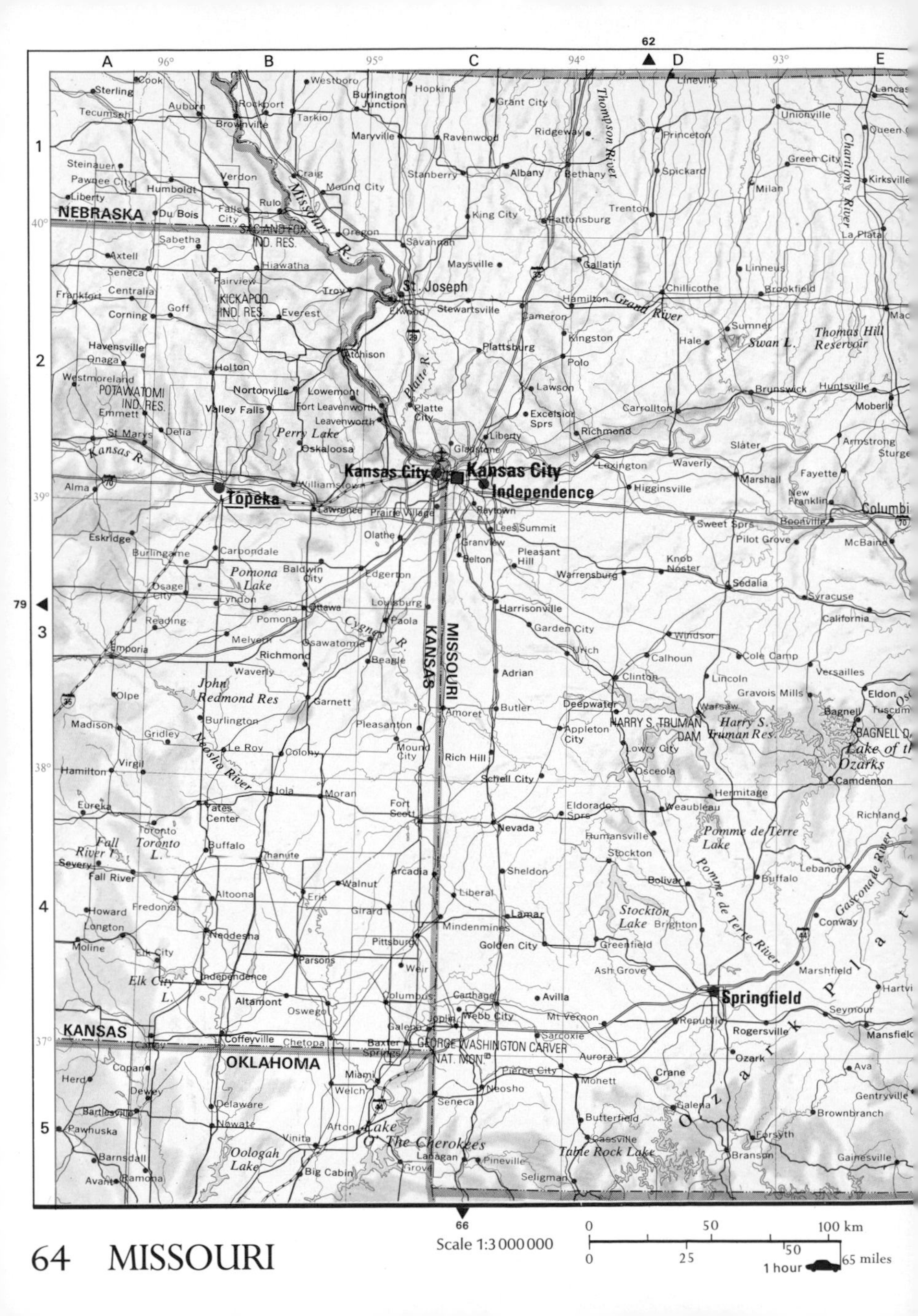

64 MISSOURI

Scale 1:3 000 000

0   50   100 km
0   25   50
1 hour   65 miles

66

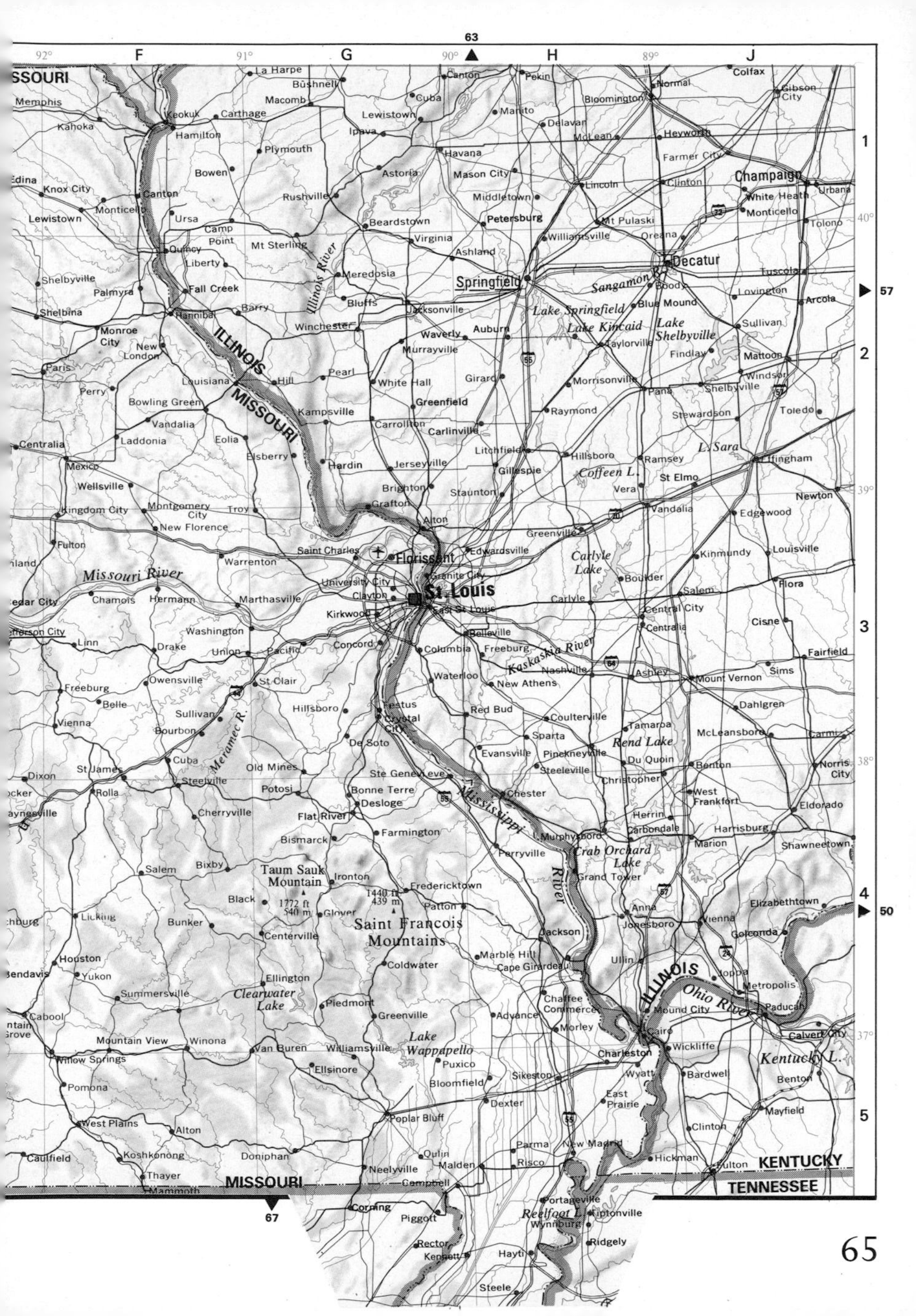

63
57
50
67
MISSOURI
ILLINOIS
KENTUCKY
TENNESSEE
St. Louis
Springfield
Decatur
Champaign
Missouri River
Illinois River
Mississippi River
Ohio River
Kaskaskia River
Meramec R.
Saint Francois Mountains
Taum Sauk Mountain
Lake Springfield
Lake Shelbyville
Carlyle Lake
Crab Orchard Lake
Rend Lake
Clearwater Lake
Lake Wappapello
Kentucky L.
Reelfoot L.

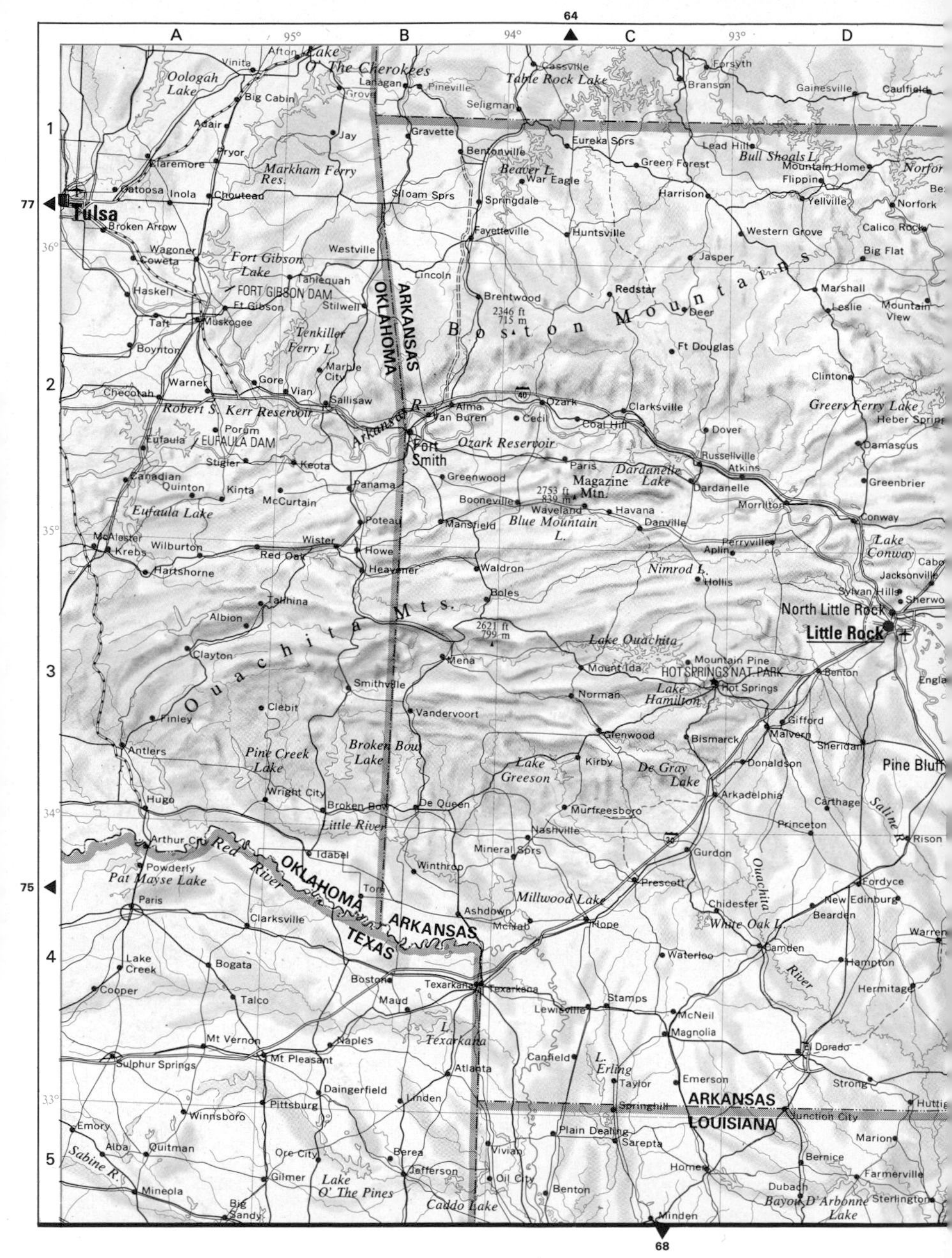

64

	A	95°	B	94° ▲	C	93°	D

Afton Lake
Oologah Lake   Vinita   O' The Cherokees
Big Cabin   Langan   Cassville   Forsyth
Grove   Pineville   Table Rock Lake   Branson   Gainesville   Caulfield

1   Adair   Jay   Gravette   Seligman   Eureka Sprs   Lead Hill   Bull Shoals L.
Pryor   Bentonville   Green Forest   Mountain Home   Norfor
Claremore   Markham Ferry   Beaver L.   War Eagle   Harrison   Flippin   Be.
Catoosa   Inola   Chouteau   Res.   Siloam Sprs   Springdale   Western Grove   Yellville   Norfork
77◄ **Tulsa**   Fayetteville   Huntsville   Calico Rock
Broken Arrow   Westville   Huntsville   Western Grove   Big Flat
Wagoner   Lincoln   Brentwood   Redstar   Jasper   Marshall
36°   Coweta   Fort Gibson   Tahlequah   2346 ft   Deer   Leslie   Mountain
Haskell   Lake   Stilwell   715 m   Ft Douglas   Clinton   View
Ft Gibson   FORT GIBSON DAM   B o s t o n M o u n t a i n s
Taft   Muskogee   Marble   Ozark   Clarksville   Dover   Greers Ferry Lake
Boynton   Tenkiller   City   Alma   Cedi   Russellville   Heber Sprs
2   Warner   Ferry L.   Vian   Sallisaw   Van Buren   Coal Hill   Atkins   Damascus
Checotah   Gore   Ozark Reservoir   Paris   Dardanelle   Morrilton   Greenbrier
Porum   Robert S. Kerr Reservoir   Greenwood   Magazine   Dardanelle   Conway
Eufaula   EUFAULA DAM   Panama   Booneville   2753 ft   Mtn.   Lake
Stigler   Keota   Poteau   839 m   Havana   Perryville   Conway   Cabo
35°   Kinta   McCurtain   Mansfield   Waveland   Danville   Aplin   Sylvan Hills   Sherwo
Canadian   Quinton   Wister   Blue Mountain   Nimrod L.   North Little Rock   Little Rock
Eufaula Lake   Red Oak   Howe   L.   Boles   Hollis   Benton   Engla
McAlester   Wilburton   Heavener   Waldron   Lake Ouachita   HOT SPRINGS NAT PARK
Krebs   Talihina   2681 ft   Mount Ida   Lake   Hot Springs   Gifford
Hartshorne   795 m   Mena   Norman   Hamilton   Bismarck   Malvern   Sheridan
3   Albion   Smithville   Glenwood   Donaldson   Pine Bluff
Clayton   O u a c h i t a   M t s.   Vandervoort   Lake   Kirby   De Gray   Carthage   Saline
Finley   Clebit   Greeson   Lake   Arkadelphia   Princeton   Rison
Antlers   Pine Creek   Broken Bow   Murfreesboro   Nashville   Gurdon   Ouachita
Lake   Lake   De Queen   Mineral Sprs   Prescott   Chidester   Fordyce
34°   Hugo   Wright City   Little River   Winthrop   Millwood Lake   New Edinburg
Arthur City   Broken Bow   Idabel   Toro   Ashdown   Hope   White Oak L.   Bearden   Warren
Powderly   Red River   Winthrop   McNab   Waterloo   Camden   Hampton
75◄ Pat Mayse Lake   OKLAHOMA   Boston   Texarkana   Lewisville   Stamps   Hermitage
Paris   ARKANSAS   Maud   Texarkana   McNeil   River
Clarksville   TEXAS   Magnolia   El Dorado   Strong
Lake   Bogata   Naples   Atlanta   Canfield   Emerson   Huttig
Creek   Talco   Texarkana   L.   Taylor   ARKANSAS
33°   Cooper   Mt Pleasant   Linden   Springhill   LOUISIANA   Junction City
Sulphur Springs   Daingerfield   Plain Dealing   Sarepta   Marion
Winnsboro   Pittsburg   Berea   Vivian   Homer   Bernice   Farmerville
Emory   Quitman   Ore City   Jefferson   Oil City   Dubach   Sterlington
5   Alba   Gilmer   Lake   Benton   Bayou D' Arbonne   Lake
Sabine R.   Mineola   O' The Pines   Caddo Lake   Minden   Lake

68

66   ARKANSAS

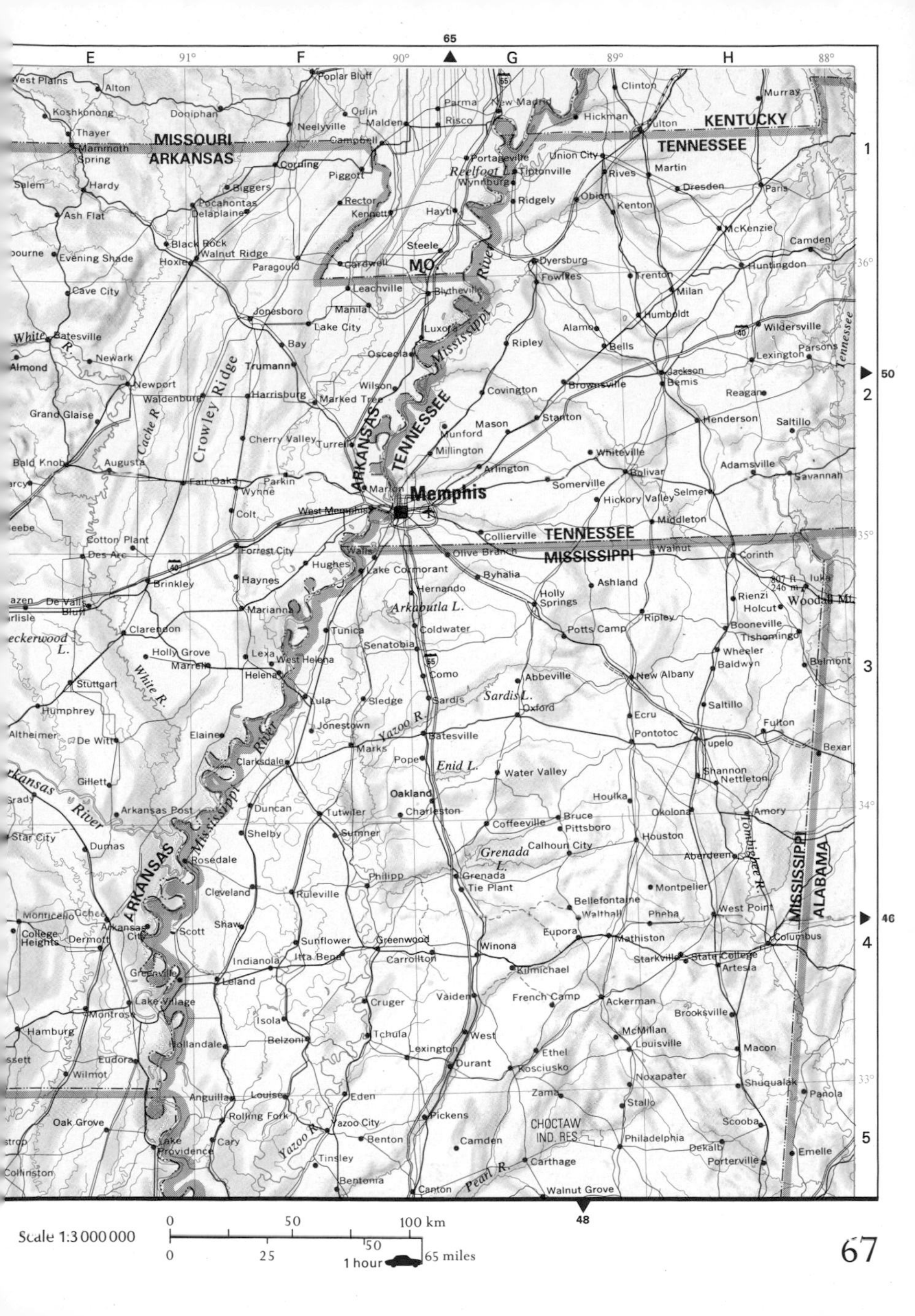

E   91°   F   90°   G   89°   H   88°

West Plains · Alton   Poplar Bluff   Clinton   Murray

Koshkonong   Doniphan   Qulin   Parma   New Madrid   Hickman   Fulton   KENTUCKY

Thayer   Neelyville · Malden   Risco   Union City   TENNESSEE

Mammoth Spring   MISSOURI   Campbell   Portageville   Martin · Dresden   Paris

Salem · Hardy   ARKANSAS   Cording   Piggott   Reelfoot L.   Tiptonville   Rives · Martin

Ash Flat   Biggers   Wynburg   Ridgely   Obion · Kenton   McKenzie

Pocahontas · Delaplaine   Rector · Kennett   Ridgely   Camden

bourne · Evening Shade   Black Rock · Hoxie   Hayti   Huntingdon

Cave City   Walnut Ridge   Steele   Dyersburg   Trenton · Milan   Wildersville

Batesville   Paragould   Cardwell   MO.   Humboldt   Lexington · Parsons

White   Newark   Jonesboro   Leachville · Blytheville   Fowlkes   Jackson · Bemis

Almond   Trumann   Manila   Luxora   Osceola   Ripley   Alamo   Bells   Reagan · Saltillo

Grand Glaise   Newport · Waldenburg   Harrisburg   Wilson   Covington   Brownsville   Henderson

Bald Knob   Augusta   Marked Tree   Mason   Stanton   Whiteville   Adamsville · Savannah

Fair Oaks · Parkin   Cherry Valley   Turrell   Munford   Arlington   Somerville   Bolivar   Selmer

eebe   Cotton Plant   Wynne   Millington   Hickory Valley   Middleton

Des Arc   Colt   Memphis   Collierville   TENNESSEE

De Valls Bluff   Forrest City   West Memphis   Walls   Olive Branch   Walnut   MISSISSIPPI   Corinth

arlisle   Brinkley   Haynes   Hughes   Lake Cormorant   Byhalia   Ashland   Rienzi · Iuka

eckerwood L.   Marianna   Hernando   Holly Springs   Holcut   Woodall Mt.

Clarendon   Arkabutla L.   Ripley   Booneville   346 m.

hazen   Holly Grove   Tunica   Coldwater   Potts Camp   Tishomingo

Stuttgart   Marvell   Senatobia   Wheeler · Baldwyn

White R.   Lexa · West Helena   Como   Abbeville   New Albany   Belmont

Humphrey   Helena   Lula   Sledge   Sardis L.   Oxford   Saltillo

Altheimer   De Witt   Jonestown   Sardis   Ecru   Fulton

Elaine   Marks   Batesville   Pontotoc   Tupelo

rkansas   Gillett   Clarksdale   Pope   Enid L.   Water Valley   Bexar

rady   Arkansas Post   Duncan   Oakland   Shannon · Nettleton

Star City   Dumas   Tutwiler   Charleston   Houlka   Okolona · Amory

Rosedale   Shelby   Sumner   Coffeeville   Bruce   Houston   Aberdeen

Cleveland   Pittsboro   Calhoun City   Montpelier   West Point

Monticello   Ruleville   Philipp   Grenada L.   Bellefontaine   Pheba

College Heights · Dermott   Arkansas City   Scott   Shaw   Grenada · Tie Plant   Walthall   Columbus

Greenville   Sunflower   Greenwood   Winona   Eupora   Mathiston   Starkville · State College   Artesia

Lake Village   Indianola · Itta Bena   Carrollton   Kilmichael   MISSISSIPPI

Montrose   Leland   Cruger   Vaiden   French Camp   Ackerman   Brooksville   ALABAMA

Hamburg   Isola   Tchula   McMillan · Louisville   Macon

ssett   Eudora   Hollandale   Belzoni   Lexington   West · Durant   Ethel   Noxapater · Shuqualak

Wilmot   Anguilla   Louise   Eden   Kosciusko   Zama   Stallo   Panola

Oak Grove   Rolling Fork   Yazoo City   Pickens   Camden   Philadelphia   Scooba

strop   Lake Providence   Cary   Benton   CHOCTAW IND. RES.   DeKalb   Emelle

olhinston   Tinsley   Carthage   Porterville

Bentonia   Canton   Walnut Grove

Scale 1:3 000 000

0   50   100 km

0   25   50   65 miles

1 hour

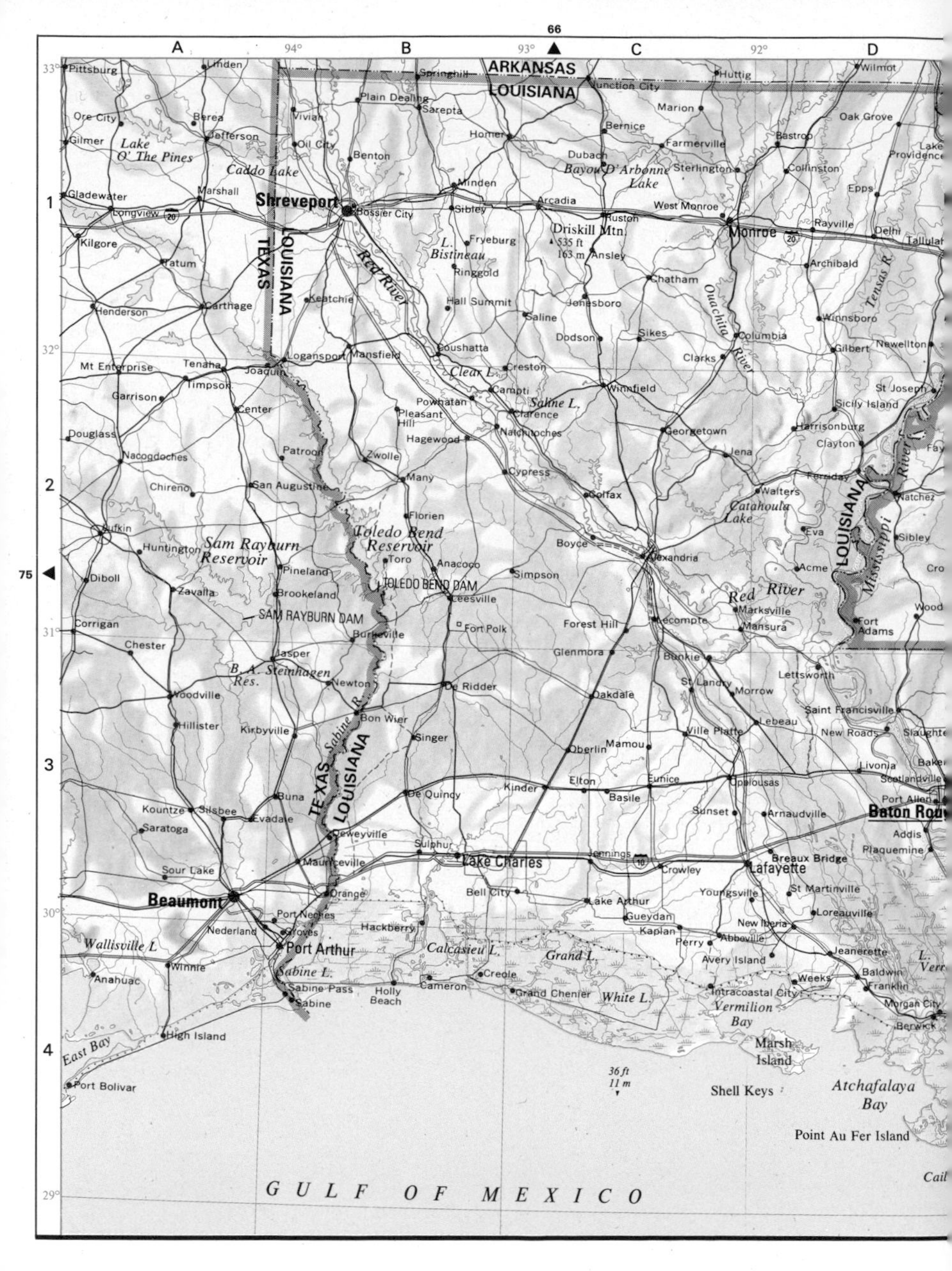

	A	94°	B	93°	C	92°	D

ARKANSAS
LOUISIANA

33°
Pittsburg   Linden   Springhill
Ore City   Berea   Plain Dealing   Junction City   Huttig   Wilmot
Gilmer   Jefferson   Sarepta   Bernice   Oak Grove   Lake
Lake   Vivian   Homer   Marion   Bastrop   Providence
O' The Pines   Oil City   Benton   Farmerville   Collinston   Epps
Gladewater   Marshall   Caddo Lake   Minden   Bayou D'Arbonne   Sterlington
1   Longview   20   Shreveport   Bossier City   Sibley   Arcadia   Ruston   West Monroe   Monroe   20   Rayville   Delhi   Tallulah
Kilgore   Red River   Fryeburg   Driskill Mtn.   Ansley   Archibald
Tatum   Carthage   L.   535 ft   163 m   Chatham   Sicily Island
32°   Keatchie   Bistineau   Ringgold   Columbia   Winnsboro   St Joseph
Henderson   Hall Summit   Saline   Jonesboro   Sikes   Clarks   Gilbert   Newellton
Mt Enterprise   Tenaha   Logansport   Mansfield   Coushatta   Dodson   Harrisonburg
Garrison   Timpson   Joaquin   Clear L.   Creston   Jena   Clayton
Douglass   Center   Powhatan   Campti   Saline L.   Winnfield   Georgetown   Ferriday   Natchez
Nacogdoches   Patroon   Pleasant   Clarence   Winnfield   Sibley
Chireno   Zwolle   Hill   Hagewood   Natchitoches   Cro
2   Lufkin   San Augustine   Many   Florien   Cypress   Colfax   Catahoula   Eva   Wood
Huntington   Toledo Bend   Boyce   Alexandria   Lake   Acme
75   Diboll   Sam Rayburn   Reservoir   Toro   Anacoco   Red   River   Fort
Reservoir   Pineland   TOLEDO BEND DAM   Simpson   River   Adams
Corrigan   Zavalla   Brookeland   Leesville   Fort Polk   Forest Hill   Lecompte   Marksville   Mansura
Chester   SAM RAYBURN DAM   Burrville   Glenmora   Bunkie
Woodville   B. A. Steinhagen   Jasper   Newton   De Ridder   St Landry   Lettsworth
Hillister   Res.   Bon Wier   Singer   Oberlin   Mamou   Ville Platte   Lebeau   Saint Francisville
Kirbyville   Oakdale   Eunice   Opelousas   New Roads   Slaughte
3   Buna   Mauriceville   De Quincy   Kinder   Elton   Basile   Livonia   Bake
Kountze   Silsbee   Evadale   Sunset   Arnaudville   Port Allen   Scotlandville
Saratoga   Neweyville   Sulphur   Jennings   Crowley   Lafayette   Baton Rou
Sour Lake   Lake Charles   Breaux Bridge   Addis
Beaumont   Orange   Bell City   Lake Arthur   Youngsville   St Martinville   Plaquemine
30°   Nederland   Port Neches   Groves   Hackberry   Gueydan   Abbeville   New Iberia   Loreauville
Wallisville L.   Winnie   Port Arthur   Sabine L.   Calcasieu L.   Kaplan   Perry   Avery Island   Jeanerette   Baldwin
Anahuac   Sabine Pass   Holly   Cameron   Creole   Grand Chenier   White L.   Intracoastal City   Weeks   Franklin
4   East Bay   High Island   Sabine   Beach   Vermilion   Morgan City   Berwick
Port Bolivar   Bay   Marsh
36 ft   Island   Atchafalaya
11 m   Shell Keys   Bay
Point Au Fer Island
29°   GULF   OF   MEXICO   Cail

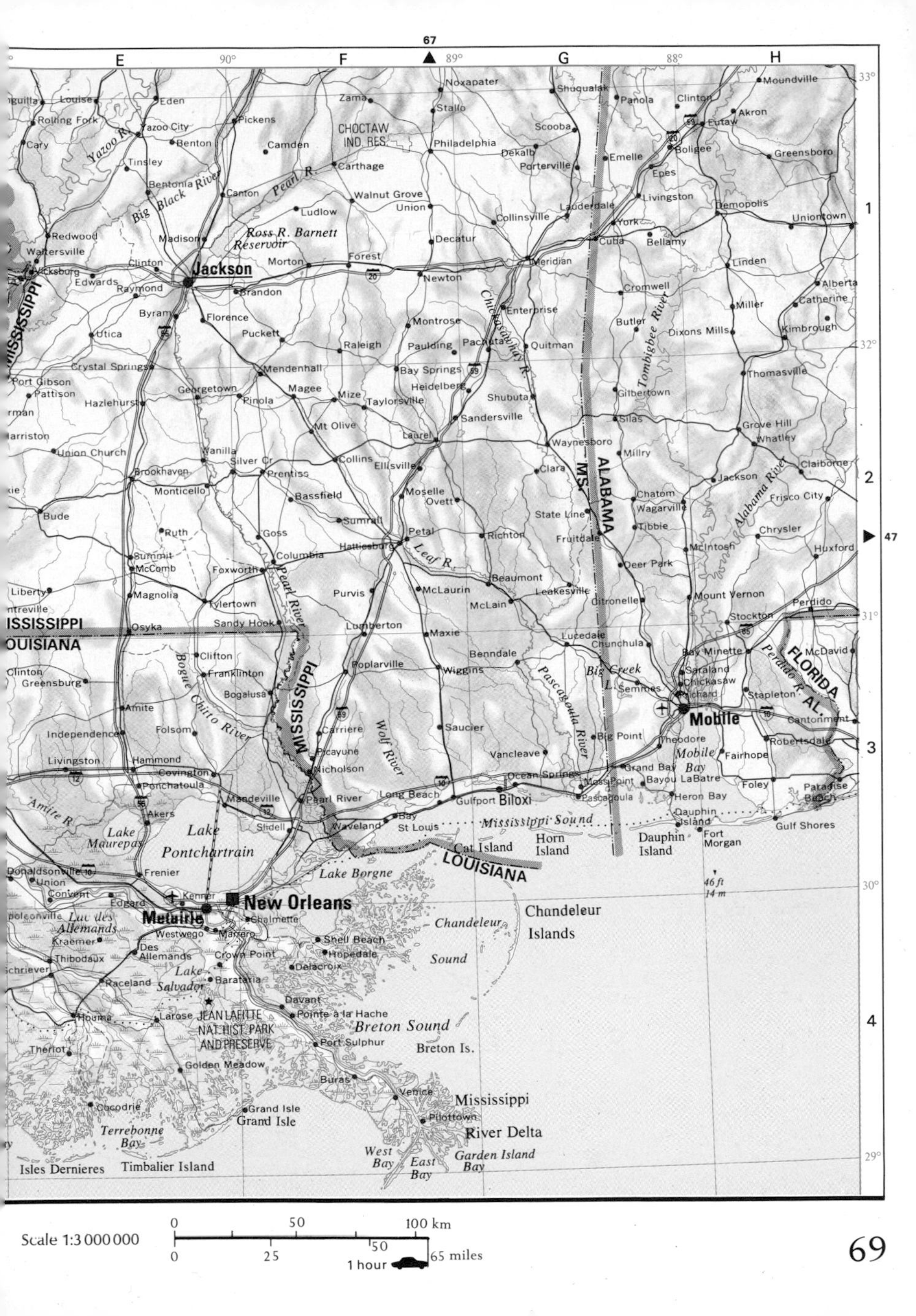

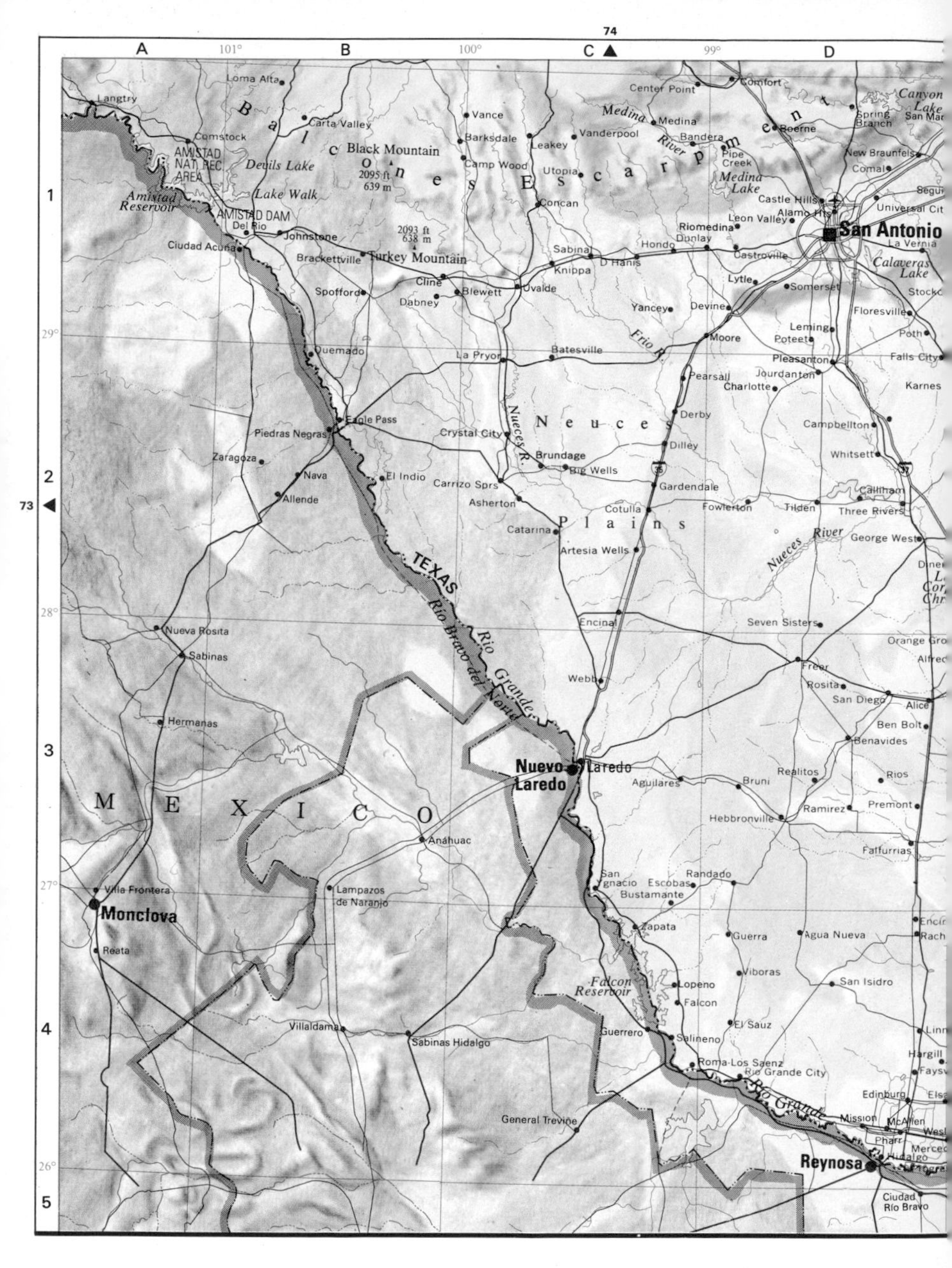

70 TEXAS-Southern

MEXICO
San Antonio
Nuevo Laredo
Laredo
Monclova
Reynosa
Balcones Escarpment
Neuces Plains
Rio Grande
Rio Bravo del Norte
Amistad Reservoir
Falcon Reservoir
Medina Lake
Calaveras Lake
Canyon Lake
Nueces River
Frio R.
Nueces R.
Medina River
Black Mountain 2095 ft 639 m
Turkey Mountain 2093 ft 638 m
Del Rio
Ciudad Acuña
Eagle Pass
Piedras Negras
Uvalde
Crystal City
Carrizo Sprs
Cotulla
Pearsall
Hondo
Castroville
Zapata
Roma-Los Saenz
Rio Grande City
Mission
McAllen
Edinburg
Hebbronville
Alice
Freer
Falfurrias
George West
Three Rivers
Pleasanton
Sabinas Hidalgo
Anáhuac
Lampazos de Naranjo
Nueva Rosita
Sabinas
Villa Frontera
Guerrero
General Treviñe

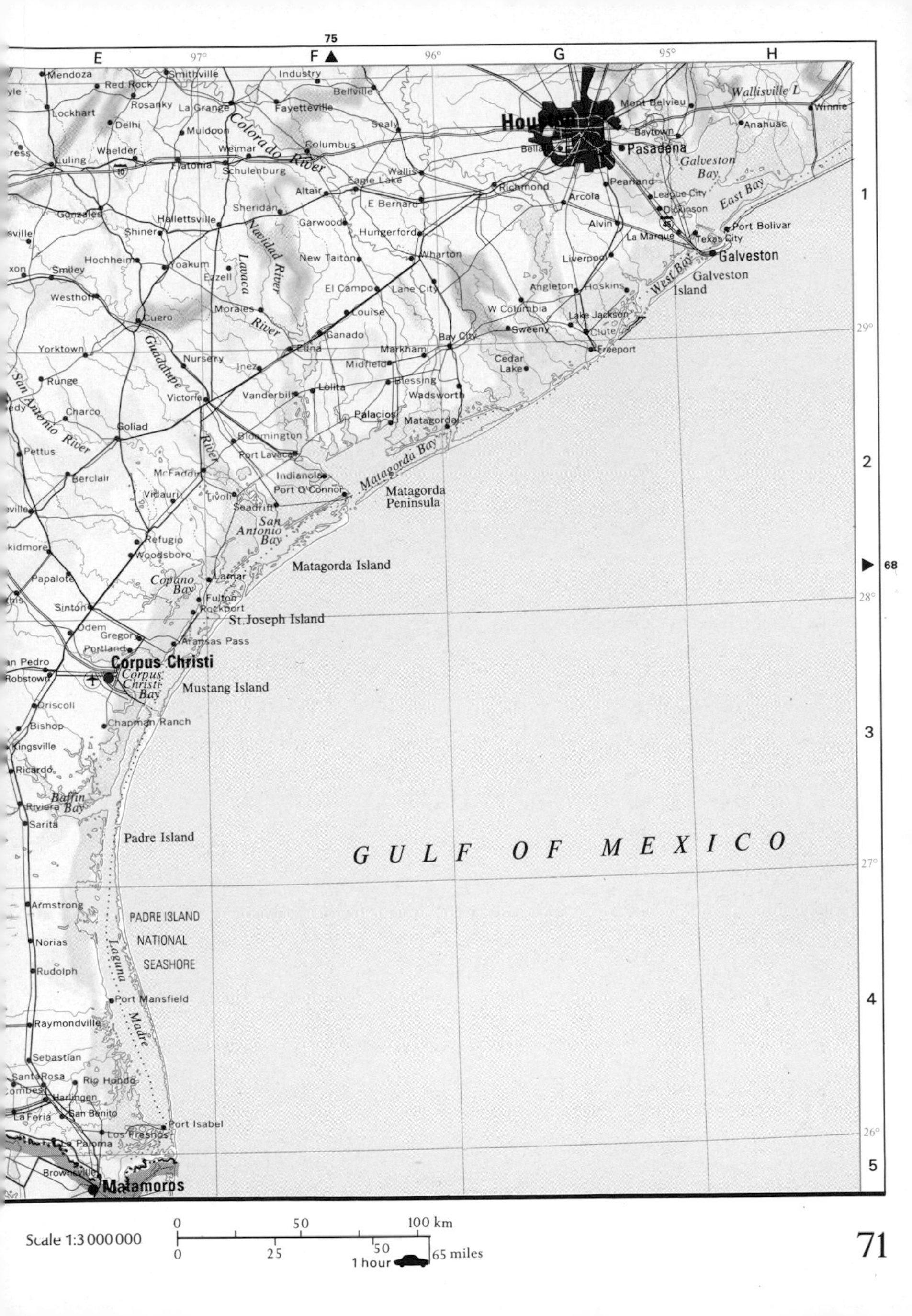

E   97°   F ▲   96°   G   95°   H

Mendoza   Smithville   Industry   Bellville   Wallisville L.
yle   Red Rock   Rosanky   La Grange   Fayetteville   Mont Belvieu   Winnie
Lockhart   Delhi   Muldoon   Columbus   Sealy   Baytown   Anahuac
ress   Luling   Waelder   Weimar   Schulenburg   Walls   Houston   Pasadena
    Gonzales   Flatonia   Altair   Eagle Lake   Richmond   Bellaire   Pearland   Galveston Bay
    Hallettsville   Sheridan   E Bernard   Arcola   Alvin   League City   Port Bolivar
sville   Shiner   Garwood   Hungerford   Liverpool   La Marque   Texas City   Dickinson   East Bay
    Hochheim   Yoakum   New Taiton   Wharton   Angleton   Hoskins   West Bay   Galveston
xon   Smiley   Ezzell   El Campo   Lane City   W Columbia   Lake Jackson   Galveston Island
    Westhoff   Cuero   Morales   Louise   Sweeny   Clute   Island
Yorktown   Nursery   Edna   Ganado   Markham   Cedar Lake   Freeport
    Runge   Inez   Midfield   Blessing
    Charco   Victoria   Vanderbilt   Lolita   Wadsworth
Pettus   Goliad   Bloomington   Palacios   Matagorda
Berclair   McFaddin   Port Lavaca   Matagorda Bay
    Vidauri   Tivoli   Indianola   Matagorda Peninsula
kidmore   Refugio   Seadrift   Port O'Connor
    Woodsboro   San Antonio Bay
Papalote   Copano Bay   Lamar   Matagorda Island
Sinton   Fulton   St.Joseph Island
    Odem   Gregor   Rockport
an Pedro   Portland   Aransas Pass
Robstown   Corpus Christi
    Corpus Christi Bay   Mustang Island
Driscoli
Bishop   Chapman Ranch
Kingsville
Ricardo
    Baffin Bay
Riviera
Sarita   Padre Island   G U L F   O F   M E X I C O
Armstrong   PADRE ISLAND
Norias   NATIONAL
Rudolph   SEASHORE
    Port Mansfield
Raymondville
Sebastian
Santa Rosa   Rio Hondo
omber   Harlingen
La Feria   San Benito
    Port Isabel
    Los Fresnos
    Palomo
Brownsville
Matamoros

San Antonio River   Guadalupe River   Lavaca River   Navidad River   Colorado River

Laguna Madre

1
29°
2
68
28°
3
27°
4
26°
5

Scale 1:3 000 000

0   50   100 km
0   25   50   65 miles
1 hour

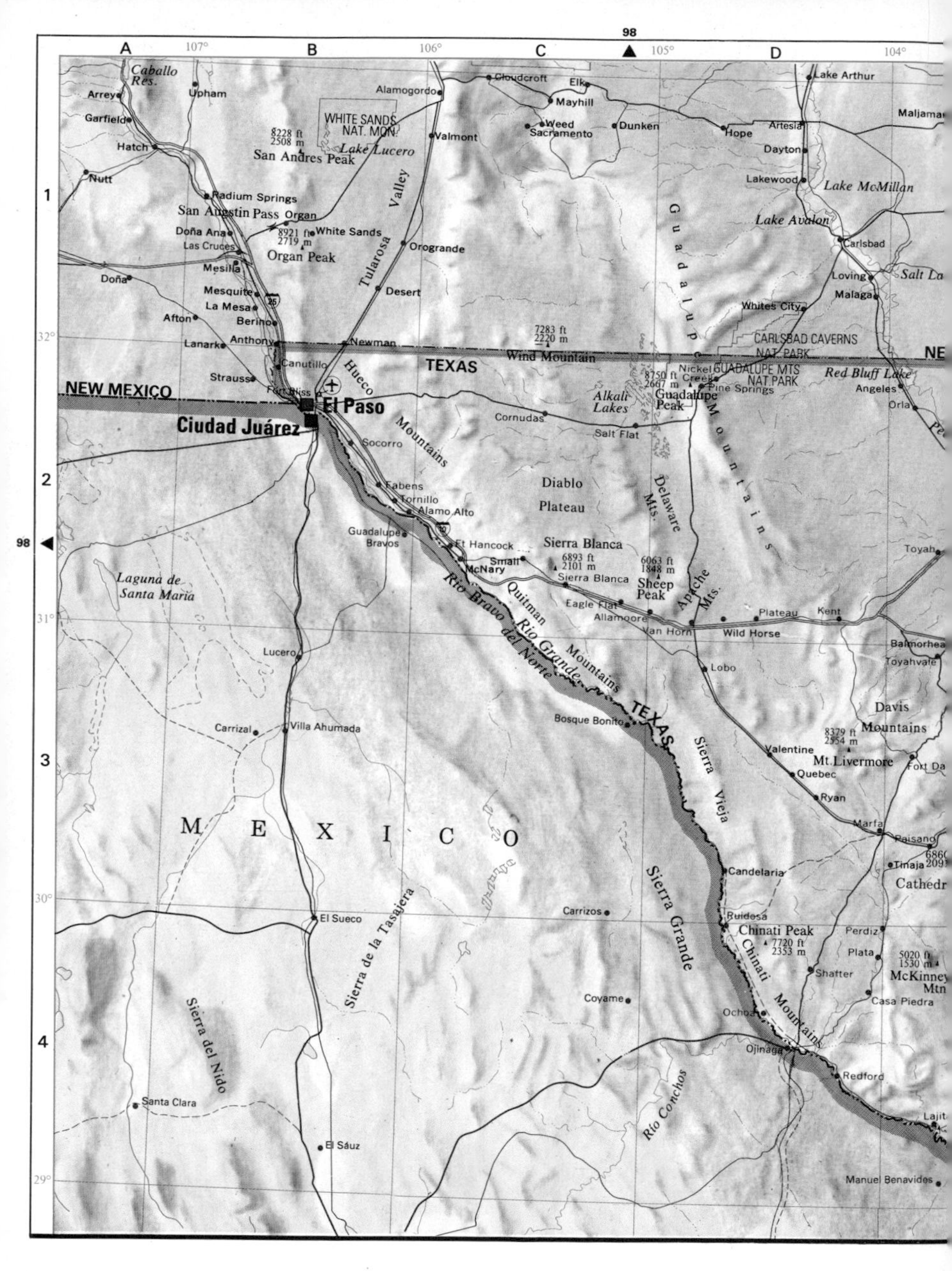
A
B
C
D
98
107°
106°
105°
104°
1
2
3
4
32°
31°
30°
29°
Caballo Res.
Arrey
Upham
Garfield
Hatch
Nutt
Radium Springs
San Augustin Pass
Organ
Doña Ana
Las Cruces
Mesilla
Doña
Mesquite
La Mesa
Afton
Berino
Lanark
Anthony
Canutillo
Strauss
Fort Bliss
NEW MEXICO
El Paso
Ciudad Juárez
Alamogordo
WHITE SANDS NAT. MON.
8228 ft 2508 m
San Andres Peak
Lake Lucero
Valmont
8921 ft 2719 m
White Sands
Organ Peak
Tularosa Valley
Orogrande
Desert
Newman
Hueco Mountains
Socorro
Fabens
Tornillo
Alamo Alto
Guadalupe Bravos
Ft Hancock
McNary
Small
Cloudcroft
Elk
Mayhill
Weed
Sacramento
Dunken
Hope
Lake Arthur
Artesia
Maljama
Dayton
Lakewood
Lake McMillan
Lake Avalon
Carlsbad
Loving
Salt La
Malaga
Whites City
Guadalupe Mountains
CARLSBAD CAVERNS NAT. PARK
GUADALUPE MTS NAT. PARK
7283 ft 2220 m
Wind Mountain
TEXAS
NE
Nickel Creek
8750 ft 2667 m
Guadalupe Peak
Pine Springs
Red Bluff Lake
Angeles
Orla
Alkali Lakes
Cornudas
Salt Flat
Diablo Plateau
Delaware Mts.
Sierra Blanca
6893 ft 2101 m
6063 ft 1848 m
Sheep Peak
Apache Mts.
Eagle Flat
Allamoore
Van Horn
Wild Horse
Plateau
Kent
Toyah
Balmorhea
Toyahvale
Lobo
Quitman Mountains
Rio Bravo del Norte
Rio Grande
TEXAS
Bosque Bonito
Sierra Vieja
Davis Mountains
8379 ft 2554 m
Mt. Livermore
Valentine
Quebec
Ryan
Fort Da
Marfa
Paisano
Tinaja
Cathedr
Laguna de Santa Maria
Lucero
Carrizal
Villa Ahumada
MEXICO
Candelaria
Sierra Grande
Carrizos
Ruidosa
Chinati Peak
7720 ft 2353 m
Chinati Mountains
Perdiz
Plata
5020 ft 1530 m
McKinney Mtn
Shafter
Casa Piedra
El Sueco
Sierra de la Tasajera
Sierra del Nido
Coyame
Ochoa
Ojinaga
Redford
Rio Conchos
Santa Clara
El Sáuz
Lajit
Manuel Benavides

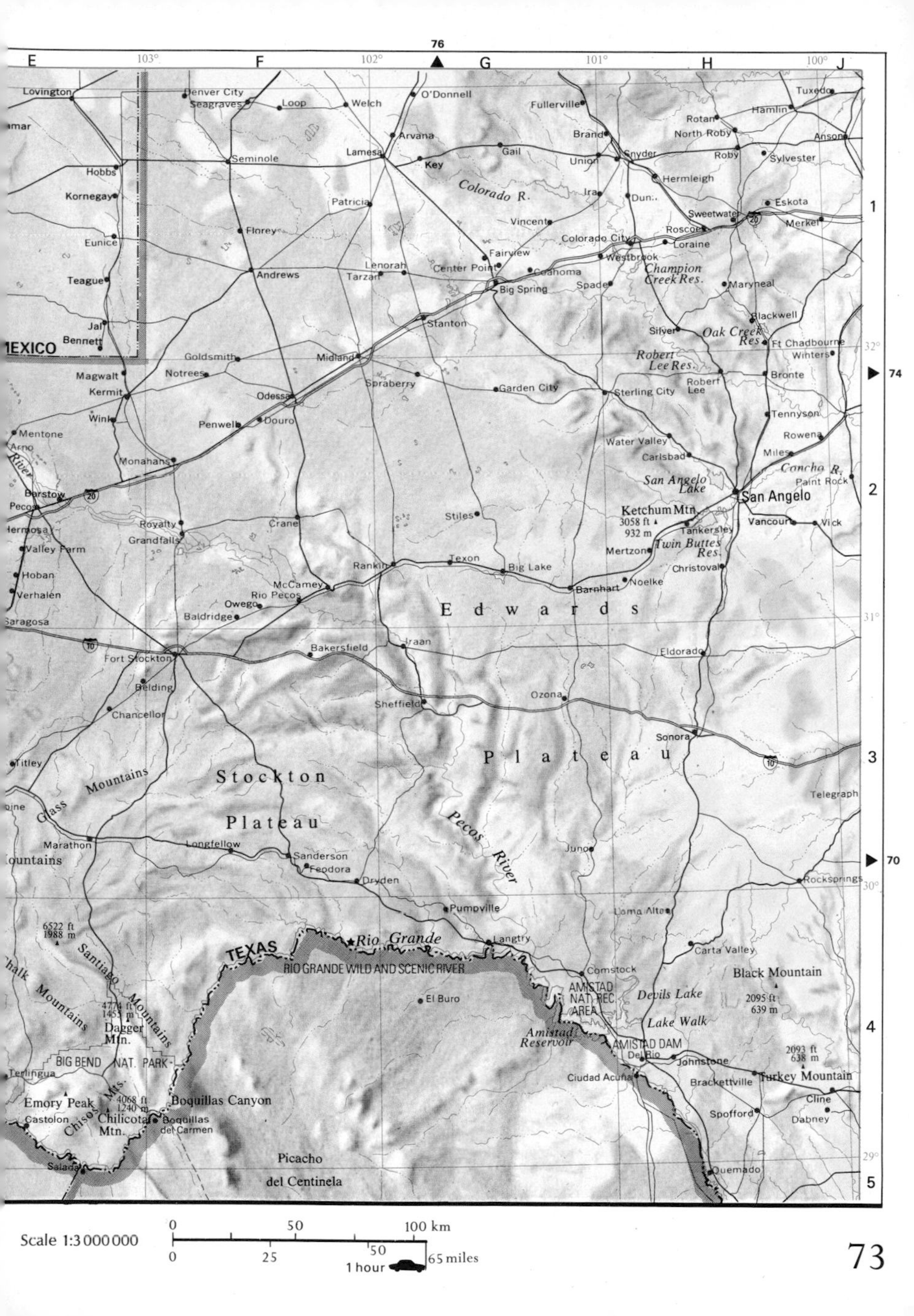

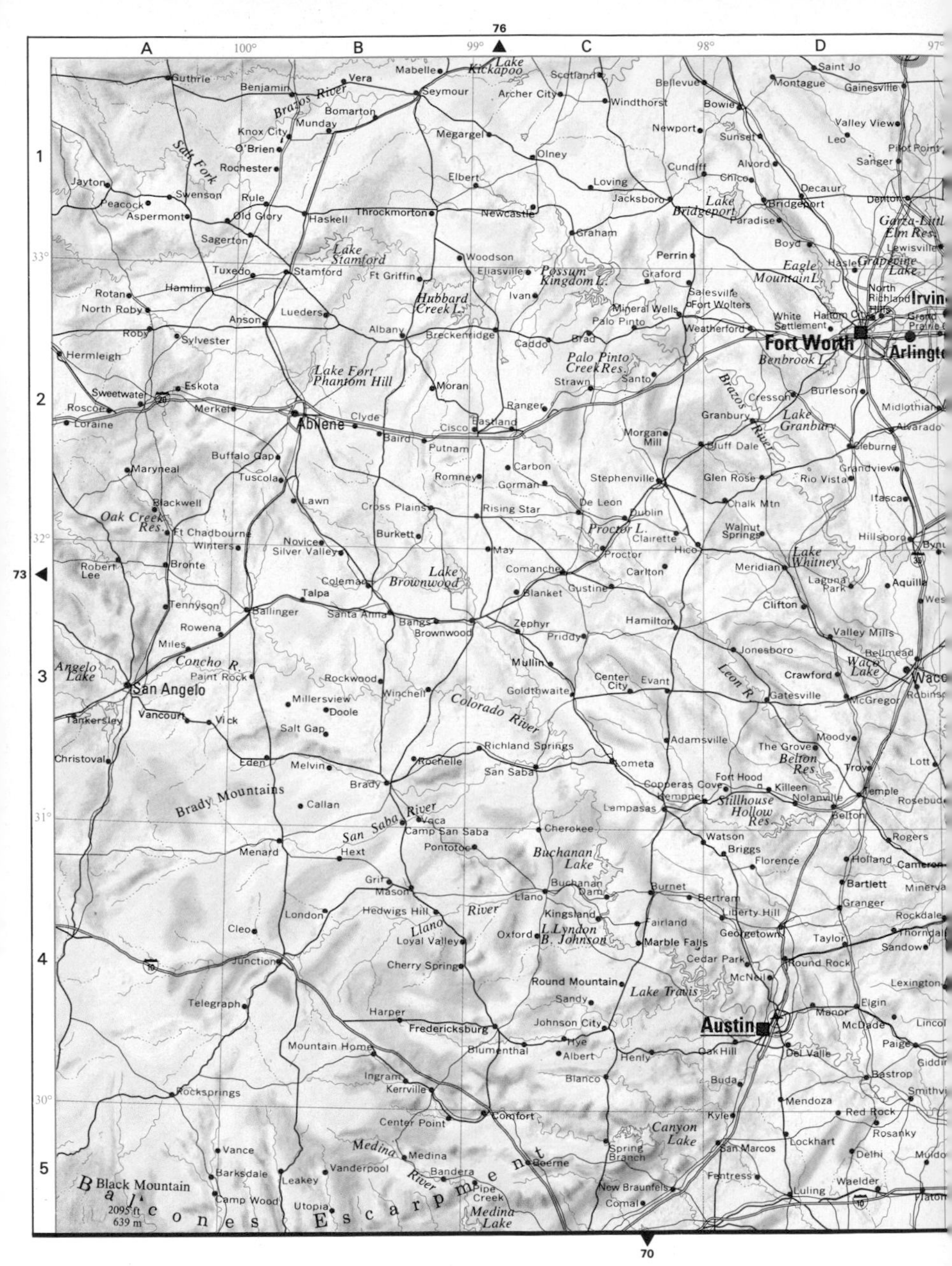

76
A
100°
B
99°
C
98°
D
97°
1
2
3
4
5
73
70
Lake Kickapoo
Mabelle
Scotland
Saint Jo
Guthrie
Vera
Benjamin
Brazos River
Seymour
Archer City
Bellevue
Montague
Gainesville
Windthorst
Bowie
Bomarton
Knox City
Munday
Newport
Sunset
Valley View
Megargel
Leo
O'Brien
Salt Fork
Pilot Point
Olney
Sanger
Rochester
Cundiff
Alvord
Elbert
Chico
Jayton
Loving
Decatur
Peacock
Swenson
Rule
Jacksboro
Lake Bridgeport
Bridgeport
Denton
Aspermont
Old Glory
Haskell
Throckmorton
Newcastle
Paradise
Garza-Little Elm Res.
Sagerton
Graham
Boyd
Lewisville
Lake Stamford
Woodson
Perrin
Tuxedo
Stamford
Ft Griffin
Eliasville
Possum Kingdom L.
Graford
Eagle Mountain L.
Hasle
Grapevine Lake
Rotan
Hamlin
Hubbard Creek L.
Ivan
Salesville
North Richland Hills
Irving
North Roby
Lueders
Mineral Wells
Fort Wolters
White Settlement
Haltom City
Anson
Palo Pinto
Weatherford
Grand Prairie
Roby
Sylvester
Albany
Breckenridge
Caddo
Brad
Fort Worth
Arlington
Hermleigh
Palo Pinto Creek Res.
Benbrook L.
Lake Fort Phantom Hill
Santo
Strawn
Moran
Brazos River
Eskota
Cresson
Burleson
Sweetwater
Ranger
Merkel
Roscoe
Abilene
Clyde
Eastland
Midlothian
Loraine
Cisco
Granbury
Lake Granbury
Alvarado
Baird
Putnam
Morgan Mill
Bluff Dale
Buffalo Gap
Cleburne
Maryneal
Carbon
Grandview
Tuscola
Romney
Stephenville
Glen Rose
Rio Vista
Gorman
Itasca
Lawn
Blackwell
De Leon
Chalk Mtn
Cross Plains
Rising Star
Dublin
Oak Creek Res.
Ft Chadbourne
Proctor L.
Walnut Springs
Burkett
Clairette
Hillsboro
Winters
Novice
Hico
Lake Whitney
Silver Valley
May
Proctor
Bronte
Robert Lee
Meridian
Coleman
Lake Brownwood
Comanche
Carlton
Laguna Park
Aquilla
Talpa
Blanket
Gustine
Tennyson
Ballinger
Santa Anna
Clifton
Bangs
Brownwood
Zephyr
Hamilton
Rowena
Priddy
Valley Mills
Miles
Jonesboro
Bellmead
Concho R.
Mullin
Angelo Lake
Paint Rock
Waco Lake
Rockwood
Crawford
Leon R.
Waco
San Angelo
Center City
Evant
Winchell
Goldthwaite
Gatesville
Millersview
McGregor
Robinson
Doole
Colorado River
Vancourt
Tankersley
Vick
Salt Gap
Adamsville
Moody
Richland Springs
The Grove
Christoval
Eden
Rochelle
Lometa
Belton Res.
Lott
Melvin
San Saba
Troy
Fort Hood
Brady
Copperas Cove
Killeen
Temple
Kempner
Brady Mountains
Stillhouse Hollow Res.
Nolanville
Rosebud
Callan
Lampasas
San Saba River
Belton
Voca
Camp San Saba
Cherokee
Rogers
Watson
Menard
Hext
Pontotoc
Buchanan Lake
Briggs
Holland
Florence
Cameron
Bartlett
Grit
Buchanan Dam
Burnet
Minerva
Mason
Llano
Bertram
Granger
Hedwigs Hill
River
Kingsland
Liberty Hill
London
Rockdale
Llano
Fairland
Cleo
Oxford
L. Lyndon B. Johnson
Georgetown
Thorndale
Loyal Valley
Marble Falls
Taylor
Sandow
Junction
Cedar Park
Round Rock
Cherry Spring
McNeil
Round Mountain
Lexington
Lake Travis
Sandy
Telegraph
Elgin
Harper
Manor
Johnson City
Austin
McDade
Lincoln
Fredericksburg
Hye
Mountain Home
Blumenthal
Oak Hill
Paige
Albert
Henly
Del Valle
Giddings
Ingram
Blanco
Bastrop
Buda
Kerrville
Rocksprings
Smithville
Mendoza
Comfort
Red Rock
Center Point
Kyle
Canyon Lake
Rosanky
Vance
Lockhart
Medina
San Marcos
Spring Branch
Delhi
Muldoon
Boerne
Barksdale
Vanderpool
Bandera
Medina River
Fentress
Waelder
Leakey
Black Mountain
Pipe Creek
New Braunfels
Luling
Camp Wood
Flatonia
2095 ft
639 m
Utopia
Comal
Medina Lake
Balcones Escarpment

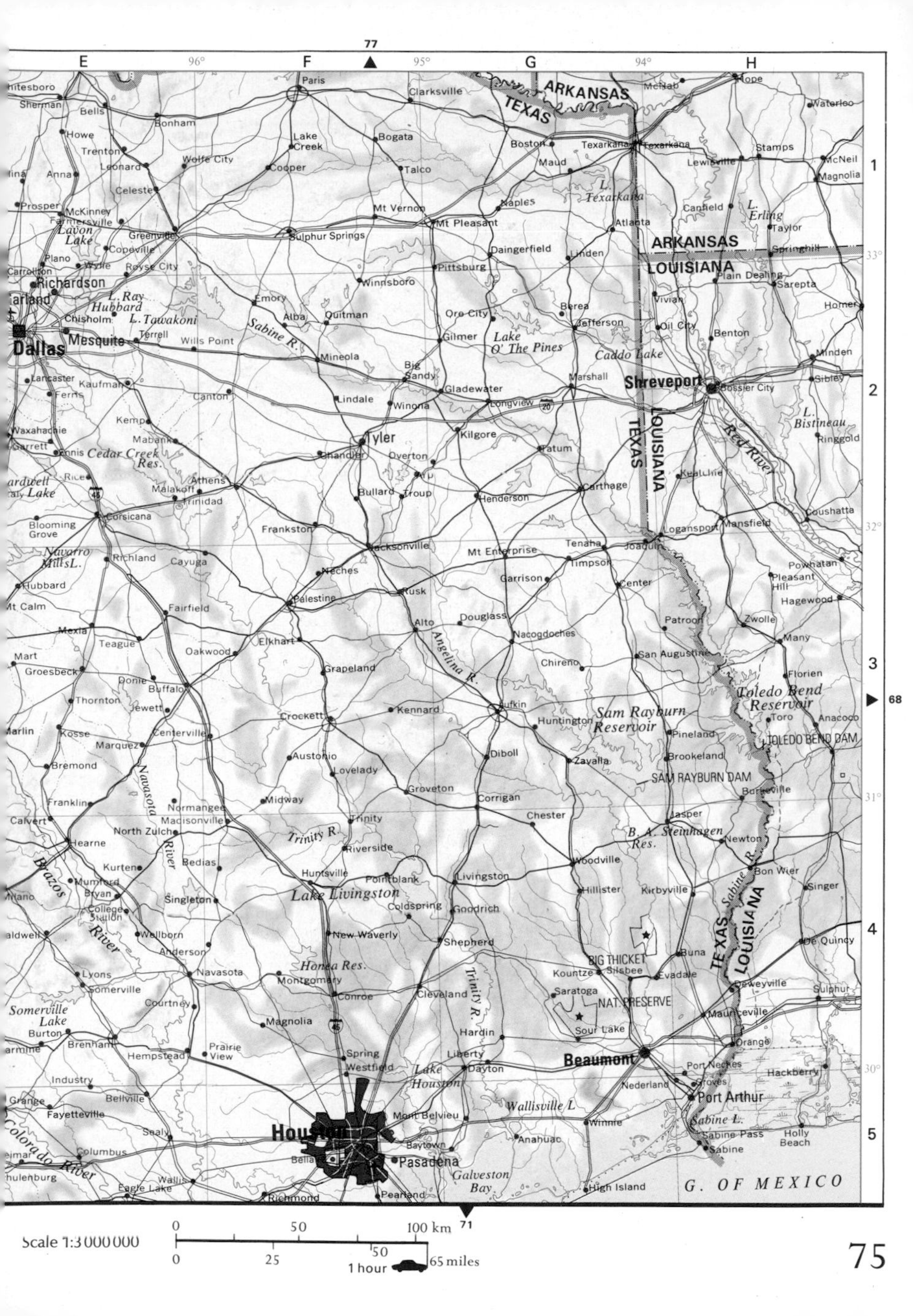

E 96° **F** 95° **G** 94° **H**

ARKANSAS
TEXAS

1

33°

ARKANSAS
LOUISIANA

2

TEXAS
LOUISIANA

32°

3

▶ 68

31°

4

TEXAS
LOUISIANA

Dallas

Mesquite

Houston
Pasadena

Beaumont

Port Arthur

Shreveport

Bossier City

Tyler

Longview

Marshall

Paris

Texarkana

Hope

5

30°

G. OF MEXICO

Galveston
Bay

Sabine L.

Lake Livingston

Sam Rayburn
Reservoir

Toledo Bend
Reservoir

Lake
O' The Pines

Caddo Lake

Scale 1:3 000 000

0   50   100 km
|----|----|----|
0   25   50
1 hour   65 miles

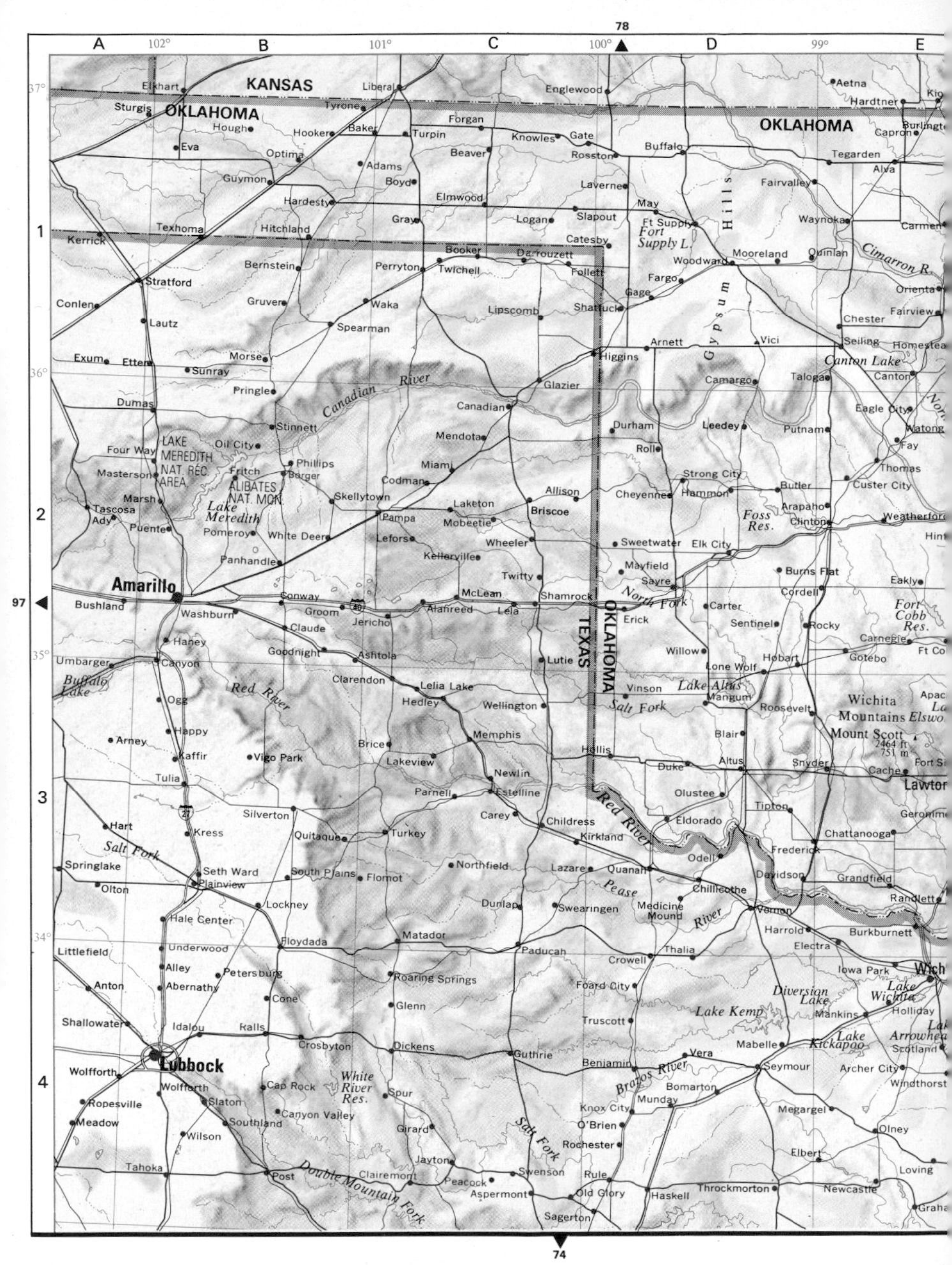
78
A
102°
B
101°
C
100°
D
99°
E
37°
KANSAS
OKLAHOMA
Elkhart
Sturgis
Hough
Eva
Liberal
Tyrone
Hooker
Baker
Turpin
Forgan
Englewood
Knowles
Gate
Beaver
Rosston
Buffalo
Aetna
Hardtner
OKLAHOMA
Capron
Tegarden
Alva
Optima
Adams
Guymon
Boyd
Hardesty
Elmwood
Laverne
Fairvalley
Gray
Logan
Slapout
May
Ft Supply
Fort Supply L.
Gypsum Hills
Waynoka
Carmen
1
Texhoma
Hitchland
Kerrick
Catesby
Booker
Darrouzett
Perryton
Twichell
Follett
Woodward
Mooreland
Quinlan
Cimarron R.
Bernstein
Stratford
Fargo
Gage
Orienta
Conlen
Gruver
Waka
Lipscomb
Shattuck
Fairview
Lautz
Spearman
Chester
Arnett
Vici
Seiling
Exum
Etter
Morse
Higgins
Canton Lake
36°
Sunray
Canton
Taloga
Camargo
Glazier
Pringle
Canadian River
Dumas
Canadian
Eagle City
Stinnett
Durham
Leedey
Putnam
Mendota
Fay
Four Way
LAKE MEREDITH NAT. REC. AREA
Oil City
Roll
Phillips
Miami
Thomas
Masterson
Fritch
Borger
Strong City
ALIBATES NAT. MON.
Codman
Cheyenne
Hammon
Butler
Custer City
Allison
Marsh
Skellytown
Laketon
Arapaho
2
Tascosa
Lake Meredith
Briscoe
Foss Res.
Ady
Puente
Pampa
Mobeetie
Clinton
Weatherford
Pomeroy
White Deer
Lefors
Wheeler
Sweetwater
Elk City
Kellerville
Mayfield
Burns Flat
Panhandle
Twitty
Sayre
Eakly
Amarillo
Conway
McLean
Shamrock
North Fork
Cordell
Fort Cobb Res.
97
Bushland
Groom
Alanreed
Lela
Carter
Washburn
Jericho
Erick
Sentinel
Rocky
Claude
TEXAS
OKLAHOMA
Haney
Carnegie
Goodnight
Ashtola
Willow
Ft Co
35°
Umbarger
Canyon
Lutie
Lone Wolf
Hobart
Gotebo
Buffalo Lake
Clarendon
Red River
Lelia Lake
Lake Altus
Vinson
Mangum
Wichita Mountains
Hedley
Ogg
Wellington
Salt Fork
Roosevelt
Happy
Memphis
Blair
Mount Scott
2464 ft
751 m
Arney
Brice
Kaffir
Vigo Park
Hollis
Lakeview
Altus
Duke
Snyder
Tulia
Newlin
Cache
3
Parnell
Estelline
Olustee
Lawton
27
Silverton
Tipton
Carey
Childress
Eldorado
Chattanooga
Hart
Kress
Quitaque
Turkey
Kirkland
Red River
Frederick
Salt Fork
Odell
Springlake
Seth Ward
Northfield
Lazare
Quanah
Davidson
Grandfield
South Plains
Flomot
Olton
Plainview
Pease
Chillicothe
Randlett
Lockney
Dunlap
Swearingen
Medicine Mound
River
Vernon
Hale Center
Harrold
Burkburnett
34°
Matador
Floydada
Electra
Littlefield
Underwood
Paducah
Thalia
Crowell
Alley
Iowa Park
Petersburg
Roaring Springs
Anton
Abernathy
Foard City
Diversion Lake
Lake Wichita
Cone
Glenn
Lake Kemp
Mankins
Holliday
Shallowater
Truscott
Idalou
Ralls
Lake Kickapoo
Crosbyton
Dickens
Mabelle
Scotland
Vera
Lubbock
Guthrie
Benjamin
Brazos River
Seymour
Wolfforth
Archer City
4
Cap Rock
White River Res.
Windthorst
Wolfforth
Bomarton
Spur
Slaton
Munday
Ropesville
Knox City
Megargel
Canyon Valley
Meadow
Southland
O'Brien
Olney
Girard
Salt Fork
Wilson
Rochester
Elbert
Jayton
Tahoka
Loving
Post
Double Mountain Fork
Swenson
Clairemont
Rule
Peacock
Throckmorton
Aspermont
Old Glory
Haskell
Newcastle
Sagerton
74

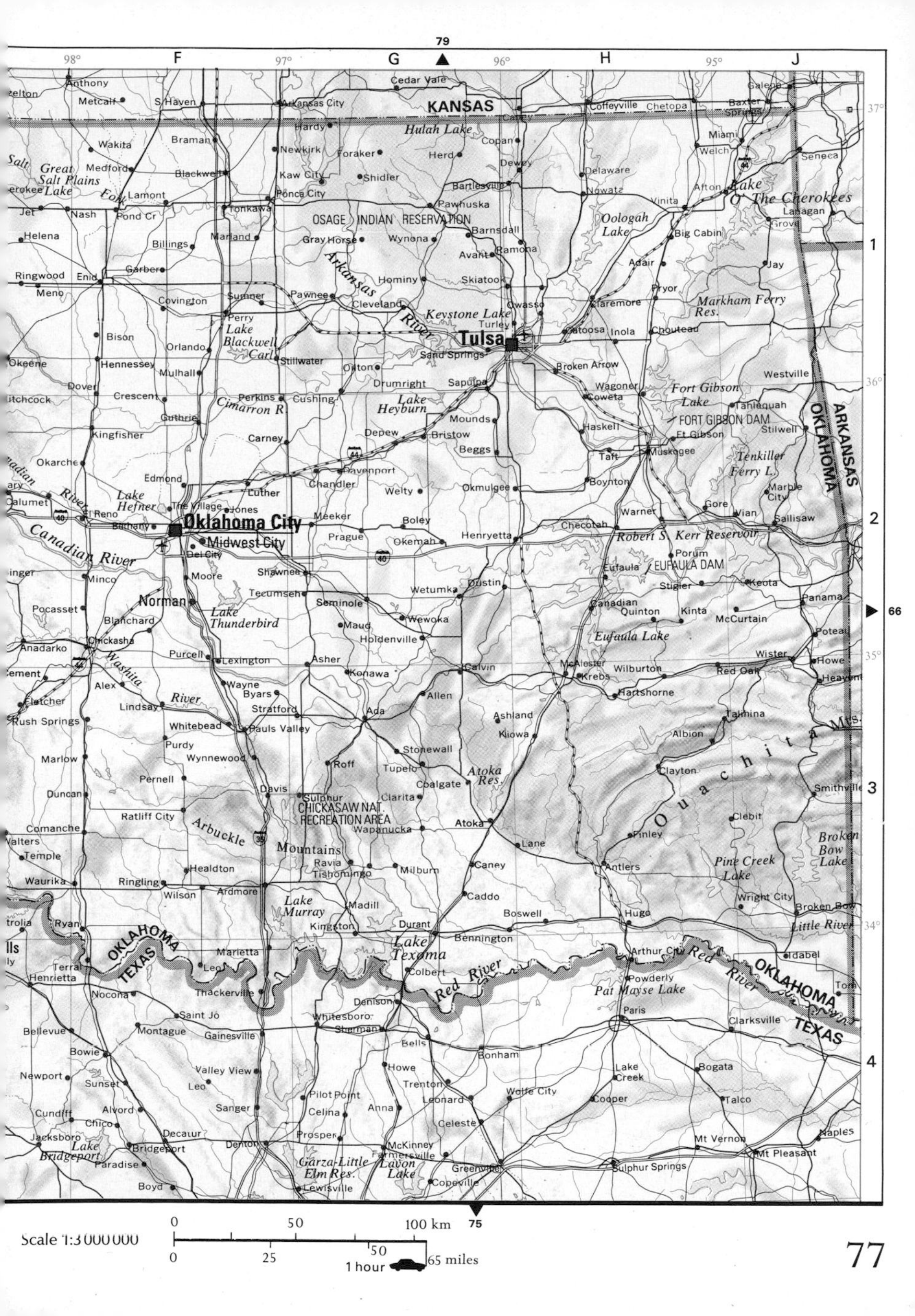
79
98°
F
97°
G
96°
H
95°
J
37°
36°
35°
34°
1
2
3
4
66
75
KANSAS
OKLAHOMA
ARKANSAS
TEXAS
Anthony
Metcalf
S.Haven
Arkansas City
Cedar Vale
Coffeyville
Chetopa
Galena
Baxter Springs
Hardy
Hulah Lake
Caney
Copan
Miami
Welch
Seneca
Wakita
Braman
Newkirk
Foraker
Herd
Dewey
Delaware
Salt Fork
Great Salt Plains Lake
Medford
Blackwell
Kaw City
Shidler
Bartlesville
Afton
Lake O' The Cherokees
Lamont
Ponca City
Nowata
Vinita
Jet
Nash
Pond Cr
Tonkawa
Pawhuska
OSAGE INDIAN RESERVATION
Oologah Lake
Langan
Grove
Helena
Marland
Gray Horse
Wynona
Barnsdall
Big Cabin
Billings
Avant
Ramona
Adair
Jay
Ringwood
Enid
Garber
Arkansas River
Hominy
Skiatook
Meno
Sumner
Pawnee
Cleveland
Pryor
Covington
Perry
Keystone Lake
Owasso
Claremore
Markham Ferry Res.
Lake Blackwell
Turley
Catoosa
Inola
Chouteau
Bison
Orlando
Carl
Tulsa
Sand Springs
Okeene
Hennessey
Stillwater
Oilton
Broken Arrow
Westville
Mulhall
Drumright
Sapulpa
Dover
Crescent
Perkins
Cushing
Wagoner
Fort Gibson Lake
Tahlequah
Coweta
Hitchcock
Cimarron R.
Lake Heyburn
FORT GIBSON DAM
Guthrie
Mounds
Haskell
Stilwell
Kingfisher
Depew
Bristow
Ft Gibson
Carney
Beggs
Muskogee
Taft
Okarche
Tenkiller Ferry L.
Davenport
Edmond
Chandler
Boynton
Marble City
Luther
Welty
Okmulgee
Canadian River
Lake Hefner
Calumet
El Reno
The Village
Jones
Meeker
Warner
Gore
Vian
Sallisaw
Bethany
Oklahoma City
Boley
Checotah
Midwest City
Prague
Okemah
Henryetta
Robert S. Kerr Reservoir
Del City
Porum
Eufaula
EUFAULA DAM
Shawnee
Minco
Moore
Stigler
Keota
Tecumseh
Wetumka
Dustin
Pocasset
Norman
Seminole
Canadian
Quinton
Kinta
McCurtain
Panama
Lake Thunderbird
Blanchard
Wewoka
Maud
Holdenville
Eufaula Lake
Poteau
Chickasha
Anadarko
Washita River
Purcell
Lexington
Asher
McAlester
Wilburton
Wister
Red Oak
Howe
Cement
Konawa
Calvin
Krebs
Heavener
Alex
Wayne
Byars
Hartshorne
Fletcher
Lindsay
Stratford
Allen
Talihina
Rush Springs
Ada
Ashland
Whitebead
Pauls Valley
Kiowa
Albion
Ouachita Mts.
Purdy
Stonewall
Marlow
Wynnewood
Roff
Tupelo
Atoka Res.
Clayton
Pernell
Coalgate
Duncan
Davis
Sulphur
Clarita
Smithville
CHICKASAW NAT. RECREATION AREA
Ratliff City
Clebit
Arbuckle Mountains
Wapanucka
Atoka
Comanche
Finley
Broken Bow Lake
Walters
Lane
Temple
Ravia
Tishomingo
Milburn
Caney
Antlers
Pine Creek Lake
Healdton
Waurika
Ringling
Wilson
Ardmore
Lake Murray
Madill
Caddo
Wright City
Boswell
Broken Bow
Ryan
Kingston
Durant
Hugo
Little River
Lake Texoma
Bennington
Terral
Marietta
Arthur City
Red River
Idabel
Henrietta
Leon
Colbert
Powderly
Pat Mayse Lake
Nocona
Thackerville
Denison
Paris
Saint Jo
Whitesboro
Clarksville
Bellevue
Montague
Gainesville
Sherman
Bells
Bonham
Bowie
Newport
Valley View
Howe
Lake Creek
Bogata
Sunset
Leo
Trenton
Wolfe City
Alvord
Pilot Point
Leonard
Cooper
Talco
Cundiff
Sanger
Celina
Anna
Chico
Celeste
Decatur
Prosper
Jacksboro
Lake Bridgeport
Bridgeport
Denton
McKinney
Farmersville
Mt Vernon
Naples
Mt Pleasant
Paradise
Garza-Little Elm Res.
Lavon Lake
Greenville
Sulphur Springs
Boyd
Lewisville
Copeville
Scale 1:3 000 000
0
50
100 km
0
25
50
65 miles
1 hour

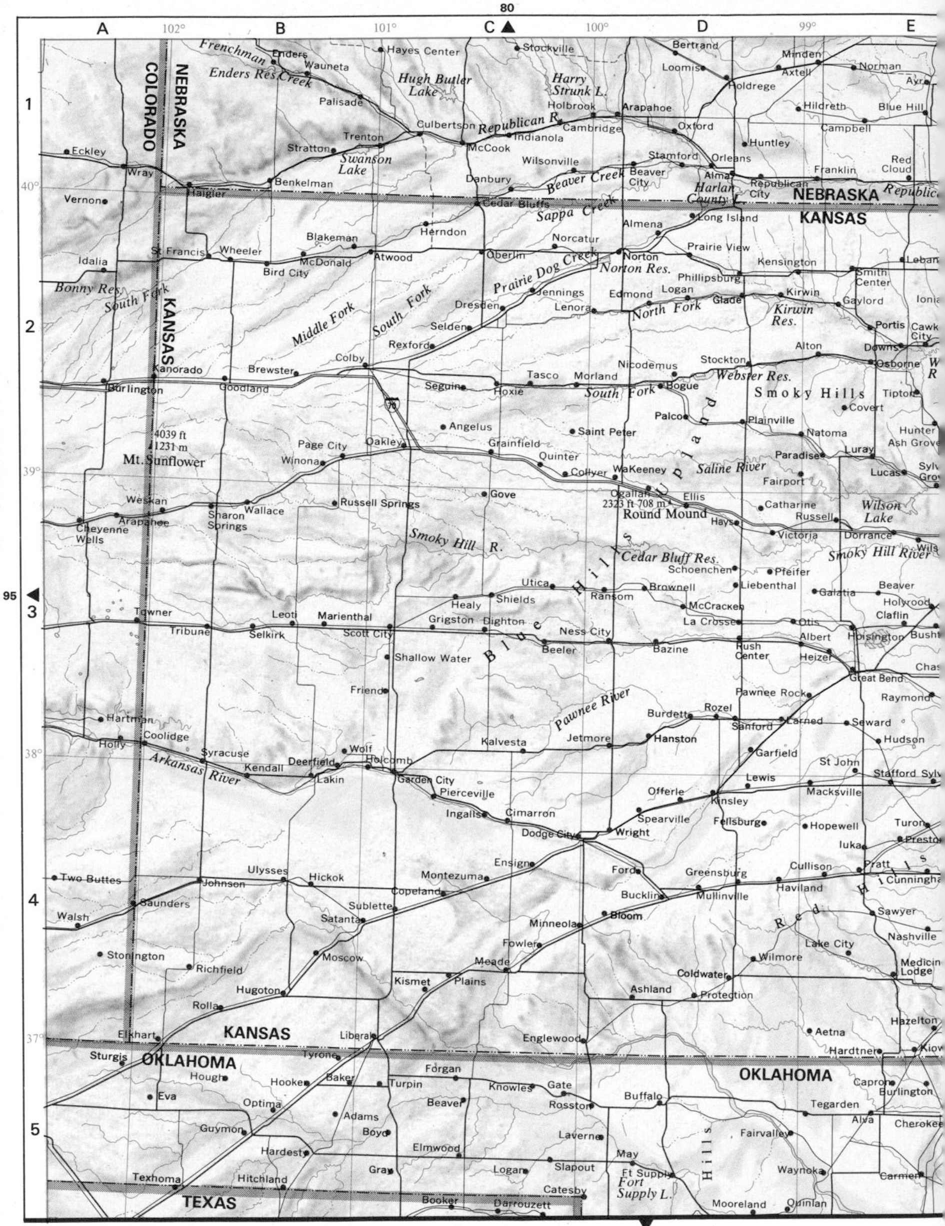
80
A
B
C
D
E
102°
101°
100°
99°
1
2
3
4
5
95
76
40°
39°
38°
37°
COLORADO
NEBRASKA
KANSAS
OKLAHOMA
TEXAS
Frenchman
Enders
Enders Res.
Creek
Wauneta
Hayes Center
Stockville
Hugh Butler Lake
Harry Strunk L.
Bertrand
Loomis
Minden
Axtell
Norman
Ayr
Holdrege
Palisade
Holbrook
Arapahoe
Hildreth
Blue Hill
Culbertson
Republican R.
Cambridge
Oxford
Campbell
Trenton
Indianola
Huntley
Eckley
Stratton
McCook
Swanson Lake
Wilsonville
Stamford
Orleans
Red Cloud
Wray
Benkelman
Haigler
Danbury
Beaver Creek
Beaver City
Alma
Harlan County L.
Franklin
Republican City
Republican
Vernon
Cedar Bluffs
Sappa Creek
Long Island
Herndon
Almena
Blakeman
Norcatur
Prairie View
St Francis
Wheeler
McDonald
Atwood
Oberlin
Norton
Norton Res.
Kensington
Leban
Idalia
Bird City
Prairie Dog Creek
Phillipsburg
Smith Center
Bonny Res.
South Fork
Jennings
Edmond
Logan
Glade
Kirwin
Gaylord
Ionia
Dresden
Lenora
North Fork
Kirwin Res.
Middle Fork
South Fork
Selden
Portis
Cawker City
Rexford
Alton
Downs
Colby
Nicodemus
Stockton
Osborne
Kanorado
Brewster
Webster Res.
Burlington
Goodland
Seguin
Hoxie
Tasco
Morland
South Fork
Bogue
Smoky Hills
Tipton
70
Covert
Angelus
Palco
Plainville
4039 ft
1231 m
Saint Peter
Natoma
Hunter
Ash Grove
Mt. Sunflower
Page City
Oakley
Grainfield
Paradise
Luray
Winona
Quinter
Saline River
Lucas
Sylvan Grove
Collyer
WaKeeney
Fairport
Upland
Weskan
Gove
Ogallah
Ellis
Catharine
Wilson Lake
Arapahoe
Sharon Springs
Wallace
Russell Springs
2323 ft 708 m
Round Mound
Russell
Cheyenne Wells
Hays
Victoria
Dorrance
Smoky Hill R.
Cedar Bluff Res.
Smoky Hill River
Wilson
Schoenchen
Pfeifer
Utica
Brownell
Liebenthal
Beaver
Healy
Shields
Ransom
Galatia
Holyrood
Towner
Leoti
Marienthal
McCracken
Claflin
Tribune
Selkirk
Scott City
Grigston
Dighton
La Crosse
Otis
Ness City
Albert
Hoisington
Bushton
Beeler
Bazine
Rush Center
Heizer
Blue Hills
Shallow Water
Great Bend
Chase
Friend
Pawnee Rock
Raymond
Pawnee River
Burdett
Rozel
Hartman
Larned
Seward
Sanford
Coolidge
Kalvesta
Jetmore
Hanston
Hudson
Holly
Syracuse
Wolf
Garfield
St John
Arkansas River
Kendall
Deerfield
Holcomb
Stafford
Lakin
Garden City
Lewis
Pierceville
Offerle
Kinsley
Macksville
Ingalls
Cimarron
Spearville
Fellsburg
Hopewell
Turon
Dodge City
Wright
Iuka
Preston
Ensign
Ford
Cullison
Pratt
Ulysses
Two Buttes
Hickok
Montezuma
Greensburg
Cunningham
Johnson
Haviland
Copeland
Bucklin
Mullinville
Saunders
Sublette
Red Hills
Walsh
Satanta
Bloom
Sawyer
Minneola
Nashville
Fowler
Lake City
Stonington
Moscow
Meade
Wilmore
Richfield
Kismet
Plains
Coldwater
Medicine Lodge
Hugoton
Ashland
Protection
Rolla
Hazelton
Aetna
Elkhart
Liberal
Englewood
Hardtner
Kiowa
Sturgis
Tyrone
Forgan
Hough
Hooker
Baker
Turpin
Knowles
Gate
Capron
Burlington
Eva
Beaver
Buffalo
Tegarden
Optima
Rosston
Adams
Alva
Cherokee
Guymon
Boyd
Laverne
Fairvalley
Hardesty
Elmwood
May
Logan
Slapout
Ft Supply
Waynoka
Texhoma
Hitchland
Fort Supply L.
Carmen
Gray
Catesby
Hills
Booker
Darrouzett
Mooreland
Quinlan

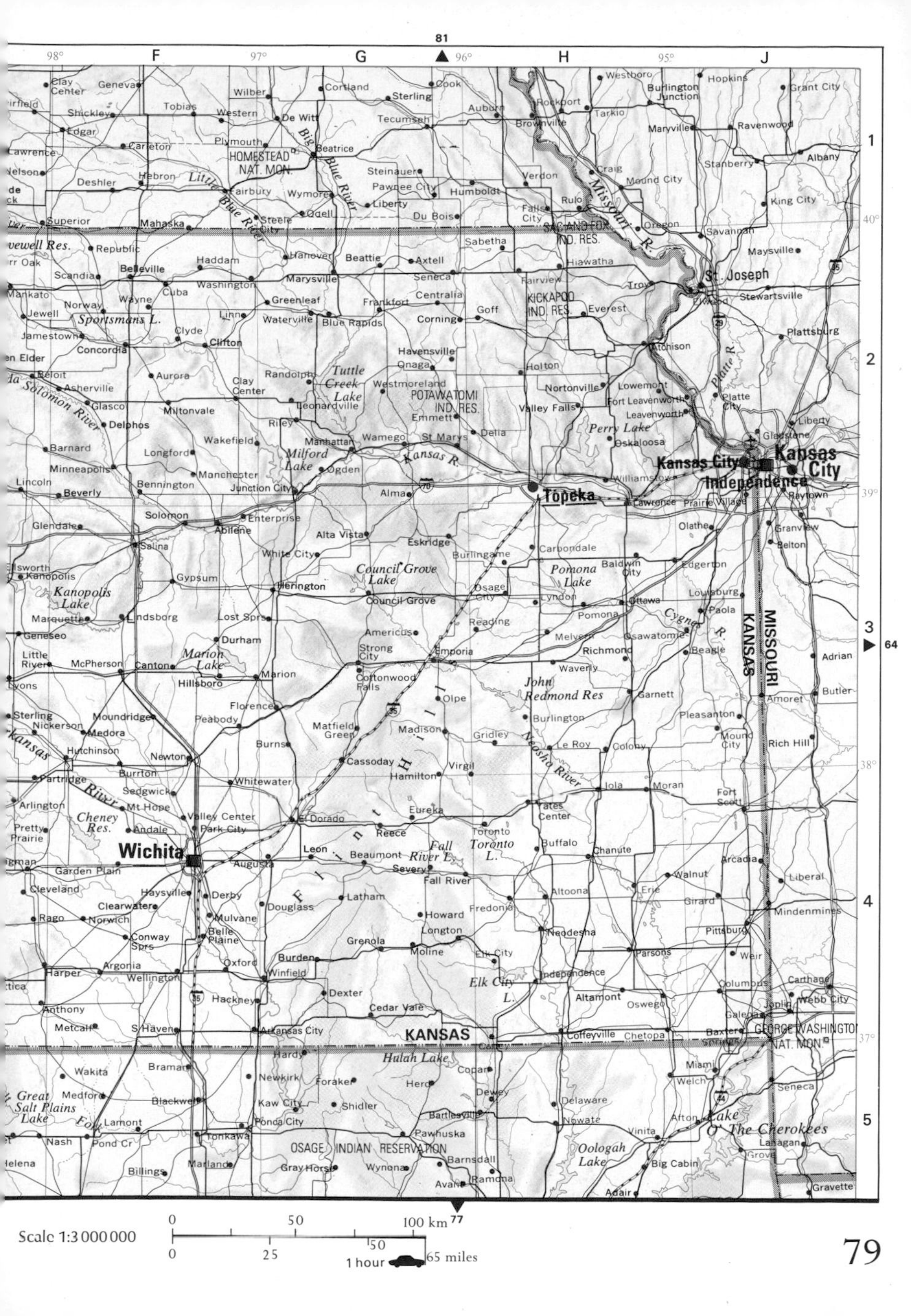

81
F
G
H
J
98°
97°
96°
95°
1
2
3
4
5
40°
39°
38°
37°
64
77
Beatrice
HOMESTEAD NAT. MON.
Big Blue River
Little Blue River
Missouri R.
SAC AND FOX IND. RES.
KICKAPOO IND. RES.
POTAWATOMI IND. RES.
St. Joseph
Tuttle Creek Lake
Milford Lake
Kansas R.
Manhattan
Junction City
Topeka
Lawrence
Kansas City
Independence
Perry Lake
Platte R.
Solomon River
Salina
Abilene
Kanopolis Lake
Council Grove Lake
Council Grove
Pomona Lake
Marion Lake
Emporia
John Redmond Res
Neosho River
Marais des Cygnes R.
Flint Hills
Hutchinson
Arkansas River
Newton
Cheney Res.
Wichita
El Dorado
Fall River L.
Toronto L.
Elk City L.
Winfield
Arkansas City
Coffeyville
Independence
Chanute
Iola
Fort Scott
Pittsburg
Parsons
Joplin
GEORGE WASHINGTON CARVER NAT. MON.
KANSAS
MISSOURI
Hulah Lake
Great Salt Plains Lake
OSAGE INDIAN RESERVATION
Ponca City
Bartlesville
Oologah Lake
Lake O' The Cherokees
Scale 1:3 000 000
0
50
100 km
0
25
50
65 miles
1 hour

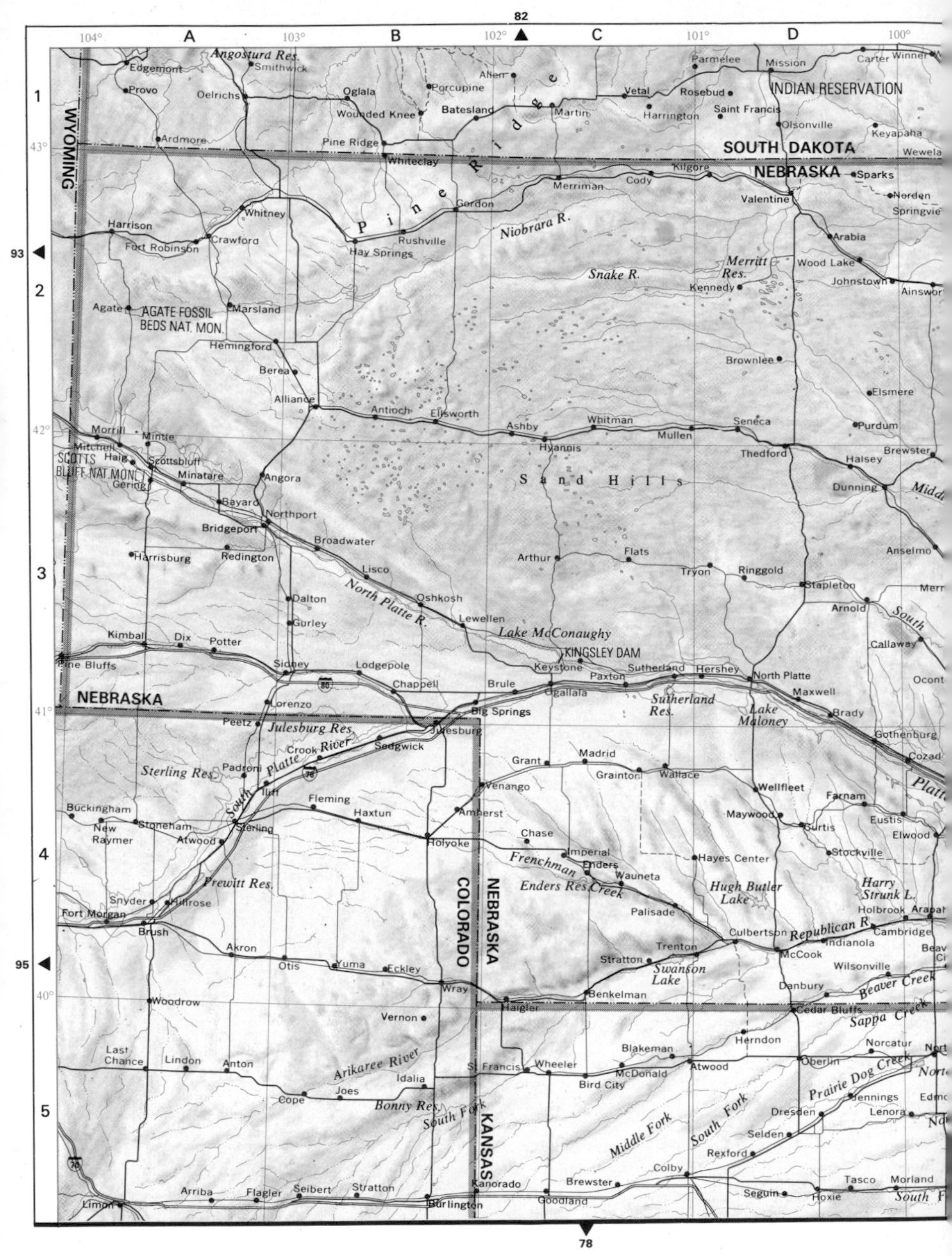
82
78
93
95
A
B
C
D
1
2
3
4
5
104°
103°
102°
101°
100°
43°
42°
41°
40°
WYOMING
SOUTH DAKOTA
NEBRASKA
COLORADO
KANSAS
INDIAN RESERVATION
Angostura Res.
Edgemont
Smithwick
Provo
Oelrichs
Oglala
Porcupine
Allen
Wounded Knee
Batesland
Martin
Vetal
Rosebud
Parmelee
Mission
Carter
Winner
Harrington
Saint Francis
Olsonville
Keyapaha
Wewela
Ardmore
Pine Ridge
Whiteclay
Kilgore
Sparks
Merriman
Cody
Valentine
Norden
Springview
Gordon
Whitney
Harrison
Crawford
Fort Robinson
Pine Ridge
Niobrara R.
Rushville
Hay Springs
Arabia
Merritt Res.
Wood Lake
Snake R.
Kennedy
Johnstown
Ainsworth
Agate
AGATE FOSSIL BEDS NAT. MON.
Marsland
Hemingford
Brownlee
Berea
Elsmere
Alliance
Antioch
Ellsworth
Whitman
Seneca
Purdum
Morrill
Mintle
Ashby
Hyannis
Mullen
Brewster
Mitchell
Haig
SCOTTS BLUFF NAT. MON.
Scottsbluff
Gering
Minatare
Angora
Thedford
Halsey
Sand Hills
Dunning
Bayard
Northport
Bridgeport
Broadwater
Harrisburg
Redington
Arthur
Flats
Anselmo
Lisco
Tryon
Ringgold
Stapleton
North Platte R.
Dalton
Oshkosh
Arnold
Gurley
Lewellen
Lake McConaughy
Callaway
Kimball
Dix
Potter
KINGSLEY DAM
Pine Bluffs
Sidney
Lodgepole
Keystone
Sutherland
Hershey
North Platte
Chappell
Brule
Paxton
Ogallala
Maxwell
Lorenzo
Sutherland Res.
Lake Maloney
Brady
Peetz
Big Springs
Julesburg Res.
Julesburg
Gothenburg
Crook
Sedgwick
Cozad
Sterling Res.
Padroni
South Platte River
Grant
Madrid
Grainton
Wallace
Venango
Wellfleet
Platte
Iliff
Fleming
Farnam
Buckingham
Stoneham
New Raymer
Atwood
Sterling
Haxtun
Amherst
Maywood
Curtis
Eustis
Chase
Elwood
Holyoke
Imperial
Stockville
Frenchman
Enders
Hayes Center
Wauneta
Enders Res.
Creek
Hugh Butler Lake
Harry Strunk L.
Prewitt Res.
Palisade
Snyder
Hillrose
Fort Morgan
Holbrook
Arapahoe
Brush
Culbertson
Republican R.
Cambridge
Akron
Trenton
Indianola
McCook
Otis
Yuma
Eckley
Stratton
Swanson Lake
Wilsonville
Wray
Benkelman
Danbury
Beaver Creek
Woodrow
Haigler
Cedar Bluffs
Sappa Creek
Vernon
Herndon
Norcatur
Last Chance
Lindon
Anton
Blakeman
Arikaree River
St. Francis
Wheeler
Atwood
Oberlin
McDonald
Bird City
Idalia
Cope
Joes
Prairie Dog Creek
Jennings
Bonny Res.
South Fork
Dresden
Lenora
Middle Fork
South Fork
Selden
Rexford
Colby
Kanorado
Brewster
Tasco
Morland
Arriba
Flagler
Seibert
Stratton
Seguin
Hoxie
Limon
Burlington
Goodland
South F
80
76
70

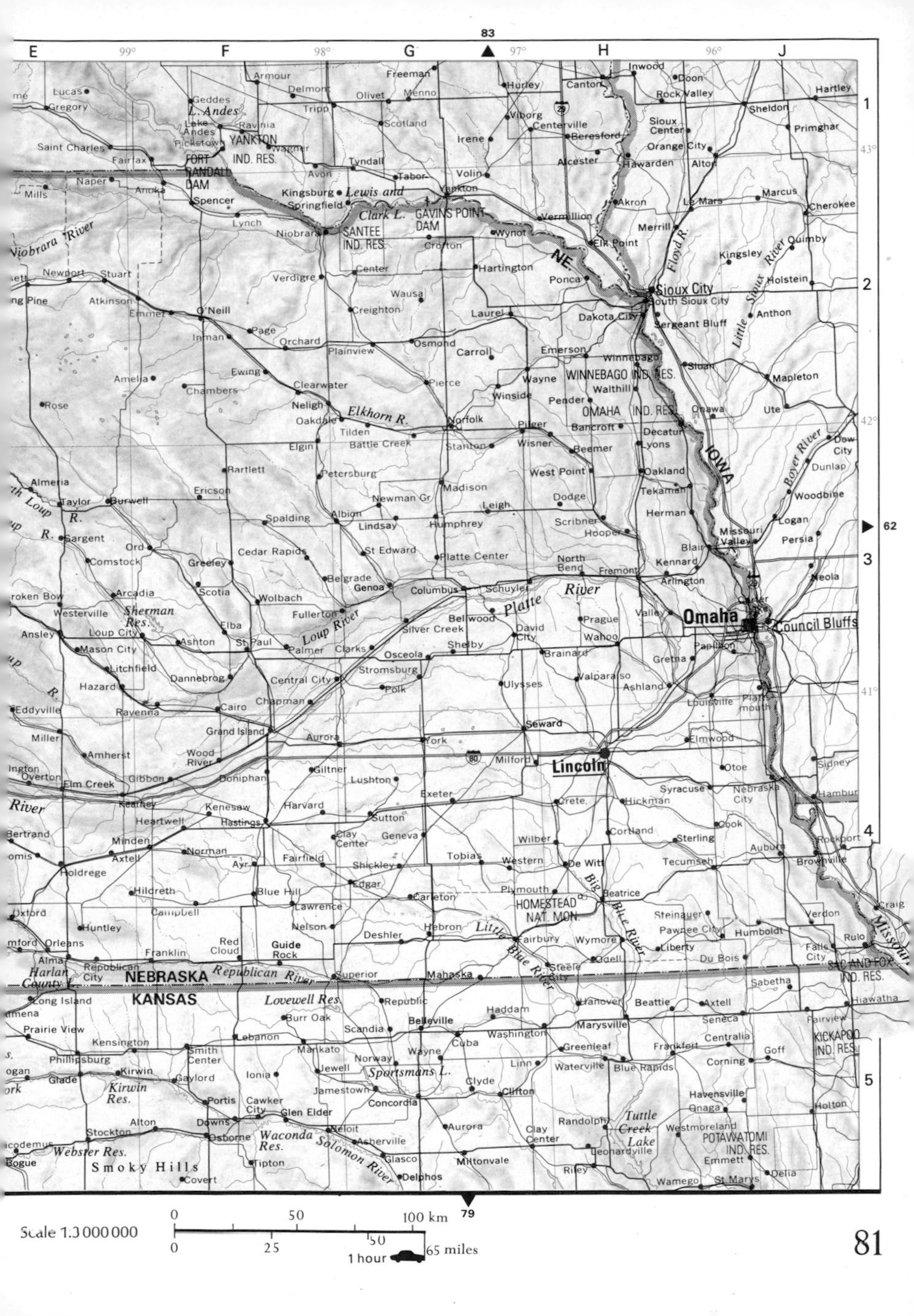

E   99°   F   98°   G   ▲ 97°   H   96°   J

1

43°

2

NE

IOWA

42°

62

3

Omaha   Council Bluffs

41°

4

NEBRASKA

KANSAS

5

Scale 1:3 000 000

0   50   100 km

0   25   50   65 miles

1 hour

79

81

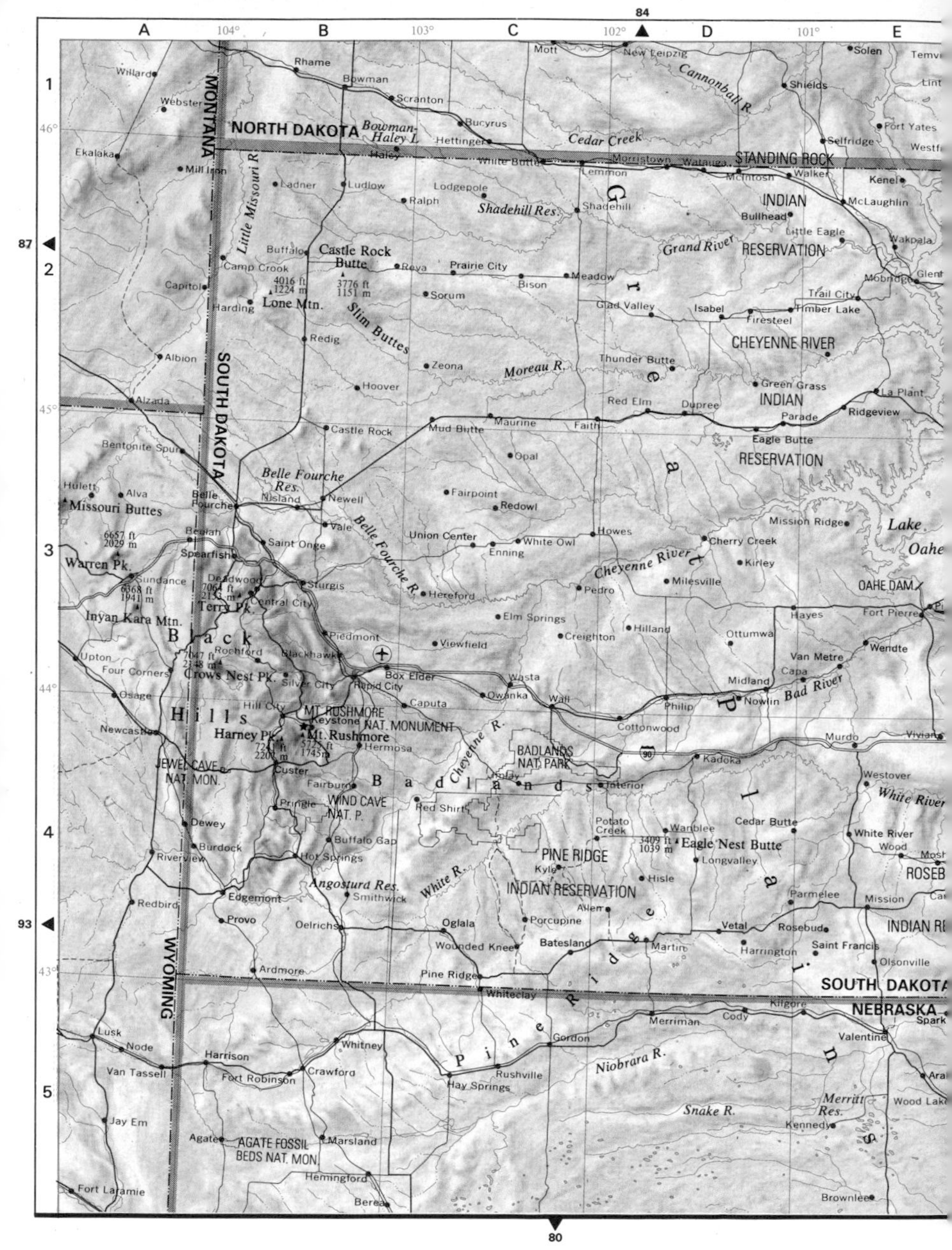
84
A
B
C
D
E
104°
103°
102°
101°
1
2
3
4
5
46°
45°
44°
43°
87
93
80
NORTH DAKOTA
SOUTH DAKOTA
MONTANA
WYOMING
NEBRASKA
Rhame
Bowman
Scranton
Bucyrus
Hettinger
Bowman-Haley L.
Haley
Mott
New Leipzig
Cannonball R.
Solen
Shields
Fort Yates
Selfridge
Cedar Creek
Willard
Webster
Ekalaka
Mill Iron
Little Missouri R.
Ladner
Ludlow
Lodgepole
Ralph
Shadehill Res.
Shadehill
White Butte
Lemmon
Morristown
Watauga
McIntosh
Walker
STANDING ROCK
INDIAN
RESERVATION
Kenel
McLaughlin
Bullhead
Little Eagle
Wakpala
Grand River
Mobridge
Glenham
Buffalo
Castle Rock Butte
Camp Crook
Capitol
Harding
Lone Mtn.
4016 ft 1224 m
3776 ft 1151 m
Reva
Prairie City
Bison
Meadow
Sorum
Glad Valley
Isabel
Firesteel
Timber Lake
Trail City
Slim Buttes
Redig
Albion
Zeona
Moreau R.
Thunder Butte
CHEYENNE RIVER
INDIAN
RESERVATION
Green Grass
La Plant
Ridgeview
Hoover
Alzada
Red Elm
Dupree
Parade
Castle Rock
Mud Butte
Maurine
Faith
Eagle Butte
Bentonite Spur
Opal
Belle Fourche Res.
Belle Fourche
Nisland
Newell
Hulett
Alva
Missouri Buttes
Fairpoint
Redowl
Vale
Mission Ridge
Lake Oahe
6657 ft 2029 m
Beulah
Saint Onge
Spearfish
Warren Pk.
Sundance
6368 ft 1941 m
Deadwood
7064 ft 2153 m
Terry Pk.
Sturgis
Central City
Belle Fourche R.
Union Center
Enning
White Owl
Howes
Cherry Creek
Kirley
Cheyenne River
Milesville
Pedro
Hereford
OAHE DAM
Inyan Kara Mtn.
Elm Springs
Hilland
Hayes
Fort Pierre
Black Hills
Piedmont
Viewfield
Creighton
Ottumwa
Wendte
Upton
Rochford
7047 ft 2148 m
Crows Nest Pk.
Blackhawk
Four Corners
Silver City
Box Elder
Rapid City
Wasta
Van Metre
Capa
Midland
Bad River
Osage
Hill City
Caputa
Owanka
Wall
Philip
Nowlin
MT. RUSHMORE NAT. MONUMENT
Keystone
Mt. Rushmore
Harney Pk.
7242 ft 2207 m
5725 ft 1745 m
Hermosa
Cheyenne R.
Cottonwood
Newcastle
BADLANDS NAT. PARK
Murdo
Vivian
Kadoka
JEWEL CAVE NAT. MON.
Custer
Fairburn
Badlands
Interior
Westover
White River
Pringle
WIND CAVE NAT. P.
Red Shirt
Dewey
Burdock
Buffalo Gap
Potato Creek
Wanblee
3409 ft 1039 m
Eagle Nest Butte
Cedar Butte
White River
Wood
Riverview
Hot Springs
PINE RIDGE INDIAN RESERVATION
Kyle
Longvalley
Hisle
ROSEBUD INDIAN RESERVATION
Angostura Res.
Smithwick
White R.
Edgemont
Redbird
Allen
Parmelee
Mission
Provo
Oelrichs
Oglala
Porcupine
Vetal
Rosebud
Wounded Knee
Batesland
Martin
Harrington
Saint Francis
Olsonville
Ardmore
Pine Ridge
Whiteclay
Great Plains
Kilgore
Merriman
Cody
Lusk
Node
Whitney
Gordon
Valentine
Sparks
Harrison
Van Tassell
Fort Robinson
Crawford
Pine Ridge
Rushville
Hay Springs
Niobrara R.
Jay Em
Snake R.
Merritt Res.
Kennedy
Wood Lake
Agate
AGATE FOSSIL BEDS NAT. MON.
Marsland
Hemingford
Fort Laramie
Berea
Brownlee

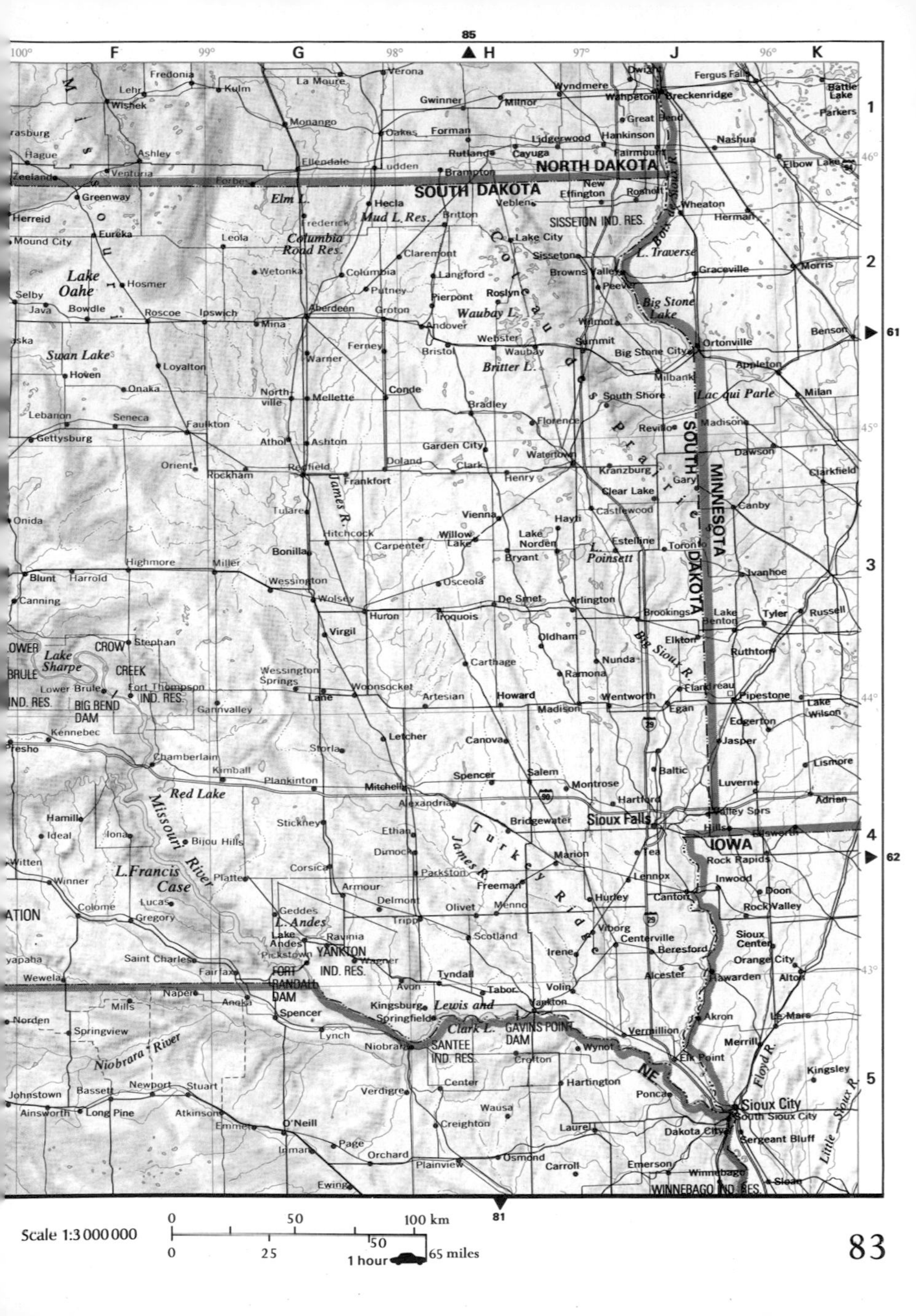
85
100°
F
99°
G
98°
H
97°
J
96°
K
1
2
3
4
5
46°
45°
44°
43°
61
62
81
NORTH DAKOTA
SOUTH DAKOTA
MINNESOTA
SOUTH DAKOTA
IOWA
NE.
Fredonia
Lehr
Wishek
Kulm
La Moure
Verona
Wyndmere
Dwight
Fergus Falls
Battle Lake
Gwinner
Milnor
Wahpeton
Breckenridge
Parkers
Monango
Great Bend
Oakes
Forman
Lidgerwood
Hankinson
Nashua
Hague
Ashley
Rutland
Cayuga
Fairmount
Ellendale
Ludden
Brampton
Elbow Lake
Zeeland
Venturia
Forbes
New Effington
Rosholt
Greenway
Elm L.
Hecla
Veblen
Wheaton
Herreid
Frederick
Mud L. Res.
Britton
SISSETON IND. RES.
Herman
Eureka
Mound City
Leola
Columbia Road Res.
Lake City
Claremont
Sisseton
L. Traverse
Bois de Sioux R.
Morris
Lake Oahe
Wetonka
Columbia
Langford
Browns Valley
Graceville
Hosmer
Putney
Roslyn
Peever
Selby
Java
Bowdle
Roscoe
Ipswich
Aberdeen
Groton
Pierpont
Waubay L.
Big Stone Lake
Mina
Andover
Wilmot
Swan Lake
Warner
Ferney
Bristol
Webster
Summit
Waubay
Big Stone City
Ortonville
Benson
Loyalton
Britter L.
Appleton
Hoven
Onaka
Milbank
Northville
Mellette
Conde
South Shore
Lac qui Parle
Milan
Lebanon
Seneca
Bradley
Faulkton
Florence
Revillo
Madison
Gettysburg
Athol
Ashton
Garden City
Dawson
Orient
Rockham
Redfield
Doland
Clark
Watertown
Kranzburg
Clarkfield
Frankfort
Henry
Gary
Clear Lake
James R.
Tulare
Castlewood
Canby
Onida
Vienna
Hayti
Hitchcock
Willow Lake
Lake Norden
Estelline
Toronto
Carpenter
Bonilla
Bryant
L. Poinsett
Highmore
Miller
Blunt
Harrold
Wessington
Osceola
Ivanhoe
Canning
Wolsey
De Smet
Arlington
Huron
Iroquois
Brookings
Lake Benton
Tyler
Russell
Virgil
Oldham
Elkton
CROW CREEK
Stephan
LOWER BRULE
Lake Sharpe
Nunda
Big Sioux R.
Ruthton
Carthage
Wessington Springs
Ramona
Lower Brule
Fort Thompson
IND. RES.
Woonsocket
Flandreau
BIG BEND DAM
Lane
Artesian
Howard
Wentworth
Pipestone
Gannvalley
Madison
Egan
Lake Wilson
Kennebec
Edgerton
Presho
Letcher
Canova
Jasper
Storla
Chamberlain
Kimball
Baltic
Lismore
Plankinton
Spencer
Salem
Red Lake
Mitchell
Montrose
Luverne
Alexandria
Hartford
Adrian
Missouri River
Hamill
Valley Sprs
Bridgewater
Sioux Falls
Stickney
Ideal
Iona
Bijou Hills
Ethan
Turkey Ridge
Hills
Ellsworth
Dimock
Marion
Tea
Rock Rapids
Witten
Corsica
James R.
L. Francis Case
Platte
Parkston
Lennox
Inwood
Winner
Armour
Freeman
Doon
Delmont
Hurley
Canton
Colome
Lucas
Olivet
Menno
Rock Valley
Geddes
Gregory
L. Andes
Tripp
Viborg
Sioux Center
Lake Andes
Ravinia
Scotland
Centerville
Pickstown
YANKTON IND. RES.
Irene
Beresford
Orange City
Saint Charles
Wagner
Fairfax
FORT RANDALL DAM
Tyndall
Alcester
Hawarden
Alton
Wewela
Avon
Tabor
Volin
Naper
Yankton
Mills
Anoka
Kingsburg
Lewis and Clark L.
Spencer
Springfield
GAVINS POINT DAM
Akron
Le Mars
Norden
Springview
Lynch
Vermillion
Niobrara River
Niobrara
SANTEE IND. RES.
Wynot
Merrill
Crofton
Elk Point
Floyd R.
Kingsley
Johnstown
Bassett
Newport
Stuart
Center
Hartington
Ponca
Verdigre
Little Sioux R.
Sioux City
Ainsworth
Long Pine
Atkinson
Wausa
South Sioux City
Emmet
O'Neill
Creighton
Laurel
Dakota City
Sergeant Bluff
Page
Inman
Orchard
Osmond
Carroll
Plainview
Emerson
Winnebago
Ewing
WINNEBAGO IND. RES.
Sloan
Scale 1:3 000 000
0
50
100 km
0
25
50
65 miles
1 hour

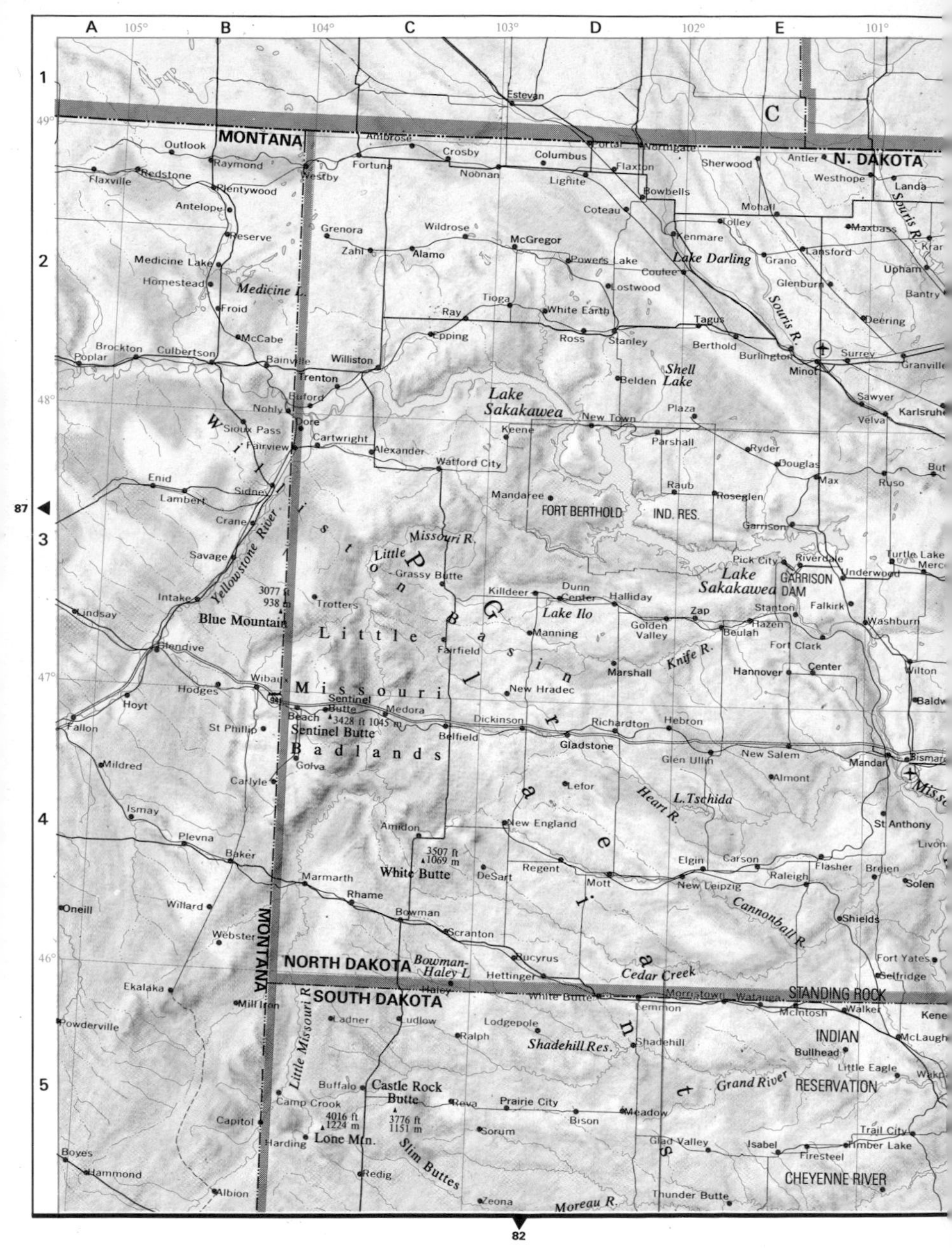

A
105°
B
104°
C
103°
D
102°
E
101°
1
2
3
4
5
49°
48°
47°
46°
87
82
C
MONTANA
N. DAKOTA
Estevan
Outlook
Raymond
Flaxville
Redstone
Plentywood
Westby
Ambrose
Fortuna
Crosby
Noonan
Columbus
Lignite
Portal
Northgate
Flaxton
Bowbells
Sherwood
Antler
Westhope
Landa
Souris R.
Mohall
Maxbass
Lansford
Grano
Upham
Glenburn
Bantry
Deering
Kenmare
Lake Darling
Coulee
Lostwood
Powers Lake
Coteau
Antelope
Reserve
Medicine Lake
Homestead
Medicine L.
Froid
McCabe
Grenora
Zahl
Alamo
Wildrose
McGregor
Tioga
Ray
White Earth
Epping
Ross
Stanley
Tagus
Berthold
Burlington
Minot
Surrey
Granville
Brockton
Poplar
Culbertson
Bainville
Williston
Trenton
Buford
Nohly
Dore
Sioux Pass
Fairview
Cartwright
Alexander
Watford City
Shell Lake
Belden
Lake Sakakawea
Keene
New Town
Plaza
Parshall
Ryder
Douglas
Sawyer
Velva
Karlsruhe
Max
Ruso
Raub
Roseglen
Mandaree
FORT BERTHOLD
IND. RES.
Garrison
Enid
Lambert
Sidney
Crane
Savage
Yellowstone River
Intake
Lindsay
Blue Mountain
3077 ft
938 m
Trotters
Little Missouri R.
Grassy Butte
Killdeer
Dunn Center
Halliday
Lake Ilo
Manning
Golden Valley
Zap
Beulah
Hazen
Stanton
Pick City
Riverdale
GARRISON DAM
Lake Sakakawea
Falkirk
Underwood
Turtle Lake
Washburn
Fort Clark
Center
Hannover
Knife R.
Marshall
Fairfield
Glendive
Wibaux
Hodges
Hoyt
Fallon
New Hradec
Wilton
Little Missouri
Williston Basin
Little Missouri Badlands
Great Plains
Sentinel Butte
3428 ft 1045 m
Beach
Medora
Belfield
Dickinson
Richardton
Hebron
Gladstone
New Salem
Glen Ullin
Mandan
Bismarck
St Phillip
Mildred
Golva
Carlyle
Lefor
Almont
Heart R.
L.Tschida
Ismay
Plevna
Baker
New England
Amidon
St Anthony
3507 ft
1069 m
White Butte
DeSart
Regent
Mott
Elgin
Carson
New Leipzig
Raleigh
Flasher
Breien
Solen
Marmarth
Rhame
Bowman
Scranton
Willard
Oneill
Webster
Cannonball R.
Shields
Fort Yates
Selfridge
Bucyrus
NORTH DAKOTA
Bowman-Haley L.
Haley
Hettinger
Cedar Creek
Ekalaka
Mill Iron
SOUTH DAKOTA
White Butte
Morristown
Watauga
Lemmon
McIntosh
Walker
STANDING ROCK
INDIAN
RESERVATION
Powderville
Ladner
Ludlow
Ralph
Lodgepole
Shadehill Res.
Shadehill
Bullhead
Little Eagle
McLaughlin
Grand River
Buffalo
Castle Rock Butte
Camp Crook
Reva
Prairie City
Bison
Meadow
Capitol
4016 ft
1224 m
3776 ft
1151 m
Harding
Lone Mtn.
Sorum
Slim Buttes
Glad Valley
Isabel
Firesteel
Timber Lake
Trail City
Boyes
Hammond
Redig
CHEYENNE RIVER
Albion
Zeona
Moreau R.
Thunder Butte

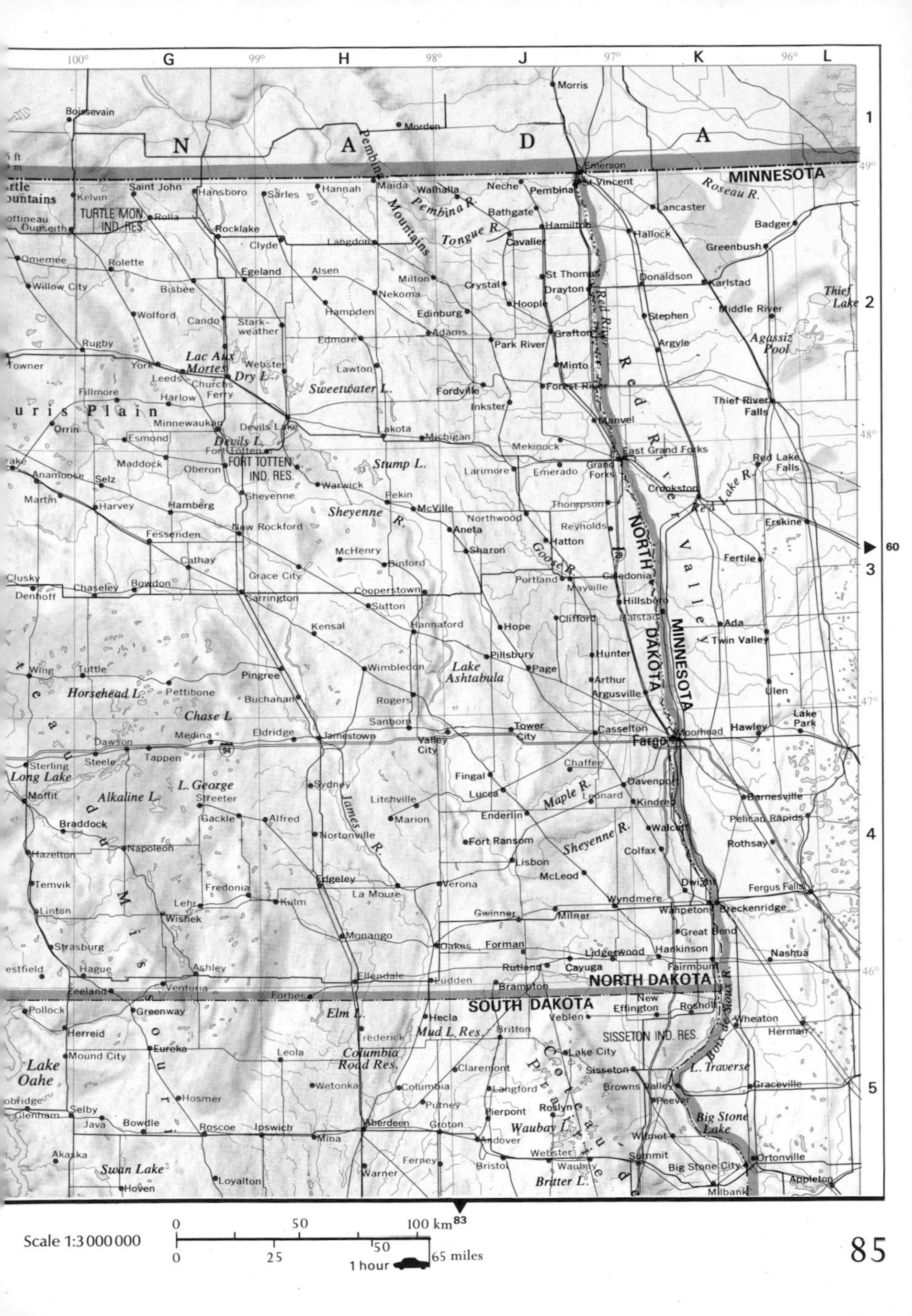
100°
G
99°
H
98°
J
97°
K
96°
L
1
2
3
4
5
49°
48°
47°
46°
60
83
N
A
D
A
MINNESOTA
NORTH DAKOTA
SOUTH DAKOTA
NORTH
DAKOTA
MINNESOTA
Morris
Boissevain
Morden
Emerson
St Vincent
Pembina
Neche
Walhalla
Maida
Hannah
Sarles
Hansboro
Saint John
Kelvin
Rolla
TURTLE MON.
IND. RES.
Dunseith
Rocklake
Clyde
Langdon
Bathgate
Hamilton
Cavalier
Lancaster
Hallock
Badger
Greenbush
Roseau R.
Pembina R.
Tongue R.
Pembina
Mountains
Omemee
Rolette
Willow City
Bisbee
Egeland
Alsen
Milton
Nekoma
Crystal
St Thomas
Drayton
Hoople
Donaldson
Karlstad
Thief
Lake
Middle River
Stephen
Wolford
Cando
Stark-
weather
Hampden
Edinburg
Adams
Edmore
Park River
Grafton
Argyle
Agassiz
Pool
Red River
Rugby
Towner
York
Leeds
Lac Aux
Mortes
Dry L.
Churchs
Ferry
Webster
Lawton
Sweetwater L.
Fordville
Minto
Forest River
Fillmore
Harlow
Inkster
Thief River
Falls
Red River Valley
Orrin
Minnewaukan
Devils Lake
Lakota
Michigan
Manvel
Esmond
Devils L.
Fort Totten
FORT TOTTEN
IND. RES.
Maddock
Oberon
Stump L.
Mekinock
East Grand Forks
Red Lake
Falls
Larimore
Emerado
Grand
Forks
Anamoose
Selz
Warwick
Crookston
Red Lake R.
Martin
Harvey
Hamberg
Sheyenne
Pekin
McVille
Thompson
Sheyenne R.
Northwood
Reynolds
Erskine
Fessenden
New Rockford
Aneta
Hatton
Sharon
Goose R.
McHenry
Binford
Fertile
Cathay
Clusky
Grace City
Portland
Mayville
Caledonia
Chaseley
Bowdon
Denhoff
Carrington
Cooperstown
Sutton
Hillsboro
Halstad
Clifford
Kensal
Hannaford
Hope
Ada
Twin Valley
Pillsbury
Hunter
Wing
Tuttle
Wimbledon
Lake
Ashtabula
Page
Pingree
Arthur
Horsehead L.
Pettibone
Buchanan
Rogers
Argusville
Ulen
Chase L.
Medina
Eldridge
Sanborn
Jamestown
Valley
City
Tower
City
Casselton
Moorhead
Fargo
Hawley
Lake
Park
Dawson
Tappen
Steele
94
Sterling
Long Lake
Chaffee
Fingal
Sydney
L. George
Streeter
Moffit
Alkaline L.
Lucca
Litchville
Leonard
Davenport
Maple R.
Kindred
Barnesville
Gackle
Alfred
Marion
Enderlin
Braddock
James R.
Pelican Rapids
Walcott
Nortonville
Sheyenne R.
Fort Ransom
Napoleon
Rothsay
Hazelton
Colfax
Lisbon
McLeod
Temvik
Edgeley
Verona
Dwight
Fergus Falls
La Moure
Fredonia
Lehr
Kulm
Wyndmere
Linton
Wishek
Gwinner
Milnor
Wahpeton
Breckenridge
Great Bend
Monango
Strasburg
Oakes
Forman
Lidgerwood
Hankinson
Nashua
Westfield
Hague
Ashley
Ellendale
Rutland
Cayuga
Fairmount
Zeeland
Venturia
Ludden
Brampton
Forbes
Pollock
Greenway
New
Effington
Rosholt
Veblen
Elm L.
Hecla
Herreid
Frederick
Mud L. Res.
Britton
SISSETON IND. RES.
Wheaton
Herman
Bois de Sioux R.
Mound City
Eureka
Leola
Columbia
Road Res.
Lake City
Claremont
Lake
Oahe
Sisseton
L. Traverse
Wetonka
Columbia
Langford
Browns Valley
Graceville
Hosmer
Putney
Peever
Mobridge
Selby
Glenham
Java
Bowdle
Roscoe
Ipswich
Mina
Aberdeen
Groton
Pierpont
Roslyn
Waubay L.
Big Stone
Lake
Wilmot
Andover
Akaska
Ferney
Webster
Summit
Swan Lake
Bristol
Waubay
Big Stone City
Ortonville
Loyalton
Warner
Britter L.
Milbank
Appleton
Hoven
Scale 1:3 000 000
0
50
100 km
0
25
50
65 miles
1 hour

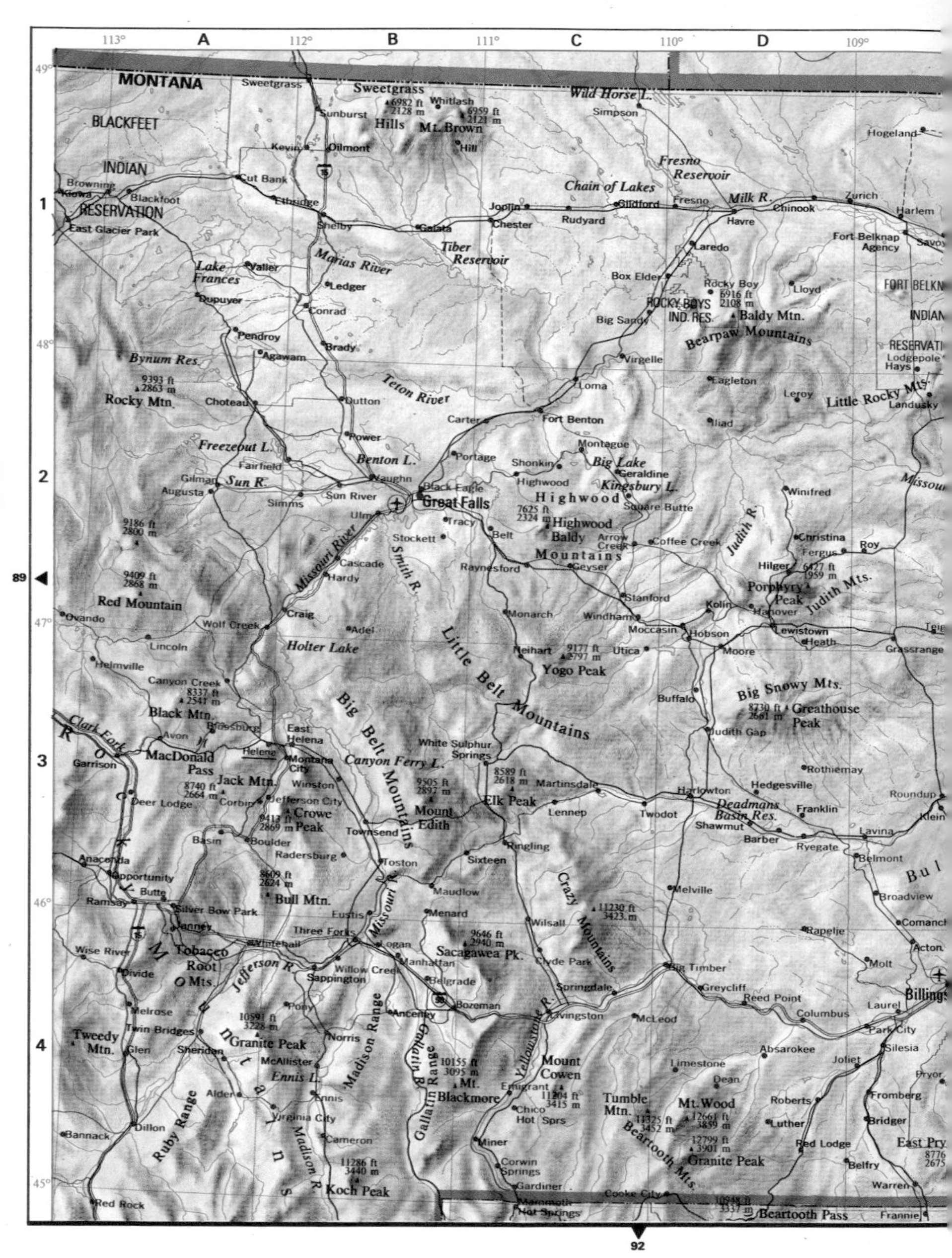

113°
A
112°
B
111°
C
110°
D
109°
49°
48°
47°
46°
45°
1
2
3
4
89
92
MONTANA
BLACKFEET
INDIAN
RESERVATION
Sweetgrass
Sweetgrass
Hills
6982 ft
2128 m
Whitlash
6959 ft
2121 m
Mt. Brown
Hill
Wild Horse L.
Simpson
Hogeland
Sunburst
Kevin
Oilmont
Cut Bank
Browning
Kiowa
Blackfoot
Ethridge
East Glacier Park
Shelby
Galata
Joplin
Chester
Rudyard
Gildford
Fresno
Fresno
Reservoir
Chain of Lakes
Milk R.
Havre
Chinook
Zurich
Harlem
Fort Belknap
Agency
Savoy
Tiber
Reservoir
Marias River
Lake
Frances
Valier
Ledger
Dupuyer
Conrad
Laredo
Box Elder
Rocky Boy
6916 ft
2108 m
ROCKY BOYS
IND. RES.
Big Sandy
Baldy Mtn.
Lloyd
FORT BELKN
INDIAN
RESERVATI
Bearpaw Mountains
Pendroy
Brady
Agawam
Bynum Res.
9393 ft
2863 m
Rocky Mtn.
Choteau
Dutton
Teton River
Virgelle
Loma
Eagleton
Lodgepole
Hays
Leroy
Little Rocky Mts.
Landusky
Carter
Fort Benton
Iliad
Power
Freezeout L.
Fairfield
Benton L.
Portage
Montague
Shonkin
Big Lake
Geraldine
Gilman
Sun R.
Augusta
Vaughn
Black Eagle
Simms
Sun River
Great Falls
Highwood
Highwood
Kingsbury L.
Square Butte
Winifred
Missou
9186 ft
2800 m
Ulm
Tracy
Belt
7625 ft
2324 m
Highwood
Baldy
Arrow
Creek
Coffee Creek
Judith R.
Christina
Stockett
Mountains
Fergus
Roy
Cascade
Smith R.
Missouri River
Raynesford
Geyser
Hilger
6427 ft
1959 m
9409 ft
2868 m
Hardy
Porphyry
Peak
Judith Mts.
Red Mountain
Stanford
Kolin
Hanover
Ovando
Craig
Monarch
Windham
Wolf Creek
Adel
Moccasin
Hobson
Lewistown
Heath
Lincoln
Holter Lake
Little Belt Mountains
Neihart
9177 ft
2797 m
Utica
Moore
Grassrange
Helmville
Yogo Peak
Canyon Creek
8337 ft
2541 m
Big Belt Mountains
Buffalo
Big Snowy Mts.
8730 ft
2661 m
Greathouse
Peak
Black Mtn.
Clark Fork
Avon
Elliston
East
Helena
Judith Gap
Garrison
MacDonald
Pass
Helena
Montana
City
Canyon Ferry L.
White Sulphur
Springs
8589 ft
2618 m
Rothiemay
Winston
Martinsdale
Harlowton
Hedgesville
Roundup
8740 ft
2664 m
Jack Mtn.
Corbin
Jefferson City
9505 ft
2897 m
Mount
Edith
Elk Peak
Lennep
Twodot
Deadmans
Basin Res.
Franklin
Klein
Deer Lodge
9413 ft
2869 m
Crowe
Peak
Townsend
Shawmut
Barber
Ryegate
Lavina
Basin
Boulder
Ringling
Radersburg
Belmont
Anaconda
Toston
Sixteen
Opportunity
Butte
8609 ft
2624 m
Crazy
Mountains
Bul
Maudlow
Melville
Broadview
Ramsay
Bull Mtn.
Silver Bow Park
11230 ft
3423 m
Eustis
Menard
Comanche
Wilsall
Rapelje
Three Forks
9646 ft
2940 m
Wise River
Whitehall
Logan
Sacagawea Pk.
Acton
Tobacco
Root
Mts.
Jefferson R.
Willow Creek
Manhattan
Clyde Park
Big Timber
Molt
Divide
Sappington
Belgrade
Greycliff
Springdale
Billings
Reed Point
Melrose
Pony
Bozeman
Livingston
Laurel
Madison Range
Anceney
McLeod
Columbus
Twin Bridges
10591 ft
3228 m
Granite Peak
Norris
Gallatin Range
Yellowstone R.
Park City
Tweedy
Mtn.
Glen
Sheridan
Absarokee
Silesia
McAllister
Ennis L.
10155 ft
3095 m
Mt.
Blackmore
Mount
Cowen
Limestone
Joliet
Pryor
Emigrant
11204 ft
3415 m
Dean
Alder
Ennis
Tumble
Mtn.
Mt. Wood
Fromberg
Chico
Hot Sprs
11325 ft
3452 m
12661 ft
3859 m
Roberts
Virginia City
Luther
Bridger
Ruby Range
Madison R.
Beartooth Mts.
Bannack
Dillon
Cameron
Gallatin R.
Miner
12799 ft
3901 m
Red Lodge
East Pry
8776
2675
Granite Peak
Belfry
11286 ft
3440 m
Corwin
Springs
Warren
45°
Koch Peak
Gardiner
Cooke City
Red Rock
Mammoth
Hot Springs
10948 ft
3337 m
Beartooth Pass
Frannie

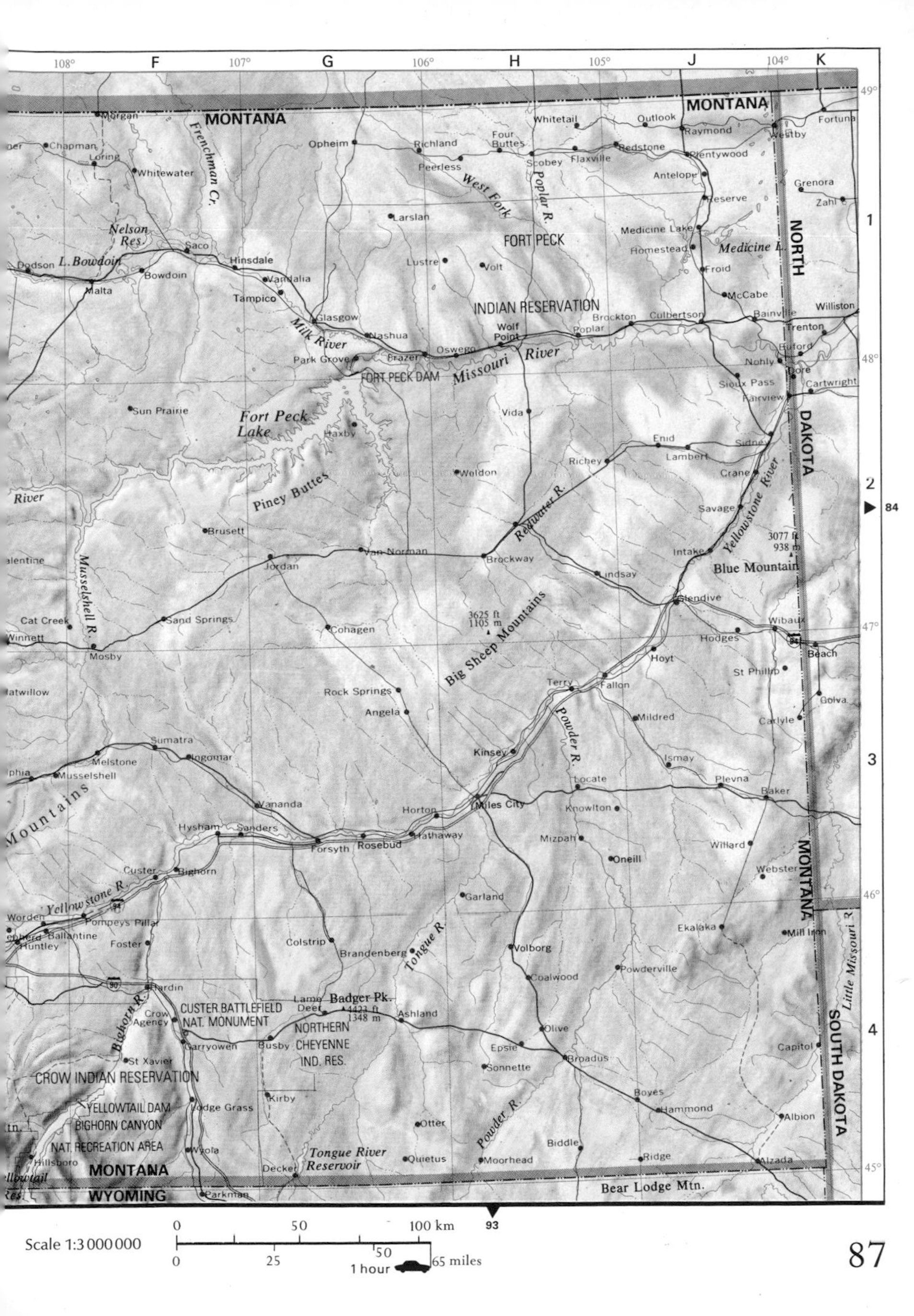

Morgan · Chapman · Loring · Whitewater · Opheim · Richland · Four Buttes · Whitetail · Outlook · Raymond · Fortuna

Peerless · Scobey · Flaxville · Redstone · Brentywood · Westby

Larslan · West Fork · Antelope · Grenora · Zahl

Nelson Res. · Saco · Hinsdale · Lustre · Volt · Reserve · Medicine Lake · Homestead · Froid · Medicine L.

Dodson L. Bowdoin · Bowdoin · Tampico · Vandalia · Glasgow · Nashua · FORT PECK · McCabe · Bainville · Williston

Malta · Milk River · Park Grove · Frazer · Oswego · INDIAN RESERVATION · Wolf Point · Brockton · Culbertson · Trenton

Sun Prairie · FORT PECK DAM · Missouri River · Poplar · Nohly · Bufford

Fort Peck Lake · Haxby · Vida · Sioux Pass · Fairview · Cartwright

River · Piney Buttes · Weldon · Richey · Enid · Lambert · Crane · Sidney · 3077 ft 938 m

Brusett · Redwater R. · Savage · Blue Mountain

Musselshell R. · Jordan · Van Norman · Brockway · Lindsay · Intake · Wibaux

Valentine · Cat Creek · Sand Springs · Cohagen · 3625 ft 1105 m · Big Sheep Mountains · Glendive · Beach

Winnett · Mosby · Rock Springs · Terry · Fallon · Hoyt · St Philip · Golva

Flatwillow · Angela · Kinsey · Mildred · Ismay · Plevna · Baker · Carlyle

Sumatra · Melstone · Ingomar · Power R. · Locate

Philia · Musselshell · Vananda · Horton · Miles City · Knowlton · Willard · Webster

Mountains · Hysham · Sanders · Forsyth · Rosebud · Hathaway · Mizpah · Oneill

Custer · Bighorn · Garland · Ekalaka · Mill Iron

Worden · Yellowstone R. · Pompeys Pillar · Foster · Colstrip · Brandenberg · Tongue R. · Volborg · Powderville

Alberta · Ballantine · Huntley · Coalwood

Hardin · CUSTER BATTLEFIELD NAT. MONUMENT · Lame Deer · Badger Pk. 1421 ft 1348 m · Ashland · Epsie · Capitol

Crow Agency · St Xavier · Garryowen · Busby · NORTHERN CHEYENNE IND. RES. · Olive · Broadus · Boyes

CROW INDIAN RESERVATION · Kirby · Sonnette · Hammond · Albion

YELLOWTAIL DAM · BIGHORN CANYON · Lodge Grass · Otter · Biddle · Ridge · Alzada

NAT. RECREATION AREA · Wyola · Decker · Tongue River Reservoir · Quietus · Moorhead

MONTANA · Parkman · Bear Lodge Mtn.

WYOMING

Scale 1:3 000 000

0 · 50 · 100 km

0 · 25 · 50 · 65 miles

1 hour

87

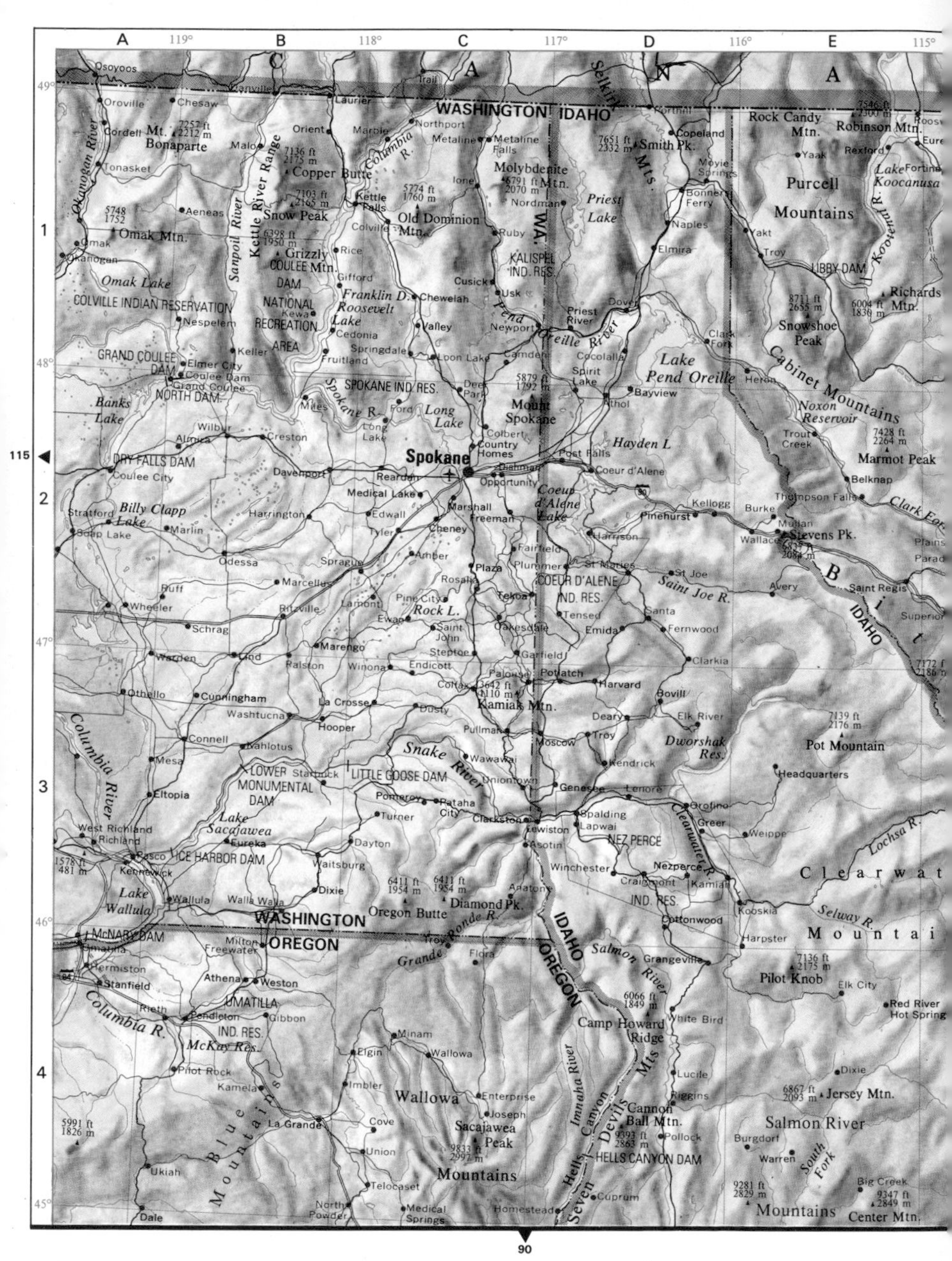

MONTANA-Western, IDAHO-Northern

119°
B
118°
C
117°
116°
115°
49°
48°
47°
46°
45°
1
2
3
4
115
90
C
WASHINGTON
WA.
Osoyoos
Oroville
Chesaw
Laurier
Trail
Northport
Metaline
Metaline Falls
Copeland
Rock Candy Mtn.
Robinson Mtn.
Cordell
Mt. Bonaparte
7257 ft 2212 m
Orient
Marble
Columbia R.
Ione
Molybdenite Mtn.
6791 ft 2070 m
7651 ft 2332 m
Smith Pk.
Selkirk Mts.
Yaak
Rexford
Okanogan River
Malo
Kettle River Range
7136 ft 2175 m
Copper Butte
Tonasket
Moyie Springs
Purcell Mountains
Lake Koocanusa
Kootenai R.
Kettle Falls
7103 ft 2165 m
Snow Peak
5774 ft 1760 m
Old Dominion Mtn.
Nordman
Priest Lake
Bonners Ferry
5748 1752
Aeneas
Sanpoil River
Naples
Omak Mtn.
Omak
Okanogan
6398 ft 1950 m
Grizzly Mtn.
Colville
Ruby
Yakt
Troy
Rice
Elmira
Omak Lake
COULEE DAM NATIONAL RECREATION AREA
Gifford
KALISPEL IND. RES.
LIBBY DAM
Franklin D. Roosevelt Lake
Chewelah
Cusick
Usk
8711 ft 2655 m
Richards Mtn.
6004 ft 1830 m
COLVILLE INDIAN RESERVATION
Kewa
Pend Oreille River
Priest River
Dover
Nespelem
Cedonia
Valley
Newport
Snowshoe Peak
Clark Fork
Keller
Springdale
Loon Lake
Camden
Cocolalla
Cabinet Mountains
GRAND COULEE DAM
Elmer City
Coulee Dam
Grand Coulee
Fruitland
Lake Pend Oreille
Spirit Lake
Heron
NORTH DAM
SPOKANE IND. RES.
Spokane R.
Deer Park
5879 ft 1792 m
Mount Spokane
Athol
Bayview
Banks Lake
Miles
Ford
Long Lake
Noxon Reservoir
Wilbur
Colbert
Country Homes
Almira
Creston
Hayden L
Trout Creek
7428 ft 2264 m
Marmot Peak
DRY FALLS DAM
Spokane
Post Falls
Coulee City
Davenport
Reardan
Coeur d'Alene
Opportunity
Belknap
Medical Lake
Coeur d'Alene Lake
Thompson Falls
Clark Fork
Stratford
Billy Clapp Lake
Harrington
Edwall
Marshall
Freeman
Kellogg
Burke
Pinehurst
Soap Lake
Marlin
Tyler
Cheney
Harrison
Mullan
Stevens Pk.
Wallace
Plains
Odessa
Amber
Sprague
Fairfield
Plummer
St. Maries
Paradise
Plaza
Rosalia
St Joe
COEUR D'ALENE IND. RES.
Saint Joe R.
Avery
Ruff
Marcellus
Saint Regis
Wheeler
Ritzville
Lamont
Pine City
Rock L.
Tekoa
Tensed
Santa
B
Superior
Schrag
Ewan
Saint John
Oakesdale
Emida
Fernwood
Warden
Marengo
Steptoe
Garfield
Ralston
Winona
Endicott
Clarkia
7172 ft 2186 m
Othello
Cunningham
Palouse
Potlatch
Harvard
Colfax
3642 ft 1110 m
Kamiak Mtn.
Bovill
La Crosse
Washtucna
Hooper
Dusty
Deary
Elk River
7139 ft 2176 m
Pot Mountain
Columbia River
Connell
Kahlotus
Pullman
Moscow
Troy
Dworshak Res.
Mesa
Snake River
Wawawai
Kendrick
Headquarters
LOWER MONUMENTAL DAM
Starbuck
LITTLE GOOSE DAM
Uniontown
Genesee
Lenore
Eltopia
Pomeroy
Pataha City
Orofino
Turner
Clarkston
Lewiston
Spalding
Lapwai
Greer
West Richland
Richland
Lake Sacajawea
Eureka
Dayton
Asotin
NEZ PERCE
Clearwater R.
Weippe
Lochsa R.
1578 ft 481 m
Pasco
Kennewick
ICE HARBOR DAM
Waitsburg
Winchester
Nezperce
Craigmont
Kamiah
Clearwat
Lake Wallula
Dixie
6411 ft 1954 m
Anatone
IND. RES.
Wallula
Walla Walla
Diamond Pk.
Oregon Butte
Kooskia
Selway R.
WASHINGTON
OREGON
OREGON
McNARY DAM
Umatilla
Milton Freewater
Troy
Grande Ronde R.
Flora
Cottonwood
Harpster
Mountai
Hermiston
Salmon River
Grangeville
7136 ft 2175 m
Pilot Knob
Stanfield
Athena
Weston
Elk City
Columbia R.
Rieth
UMATILLA
Pendleton
IND. RES.
Gibbon
6066 ft 1849 m
Camp Howard Ridge
White Bird
Red River Hot Spring
McKay Res.
Minam
Elgin
Wallowa
Imnaha River
Mts
Pilot Rock
Kamela
Imbler
Enterprise
Lucile
Dixie
Blue Mountains
Wallowa
Joseph
Riggins
6867 ft 2093 m
Jersey Mtn.
5991 ft 1826 m
La Grande
Cove
Sacajawea Peak
Hells Canyon
Devils
Cannon Ball Mtn.
9393 ft 2863 m
Pollock
Salmon River
Burgdorf
Union
9833 ft 2997 m
HELLS CANYON DAM
Warren
South Fork
Ukiah
Mountains
Seven
Telocaset
Cuprum
9281 ft 2829 m
Big Creek
9347 ft 2849 m
Mountains
Center Mtn.
North Powder
Medical Springs
Homestead
Dale

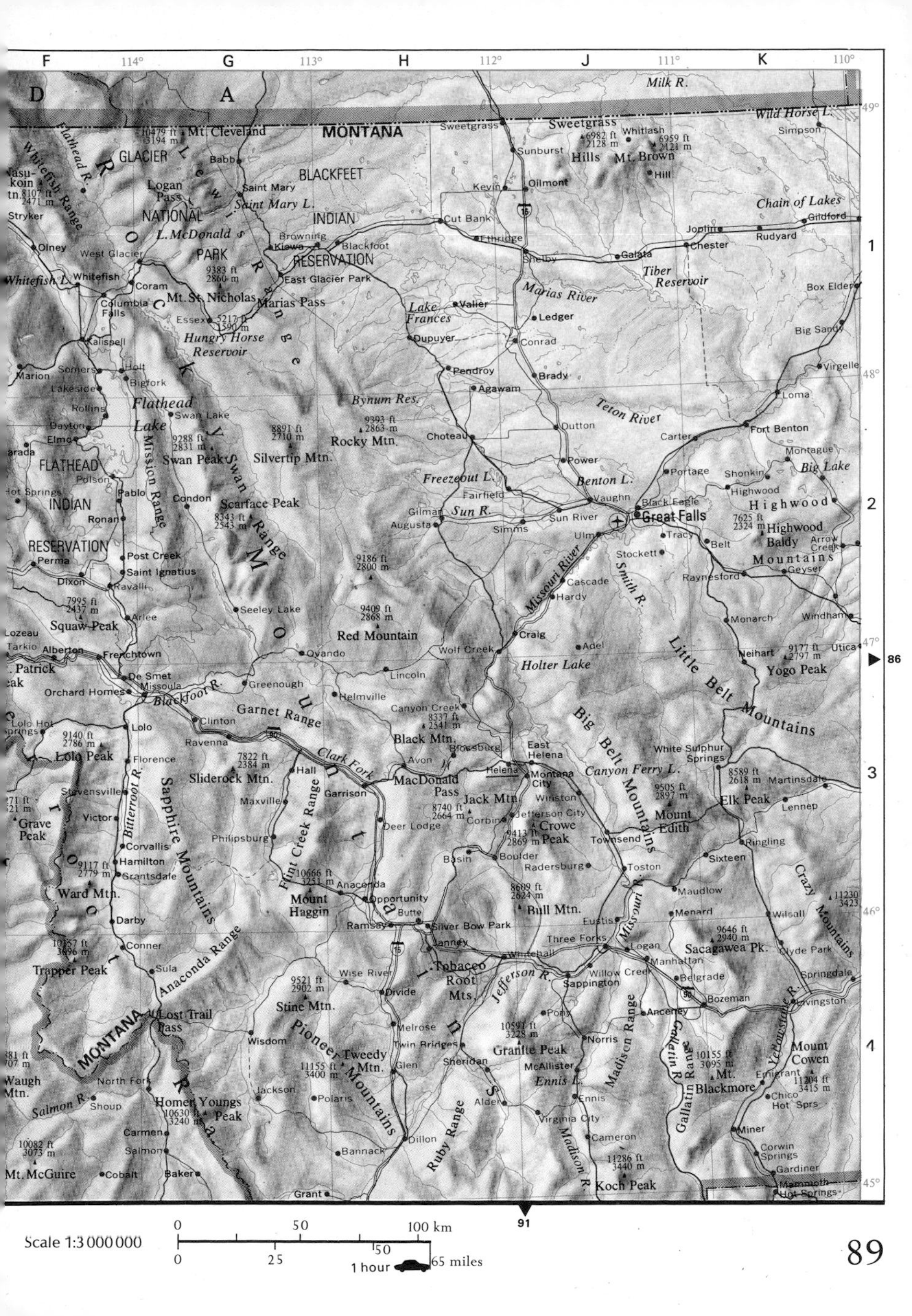

F 114° G 113° H 112° J 111° K 110°

D A N A Milk R.

MONTANA

Wild Horse L.
Simpson

Sweetgrass
Sunburst Sweetgrass Whitlash 6959 ft Chain of Lakes
Hills Mt. Brown 2123 m 2121 m Gildford
Mt Cleveland 6082 ft Hill Joplin Rudyard
GLACIER Logan Babb Saint Mary Kevin Oilmont Shelby Galata Chester Box Elder
Pass NATIONAL Saint Mary L. Browning Blackfoot Cut Bank Ethridge Tiber Big Sandy
L. McDonald PARK East Glacier Park Lake Valier Ledger Reservoir Virgelle
West Glacier 9383 ft Frances Conrad Loma
Coram 2860 m Marias Pass Dupuyer Marias River Dutton Fort Benton
Columbia Mt. St. Nicholas Pendroy Brady Teton River Carter Montague
Falls Essex 5217 Agawam Benton L. Portage Shonkin Big Lake
Hungry Horse 1590 m Bynum Res. Choteau Power Vaughn Black Eagle Highwood
Reservoir 9393 ft Fairfield Simms Sun River GREAT FALLS Highwood Arrow
Rocky Mtn. Freezeout L. Gilman Augusta Belt Baldy Geyser
8891 ft Sun R. Stockett Raynesford Mountains Windham
2710 m 9186 ft Cascade Smith R. Monarch
9400 ft 2800 m Hardy 9177 ft Utica 86
Red Mountain Ovando Wolf Creek Craig Adel Neihart 2797 m Yogo Peak
Helmville Lincoln Holter Lake Little Belt
Canyon Creek 8337 ft Mountains
Black Mtn. 2541 m East White Sulphur 8589 ft Martinsdale
Avon Stoncburg Helena Springs 2618 m Lennep
Clark Fork Helena Montana Canyon Ferry L. Elk Peak Ringling
MacDonald Garrison City Winston 9505 ft Mount Sixteen 11430
Pass Deer Lodge 8740 ft Corbin Jefferson R. 2897 m Edith Townsend 3423
Jack Mtn. 2664 m Crowe Radersburg Toston Maudlow Menard
Anaconda 9413 Peak Boulder Bull Mtn. 9646 ft Sacagawea Pk. Clyde Park
Mount Opportunity Basin 2869 m 8609 ft Logan 2940 m Wilsall Springdale
Haggin Butte Three Forks Manhattan Belgrade Livingston
Ramsay Silver Bow Park Whitehall Willow Creek Bozeman Mount
9521 ft Wise River Tobacco Sappington Ancency 10155 ft Cowen
Stine Mtn. 2902 m Divide Root Pony Norris Gallatin Mt. 3095 m 11304
Melrose Mts. McAllister Range Blackmore 3415 m
Tweedy Twin Bridges 10571 ft Granite Peak Ennis Emigrant Chico
Pioneer Mtn. Glen Sheridan Ennis Virginia City Miner Hot Sprs.
11155 ft Jackson Polaris Madison R. Cameron Corwin
3400 m Bannack Dillon 11286 ft Springs
Homer Youngs Koch Peak 3440 m Gardiner
Peak Grant Mammoth

Scale 1:3 000 000

0   50   100 km
0   25   50
1 hour   65 miles

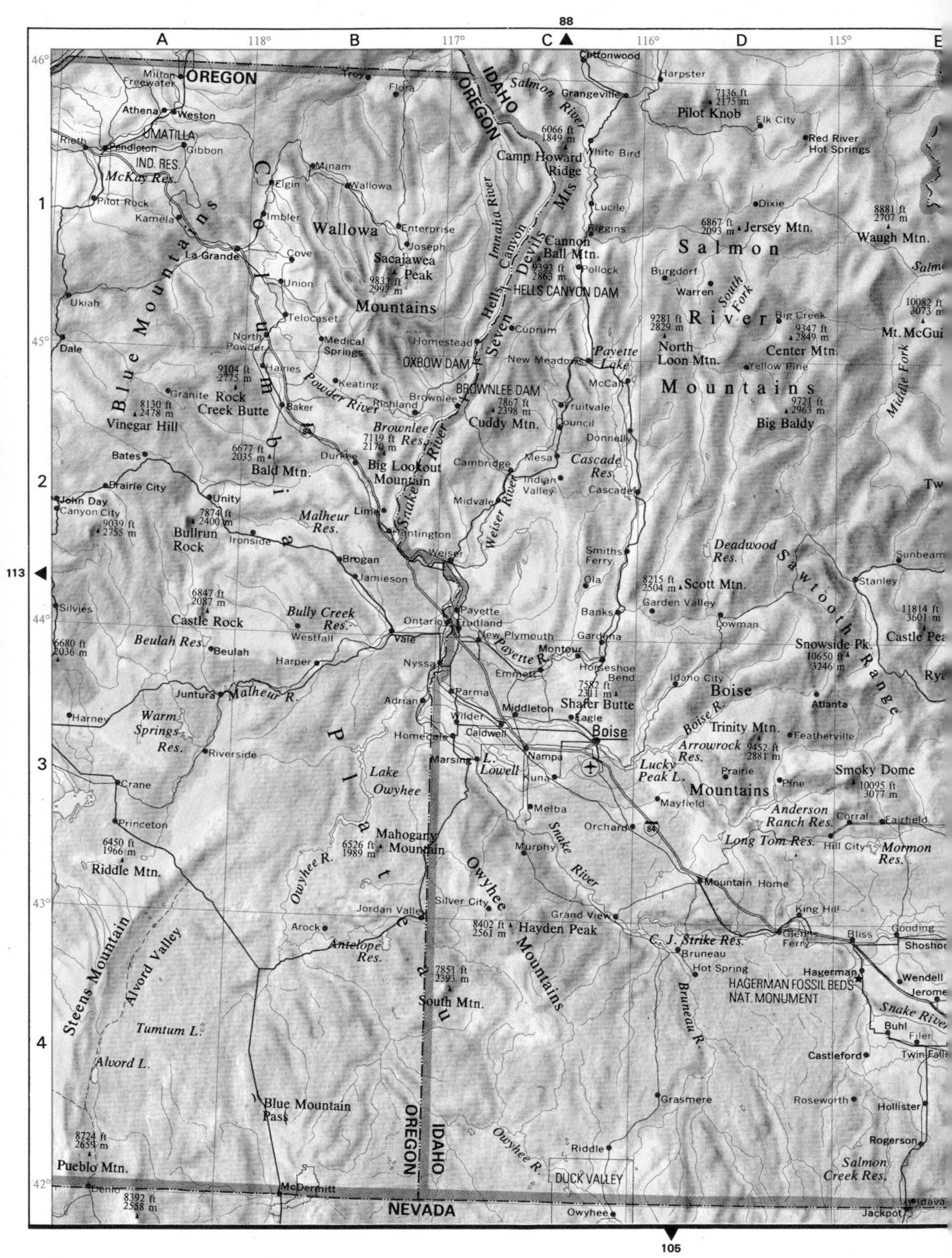

46° **OREGON**

A   118°   B   117°   C ▲   116°   D   115°   E

Milton
Freewater
Athena
Weston
Troy
Flora
Cottonwood
Grangeville
Harpster
1136 ft
2175 m
Rieth
Pendleton
Gibbon
UMATILLA
IND. RES.
McKay Res.
Pilot Rock
Kamela
Minam
Wallowa
Imbler
Elgin
Wallowa
Enterprise
Joseph
Cove
La Grande
Union
Medical
Springs
Telocaset
Keating
North
Powder
Richland
Baker
Hamer
Granite
Rock
Creek Butte
Bates
Prairie City
John Day
Canyon City
Unity
Ironside
Brogan
Jamieson
Westfall
Vale
Harper
Beulah
Juntura
Harney
Riverside
Crane
Princeton
Riddle Mtn.
Silvies
Camp Howard
Ridge
White Bird
Lucile
Riggins
Pollock
Warren
Dixie
Jersey Mtn.
Waugh Mtn.
Burgdorf
Big Creek
Center Mtn.
Yellow Pine
Big Baldy
Deadwood
Res.
Stanley
Sunbeam
Scott Mtn.
Garden Valley
Lowman
Idaho City
Featherville
Atlanta
Trinity Mtn.
Smoky Dome
Fairfield
Corral
Hill City
Mormon
Res.
King Hill
Gooding
Bliss
Shoshone
Wendell
Jerome
Hagerman
Buhl
Filer
Twin Falls
Castleford
Hollister
Rogerson
Jackpot

OREGON
IDAHO

90 IDAHO-Southern

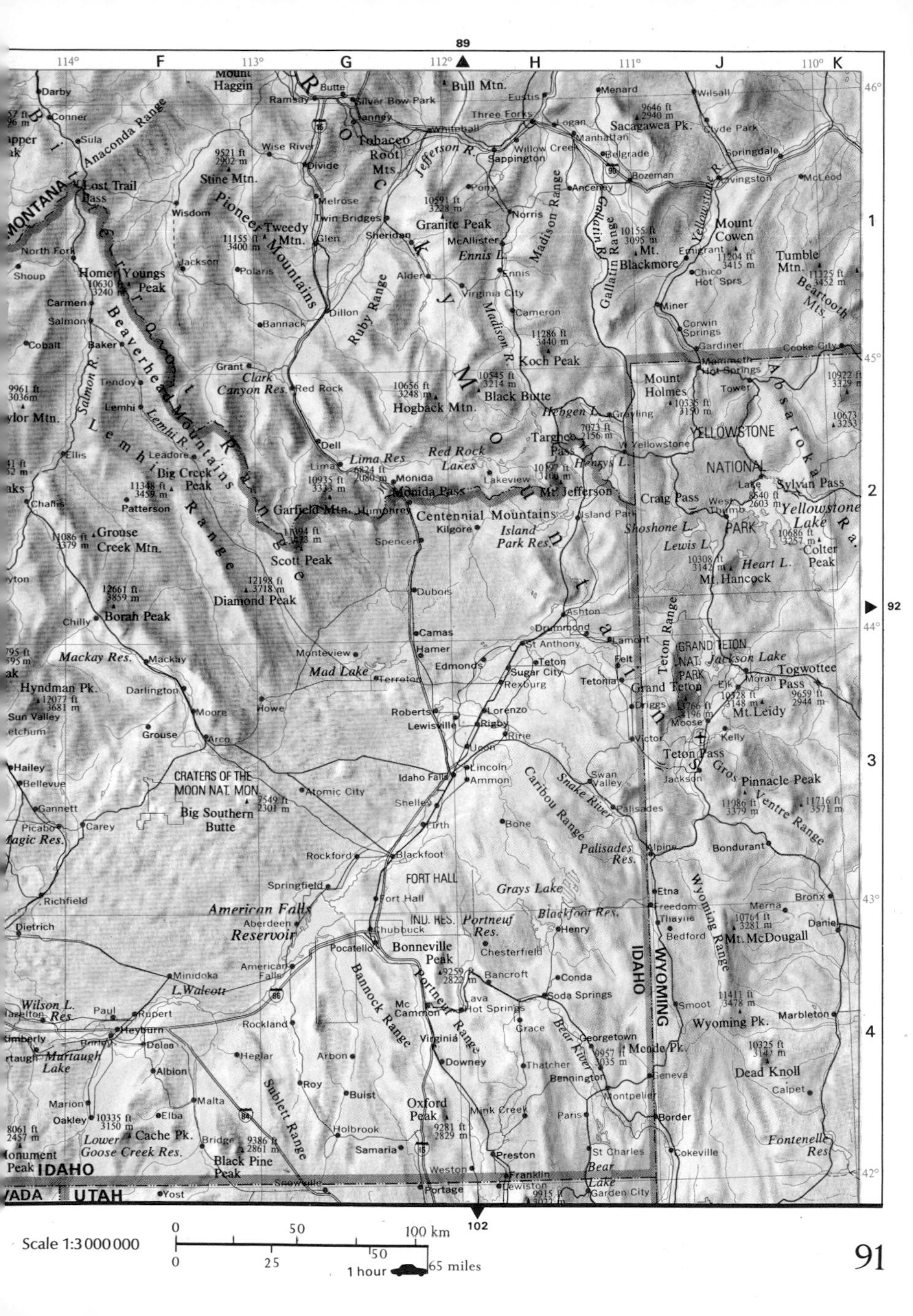

114° F 113° G 112° H 111° J 110° K

46°
45°
44°
43°
42°

1
2
3
4

Scale 1:3 000 000

| 0 | | 50 | | 100 km |

| 0 | | 25 | | 50 | 65 miles |

1 hour

91

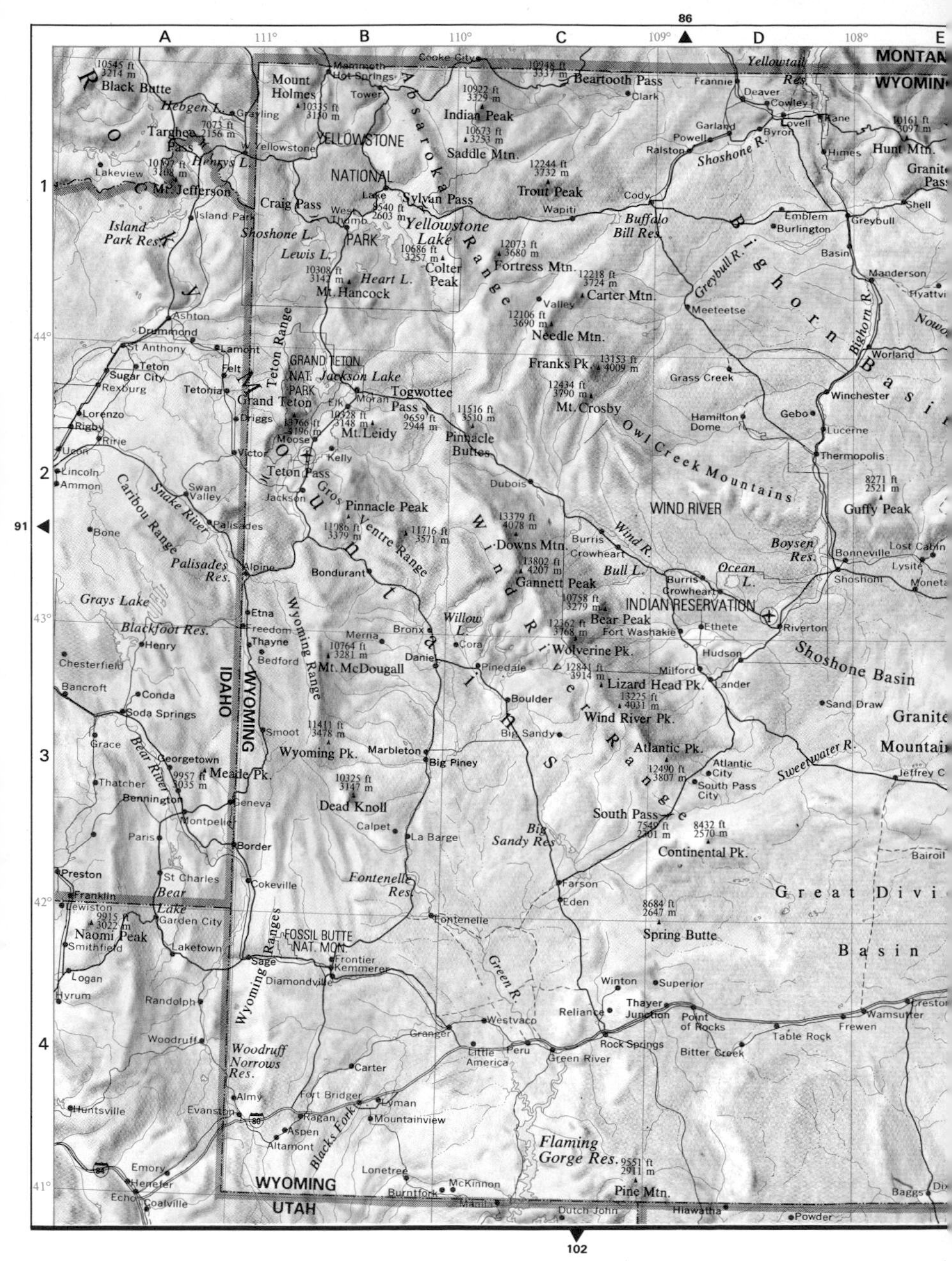

MONTANA
WYOMING
IDAHO
UTAH
YELLOWSTONE NATIONAL PARK
GRAND TETON NAT. PARK
FOSSIL BUTTE NAT. MON.
WIND RIVER INDIAN RESERVATION
Rocky Mountains
Absaroka Range
Bighorn Basin
Owl Creek Mountains
Wind River Range
Teton Range
Gros Ventre Range
Wyoming Range
Caribou Range
Shoshone Basin
Great Divide Basin
Yellowstone Lake
Jackson Lake
Flaming Gorge Res.
Gannett Peak
Grand Teton
Cody
Jackson
Riverton
Lander
Rock Springs
Green River
Evanston
Kemmerer
Pinedale
Thermopolis
Worland
Greybull
Powell
Dubois

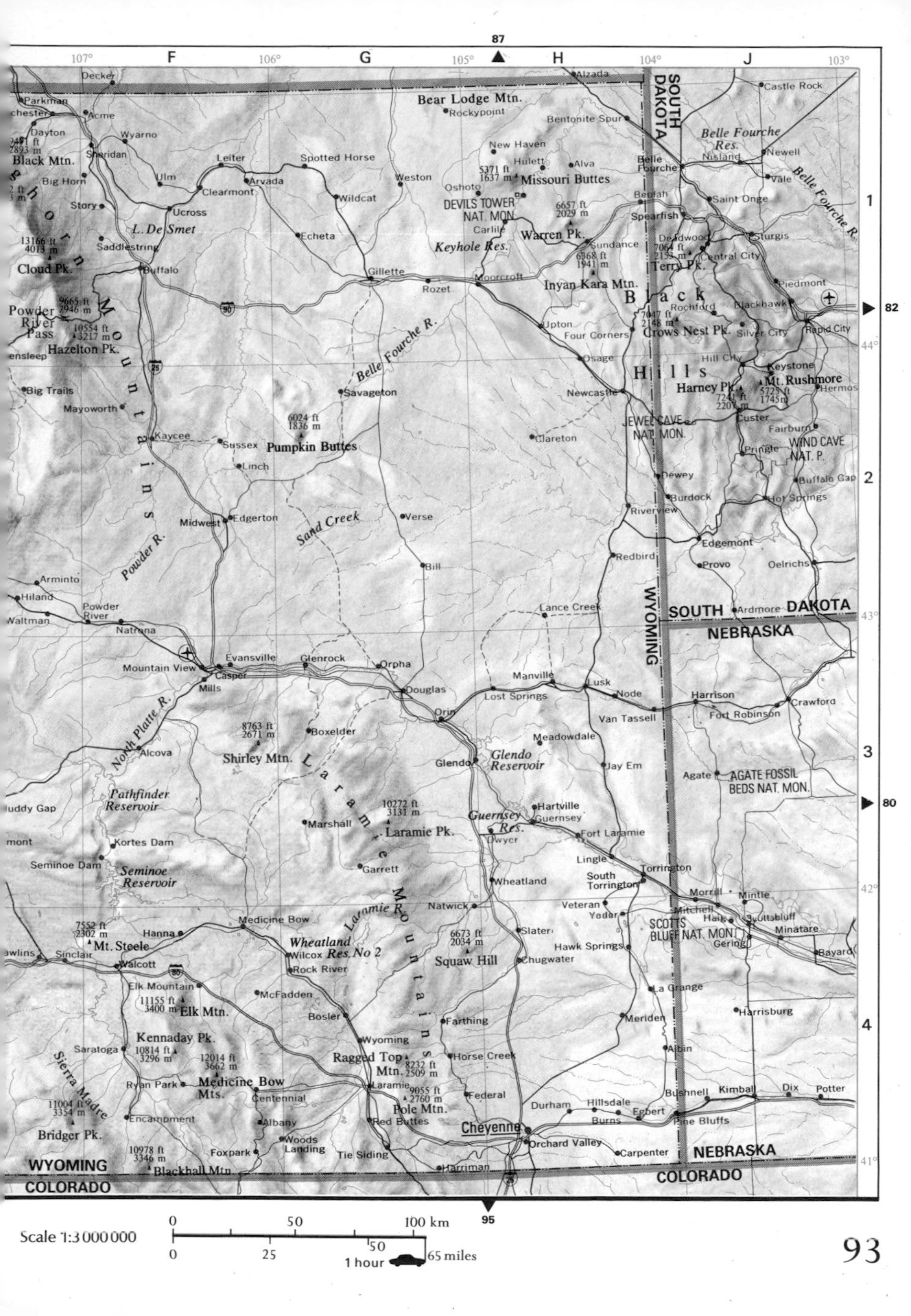

87
95
82
80
107°
106°
105°
104°
103°
F
G
H
J
1
2
3
4
44°
43°
42°
41°
SOUTH DAKOTA
WYOMING
SOUTH DAKOTA
NEBRASKA
COLORADO
Bear Lodge Mtn.
Rockypoint
Alzada
Castle Rock
Bentonite Spur
Belle Fourche Res.
Belle Fourche R.
New Haven
Hulett
Alva
Missouri Buttes
DEVILS TOWER NAT. MON.
Oshoto
Carlile
Warren Pk.
Keyhole Res.
Sundance
Inyan Kara Mtn.
Belle Fourche
Nisland
Newell
Vale
Saint Onge
Beulah
Spearfish
Deadwood
Sturgis
Central City
Terry Pk.
Piedmont
Blackhawk
Rapid City
Rochford
Black Hills
Crows Nest Pk.
Silver City
Hill City
Keystone
Mt. Rushmore
Harney Pk.
Hermosa
Custer
Fairburn
JEWEL CAVE NAT. MON.
WIND CAVE NAT. P.
Pringle
Dewey
Buffalo Gap
Burdock
Hot Springs
Riverview
Edgemont
Provo
Oelrichs
Redbird
Ardmore
Decker
Parkman
Ranchester
Acme
Dayton
Black Mtn.
Wyarno
Sheridan
Big Horn
Story
Leiter
Spotted Horse
Ulm
Clearmont
Arvada
Weston
Wildcat
Ucross
L. De Smet
Echeta
Saddlestring
Cloud Pk.
Buffalo
Gillette
Rozet
Moorcroft
Upton
Four Corners
Osage
Newcastle
Powder River Pass
Hazelton Pk.
Tensleep
Big Horn Mountains
Big Trails
Mayoworth
Kaycee
Sussex
Pumpkin Buttes
Linch
Savageton
Belle Fourche R.
Clareton
Midwest
Edgerton
Sand Creek
Verse
Powder R.
Bill
Arminto
Hiland
Waltman
Powder River
Natrona
Lance Creek
Evansville
Glenrock
Orpha
Mountain View
Casper
Mills
Douglas
Manville
Lusk
Node
Lost Springs
Harrison
Crawford
Van Tassell
Fort Robinson
Orin
Boxelder
North Platte R.
Alcova
Shirley Mtn.
Laramie Mountains
Meadowdale
Glendo
Glendo Reservoir
Jay Em
Agate
AGATE FOSSIL BEDS NAT. MON.
Pathfinder Reservoir
Muddy Gap
Marshall
Laramie Pk.
Hartville
Guernsey
Guernsey Res.
Dwyer
Fort Laramie
Kortes Dam
Lingle
Torrington
Seminoe Dam
Seminoe Reservoir
Garrett
South Torrington
Wheatland
Morrill
Mintle
Veteran
Natwick
Yoder
Mitchell
Scottsbluff
Medicine Bow
Laramie R.
Slater
SCOTTS BLUFF NAT. MON.
Minatare
Mt. Steele
Hanna
Wheatland Res. No 2
Wilcox
Squaw Hill
Hawk Springs
Gering
Bayard
Rawlins
Sinclair
Walcott
Rock River
Chugwater
Elk Mountain
Elk Mtn.
McFadden
La Grange
Bosler
Farthing
Meriden
Harrisburg
Kennaday Pk.
Wyoming
Saratoga
Horse Creek
Albin
Ragged Top Mtn.
Sierra Madre
Ryan Park
Medicine Bow Mts.
Laramie
Centennial
Federal
Pole Mtn.
Bushnell
Kimball
Dix
Potter
Durham
Hillsdale
Egbert
Encampment
Albany
Red Buttes
Burns
Pine Bluffs
Bridger Pk.
Cheyenne
Orchard Valley
Woods Landing
Foxpark
Tie Siding
Carpenter
Blackhall Mtn.
Harriman
NEBRASKA
WYOMING
COLORADO
9471 ft 2893 m
13166 ft 4013 m
9665 ft 2946 m
10554 ft 3217 m
5371 ft 1637 m
6657 ft 2029 m
6368 ft 1941 m
7064 ft 2155 m
7047 ft 2148 m
7241 ft 2207 m
5725 ft 1745 m
6024 ft 1836 m
8763 ft 2671 m
10272 ft 3131 m
7552 ft 2302 m
6673 ft 2034 m
11155 ft 3400 m
10814 ft 3296 m
12014 ft 3662 m
8232 ft 2509 m
9055 ft 2760 m
11004 ft 3354 m
10978 ft 3346 m
Scale 1:3 000 000
0
50
100 km
0
25
50
65 miles
1 hour

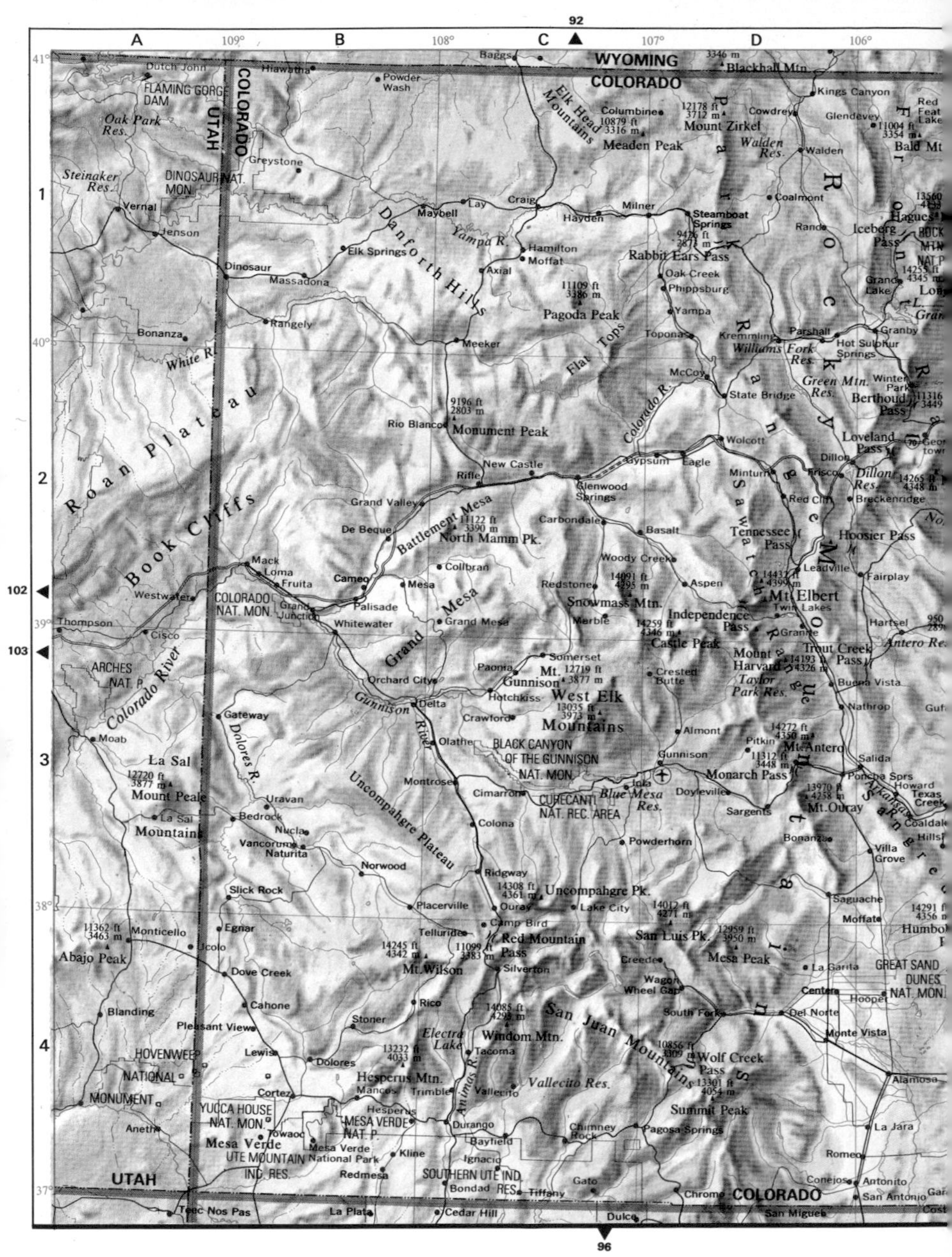

92
A
B
C
D
109°
108°
107°
106°
41°
40°
39°
38°
37°
1
2
3
4
102
103
96
WYOMING
COLORADO
UTAH
Baggs
Dutch John
Hiawatha
Powder Wash
FLAMING GORGE DAM
Oak Park Res.
Elk Head Mountains
3346 m
Blackhall Mtn.
Kings Canyon
Columbine
12178 ft 3712 m
Mount Zirkel
Cowdrey
Glendevey
10879 ft 3316 m
Meaden Peak
Walden Res.
Walden
11004 ft 3354 m
Bald Mt
Red Feat Lake
Greystone
Steinaker Res.
DINOSAUR NAT. MON.
Vernal
Jenson
Maybell
Lay
Craig
Danforth Hills
Yampa R.
Hayden
Milner
Steamboat Springs
9426 ft 2873 m
Rabbit Ears Pass
Coalmont
Rand
Iceberg Pass
Hagues
ROCKY MTN. NAT. P.
Elk Springs
Hamilton
Moffat
Axial
Dinosaur
Massadona
11109 ft 3386 m
Pagoda Peak
Oak Creek
Phippsburg
Yampa
Grand Lake
14255 ft 4345 m
Bonanza
Rangely
White R.
Meeker
Flat Tops
Topona
Kremmling
Williams Fork Res.
Parshall
Hot Sulphur Springs
Granby
McCoy
State Bridge
Green Mtn. Res.
Winter Park
Berthoud Pass
Roan Plateau
9196 ft 2803 m
Rio Blanco
Monument Peak
Colorado R.
Wolcott
Loveland Pass
New Castle
Rifle
Gypsum
Eagle
Dillon
Minturn
Frisco
Dillon Res.
14265 ft 4348 m
Book Cliffs
Glenwood Springs
Red Cliff
Breckenridge
Grand Valley
Battlement Mesa
11122 ft 3390 m
North Mamm Pk.
De Beque
Carbondale
Basalt
Tennessee Pass
Sawatch Range
Hoosier Pass
Mack
Loma
Fruita
Collbran
Woody Creek
Cameo
Mesa
Grand Mesa
Redstone
14091 ft 4295 m
Aspen
14433 ft 4399 m
Leadville
Fairplay
Westwater
COLORADO NAT. MON.
Grand Junction
Palisade
Snowmass Mtn.
Independence Pass
Mt. Elbert
Twin Lakes
Thompson
Cisco
Whitewater
Marble
14259 ft 4346 m
Castle Peak
Granite
Hartsel
Antero Res.
ARCHES NAT. P.
Colorado River
Somerset
Paonia
Mt. Gunnison
12719 ft 3877 m
Mount Harvard
14193 ft 4326 m
Trout Creek Pass
Orchard City
Hotchkiss
Crested Butte
Taylor Park Res.
Buena Vista
Gunnison River
Delta
West Elk Mountains
13035 ft 3973 m
Nathrop
Gateway
Crawford
Almont
14272 ft 4350 m
Pitkin
Mt. Antero
Moab
Dolores R.
Olathe
BLACK CANYON OF THE GUNNISON NAT. MON.
Gunnison
La Sal
12720 ft 3877 m
Mount Peale
Uncompahgre Plateau
Montrose
Monarch Pass
12312 ft 3448 m
Salida
Poncha Sprs
Howard
Texas Creek
Arkansas R.
Cimarron
CURECANTI NAT. REC. AREA
Blue Mesa Res.
Doyleville
Sargents
13970 ft 4258 m
Mt. Ouray
Uravan
La Sal
Bedrock
Mountains
Nucla
Colona
Vancorum
Naturita
Powderhorn
Coaldale
Bonanza
Villa Grove
Norwood
Ridgway
14308 ft 4361 m
Uncompahgre Pk.
Slick Rock
Placerville
Ouray
Lake City
14012 ft 4271 m
Saguache
Moffat
14291 ft 4356 m
11362 ft 3463 m
Monticello
Egnar
Telluride
Camp Bird
Red Mountain Pass
San Luis Pk.
12959 ft 3950 m
Abajo Peak
Ucolo
14245 ft 4342 m
11099 ft 3383 m
Mesa Peak
Mt. Wilson
Dove Creek
Silverton
Creede
La Garita
GREAT SAND DUNES NAT. MON.
Wagon Wheel Gap
Center
Hooper
Blanding
Cahone
Rico
14085 ft 4293 m
San Juan Mountains
South Fork
Del Norte
Pleasant View
Stoner
Electra Lake
Windom Mtn.
Monte Vista
HOVENWEEP NATIONAL MONUMENT
Lewis
Dolores
13232 ft 4033 m
Tacoma
10856 ft 3309 m
Wolf Creek Pass
Hesperus Mtn.
Animas R.
Vallecito Res.
13301 ft 4054 m
Alamosa
Cortez
Mancos
Trimble
Vallecito
Summit Peak
YUCCA HOUSE NAT. MON.
Hesperus
MESA VERDE NAT. P.
Aneth
Towaoc
Durango
Chimney Rock
Pagosa Springs
La Jara
Mesa Verde
UTE MOUNTAIN IND. RES.
Mesa Verde National Park
Kline
Bayfield
Ignacio
Romeo
Redmesa
SOUTHERN UTE IND. RES.
Gato
Conejos
Antonito
Bondad
Tiffany
Chromo
San Antonio
Teec Nos Pas
La Plata
Cedar Hill
Dulce
San Miguel

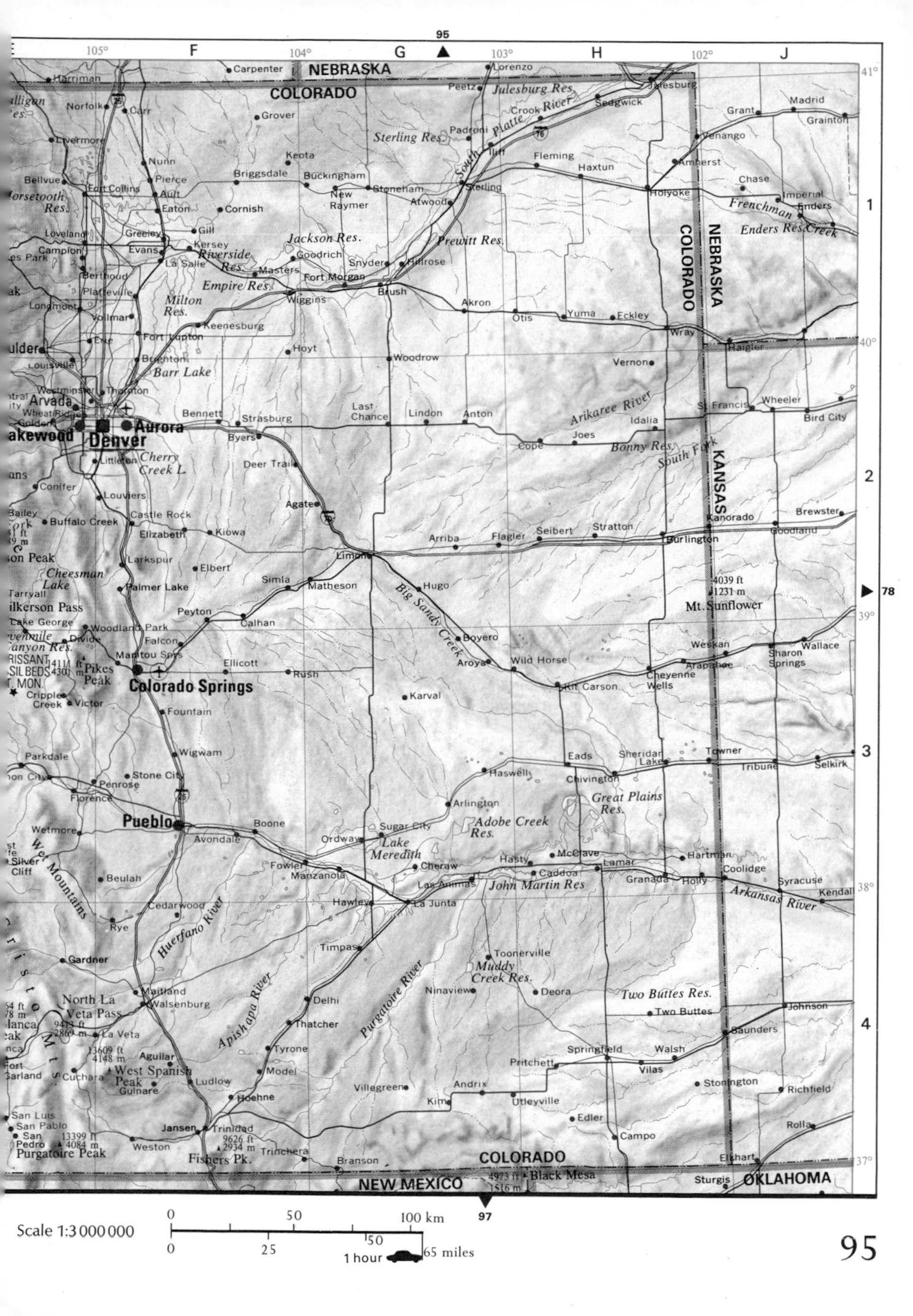

105° F 104° G ▲ 103° H 102° J 41°

NEBRASKA
COLORADO

Carpenter
Harriman
Norfolk
Carr
Grover
Lorenzo
Peetz
Julesburg Res.
Crook River
Sedgwick
Julesburg
Grant
Madrid
Grainton

Livermore
Keota
Padroni
South Platte
Fleming
Haxtun
Venango

Sterling Res.
Ovid
Amherst
Chase
Imperial
Enders

Bellvue
Fort Collins
Nunn
Pierce
Ault
Briggsdale
Buckingham
Stoneham
Atwood
Sterling
Holyoke
Frenchman
Enders Res.
Creek

Loveland
Eaton
Cornish
New
Raymer
COLORADO
NEBRASKA
1

Campion
Greeley
Gill
Jackson Res.
Prewitt Res.

Estes Park
Berthoud
La Salle
Kersey
Riverside
Res.
Goodrich
Snyder
Melrose

Longmont
Placerville
Evans
Masters
Fort Morgan
Brush
Akron
Yuma
Eckley
Wray
Haigler
40°

Boulder
Erie
Fort Lupton
Milton
Res.
Wiggins
Otis

Louisville
Brighton
Keenesburg
Hoyt
Vernon

Arvada
Thornton
Barr Lake
Woodrow

Wheat Ridge
Bennett
Strasburg
Last
Chance
Lindon
Anton
Arikaree River
St. Francis
Wheeler

Lakewood
Denver
Aurora
Byers
Cope
Joes
Idalia
Bird City

Littleton
Cherry
Creek L.
Deer Trail
Bonny Res.
South Fork
KANSAS
2

Conifer
Louviers
Castle Rock
Agate
Brewster

Buffalo Creek
Elizabeth
Kiowa
Arriba
Flagler
Seibert
Stratton
Kanorado
Goodland

son Peak
Larkspur
Elbert
Limon
Burlington

Cheesman
Lake
Palmer Lake
Simla
Matheson
Hugo
4039 ft
1231 m
Mt. Sunflower
▶ 78
39°

Tarryall
Wilkerson Pass
Woodland Park
Peyton
Big Sandy Creek
Boyero

Lake George
Divide
Falcon
Calhan
Weskan
Wallace

FLORISSANT
FOSSIL BEDS
NAT. MON.
Manitou Spgs
Ellicott
Rush
Aroya
Wild Horse
Cheyenne
Wells
Arapahoe
Sharon
Springs

Pikes
Peak
4301 m
Colorado Springs
Karval
Kit Carson

Cripple
Creek
Victor
Fountain

Parkdale
Wigwam
Eads
Sheridan
Lake
Towner
Selkirk
3

Cañon City
Stone City
Penrose
Haswell
Chivington
Tribune

Florence
Arlington
Great Plains
Res.

Wetmore
Pueblo
Boone
Avondale
Ordway
Sugar City
Lake
Meredith
Adobe Creek
Res.
Hasty
McClave
Lamar
Hartman
Coolidge

Silver
Cliff
Beulah
Fowler
Manzanola
Cheraw
Caddoa
Granada
Holly
Syracuse
Kendall
38°

Cedarwood
Huerfano River
Las Animas
John Martin Res.
Arkansas River

Rye
Hawley
La Junta

Gardner
Timpas
Toonerville

North La
Veta Pass
Maitland
Walsenburg
Delhi
Muddy
Creek Res.
Deora
Two Buttes Res.

La Veta
Aguilar
Thatcher
Apishapa River
Ninaview
Two Buttes
Johnson
4

West Spanish
Peak
Model
Tyrone
Purgatoire River
Springfield
Walsh
Saunders

Gulnare
Ludlow
Boehne
Villegreen
Andrix
Pritchett
Vilas
Stonington
Richfield

San Luis
San Pablo
Jansen
Weston
Kim
Utleyville
Edler
Campo
Rolla

Purgatoire Peak
4084 m
Trinidad
Fishers Pk.
Trinchera
Branson
Black Mesa
1516 m
Elkhart
Sturgis
OKLAHOMA
37°

NEW MEXICO
COLORADO
97

Scale 1:3 000 000

0   50   100 km
97
0   25   50   65 miles
1 hour

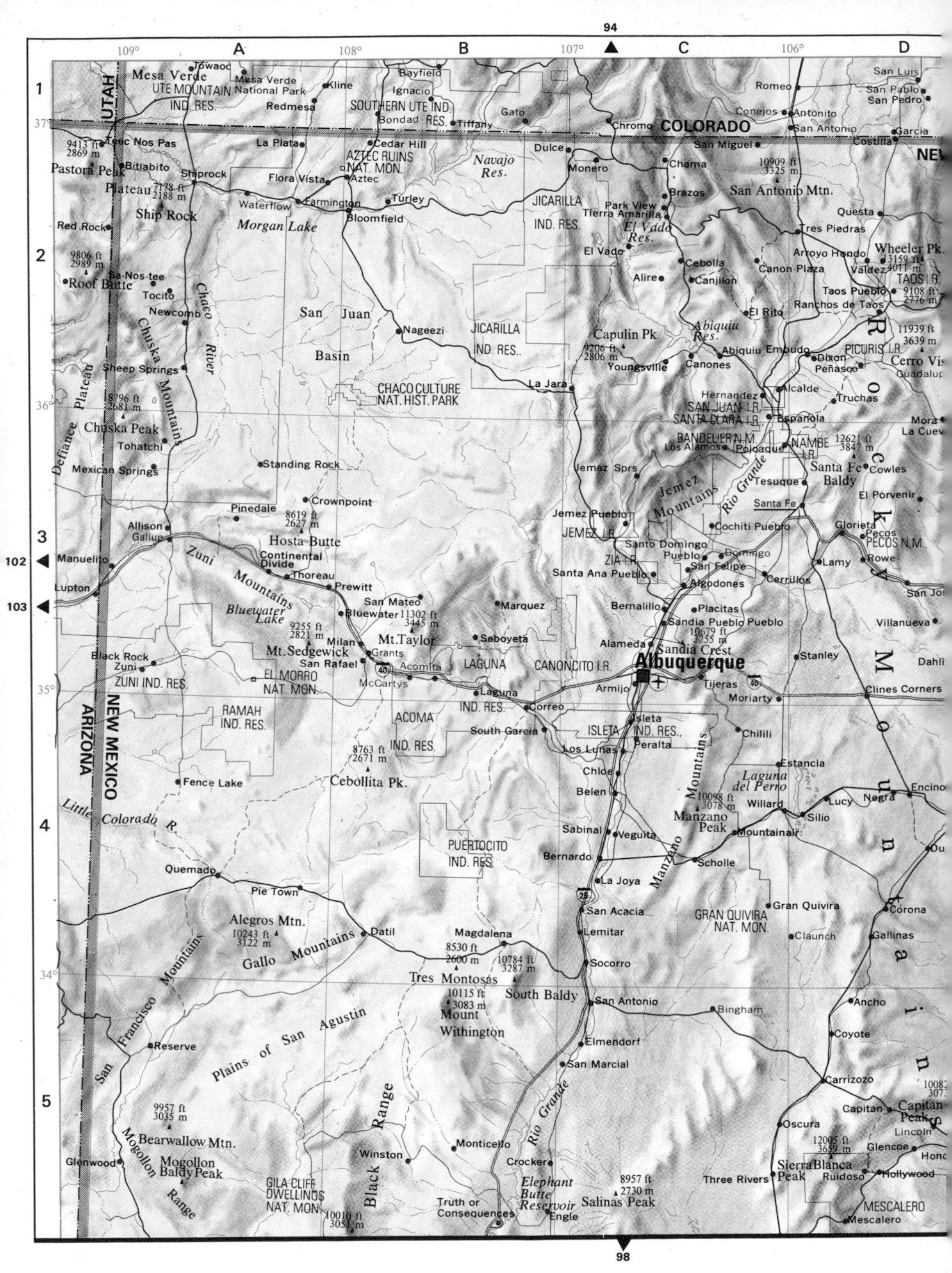
94
109°
A
108°
B
107°
C
106°
D
1
2
3
4
5
Towaoc
Mesa Verde
Mesa Verde National Park
UTE MOUNTAIN IND. RES.
UTAH
Redmesa
Kline
Bayfield
Ignacio
SOUTHERN UTE IND. RES.
Bondad
Tiffany
Gato
Chromo
COLORADO
Romeo
San Luis
San Pablo
San Pedro
Conejos
Antonito
San Antonio
Garcia
Costilla
37°
9413 ft
2869 m
Teec Nos Pas
Pastora Peak
Bitlabito
Shiprock
Plateau
7178 ft
2188 m
Ship Rock
La Plata
Cedar Hill
AZTEC RUINS NAT. MON.
Aztec
Flora Vista
Farmington
Waterflow
Turley
Bloomfield
Morgan Lake
Navajo Res.
Dulce
Monero
JICARILLA IND. RES.
Chama
San Miguel
10909 ft
3325 m
San Antonio Mtn.
Brazos
Park View
Tierra Amarilla
El Vado Res.
El Vado
Questa
Tres Piedras
Red Rock
9806 ft
2989 m
Sa-Nos-tee
Roof Butte
Tocito
Newcomb
Chaco River
Chuska Mountains
San Juan Basin
Nageezi
JICARILLA IND. RES.
Alire
Cebolla
Canjilon
Arroyo Hondo
Canon Plaza
Wheeler Pk.
13159 ft
4011 m
Valdez
TAOS I.R.
Taos Pueblo
Ranchos de Taos
9108 ft
2776 m
El Rito
Abiquiu Res.
Capulin Pk
9206 ft
2806 m
Youngsville
Abiquiu
Embudo
Canones
Dixon
PICURIS I.R.
Peñasco
11939 ft
3639 m
Cerro Vis
Guadalup
Sheep Springs
Defiance Plateau
8796 ft
2681 m
36°
Chuska Peak
Tohatchi
La Jara
CHACO CULTURE NAT. HIST. PARK
Hernandez
Alcalde
SAN JUAN I.R.
SANTA CLARA I.R.
Española
Truchas
BANDELIER N.M.
Los Alamos
Pojoaque
NAMBE I.R.
12621 ft
3847 m
Mora
La Cuev
Mexican Springs
Standing Rock
Jemez Sprs
Jemez Mountains
Rio Grande
Tesuque
Santa Fe Baldy
Cowles
Santa Fe
El Porvenir
Crownpoint
Pinedale
8619 ft
2627 m
Hosta Butte
Allison
Gallup
Jemez Pueblo
JEMEZ I.R.
Cochiti Pueblo
Glorieta
Pecos
PECOS N.M.
102
Manuelito
Continental Divide
Zuni Mountains
Thoreau
Santo Domingo Pueblo
Domingo
ZIA I.R.
San Felipe
Santa Ana Pueblo
Lamy
Rowe
Lupton
Prewitt
Algodones
Cerrillos
San Jos
103
San Mateo
Bluewater
11302 ft
3445 m
Marquez
Bluewater Lake
Bernalillo
Placitas
9255 ft
2821 m
Milan
Mt. Taylor
Seboyeta
Sandia Pueblo
Pueblo
10679 ft
3255 m
Villanueva
Black Rock
Zuni
Mt. Sedgewick
Grants
San Rafael
Acomita
LAGUNA
CANONCITO I.R.
Alameda
Sandia Crest
Albuquerque
Stanley
Dahl
ZUNI IND. RES.
EL MORRO NAT. MON.
McCartys
40
Laguna
Armijo
Tijeras
Moriarty
Clines Corners
35°
RAMAH IND. RES.
LAGUNA IND. RES.
Correo
ACOMA IND. RES.
South Garcia
Isleta
ISLETA IND. RES.
Chilili
NEW MEXICO
ARIZONA
8763 ft
2671 m
Los Lunas
Peralta
Manzano Mountains
Estancia
Cebollita Pk.
Chloe
Laguna del Perro
Fence Lake
Belen
10098 ft
3078 m
Willard
Lucy
Negra
Encino
Little Colorado R.
Manzano Peak
Silio
PUERTOCITO IND. RES.
Sabinal
Veguita
Mountainair
Bernardo
Scholle
Quemado
La Joya
Pie Town
25
San Acacia
Gran Quivira
GRAN QUIVIRA NAT. MON.
Corona
Alegros Mtn.
10243 ft
3122 m
Datil
Magdalena
Lemitar
Claunch
Gallinas
Gallo Mountains
8530 ft
2600 m
10784 ft
3287 m
Socorro
34°
Tres Montosas
10115 ft
3083 m
South Baldy
Mount Withington
San Antonio
Bingham
Ancho
San Francisco Mountains
Plains of San Agustin
Reserve
Elmendorf
Coyote
San Marcial
Carrizozo
Rocky Mountains
10083
3073
9957 ft
3035 m
Black Range
Rio Grande
Capitan
Capitan Peak
Oscura
Lincoln
Bearwallow Mtn.
Monticello
12005 ft
3659 m
Glencoe
Hondo
Glenwood
Mogollon Baldy Peak
Winston
Crocker
Sierra Blanca Peak
Ruidoso
Hollywood
Three Rivers
Mogollon Range
GILA CLIFF DWELLINGS NAT. MON.
Elephant Butte Reservoir
8957 ft
2730 m
Salinas Peak
Truth or Consequences
MESCALERO
10010 ft
3051 m
Engle
Mescalero
98

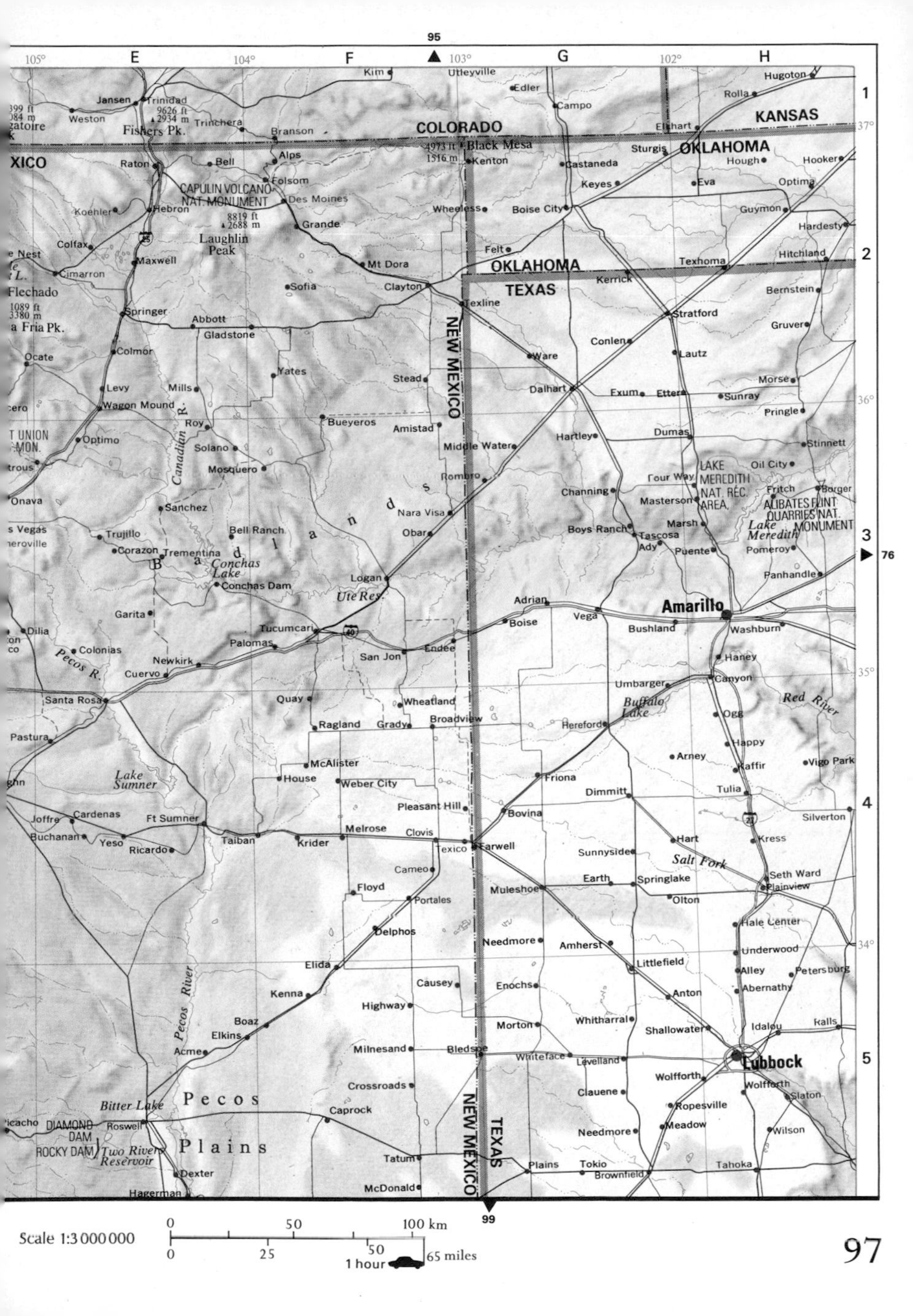

95
105°
E
104°
F
103°
G
102°
H
1
2
3
4
5
37°
36°
35°
34°
KANSAS
COLORADO
OKLAHOMA
TEXAS
NEW MEXICO
Kim
Utleyville
Edler
Campo
Hugoton
Rolla
Elkhart
Jansen
Trinidad
9626 ft
2934 m
Fishers Pk.
Weston
Trinchera
Branson
4973 ft
1516 m
Black Mesa
Kenton
Sturgis
Hough
Hooker
Raton
Bell
Alps
Folsom
Castaneda
Keyes
Eva
Optima
CAPULIN VOLCANO NAT. MONUMENT
Des Moines
Koehler
Hebron
8819 ft
2688 m
Laughlin Peak
Grande
Wheeless
Boise City
Guymon
Hardesty
Colfax
Maxwell
Felt
Hitchland
Cimarron
Mt Dora
Texhoma
Kerrick
Flechado
Sofia
Clayton
Bernstein
Texline
Stratford
Springer
Abbott
Gladstone
Gruver
Conlen
Colmor
Ocate
Lautz
Ware
Yates
Stead
Levy
Mills
Dalhart
Exum
Etter
Sunray
Morse
Wagon Mound
Canadian R.
Roy
Bueyeros
Amistad
Pringle
Optimo
Solano
Middle Water
Hartley
Dumas
Stinnett
Mosquero
Rombro
Four Way
LAKE MEREDITH NAT. REC. AREA
Oil City
Onava
Sanchez
Channing
Masterson
Fritch
Borger
Nara Visa
ALIBATES FLINT QUARRIES NAT. MONUMENT
Bell Ranch
Obar
Boys Ranch
Marsh
Tascosa
Lake Meredith
Trujillo
Corazon
Trementina
Ady
Puente
Pomeroy
Conchas Lake
Conchas Dam
B a d l a n d s
Logan
Ute Res.
Panhandle
Adrian
Vega
Amarillo
Garita
Boise
Bushland
Washburn
Dilia
Tucumcari
Colonias
Palomas
San Jon
Endee
Haney
Pecos R.
Newkirk
Cuervo
Umbarger
Canyon
Santa Rosa
Quay
Wheatland
Buffalo Lake
Red River
Ragland
Grady
Broadview
Hereford
Ogg
Pastura
Happy
McAlister
Arney
Vigo Park
House
Weber City
Friona
Kaffir
Lake Sumner
Dimmitt
Tulia
Pleasant Hill
Bovina
Silverton
Joffre
Cardenas
Ft Sumner
Buchanan
Yeso
Ricardo
Taiban
Krider
Melrose
Clovis
Texico
Farwell
Hart
Kress
Sunnyside
Salt Fork
Cameo
Earth
Springlake
Seth Ward
Plainview
Floyd
Portales
Muleshoe
Olton
Hale Center
Delphos
Needmore
Amherst
Underwood
Elida
Littlefield
Alley
Petersburg
Causey
Enochs
Abernathy
Kenna
Anton
Pecos River
Highway
Boaz
Elkins
Morton
Whitharral
Shallowater
Idalou
Ralls
Acme
Milnesand
Bledsoe
Whiteface
Levelland
Lubbock
Wolfforth
Crossroads
Clauene
Pecos
Slaton
Bitter Lake
Ropesville
Caprock
Roswell
DIAMOND DAM
ROCKY DAM
Two Rivers Reservoir
Plains
Meadow
Wilson
Needmore
Tatum
Plains
Tokio
Brownfield
Tahoka
Dexter
McDonald
Hagerman
76
99
Scale 1:3 000 000
0
50
100 km
0
25
50
65 miles
1 hour

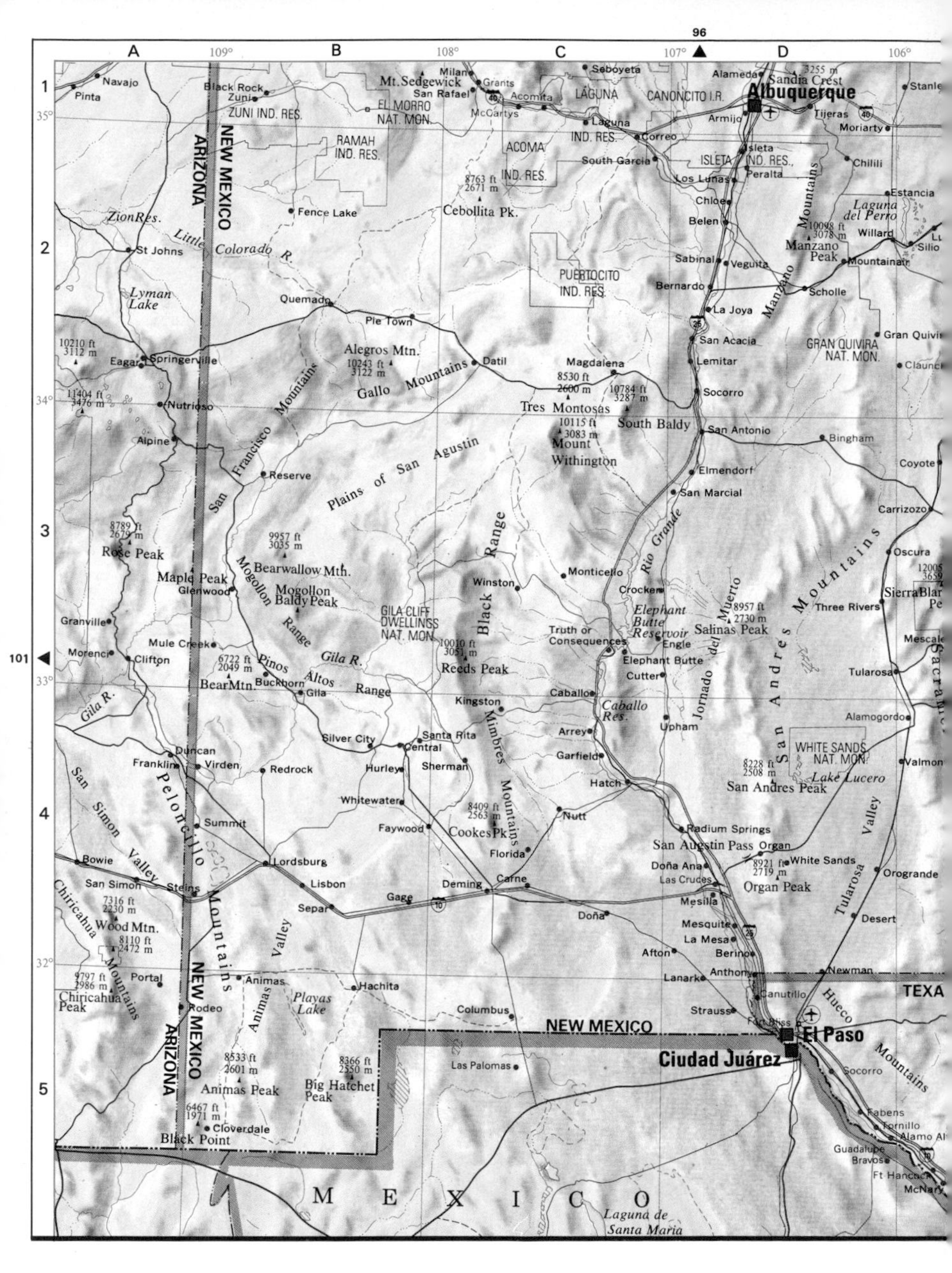

| | A | 109° | B | 108° | C | 107° | ▲ | D | 106° |

Navajo
Pinta
Black Rock
Zuni
Mt. Sedgewick
Milan
Grants
Sebóyeta
Alameda
Sandia Crest
3255 m
Albuquerque
Stanle

ZUNI IND. RES.
San Rafael
Acomita
LAGUNA
CANONCITO I.R.
Armijo
Tijeras
Moriarty

EL MORRO
NAT. MON.
McCartys
LAGUNA
IND. RES.
Correo
ISLETA IND. RES.
Peralta
Chilili

RAMAH
IND. RES.
ACOMA
IND. RES.
South Garcia
Los Lunas
Chloe
Estancia
Willard
LL
Silio

Fence Lake
8763 ft
2671 m
Cebollita Pk.
PUERTOCITO
IND. RES.
Belen
Sabinal
Veguita
Manzano
Peak
10098 ft
3078 m
Mountainair

Zion Res.
St Johns
Little
Colorado R.
Quemado
Bernardo
Scholle
GRAN QUIVIRA
NAT. MON.
Gran Quivi

Lyman
Lake
Pie Town
La Joya
San Acacia
Lemitar
Clauncl

10210 ft
3112 m
Eagar
Springerville
Alegros Mtn.
10243 ft
3122 m
Datil
Magdalena
8530 ft
2600 m
10784 ft
3287 m
Socorro

11404 ft
3476 m
Nutrioso
Gallo
Mountains
Tres Montosas
10115 ft
3083 m
Mount
Withington
South Baldy
San Antonio
Bingham

Alpine
San
Francisco
Mountains
Plains of San Agustin
Elmendorf
Coyote

Reserve
San Marcial
Carrizozo

8789 ft
2679 m
Rose Peak
9957 ft
3035 m
Bearwallow Mtn.
Winston
Monticello
Oscura
12005
3659

Maple Peak
Glenwood
Mogollon
Baldy Peak
Crocker
Elephant
Butte
Reservoir
8957 ft
2730 m
Salinas Peak
Three Rivers
Sierra Blar
Pe

Granville
Morenci
Mule Creek
Clifton
Mogollon
Range
GILA CLIFF
DWELLINGS
NAT. MON.
Black
Range
Reeds Peak
10010 ft
3051 m
Truth or
Consequences
Elephant Butte
Cutter
Tularosa
Mescale

6722 ft
2049 m
Bear Mtn
Buckhorn
Gila
Pinos
Altos
Range
Gila R.
Kingston
Caballo
Caballo
Res.
Upham
Jornada
del
Muerto
San Andres
Mountains
Alamogordo

Gila R.
Duncan
Franklin
Virden
Redrock
Silver City
Santa Rita
Central
Hurley
Sherman
Arrey
Garfield
Hatch
WHITE SANDS
NAT. MON.
8228 ft
2508 m
San Andres Peak
Lake Lucero
Valmon

San
Simon
Valley
Bowie
San Simon
Steins
Summit
Lordsburg
Lisbon
Separ
Gage
Deming
Carne
Doña
Whitewater
Faywood
Florida
Cookes Peak
8409 ft
2563 m
Nutt
Radium Springs
San Augustin Pass
Doña Ana
Las Cruces
Mesilla
Organ
8921 ft
2719 m
Organ Peak
White Sands
Desert
Orogrande
Tularosa
Valley

7316 ft
2230 m
San Simon
Chiricahua
Wood Mtn.
8110 ft
2472 m
Peloncillo
Mountains
Mimbres
Mountains
Mesquite
La Mesa
Afton
Berino
Newman

4797 ft
2986 m
Chiricahua
Peak
Portal
Rodeo
Animas
Valley
Hachita
Playas
Lake
Columbus
Lanark
Anthony
TEXA

NEW MEXICO
ARIZONA
8533 ft
2601 m
Animas Peak
8366 ft
2550 m
Big Hatchet
Peak
Las Palomas
NEW MEXICO
Strauss
Canutillo
El Paso
Socorro
Fabens

6467 ft
1971 m
Cloverdale
Black Point
Ciudad Juárez
Hueco
Mountains
Guadalupe
Bravose
Ft Hanco
McNary
Alamo Al

M   E   X   I   C   O
Laguna de
Santa Maria

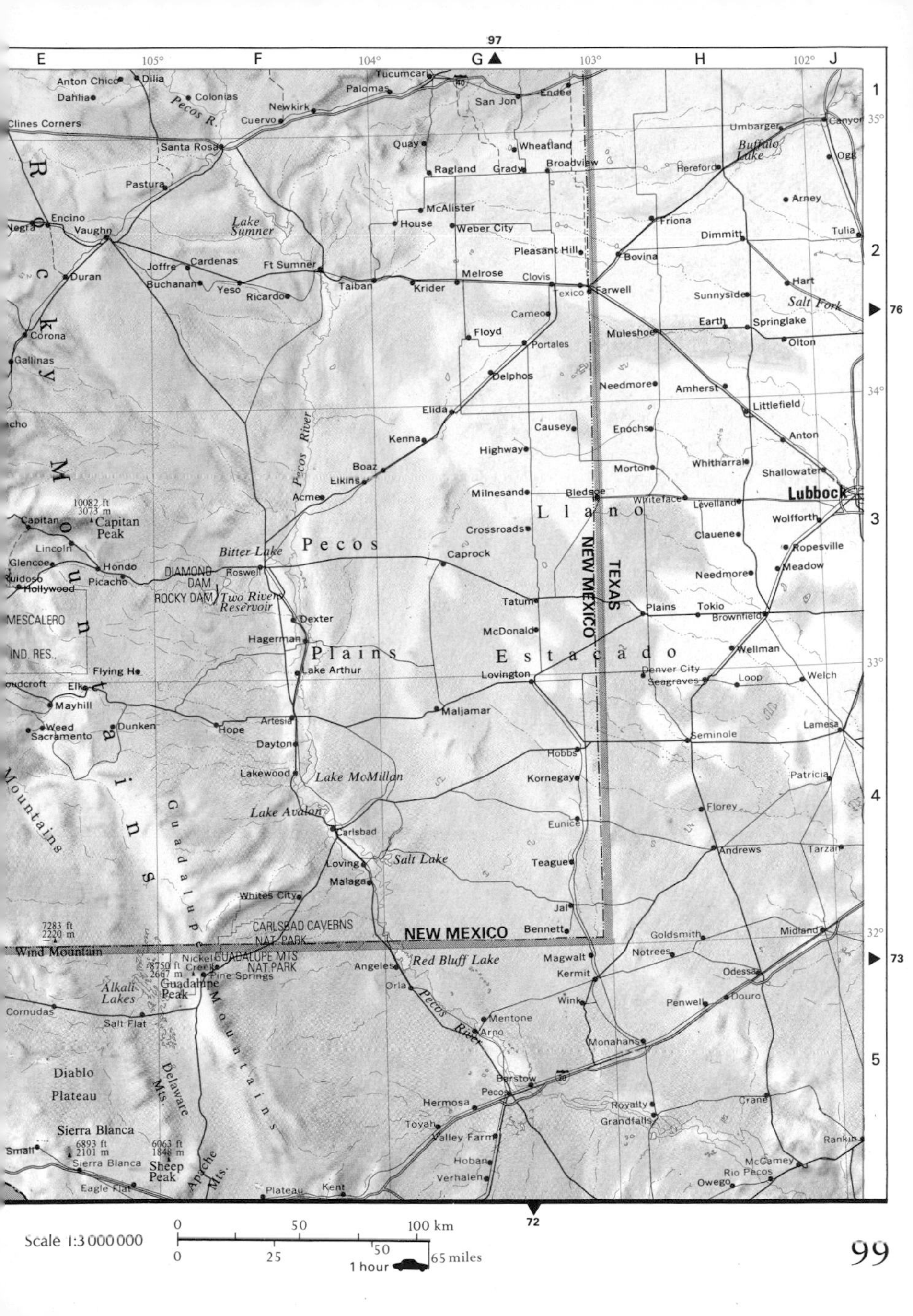
97
E
105°
F
104°
G
103°
H
102°
J
1
2
3
4
5
76
73
72
35°
34°
33°
32°
Anton Chico
Dilia
Dahlia
Colonias
Pecos R.
Newkirk
Cuervo
Clines Corners
Santa Rosa
Tucumcari
Palomas
40
San Jon
Endee
Quay
Wheatland
Ragland
Grady
Broadview
Pastura
McAlister
House
Weber City
Encino
Negra
Vaughn
Lake Sumner
Pleasant Hill
Duran
Joffre
Cardenas
Ft Sumner
Buchanan
Yeso
Ricardo
Taiban
Krider
Melrose
Clovis
Texico
Farwell
Cameo
Corona
Floyd
Portales
Gallinas
Delphos
Elida
Kenna
Boaz
Elkins
Acme
Pecos River
Causey
Highway
Milnesand
Bledsoe
Crossroads
Caprock
Tatum
McDonald
Lovington
Maljamar
Bitter Lake
Roswell
DIAMOND DAM
ROCKY DAM
Two Rivers Reservoir
Dexter
Hagerman
Lake Arthur
Artesia
Dayton
Lakewood
Lake McMillan
Lake Avalon
Carlsbad
Loving
Salt Lake
Malaga
Whites City
CARLSBAD CAVERNS NAT. PARK
NEW MEXICO
Pecos
Plains
Llano
Estacado
NEW MEXICO
TEXAS
10082 ft
3073 m
Capitan
Capitan Peak
Lincoln
Glencoe
Hondo
Ruidoso
Hollywood
Picacho
MESCALERO IND. RES.
Flying H
Cloudcroft
Elk
Mayhill
Weed
Sacramento
Dunken
Hope
Rocky
Mountains
Sacramento Mountains
Guadalupe
Guadalupe Mountains
7283 ft
2220 m
Wind Mountain
8750 ft
2667 m
Nickel Creek
GUADALUPE MTS NAT. PARK
Pine Springs
Guadalupe Peak
Alkali Lakes
Cornudas
Salt Flat
Diablo Plateau
Delaware Mts.
Sierra Blanca
6893 ft
2101 m
Small
Sierra Blanca
6063 ft
1848 m
Sheep Peak
Apache Mts.
Eagle Flat
Plateau
Kent
Umbarger
Canyon
Buffalo Lake
Ogg
Hereford
Arney
Friona
Dimmitt
Tulia
Bovina
Hart
Sunnyside
Salt Fork
Earth
Springlake
Muleshoe
Olton
Needmore
Amherst
Littlefield
Enochs
Anton
Morton
Whitharral
Shallowater
Whiteface
Levelland
Lubbock
Wolfforth
Clauene
Ropesville
Meadow
Needmore
Plains
Tokio
Brownfield
Wellman
Denver City
Seagraves
Loop
Welch
Lamesa
Seminole
Hobbs
Kornegay
Patricia
Florey
Eunice
Andrews
Tarzan
Teague
Jal
Bennett
Goldsmith
Midland
Notrees
Magwalt
Kermit
Odessa
Angeles
Red Bluff Lake
Orla
Wink
Penwell
Douro
Pecos River
Mentone
Arno
Monahans
Barstow
20
Pecos
Hermosa
Crane
Royalty
Grandfalls
Toyah
Valley Farm
Rankin
Hoban
McCamey
Rio Pecos
Verhalen
Owego
Scale 1:3 000 000
0
50
100 km
0
25
50
65 miles
1 hour

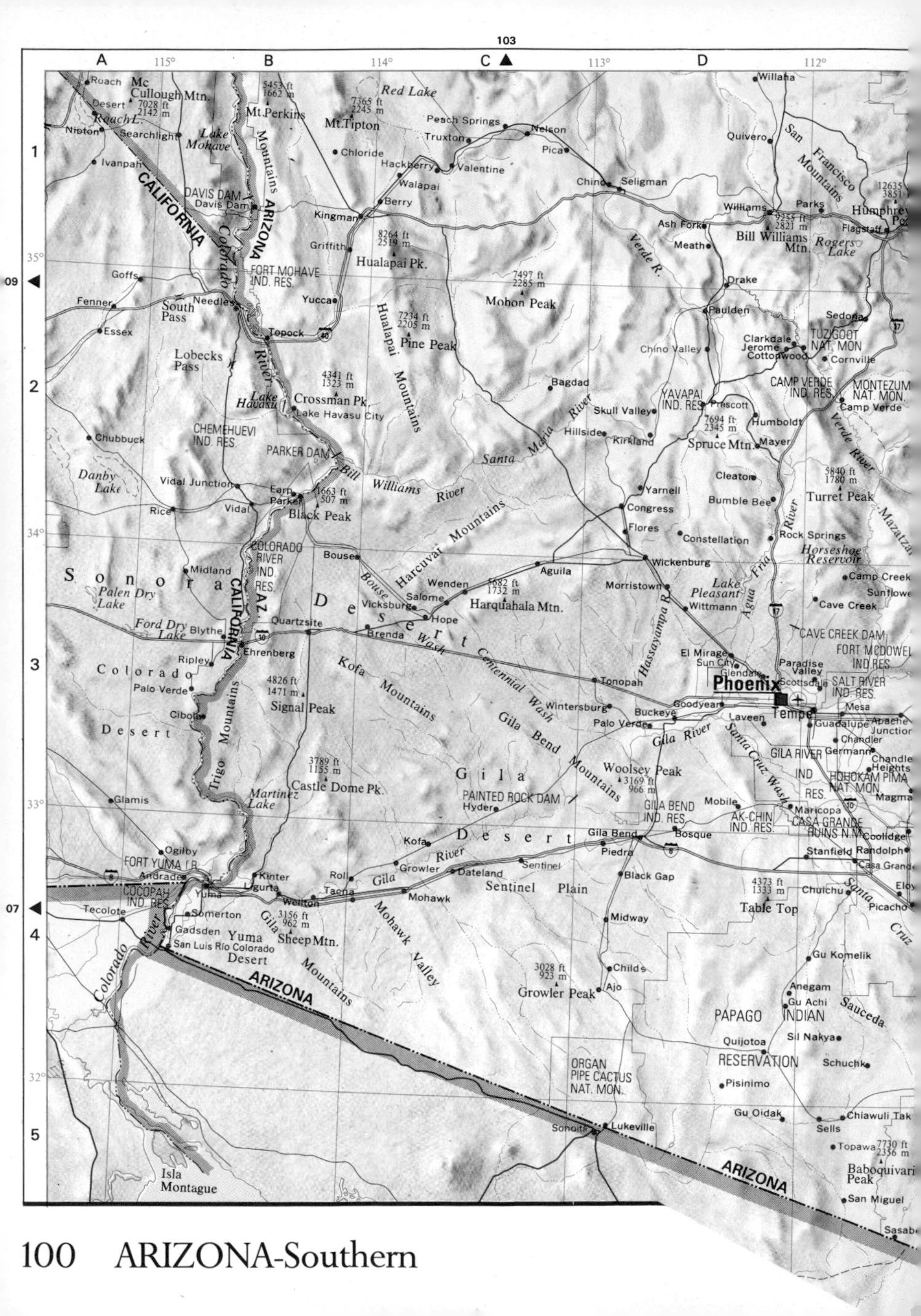

100 ARIZONA-Southern

103
B
C
D
115°
114°
113°
112°
2
3
4
5
09
07
35°
34°
33°
32°
Roach
Mc Cullough Mtn.
Desert
7028 ft
2142 m
Roach L.
Nipton
Searchlight
Ivanpah
Lake Mohave
5453 ft
1662 m
Mt.Perkins
Red Lake
7365 ft
2245 m
Mt.Tipton
Peach Springs
Truxton
Nelson
Pica
Chloride
Hackberry
Valentine
Walapai
Chino
Seligman
Willaha
Quivero
San Francisco Mountains
12635
3851
Humphreys Pk.
Parks
Williams
9255 ft
2821 m
Bill Williams Mtn.
Flagstaff
Rogers Lake
Ash Fork
Meath
CALIFORNIA
DAVIS DAM
Davis Dam
Mountains
Kingman
Berry
Griffith
8264 ft
2519 m
Hualapai Pk.
Colorado
Verde R.
FORT MOHAVE IND. RES.
Goffs
Fenner
South Pass
Needles
Yucca
7497 ft
2285 m
Mohon Peak
Drake
Paulden
Sedona
Essex
Topock
40
7234 ft
2205 m
Pine Peak
Hualapai Mountains
Chino Valley
Clarkdale
Jerome
Cottonwood
TUZIGOOT NAT. MON.
Cornville
17
Lobecks Pass
River
4341 ft
1323 m
Crossman Pk.
Lake Havasu
Lake Havasu City
Bagdad
CAMP VERDE IND. RES.
MONTEZUMA NAT. MON.
Camp Verde
YAVAPAI IND. RES.
Prescott
Skull Valley
Humboldt
7694 ft
2345 m
Spruce Mtn.
Mayer
Santa Maria River
Hillside
Kirkland
CHEMEHUEVI IND. RES.
Chubbuck
PARKER DAM
Bill Williams River
Verde River
Danby Lake
Vidal Junction
Earp
Parker
1663 ft
507 m
Black Peak
5840 ft
1780 m
Turret Peak
Cleator
Yarnell
Bumble Bee
Rice
Vidal
Congress
Harcuvar Mountains
Flores
Constellation
Rock Springs
Mazatzal
Agua Fria River
COLORADO RIVER IND. RES.
Bouse
Wickenburg
Horseshoe Reservoir
Sonora
Midland
Palen Dry Lake
AZ.
Aguila
5682 ft
1732 m
Harquahala Mtn.
Wenden
Salome
Vicksburg
Hope
Bouse Wash
Desert
Morristown
Lake Pleasant
Wittmann
Camp Creek
Sunflower
Cave Creek
Ford Dry Lake
Blythe
Quartzsite
Brenda
Centennial Wash
Hassayampa R.
CAVE CREEK DAM
FORT MCDOWELL IND. RES.
Ehrenberg
Ripley
El Mirage
Sun City
Glendale
Paradise Valley
Scottsdale
SALT RIVER IND. RES.
Colorado
Palo Verde
4826 ft
1471 m
Signal Peak
Kofa Mountains
Tonopah
Phoenix
Wintersburg
Goodyear
Tempe
Mesa
Cibola
Buckeye
Laveen
Apache Junction
Guadalupe
Chandler
Desert
Trigo Mountains
Gila Bend Mountains
Palo Verde
Gila River
Santa Cruz Wash
GILA RIVER IND. RES.
Germann
Chandler Heights
HOHOKAM PIMA NAT. MON.
3789 ft
1155 m
Castle Dome Pk.
Gila
Woolsey Peak
3169 ft
966 m
Magma
Glamis
Martinez Lake
PAINTED ROCK DAM
Hyder
GILA BEND IND. RES.
Mobile
Maricopa
AK-CHIN IND. RES.
CASA GRANDE RUINS N.M.
Coolidge
Kofa
Gila Bend
Bosque
Randolph
Ogilby
Piedra
Stanfield
Casa Grande
FORT YUMA I.R.
8
Andrade
Kinter
Growler
Dateland
Sentinel
Black Gap
Roll
Ligurta
Tacna
Mohawk
Sentinel Plain
4373 ft
1333 m
Chuichu
Eloy
COCOPAH IND. RES.
Yuma
Wellton
Table Top
Picacho
Tecolote
Somerton
3156 ft
962 m
Gila Sheep Mtn.
Mohawk Valley
Midway
Gadsden
Yuma
San Luis Rio Colorado
Desert
Santa Cruz
Gu Komelik
Colorado River
Mountains
3028 ft
923 m
Growler Peak
Child's
Ajo
Anegam
Gu Achi
PAPAGO INDIAN RESERVATION
Sauceda
Sil Nakya
Quijotoa
Schuchk
ORGAN PIPE CACTUS NAT. MON.
Pisinimo
Gu Oidak
Chiawuli Tak
Sells
Sonoita
Lukeville
Topawa
7730 ft
2356 m
Baboquivari Peak
Isla Montague
San Miguel
Sasabe

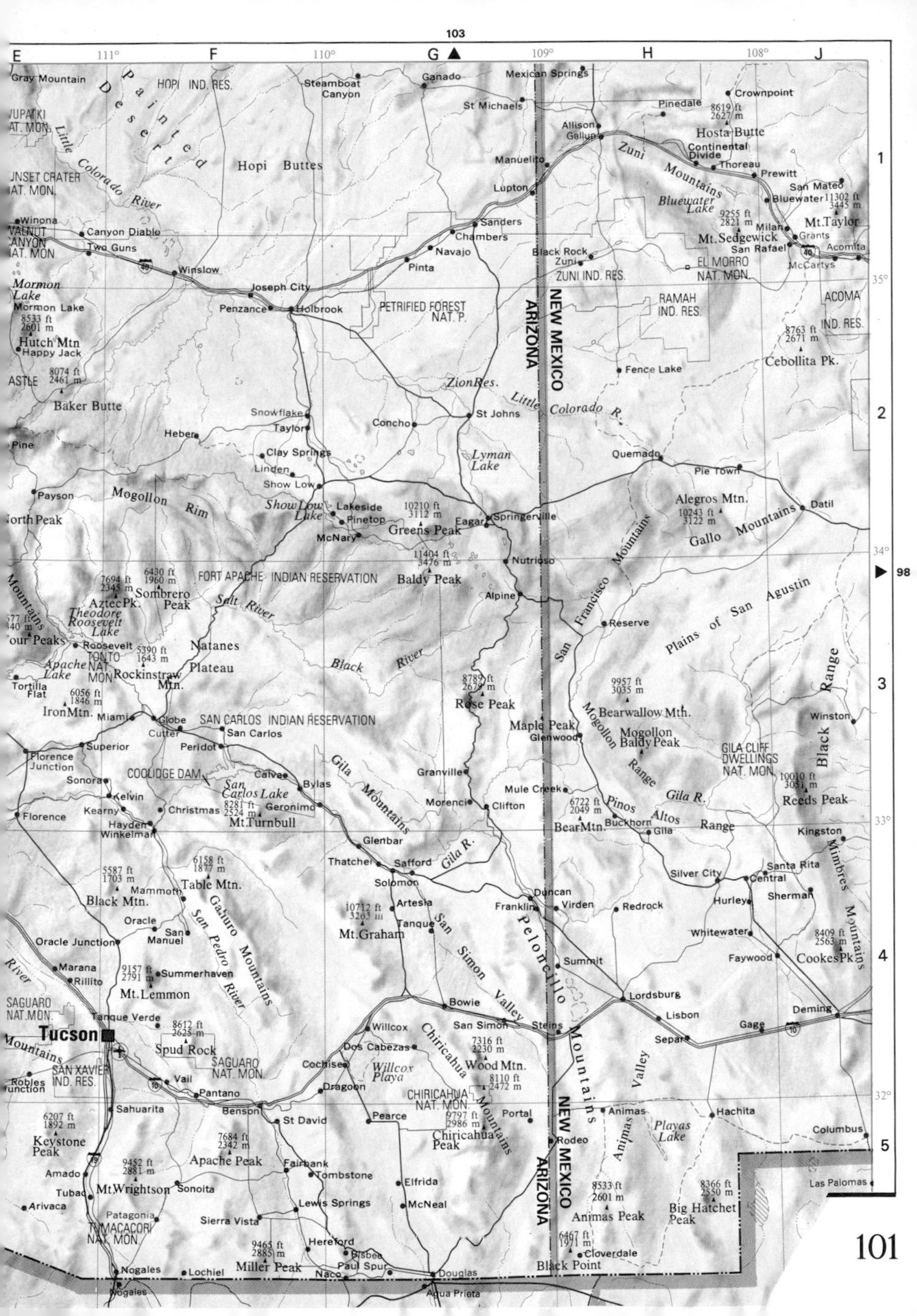
103
E
111°
F
110°
G
109°
H
108°
J
Gray Mountain
Painted Desert
HOPI IND. RES.
Steamboat Canyon
Ganado
Mexican Springs
Crownpoint
WUPATKI NAT. MON.
St Michaels
Pinedale
8619 ft 2627 m
Hosta Butte
Little Colorado River
Hopi Buttes
Allison
Gallup
Continental Divide
Zuni Mountains
Manuelito
Thoreau
Prewitt
1
SUNSET CRATER NAT. MON.
Lupton
San Mateo
Bluewater
11302 ft 3445 m
Bluewater Lake
9255 ft 2821 m
Winona
WALNUT CANYON NAT. MON.
Canyon Diablo
Two Guns
Sanders
Chambers
Navajo
Mt.Taylor
Milan
Grants
Mt. Sedgewick
San Rafael
Black Rock
Zuni
Acomita
McCartys
Winslow
Pinta
EL MORRO NAT. MON.
ZUNI IND. RES.
Mormon Lake
Mormon Lake
Joseph City
35°
ACOMA IND. RES.
NEW MEXICO
ARIZONA
RAMAH IND. RES.
Penzance
Holbrook
PETRIFIED FOREST NAT. P.
8533 ft 2601 m
Hutch Mtn
Happy Jack
8763 ft 2671 m
Cebollita Pk.
8074 ft 2461 m
Fence Lake
Baker Butte
Zion Res.
Little Colorado R.
Snowflake
Taylor
Concho
St Johns
2
Heber
Pine
Clay Springs
Lyman Lake
Quemado
Linden
Pie Town
Show Low
Payson
Mogollon Rim
Alegros Mtn.
10243 ft 3122 m
Datil
North Peak
Show Low Lake
Lakeside
Pinetop
10210 ft 3112 m
Springerville
Eagar
Greens Peak
Gallo Mountains
McNary
San Francisco Mountains
34°
11404 ft 3476 m
Nutrioso
98
7694 ft 2345 m
6430 ft 1960 m
FORT APACHE INDIAN RESERVATION
Baldy Peak
Aztec Pk.
Sombrero Peak
Alpine
Plains of San Agustin
Theodore Roosevelt Lake
Salt River
Reserve
Four Peaks
Roosevelt
Natanes Plateau
TONTO NAT. MON.
5390 ft 1643 m
Apache Lake
Rockinstraw Mtn.
Black River
Black Range
Tortilla Flat
6056 ft 1846 m
8789 ft 2679 m
9957 ft 3035 m
3
Iron Mtn.
Rose Peak
Bearwallow Mtn.
Miami
Globe
SAN CARLOS INDIAN RESERVATION
Winston
Cutter
San Carlos
Maple Peak
Glenwood
Mogollon Baldy Peak
Florence Junction
Superior
Peridot
GILA CLIFF DWELLINGS NAT. MON.
COOLIDGE DAM
Gila Mountains
Calva
Granville
Mogollon Range
Sonora
San Carlos Lake
Bylas
10010 ft 3051 m
Kelvin
Mule Creek
Gila R.
Reeds Peak
Florence
Kearny
Christmas
8281 ft 2524 m
Geronimo
Morenci
Clifton
6722 ft 2049 m
Pinos Altos Range
Hayden
Mt.Turnbull
Bear Mtn.
Buckhorn
Gila
33°
Winkelman
Kingston
Glenbar
Mimbres Mountains
Thatcher
Safford
Gila R.
Santa Rita
5587 ft 1703 m
6158 ft 1877 m
Central
Silver City
Table Mtn.
Solomon
Mammoth
Duncan
Sherman
Black Mtn.
Galiuro Mountains
10712 ft 3263 m
Artesia
Virden
Redrock
Hurley
Franklin
Oracle
San Pedro River
Tanque
Mt.Graham
San Simon Valley
Peloncillo Mountains
San Manuel
Whitewater
Oracle Junction
8409 ft 2563 m
Faywood
Cookes Pk
4
Summit
Marana
9157 ft 2791 m
Summerhaven
Rillito
River
Mt.Lemmon
Lordsburg
SAGUARO NAT. MON.
Bowie
Lisbon
Deming
Tanque Verde
Willcox
San Simon
Steins
Tucson
8612 ft 2625 m
Gage
Mountains
Spud Rock
Dos Cabezas
Chiricahua Mountains
7316 ft 2230 m
Separ
SAGUARO NAT. MON.
Wood Mtn.
SAN XAVIER IND. RES.
Cochise
Willcox Playa
Valley
Robles Junction
Vail
8110 ft 2472 m
Pantano
Dragoon
CHIRICAHUA NAT. MON.
32°
Sahuarita
Benson
Portal
Animas
Hachita
6207 ft 1892 m
St David
Pearce
9797 ft 2986 m
Playas Lake
Keystone Peak
Chiricahua Peak
Rodeo
Animas
Columbus
5
7684 ft 2342 m
Apache Peak
9452 ft 2881 m
Amado
Fairbank
Tombstone
Las Palomas
Mt.Wrightson
Sonoita
Elfrida
8533 ft 2601 m
8366 ft 2550 m
Tubac
Lewis Springs
McNeal
Arivaca
Patagonia
Animas Peak
Big Hatchet Peak
Sierra Vista
TUMACACORI NAT. MON.
Hereford
6467 ft 1971 m
9465 ft 2885 m
Bisbee
Cloverdale
Miller Peak
Paul Spur
Black Point
Nogales
Lochiel
Naco
Douglas
Nogales
Agua Prieta

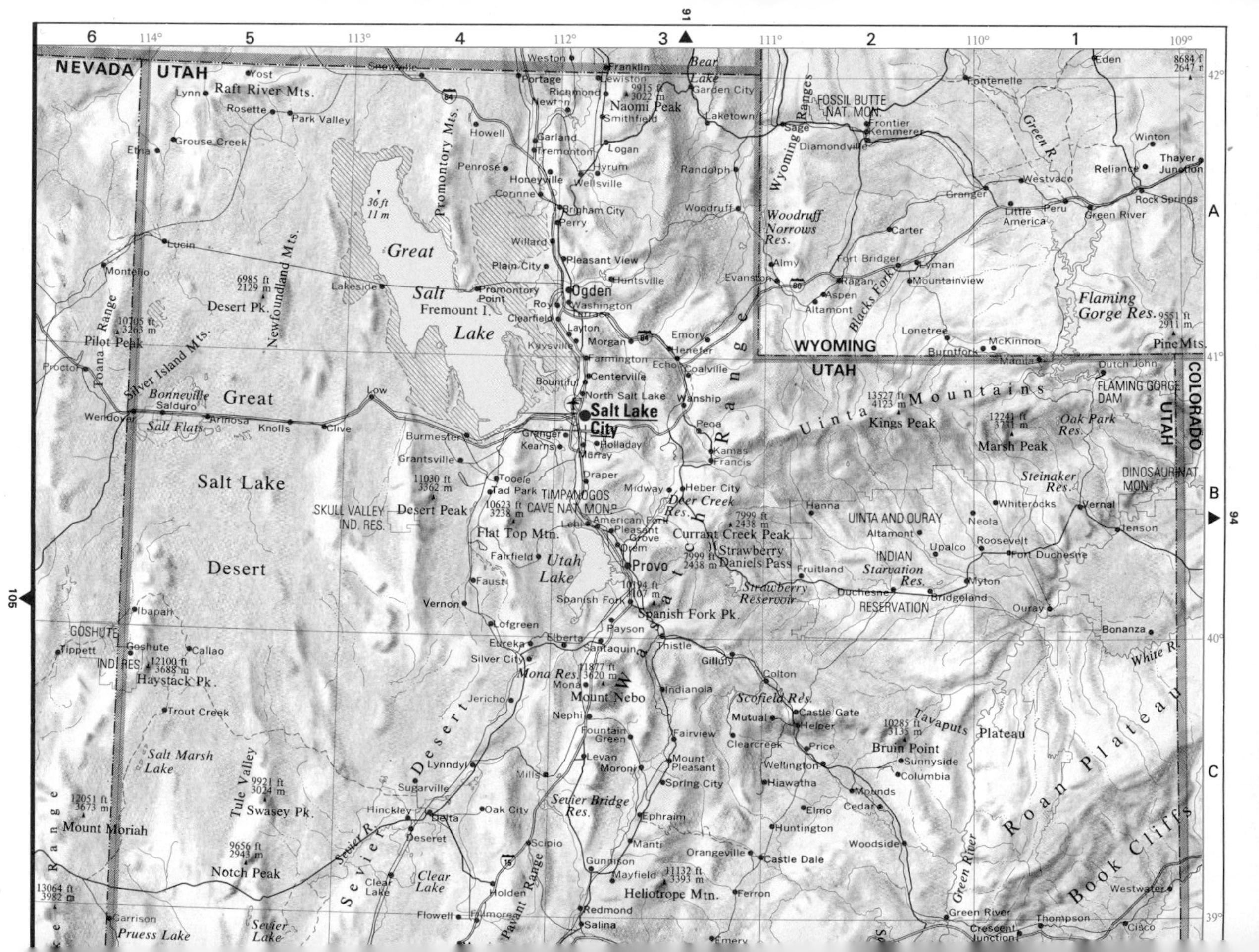
NEVADA
UTAH
WYOMING
COLORADO
Salt Lake City
Ogden
Provo
Great Salt Lake
Fremont I.
Utah Lake
Great Salt Lake Desert
Bonneville Salt Flats
Uinta Mountains
Wasatch Range
Kings Peak
Marsh Peak
Flaming Gorge Res.
FLAMING GORGE DAM
Roan Plateau
Book Cliffs
Tavaputs Plateau
Bruin Point
Sevier Desert
Sevier R.
Sevier Lake
Sevier Bridge Res.
Clear Lake
Pruess Lake
Salt Marsh Lake
Tule Valley
Swasey Pk.
Notch Peak
Mount Moriah
Haystack Pk.
Pilot Peak
Toana Range
Silver Island Mts.
Desert Pk.
Newfoundland Mts.
Promontory Mts.
Raft River Mts.
Naomi Peak
Bear Lake
Wyoming Ranges
Woodruff Narrows Res.
Blacks Fork
Green R.
Green River
White R.
Steinaker Res.
Oak Park Res.
Strawberry Reservoir
Starvation Res.
Scofield Res.
Deer Creek Res.
Mona Res.
Mount Nebo
Spanish Fork Pk.
Currant Creek Peak
Strawberry Daniels Pass
Heliotrope Mtn.
Desert Peak
Flat Top Mtn.
Pavant Range
FOSSIL BUTTE NAT. MON.
DINOSAUR NAT. MON.
TIMPANOGOS CAVE NAT. MON.
UINTA AND OURAY INDIAN RESERVATION
SKULL VALLEY IND. RES.
GOSHUTE IND. RES.
Wendover
Logan
Brigham City
Vernal
Price
Nephi
Tooele
Delta
Evanston
Rock Springs
Kemmerer
Heber City
Duchesne
Roosevelt
Spanish Fork
Payson
Richfield
Green River
Thompson
6
5
4
3
2
1
A
B
C
91
94
105

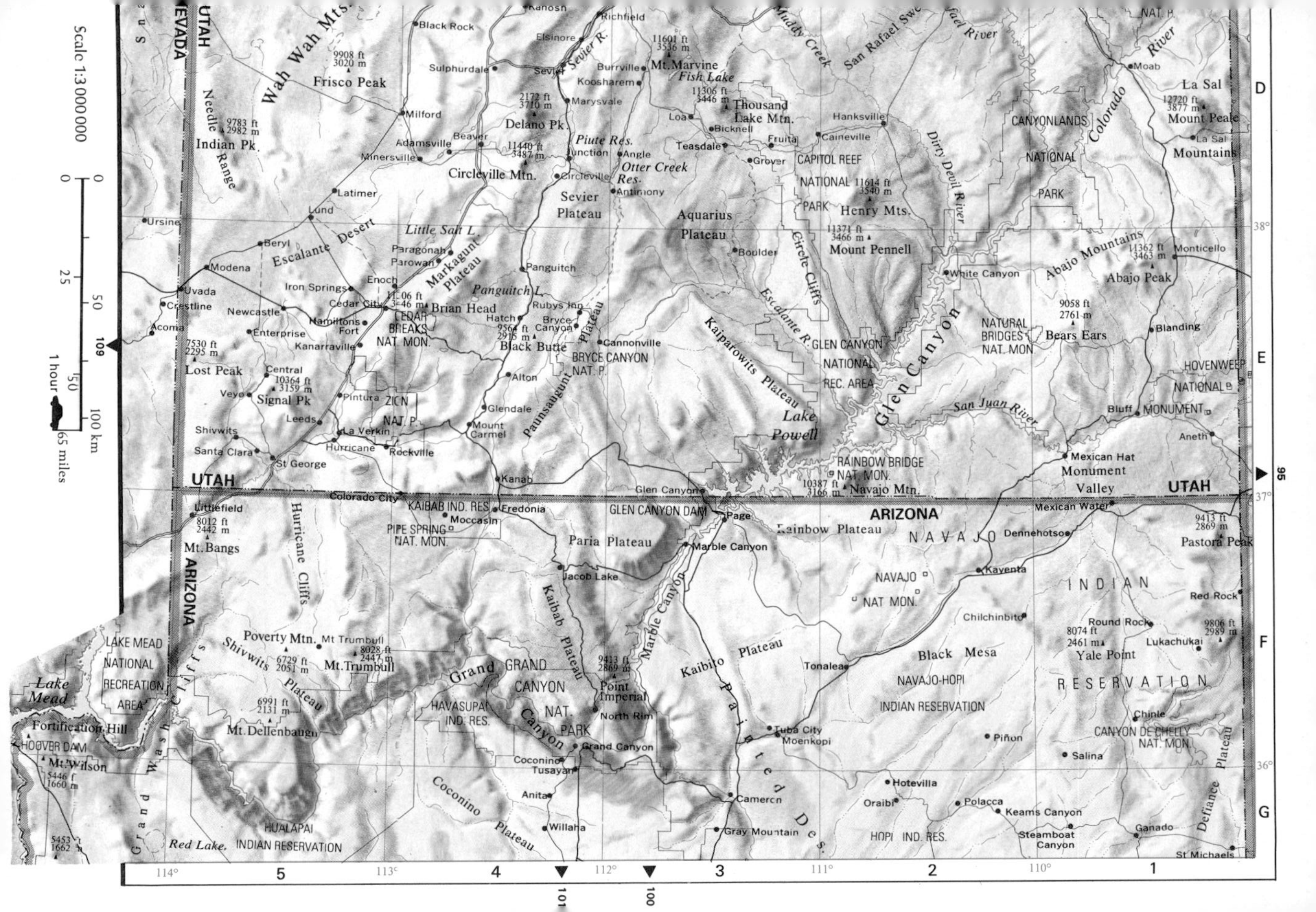
UTAH
NEVADA
ARIZONA
Scale 1:3 000 000
0 25 50 100 km
0 50 65 miles
1 hour
109
95
101
100
D
E
F
G
1
2
3
4
5
38°
37°
36°
110°
111°
112°
113°
114°
Wah Wah Mts.
Frisco Peak
9908 ft
3020 m
Needle Range
Indian Pk.
9783 ft
2982 m
Black Rock
Sulphurdale
Milford
Adamsville
Minersville
Beaver
Richfield
Elsinore
Sevier
Sevier R.
Marysvale
Delano Pk.
2172 ft
3710 m
11440 ft
3487 m
Circleville Mtn.
Junction
Piute Res.
Circleville
Angle
Otter Creek Res.
Antimony
Sevier Plateau
Burrville
Koosharem
Mt. Marvine
11601 ft
3536 m
Fish Lake
Thousand Lake Mtn.
11306 ft
3446 m
Loa
Bicknell
Teasdale
Grover
Fruita
Caineville
Hanksville
CAPITOL REEF NATIONAL PARK
Henry Mts.
11614 ft
3540 m
Mount Pennell
11371 ft
3466 m
Aquarius Plateau
Boulder
Circle Cliffs
Muddy Creek
San Rafael River
Dirty Devil River
Moab
Colorado River
La Sal Mountains
Mount Peale
12720 ft
3877 m
La Sal
CANYONLANDS NATIONAL PARK
Abajo Mountains
Abajo Peak
11362 ft
3463 m
Monticello
Blanding
White Canyon
NATURAL BRIDGES NAT. MON.
Bears Ears
9058 ft
2761 m
HOVENWEEP NATIONAL MONUMENT
Bluff
Aneth
San Juan River
Glen Canyon
Mexican Hat
Monument Valley
Ursine
Latimer
Lund
Beryl
Escalante Desert
Modena
Uvada
Crestline
Acoma
Little Salt L.
Paragonah
Parowan
Markagunt Plateau
Enoch
Iron Springs
Cedar City
Newcastle
Hamiltons Fort
Enterprise
Kanarraville
Brian Head
CEDAR BREAKS NAT. MON.
Panguitch
Panguitch L.
Hatch
Rubys Inn
Bryce Canyon
Black Butte
9564 ft
2915 m
Cannonville
BRYCE CANYON NAT. P.
Paunsaugunt Plateau
Alton
Glendale
Mount Carmel
Kanab
Lost Peak
7530 ft
2295 m
Central
Signal Pk
10364 ft
3159 m
Veyo
Pintura
ZION NAT. P.
Leeds
La Verkin
Hurricane
Rockville
Shivwits
Santa Clara
St George
Kaiparowits Plateau
Escalante R.
GLEN CANYON NATIONAL REC. AREA
Lake Powell
RAINBOW BRIDGE NAT. MON.
Navajo Mtn.
10387 ft
3166 m
Glen Canyon
Colorado City
KAIBAB IND. RES.
Fredonia
Moccasin
PIPE SPRING NAT. MON.
GLEN CANYON DAM
Page
Plateau
Paria Plateau
Marble Canyon
Jacob Lake
Kaibab Plateau
Littlefield
8012 ft
2442 m
Mt. Bangs
Hurricane Cliffs
LAKE MEAD NATIONAL RECREATION AREA
Lake Mead
Fortification Hill
HOOVER DAM
Mt. Wilson
5446 ft
1660 m
5453
1662
Grand Wash Cliffs
Poverty Mtn.
6729 ft
2051 m
Mt Trumbull
Mt. Trumbull
8028 ft
2447 m
Shivwits Plateau
Mt. Dellenbaugh
6991 ft
2131 m
Grand Canyon
GRAND CANYON NAT. PARK
HAVASUPAI IND. RES.
Point Imperial
9413 ft
2869 m
North Rim
Grand Canyon
Coconino
Tusayan
Anita
Willaha
Coconino Plateau
HUALAPAI INDIAN RESERVATION
Red Lake
Kaibito Plateau
Painted Des.
Tonalea
Tuba City
Moenkopi
Cameron
Gray Mountain
ARIZONA
NAVAJO INDIAN RESERVATION
Mexican Water
Dennehotso
Kayenta
NAVAJO NAT. MON.
Chilchinbito
Black Mesa
NAVAJO-HOPI INDIAN RESERVATION
Round Rock
8074 ft
2461 m
Yale Point
Lukachukai
9806 ft
2989 m
Red Rock
Pastora Peak
9413 ft
2869 m
Chinle
CANYON DE CHELLY NAT. MON.
Piñon
Salina
Hotevilla
Oraibi
Polacca
Keams Canyon
HOPI IND. RES.
Steamboat Canyon
Ganado
Defiance Plateau
St Michaels

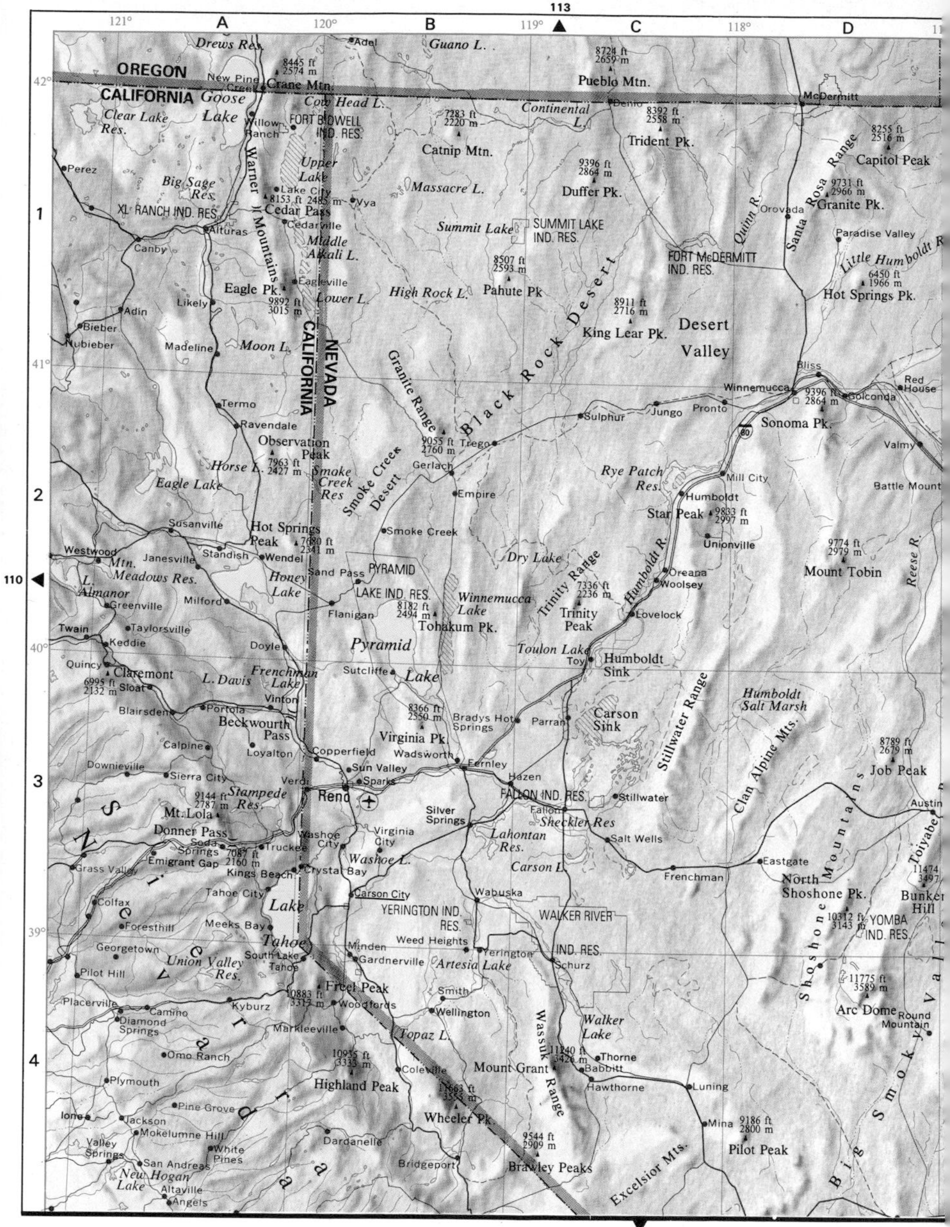
113
121°
A
120°
B
119°
C
118°
D
Drews Res.
Adel
Guano L.
8445 ft
2574 m
8724 ft
2659 m
OREGON
New Pine Creek
Crane Mtn.
Pueblo Mtn.
42°
CALIFORNIA
Goose Lake
Cow Head L.
Continental L.
Denio
McDermitt
Clear Lake Res.
Willow Ranch
FORT BIDWELL IND. RES.
7283 ft
2220 m
8392 ft
2558 m
Trident Pk.
8255 ft
2516 m
Catnip Mtn.
Santa Rosa Range
Capitol Peak
Perez
Warner Mountains
Upper Lake
9396 ft
2864 m
Big Sage Res.
Lake City
Massacre L.
Duffer Pk.
9731 ft
2966 m
8153 ft
2485 m
Cedar Pass
Vya
Orovada
Granite Pk.
1
XL RANCH IND. RES.
Quinn R.
Alturas
Cedarville
Summit Lake
SUMMIT LAKE IND. RES.
Paradise Valley
Canby
Middle Alkali L.
FORT McDERMITT IND. RES.
Little Humboldt R.
8507 ft
2593 m
6450 ft
1966 m
Eagleville
Eagle Pk.
High Rock L.
Pahute Pk
Hot Springs Pk.
9892 ft
3015 m
Lower L.
Likely
Black Rock Desert
8911 ft
2716 m
Adin
King Lear Pk.
Desert Valley
Bieber
Nubieber
Madeline
Moon L.
NEVADA
CALIFORNIA
Granite Range
41°
Bliss
Winnemucca
Red House
9396 ft
2864 m
Golconda
Termo
Jungo
Pronto
Sulphur
Sonoma Pk.
Ravendale
9055 ft
2760 m
Trego
80
Observation Peak
Valmy
Smoke Creek Desert
Gerlach
7963 ft
2427 m
Horse L.
Smoke Creek Res
Rye Patch Res.
Mill City
Eagle Lake
2
Empire
Humboldt
Battle Mount
Star Peak
9833 ft
2997 m
Susanville
Hot Springs Peak
Smoke Creek
7680 ft
2341 m
Unionville
Westwood
Standish
Wendel
Dry Lake
Trinity Range
9774 ft
2979 m
Janesville
Humboldt R.
Oreana
Mount Tobin
Mtn. Meadows Res.
Sand Pass
PYRAMID LAKE IND. RES.
Woolsey
Reese R.
110
L. Almanor
Honey Lake
7336 ft
2236 m
Milford
Winnemucca Lake
Greenville
Flanigan
8182 ft
2494 m
Trinity Peak
Lovelock
Tohakum Pk.
Twain
Taylorsville
Keddie
Doyle
Pyramid Lake
Toulon Lake
40°
Toy
Humboldt Sink
Quincy
Frenchman Lake
Sutcliffe
Claremont
L. Davis
Stillwater Range
6995 ft
2132 m
Sloat
Humboldt Salt Marsh
Vinton
Blairsden
Portola
8366 ft
2550 m
Bradys Hot Springs
Parran
Carson Sink
Beckwourth Pass
Virginia Pk.
Clan Alpine Mts.
8789 ft
2679 m
Loyalton
Calpine
Copperfield
Wadsworth
Job Peak
Downieville
Sun Valley
Fernley
3
Sierra City
Sparks
Hazen
Verdi
Reno
FALLON IND. RES.
Stillwater
Austin
Stampede Res.
9144 ft
2787 m
Silver Springs
Fallon
Sheckler Res
Mt. Lola
Donner Pass
Virginia City
Lahontan Res.
Salt Wells
Toiyabe
Soda Springs
7087 ft
2160 m
Truckee
Washoe City
Grass Valley
Emigrant Gap
Washoe L.
Carson L.
Eastgate
Frenchman
11474
3497
Kings Beach
Crystal Bay
North Shoshone Pk.
Tahoe City
Carson City
Wabuska
Bunker Hill
Colfax
Lake Tahoe
YERINGTON IND. RES.
WALKER RIVER IND. RES.
10312 ft
3143 m
YOMBA IND. RES.
Meeks Bay
Foresthill
39°
Weed Heights
Shoshone Mountains
Georgetown
Minden
Yerington
South Lake Tahoe
Gardnerville
Artesia Lake
Schurz
Union Valley Res.
Pilot Hill
11775 ft
3589 m
Freel Peak
10883 ft
3317 m
Smith
Placerville
Woodfords
Kyburz
Camino
Wellington
Arc Dome
Round Mountain
Diamond Springs
Walker Lake
Markleeville
Topaz L.
Wassuk Range
10935 ft
3333 m
11240 ft
3426 m
Thorne
4
Omo Ranch
Mount Grant
Babbitt
Coleville
Plymouth
Highland Peak
11663 ft
3555 m
Hawthorne
Luning
Pine Grove
Wheeler Pk.
Ione
Jackson
Mina
9186 ft
2800 m
Mokelumne Hill
Dardanelle
9544 ft
2909 m
Valley Springs
White Pines
Pilot Peak
San Andreas
Bridgeport
Brawley Peaks
Excelsior Mts.
New Hogan Lake
Big Smoky Valley
Altaville
Angels
Sierra Nevada
108

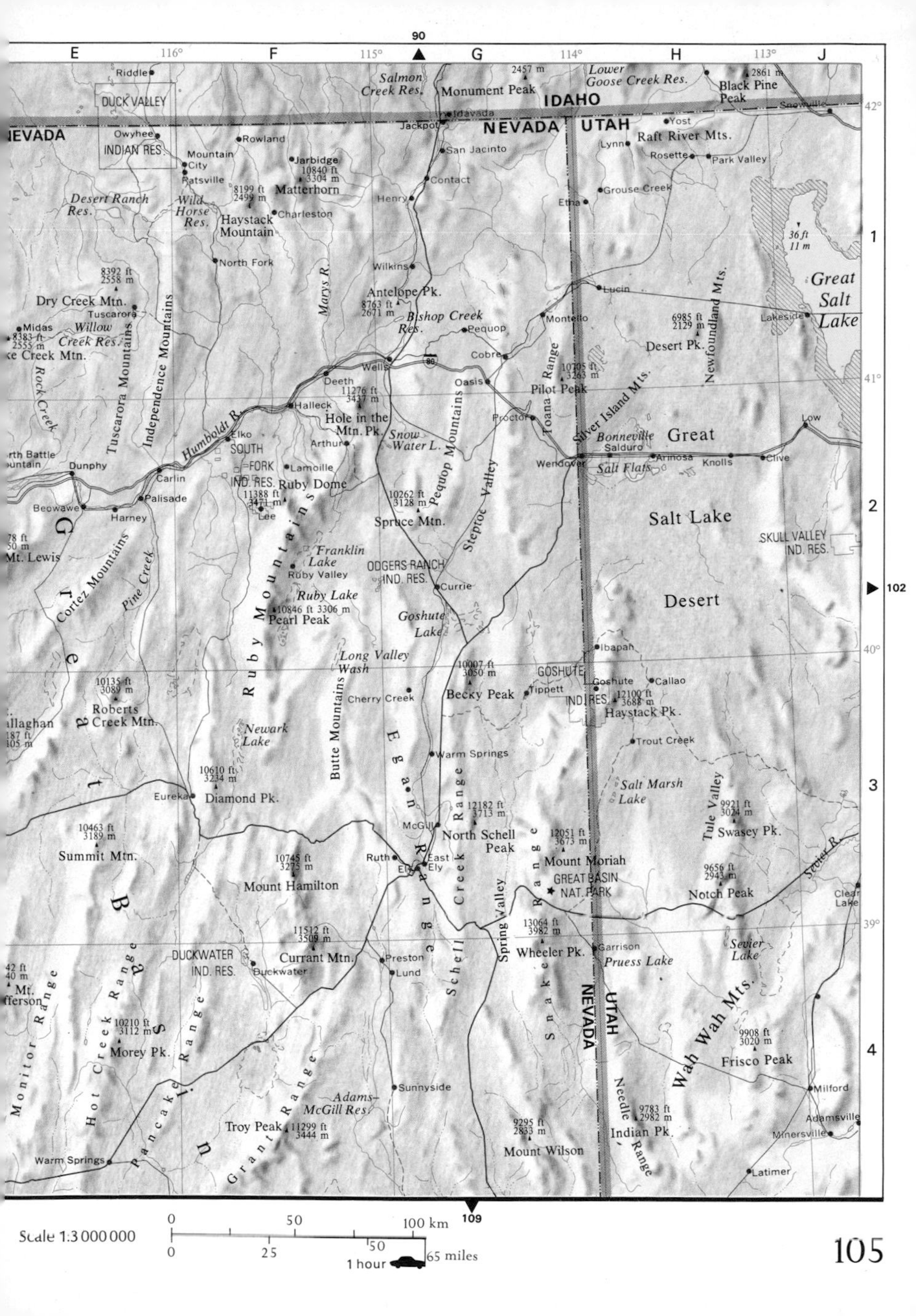

Riddle

DUCK VALLEY

Owyhee

NEVADA

INDIAN RES.

Salmon
Creek Res.
Monument Peak

2457 m

Lower
Goose Creek Res.

Black Pine
Peak

2861 m

Snowville

IDAHO

Idavada

Jackpot

NEVADA UTAH

42°

Yost

36 ft
11 m

1

Mountain
City
Patsville

Rowland

Jarbidge
10840 ft
3304 m

8199 ft
2499 m

Matterhorn

San Jacinto

Lynn

Raft River Mts.

Rosette

Park Valley

Contact

Wild
Horse
Res.

Haystack
Mountain

Charleston

Henry

Etna

Grouse Creek

Desert Ranch
Res.

North Fork

Wilkins

Lucin

Lakeside

Great
Salt
Lake

8392 ft
2558 m

Dry Creek Mtn.

Tuscarora

Antelope Pk.

8763 ft
2671 m

Bishop Creek
Res.

Pequop

Montello

6985 ft
2129 m

Desert Pk.

Newfoundland Mts.

Midas

8183 ft
2353 m

Willow
Creek Res.

Tuscarora Mountains

Independence Mountains

Marys R.

Wells

90

Cobre

8073 ft
2335 m

Pilot Peak

Silver Island Mts.

ce Creek Mtn.

Rock Creek

Deeth

Oasis

41°

Humboldt R.

Halleck

1276 ft
1147 m

Hole in the
Mtn. Pk.

Snow
Water L.

Proctor

Toana Range

Bonneville
Saldura

Great

78 ft
50 m

Mt. Lewis

Elko

SOUTH

FORK

Arthur

Lamoille

Ruby Dome

Spruce Mtn.

Wendover

Salt Flats

Armosa

Knolls

Clive

Low

Dunphy

Carlin

IND. RES.

11388 ft
3471 m

Lee

10262 ft
3128 m

Pequop Mountains

Salt Lake

SKULL VALLEY
IND. RES.

2

Beowawe

Palisade

Harney

Franklin
Lake

Ruby Valley

Steptoe Valley

102

Pine Creek

Cortez Mountains

Ruby Mountains

Ruby Lake

10846 ft 3306 m

Pearl Peak

ODGERS RANCH
IND. RES.

Currie

Goshute
Lake

Desert

Ibapah

40°

G

r

e

a

t

Long Valley
Wash

10007 ft
3050 m

GOSHUTE
Tippett

Goshute
12100 ft
3688 m

Callao

INDI RES.

Haystack Pk.

10135 ft
3089 m

Roberts
Creek Mtn.

Newark
Lake

Cherry Creek

Becky Peak

Warm Springs

Trout Creek

3

llaghan

187 ft
105 m

Butte Mountains

Egan Range

Salt Marsh
Lake

Tule Valley

9921 ft
3024 m

Swasey Pk.

Eureka

10610 ft
3234 m

Diamond Pk.

12182 ft
3713 m

McGill

North Schell
Peak

12051 ft
3673 m

Mount Moriah

9656 ft
2943 m

Notch Peak

Sevier R.

Clear
Lake

10463 ft
3189 m

Summit Mtn.

Ruth

East
Ely

Ely

GREAT BASIN
NAT. PARK

39°

10745 ft
3275 m

Mount Hamilton

Schell Creek Range

Spring Valley

13064 ft
3982 m

Wheeler Pk.

Garrison

Pruess Lake

Sevier
Lake

42 ft
40 m

Mt.
fferson

DUCKWATER
IND. RES.

11512 ft
3509 m

Currant Mtn.

Duckwater

Preston

Lund

Snake Range

Wah Wah Mts.

9908 ft
3020 m

Frisco Peak

4

Monitor Range

Hot Creek Range

Pancake Range

10210 ft
3112 m

Morey Pk.

Grant Range

Adams-
McGill Res.

Sunnyside

Needle Range

NEVADA

UTAH

9783 ft
2982 m

Indian Pk.

Milford

Adamsville

Warm Springs

Troy Peak

11299 ft
3444 m

9295 ft
2833 m

Mount Wilson

Minersville

Latimer

Scale 1:3 000 000

0   50   100 km

109

0   25   50   65 miles

1 hour

105

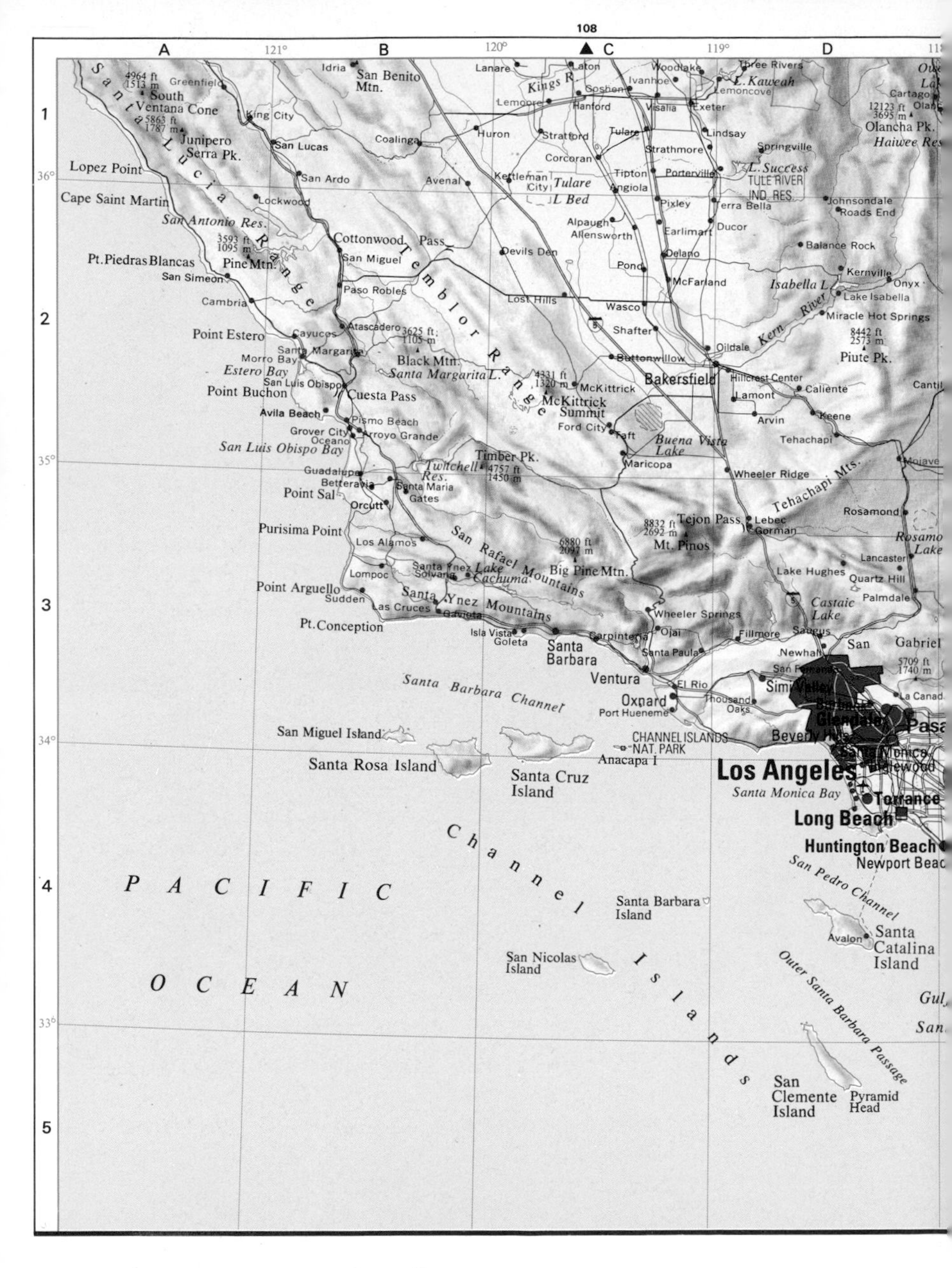

106 CALIFORNIA-Southern

108
B
D
121°
120°
119°
2
3
4
5
36°
35°
34°
33°
Santa Lucia Range
Greenfield
4964 ft
1513 m
Ventana Cone
5863 ft
1787 m
Junipero
Serra Pk.
King City
San Lucas
Lopez Point
San Ardo
Cape Saint Martin
Lockwood
San Antonio Res.
3593 ft
1095 m
Pine Mtn.
Pt. Piedras Blancas
San Simeon
Cambria
Idria
San Benito
Mtn.
Coalinga
Avenal
Cottonwood Pass
San Miguel
Paso Robles
Temblor Range
Point Estero
Cayucos
Atascadero
3625 ft
1105 m
Morro Bay
Santa Margarita
Estero Bay
Black Mtn.
Santa Margarita L.
San Luis Obispo
Point Buchon
Cuesta Pass
Avila Beach
Pismo Beach
Grover City
Oceano
Arroyo Grande
San Luis Obispo Bay
Guadalupe
Betteravia
Santa Maria
Point Sal
Orcutt
Gates
Twitchell Res.
Timber Pk.
4757 ft
1450 m
Purisima Point
Los Alamos
San Rafael Mountains
Lompoc
Santa Ynez
Solvang
Lake Cachuma
Point Arguello
Sudden
Las Cruces
Gaviota
Santa Ynez Mountains
Pt. Conception
Isla Vista
Goleta
Santa Barbara
Carpinteria
Lanare
Laton
Kings R.
Lemoore
Goshen
Hanford
Huron
Stratford
Corcoran
Kettleman City
Tulare L Bed
Devils Den
Lost Hills
4331 ft
1320 m
McKittrick
McKittrick Summit
Ford City
Taft
Buena Vista Lake
Maricopa
6880 ft
2097 m
Big Pine Mtn.
8832 ft
2692 m
Mt. Pinos
Tejon Pass
Lebec
Gorman
Woodlake
Ivanhoe
Visalia
Exeter
Three Rivers
L. Kaweah
Lemoncove
Tulare
Lindsay
Strathmore
Springville
Tipton
Porterville
L. Success
TULE RIVER
IND. RES.
Angiola
Pixley
Terra Bella
Alpaugh
Allensworth
Earlimart
Ducor
Delano
Pond
McFarland
Wasco
Shafter
Buttonwillow
Oildale
Bakersfield
Hillcrest Center
Lamont
Arvin
Wheeler Ridge
Kern River
Isabella L.
Kernville
Onyx
Lake Isabella
Miracle Hot Springs
8442 ft
2573 m
Piute Pk.
Caliente
Keene
Tehachapi
Tehachapi Mts.
Johnsondale
Roads End
Balance Rock
12123 ft
3695 m
Olancha Pk.
Cartago
Haiwee Res.
Mojave
Rosamond
Rosamond Lake
Lancaster
Lake Hughes
Quartz Hill
Palmdale
Castaic Lake
Wheeler Springs
Ojai
Fillmore
Saugus
Santa Paula
Newhall
San Gabriel
5709 ft
1740 m
Ventura
El Rio
Simi Valley
Oxnard
Port Hueneme
Thousand Oaks
La Canada
Glendale
Beverly Hills
Santa Monica
Inglewood
Los Angeles
Santa Monica Bay
Torrance
Long Beach
Huntington Beach
Newport Beach
Santa Barbara Channel
San Miguel Island
Santa Rosa Island
Santa Cruz Island
CHANNEL ISLANDS NAT. PARK
Anacapa I
Channel Islands
PACIFIC
OCEAN
Santa Barbara Island
San Nicolas Island
San Pedro Channel
Avalon
Santa Catalina Island
Outer Santa Barbara Passage
San Clemente Island
Pyramid Head

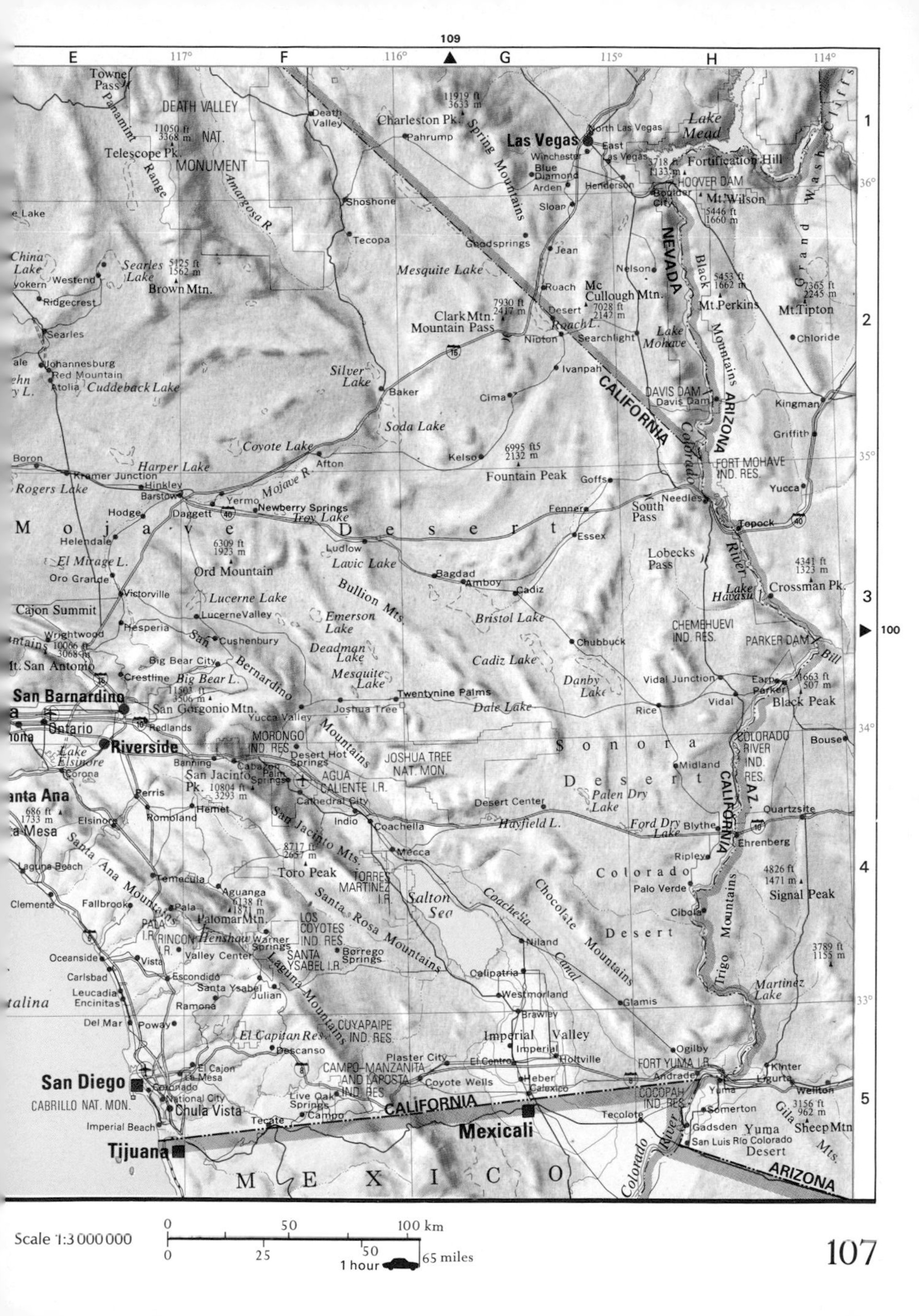

E · 117° · F · 116° · ▲ · G · 115° · H · 114°

1

Towne
Pass
DEATH VALLEY
Telescope Pk.
11050 ft
3368 m   NAT.
MONUMENT
Panamint Range
Amargosa R.
Death
Valley
Charleston Pk.
11919 ft
3633 m
Spring Mountains
Pahrump
Shoshone
Las Vegas
North Las Vegas
East
Las Vegas
Winchester
Blue
Diamond
Arden
Henderson
Boulder
City
718 ft
1133 m   Fortification Hill
HOOVER DAM
Mt. Wilson
5446 ft
1660 m
Lake
Mead
Grand Wash Cliffs

2

China
Lake
yokern
Westend
Ridgecrest
Searles
Searles
Lake
5125 ft
1562 m
Brown Mtn.
Johannesburg
Red Mountain
Atolia
Cuddeback Lake
ahn
L.
Silver
Lake
Baker
Cima
Ivanpah
Mesquite Lake
Goodsprings
Jean
Roach
Mc
Cullough Mtn.
7930 ft
2417 m
7028 ft
2142 m
Clark Mtn.
Mountain Pass
Roach L.
Nipton
Searchlight
Desert
Tecopa
Sloan
NEVADA
5453 ft
1662 m   Mt. Perkins
7365 ft
2245 m   Mt. Tipton
Chloride
Kingman
Griffith
Lake
Mohave
Davis Dam
DAVIS DAM
Black Mountains
Colorado
ARIZONA
CALIFORNIA

3

ale
chn
L.
Boron
Rogers Lake
Kramer Junction
Harper Lake
Hinkley
Barstow
Yermo
Daggett
Hodge
Helendale
El Mirage L.
Oro Grande
Victorville
Lucerne Lake
LucerneValley
Cajon Summit
Wrightwood
9006 ft
3068 m
Mt. San Antonio
Hesperia
Cushenbury
San
Bernardino
Big Bear City
Mojave R.
Afton
Coyote Lake
Soda Lake
Newberry Springs
Troy Lake
Ludlow
Lavic Lake
Bagdad
Amboy
Cadiz
Ord Mountain
6309 ft
1923 m
Bullion Mts.
Emerson
Lake
Deadman
Lake
Mesquite
Lake
Kelso
6995 ft
2132 m
Fountain Peak
Fenner
Essex
Goffs
South
Pass
Lobecks
Pass
Chubbuck
Bristol Lake
Cadiz Lake
Danby
Lake
CHEMEHUEVI
IND. RES.
Needles
Topock
Yucca
FORT MOHAVE
IND. RES.
4341 ft
1323 m
Lake
Havasu
Crossman Pk.
PARKER DAM
Colorado River
Bill

▶ **100**

4

Cajon Summit
Crestline
Big Bear L.
5803 ft
1562 m
Mt. San Gorgonio Mtn.
San Barnardino
Ontario
Redlands
Riverside
Lake
Elsinore
Corona
Santa Ana
Mesa
686 ft
1733 m
Elsinore
Perris
Romoland
Hemet
Banning
San Jacinto
Pk. 10804 ft
3293 m
Desert Hot
Springs
Palm
Springs
Cathedral City
AGUA
CALIENTE I.R.
MORONGO
IND. RES.
Yucca Valley
Joshua Tree
Twentynine Palms
Dale Lake
Rice
Vidal
Vidal Junction
Earp
Parker
3663 ft
507 m
Black Peak
COLORADO
RIVER
IND.
RES.
Bouse
Quartzsite
CALIFORNIA
AZ.
Signal Peak
4826 ft
1471 m
Ehrenberg
Blythe
Ripley
Palo Verde
Cibola
JOSHUA TREE
NAT. MON.
Indio
Coachella
Mecca
8717 ft
2657 m
San Jacinto Mts.
Toro Peak
TORRES
MARTINEZ
I.R.
Salton
Sea
Desert Center
Hayfield L.
Ford Dry
Lake
Palen Dry
Lake
Midland
Sonora
Desert
Colorado
Chocolate Mountains
Desert

5

Santa Ana
anta Ana
Laguna Beach
Clemente
Fallbrook
Oceanside
Carlsbad
Leucadia
Encinitas
atalina
Del Mar
Poway
Temecula
Aguanga
Pala
PALA
I.R.
RINCON I.R.
Valley Center
Vista
Escondido
Santa Ysabel
Ramona
Julian
6138 ft
1871 m   PalomarMt.
Warner
Springs
Henshaw
Springs
SANTA
YSABEL I.R.
LOS
COYOTES I.R.
Borrego
Springs
CUYAPAIPE
IND. RES.
El Capitan Res.
Descanso
Santa Rosa Mountains
Coachella Canal
Niland
Calipatria
Westmorland
Brawley
Imperial
Imperial
Holtville
Glamis
3789 ft
1155 m
Trigo Mountains
Martinez
Lake
3156 ft
962 m
San Diego
CABRILLO NAT. MON.
Coronado
El Cajon
La Mesa
National City
Chula Vista
Imperial Beach
Spring
Valley
Live Oak
Springs
CAMPO-MANZANITA
AND LA POSTA
IND. RES.
Plaster City
El Centro
Heber
Coyote Wells
Tecate
Campo
Valley
Calexico
Mexicali
CALIFORNIA
FORT YUMA I.R.
Andrade
COCOPAH
IND. RES.
Ogilby
Tecolote
San Luis Rio Colorado
Gadsden
Yuma
Kinter
Ligurta
Colorado River
Gila River
Yuma
3156 ft
962 m
Sheep Mtn.
Wellton
ARIZONA
DESERT
Tijuana
M   E   X   I   C   O

Scale 1:3 000 000

0 — 50 — 100 km

0 — 25 — 50 — 65 miles
1 hour

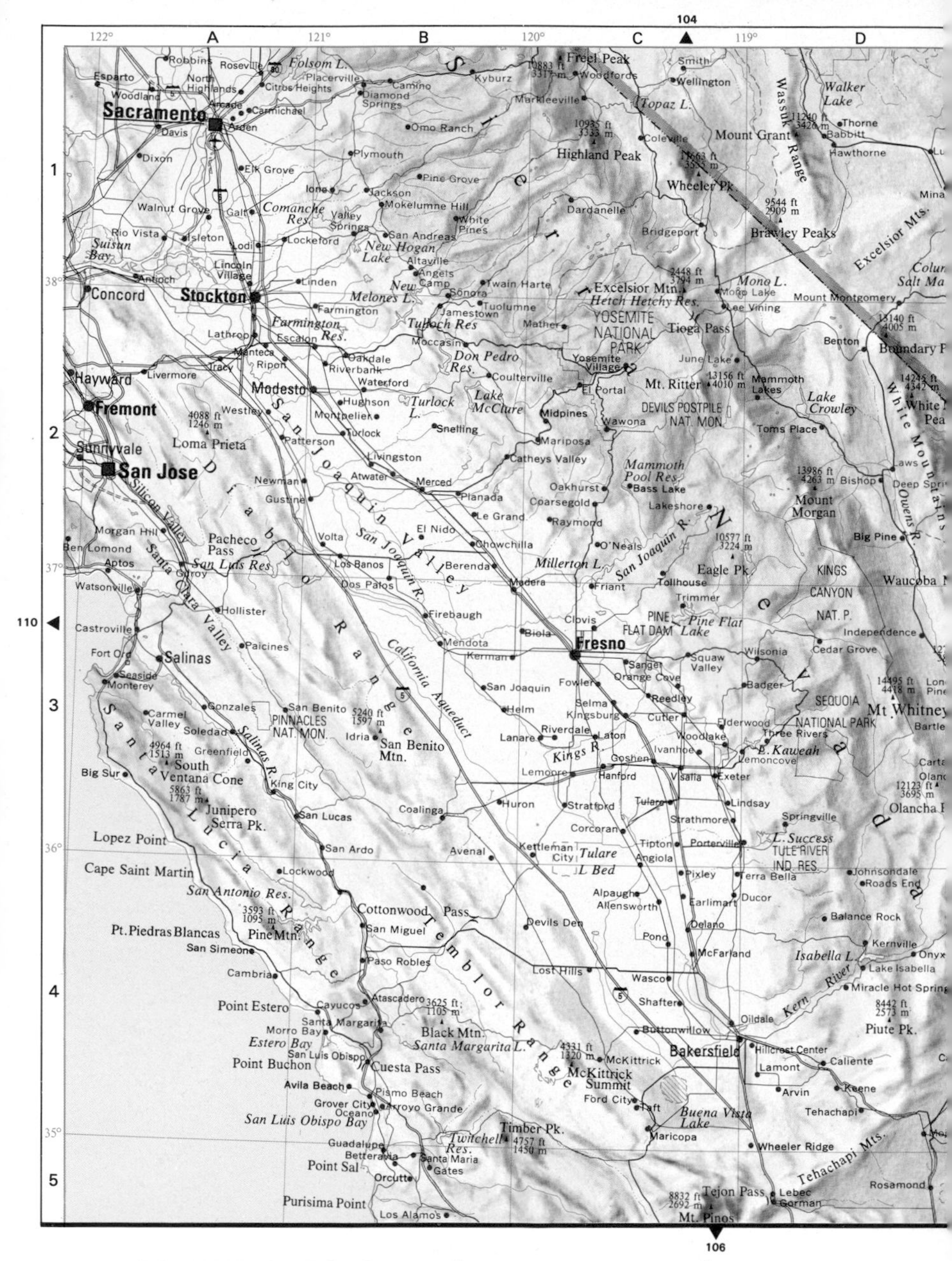

CALIFORNIA-Central, NEVADA-Southern

104
122°
121°
B
120°
119°
1
2
3
4
5
38°
37°
36°
35°
110
106
Sacramento
Stockton
Modesto
Fremont
Hayward
Sunnyvale
San Jose
Concord
Fresno
Bakersfield
Robbins
Roseville
Folsom L.
Esparto
North Highlands
Citrus Heights
Woodland
Arcade
Carmichael
Arden
Davis
Dixon
Elk Grove
Placerville
Camino
Diamond Springs
Kyburz
Omo Ranch
Plymouth
Pine Grove
Ione
Jackson
Mokelumne Hill
White Pines
Walnut Grove
Galt
Comanche Res.
Valley Springs
San Andreas
Rio Vista
Isleton
Lodi
Lockeford
New Hogan Lake
Altaville
Angels Camp
Suisun Bay
Antioch
Lincoln Village
Linden
New Melones L.
Sonora
Twain Harte
Tuolumne
Jamestown
Farmington
Farmington Res.
Tulloch Res
Lathrop
Escalon
Manteca
Ripon
Tracy
Livermore
Moccasin
Oakdale
Riverbank
Don Pedro Res.
Coulterville
Waterford
Hughson
Turlock L.
Lake McClure
Montpelier
Turlock
Snelling
Westley
4088 ft
1246 m
Loma Prieta
Patterson
Livingston
Atwater
Merced
Newman
Gustine
Planada
Le Grand
El Nido
Chowchilla
Morgan Hill
Ben Lomond
Aptos
Watsonville
Pacheco Pass
San Luis Res
Gilroy
Volta
Los Banos
Dos Palos
Berenda
Madera
San Joaquin Valley
San Joaquin R.
Diablo Range
Silicon Valley
Santa Clara Valley
Hollister
Castroville
Fort Ord
Salinas
Seaside
Monterey
Paicines
Firebaugh
Mendota
Kerman
Biola
California Aqueduct
San Joaquin
Helm
Carmel Valley
Gonzales
San Benito
PINNACLES NAT. MON.
5240 ft
1597 m
Idria
San Benito Mtn.
Soledad
Greenfield
Salinas R.
4964 ft
1513 m
South Ventana Cone
Big Sur
5863 ft
1787 m
Junipero Serra Pk.
King City
Santa Lucia Range
San Lucas
Coalinga
Huron
Lopez Point
San Ardo
Avenal
Cape Saint Martin
Lockwood
San Antonio Res.
3593 ft
1095 m
Pine Mtn.
Pt. Piedras Blancas
San Simeon
Cottonwood Pass
San Miguel
Temblor Range
Paso Robles
Cambria
Atascadero
3625 ft
1105 m
Point Estero
Cayucos
Santa Margarita
Morro Bay
Black Mtn.
Santa Margarita L.
Estero Bay
San Luis Obispo
Point Buchon
Cuesta Pass
Avila Beach
Pismo Beach
Grover City
Oceano
Arroyo Grande
San Luis Obispo Bay
Guadalupe
Betteravia
Santa Maria
Gates
Point Sal
Orcutt
Purisima Point
Los Alamos
Twitchell Res.
Timber Pk.
4757 ft
1450 m
Freel Peak
10883 ft
3317 m
Woodfords
Smith
Wellington
Markleeville
Topaz L.
10935 ft
3333 m
Coleville
Highland Peak
11663 ft
3555 m
Wheeler Pk.
Walker Lake
Wassuk Range
11240 ft
3426 m
Thorne
Mount Grant
Babbitt
Hawthorne
Dardanelle
Bridgeport
9544 ft
2909 m
Brawley Peaks
Excelsior Mts.
Mina
Sierra Nevada
2448 ft
3794 m
Excelsior Mtn.
Hetch Hetchy Res.
Mono L.
Mono Lake
Lee Vining
Mount Montgomery
Mather
YOSEMITE NATIONAL PARK
Tioga Pass
Yosemite Village
June Lake
Benton
13140 ft
4005 m
Boundary P
El Portal
Mt. Ritter
13156 ft
4010 m
Mammoth Lakes
14246 ft
4342 m
White Mountains
Midpines
DEVILS POSTPILE NAT. MON.
Lake Crowley
Wawona
Toms Place
Mariposa
Catheys Valley
Mammoth Pool Res.
Bass Lake
13986 ft
4263 m
Bishop
Laws
Oakhurst
Coarsegold
Lakeshore
Mount Morgan
Owens R.
Raymond
O'Neals
10577 ft
3224 m
Big Pine
Millerton L.
Eagle Pk.
KINGS CANYON NAT. P.
Friant
Tollhouse
Trimmer
Clovis
PINE FLAT DAM
Pine Flat Lake
Independence
Squaw Valley
Wilsonia
Cedar Grove
Sanger
Orange Cove
Fowler
Reedley
Badger
14495 ft
4418 m
Mt Whitney
Selma
Kingsburg
Cutler
SEQUOIA NATIONAL PARK
Riverdale
Laton
Elderwood
Woodlake
Three Rivers
Lanare
Kings R.
Ivanhoe
L. Kaweah
Lemoncove
Goshen
Lemoore
Hanford
Visalia
Exeter
12123 ft
3695 m
Olancha
Stratford
Tulare
Lindsay
Springville
Corcoran
Strathmore
Tipton
Porterville
L. Success
TULE RIVER IND. RES.
Kettleman City
Tulare L Bed
Angiola
Pixley
Terra Bella
Johnsondale
Roads End
Alpaugh
Allensworth
Earlimart
Ducor
Devils Den
Delano
Balance Rock
Pond
McFarland
Kernville
Isabella L.
Lake Isabella
Lost Hills
Wasco
Miracle Hot Spring
Shafter
8442 ft
2573 m
Piute Pk.
Oildale
Kern River
Buttonwillow
4331 ft
1320 m
McKittrick
McKittrick Summit
Hillcrest Center
Caliente
Lamont
Arvin
Keene
Ford City
Taft
Buena Vista Lake
Tehachapi
Maricopa
Wheeler Ridge
Tehachapi Mts.
8832 ft
2692 m
Tejon Pass
Mt. Pinos
Lebec
Gorman
Rosamond

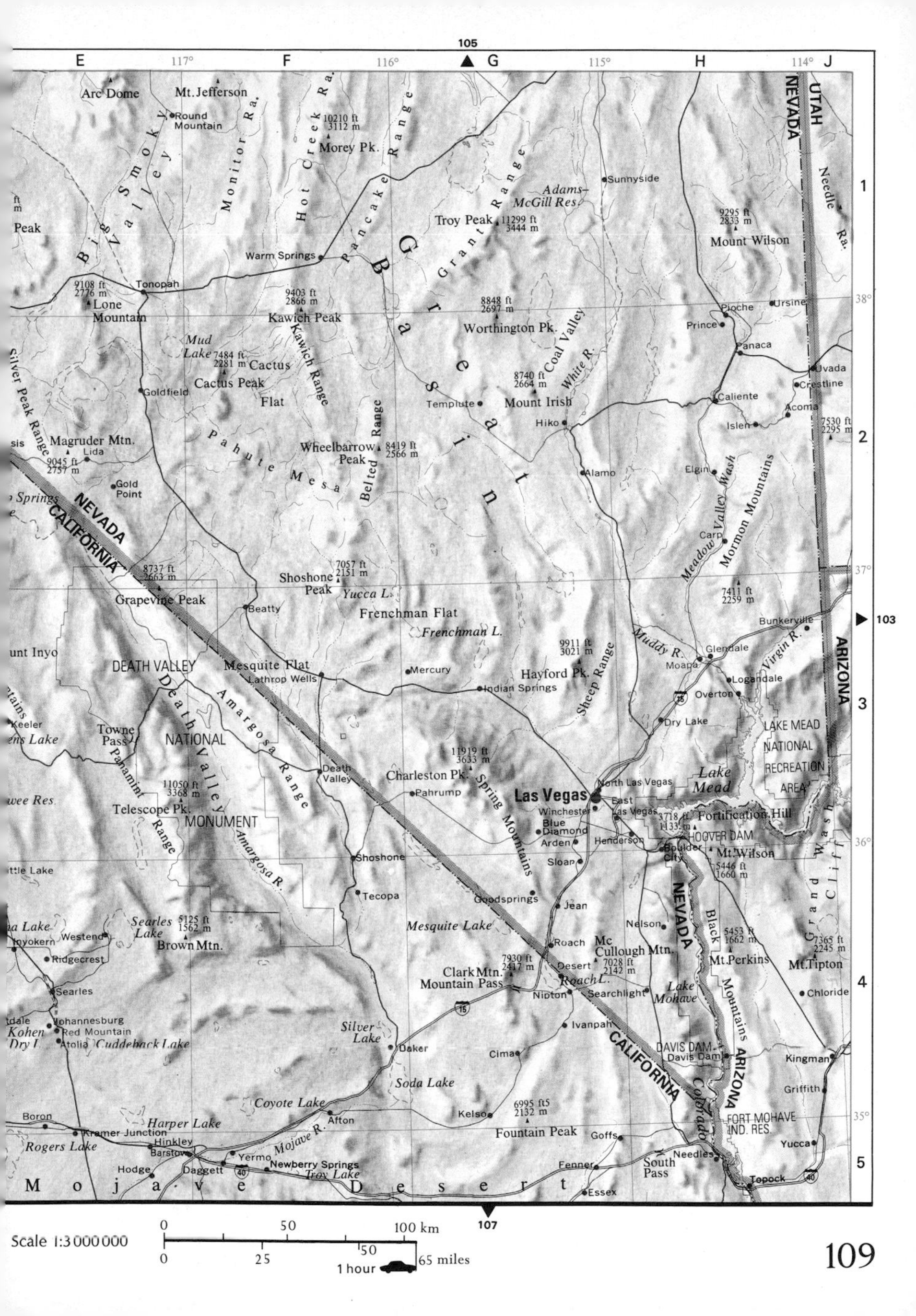

E   117°   F   116°   ▲   G   115°   H   114°   J

NEVADA   UTAH

Arc Dome   Mt. Jefferson   Hot Creek Ra.   Pancake Range   Needle Ra.

Round   Mountain   10210 ft   3112 m   Morey Pk.

Peak   Monitor Ra.   Adams-   McGill Res   Sunnyside   1

Big Smoky   Valley   Troy Peak   11299 ft   3444 m   9295 ft   2833 m   Mount Wilson

Warm Springs   Grant Range   Basin

9108 ft   2776 m   Tonopah   Lone   Mountain   9403 ft   2866 m   8848 ft   2697 m   Pioche   Ursine   38°

Mud   Lake   Kawich Peak   Kawich Range   Worthington Pk.   White R.   Coal Valley   Prince   Panaca

7484 ft   2281 m   Cactus   8740 ft   2664 m   Caliente   Ovada   Crestline

Goldfield   Cactus Peak   Flat   Mount Irish   Islen   Acoma   2

Pahute Mesa   Wheelbarrow   Peak   8419 ft   2566 m   Temple ute   Hiko   Elgin   7530 ft   2295 m

Magruder Mtn.   Lida   Belted Range   Alamo   Mormon Mountains   Meadow Valley Wash

9045 ft   2757 m   Gold   Point   Cary

Silver Peak Range   NEVADA   CALIFORNIA   7057 ft   2151 m   Shoshone   Peak   Yucca L.   7411 ft   2259 m   Bunkerville   ARIZONA   103

8737 ft   2663 m   Grapevine Peak   Frenchman Flat   Virgin R.   Glendale

Beatty   Frenchman L.   9911 ft   3021 m   Muddy R.   Moapa   Logandale

mt Inyo   DEATH VALLEY   Mesquite Flat   Lathrop Wells   Mercury   Hayford Pk.   Sheep Range   Overton   3

Keeler   Towne   Pass   NATIONAL   Amargosa Range   Death Valley   Indian Springs   Dry Lake   LAKE MEAD   NATIONAL   RECREATION   AREA

ens Lake   Panamint Range   11050 ft   3368 m   Death   Valley   11919 ft   3633 m   Lake   Mead

wee Res.   Telescope Pk.   MONUMENT   Charleston Pk.   Spring Mountains   North Las Vegas   Fortification Hill

little Lake   Amargosa R.   Pahrump   Las Vegas   East   Las Vegas   3718 ft   1135 m   36°

Searles   Lake   5125 ft   1562 m   Shoshone   Winchester   Blue   Diamond   Henderson   HOOVER DAM   Mt. Wilson

a Lake   Westend   Brown Mtn.   Tecopa   Arden   Sloan   Boulder   City   5446 ft   1660 m

nyokern   Ridgecrest   Mesquite Lake   Goodsprings   Jean   Black   Mountains

Searles   Clark Mtn.   Mountain Pass   7930 ft   2417 m   Roach   Desert   Mc   Cullough Mtn.   7028 ft   2142 m   Nelson   Mt. Perkins   5453 ft   1662 m   2365 ft   2245 m   Mt. Tipton   4

dale   Johannesburg   Red Mountain   atolia   Cuddeback Lake   Silver   Lake   Roach L.   Nipton   Searchlight   Lake   Mohave   Chloride

Kohen   Dry l.   Baker   Cima   Ivanpah   DAVIS DAM   Davis Dam   Kingman   ARIZONA

Boron   Coyote Lake   Soda Lake   Kelso   6995 ft5   2132 m   Goffs   FORT MOHAVE   IND. RES.   Griffith   35°

Rogers Lake   Harper Lake   Afton   Mojave R.   Fountain Peak   South   Pass   Needles   Yucca

Kramer Junction   Hinkley   Barstow   Yermo   Newberry Springs   Troy Lake   Fenner   Essex   Topock   5

Hodge   Daggett   M o j a v e   D e s e r t

Scale 1:3 000 000

0   50   100 km
0   25   50   65 miles
1 hour

109

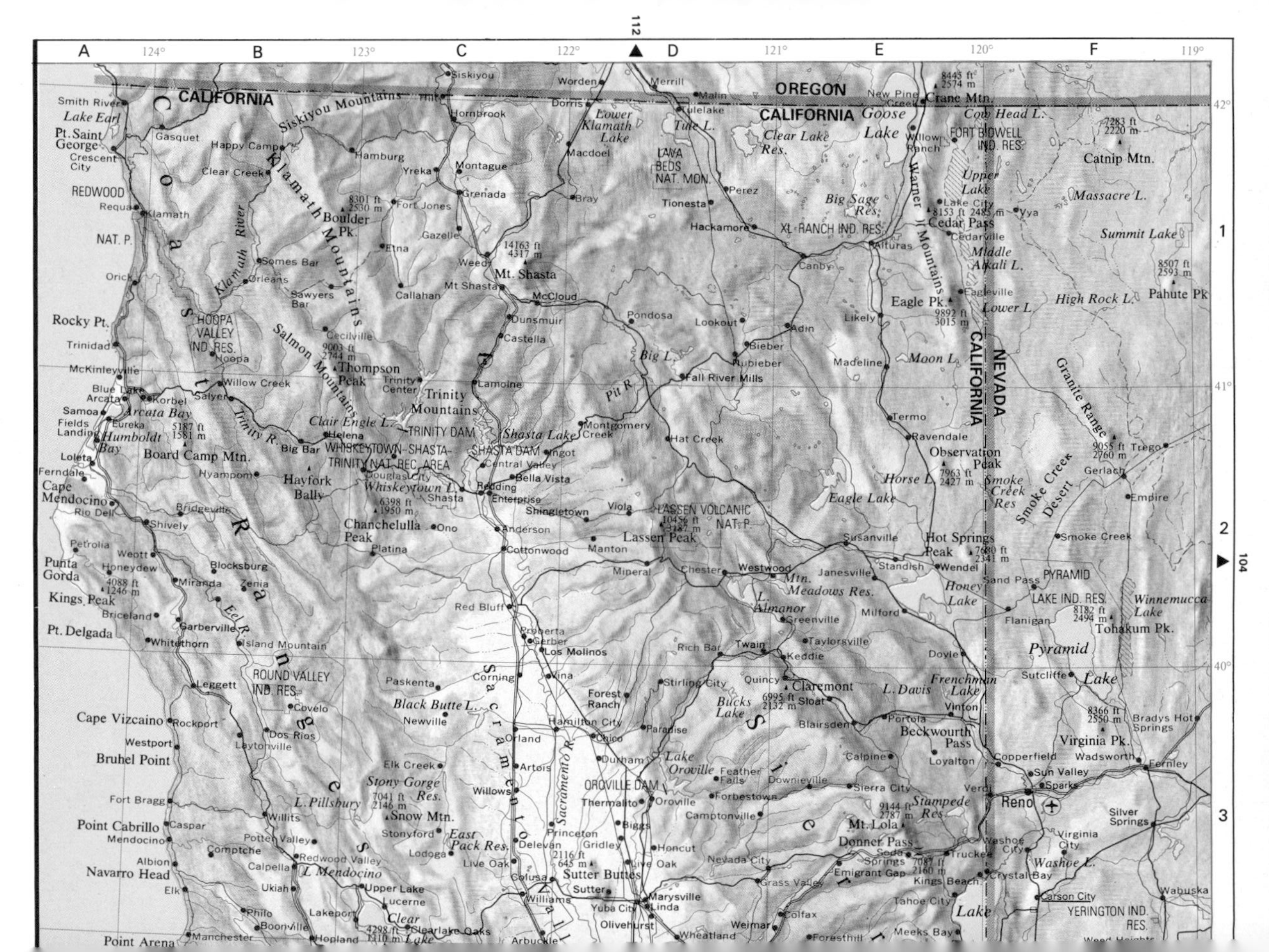
OREGON
CALIFORNIA
NEVADA
Klamath Mountains
Siskiyou Mountains
Salmon Mountains
Trinity Mountains
Warner Mountains
Granite Range
Smoke Creek Desert
Mt. Shasta
Lassen Peak
LASSEN VOLCANIC NAT. P.
LAVA BEDS NAT. MON.
REDWOOD NAT. P.
HOOPA VALLEY IND. RES.
ROUND VALLEY IND. RES.
PYRAMID LAKE IND. RES.
FORT BIDWELL IND. RES.
XL RANCH IND. RES.
YERINGTON IND. RES.
WHISKEYTOWN-SHASTA-TRINITY NAT. REC. AREA
Goose Lake
Lower Klamath Lake
Tule L.
Clear Lake Res.
Eagle Lake
Honey Lake
Pyramid Lake
L. Almanor
Shasta Lake
Clair Engle L.
Lake Oroville
Clear Lake
Sacramento R.
Klamath River
Trinity R.
Eel R.
Pit R.
Humboldt Bay
Arcata Bay
Cape Mendocino
Point Arena
Cape Vizcaino
Redding
Eureka
Reno
Chico
Yreka
Ukiah
Marysville
Coast Ranges
Sacramento Valley
Sierra
104
112

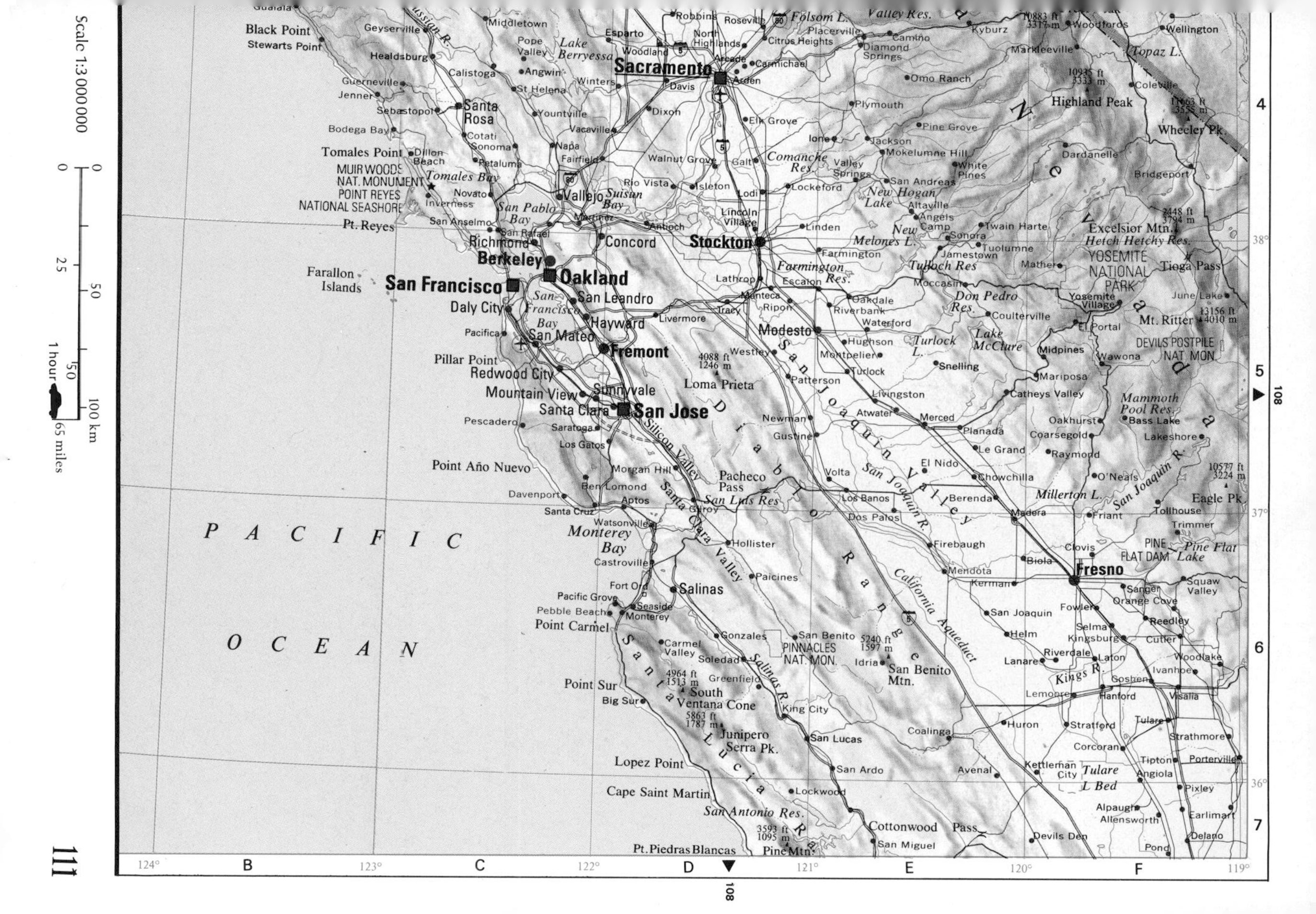

108
4
5
6
7
38°
37°
36°
119°
120°
121°
122°
123°
124°
B
C
D
E
F
Scale 1:3 000 000
0
50
100 km
0
25
50
65 miles
1 hour
Sacramento
Stockton
Modesto
Fresno
San Jose
Oakland
Berkeley
San Francisco
Fremont
Hayward
San Leandro
Concord
Richmond
Daly City
Santa Rosa
Salinas
Monterey
Monterey Bay
Santa Cruz
Sunnyvale
Mountain View
Santa Clara
Redwood City
San Mateo
Silicon Valley
San Francisco Bay
San Pablo Bay
Suisun Bay
Vallejo
Napa
Petaluma
Novato
San Rafael
Davis
Woodland
Dixon
Vacaville
Fairfield
Merced
Turlock
Madera
Visalia
Tulare
Hanford
Porterville
Delano
Coalinga
Hollister
Gilroy
Watsonville
Lake Berryessa
Folsom L.
Russian R.
San Joaquin R.
San Joaquin Valley
California Aqueduct
Diablo Range
Santa Lucia Range
Sierra Nevada
YOSEMITE NATIONAL PARK
DEVILS POSTPILE NAT. MON.
PINNACLES NAT. MON.
MUIR WOODS NAT. MONUMENT
POINT REYES NATIONAL SEASHORE
Pt. Reyes
Tomales Point
Tomales Bay
Bodega Bay
Farallon Islands
Pillar Point
Point Año Nuevo
Point Sur
Point Carmel
Lopez Point
Cape Saint Martin
Pt. Piedras Blancas
Black Point
Stewarts Point
Highland Peak
Wheeler Pk.
Mt. Ritter
Eagle Pk.
Excelsior Mtn.
Tioga Pass
Pacheco Pass
Cottonwood Pass
Loma Prieta
San Benito Mtn.
Junipero Serra Pk.
South Ventana Cone
Pine Mtn.
Hetch Hetchy Res.
Mammoth Pool Res.
Millerton L.
Pine Flat Lake
Tulare L. Bed
Kings R.
Salinas R.
San Luis Res.
San Antonio Res.
Don Pedro Res.
Lake McClure
Melones L.
New Hogan Lake
Comanche Res.
Farmington Res.
Turlock L.
Tulloch Res.
Topaz L.
PACIFIC OCEAN

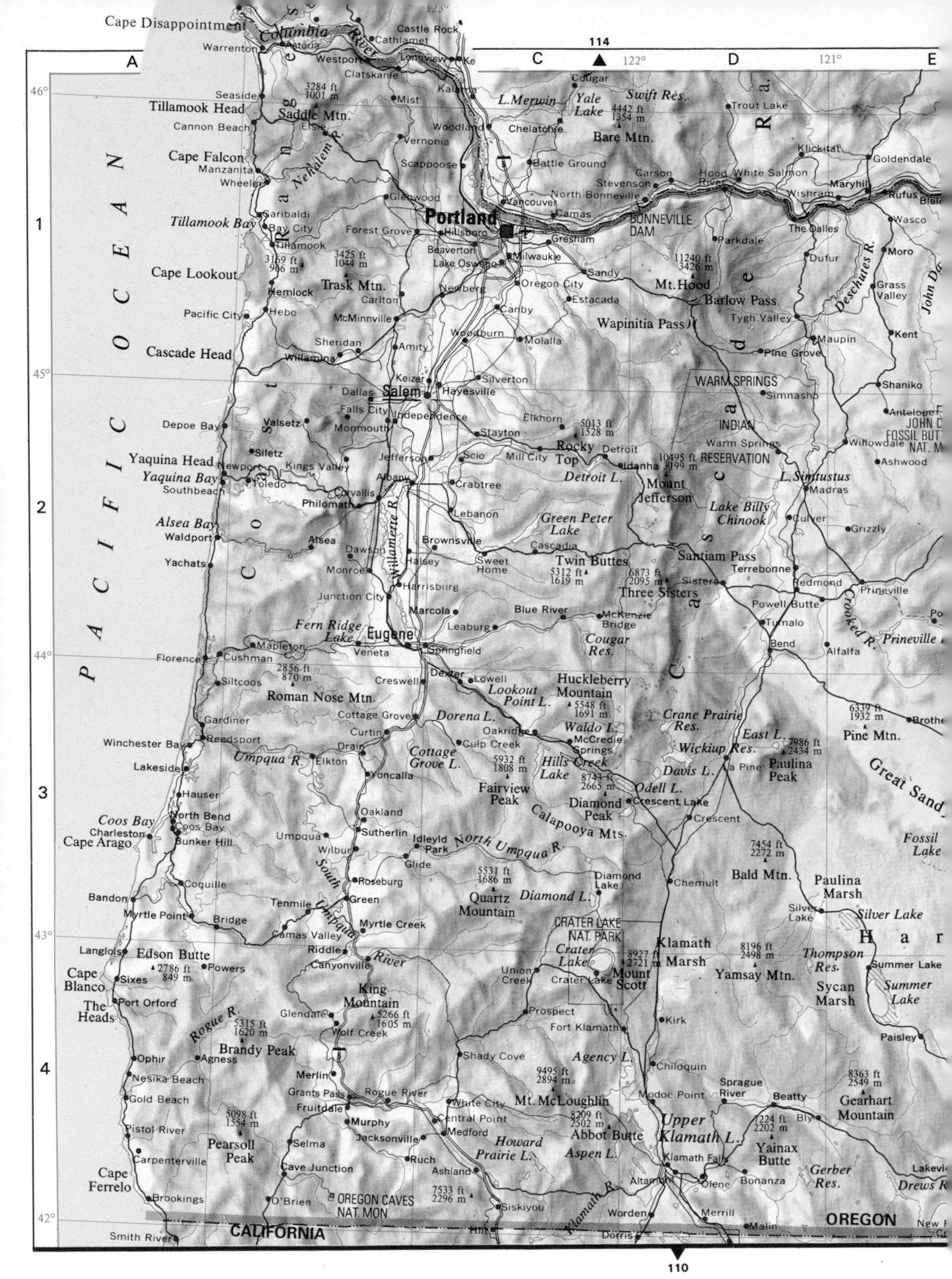
PACIFIC OCEAN
Portland
Salem
Eugene
Columbia River
Willamette R.
Coast Range
Cascade Range
Mt. Hood
Three Sisters
Mount Jefferson
Crater Lake
CRATER LAKE NAT. PARK
WARM SPRINGS INDIAN RESERVATION
OREGON CAVES NAT. MON
BONNEVILLE DAM
Upper Klamath L.
Rogue R.
Umpqua R.
North Umpqua R.
Great Sandy
CALIFORNIA
OREGON
114
110

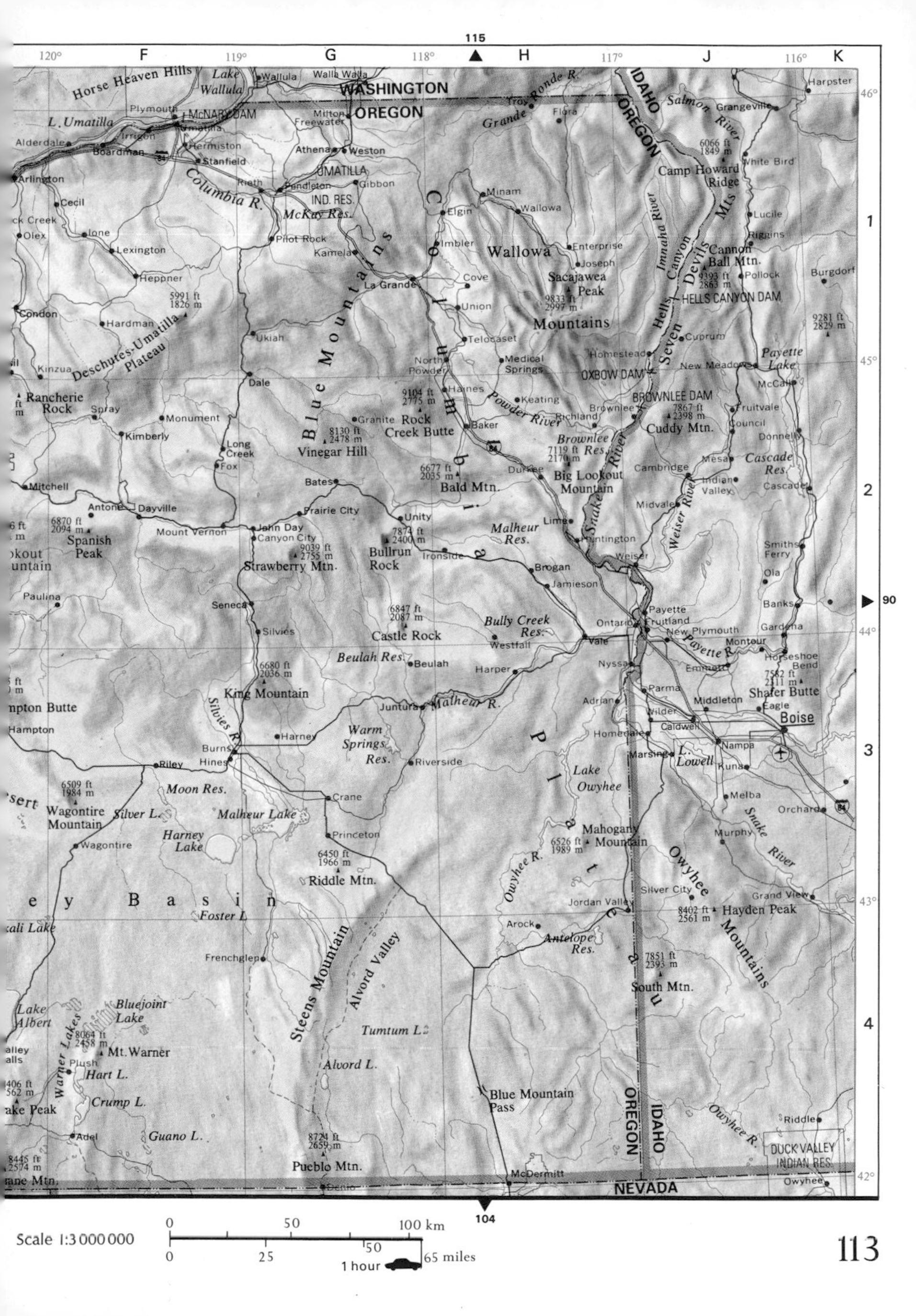
115
120°
F
119°
G
118°
H
117°
J
116°
K
46°
45°
44°
43°
42°
1
2
3
4
90
104
WASHINGTON
OREGON
IDAHO
NEVADA
Horse Heaven Hills
Lake Wallula
Wallula
Walla Walla
Plymouth
McNARY DAM
L. Umatilla
Umatilla
Irrigon
Alderdale
Boardman
Hermiston
Stanfield
Milton-Freewater
Athena
Weston
Arlington
Columbia R.
Rieth
Pendleton
UMATILLA IND. RES.
Gibbon
McKay Res.
Cecil
Ione
Olex
Lexington
Pilot Rock
Kamela
Heppner
Condon
5991 ft
1826 m
Hardman
Deschutes-Umatilla Plateau
Kinzua
Ukiah
Dale
Rancherie Rock
Spray
Monument
Kimberly
Long Creek
Fox
Mitchell
Antone
Dayville
6870 ft
2094 m
Spanish Peak
Mount Vernon
John Day
Canyon City
Paulina
Seneca
Silvies
Troy
Grande Ronde R.
Flora
Minam
Wallowa
Elgin
Imbler
Cove
La Grande
Union
Telocaset
Blue Mountains
Columbia Plateau
Wallowa Mountains
Enterprise
Joseph
Sacajawea Peak
9833 ft
2997 m
Medical Springs
North Powder
Haines
9104 ft
2775 m
Rock Creek Butte
Granite
8130 ft
2478 m
Vinegar Hill
Baker
Keating
Powder River
Richland
6677 ft
2035 m
Bald Mtn.
Bates
Prairie City
Unity
7874 ft
2400 m
Bullrun Rock
9039 ft
2755 m
Strawberry Mtn.
Ironside
Durkee
7119 ft
2170 m
Big Lookout Mountain
Brownlee Res.
Malheur Res.
Lime
Huntington
Brogan
Jamieson
6847 ft
2087 m
Castle Rock
Bully Creek Res.
Westfall
Vale
Ontario
Beulah Res.
Beulah
Harper
6680 ft
2036 m
King Mountain
Juntura
Malheur R.
Silvies R.
Hampton Butte
Hampton
Harney
Warm Springs Res.
Burns
Hines
Riley
Riverside
6509 ft
1984 m
Wagontire Mountain
Moon Res.
Silver L.
Malheur Lake
Harney Lake
Crane
Princeton
Wagontire
6450 ft
1966 m
Riddle Mtn.
Foster L.
Frenchglen
Steens Mountain
Alvord Valley
Tumtum L.
Alvord L.
Lake Albert
Bluejoint Lake
Warner Lakes
8064 ft
2458 m
Mt. Warner
Plush
Hart L.
Crump L.
Adel
Guano L.
8724 ft
2659 m
Pueblo Mtn.
Denio
McDermitt
Blue Mountain Pass
Harpster
Salmon River
Grangeville
6066 ft
1849 m
White Bird
Camp Howard Ridge
Lucile
Riggins
Imnaha River
Hells Canyon
Seven Devils Mts
Cannon Ball Mtn.
9393 ft
2863 m
Pollock
Burgdorf
HELLS CANYON DAM
9281 ft
2829 m
Cuprum
Homestead
Payette Lake
New Meadows
McCall
OXBOW DAM
BROWNLEE DAM
Brownlee
7867 ft
2398 m
Cuddy Mtn.
Fruitvale
Council
Donnelly
Cambridge
Mesa
Cascade Res.
Indian Valley
Cascade
Midvale
Weiser River
Snake River
Weiser
Smiths Ferry
Ola
Banks
Payette
Fruitland
New Plymouth
Gardena
Montour
Payette R.
Horseshoe Bend
Nyssa
Emmett
7582 ft
2311 m
Shafer Butte
Parma
Adrian
Middleton
Eagle
Wilder
Caldwell
Boise
Homedale
Nampa
Marsing
L. Lowell
Kuna
Lake Owyhee
Melba
Orchard
Mahogany Mountain
6526 ft
1989 m
Murphy
Owyhee R.
Owyhee Mountains
Silver City
Grand View
Jordan Valley
8402 ft
2561 m
Hayden Peak
Arock
Antelope Res.
7851 ft
2393 m
South Mtn.
Riddle
DUCK VALLEY INDIAN RES.
Owyhee
Scale 1:3 000 000
0
50
100 km
0
25
50
65 miles
1 hour

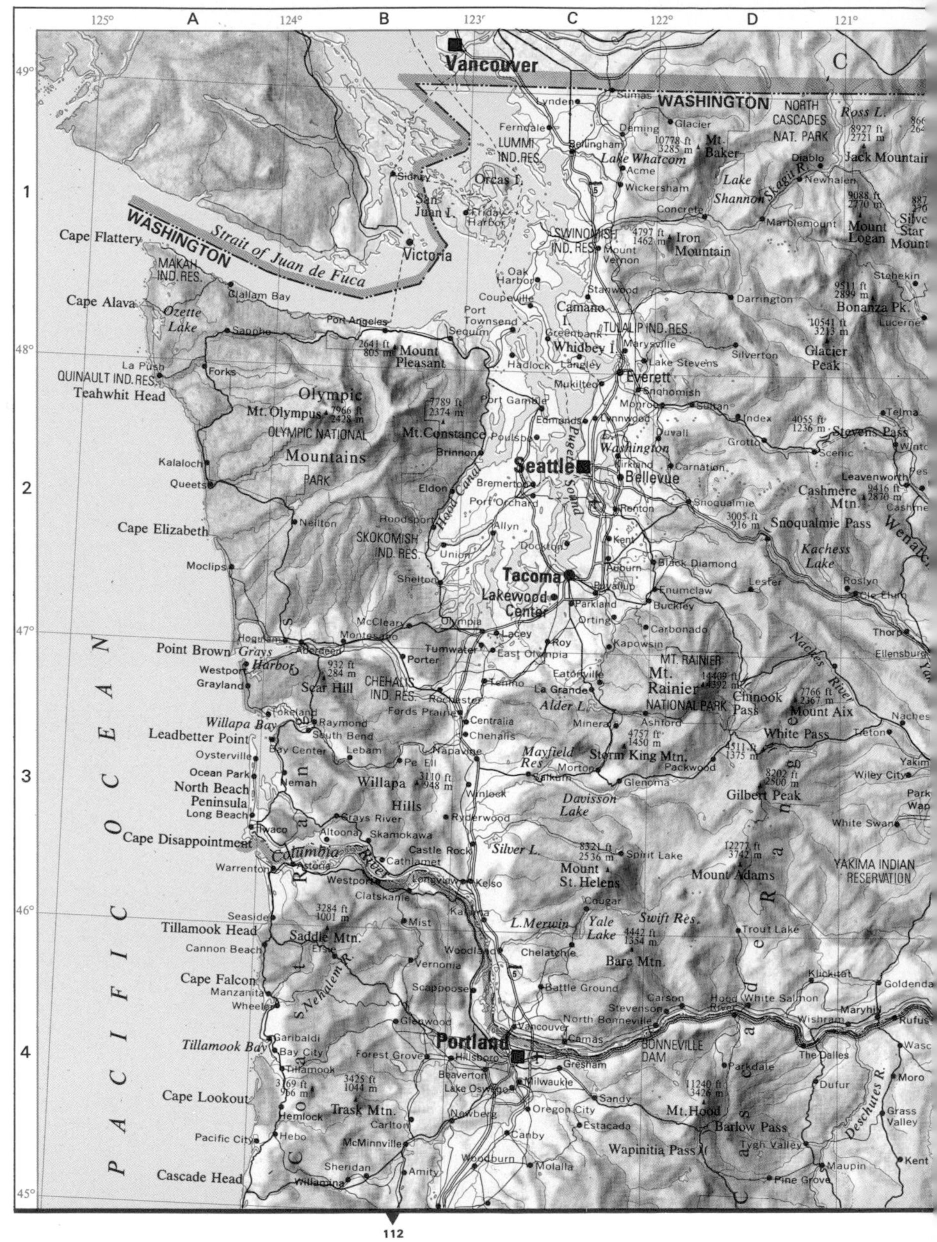

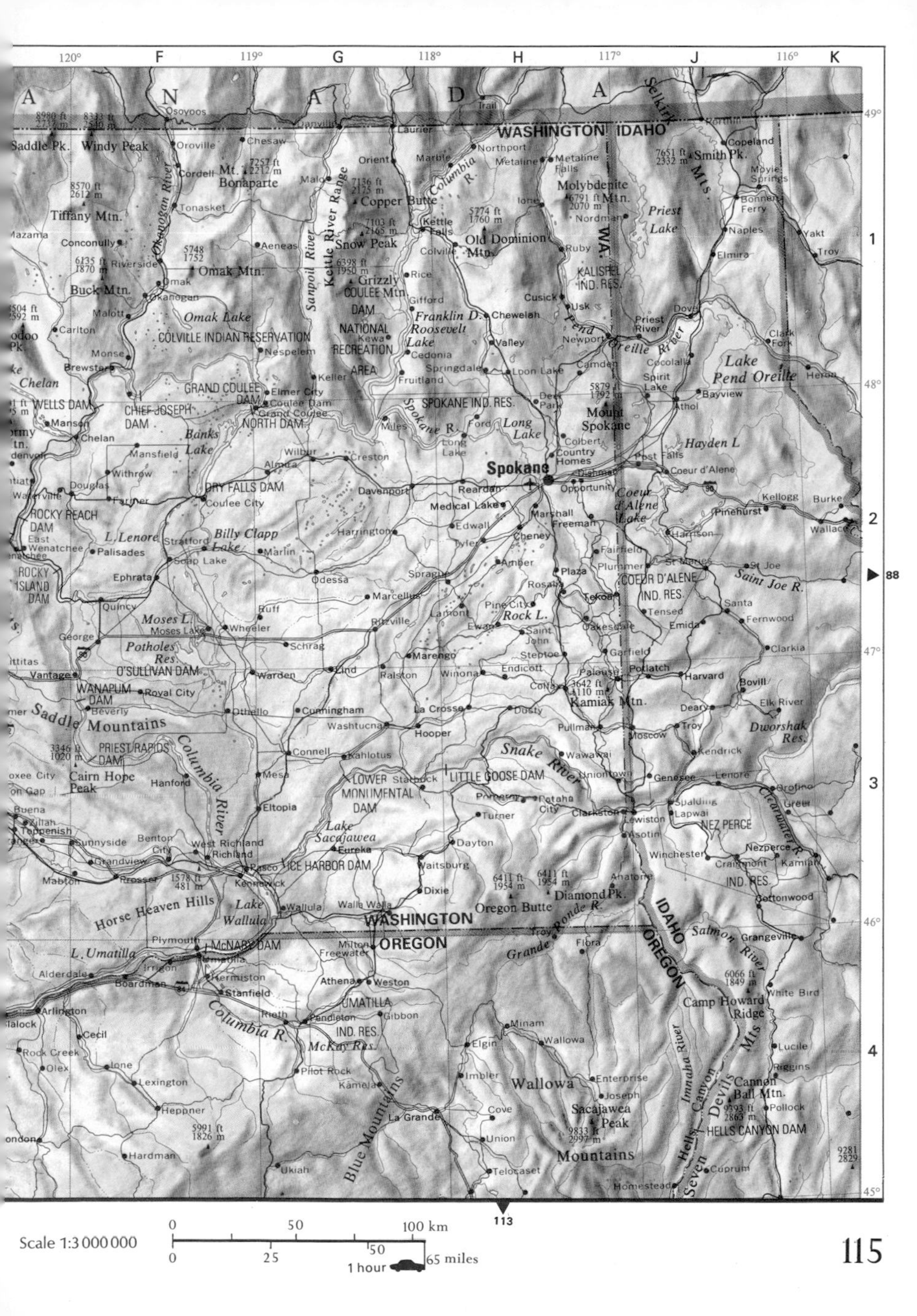

120°
F
119°
G
118°
H
117°
J
116°
K
49°
48°
47°
46°
45°
1
2
3
4
88
113
C A N A D A
WASHINGTON
IDAHO
WA.
OREGON
Osoyoos
Saddle Pk.
Windy Peak
Oroville
Chesaw
Danville
Laurier
Trail
Northport
Metaline
Metaline Falls
Marble
Orient
Copeland
Smith Pk.
Selkirk Mts.
Moyie Springs
Bonners Ferry
Cordell
Mt. Bonaparte
Malo
Kettle River Range
Copper Butte
Columbia R.
Molybdenite Mtn.
Ione
Nordman
Priest Lake
Naples
Yakt
Troy
Tonasket
Tiffany Mtn.
Okanogan River
Conconully
Aeneas
Sanpoil River
Snow Peak
Kettle Falls
Colville
Old Dominion Mtn.
Ruby
Elmira
Riverside
Omak Mtn.
Omak
Okanogan
Buck Mtn.
Grizzly
Rice
KALISPEL IND. RES.
Malott
Omak Lake
COULEE DAM NATIONAL RECREATION AREA
Gifford
Franklin D. Roosevelt Lake
Chewelah
Cusick
Usk
Pend Oreille River
Priest River
Dover
Carlton
COLVILLE INDIAN RESERVATION
Nespelem
Kewa
Cedonia
Valley
Newport
Clark Fork
Monse
Brewster
Chelan
Lake Chelan
Keller
Springdale
Fruitland
Loon Lake
Camden
Cocolalla
Lake Pend Oreille
Hope
GRAND COULEE DAM
Elmer City
Coulee Dam
Grand Coulee
NORTH DAM
WELLS DAM
CHIEF JOSEPH DAM
Manson
SPOKANE IND. RES.
Spokane R.
Miles
Ford
Long Lake
Deer Park
Mount Spokane
Spirit Lake
Bayview
Athol
Banks Lake
Mansfield
Withrow
Wilbur
Almira
Creston
Colbert
Country Homes
Hayden L
Post Falls
Coeur d'Alene
Spokane
Dishman
Opportunity
Douglas
Waterville
Farmer
DRY FALLS DAM
Coulee City
Davenport
Reardan
Medical Lake
Coeur d'Alene Lake
Kellogg
Burke
Pinehurst
Wallace
ROCKY REACH DAM
East Wenatchee
Wenatchee
L. Lenore
Stratford
Billy Clapp Lake
Harrington
Edwall
Marshall
Freeman
Cheney
Tyler
Harrison
Palisades
Marlin
Soap Lake
Fairfield
Ephrata
Odessa
Sprague
Amber
Plaza
Plummer
St Maries
St Joe
Saint Joe R.
ROCKY ISLAND DAM
Quincy
Rosalia
COEUR D'ALENE IND. RES.
Tekoa
Marcellus
Pine City
Tensed
Santa
Fernwood
Moses L.
Moses Lake
Wheeler
Ruff
Ritzville
Lamont
Rock L.
Ewan
Saint John
Oakesdale
Emida
George
Potholes Res.
Schrag
Marengo
Steptoe
Garfield
Clarkia
O'SULLIVAN DAM
Vantage
Warden
Lind
Ralston
Winona
Endicott
Colfax
Palouse
Potlatch
Harvard
Bovill
WANAPUM DAM
Royal City
Beverly
Kamiak Mtn.
Elk River
Saddle Mountains
Othello
Cunningham
La Crosse
Dusty
Deary
Washtucna
Hooper
Pullman
Moscow
Troy
Dworshak Res.
PRIEST RAPIDS DAM
Connell
Kahlotus
Snake River
Wawawai
Kendrick
Cairn Hope Peak
Hanford
Columbia River
Mesa
LOWER MONUMENTAL DAM
Starbuck
LITTLE GOOSE DAM
Uniontown
Genesee
Lenore
Orofino
Greer
Buena
Toppenish
Eltopia
Pomeroy
Potaha City
Turner
Clarkston
Lewiston
Spalding
Lapwai
NEZ PERCE IND. RES.
Clearwater R.
Sunnyside
Benton City
West Richland
Richland
Lake Sacajawea
Eureka
Dayton
Asotin
Nezperce
Grandview
Prosser
Mabton
Pasco
ICE HARBOR DAM
Kennewick
Waitsburg
Winchester
Craigmont
Kamiah
Horse Heaven Hills
Lake Wallula
Wallula
Walla Walla
Dixie
Anatone
Diamond Pk.
Oregon Butte
Grande Ronde R.
Cottonwood
WASHINGTON
OREGON
IDAHO
OREGON
Salmon River
Grangeville
Troy
Flora
Plymouth
McNARY DAM
Umatilla
L. Umatilla
Milton-Freewater
Alderdale
Irrigon
Hermiston
Boardman
Stanfield
Athena
Weston
White Bird
Camp Howard Ridge
Arlington
UMATILLA IND. RES.
Pendleton
Gibbon
Rieth
Columbia R.
McKay Res.
Minam
Wallowa
Cecil
Rock Creek
Olex
Elgin
Lucile
Riggins
Ione
Lexington
Pilot Rock
Kamela
Imbler
Wallowa Mountains
Enterprise
Joseph
Imnaha River
Cannon Ball Mtn.
Heppner
Blue Mountains
La Grande
Cove
Sacajawea Peak
Hells Canyon
Seven Devils Mts.
Pollock
HELLS CANYON DAM
Union
Hardman
Ukiah
Telocaset
Cuprum
Homestead
Scale 1:3 000 000
0
50
100 km
0
25
50
65 miles
1 hour

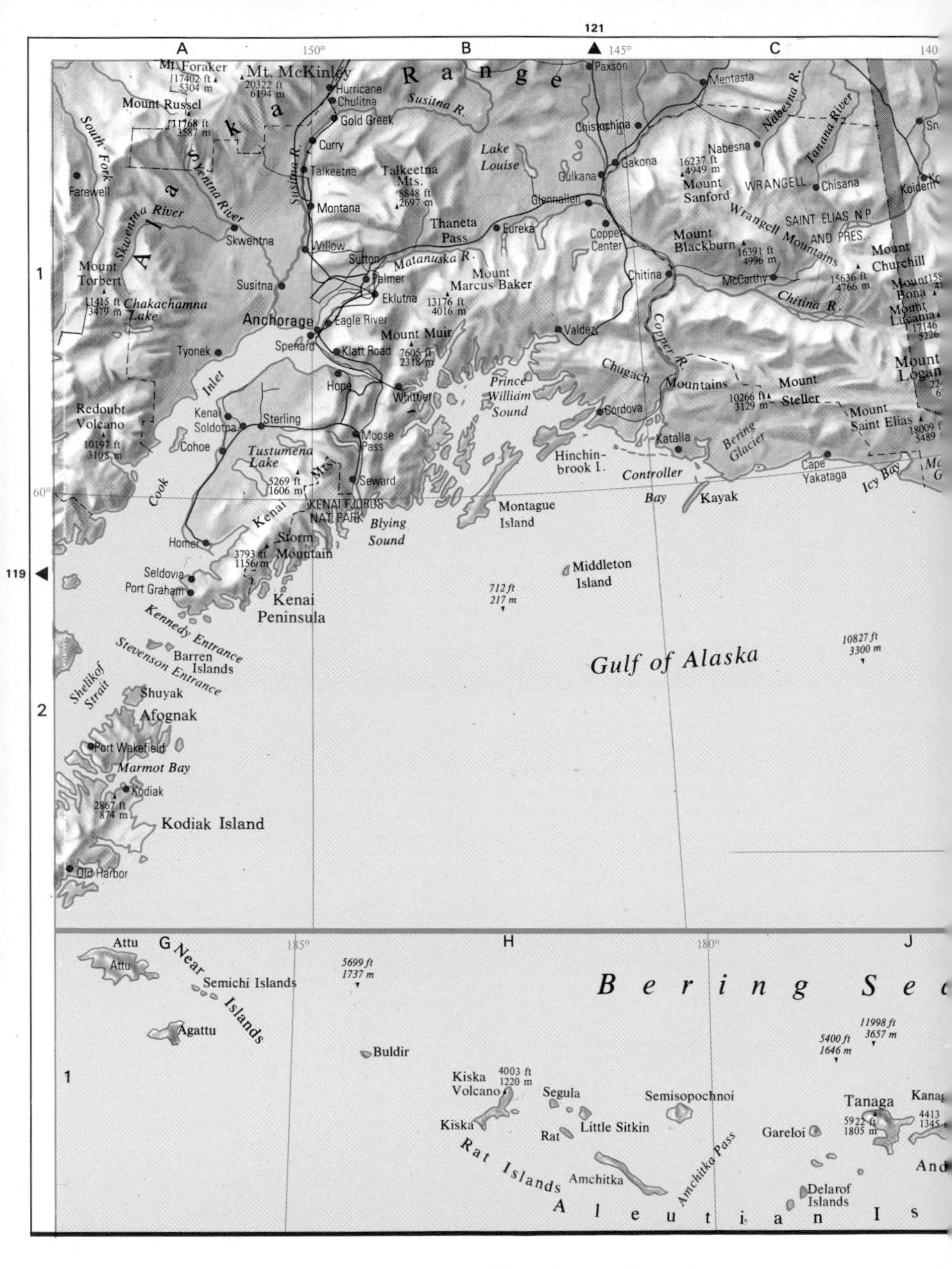

121
119
A
B
C
G
H
J
1
2
Mt. Foraker
17402 ft
5304 m
Mt. McKinley
20322 ft
6194 m
Alaska Range
Mount Russel
11768 ft
3587 m
South Fork
Farewell
Skwentna River
Yentna River
Susitna R.
Susitna R.
Hurricane
Chulitna
Gold Greek
Curry
Talkeetna
Talkeetna Mts.
8848 ft
2697 m
Montana
Skwentna
Willow
Sutton
Palmer
Eklutna
Susitna
Mount Torbert
11415 ft
3479 m
Chakachamna Lake
Anchorage
Eagle River
Spenard
Klatt Road
Tyonek
Inlet
Hope
Whittier
Redoubt Volcano
10197 ft
3108 m
Kenai
Soldotna
Sterling
Cohoe
Tustumena Lake
Moose Pass
Seward
5269 ft
1606 m
Kenai Mts.
Cook
KENAI FJORDS NAT. PARK
Homer
3793 ft
1156 m
Storm Mountain
Seldovia
Port Graham
Kenai Peninsula
Kennedy Entrance
Barren Islands
Stevenson Entrance
Shelikof Strait
Shuyak
Afognak
Port Wakefield
Marmot Bay
Kodiak
2867 ft
874 m
Kodiak Island
Old Harbor
Paxson
Mentasta
Nabesna R.
Tanana River
Chistochina
Lake Louise
Gakona
Gulkana
Glennallen
Nabesna
16237 ft
4949 m
Mount Sanford
WRANGELL
Chisana
Wrangell Mountains
SAINT ELIAS N.P. AND PRES.
Thaneta Pass
Eureka
Copper Center
Matanuska R.
Mount Marcus Baker
13176 ft
4016 m
Mount Muir
7605 ft
2318 m
Mount Blackburn
16391 ft
4996 m
Chitina
McCarthy
Chitina R.
Mount Churchill
15636 ft
4766 m
Mount Bona
Mount Lucania
17146
Mount Logan
Valdez
Copper R.
Chugach Mountains
Mount Steller
10266 ft
3129 m
Prince William Sound
Cordova
Katalla
Bering Glacier
Mount Saint Elias
18009 ft
5489
Hinchinbrook I.
Controller Bay
Kayak
Cape Yakataga
Icy Bay
Montague Island
Blying Sound
Middleton Island
712 ft
217 m
Gulf of Alaska
10827 ft
3300 m
Koidern
150°
145°
140°
60°
185°
180°
Attu
Near Islands
Semichi Islands
5699 ft
1737 m
Agattu
Buldir
Bering Sea
11998 ft
3657 m
5400 ft
1646 m
Kiska Volcano
4003 ft
1220 m
Segula
Semisopochnoi
Tanaga
Kiska
Rat
Little Sitkin
Gareloi
5922 ft
1805 m
Rat Islands
Amchitka
Amchitka Pass
Delarof Islands
Aleutian Is

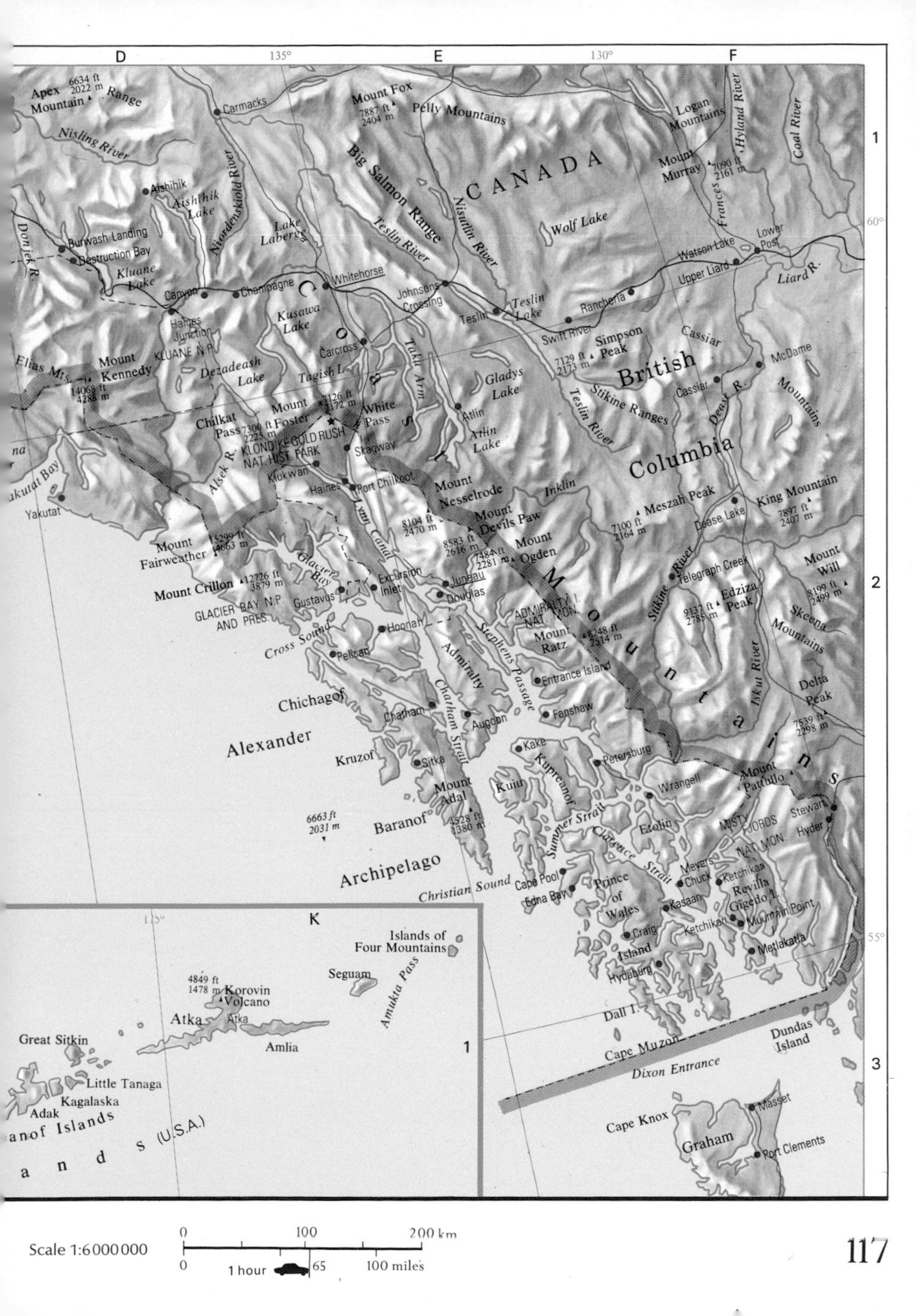

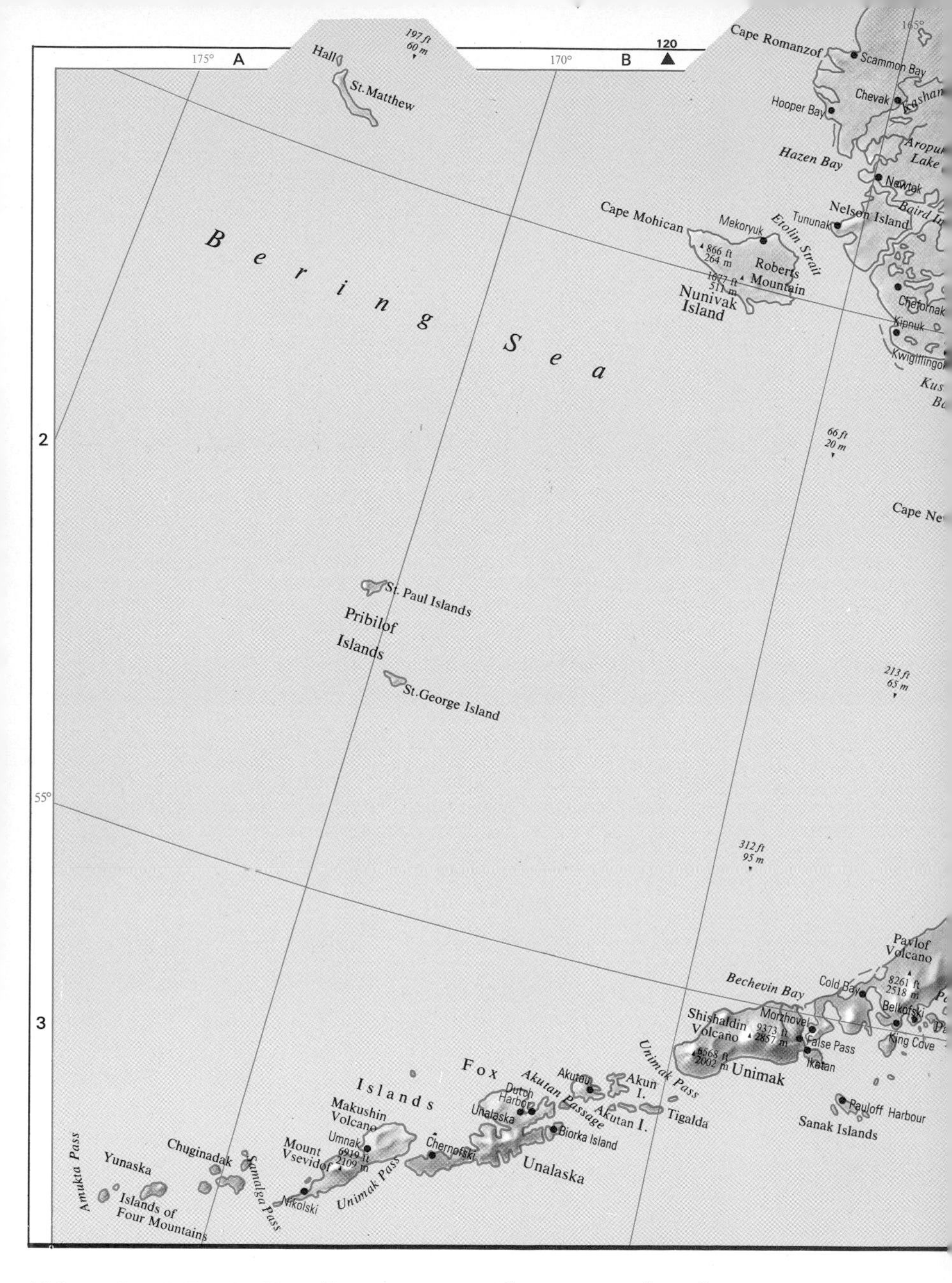

175°
A
170°
B
120
165°
Hall
197 ft
60 m
St. Matthew
Cape Romanzof
Scammon Bay
Chevak
Hooper Bay
Hazen Bay
Newtok
Nelson Island
Tununak
Cape Mohican
Mekoryuk
Etolin Strait
866 ft
264 m
Roberts Mountain
1677 ft
511 m
Nunivak Island
Kipnuk
Bering Sea
66 ft
20 m
2
St. Paul Islands
Pribilof Islands
St. George Island
213 ft
65 m
55°
312 ft
95 m
Pavlof Volcano
8261 ft
2518 m
Cold Bay
Bechevin Bay
Belkofski
King Cove
Morzhovoi
Shishaldin Volcano
9373 ft
2857 m
False Pass
Ikatan
6568 ft
2002 m
Unimak
3
Unimak Pass
Fox Islands
Akutan
Akun I.
Akutan Passage
Akutan I.
Tigalda
Pauloff Harbour
Sanak Islands
Makushin Volcano
Dutch Harbor
Unalaska
Biorka Island
Umnak
6919 ft
2109 m
Mount Vsevidof
Chernofski
Unalaska
Chuginadak
Samalga Pass
Yunaska
Amukta Pass
Islands of Four Mountains
Nikolski
Umnak Pass

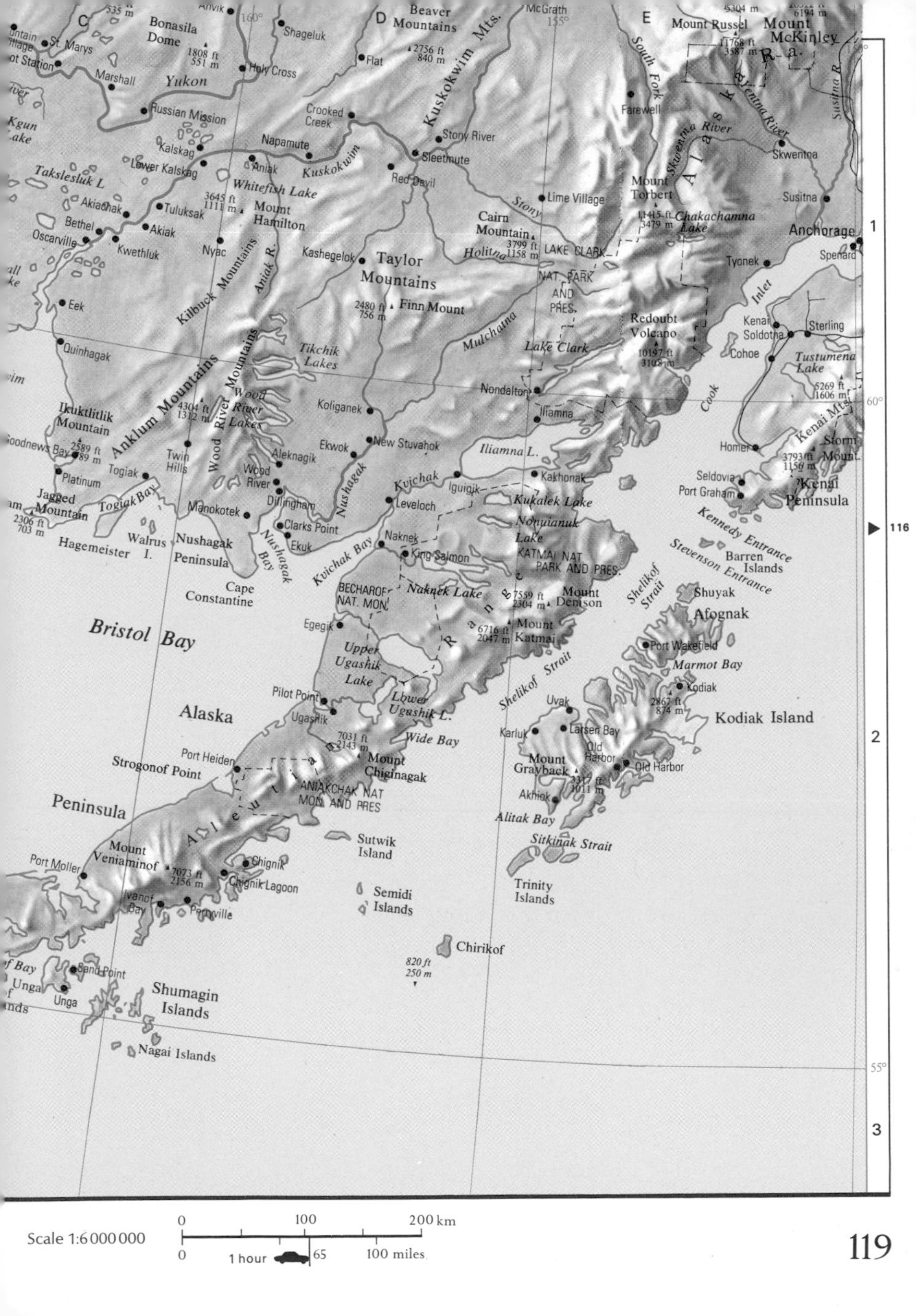

Scale 1:6 000 000

0   100   200 km

0   1 hour ⚓ 65   100 miles

119

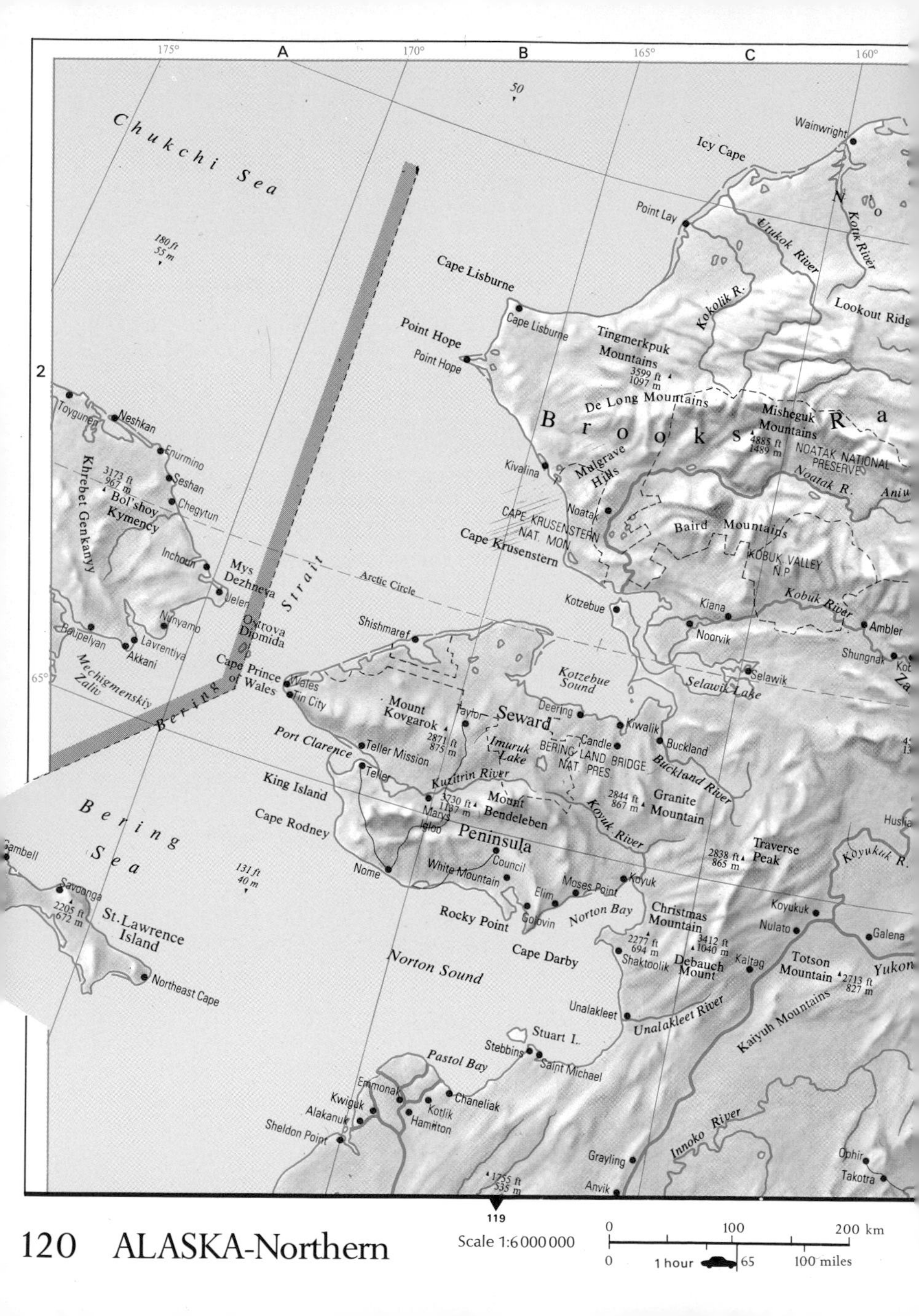

175°   A   170°   B   165°   C   160°

Chukchi Sea

Wainwright

Icy Cape

N Kotik River

Point Lay

Uliuok River

Lookout Ridge

180 ft
55 m

Cape Lisburne

Tingmerkpuk
Mountains
3599 ft
1097 m

Kokolik R.

Point Hope
Point Hope

Cape Lisburne

B r o o k s

De Long Mountains

Misheguk
Mountains
4885 ft
1489 m

R a

NOATAK NATIONAL
PRESERVE

Toygunen

Neshkan

Enurmino

Kivalina

Malgrave
Hills

Noatak R.

Aniu

Seshan

3173 ft
967 m

Bol'shoy
Kymency

Chegytun

Noatak

CAPE KRUSENSTERN
NAT. MON.

Cape Krusenstern

Baird Mountains

KOBUK VALLEY
N.P.

Kobuk River

Ambler

Shungnak

Kot

Za

Inchoun

Mys
Dezhneva

Uelen

Arctic Circle

Kotzebue

Kiana

Noorvik

Selawik

Khrebet Genkanry

Ninyamo

Lavrentiya

Akkani

Ostrova
Dipmida

Shishmaref

Selawik Lake

65°

Mechigmenskiy
Zaliv

Baupelyan

Cape Prince
of Wales

Wales

Tin City

Kotzebue
Sound

Deering

Kiwalik

Buckland

Mount
Kovgarok
2871 ft
875 m

Taylor

Seward

Candle

BERING
LAND BRIDGE
NAT. PRES.

Buckland River

Granite
Mountain
2844 ft
807 m

Port Clarence

Teller Mission

Imuruk
Lake

King Island

Bering
Strait

Teller

Kuzitrin River

1730 ft
527 m

Mount
Bendeleben

Kobuk River

2838 ft
865 m

Traverse
Peak

Husha

Koyukuk R.

Cape Rodney

Mary's
Igloo

Peninsula

Council

Gambell

Bering
Sea

131 ft
40 m

Nome

White Mountain

Elim

Moses Point

Koyuk

Christmas
Mountain

Koyukuk

Nulato

Galena

Savoonga

2205 ft
672 m

St. Lawrence
Island

Rocky Point

Golovin

Norton Bay

2277 ft
694 m

2412 ft
1040 m

Debauch
Mount

Kaltag

Totson
Mountain

2713 ft
827 m

Yukon

Cape Darby

Shaktoolik

Northeast Cape

Norton Sound

Unalakleet

Unalakleet River

Karyuh Mountains

Stuart I.

Pastol Bay

Stebbins

Saint Michael

Kwiguk

Emmonak

Alakanuk

Kotlik

Hamilton

Chaneliak

Sheldon Point

1755 ft
535 m

Grayling

Innoko River

Anvik

Ophir

Takotra

119

120   ALASKA-Northern

Scale 1:6 000 000

| 0 | 100 | 200 km |

1 hour 65

| 0 | 100 miles |

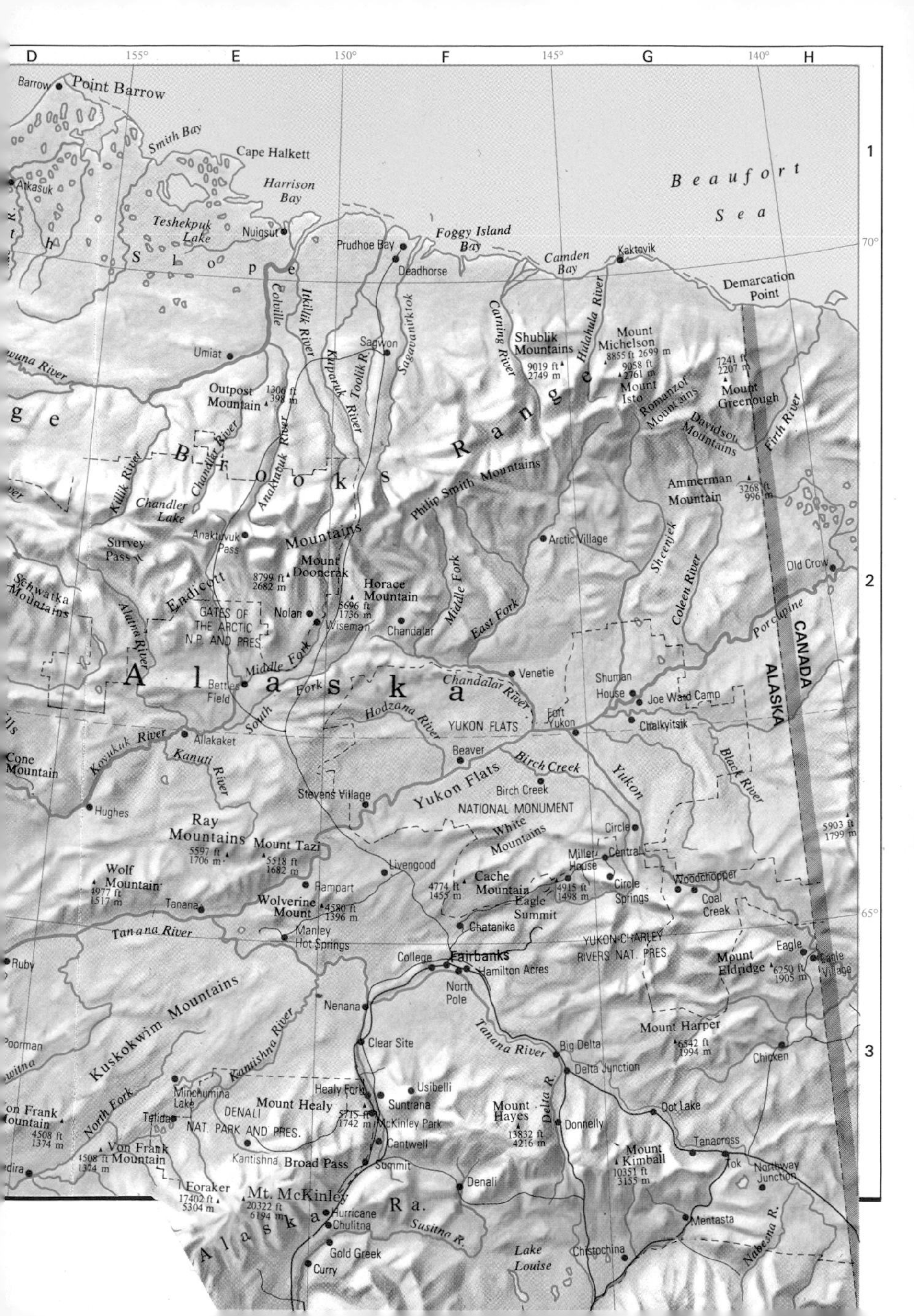
D
E
F
G
H
155°
150°
145°
140°
70°
65°
1
2
3
Barrow
Point Barrow
Smith Bay
Cape Halkett
Harrison Bay
Atkasuk
Teshekpuk Lake
Nuigsut
Slope
Colville
Ikpikpuk River
Prudhoe Bay
Deadhorse
Foggy Island Bay
Camden Bay
Kaktovik
Beaufort Sea
Demarcation Point
Sagavanirktok
Kuparuk River
Toolik R.
Sagwon
Umiat
Canning River
Hulahula River
Shublik Mountains
9019 ft 2749 m
Mount Michelson
8855 ft 2699 m
9058 ft 2761 m
Mount Isto
Romanzof Mountains
7241 ft 2207 m
Mount Greenough
Davidson Mountains
Firth River
Outpost Mountain
1306 ft 398 m
Brooks Range
Chandler River
Anaktuvuk River
Killik River
Chandler Lake
Philip Smith Mountains
Ammerman Mountain
3268 ft 996 m
Anaktuvuk Pass
Survey Pass
Mountains
Mount Doonerak
8799 ft 2682 m
Horace Mountain
5696 ft 1736 m
Arctic Village
Sheenjek
Coleen River
Old Crow
Schwatka Mountains
Endicott
Alatna River
GATES OF THE ARCTIC N.P. AND PRES.
Nolan
Wiseman
Chandalar
Middle Fork
East Fork
Porcupine
CANADA
ALASKA
Alaska
Bettles Field
Middle Fork
South Fork
Chandalar River
Venetie
Shuman House
Joe Ward Camp
Hodzana River
YUKON FLATS
Fort Yukon
Chalkyitsik
Koyukuk River
Allakaket
Kanuti River
Cone Mountain
Beaver
Birch Creek
Yukon
Black River
Yukon Flats
Stevens Village
Birch Creek
NATIONAL MONUMENT
Hughes
Ray Mountains
Mount Tazi
5597 ft 1706 m
5518 ft 1682 m
White Mountains
Circle
5903 ft 1799 m
Wolf Mountain
4977 ft 1517 m
Livengood
Miller House
Central
Rampart
4774 ft 1455 m
Cache Mountain
4915 ft 1498 m
Circle Springs
Woodchopper
Coal Creek
Tanana
Wolverine Mount
4580 ft 1396 m
Eagle Summit
Chatanika
Tanana River
Manley Hot Springs
YUKON-CHARLEY RIVERS NAT. PRES.
Ruby
College
Fairbanks
Hamilton Acres
Mount Eldridge
6250 ft 1905 m
Eagle
Eagle Village
North Pole
Kuskokwim Mountains
Nenana
Mount Harper
6542 ft 1994 m
Poorman
Kantishna River
Clear Site
Tanana River
Big Delta
Chicken
Delta Junction
North Fork
Minchumina Lake
Healy Fork
Usibelli
Mount Healy
Suntrana
Von Frank Mountain
4508 ft 1374 m
Telida
DENALI NAT. PARK AND PRES.
5715 ft 1742 m
McKinley Park
Mount Hayes
13832 ft 4216 m
Delta R.
Donnelly
Dot Lake
Cantwell
Tanacross
Kantishna
Broad Pass
Summit
Mount Kimball
10351 ft 3155 m
Tok
Northway Junction
Foraker
17402 ft 5304 m
Mt. McKinley
20322 ft 6194 m
Denali
Alaska Ra.
Hurricane
Chulitna
Susitna R.
Mentasta
Nabesna R.
Gold Creek
Lake Louise
Chistochina
Curry

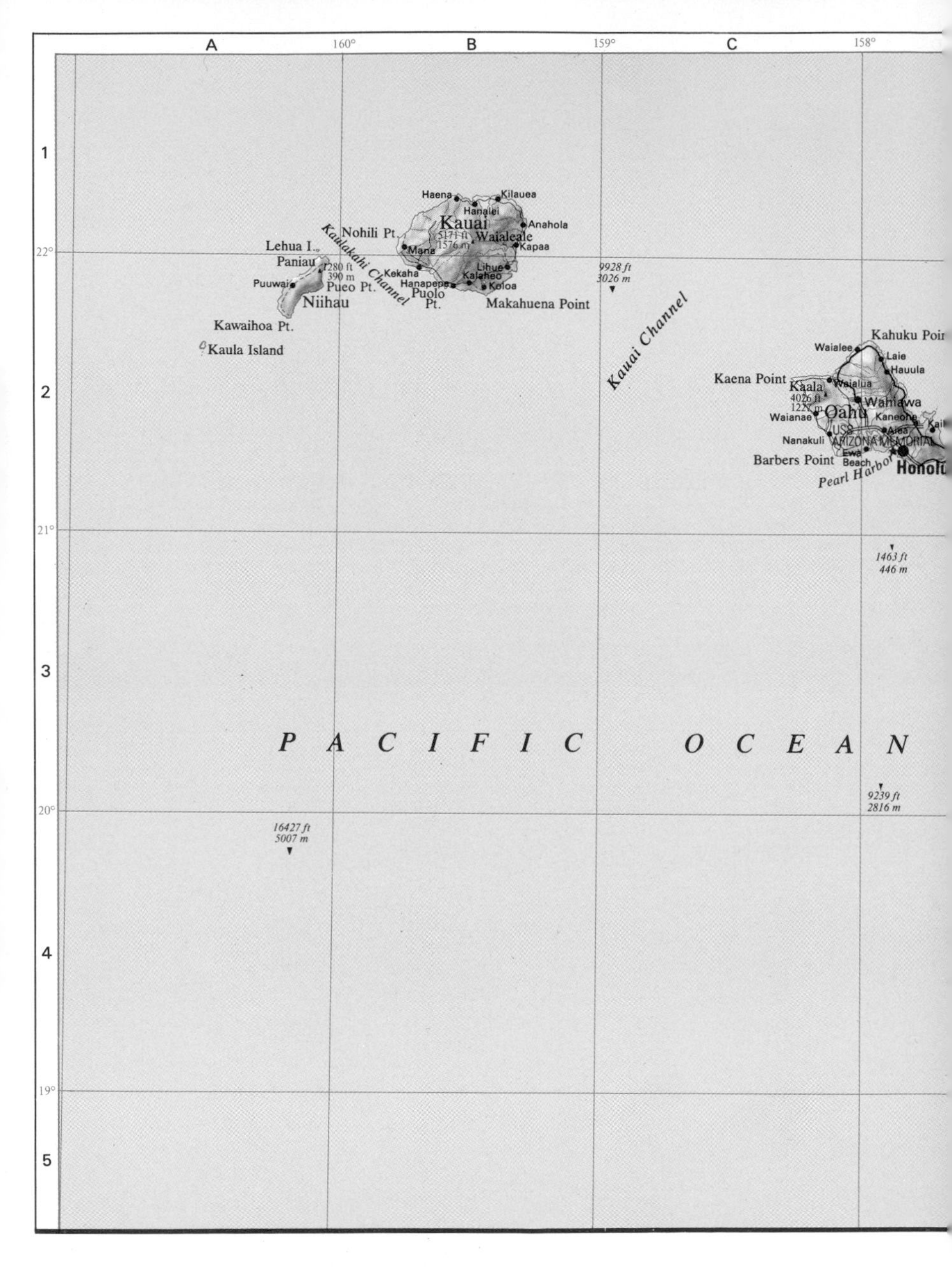

A
B
C
160°
159°
158°
1
2
3
4
5
22°
21°
20°
19°
Haena
Kilauea
Hanalei
Kauai
Anahola
Nohili Pt.
5171 ft
1576 m
Waialeale
Kapaa
Mana
Kaulakahi Channel
Lehua I.
Paniau
1280 ft
390 m
Puuwai
Pueo Pt.
Niihau
Kekaha
Hanapepe
Puolo Pt.
Lihue
Kalaheo
Koloa
Makahuena Point
9928 ft
3026 m
Kawaihoa Pt.
Kaula Island
Kauai Channel
Kahuku Point
Waialee
Laie
Hauula
Kaena Point
Kaala
4026 ft
Waialua
Wahiawa
Oahu
Waianae
Kaneohe
USS ARIZONA MEMORIAL
Aiea
Nanakuli
Ewa Beach
Barbers Point
Pearl Harbor
1463 ft
446 m
P A C I F I C O C E A N
9239 ft
2816 m
16427 ft
5007 m

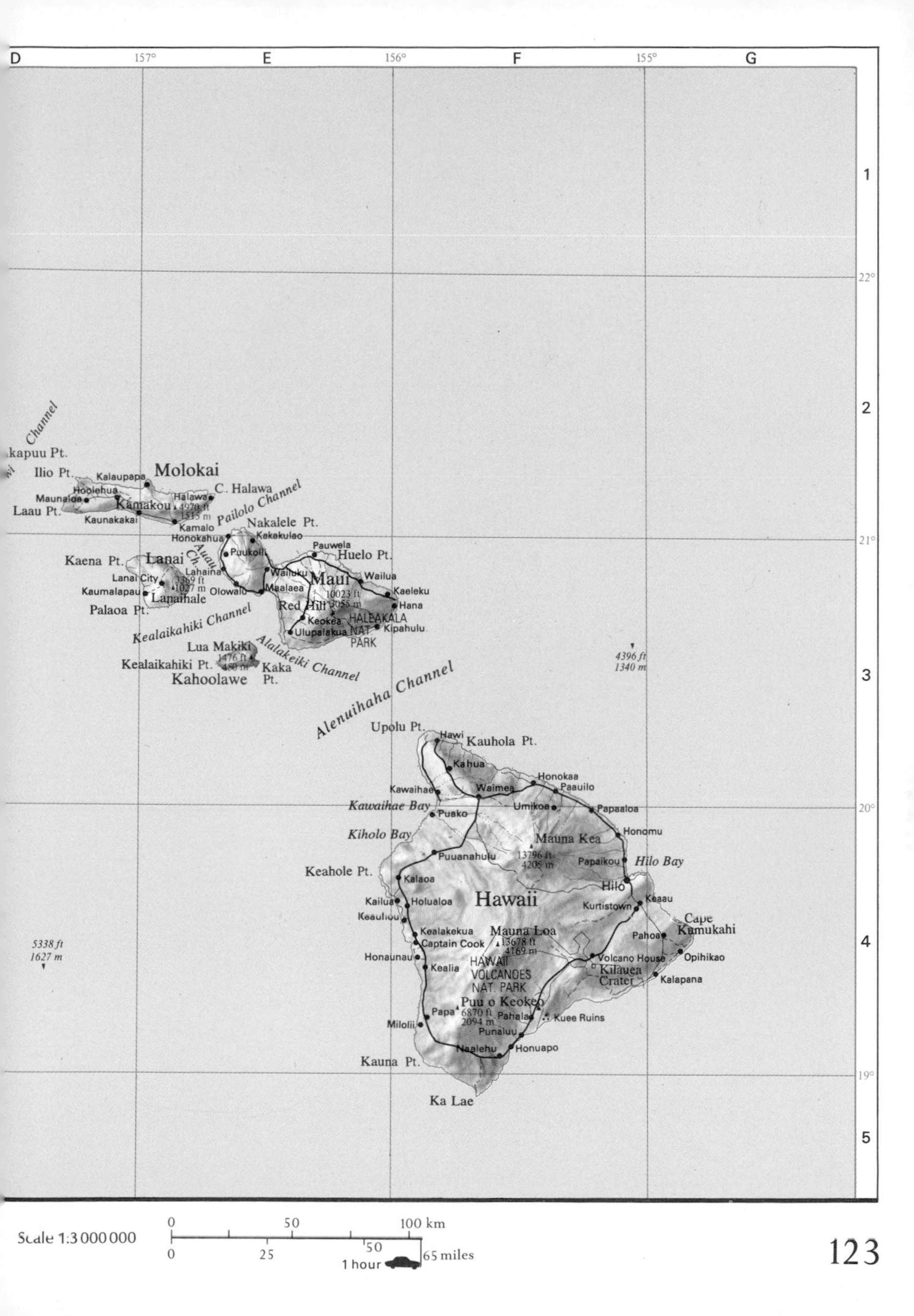

D   157°   E   156°   F   155°   G

1

22°

2

kapuu Pt.
Ilio Pt.
Hoolehua
Kalaupapa
Molokai
Maunaloa
Kaunakakai
Kamakou
1513 m
C. Halawa
Halawa
Laau Pt.
Kamalo
Honokahua
Nakalele Pt.
Kakakuleo
Pailolo Channel

Kaena Pt.
Lanai
Puukoli
Pauwela
Huelo Pt.
Lanai City
1026 ft
1027 m
Olowalu
Waihee
Wailuku
Maui
Wailua
Kaumalapau
Lahaina
Maalaea
Kaeleku
Lanaihale
Red Hill
10023 ft
3055 m
Keokea
Hana
Palaoa Pt.
Ulupalakua
HALEAKALA NAT. PARK
Kipahulu

Kealaikahiki Channel
Lua Makiki
1476 ft
450 m
Alalakeiki Channel
Kealaikahiki Pt.
Kaka
Pt.
Kahoolawe

4396 ft
1340 m

3

Alenuihaha Channel

Upolu Pt.
Hawi
Kauhola Pt.
Kahua
Honokaa
Paauilo
Kawaihae
Waimea
Umikoa
Papaaloa
Kawaihae Bay
Puako
Honomu
Kiholo Bay
Mauna Kea
Papaikou
Hilo Bay
Puuanahulu
13796 ft
4205 m
Papaloa
Keahole Pt.
Kalaoa
Hilo
Kailua
Holualoa
Hawaii
Kurtistown
Keaau
Keauhou
Kealakekua
Mauna Loa
Pahoa
**Cape
Kamukahi**
Captain Cook
13678 ft
4169 m
Volcano House
Opihikao
Honaunau
Kealia
**Kilauea
Crater**
Kalapana
**HAWAII
VOLCANOES
NAT PARK**
Puu o Keokeo
Milolii
Papa
6870 ft
2094 m
Pahala
Kuee Ruins
Punaluu
Naalehu
Honuapo
Kauna Pt.

4

5338 ft
1627 m

4

Ka Lae

19°

5

123

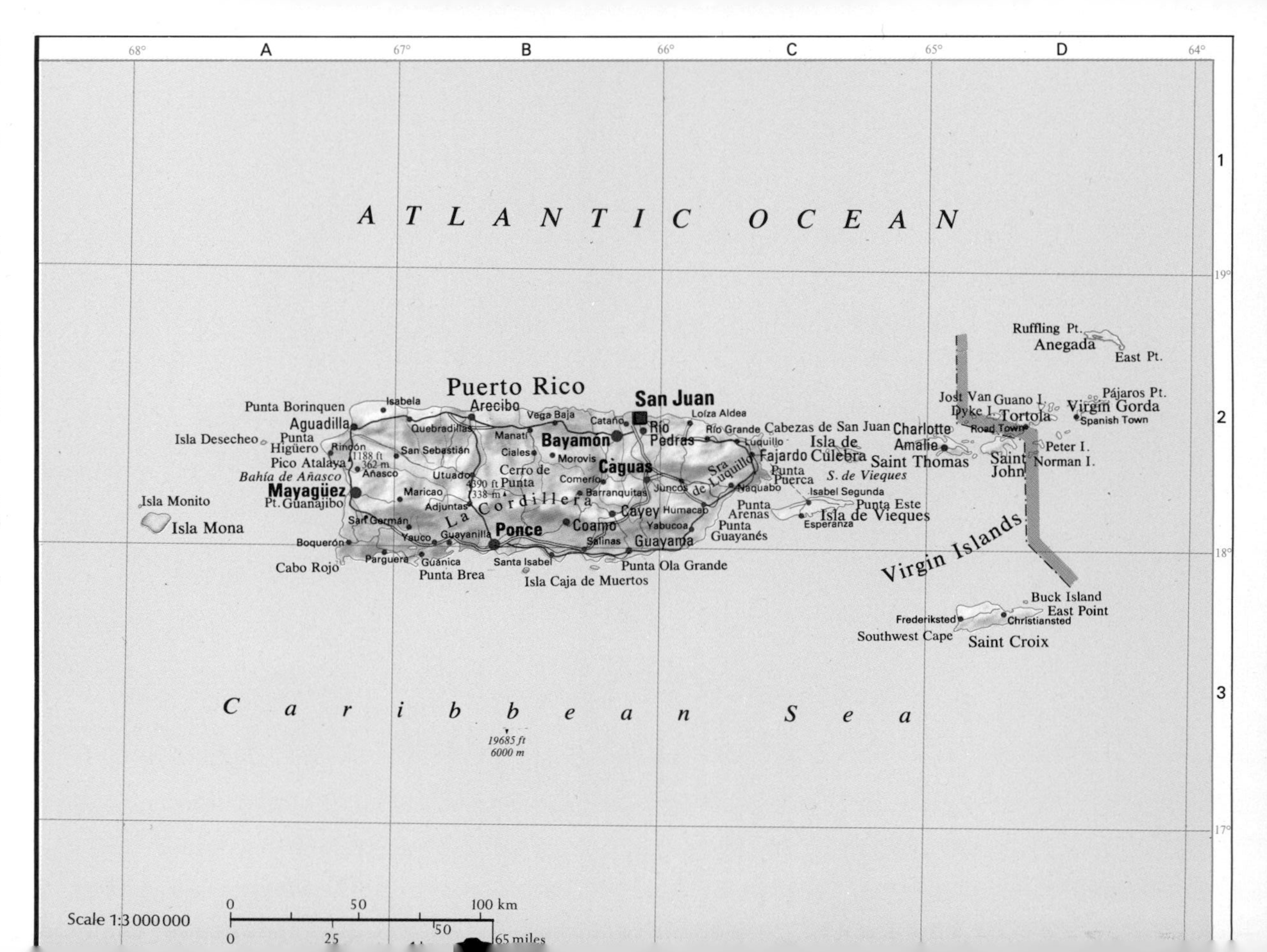

ATLANTIC OCEAN

Puerto Rico

San Juan

Ruffling Pt.
Anegada
East Pt.

Josh Van Guano I.
Virgin Gorda
Spanish Town
Jost Van Dyke I.
Peter I.
Tortola
Road Town
John Norman I.
Saint Thomas
Saint John
Charlotte Amalie

Virgin Islands

Buck Island
East Point
Christiansted
Saint Croix
Frederiksted
Southwest Cape

Caribbean Sea

Aguadilla
Isabela
Quebradillas
San Sebastián
Utuado
Adjuntas
Maricao
Sabana Grande
Yauco
Parguera
Guánica
Punta Brea

Arecibo
Manatí
Vega Baja
Cataño
Morovis
Ciales
Cerro de
Punta
1330 m
Comerío
Barranquitas
Aibonito
Santa Isabel

Bayamón
Caguas
Ponce
Coamo
Salinas
Guayama

Río Piedras
Lota Aldea
Río Grande
Luquillo
Cabezas de San Juan
Fajardo
Junco
Humacao
Yabucoa
Cayey
Punta Ola Grande
Isla Caja de Muertos

Isla de
Culebra
Punta
Puerca
Isabel Segunda
S. de Vieques
Isla de Vieques
Esperanza
Punta Este
Punta
Arenas
Guayanés

Cordillera
La

Punta Borinquen
Aguadilla
Punta
Higüero
Rincón
Pico Atalaya
1303 m
Bahía de Añasco
Añasco
Mayagüez
Pt. Guanajibo
San Germán
Boquerón
Cabo Rojo

Isla Desecheo

Isla Monito

Isla Mona

19685 ft
6000 m

Scale 1:3 000 000

0   25   50   65 miles

0   50   100 km

64°
65°
66°
67°
68°
18°
19°
17°

1
2
3
A
B
C
D

124   Puerto Rico, U.S. Virgin Islands

How to use the index

After each name in this Index there are some numbers and letters. The number in **bold** type immediately after the name tells you which page to look at in the atlas. The letter and number after the page number tell you which grid square to look at. For example, suppose you look up Broadwater in the Index. You will see Broadwater (NE.) **80** B 3. So to find Broadwater you need to turn to page 80 and look in square B 3.

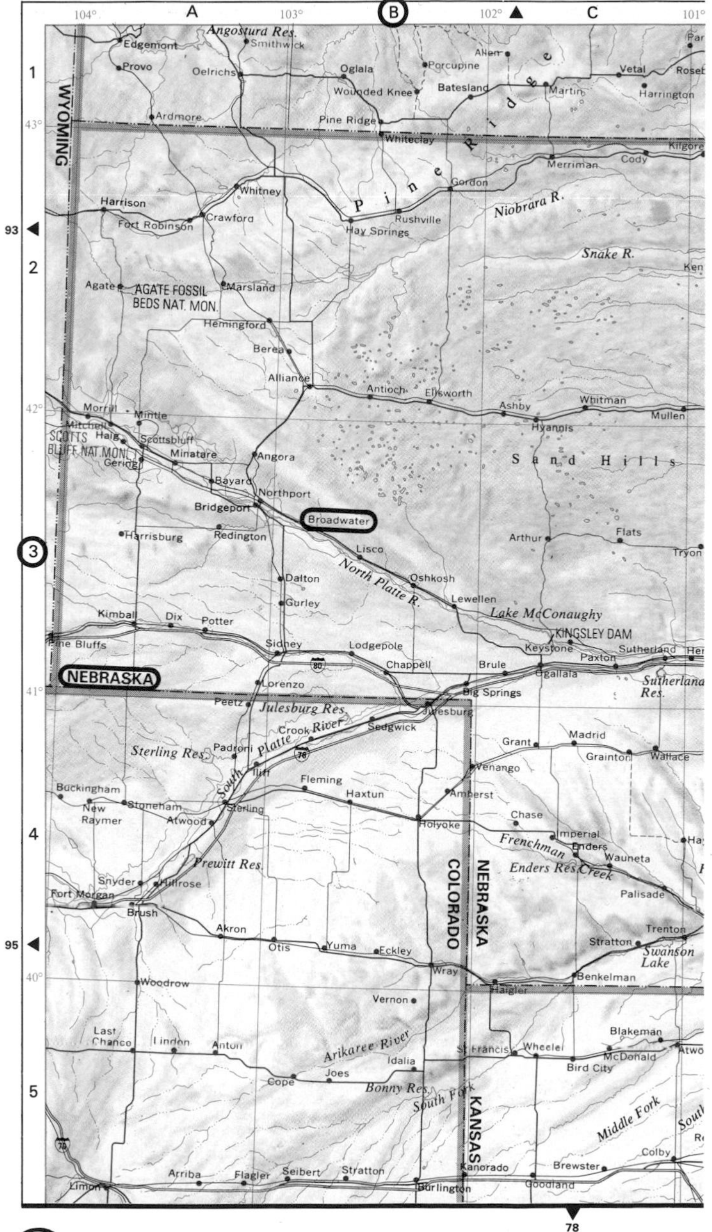

Brilliant (AL.) **46** B 5
Brillon (WI.) **59** E 1–2
Brinford (N.D.) **85** H 3
Brinkley (AR.) **67** E 3
Brinnon (WA.) **114** BC 2
Briscoe (TX.) **76** C 2
Bristol (CT.) **35** H 2
Bristol (FL.) **47** F 2
Bristol (S.D.) **83** H 2
Bristol (TN.) **51** H 4
Bristol (VA.) **36** B 5
Bristol Bay (AL.) **119** CD 2
Bristol Lake **107** G 3
Bristow (OK.) **77** G 2
British Columbia (AL.)
   117 E 2
British Mountains (AL.)
   121 GH 2
Britter Lake (S.D.) **83** H 2
Britton (S.D.) **83** H 2
Broad Pass **121** EF 3
Broad River **40** D 2
Broadalbin (N.Y.) **33** F 2
Broadview (MT.) **88** E 3
Broadview (N.M.) **97** G 4
Broadwater (NE.) **80** B 3
Broadway (VA.) **37** E 3
Broadys (MT.) **89** H 4
Brockton (MA.) **31** E 3
Brockton (MT.) **89** H 1
Brockville (Can.) **32** E 1
Brockway (MT.) **89** H 2
Brockway (PA.) **34** C 2
Brodhead (WI.) **59** G 3
Brogan (OR.) **113** H 2
Broken Arrow (OK.) **77** H 1
Broken Bow (NE.)
   80–81 E 3
Broken Bow (OK.) **77** J 3
Broken Bow Lake **77** J 3
Brønte (TX.) **73** H 2
Bronx (WY.) **92** B 3
Brookeland (TX.) **75** H 3
Brookfield (MO.) **64** D 2
Brookhaven (MS.) **49** E 4

Abajo Mountains **103** E 1
Abajo Peak **103** E 1
Abbeville (AL.) **47** E 3
Abbeville (GA.) **43** D 4
Abbeville (LA.) **68** C 4
Abbeville (MS.) **48** B 3
Abbeville (S.C.) **40** C 2
Abbot Butte **112** C 4
Abbotsford (WI.) **59** E 4
Abbott (N.M.) **97** F 2
Aberdeen (MD.) **37** H 2
Aberdeen (MS.) **48** C 2
Aberdeen (N.C.) **39** E 3
Aberdeen (S.D.) **83** G 2
Aberdeen (WA.) **114** B 2–3
Abernant (AL.) **46** C 5
Abernathy (TX.) **76** B 4
Abilene (KS.) **79** F 3
Abilene (TX.) **74** B 2
Abingdon (VA.) **36** B 5
Abiquiu (N.M.) **96** D 2
Abiquiu Reservoir **96** D 2
Absaroka Range **92** BC 1
Absarokee (MT.) **86** D 4
Acadia National Park
    29 D 3
Accomac (VA.) **37** J 4
Ackerman (MS.) **48** C 3
Ackley (IA.) **63** E 3
Acme (LA.) **68** D 2
Acme (N.M.) **99** F 3
Acme (WA.) **114** C 1
Acme (WY.) **93** F 1
Acoma (NV.) **109** H 2
Acoma Indian Reservation
    96 C 4
Acomita (N.M.) **96** C 3
Acton (MT.) **86** E 4
Ada (MN.) **60** C 6
Ada (OK.) **77** G 3
Ada (WI.) **59** F 1
Adair (IA.) **62** D 4
Adair (OK.) **77** H 1
Adairsville (GA.) **42** B 5
Adak (AL.) **117** J 1
Adal, Mount **117** DE 2
Adams (MA.) **30** C 3
Adams (N.D.) **85** HJ 2
Adams (N.Y.) **32** E 2
Adams (OK.) **76** B 1
Adams (TN.) **50** C 4
Adams (WI.) **59** F 3
Adams, Mount **114** D 3
Adams–McGill Reservoir
    105 F 4
Adamsville (TN.) **50** B 5
Adamsville (TX.) **74** C 3
Adamsville (UT.)
    103 D 4–5
Addis (LA.) **68** D 3
Addison (N.Y.) **32** C 3
Adel (GA.) **43** E 4
Adel (MT.) **86** B 2
Adel (OR.) **113** F 4
Adin (CA.) **110** A 2
Adirondack Mountains
    33 EF 1–2
Adjuntas (P.R.) **124** B 2
Admiralty (AL.) **117** E 2

Admiralty I. Nat. Mon. (AL.)
    117 E 2
Adobe Creek Reservoir
    95 G 3
Adrian (GA.) **43** D 3
Adrian (MI.) **55** G 2
Adrian (MN.) **61** G 5
Adrian (MO.) **64** C 3
Adrian (OR.) **113** H 3
Adrian (TX.) **97** H 3
Advance (MO.) **65** H 4
Ady (TX.) **97** H 3
Aeneas (WA.) **115** G 1
Aetna (KS.) **78** E 4
Afognak (AL.) **119** E 2
Afton (CA.) **107** F 2
Afton (IA.) **62** D 4
Afton (KS.) **77** H 1
Afton (N.M.) **98** C 4
Afton (NV.) **107** F 2
Agassiz Pool **60** B 6
Agate (CO.) **95** F 2
Agate (NE.) **80** A 2
Agate Fossil Beds National
    Monument **80** A 2
Agattu (AL.) **116** G 1
Agawa Bay (MI.) **54** A 3
Agawam (MT.) **86** AB 2
Agency Lake **112** CD 4
Agness (OR.) **112** AB 4
Agua Caliente Indian
    Reservation **107** F 4
Agua Fria Peak **96–97** E 2
Agua Fria River **100** D 2–3
Agua Nueva (TX.) **70** D 4
Agua Prieta (Mex.) **98** A 5
Aguadilla (P.R.) **124** A 2
Aguanga (CA.) **107** F 4
Aguila (AZ.) **100** C 3
Aguilar (CO.) **95** F 4
Ahoskie (N.C.) **39** H 2
Aiea (HI.) **122** D 2
Aiken (S.C.) **40** D 3
Ainsworth (NE.) **80** E 2
Aishihik **117** D 1
Aishihik Lake (AL.) **117** D 1
Aitkin (MN.) **60** D 3
Aix, Mount **114** D 3
Ajo (AZ.) **100** D 4
Ak-Chin Indian Reservation
    100 D 3
Akaska (SD.) **83** E 2
Akeley (MN.) **60** C 4
Akers (LA.) **69** E 3
Akhiok **119** E 2
Akiachak **118** C 1
Akiak **118** C 1
Akkani **120** A 2
Akron (AL.) **46** D 5
Akron (CO.) **95** G 1
Akron (IA.) **62** B 3
Akron (N.Y.) **32** B 2
Akron (OH.) **53** H 1
Akun I. (AL.) **118** B 3
Akutan I. (AL.) **118** B 3
Akutan Passage **118** B 3
Akutau **118** B 3
Alabama (North) **53** F 2
Alabama (South) **46–47**
Alabama River **47** E 5
Alabaster (AL.) **46** C 4
Alachua (FL.) **44** B 4
Alakanuk **120** BC 3
Alalakeiki Channel **123** E 3
Alama (NV.) **109** G 2
Alameda (N.M.) **96** D 3

Alamo (GA.) **43** D 3
Alamo (ND.) **84** C 2
Alamo (TN.) **50** A 5
Alamo Alto (TX.) **72** C 2
Alamo Heights (TX.) **70** D 1
Alamogordo (N.M.) **99** E 4
Alamosa (CO.) **94** E 4
Alanreed (TX.) **76** C 2
Alanson (MI.) **54** C 3
Alapaha (GA.) **43** E 4
Alaska (AL.) **121** EF 2
Alaska Peninsula (AL.)
    119 CD 2
Alaska Range (AL.)
    116 AB 1
Alatna River (AL.) **121** E 2
Alava, Cape **114** A 1
Alba (TX.) **75** F 2
Albany (GA.) **43** E 5
Albany (KY.) **51** E 4
Albany (MN.) **61** E 4
Albany (MO.) **64** C 1
Albany (N.Y.) **33** F 3
Albany (OH.) **53** G 3
Albany (OR.) **112** B 2
Albany (TX.) **74** B 2
Albany (WY.) **93** F 4
Albany (WY.) **93** F 4
Albemarle (N.C.) **38** D 3
Albemarle Sound **39** HJ 2
Alberene (VA.) **37** F 4
Albert (KS.) **78** E 3
Albert (TX.) **74** C 4
Albert City (IA.) **62** D 3
Albert Lea (MN.) **61** G 3
Alberta (AL.) **46** D 5
Alberta (VA.) **37** G 5
Albert,Lake (OR.) **112** E 4
Alberton (MT.) **89** F 2
Albertville (AL.) **46** B 4
Albia (AL.) **63** F 4
Albin (WY.) **93** HJ 4
Albion (CA.) **110** C 5
Albion (IA.) **63** E 3
Albion (ID.) **91** F 4
Albion (IL.) **57** E 3
Albion (IN.) **52** D 1
Albion (MI.) **55** F 3
Albion (MT.) **87** J 4
Albion (NE.) **81** G 3
Albion (N.Y.) **32** B 2
Albion (OK.) **77** H 3
Albion (PA.) **34** A 2
Alborn (MN.) **60** D 2
Albuquerque (N.M.) **96** D 3
Alcalde (N.M.) **96** DE 2
Alcester (S.D.) **83** J 4–5
Alcova (WY.) **93** F 3
Alden (MN.) **61** G 3
Alder (MT.) **86** A 4
Alder Lake **114** C 3
Alderdale (WA.) **115** EF 4
Aledo (IL.) **56** B 5
Alegros Mountain **96** B 4
Aleknagik (AL.) **119** D 2
Alenuihaha Channel
    123 EF 3
Aleutian Island (AL.)
    116–117 HJ 1
Aleutian Range (AL.)
    119 D 2
Alex (OK.) **77** F 3
Alexander (ND.) **84** C 3
Alexander Archipelago
    (AL.) **117** D 2
Alexander City (AL.) **46** D 3

Alexandria (IN.) **52** D 2
Alexandria (KY.) **51** F 2
Alexandria (LA.) **68** C 2
Alexandria (MN.) **61** E 5
Alexandria (S.D.) **83** GH 4
Alexandria (TN.) **50** D 4
Alexandria (VA.) **37** G 3
Alexandria Bay (N.Y.)
    32 E 1
Alexis (IL.) **56** B 5
Alfalfa (OR.) **112** DE 2
Alfred (ME.) **29** E 5
Alfred (ND.) **85** H 4
Alfred (TX.) **70** D 3
Algodones (N.M.) **96** D 3
Algoma (WI.) **59** E 1
Algona (IA.) **62** D 2
Algood (TN.) **51** E 4
Alibates Flint Quarries
    National Monument
    (TX.) **76** B 2
Alibates National
    Monument **76** B 2
Alice (TX.) **70** D 3
Aliceville (AL.) **46** C 6
Aliquippa (PA.) **34** A 3
Alire (N.M.) **96** D 2
Alitak Bay **119** E 2
Alkali Lake **113** E 4
Alkali Lakes **72** C 2
Alkaline Lake **85** G 4
Alkavista (VA.) **37** E 4
Allagash River **28** B 4
Allakaket (AL.) **121** E 2
Allamoore (TX.) **72** C 2
Allatoona Lake **42** B 5
Allegan (MI.) **55** F 4
Allegany (N.Y.) **32** B 3
Allegany Indian
    Reservation **32** B 3
Allegheny Mountains
    36–37 DE 3–4
Allegheny Plateau
    36 D 2–3
Allegheny Reservoir **34** C 2
Allegheny River **34** B 2
Allen (OK.) **77** G 3
Allen (SD.) **82** D 4
Allendale (IL.) **57** E 2
Allendale (S.C.) **40** D 3
Allende (Mex.) **70** B 2
Allensworth (CA.) **106** C 2
Allentown (PA.) **34** E 3
Alley (TX.) **76** B 4
Alliance (NE.) **80** AB 2
Alliance (OH.) **53** H 2
Allison (IA.) **63** F 3
Allison (N.M.) **96** B 3
Allouez (WI.) **59** E 1
Allyn (WA.) **114** C 2
Alma (AR.) **66** B 2
Alma (GA.) **43** E 3
Alma (KS.) **79** G 2
Alma (MI.) **55** E 3
Alma (NE.) **81** E 4
Alma (WI.) **59** E 5
Alma Center (WI.) **59** E 5
Almanor, Lake **110** B 3
Almena (KS.) **78** D 2
Almeria (NE.) **81** E 3
Almira (WA.) **115** G 2
Almond (AR.) **67** E 2
Almont (CO.) **94** D 3
Almont (MI.) **55** F 1
Almont (ND.) **84** E 4
Almy (WY.) **92** B 4

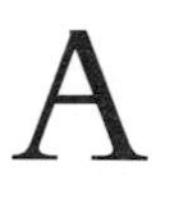

Alpaugh (CA.) **106** C 2
Alpena (MI.) **54** C 2
Alpha (IL.) **56** B 5
Alpha (MI.) **58** C 2
Alpine (AZ.) **101** G 3
Alpine (ID.) **92** B 2
Alpine (TX.) **72–73** E 3
Alps (N.M.) **97** G 2
Alsea (OR.) **112** B 2
Alsea Bay **112** A 2
Alsek R. (AL.) **117** D 2
Alsen (N.D.) **85** H 2
Alta (IA.) **62** C 3
Alta Vista (KS.) **79** G 3
Altair (TX.) **71** F 1
Altamaha River **43** E 3
Altamont (KS.) **79** H 4
Altamont (OR.) **112** D 4
Altamont (TN.) **50** E 5
Altamont (UT.) **102** B 2
Altamont (WY.) **92** B 4
Altaville (CA.) **111** D 2
Altheimer (AR.) **67** E 3
Alto (TX.) **75** F 3
Alton (IA.) **62** B 3
Alton (IL.) **57** E 5
Alton (KS.) **78** DE 2
Alton (MO.) **65** F 5
Alton (N.H.) **29** E 6
Alton (UT.) **103** E 4
Altoona (FL.) **44** C 3
Altoona (KS.) **79** H 4
Altoona (PA.) **34** C 3
Altoona (WA.) **114** B 3
Alturas (CA.) **110** A 2
Altus (OK.) **76** D 3
Altus, Lake **76** D 3
Alva (OK.) **76** E 1
Alva (WY.) **93** H 1
Alvarado (TX.) **74** D 2
Alvin (TX.) **71** G 1
Alvord (TX.) **74** D 1
Alvord Lake **113** G 4
Alvord Valley **113** G 4
Alzada (MT.) **87** J 4
Amado (AZ.) **101** E 5
Amagansett (N.Y.) **35** J 2–3
Amargosa Range **109** F 3
Amargosa River **107** F 1–2
Amarillo (TX.) **76** B 2
Amasa (MI.) **58** C 2
Amber (WA.) **115** H 2
Amberg (WI.) **59** D 2
Ambler **120** D 2
Amboy (CA.) **107** G 3
Amboy (IL.) **56** B 4
Amboy (MN.) **61** G 4
Ambridge (PA.) **34** A 3
Ambrose (ND.) **84** C 2
Amchitka (AL.) **116** H 1
Amchitka Pass (AL.)
 116 HJ 1
Amelia (NE.) **81** E 2
Amelia CH (VA.) **37** G 4
Amelia City (FL.) **44** A 3
Amelia Island **44** A 3
American Falls (ID.)
 91 FG 4
American Falls Reservoir
 91 G 4
American Fork (UT.)
 102 B 3
Americus (GA.) **43** D 5
Americus (KS.) **79** G 3
Ames (IA.) **63** E 3
Amherst (CO.) **95** H 1

Amherst (MA.) **30** D 3
Amherst (ME.) **28** D 3
Amherst (NE.) **81** E 4
Amherst (N.Y.) **32** B 2–3
Amherst (TX.) **97** H 4
Amherst (VA.) **37** EF 4
Amherst Junction (WI.)
 59 E 3
Amidon (ND.) **84** C 4
Amistad (N.M.) **97** G 3
Amistad Dam **73** GH 4
Amistad National
 Recreation Area **73** GH 4
Amistad Reservoir **73** GH 4
Amite (LA.) **69** E 3
Amite River **69** E 3
Amity (OR.) **112** B 1
Amlia (AL.) **117** K 1
Ammerman Mountain
 121 G 2
Ammon (ID.) **91** H 3
Amoret (MO.) **64** C 3
Amory (MS.) **48** C 2
Amsterdam (N.Y.) **33** F 3
Amukta Pass (AL.) **117** K 1
Amukta Pass (AL.) **118** A 3
Anacapa Island **106** C 3–4
Anacoco (LA.) **68** B 2
Anaconda (MT.) **86** A 3
Anaconda Range **89** G 4
Anadarko (OK.) **77** E 2
Anahola (HI.) **88** B 2
Anahuac (Mex.) **70** B 3
Anahuac (TX.) **75** G 5
Anaktuvuk Pass **121** E 2
Anaktuvuk River **121** E 2
Anamoose (ND.) **85** F 3
Anamosa (IA.) **63** G 3
Añasco (P.R.) **124** A 2
Añasco, Bahía de **124** A 2
Anatone (WA.) **115** H 3
Anceney (MT.) **86** B 4
Ancho (N.M.) **99** E 3
Anchorage (AL.) **116** A 1
Anclote Keys **44** C 5
Andale (KS.) **79** F 4
Andalusia (AL.) **47** E 4
Anderson (CA.) **110** B 4
Anderson (IN.) **52** D 2
Anderson (S.C.) **40** C 2
Anderson (TX.) **75** E 4
Anderson Ranch Reservoir
 90 D 3
Andes, Lake **83** G 4
Andover (N.Y.) **32** C 3
Andover (OH.) **53** J 1
Andover (S.D.) **83** H 2
Andrade (CA.) **107** G 5
Andreafsky River **120** C 3
Andreanof Islands (AL.)
 116–117 J 1
Andrews (S.C.) **41** F 3
Andrews (TX.) **73** F 1
Andrix (CO.) **95** G 4
Androscoggin River
 28 D 5–6
Anegada (AZ.) **100** DE 4
Anegam (AZ.) **100** DE 4
Aneta (N.D.) **85** J 3
Aneth (UT.) **103** E 1
Angela (MT.) **87** E 2
Angeles (TX.) **72** D 2
Angelina River **75** G 3
Angels Camp (CA.) **111** D 2
Angelus (KS.) **78** C 2
Angiola (CA.) **111** F 1

Angle (UT.) **103** D 3
Angle Inlet (MN.) **60** A 5
Angleton (TX.) **71** G 1
Angola (IN.) **52** E 1
Angora (NE.) **80** A 3
Angostura Reservoir
 82 B 4
Anguilla (MS.) **48** CD 4
Angwin (CA.) **111** D 4
Aniak River **119** D 1
Aniakchak Nat. Mon. and
 Pres. (AL.) **119** D 2
Animas (N.M.) **98** B 5
Animas Peak **98** B 5
Animas River **94** C 4
Animas Valley **98** B 4–5
Anita (AZ.) **103** G 4
Aniuk River **120** D 2
Aniwa (WI.) **59** D 3
Ankeny (IA.) **63** E 4
Anklum Mountains **119** C 2
Ann Arbor (MI.) **55** F 3
Anna (IL.) **57** F 4
Anna (TX.) **75** E 1
Anna, Lake **37** G 3
Annandale (MN.) **61** E 4
Annapolis (MD.) **37** H 3
Anniston (AL.) **46** C 3
Anoka (MN.) **61** E 3
Anoka (NE.) **81** F 2
Anselmo (NE.) **80** E 3
Ansley (LA.) **68** C 1
Ansley (NE.) **81** E 3
Anson (TX.) **74** B 2
Ansonville (N.C.) **38** D 3
Antelope (MT.) **87** J 1
Antelope (OR.) **112** E 2
Antelope Peak **105** G 1
Antelope Reservoir **113** H 4
Antero, Mount **94** D 3
Antero Reservoir **94** D 3
Anthon (IA.) **62** C 3
Anthony (KS.) **79** EF 4
Anthony (N.M.) **98** D 4
Antietam (MD.) **37** G 2
Antigo (WI.) **59** D 3
Antimony (UT.) **103** D 3
Antioch (CA.) **111** D 3
Antioch (NE.) **80** B 2
Antler (ND.) **84** E 2
Antlers (OK.) **77** H 3
Anton (CO.) **95** G 2
Anton (TX.) **99** H 3
Anton Chico (N.M.) **96** E 3
Antone (OR.) **113** F 2
Antonito (CO.) **94** E 4
Antwerp (N.Y.) **32** E 1
Anvik (AL.) **120** C 3
Apache (OK.) **77** E 3
Apache Junction (AZ.)
 100 E 3
Apache Lake **101** E 3
Apache Mountains **72** D 2
Apache Peak **101** F 5
Apalachee (GA.) **42** C 4
Apalachee Bay **47** G 2
Apalachicola (FL.)
 47 G 2
Apalachicola Bay **47** G 2–3
Apalachicola River **47** F 3
Apex Mountain **111** F 1
Apishapa River **95** F 4
Aplin (AR.) **66** C 2–3
Apopka (FL.) **44** C 3
Apopka, Lake **44** C 3
Apostle Islands **58** B 4

Apostle Islands National
 Lakeshore **58** C 4
Appalachia (VA.) **36** B 2
Apple Creek (OH.) **53** H 2
Apple Grove (VA.) **37** G 4
Appleton (MN.) **61** E 6
Appleton (WI.) **59** E 2
Appleton City (MO.) **64** C 3
Appling (GA.) **42** C 3
Appomattox (VA.) **37** F 4
Appomattox River **37** F 4
Aptos (CA.) **111** E 3
Aquarius Plateau **103** DE 3
Aquilares (TX.) **70** C 3
Aquilla (TX.) **74** D 3
Arab (AL.) **46** B 4
Arabia (NE.) **80** D 2
Arago, Cape **112** A 3
Aransas Pass (TX.) **71** E 3
Arapaho (OK.) **76** D 2
Arapahoe (CO.) **95** H 3
Arapahoe (N.C.) **39** H 3–4
Arapahoe (NE.) **80** E 4
Arbon (ID.) **91** G 4
Arbuckle (CA.) **110** C 4
Arbuckle, Lake **44–45** D 3
Arbuckle Mountains
 77 FG 3
Arbuckle National
 Recreation Area **77** G 3
Arc Dome **104** D 4
Arcade (CA.) **111** D 3
Arcade (N.Y.) **32** B 3
Arcadia (FL.) **45** D 3
Arcadia (KS.) **79** J 4
Arcadia (LA.) **68** C 1
Arcadia (MI.) **55** D 5
Arcadia (NE.) **81** E 3
Arcata (CA.) **110** B 6
Arcata Bay **110** B 6
Archer (FL.) **44** B 4
Archer City (TX.) **76** E 4
Arches National Park
 103 D 1
Archibald (LA.) **68** D 1
Arco (ID.) **91** F 3
Arcola (IL.) **56** D 3
Arcola (TX.) **71** G 1
Arctic Village (AL.)
 121 FG 2
Arden (CA.) **111** D 3
Arden (NV.) **109** G 3
Ardenvoir (WA.) **115** E 2
Ardmore (OK.) **77** F 3
Ardmore (SD.) **82** B 4
Ardmore (TN.) **50** D 5
Arecibo (P.R.) **124** B 2
Arena, Point **110** D 5
Arenas, Punta **124** C 2
Argonia (KS.) **79** F 4
Argos (IN.) **52** C 1
Arguello, Point **106** B 3
Argusville (N.D.) **85** J 3
Argyle (MN.) **60** B 6
Arikaree River **95** H 2
Arinosa (UT.) **102** B 5
Ariton (AL.) **47** E 3
Arkabutla Lake **48** B 3–4
Arkadelphia (AR.) **66** D 3
Arkansas **66–67**
Arkansas City (AR.) **67** E 4
Arkansas City (KS.) **79** G 4
Arkansas Post (AR.) **67** E 3
Arkansas River **67** E 3
Arlee (MT.) **89** F 2
Arlington (CO.) **95** G 3

Arlington (GA.) **43** E 5
Arlington (KS.) **79** E 4
Arlington (MN.) **61** F 4
Arlington (NE.) **81** H 3
Arlington (OR.) **113** E 1
Arlington (S.D.) **83** H 3
Arlington (TN.) **67** G 2
Arlington (TX.) **74** D 2
Arlington (VA.) **37** G 3
Arlington Hights (IL.)
   56 A 3
Armijo (N.M.) **96** D 3
Arminto (WY.) **93** E 2
Armour (S.D.) **83** G 4
Armstrong (MO.) **64** E 2
Armstrong (TX.) **71** E 4
Arnaudville (LA.)
   68 D 3
Arnett (OK.) **76** D 1
Arney (TX.) **97** H 4
Arno (TX.) **73** E 2
Arnold (MN.) **60** D 2
Arnold (NE.) **80** D 3
Arock (OR.) **113** H 4
Aropuk Lake **118** C 1
Aroya (CO.) **95** G 3
Arp (TX.) **75** F 2
Arrey (N.M.) **98** C 4
Arriba (CO.) **95** G 2
Arrow Creek (MT.) **86** C 2
Arrowhead, Lake **76** E 4
Arrowrock Reservoir
   90 D 3
Arroyo Grande (CA.)
   106 B 2
Arroyo Hondo (N.M.)
   96 E 2
Artesia (AZ.) **101** G 4
Artesia (MS.) **48** C 2
Artesia (N.M.) **99** F 4
Artesia Lake **104** B 4
Artesia Wells (TX.)
   70 C 2
Artesian (S.D.) **83** H 3
Arthur (N.D.) **85** J 3
Arthur (NE.) **80** C 3
Arthur (NV.) **105** F 2
Arthur (TN.) **51** G 4
Arthur City (TX.) **77** H 4
Artois (CA.) **110** C 4
Arvada (CO.) **95** E 2
Arvada (WY.) **93** F 1
Arvana (TX.) **73** G 1
Arvin (CA.) **106** D 2
Ascutney, Mount **30** D 2
Ash Flat (AR.) **67** E 1
Ash Fork (AZ.) **100** D 1
Ash Grove (KS.)
   78–79 E 2
Ash Grove (MO.) **64** D 4
Ashburn (GA.) **43** E 4
Ashbury Park (N.J.)
   35 H 3
Ashby (NE.) **80** C 2
Ashdown (AR.) **66** B 4
Asheboro (N.C.) **38** E 3
Asher (OK.) **77** G 2
Asherton (TX.) **70** C 2
Asherville (KS.)
   79 F 2
Asheville (N.C.)
   51 H 5
Ashford (WA.) **114** CD 3
Ashland (AL.) **46** C 3
Ashland (IL.) **56** D 4
Ashland (KS.) **78** D 4

Ashland (KY.) **51** H 2
Ashland (ME.) **28** B 3
Ashland (MO.) **65** E 3
Ashland (MS.) **48** B 3
Ashland (MT.) **87** G 4
Ashland (NE.) **81** H 3
Ashland (OH.) **53** G 2
Ashland (OK.) **77** G 3
Ashland (OR.) **112** C 4
Ashland (VA.) **37** G 4
Ashland (WI.) **58** C 4
Ashland City (TN.)
   50 C 4
Ashley (IL.) **57** E 5
Ashley (MI.) **55** E 3
Ashley (ND.) **85** G 4
Ashokan Res. **33** F 3–4
Ashtabula (OH.) **53** J 1
Ashtabula, Lake **85** J 3
Ashtola (TX.) **76** BC 2
Ashton (ID.) **91** H 2
Ashton (NE.) **81** F 3
Ashton (S.D.) **83** G 3
Ashville (AL.) **46** C 4
Ashwood (OR.) **112** E 2
Asotin (WA.) **115** HJ 3
Aspen (CO.) **94** D 2
Aspen (WY.) **92** B 4
Aspen Lake **112** C 4
Aspermont (TX.) **76** C 4
Assateague Island
   37 J 3
Assateague Island National
   Seashore **37** J 3
Astoria (IL.) **56** C 5
Astoria (OR.) **114** B 3
Atalaya, Pico **124** A 2
Atascadero (CA.) **106** B 2
Atchafalaya Bay **68** D 4
Atchison (KS.) **79** H 2
Athena (OR.) **113** G 1
Athens (AL.) **46** B 4
Athens (GA.) **42** C 4
Athens (OH.) **53** G 3
Athens (PA.) **34** E 2
Athens (TN.) **51** F 5
Athens (TX.) **75** EF 2
Athens (WI.) **59** D 4
Athol (ID.) **88** D 2
Athol (MA.) **30** D 3
Athol (S.D.) **83** G 3
Atikokan (Can.) **60** B 1
Atka (AL.) **117** K 1
Atkasuk (AL.) **121** D 1
Atkins (AR.) **66** D 2
Atkinson (GA.) **43** E 2
Atkinson (N.C.) **39** F 4
Atkinson (NE.) **81** E 2
Atlanta (GA.) **42** C 5
Atlanta (ID.) **90** D 3
Atlanta (MI.) **54** C 3
Atlanta (TX.) **75** G 1
Atlantic (IA.) **62** CD 4
Atlantic (N.C.) **39** H 4
Atlantic Beach (FL.)
   44 A 3
Atlantic City (N.J.)
   35 G 4
Atlantic City (WY.) **92** D 3
Atlantic Peak **92** D 3
Atlin (AL.) **117** E 2
Atlin Lake (AL.) **117** E 2
Atoka (OK.) **77** G 3
Atoka Reservoir **77** G 3
Atolia (CA.) **107** E 2
Atomic City (ID.) **91** G 3

Attalla (AL.) **46** B 4
Attica (KS.) **79** E 4
Attica (OH.) **53** G 1
Attleboro (MA.) **31** E 4
Attu (AL.) **116** G 1
Atwater (CA.) **111** E 2
Atwood (CO.) **95** G 1
Atwood (KS.) **78** BC 2
Atwood Lake **53** H 2
Au Gres (MI.) **55** D 2
Au Sable Forks (N.Y.)
   33 G 1
Au Sable Point **55** D 2
Auau Channel **123** E 3
Auburn (AL.) **46** D 3
Auburn (CA.) **110** D 3
Auburn (IL.) **57** D 4
Auburn (IN.) **52** D 1
Auburn (KY.) **50** D 4
Auburn (MA.) **30** E 3
Auburn (ME.) **29** D 5
Auburn (NE.) **81** J 4
Auburn (N.Y.) **32** D 3
Auburn (WA.) **114** C 2
Aucilla River **44** A 5
Audubon (IA.) **62** D 4
Augoon **117** E 2
Augusta (AR.) **67** E 2
Augusta (GA.) **42** C 3
Augusta (KS.) **79** F 4
Augusta (KY.) **51** F 2
Augusta (ME.) **29** D 4
Augusta (MT.) **86** A 2
Augusta (WI.) **59** E 5
Ault (CO.) **95** F 1
Aurora (CO.) **95** F 2
Aurora (IL.) **56** B 3
Aurora (IN.) **52** D 3
Aurora (KS.) **79** F 2
Aurora (KY.) **50** B 4
Aurora (MN.) **60** C 2
Aurora (MO.) **64** D 4–5
Aurora (N.C.) **39** H 3
Aurora (NE.) **81** F 4
Aurora (W.V.) **36** E 2
Austin (IN.) **52** D 4
Austin (KY.) **50** E 4
Austin (MN.) **61** G 2
Austin (PA.) **34** C 2
Austin (TX.) **74** D 4
Austintown (OH.) **53** J 1
Austinville (VA.) **36** D 5
Austonio (TX.) **75** F 3
Australia Mountain **117** D 1
Ava (MO.) **64** E 5
Avalon (CA.) **106** D 4
Avalon, Lake **99** F 4
Avant (OK.) **77** G 1
Avenal (CA.) **111** F 2
Avery (ID.) **88** E 2
Avery Island (LA.) **68** C 4
Avila Beach (CA.) **106** B 2
Avilla (MO.) **64** C 4
Avis (PA.) **34** D 2
Avoca (IA.) **62** C 4
Avon (MT.) **86** A 3
Avon (N.C.) **39** J 3
Avon (S.D.) **83** G 5
Avon Park (FL.) **45** D 3
Avondale (CO.) **95** F 3
Avondale (PA.) **35** F 4
Awuna River **121** D 2
Axial (CO.) **94** C 1
Axtell (NE.) **79** G 2
Axtell (NE.) **81** E 4
Aynor (S.C.) **41** F 2–3

Ayr (NE.) **81** F 4
Aziscohos Lake **28** C 5
Aztec (N.M.) **96** C 2
Aztec Peak **101** F 3
Aztec Ruins National
   Monument **96** C 2

B

B. A. Steinhagen Reservoir
   75 G 4
Babb (MT.) **89** G 1
Babbitt (NV.) **104** C 4
Baboquivari Peak **100** E 5
Backbone Mountain **36** E 2
Backbone Range **117** E 1
Backus (MN.) **60** D 4
Baconton (GA.) **43** E 5
Bad Axe (MI.) **55** E 1
Bad River **82** DE 3
Bad River Indian
   Reservation **58** C 4
Badger (CA.) **108** D 3
Badger (MN.) **60** B 6
Badger Peak **87** G 4
Badin (N.C.) **38** D 3
Badin Lake **38** D 3
Badlands **97** FG 3
Badlands **82** BC 4
Badlands National
   Monument **82** C 4
Badlands National Park
   (S.D.) **82** C 4
Baffin Bay (TX.) **71** E 3
Bagdad (AZ.) **100** C 2
Bagdad (CA.) **107** G 3
Baggs (WY.) **92** E 4
Bagley (MN.) **60** C 5
Bagnell (MO.) **64** E 3
Bagnell Dam **64** E 3
Bahia de Añasco **124** A 2
Bailey (CO.) **95** E 2
Baileys Harbor (WI.) **54** C 6
Bainbridge (GA.) **43** F 5
Bainbridge (OH.) **53** F 3
Bainville (MT.) **87** J 1
Baird (TX.) **74** B 2
Baird Inlet (AL.) **118** C 1
Baird Mountains (AL.)
   120 CD 2
Bairoil (WY.) **92** E 3
Baker (CA.) **107** F 2
Baker (FL.) **47** F 4
Baker (LA.) **68** D 3
Baker (MT.) **89** G 4
Baker (MT.) **87** J 3
Baker (OK.) **76** B 1
Baker (OR.) **113** H 2
Baker Butte **101** F 2
Baker, Mount **114** D 1
Bakersfield (CA.) **106** C 2
Bakersfield (TX.) **73** F 3
Bakersville (N.C.) **51** H 4
Balance Rock (CA.) **106** D 2
Balcones Escarpment
   70 BD 1
Bald Knob (AR.) **67** E 2
Bald Mountain **112** D 3

Bald Mountain **113** H 2
Bald Mountain **94** E 1
Bald Point **47** G 2
Baldridge (TX.) **73** F 2
Baldwin (FL.) **44** A 3
Baldwin (LA.) **68** D 4
Baldwin (MI.) **55** E 5
Baldwin (ND.) **84** F 3
Baldwin (WI.) **59** E 6
Baldwin City (KS.) **79** H 3
Baldwinsville (N.Y.) **32** D 2
Baldwyn (MS.) **48** B 2
Baldy Mountain **86** D 1
Baldy Peak **101** G 3
Ballantine (MT.) **87** E 4
Ballinger (TX.) **74** B 3
Ballston Spa (N.Y.) **33** G 2–3
Balltown (IA.) **63** H 3
Balmorhea (TX.) **72** E 3
Baltic (S.D.) **83** J 4
Baltimore (MD.) **37** H 2
Baltimore (OH.) **53** G 3
Bamberg (SC.) **40** D 3
Bancroft (ID.) **91** H 4
Bancroft (NE.) **81** H 2
Bandelier National Monument **96** D 3
Bandera (TX.) **70** C 1
Bandon (OR.) **112** A 3
Bangor (ME.) **28** D 3
Bangor (MI.) **55** F 5
Bangs (TX.) **74** B 3
Bangs, Mount **103** F 5
Banks (ID.) **90** C 2
Banks (ID.) **90** C 2
Banks Lake **115** F 2
Banks Lake **43** E 4
Bannack (MT.) **86** A 4
Banning (CA.) **107** F 4
Bannock Range **91** G 4
Bantry (ND.) **84** F 2
Bar Harbor (ME.) **28** D 3
Baraboo (WI.) **59** F 3
Baraga (MI.) **58** C 2
Baranof (AL.) **117** D 2
Barataria (LA.) **69** E 4
Barber (MT.) **86** D 3
Barbers Point **122** C 2
Barberton (OH.) **53** H 1–2
Barberville (FL.) **44** B 3
Barboursville (W.V.) **36** B 3
Barbourville (KY.) **51** G 4
Barco (N.C.) **39** J 2
Bardwell (KY.) **50** B 4
Bardwell Lake **75** E 2
Bare Mountain **114** C 4
Bark Point **58** C 5
Barker Heights (N.C.) **51** H 5
Barkhamsted Reservoir **35** HJ 2
Barkley, Lake **50** C 4
Barksdale (TX.) **70** C 1
Barlow Pass **112** D 1
Barnard (KS.) **78** EF 2
Barnegat (N.J.) **35** G 4
Barnesville (GA.) **42** C 5
Barnesville (MN.) **60** D 6
Barnesville (OH.) **53** H 3
Barnhart (TX.) **73** G 2
Barnsdall (OK.) **77** G 1
Barnwell (S.C.) **40** D 3
Barr Lake **95** F 2
Barranquitas (P.R.) **124** B 2
Barre (VT.) **30** D 1
Barren Island (AL.) **119** E 2
Barren River Lake **50** D 4
Barrie (Can.) **32** A 1
Barrow (AL.) **121** D 1
Barry (IL.) **56** D 5
Barryton (MI.) **55** E 4
Barstow (CA.) **107** E 3
Barstow (TX.) **73** E 2
Bartlesville (OK.) **77** G 1
Bartlett (CA.) **108** D 3
Bartlett (NE.) **81** F 3
Bartlett (TX.) **74** D 4
Bartow (FL.) **44** D 3
Bartow (GA.) **42** D 3
Basalt (CO.) **94** D 2
Basile (LA.) **68** C 3
Basin (MT.) **86** A 3
Basin (WY.) **92** D 1
Baskahegan Lake **28** C 2
Bass Lake (CA.) **111** E 1
Bassett (NE.) **81** E 2
Bassett (VA.) **36** E 5
Bassfield (MS.) **49** E 3
Basswood Lake **60** B 1
Bastrop (LA.) **68** D 1
Bastrop (TX.) **74** D 4
Batavia (N.Y.) **32** B 2
Batavia (OH.) **53** E 3
Batchawana Mountain (Can.) **54** A 3
Bates (OR.) **113** G 2
Batesburg (S.C.) **40** D 3
Batesland (SD.) **82** C 4
Batesville (AR.) **67** E 2
Batesville (MS.) **48** B 3
Batesville (TX.) **70** C 1
Bath (ME.) **29** E 4
Bath (N.Y.) **32** C 3
Bathgate (N.D.) **85** J 2
Baton Rouge (LA.) **68–69** D 3
Battle Creek (MI.) **55** F 4
Battle Creek (NE.) **81** G 3
Battle Ground (WA.) **114** C 4
Battle Lake (MN.) **61** D 5
Battle Mountain (NV.) **104** D 2
Battlement Mesa **94** BC 2
Battles Field (AL.) **121** E 2
Baudette (MN.) **60** B 4
Baxley (GA.) **43** E 3
Baxter (IA.) **63** E 4
Baxter (MN.) **60** D 4
Baxter Springs (KS.) **79** J 4
Bay (AR.) **67** F 2
Bay Center (WA.) **114** B 3
Bay City (MI.) **55** E 2
Bay City (OR.) **112** B 1
Bay City (TX.) **71** G 1
Bay Minette (AL.) **47** F 6
Bay Port (MI.) **55** E 2
Bay Saint Louis (MS.) **49** F 3
Bay Springs (MS.) **49** E 3
Bayamón (P.R.) **124** B 2
Bayard (IA.) **62** D 4
Bayard (NE.) **80** A 3
Bayboro (N.C.) **39** H 3
Bayfield (CO.) **94** C 4
Bayfield (WI.) **58** C 4
Bayou D'Arbonne Lake **68** C 1
Bayou La Batre (AL.) **47** F 6
Bayport (FL.) **44** C 4
Baytown (TX.) **71** G 1
Bayview (ID.) **88** D 2
Bazine (KS.) **78** D 3
Beach (ND.) **84** C 4
Beacon (N.Y.) **33** G 4
Beafort (NC.) **39** H 4
Beagle (KS.) **79** J 3
Bear Lake **91** H 4–5
Bear Lodge Mountains **93** GH 1
Bear Mountain **98** B 3
Bear Peak **92** C 2
Bear River **91** H 4
Bearden (AR.) **66** D 4
Beardstown (IL.) **56** C 5
Bearpaw Mountains **86** D 1
Bears Ears **103** E 1
Beartooth Mountains **86** CD 4
Beartooth Pass **92** C 1
Bearwallow Mountain **98** B 3
Beatrice (AL.) **47** E 5
Beatrice (NE.) **81** H 4
Beattie (NE.) **79** G 2
Beatty (NV.) **109** F 3
Beatty (OR.) **112** D 4
Beattyville (KY.) **51** G 3
Beaufort (S.C.) **41** E 4
Beaufort Sea (AL.) **121** GH 1
Beaulieu (MN.) **60** C 5
Beaumont (KS.) **79** G 4
Beaumont (MS.) **49** E 2
Beaumont (TX.) **75** G 4
Beaupré (Can.) **28** A 6
Beaver (AL.) **121** F 2
Beaver (KS.) **78** E 3
Beaver (OK.) **76** C 1
Beaver (PA.) **34** A 3
Beaver (UT.) **103** D 4
Beaver City (NE.) **80** E 4
Beaver Creek **80** DE 4
Beaver Dam (WI.) **59** F 2
Beaver Falls (PA.) **34** A 3
Beaver Island **54** C 4
Beaver Lake (AR.) **66** BC 1
Beaver Mountains **119** D 1
Beaverdam Lake **59** F 2
Beaverhead Mountains **89** G 4
Beaverton (MI.) **55** E 3
Beaverton (OR.) **112** C 1
Becharof Nat. Mon. (AL.) **119** D 2
Bechevin Bay (AL.) **118** C 2
Becker (MN.) **61** E 3
Beckley (W.V.) **36** C 4
Beckwourth Pass **110** C 2
Becky Peak **105** G 3
Bedford (IA.) **62** D 5
Bedford (IN.) **52** C 4
Bedford (KY.) **51** E 2
Bedford (OH.) **53** H 1
Bedford (PA.) **34** C 3–4
Bedford (VA.) **36** E 4
Bedford (WY.) **92** B 3
Bedias (TX.) **75** E 4
Bedrock (CO.) **94** B 3
Bee Ridge (FL.) **45** D 4
Bee Spr (KY.) **50** D 3
Beebe (AR.) **67** E 2
Beech Grove (IN.) **52** C 3
Beecher (MI.) **55** E 2
Beecher Falls (N.H.) **28** D 6
Beeler (KS.) **78** C 3
Beemer (NE.) **81** H 3
Beeville (TX.) **71** E 2
Beggs (OK.) **77** G 2
Bel Air (MD.) **37** H 2
Belden (ND.) **84** C 2
Belding (MI.) **55** E 4
Belding (TX.) **73** EF 3
Belen (N.M.) **96** D 4
Belfield (ND.) **84** C 4
Belfry (MT.) **86** E 4
Belgrade (MN.) **61** E 4
Belgrade (MT.) **86** B 4
Belgrade (NE.) **81** FG 3
Belhaven (N.C.) **39** H 3
Beliot (WI.) **59** G 2
Belknap (MT.) **88** E 2
Belkofski **118** C 2
Bell (FL.) **44** B 4
Bell (N.M.) **97** F 2
Bell City (LA.) **68** B 3
Bell Ranch (N.M.) **97** F 3
Bella Vista (CA.) **110** B 4
Bellaire (MI.) **54** D 4
Bellaire (OH.) **53** J 2
Bellaire (TX.) **71** G 1
Bellamy (AL.) **46** D 6
Bellamy (VA.) **37** H 4
Belle (MO.) **65** F 3
Belle Fourche (SD.) **82** B 3
Belle Fourche Reservoir **82** B 3
Belle Fourche River **82** BC 3
Belle Glade (FL.) **45** E 2
Belle Isle (FL.) **44** C 3
Belle Plain (KS.) **79** F 4
Belle Plaine (IA.) **63** F 4
Belle Plaine (MN.) **61** F 3
Bellefontaine (MS.) **48** C 3
Bellefontaine (OH.) **53** E 2
Bellefonte (PA.) **34** D 3
Belleview (FL.) **44** B 4
Belleville (Can.) **32** C 1
Belleville (IL.) **57** E 5
Belleville (KS.) **79** F 2
Bellevue (IA.) **63** H 3
Bellevue (ID.) **91** E 3
Bellevue (MI.) **55** F 4
Bellevue (OH.) **53** G 1
Bellevue (TX.) **74** C 1
Bellevue (WA.) **114** C 2
Bellingham (WA.) **114** C 1
Bellmead (TX.) **74** D 3
Bellows Falls (VT.) **30** D 2
Bells (TN.) **50** A 5
Bells (TX.) **75** E 1
Bellville (OH.) **53** G 2
Bellville (TX.) **75** E 5
Bellvue (CO.) **95** E 1
Bellwood (NE.) **81** G 3
Belmar (N.J.) **35** H 3
Belmond (IA.) **63** E 3
Belmont (MS.) **48** B 2
Belmont (MT.) **86** E 3
Belmont (N.Y.) **32** C 3
Belmont (WI.) **59** G 4
Beloit (KS.) **78** E 2
Belt (MT.) **86** C 2
Belted Range **109** F 2
Belton (MO.) **64** C 3
Belton (S.C.) **40** C 2
Belton (TX.) **74** D 3
Belton Reservoir **74** D 3
Belvidere (IL.) **56** A 3
Belzoni (MS.) **48** C 4
Bemidji (MN.) **60** C 4
Bemis (TN.) **50** B 5

Bemis (W.V.) **36** E 3
Ben Bolt (TX.) **70** D 3
Ben Lomond (CA.) **111** E 4
Benavides (TX.) **70** D 3
Benbrook Lake **74** D 2
Bend (OR.) **112** D 2
Bendavis (MO.) **65** E 4
Bendeleben, Mount **120** C 2
Benedict (MN.) **60** C 4
Benjamin (TX.) **76** D 4
Benkelman (NE.) **80** C 4
Benkelman (NE.) **80** C 4
Benndale (MS.) **49** F 2
Bennett (CO.) **95** F 2
Bennett (N.M.) **99** G 4
Bennettsville (S.C.) **41** F 2
Bennington (ID.) **91** H 4
Bennington (KS.) **79** F 2
Bennington (TX.) **77** G 4
Benson (AZ.) **101** F 5
Benson (MN.) **61** E 5
Benson (N.C.) **39** F 3
Benton (AR.) **66** D 3
Benton (CA.) **108** D 2
Benton (IL.) **57** F 3
Benton (KY.) **50** B 4
Benton (LA.) **68** B 1
Benton (MS.) **48** D 4
Benton (TN.) **51** F 5
Benton (WI.) **59** G 4
Benton City (WA.) **115** F 3
Benton Harbor (MI.) **55** F 5
Benton Lake **86** B 2
Bentonia (MS.) **48** D 4
Bentonite Spur (WY.) **93** H 1
Bentonville (AR.) **66** B 1
Beowawe (NV.) **105** E 2
Berclair (TX.) **71** E 2
Berea (KY.) **51** F 3
Berea (NE.) **80** A 2
Berea (TX.) **75** G 2
Berenda (CA.) **111** E 2
Beresford (S.D.) **83** J 4
Bergen (N.Y.) **32** B 2
Bergland (MI.) **58** C 3
Bering Glacier (AL.) **116** C 1
Bering Land Bridge Nat. Pres. (AL.) **120** C 2
Bering Sea (AL.) **116** HJ 1
Berino (N.M.) **98** D 4
Berkeley (CA.) **111** E 4
Berkshire Hills **30** CD 3
Berlin (N.H.) **28** D 6
Berlin (WI.) **59** F 3
Berlin Lake **53** H 1
Bernalillo (N.M.) **96** D 3
Bernardo (N.M.) **96** CD 4
Berne (IN.) **52** E 2
Bernice (LA.) **68** C 1
Bernstein (TX.) **76** B 1
Berry (AZ.) **100** C 1
Berrydale (FL.) **47** F 5
Berryessa, Lake **111** D 4
Berthold (ND.) **84** E 2
Berthoud (CO.) **95** E 1
Berthoud Pass **94** E 2
Bertram (IA.) **63** G 4
Bertram (TX.) **74** D 4
Bertrand (NE.) **81** E 4
Berwick (LA.) **68** D 4
Berwick (ME.) **29** E 5
Berwick (PA.) **34** E 2
Beryl (UT.) **103** E 5

Bessemer (AL.) **46** C 5
Bethany (MO.) **64** C 1
Bethany (OK.) **77** F 2
Bethel **119** C 1
Bethel (ME.) **28** D 5
Bethel (N.C.) **39** G 3
Bethel (VT.) **30** D 2
Bethlehem (PA.) **35** F 3
Bettendorf (IA.) **63** H 4
Betteravia (CA.) **106** B 3
Beulah (CO.) **95** F 3
Beulah (MI.) **55** D 5
Beulah (ND.) **84** E 2
Beulah (OR.) **113** G 3
Beulah (WY.) **93** H 1
Beulah Reservoir **113** G 3
Beverly (KS.) **79** F 2
Beverly (WA.) **115** F 3
Beverly Hills (CA.) **106** D 3
Beving Strait (AL.) **120** B 2
Bexar (AL.) **46** B 6
Bexar (AR.) **66** DE 1
Bicknell (UT.) **103** D 3
Biddeford (ME.) **29** E 5
Biddle (MT.) **87** H 4
Bieber (CA.) **110** A 3
Big Baldy **90** D 2
Big Bar (CA.) **110** B 5
Big Bay (MI.) **54** B 6
Big Bay De Noc **54** C 5
Big Bear City (CA.) **107** E 4
Big Bear Lake **107** F 3
Big Belt Mountains **86** B 3
Big Bend Dam **83** F 3–4
Big Bend National Park **73** E 4
Big Black River **48** D 4
Big Blue River **81** H 4
Big Cabin (KS.) **77** H 1
Big Clifty (KY.) **50** D 3
Big Creek (ID.) **88** E 4
Big Creek Lake **47** F 6
Big Creek Peak **91** F 2
Big Cypress Indian Reservation **45** E 2–3
Big Cypress Swamp **45** E 3
Big Delta (AL.) **121** F 3
Big Eau Pleine Reservoir **59** E 3–4
Big Falls (MN.) **60** B 3
Big Flat (AR.) **66** D 1
Big Hatchet Peak **98** B 5
Big Horn (WY.) **93** E 1
Big Island (VA.) **36–37** E 4
Big Lake **28** C 2
Big Lake (CA.) **110** A 3
Big Lake (MN.) **61** E 3
Big Lake (MT.) **86** C 2
Big Lake (TX.) **73** G 2
Big Lookout Mountain **113** H 2
Big Pine (CA.) **108** D 2
Big Pine (FL.) **45** G 3
Big Pine Mountain **106** C 3
Big Piney (WY.) **92** B 3
Big Point (MS.) **49** F 2
Big Rapids (MI.) **55** E 4
Big Sable Point **55** D 5
Big Sage Reservoir **110** A 2
Big Salmon Range (AL.) **117** E 1
Big Sandy (MT.) **86** C 1
Big Sandy (TN.) **50** B 4
Big Sandy (TX.) **75** F 2
Big Sandy (WY.) **92** C 3
Big Sandy Creek **95** G 2–3

Big Sandy Lake **60** D 3
Big Sandy Reservoir **92** C 3
Big Sheep Mountains **87** H 2–3
Big Sioux River **83** J 3
Big Smoky Valley **104** DE 4
Big Snowy Mountains **86** D 3
Big Southern Butte **91** F 3
Big Spring (TX.) **73** G 1
Big Springs (NE.) **80** B 3
Big Stone City (S.D.) **83** J 2
Big Stone Gap (VA.) **36** B 2
Big Stone Lake **61** E 6
Big Sur (CA.) **111** F 3
Big Thicket National Preserve (TX.) **75** G 4
Big Timber (MT.) **86** D 4
Big Trails (WY.) **93** E 2
Big Wells (TX.) **70** C 2
Bigfork (MN.) **60** C 3
Bigfork (MT.) **89** FG 1
Biggers (AR.) **67** F 1
Biggs (CA.) **110** C 3
Bighorn (MT.) **87** F 3
Bighorn Basin **92** D 1–2
Bighorn Canyon National Recreation Area **87** EF 4
Bighorn Mountains **93** EF 1–2
Bighorn River **87** F 4
Bijou Hills (SD.) **83** F 4
Bill (WY.) **93** G 2
Bill Williams Mountain **100** D 1
Bill Williams River **100** BC 2
Billings (MT.) **86–87** E 4
Billings (OK.) **77** F 1
Billy Chinook, Lake **112** D 2
Billy Clapp Lake **115** F 2
Biloxi (MS.) **49** F 2
Binger (OK.) **77** E 2
Bingham (ME.) **28** C 4
Bingham (N.M.) **98** D 3
Binghamton (N.Y.) **32** E 3
Biola (CA.) **111** F 1
Biorka Island **118** B 3
Birch Creek **121** F 2
Birch Creek (AL.) **121** F 2
Birch Run (MI.) **55** E 2
Birchwood (WI.) **58** D 5
Bird City (KS.) **78** B 2
Birmingham (AL.) **46** C 5
Birmingham (MI.) **55** F 2
Bisbee (ND.) **85** G 2
Biscayne Bay **45** F 2
Biscayne National Monument **45** F 2
Biscayne National Park (FL.) **45** E 6
Bishop (CA.) **108** D 2
Bishop (TX.) **71** E 3
Bishop Creek Reservoir **105** G 1
Bishopville (S.C.) **41** E 2
Bismarck (AR.) **66** C 3
Bismarck (MO.) **65** G 4
Bismarck (N.D.) **84** F 4
Bison (OK.) **77** F 1
Bison (SD.) **82** C 2
Bison Peak **94–95** E 2
Bistineau, Lake **68** B 1
Bitely (MI.) **55** E 4
Bitlabito (N.M.) **96** B 2
Bitter Creek (WY.) **92** D 4

Bitter Lake (N.M.) **99** F 3
Bitterroot Range **88–89** EG 2–4
Bitterroot River **89** F 3
Bixby (MO.) **65** F 4
Black (MO.) **65** F 4
Black Butte **91** H 2
Black Butte **103** E 4
Black Butte Lake **110** C 4
Black Canyon of the Gunnison National Monument **94** C 3
Black Diamond (WA.) **114** D 2
Black Eagle (MT.) **86** B 2
Black Gap (AZ.) **100** D 4
Black Hills **H 1–2**
Black Lake (MI.) **54** C 3
Black Lake (N.Y.) **32–33** E 1
Black Mesa **103** F 2
Black Mesa **97** G 2
Black Mountain **106** B 2
Black Mountain **86** A 3
Black Mountain **93** E 1
Black Mountain **101** F 4
Black Mountain **70** B 1
Black Mountain **51** H 4
Black Mountains **100** B 1
Black Peak **100** B 2
Black Pine Peak **91** F 4
Black Point **111** D 5
Black Point **98** B 5
Black Range **98** C 3
Black River **101** G 3
Black River **33** E 2
Black River **41** F 3
Black River (AK.) **121** G 2
Black Rock (AR.) **67** E 1
Black Rock (N.M.) **96** B 3
Black Rock (UT.) **103** D 4
Black Rock Desert **104** BC 1–2
Black Warrior River **46** C 5
Blackbeard Island **43** E 2
Blackfeet Indian Reservation **86** A 1
Blackfoot (MT.) **86** A 1
Blackfoot Reservoir **91** H 4
Blackfoot River **89** G 3
Blackford (ID.) **91** G 3
Blackhall Mountain **93** F 4
Blackhawk (SD.) **82** B 3
Blackman (FL.) **47** F 4
Blackmore, Mount **86** BC 4
Blacks Fork **92** B 4
Blacksburg (VA.) **36** D 4
Blackshear (GA.) **43** E 3
Blackshear, Lake **43** E 5
Blackstone (VA.) **37** F 4
Blackville (S.C.) **40** D 3
Blackwell (OK.) **77** F 1
Blackwell (TX.) **34** D 2
Blackwell (TX.) **73** H 1
Blackwood (N.J.) **35** F 4
Blaine (MN.) **61** E 3
Blair (NE.) **81** H 3
Blair (OK.) **76** D 3
Blair (WI.) **59** E 5
Blairsden (CA.) **110** C 2
Blairsville (GA.) **42** B 5
Blairsville (PA.) **34** B 3
Blake Point **58** A 2
Blakely (GA.) **43** E 5
Blakely (W.V.) **36** C 3
Blakeman (KS.) **78** B 2
Blalock (OR.) **112** E 1

Blanca (CO.) **94** E 4
Blanca Peak **94–95** E 4
Blanchard (OK.) **77** F 2
Blanco (TX.) **74** C 4
Blanco, Cape **112** A 4
Bland (VA.) **36** C 4
Blaney Park (MI.) **54** B 5
Blanket (TX.) **74** C 3
Bledsoe (TX.) **99** G 3
Bleecker (AL.) **46** D 3
Blessing (TX.) **71** F 2
Blewett (TX.) **70** C 1
Blewett Falls Lake **38** E 3
Blind River (Can.) **54** B 1
Bliss (ID.) **90** E 4
Bliss (NV.) **104** D 1
Blissfield (MI.) **55** G 2
Blitchton (GA.) **43** D 2
Block Island **30** E 4
Block Island (N.Y.) **31** E 4
Block Island Sound **35** JK 2
Blocksburg (CA.) **110** B 5
Bloom (KS.) **95** D 4
Bloomer (WI.) **59** D 5
Bloomfield (IA.) **63** F 5
Bloomfield (IN.) **52** C 3
Bloomfield (KY.) **51** E 3
Bloomfield (MO.) **65** G 5
Bloomfield (N.M.) **96** C 2
Blooming Grove (TX.) **75** E 2
Blooming Prairie (MN.) **61** G 2–3
Bloomington (IL.) **56** C 4
Bloomington (IN.) **52** C 3
Bloomington (MN.) **61** F 3
Bloomington (TX.) **71** F 2
Bloomington (WI.) **59** G 4
Bloomsburg (PA.) **34** E 2
Blossburg (MT.) **86** A 3
Blossburg (PA.) **34** D 2
Blountstown (FL.) **47** F 3
Blountville (TN.) **51** H 4
Blowing Rock (N.C.) **38** C 2
Blue Cypress Lake **45** D 2
Blue Diamond (NV.) **109** G 3
Blue Earth (MN.) **61** G 4
Blue Hill (ME.) **28** D 3
Blue Hill (NE.) **81** F 4
Blue Hills Upland **78** CD 3
Blue Lake (CA.) **110** B 6
Blue Mesa Reservoir **94** C 3
Blue Mound (IL.) **56** D 4
Blue Mountain (MT.) **87** J 2
Blue Mountain (PA.) **34–35** E 3
Blue Mountain Lake **66** C 2
Blue Mountain Pass **113** H 4
Blue Mountains (OR.) **113** G 1–2
Blue Rapids (NE.) **79** G 2
Blue Ridge **38** CD 2
Blue Ridge (GA.) **42** B 5
Blue Ridge (VA.) **36** D 4
Blue River (OR.) **112** C 2
Bluefield (W.V.) **36** C 4
Bluejoint Lake **113** F 4
Bluestone Lake **36** D 4
Bluewater (N.M.) **96** C 3
Bluewater Lake **96** B 3
Bluff City (TN.) **51** H 4
Bluff Dale (TX.) **74** D 2
Bluff Park (AL.) **46** C 4
Bluffs (IL.) **56** D 5

Bluffton (IN.) **52** D 2
Blumenthal (TX.) **74** C 4
Blunt (SD.) **83** F 3
Bly (OR.) **112** D 4
Blying Sound **116** B 2
Blying Sound (AL.) **116** B 2
Blythe (CA.) **107** H 4
Blytheville (AR.) **67** G 2
Board Camp Mountain **110** B 5
Boardman (OH.) **53** J 1
Boardman (OR.) **113** F 1
Boaz (AL.) **46** B 4
Boaz (N.M.) **99** F 3
Boca Grande (FL.) **45** E 4
Boca Raton (FL.) **45** E 2
Bodega Bay (CA.) **111** D 5
Boerne (TX.) **70** D 1
Bogalusa (LA.) **69** E 3
Bogata (TX.) **75** F 1
Bogue (KS.) **78** D 2
Bogue Chitto River **69** E 3
Bois Blanc Island **54** C 3
Boise (ID.) **90** C 3
Boise (TX.) **97** H 3
Boise City (OK.) **97** G 2
Boise Mountains **90** D 3
Boise River **90** D 3
Boissevain (ND.) **85** F 1
Boix de Sioux River **61** E 6
Bokeelia (FL.) **45** E 4
Boles (AR.) **66** BC 3
Boley (OK.) **77** G 2
Boligee (AL.) **46** D 5–6
Bolivar (MO.) **64** D 4
Bolivar (N.Y.) **32** B 3
Bolivar (TN.) **50** B 5
Bol'shoy Kymency **120** A 2
Bolton (N.C.) **39** F 4
Bomarton (TX.) **76** D 4
Bon Air (VA.) **37** G 4
Bon Wier (TX.) **75** H 4
Bonanza (CO.) **94** D 3
Bonanza (OR.) **112** D 4
Bonanza (UT.) **102** B 1
Bonanza Peak **114** E 1
Bonaparte (IA.) **63** G 5
Bonaparte, Mount **115** F 1
Bonasila Dome **119** C 1
Bondad (CO.) **94** C 4
Bondurant (WY.) **92** B 2
Bone (ID.) **91** H 3
Bonham (TX.) **75** E 1
Bonifay (FL.) **47** F 3
Bonilla (S.D.) **83** G 3
Bonita Springs (FL.) **45** E 3
Bonne Terre (MO.) **65** G 4
Bonners Ferry (ID.) **88** D 1
Bonneville (WY.) **92** D 2
Bonneville Dam **112** D 1
Bonneville Peak **91** G 4
Bonneville Salt Flats **102** B 5
Bonny Reservoir **95** H 2
Boody (IL.) **56** D 3
Book Cliffs **102** C 1
Booker (TX.) **76** C 1
Boone (CO.) **95** F 3
Boone (IA.) **62** E 3
Boone (N.C.) **38** C 2
Boone Reservoir **51** H 4
Boones Mill (VA.) **36** E 4
Booneville (AR.) **66** B 2
Booneville (KY.) **51** G 3
Booneville (MS.) **48** B 2
Boonville (CA.) **110** C 5

Boonville (IN.) **52** B 4
Boonville (MO.) **64** E 3
Boonville (N.Y.) **33** E 2
Booth (AL.) **46** D 4
Boquerón (P.R.) **124** A 2
Boquillas Canyon **73** F 4
Boquillas del Carmen (TX.) **73** F 4
Borah Peak **91** F 2
Border (WY.) **92** B 3
Borger (TX.) **76** B 2
Borgne, Lake **69** E 3
Borinquen, Punta **124** A 2
Boron (CA.) **107** E 2
Borrego Springs (CA.) **107** F 4
Boscobel (WI.) **59** F 4
Bosler (WY.) **93** G 4
Bosque (AZ.) **100** D 4
Bosque Bonito (Mex.) **72** C 3
Bossier City (LA.) **68** B 1
Boston (GA.) **43** F 4
Boston (MA.) **31** E 3
Boston (TX.) **75** G 1
Boston Mountains **66** BD 2
Boswell (IN.) **52** D 2
Boswell (OK.) **77** G 3
Boswell (PA.) **34** B 3
Bottineau (ND.) **84–85** F 2
Boulder (CO.) **95** E 1
Boulder (IL.) **57** E 5
Boulder (MT.) **86** A 3
Boulder (UT.) **103** E 3
Boulder (WY.) **92** C 3
Boulder City (NV.) **107** H 2
Boulder Peak **110** A 5
Boundary **121** G 3
Boundary Peak **108** D 2
Bountiful (UT.) **102** B 3
Bourbon (MO.) **65** F 3
Bouse (AZ.) **100** B 3
Bouse Wash **100** C 3
Bovill (ID.) **88** D 3
Bovina (TX.) **97** H 4
Bowbells (ND.) **84** D 2
Bowdle (SD.) **83** F 2
Bowdoin (MT.) **87** F 1
Bowdoin, Lake **87** F 1
Bowdon (ND.) **85** G 3
Bowen (IL.) **56** C 6
Bowie (AZ.) **101** G 4
Bowie (MD.) **37** H 2
Bowie (TX.) **74** D 1
Bowling Green (FL.) **45** D 3
Bowling Green (KY.) **50** D 4
Bowling Green (MO.) **65** F 2
Bowling Green (OH.) **53** F 1
Bowling Green (VA.) **37** G 3
Bowman (ND.) **84** C 4
Bowman-Haley Lake **82** B 1
Box Elder (MT.) **86** C 1
Box Elder (SD.) **82** B 3
Boxelder (WY.) **93** G 3
Boyce (LA.) **68** C 2
Boyd (OK.) **76** C 1
Boyd (TX.) **74** D 1
Boydton (VA.) **37** F 5
Boyer River **62** C 4
Boyero (CO.) **95** G 3
Boyes (MT.) **87** HJ 4
Boykins (VA.) **37** G 5
Boyne City (MI.) **54** C 3
Boynton (OK.) **77** H 2

Boynton Beach (FL.) **45** E 2
Boys Ranch (TX.) **97** H 3
Boysen Reservoir **92** D 2
Bozeman (MT.) **86** B 4
Brackettville (TX.) **70** B 1
Brad (TX.) **74** C 2
Braddock (ND.) **85** F 4
Bradenton (FL.) **45** D 4
Bradford (PA.) **34** C 2
Bradley (AL.) **47** E 4
Bradley (FL.) **44** D 4
Bradley (IL.) **56** B 3
Bradley (S.D.) **83** H 2
Brady (MT.) **86** B 1
Brady (NE.) **80** D 3
Brady (TX.) **74** B 3
Brady Mountains **74** AB 3
Bradys Hot Springs (NV.) **104** B 3
Braham (MN.) **61** E 3
Braidwood (IL.) **56** B 3
Brainard (NE.) **81** H 3
Brainerd (MN.) **60** D 4
Braman (OK.) **77** F 1
Brampton (N.D.) **83** H 2
Branchville (S.C.) **41** E 3
Brand (TX.) **73** G 1
Brandenberg (MT.) **87** G 4
Brandenburg (KY.) **50** D 3
Brandon (FL.) **44** D 4
Brandon (MS.) **48** D 3
Brandon (VT.) **30** C 2
Brandy Peak **112** B 4
Branford (FL.) **44** AB 4
Branson (CO.) **95** G 4
Branson (MO.) **64** D 5
Brant Lake (N.Y.) **33** G 2
Brantley (AL.) **47** E 4
Brasstown Bald **42** B 4
Brattleboro (VT.) **30** D 3
Brave (PA.) **34** A 4
Brawley (CA.) **107** G 5
Brawley Peaks **104** C 4
Bray (CA.) **110** A 3
Brazil (IN.) **52** B 3
Brazos (N.M.) **96** D 2
Brazos River **75** E 4
Brea, Punta **124** B 3
Breaux Bridge (LA.) **68** D 3
Breckenridge (CO.) **94** E 2
Breckenridge (MN.) **61** D 6
Breckenridge (TX.) **74** C 2
Breien (ND.) **84** F 4
Bremen (GA.) **42** C 6
Bremen (IN.) **52** C 1
Bremerton (WA.) **114** C 2
Bremond (TX.) **75** E 3
Brenda (AZ.) **100** C 3
Brenham (TX.) **75** E 4
Brent (AL.) **46** D 5
Brentwood (AR.) **66** B 2
Brentwood (N.Y.) **35** H 3
Brentwood (TN.) **50** D 4
Breton Islands **69** F 4
Breton Sound **69** F 4
Brevard (N.C.) **51** H 5
Brevort (MI.) **54** B 4
Brewer (ME.) **28** D 3
Brewster (KS.) **78** B 2
Brewster (MN.) **61** G 5
Brewster (NE.) **80** E 3
Brewster (WA.) **115** EF 1
Brewton (AL.) **47** E 5
Brian Head **103** E 4
Brice (TX.) **76** C 3
Briceland (CA.) **110** B 6

Bricelyn (MN.) **61** G 3
Bridge (ID.) **91** F 4
Bridge (OR.) **112** AB 3
Bridgeboro (GA.) **43** E 4
Bridgeland (UT.) **102** B 2
Bridgeport (AL.) **46** B 3
Bridgeport (CA.) **111** D 1
Bridgeport (CT.) **35** H 2
Bridgeport (NE.) **80** A 3
Bridgeport (TX.) **74** D 1
Bridgeport, Lake **74** D 1
Bridger (MT.) **86** E 4
Bridger Peak **93** E 4
Bridgeton (N.J.) **35** F 4
Bridgeville (CA.) **110** B 5
Bridgeville (DE.) **37** J 3
Bridgewater (ME.) **28** B 3
Bridgewater (S.D.) **83** H 4
Bridgman (MI.) **55** G 5
Bridgton (ME.) **29** D 5
Briggs (TX.) **74** D 4
Briggsdale (CO.) **95** F 1
Brigham City (UT.) **102** A 3
Brighton (CO.) **95** F 2
Brighton (FL.) **45** D 3
Brighton (IA.) **63** G 4
Brighton (IL.) **57** D 5
Brighton (MI.) **55** F 2
Brighton (MO.) **64** D 4
Brighton (N.Y.) **32** C 2
Brighton Indian Reservation **45** D 3
Brilliant (AL.) **46** B 5
Brillon (WI.) **59** E 1–2
Brinford (N.D.) **85** H 3
Brinkley (AR.) **67** E 3
Brinnon (WA.) **114** BC 2
Briscoe (TX.) **76** C 2
Bristol (CT.) **35** H 2
Bristol (FL.) **47** F 2
Bristol (S.D.) **83** H 2
Bristol (TN.) **51** H 4
Bristol (VA.) **36** B 5
Bristol Bay (AL.) **119** CD 2
Bristol Lake **107** G 3
Bristow (OK.) **77** G 2
British Columbia (AL.) **117** E 2
British Mountains (AL.) **121** GH 2
Britter Lake (S.D.) **83** H 2
Britton (S.D.) **83** H 2
Broad Pass **121** EF 3
Broad River **40** D 2
Broadalbin (N.Y.) **33** F 2
Broadview (MT.) **86** E 3
Broadview (N.M.) **97** G 4
Broadwater (NE.) **80** B 3
Broadway (VA.) **37** E 3
Broadys (MT.) **87** H 4
Brockton (MA.) **31** E 3
Brockton (MT.) **87** H 1
Brockville (Can.) **32** E 1
Brockway (MT.) **87** H 2
Brockway (PA.) **34** C 2
Brodhead (WI.) **59** G 3
Brogan (OR.) **113** H 2
Broken Arrow (OK.) **77** H 1
Broken Bow (NE.) **80–81** E 3
Broken Bow (OK.) **77** J 3
Broken Bow Lake **77** J 3
Bronte (TX.) **73** H 2
Bronx (WY.) **92** B 3
Brookeland (TX.) **75** H 3
Brookfield (MO.) **64** D 2
Brookhaven (MS.) **49** E 4
Brookings (OR.) **112** A 4
Brookings (S.D.) **83** J 3
Brooklyn (IA.) **63** F 4
Brooklyn Park (MN.) **61** E 3
Brookneal (VA.) **37** F 4
Brooks Range (AL.) **120–121** CD 2
Brookston (MN.) **60** D 2
Brooksville (AL.) **46** B 4
Brooksville (FL.) **44** C 4
Brooksville (KY.) **51** F 2
Brooksville (MS.) **48** C 2
Brookville (IN.) **52** D 3
Brookville (PA.) **34** B 2
Brothers (OR.) **112** E 3
Browerville (MN.) **61** D 4
Brown City (MI.) **55** E 1
Brown City (MI.) **55** E 2
Brown Deer (WI.) **59** F 1
Brown, Mount **86** B 1
Brown Mountain **107** E 2
Brown, Point **114** A 3
Brownbranch (MO.) **64** E 5
Brownell (KS.) **78** D 3
Brownfield (TX.) **99** H 3
Browning (MT.) **89** G 1
Brownlee (NE.) **80** D 2
Brownlee (OR.) **113** HJ 2
Brownlee Dam **90** C 2
Brownlee Reservoir **113** H 2
Browns Valley (S.D.) **83** H 2
Brownstown (IN.) **52** D 4
Brownsville (OR.) **112** C 2
Brownsville (PA.) **34** B 4
Brownsville (TN.) **50** A 5
Brownsville (TX.) **71** E 5
Brownton (MN.) **61** F 4
Brownville (AL.) **46** C 5
Brownville (ME.) **28** C 3
Brownville (NE.) **81** J 4
Brownwood (TX.) **74** C 3
Brownwood, Lake **74** B 3
Broxton (GA.) **43** E 3
Bruce (MS.) **48** BC 3
Bruce (WI.) **59** D 5
Bruce Crossing (MI.) **58** C 3
Bruhel Point **110** C 5
Bruin Point **102** C 2
Brule (NE.) **80** C 3
Brule (WI.) **58** C 5
Brundage (TX.) **70** C 2
Bruneau (ID.) **90** D 4
Bruneau River **90** D 4
Bruni (TX.) **70** D 3
Brunswick (GA.) **43** E 2
Brunswick (ME.) **29** E 5
Brunswick (MO.) **64** D 2
Brunswick (OH.) **53** H 1
Brusett (MT.) **87** F 2
Brush (CO.) **95** G 1
Bryan (OH.) **52** E 1
Bryan (TX.) **75** E 4
Bryant (S.D.) **83** H 3
Bryce Canyon (UT.) **103** E 4
Bryce Canyon National Park **103** E 4
Bryson City (N.C.) **51** G 5
Buchanan (GA.) **42** C 6
Buchanan (ND.) **85** G 3
Buchanan (N.M.) **97** F 4
Buchanan (VA.) **36** E 4
Buchanan Dam (TX.) **74** C 4
Buchanan Lake **74** C 4
Buchon, Point **106** B 2
Buck Island **124** D 3
Buck Mountain **115** F 1
Buckeye (AZ.) **100** D 3
Buckhannon (W.V.) **36** D 2–3
Buckhorn Lake **51** G 3
Buckingham (CO.) **95** G 1
Buckingham (VA.) **37** F 4
Buckland (AL.) **120** C 2
Buckland River **120** C 2
Buckley (WA.) **114** D 2
Bucklin (KS.) **95** D 4
Bucks Lake **110** C 3
Bucksport (ME.) **28** D 3
Bucyrus (ND.) **84** D 4
Bucyrus (OH.) **53** F 2
Buda (IL.) **56** B 4
Buda (TX.) **74** D 4
Bude (MS.) **49** E 4
Buena (WA.) **115** E 3
Buena Vista (CO.) **94** D 3
Buena Vista (GA.) **43** D 5
Buena Vista (VA.) **36–37** E 4
Buena Vista Lake **106** C 2
Bueryeros (N.M.) **97** G 3
Buffalo (KS.) **79** H 4
Buffalo (MO.) **64** D 4
Buffalo (MT.) **86** D 3
Buffalo (N.Y.) **32** A 3
Buffalo (OH.) **53** H 3
Buffalo (OK.) **76** D 1
Buffalo (SD.) **82** B 2
Buffalo (TX.) **75** E 3
Buffalo (WY.) **93** F 1
Buffalo Bill Reservoir **92** C 1
Buffalo Center (IA.) **62** E 2
Buffalo Creek (CO.) **95** E 2
Buffalo Gap (SD.) **82** B 4
Buffalo Gap (TX.) **74** A 2
Buffalo Lake **97** H 4
Buffalo Valley (TN.) **50** D 4
Buford (GA.) **42** B 5
Buford (ND.) **84** C 2
Buhl (ID.) **90** E 4
Buist (ID.) **91** G 4
Buldir (AL.) **116** H 1
Bull Island **41** F 4
Bull Lake **92** C 2
Bull Mountain **86** B 3
Bull Mountains **86–87** EF 3
Bull Shoals Lake **66** D 1
Bullard (TX.) **75** F 2
Bullhead (SD.) **82** D 2
Bullion Mountains **107** F 3
Bullrun Rock **113** G 2
Bully Creek Reservoir **113** H 2
Bumble Bee (AZ.) **100** D 2
Buna (TX.) **75** H 4
Bunker (MO.) **65** F 4
Bunker Hill **104** D 3
Bunker Hill (IN.) **52** C 2
Bunker Hill (OR.) **112** A 3
Bunkerville (NV.) **109** H 3
Bunkie (LA.) **68** C 3
Bunn (N.C.) **39** F 3
Bunnell (FL.) **44** B 3
Buras (LA.) **69** F 4
Burbank (CA.) **106** D 3
Burden (KS.) **79** G 4
Burdett (KS.) **78** D 3
Burdock (SD.) **82** B 4
Burgaw (N.C.) **39** G 4
Burgdorf (ID.) **88** E 4
Burkburnett (TX.) **76** E 3
Burke (ID.) **88** E 2
Burkesville (KY.) **51** E 4
Burkett (TX.) **74** B 2
Burkeville (TX.) **75** H 3
Burkeville (VA.) **37** F 4
Burleson (TX.) **74** D 2
Burley (ID.) **91** F 4
Burlingame (NE.) **79** G 3
Burlington (CO.) **95** H 2
Burlington (IA.) **63** G 5
Burlington (KS.) **79** H 3
Burlington (N.C.) **39** E 2
Burlington (ND.) **84** E 2
Burlington (OK.) **76–77** E 1
Burlington (VT.) **30** C 1
Burlington (WI.) **59** G 2
Burlington (WY.) **92** D 1
Burlington Junction (MO.) **64** B 1
Burmester (UT.) **102** B 4
Burnet (TX.) **74** C 4
Burns (KS.) **79** FG 3
Burns (OR.) **113** F 3
Burns (WY.) **93** H 4
Burns Flat (OK.) **76** D 2
Burnside (KY.) **51** F 4
Burnsville (N.C.) **51** H 5
Burnsville (W.V.) **36** D 3
Burntfork (WY.) **92** B 4
Burr Oak (KS.) **79** E 2
Burris (WY.) **92** C 2
Burris (WY.) **92** D 2
Burrton (KS.) **79** F 3
Burrville (UT.) **103** D 4
Burt Lake **54** C 3
Burton (TX.) **75** E 4
Burton, Lake **42** B 4
Burwash Landing **117** D 1
Burwell (NE.) **81** E 3
Busby (MT.) **87** G 4
Bushland (TX.) **97** H 3
Bushnell (FL.) **44** C 4
Bushnell (IL.) **56** C 5
Bushnell (NE.) **80** A 3
Bushton (KS.) **78** E 3
Bussey (IA.) **63** F 4
Bustamante (TX.) **70** C 3
Butler (AL.) **47** D 6
Butler (GA.) **43** D 5
Butler (IN.) **52** E 1
Butler (MO.) **64** C 3
Butler (OK.) **76** D 2
Butler (PA.) **34** B 3
Butte (MT.) **86** A 3
Butte (ND.) **84** F 3
Butte Mountains **105** F 3
Butterfield (MN.) **61** G 4–5
Butterfield (MO.) **64** D 5
Butternut (WI.) **58** C 4
Buttonwillow (CA.) **106** C 2
Buxton (N.C.) **39** J 3

Buzzards Bay **31** F 4
Byars (OK.) **77** F 3
Byers (CO.) **95** F 2
Byhalia (MS.) **48** B 3
Bylas (AZ.) **101** F 3
Bynum (N.C.) **39** E 3
Bynum (TX.) **74** D 3
Bynum Reservoir **86** A 2
Byram (MS.) **48** D 4
Byrdstown (TN.) **51** E 4
Byron (IL.) **56** A 4
Byron (WY.) **92** D 1

C

C. J. Strike Reservoir **90** D 4
Caballo (N.M.) **98** C 3–4
Caballo Reservoir **98** C 4
Cabazon (CA.) **107** F 4
Cabezas de San Juan **124** C 2
Cabinet Mountains **88** E 1–2
Cable (WI.) **58** C 5
Cabo Rojo **124** A 3
Cabool (MO.) **65** E 4
Cabot (AR.) **66** D 3
Cabot, Mount **28** D 6
Cabrillo National Monument **107** E 5
Cabrillo, Point **110** C 5
Cache (OK.) **76** E 3
Cache Mountain **121** F 2
Cache Peak **91** F 4
Cache River **67** E 2
Cachuma, Lake **106** C 3
Cactus Flat **109** F 2
Cactus Peak **109** F 2
Caddo (OK.) **77** G 3
Caddo (TX.) **74** C 2
Caddo Lake **75** G 2
Caddoa (CO.) **95** H 3
Cadillac (MI.) **55** D 4
Cadiz (CA.) **107** G 3
Cadiz (KY.) **50** C 4
Cadiz (OH.) **53** J 2
Cadiz Lake **107** G 3
Cadott (WI.) **59** E 5
Cadwell (GA.) **43** D 3–4
Caguas (P.R.) **124** B 2
Cahaba Heights (AL.) **46** C 4
Cahone (CO.) **94** B 4
Caillou Bay **68–69** D 4
Caineville (UT.) **103** D 2
Cairn Hope Peak **115** E 3
Cairn Mountain **119** D 1
Cairo (GA.) **43** F 5
Cairo (IL.) **57** F 4
Cairo (NE.) **81** F 3
Caja de Muertos, Isla **124** B 3
Cajon Summit **107** E 3
Calais (ME.) **28** C 2
Calapooya Mountains **112** C 3
Calaveras Lake **70** D 1
Calcasieu Lake **68** B 4
Caldwell (ID.) **90** C 3
Caldwell (OH.) **53** H 3
Caldwell (TX.) **75** E 4
Caldwell (W.V.) **36** D 4
Caledonia (MN.) **61** G 1
Caledonia (N.D.) **85** J 3
Caledonia (N.Y.) **32** C 3
Caledonia (WI.) **59** G 1
Calera (AL.) **46** C 4
Calexico (CA.) **107** G 5
Calhan (CO.) **95** F 2
Calhoun (AL.) **47** D 4
Calhoun (GA.) **42** B 5
Calhoun (KY.) **50** C 3
Calhoun (MO.) **64** D 3
Calhoun (TN.) **51** F 5
Calhoun City (MS.) **48** C 3
Calhoun Falls (S.C.) **40** C 2
Calico Rock (AR.) **66** D 1
Caliente (CA.) **106** D 2
Caliente (NV.) **109** H 2
California **110**
California (MO.) **64** E 3
California Aqueduct **111** F 2
Calipatria (CA.) **107** G 4
Calistoga (CA.) **111** D 4
Callaghan, Mount **105** E 3
Callahan (CA.) **110** A 4
Callahan (FL.) **44** A 3
Callan (TX.) **74** B 3
Callao (UT.) **102** C 5
Callaway (NE.) **80** E 3
Calliham (TX.) **70** D 2
Calmar (IA.) **63** G 2
Caloosahatchee River **53** N 8
Calpella (CA.) **110** C 5
Calpet (WY.) **92** B 3
Calpine (CA.) **110** C 2
Calumet (MN.) **60** C 3
Calumet (OK.) **77** E 2
Calva (AZ.) **101** F 3
Calvert (TX.) **75** E 4
Calvet City (KY.) **50** B 4
Calvin (OK.) **77** G 3
Camano Island **114** C 1
Camargo (OK.) **78** D 1
Camas (ID.) **91** G 2
Camas (WA.) **114** C 4
Camas Valley (OR.) **112** B 3
Cambria (CA.) **106** A 2
Cambridge (IA.) **63** E 4
Cambridge (ID.) **90** C 2
Cambridge (IL.) **56** B 5
Cambridge (MA.) **30–31** E 3
Cambridge (MD.) **37** H 3
Cambridge (MN.) **61** E 3
Cambridge (NE.) **80** D 4
Cambridge (OH.) **53** H 2
Cambridge City (IN.) **52** D 3
Cambridge Sprs (PA.) **34** B 2
Camden (AL.) **47** E 5
Camden (AR.) **66** D 4
Camden (ME.) **29** D 4
Camden (MS.) **48** D 3
Camden (N.C.) **39** H 2
Camden (N.J.) **35** F 4
Camden (N.Y.) **32** E 2
Camden (OH.) **52** E 3
Camden (S.C.) **41** E 2
Camden (TN.) **50** B 4
Camden (WA.) **115** H 1
Camden Bay (AL.) **121** FG 1
Camdenton (MO.) **64** E 3–4
Cameo (CO.) **94** B 2
Cameo (N.M.) **97** G 4
Cameron (AZ.) **103** G 3
Cameron (LA.) **68** B 4
Cameron (MO.) **64** C 2
Cameron (MT.) **86** B 4
Cameron (TX.) **74** D 4
Cameron (WI.) **59** D 5
Cameron (W.V.) **36** D 2
Camilla (GA.) **43** E 5
Camino (CA.) **111** D 2
Camp Bird (CO.) **94** C 4
Camp Creek (AZ.) **100** E 3
Camp Creek (W.V.) **36** C 4
Camp Crook (SD.) **82** B 2
Camp Hill (PA.) **34** D 3
Camp Howard Ridge **88** D 4
Camp Point (IL.) **56** CD 6
Camp San Saba (TX.) **74** B 3–4
Camp Verde (AZ.) **100** E 2
Camp Verde Indian Reservation **100** DE 2
Camp Wood (TX.) **70** C 1
Campbell (MO.) **65** G 5
Campbell (NE.) **81** F 4
Campbell Hill **53** F 2
Campbellsport (WI.) **59** F 2
Campbellsville (KY.) **50–51** E 3
Campbellton (FL.) **47** F 3
Campbellton (TX.) **70** D 2
Campion (CO.) **95** E 1
Campo (CA.) **107** F 5
Campo (CO.) **95** H 4
Campo-Manzanita and Laposta Indian Reservation **107** F 5
Campti (LA.) **68** B 2
Campton (KY.) **51** G 3
Camptonville (CA.) **110** C 3
Canaan (CT.) **35** H 1
Canadian (OK.) **77** H 2
Canadian (TX.) **76** C 2
Canadian River **77** EF 2
Canandaigua Lake **32** C 3
Canandaiqua (N.Y.) **32** C 3
Canaseraga (N.Y.) **32** C 3
Canaveral, Cape **44** C 2
Canby (CA.) **110** A 2
Canby (MN.) **61** F 6
Canby (OR.) **112** C 1
Candelaria (TX.) **72** D 3
Candle **120** C 2
Cando (ND.) **85** G 2
Candor (N.C.) **38** E 3
Caney (OK.) **77** G 3
Canfield (AR.) **66** C 4
Canisteo (N.Y.) **32** C 3
Canjilon (N.M.) **96** D 2
Cannel City (KY.) **51** G 3
Cannelton (IN.) **52** C 5
Canning (SD.) **83** F 3
Cannon Ball Mountain **88** D 4
Cannon Beach (OR.) **112** A 1
Cannon Falls (MN.) **61** F 2
Cannonball River **84** E 4
Cannonsville Reservoir **32–33** E 3
Cannonville (UT.) **103** E 4
Canon City (CO.) **95** E 3
Canon Plaza (N.M.) **96** D 2
Canoncito Indian Reservation **96** CD 3
Canones (N.M.) **96** D 2
Canoochee River **43** DE 2
Canova (S.D.) **83** H 4
Cantil (CA.) **106** D 2
Canton (GA.) **42** B 5
Canton (IL.) **56** C 5
Canton (KS.) **79** F 3
Canton (MO.) **65** F 1
Canton (MS.) **48** D 3
Canton (N.C.) **51** H 5
Canton (N.Y.) **33** E 1
Canton (OH.) **53** H 2
Canton (OK.) **76** E 1
Canton (PA.) **34** E 2
Canton (S.D.) **83** J 4
Canton (TX.) **75** F 2
Canton Lake **76** E 1
Cantonment (FL.) **47** F 5
Cantwell (AL.) **121** F 3
Canutillo (TX.) **72** B 2
Canyon **117** D 1
Canyon (MN.) **60** C 2
Canyon (TX.) **76** B 2–3
Canyon City (OR.) **113** G 2
Canyon Creek (MT.) **86** A 3
Canyon de Chelly National Monument **103** F 1
Canyon Diablo (AZ.) **101** E 1
Canyon Ferry Lake **86** B 3
Canyon Lake **74** C 5
Canyon Valley (TX.) **76** B 4
Canyonlands National Park **103** D 1–2
Canyonville (OR.) **112** B 4
Cap-de-la-Madeleine (Can.) **28** B 7
Cap Rock (TX.) **76** B 4
Capa (SD.) **82** D 3
Cape Alava **114** A 1
Cape, Ann **31** F 3
Cape Ann **31** F 3
Cape Arago **112** A 3
Cape Blanco **112** A 4
Cape Canaveral **44** C 2
Cape Charles **37** J 4
Cape Charles (VA.) **37** J 4
Cape Cod **31** G 4
Cape Cod Bay **31** F 4
Cape Constantine (AL.) **119** D 2
Cape Coral (FL.) **45** E 3
Cape Darby **120** C 3
Cape Disappointment **114** A 3
Cape Elizabeth **114** A 2
Cape Elizabeth (ME.) **29** E 5
Cape Falcon **112** A 1
Cape Fear **39** G 5
Cape Fear River **39** F 4
Cape Ferrelo **112** A 4
Cape Flattery **114** A 1
Cape Girardeau (MO.) **65** H 4
Cape Halawa **123** E 2
Cape Halkett (AL.) **121** E 1
Cape Hatteras **39** J 3
Cape Hatteras National Seashore **39** J 3
Cape Henlopen **37** JK 3
Cape Henry **37** J 2
Cape Island **41** F 3
Cape Knox (AL.) **117** E 3

Cape Krusenstern **120** C 2
Cape Krusenstern
  Nat.Mon. (AL.) **120** C 2
Cape Kumukahi **123** G 4
Cape Lisburne (AL.)
  120 B 2
Cape, Lookout **39** H 4
Cape Lookout **112** A 1
Cape Lookout National
  Seashore **39** H 4
Cape May **35** G 5
Cape May (N.J.) **35** F 4–5
Cape May CH (N.J.) **35** G 4
Cape Mendocino **110** B 6
Cape Mohican (AL.)
  118 B 1
Cape Muzon (AL.) **117** E 3
Cape Newenham (AL.)
  118–119 C 2
Cape Pool **117** E 2
Cape Prince of Wales (AL.)
  120 B 2
Cape Rodney (AL.) **120** B 3
Cape Romain **41** F 4
Cape Romano **45** F 3
Cape Romanzof (AL.)
  118 B 1
Cape Sable **45** F 3
Cape Saint Martin **109** H 3
Cape San Blas **47** G 3
Cape Small **29** E 4
Cape Vincent (N.Y.) **32** D 1
Cape Vizcaino **110** C 5
Cape Yakataga (AL.)
  116 C 1–2
Capitan (N.M.) **99** E 3
Capitan Peak **99** E 3
Capitol (MT.) **87** J 4
Capitol Peak **104** D 1
Capitol Reef National Park
  103 D 3
Capps (FL.) **44** A 5
Caprock (N.M.) **99** G 3
Capron (OK.) **76** E 1
Captain Cook (HI.) **123** F 4
Captiva (FL.) **45** E 4
Capulin Mountain National
  Monument **97** F 2
Capulin Peak **96** D 2
Capulin Volcano National
  Monument (N.M.)
  97 EF 2
Caputa (SD.) **82** C 3
Carbon (TX.) **74** C 2
Carbon Hill (AL.) **46** C 5
Carbonado (WA.) **114** D 2
Carbondale (CO.) **94** C 2
Carbondale (IL.) **57** F 4
Carbondale (KS.) **79** H 3
Carbondale (PA.) **35** F 2
Carcross (AL.) **117** DE 1
Cardenas (N.M.) **97** F 4
Cardwell (MO.) **67** F 1
Carey (ID.) **91** F 3
Carey (OH.) **53** F 2
Carey (TX.) **76** C 3
Caribou (ME.) **28** B 3
Caribou Range **91** H 3
Carl Blackwell, Lake **77** F 1
Carleton (NE.) **81** G 4
Carlile (WY.) **93** H 1
Carlin (NV.) **105** E 2
Carlinville (IL.) **57** D 5
Carlisle (AR.) **67** E 3
Carlisle (IA.) **63** E 4
Carlisle (KY.) **51** G 2

Carlisle (S.C.) **40** D 2
Carlistle (PA.) **34** D 3
Carlsbad (CA.) **107** E 4
Carlsbad (N.M.) **99** F 4
Carlsbad (TX.) **73** H 2
Carlsbad Caverns National
  Park **99** F 4
Carlton (MN.) **60** D 2
Carlton (OR.) **112** B 1
Carlton (TX.) **74** C 3
Carlton (WA.) **115** E 1
Carlyle (IL.) **57** E 5
Carlyle (MT.) **87** J 3
Carlyle Lake **57** E 5
Carmacks (AL.) **117** D 1
Carmel, Point **111** F 3–4
Carmel Valley (CA.) **111** F 3
Carmen (ID.) **89** FG 4
Carmen (OK.) **76** E 1
Carmi (IL.) **57** E 3
Carmichael (CA.) **111** D 3
Carmine (TX.) **75** E 4
Carnation (WA.) **114** D 2
Carne (N.M.) **98** C 4
Carnegie (OK.) **76** E 2
Carnesville (GA.) **42** B 4
Carney (OK.) **77** F 2
Carning River **121** F 2
Caro (MI.) **55** E 2
Carol City (FL.) **45** F 2
Carolina Beach (N.C.)
  39 G 4
Carp (NV.) **109** H 2
Carpenter (S.D.) **83** G 3
Carpenter (WY.) **93** H 4
Carpenterville (OR.)
  112 A 4
Carpinteria (CA.) **106** C 3
Carr (CO.) **95** F 1
Carrabelle (FL.) **47** G 2
Carriere (MS.) **49** F 3
Carrington (ND.) **85** G 3
Carrizal (Mex.) **72** B 3
Carrizo Plateau **103** F 1
Carrizo Springs (TX.)
  70 B 2
Carrizos (Mex.) **72** C 3
Carrizozo (N.M.) **98** E 3
Carroll (IA.) **62** D 3
Carroll (NE.) **81** G 2
Carrollton (AL.) **46** C 6
Carrollton (GA.) **42** C 6
Carrollton (IL.) **57** D 5
Carrollton (KY.) **51** E 2
Carrollton (MO.) **64** D 2
Carrollton (MS.) **48** C 3–4
Carrollton (TX.) **74–75** D 1
Carry Falls Reservoir **33** F 1
Carson (ND.) **84** E 4
Carson (WA.) **114** D 4
Carson City (MI.) **55** E 3
Carson City (NV.) **104** B 3
Carson City (NV.) **104** B 3
Carson Lake **104** C 3
Carson Sink **104** C 3
Carta Valley (TX.) **73** H 4
Cartago (CA.) **109** E 3
Carter (MT.) **86** B 2
Carter (OK.) **76** D 2
Carter (SD.) **82** E 4
Carter (WI.) **59** D 2
Carter (WY.) **92** B 4
Carter Lake (NE.) **81** J 3
Carter Mountain **92** C 1
Carters Lake **42** B 5
Cartersville (GA.) **42** B 6

Carthage (AR.) **66** D 3
Carthage (IL.) **56** C 6
Carthage (MO.) **64** C 4
Carthage (MS.) **48** D 3
Carthage (N.C.) **38** E 3
Carthage (N.Y.) **32** E 2
Carthage (S.D.) **83** H 3
Carthage (TN.) **50** E 4
Carthage (TX.) **75** G 2
Cartwright (ND.) **84** C 3
Cary (MS.) **48** D 4
Cary (N.C.) **39** F 3
Caryville (TN.) **51** F 4
Casa Grande (AZ.) **100** E 4
Casa Grande Ruins
  National Monument
  100 E 3–4
Casa Piedra (TX.) **72** DE 4
Cascade (IA.) **63** H 3
Cascade (ID.) **90** C 2
Cascade (MT.) **86** B 2
Cascade Head **112** A 1
Cascade Range **114** D 3–4
Cascade Reservoir **90** C 2
Cascadia (OR.) **112** C 2
Casco Bay **29** E 4–5
Caseville (MI.) **55** E 2
Cashmere (WA.) **114** E 2
Cashmere Mountain
  114 DE 2
Caspar (CA.) **110** C 5
Casper (WY.) **93** F 3
Cass (W.V.) **36** D 3
Cass City (MI.) **55** E 2
Cass Lake (MN.) **60** C 4
Casselton (N.D.) **85** J 4
Cassiar (AL.) **117** E 2
Cassiar Mountains (AL.)
  117 F 2
Cassoday (KS.) **79** G 3
Cassopolis (MI.) **55** G 5
Cassville (MO.) **64** D 5
Cassville (WI.) **59** G 4
Castaic Lake **106** D 3
Castaneda (OK.) **97** G 2
Castella (CA.) **110** A 4
Castillo de San Marcos
  National Monument
  44 B 3
Castle Dale (UT.) **102** C 2
Castle Dome Peak **100** B 3
Castle Gate (UT.) **102** C 2
Castle Hayne (N.C.) **39** G 4
Castle Hills (TX.) **70** D 1
Castle Peak **90**–**91** F 2
Castle Peak **94** D 2–3
Castle Rock **113** G 2
Castle Rock (CO.) **95** F 2
Castle Rock (SD.) **82** J 3
Castle Rock (WA.) **114** BC 3
Castle Rock Butte **82** B 2
Castle Rock Lake **59** F 3
Castleberry (AL.) **47** E 4
Castleford (ID.) **90** D 4
Castlewood (S.D.) **83** J 3
Castolon (TX.) **73** E 4
Castroville (CA.) **111** F 3
Castroville (TX.) **70** D 1
Cat Creek (MT.) **87** E 2
Cat Island (MS.) **49** F 3
Catahoula Lake **68** C 2
Cataño (P.R.) **124** B 2
Cataract Lake **52** C 3
Catarina (TX.) **70** C 2
Catawba River **41** E 2
Catawissa (PA.) **34** E 3

Catesbu (OK.) **76** D 1
Catharine (KS.) **78** D 3
Cathay (ND.) **85** G 3
Cathedral City (CA.) **107** F 4
Cathedral Mountain
  72–73 E 3
Catherine (AL.) **46** D 5
Catheys Valley (CA.)
  111 E 1–2
Cathlamet (WA.) **114** B 3
Catlettsburg (KY.) **51** H 2
Catnip Mountain **104** B 1
Catonsville (MD.) **37** H 2
Catoosa (OK.) **77** H 1
Catskill (N.Y.) **33** F 3
Catskill Mountains **33** F 3
Cattaraugus Indian
  Reservation **32** B 3
Caucomgomoc Lake **28** B 4
Cauga (TX.) **75** E 3
Caulfield (MO.) **65** E 5
Causey (N.M.) **99** G 3
Cavalier (N.D.) **85** J 2
Cave City (AR.) **67** E 2
Cave City (KY.) **50** E 3
Cave Creek (AZ.) **100** E 3
Cave Creek Dam **100** DE 3
Cave Junction (OR.)
  112 B 4
Cavour (WI.) **58** D 2
Cawker City (KS.) **78** E 2
Cayey (P.R.) **124** B 2
Cayucos (CA.) **106** B 2
Cayuga (N.D.) **85** J 4
Cayuga Lake **32** D 3
Cazenovia (N.Y.) **32** E 3
Cebolla (N.M.) **96** D 2
Cebollita Peak **96** C 4
Cecil (AR.) **66** C 2
Cecil (OR.) **113** F 1
Cecilia (KY.) **50** D 3
Cecilville (CA.) **110** A 5
Cedar (UT.) **102** C 2
Cedar Bluff Reservoir
  78 D 3
Cedar Bluffs (KS.) **78** C 2
Cedar Breaks National
  Monument **103** E 4
Cedar Butte (SD.) **82** D 4
Cedar City (MO.) **65** E 3
Cedar City (UT.) **103** E 5
Cedar Creek **84** DE 4
Cedar Creek Reservoir
  75 E 2
Cedar Falls (IA.) **63** F 3
Cedar Grove (CA.) **108** D 3
Cedar Grove (W.V.) **36** C 3
Cedar Hill (N.M.) **96** C 2
Cedar Key (FL.) **44** B 4
Cedar Keys **44** B 5
Cedar Lake (TX.) **71** G 2
Cedar Mills (MN.) **61** F 4
Cedar Park (TX.) **74** CD 4
Cedar Pass **110** A 2
Cedar Rapids (IA.) **63** G 4
Cedar Rapids (NE.) **81** F 3
Cedar River (IA.) **63** F 2
Cedar River (MI.) **54** C 6
Cedar Vale (KS.) **79** G 4
Cedartown (GA.) **42** B 6
Cedarville (CA.) **110** A 2
Cedarwood (CO.) **95** F 4
Ceder Springs (MI.) **55** E 4
Cedonia (WA.) **115** G 1
Celeste (TX.) **75** E 1
Celina (OH.) **52** E 2

Celina (TN.) **50** E 4
Celina (TX.) **75** E 1
Cement (OK.) **77** E 3
Cement City (MI.) **55** F 3
Centennial (WY.) **93** F 4
Centennial Mountains
91 GH 2
Centennial Wash **100** C 3
Center (CO.) **94** D 4
Center (ND.) **84** E 3
Center (NE.) **81** G 2
Center (TX.) **75** G 3
Center City (MN.) **61** E 2
Center City (TX.) **74** C 3
Center Hill (FL.) **44** C 3
Center Hill Reservoir
50–51 E 4
Center Mountain **88** E 4
Center Point (AL.) **46** C 4
Center Point (IN.) **52** B 3
Center Point (TX.) **73** G 1
Center Point (TX.) **74** B 5
Centerburg (OH.) **53** G 2
Centerville (IA.) **63** E 5
Centerville (PA.) **34** A 3
Centerville (S.D.) **83** J 4
Centerville (TN.) **50** C 5
Centerville (TX.) **75** E 3
Centerville (UT.) **102** B 3
Central (AK.) **121** G 2
Central (N.M.) **98** B 4
Central (UT.) **103** E 5
Central City (CO.) **95** E 2
Central City (IA.) **63** G 3
Central City (IL.) **57** E 5
Central City (KY.) **50** C 3
Central City (NE.) **81** F 3
Central City (PA.) **34** C 3
Central City (SD.) **82** B 3
Central Lake (MI.) **54** C 4
Central Point (OR.) **112** C 4
Central Square (N.Y.)
32 D 2
Central Valley (CA.) **110** B 4
Centralia (IL.) **57** E 5
Centralia (MO.) **65** E 2
Centralia (NE.) **79** G 2
Centralia (WA.) **114** C 3
Centre (AL.) **46** B 3
Centre Hall (PA.) **34** D 3
Centreville (AL.) **46** D 5
Centreville (MD.) **37** HJ 2
Centreville (MI.) **55** G 4
Centreville (MO.) **65** G 4
Centreville (MS.) **49** E 5
Cerrillos (N.M.) **96** D 3
Cerro de Punto **124** B 2
Cerro Vista Peak **96** E 2
Ceylon (MN.) **61** G 4
Chaco Canyon National
Monument **96** BC 2
Chaco Culture National
Historic Park (N.M.)
96 B 2
Chaco River **96** B 2
Chadbourn (N.C.) **39** F 4
Chaffee (MO.) **65** H 4
Chaffee (N.D.) **85** J 4
Chaffey (WI.) **58** C 6
Chain of Lakes **86** C 1
Chakachamna Lake **119** E 1
Chalk Mountain (TX.)
74 D 2
Chalk Mountains **73** E 4
Chalkyitsik **121** G 2
Challis (ID.) **91** E 2

Chalmette (LA.) **69** F 4
Chama (N.M.) **96** D 2
Chamberlain (SD.) **83** F 4
Chamberlain Lake **28** B 3–4
Chambers (AZ.) **101** F 1
Chambers (NE.) **81** F 2
Chambers Island **59** D 1
Chambersburg (PA.) **34** D 4
Chamois (MO.) **65** F 3
Champagne (Yukon, Can.)
117 D 1
Champaign (IL.) **56** C 3
Champion (MI.) **58** C 2
Champion Creek Reservoir
73 H 1
Champlain, Lake **30** C 1
Chancellor (TX.) **73** E 3
Chanchelulla Peak **110** B 4
Chandalar (AL.) **121** F 2
Chandalar River (AL.)
121 F 2
Chandeleur Islands **49** G 2
Chandeleur Sound **69** F 4
Chandler (AZ.) **100** E 3
Chandler (IN.) **52** B 4
Chandler (OK.) **77** G 2
Chandler (TX.) **75** F 2
Chandler Heights (AZ.)
100 E 3
Chandler Lake **121** E 2
Chandler River **121** E 2
Chaneliak **120** C 3
Channel Islands National
Monument **106** C 3
Channel Islands National
Park (CA.) **106** C 3
Channing (MI.) **58** C 2
Channing (TX.) **97** H 3
Chanute (KS.) **79** H 4
Chapel Hill (N.C.) **39** E 3
Chapel Hill (TN.) **50** D 5
Chapleau (Can.) **54** A 2
Chapman (MT.) **87** E 1
Chapman (NE.) **81** F 3
Chapman Ranch (TX.)
71 E 3
Chapmanville (W.V.) **36** B 4
Chappell (NE.) **80** B 3
Charco (TX.) **71** E 2
Chardon (OH.) **53** H 1
Charham Strait (AL.)
117 E 2
Chariton (IA.) **63** E 4
Chariton River **64** E 1
Charles, Cape (VA.) **37** H 4
Charles City (IA.) **63** F 2
Charles City (VA.) **37** G 4
Charles Mill Lake **53** G 2
Charles Town (W.V.)
37 G 2
Charlesbourg (Can.) **28** B 6
Charleston (IL.) **57** D 3
Charleston (MO.) **65** H 5
Charleston (MS.) **48** B 3–4
Charleston (NV.) **105** F 1
Charleston (OR.) **112** A 3
Charleston (S.C.) **41** E 4
Charleston (TN.) **51** F 5
Charleston (W.V.) **36** C 3
Charleston Peak **109** G 3
Charlestown (IN.) **52** D 4
Charlestown (N.H.) **29** E 7
Charlevoix (MI.) **54** C 4
Charlotte (MI.) **55** F 3
Charlotte (N.C.) **38** D 3
Charlotte (TN.) **50** C 4

Charlotte (TX.) **70** D 2
Charlotte Amalie **124** CD 2
Charlotte Beach (FL.)
45 E 4
Charlotte Cort House (VA.)
37 F 4
Charlotte Harbour **45** E 4
Charlottesville (VA.) **37** F 3
Chase (AL.) **46** B 4
Chase (KS.) **78** E 3
Chase (NE.) **80** C 4
Chase (NE.) **80** C 4
Chase City (VA.) **37** F 5
Chase Lake **85** G 3–4
Chaseley (ND.) **85** G 3
Chaska (MN.) **61** F 3
Chassahowitzka (FL.)
44 C 4
Chatanika **121** F 2
Chateangay (N.Y.) **33** F 1
Chatfield (MN.) **61** G 2
Chatham (AK.) **117** D 2
Chatham (LA.) **68** C 1
Chatham (MA.) **31** G 4
Chatham (MI.) **54** B 5
Chatham (N.Y.) **33** G 3
Chatham (VA.) **36** E 5
Chatom (AL.) **47** E 6
Chatsworth (GA.) **42** B 5
Chattahoochee (FL.) **47** F 2
Chattahoochee River
47 E 3
Chattanooga (OK.) **76** E 3
Chattanooga (TN.) **51** E 5
Chauncey (OH.) **53** G 3
Chautauqua Lake **32** A 3
Cheaha Mountain **46** C 3
Cheboygan (MI.) **54** C 3
Checotah (OK.) **77** H 4
Cheektowaga (N.Y.) **32** A 3
Cheesman Lake **95** E 2
Chefornak **118** C 1
Chegytun (AL.) **120** A 2
Chehalis (WA.) **114** C 3
Chehalis Indian
Reservation **114** B 3
Chelan (WA.) **115** F 2
Chelan, Lake **115** E 1
Chelatchie (WA.) **114** C 4
Chelsea (MI.) **55** F 3
Chelsea (VT.) **30** D 2
Chelsea (WI.) **59** D 4
Chelyan (W.V.) **36** C 3
Chemehuevi Indian
Reservation **107** H 3
Chemult (OR.) **112** D 3
Chenango Bridge (N.Y.)
32 E 3
Cheney (WA.) **115** H 2
Cheney Reservoir **79** F 4
Chenoa (IL.) **56** C 3
Cheraw (CO.) **95** G 3
Cheraw (S.C.) **41** F 2
Chernofski **118** B 3
Cherokee (IA.) **62** C 3
Cherokee (N.C.) **51** G 5
Cherokee (OK.) **76–77** F 1
Cherokee (TX.) **74** C 3–4
Cherokee Indian
Reservation **51** G 5
Cherokee Lake **51** G 4
Cherry Creek (NV.) **105** F 3
Cherry Creek (SD.) **82** D 3
Cherry Creek Lake **95** F 2
Cherry Spring (TX.) **74** B 4
Cherry Tree (PA.) **34** C 3

Cherry Valley (AR.) **67** F 2
Cherryville (MO.) **65** F 4
Chesapeake (VA.) **37** H 5
Chesapeake and Ohio
Canal National Historic
Park (MD.) **37** G 2
Chesapeake Bay **37** H 3–4
Chesaw (WA.) **115** FG 1
Chesnee (S.C.) **40** D 1
Chester (CA.) **110** B 3
Chester (IL.) **57** F 4
Chester (MT.) **86** C 1
Chester (OK.) **76** E 1
Chester (PA.) **35** F 4
Chester (S.C.) **40** D 2
Chester (TX.) **75** G 4
Chester (VA.) **37** G 4
Chesterfield (ID.) **91** H 4
Chesterfield (S.C.) **41** E 2
Chesterfield (VA.) **37** G 4
Chestertown (MD.) **37** HJ 2
Chestnut Mountain (GA.)
42 B 4
Chesuncook (ME.) **28** B 4
Chesuncook Lake **28** BC 4
Chetek (WI.) **59** D 5
Chetopa (KS.) **79** H 4
Chevak **118** B 1
Chevak (AL.) **118** B 1
Chewelah (WA.) **115** H 1
Cheyenne (OK.) **76** D 2
Cheyenne (WY.) **93** H 4
Cheyenne River **82** D 3
Cheyenne River Indian
Reservation **82** DE 2
Cheyenne Wells (CO.)
95 H 3
Chiawuli (AZ.) **100** E 5
Chicago (IL.) **56** B 2
Chicago Heights (IL.)
56 B 2
Chichagof (AL.) **117** D 2
Chickamauga Lake **51** EF 5
Chickasaw (AL.) **47** F 6
Chickasaw National
Recreation Area (OK.)
77 G 4
Chickasawhay River
48–49 DE 2
Chickasha (OK.) **77** F 2
Chicken (AL.) **121** G 3
Chico (CA.) **110** C 3
Chico (TX.) **74** D 1
Chico Hot Springs (MT.)
86 C 4
Chicopee (MA.) **30** D 3
Chidester (AR.) **66** C 4
Chief Joseph Dam **115** F 2
Chiefland (FL.) **44** B 4
Chiginagak, Mount **119** D 2
Chignik (AL.) **119** D 2
Chignik Lagoon **119** D 2
Chilchinbito (AZ.) **103** F 2
Childersburg (AL.) **46** C 4
Childress (TX.) **76** C 3
Childs (AZ.) **100** D 4
Chilicotal Mountain **73** E 4
Chilili (N.M.) **96** D 4
Chilkat Pass **117** D 2
Chillicothe (IL.) **56** C 4
Chillicothe (MO.) **64** D 2
Chillicothe (OH.) **53** G 3
Chillicothe (TX.) **76** D 3
Chilly (ID.) **91** F 2
Chiloquin (OR.) **112** D 4
Chimney Rock (CO.) **94** C 4

China Lake **107** E 2
Chinati Mountains **72** D 4
Chinati Peak **72** D 4
Chincoteague (VA.) **37** J 4
Chinle (AZ.) **103** F 1
Chino (AZ.) **100** C 1
Chino Valley (AZ.) **100** D 2
Chinook (MT.) **86** D 1
Chinook Pass **114** D 3
Chipley (FL.) **47** F 3
Chippewa Falls (WI.) **59** E 5
Chippewa, Lake **58** D 5
Chippewa River **59** E 5–6
Chiputneticook Lakes
  28 C 2
Chireno (TX.) **75** G 3
Chiricahua Mountains
  101 G 4–5
Chiricahua National
  Monument **101** G 4–5
Chiricahua Peak **101** F 5
Chirikof (AL.) **119** DE 2
Chisana **116** C 1
Chisholm (MN.) **60** C 2
Chisholm (TX.) **75** E 2
Chisos Mountains **73** E 4
Chistochina **116** B 1
Chitina (AL.) **116** BC 1
Chitina R. (AL.) **116** C 1
Chivington (CO.) **95** H 3
Chloe (N.M.) **96** D 4
Chloride (AZ.) **100** B 1
Chocolate Mountains
  107 G 4
Choctaw Indian
  Reservation **48** D 3
Choctawhatchee Bay
  47 F 4
Chokoloskee (FL.) **45** F 3
Choteau (MT.) **86** A 2
Chouteau (OK.) **77** H 1
Chowan River **39** H 2
Chowchilla (CA.) **111** E 2
Chrisman (IL.) **56** D 2
Christian Sound (AL.)
  117 DE 2
Christiansburg (VA.) **36** D 4
Christiansted **124** D 3
Christina (MT.) **86** D 2
Christmas (AZ.) **101** F 3
Christmas Mountain
  120 C 3
Christopher (IL.) **57** F 4
Christoval (TX.) **73** H 2
Chromo (CO.) **94** D 4
Chrysler (AL.) **47** E 5
Chrystal Falls (MI.) **58** C 2
Chubbuck (CA.) **107** G 3
Chubbuck (ID.) **91** G 4
Chugach Mountains (AL.)
  116 BC 1
Chuginadak (AL.) **118** A 3
Chugwater (WY.) **93** H 4
Chuichu (AZ.) **100** E 4
Chukchi Sea (AL.) **120** A 2
Chula Vista (CA.) **107** E 5
Chulitna (AL.) **116** B 1
Chuluota (FL.) **44** C 3
Chunchula (AL.) **47** F 6
Church Ferry (ND.) **85** G 2
Churchill, Mount **116** C 1
Churchville (VA.) **37** E 3
Chuska Mountains
  96 B 2–3
Chuska Peak **96** B 3
Ciales (P.R.) **124** B 2

Cibola (AZ.) **100** B 3
Cima (CA.) **107** G 2
Cimarron (CO.) **94** C 3
Cimarron (KS.) **78** C 4
Cimarron (N.M.) **97** F 2
Cimarron River **76** E 1
Cincinnati (OH.) **52** E 3
Circle Cliffs **103** E 3
Circle Springs **121** G 2
Circleville (OH.) **53** G 3
Circleville (UT.) **103** D 4
Circleville Mountain
  103 D 4
Cirkle (AL.) **121** G 2
Cisco (TX.) **74** B 2
Cisco (UT.) **102** D 1
Cisne (IL.) **57** E 3
Citra (FL.) **44** B 4
Citronelle (AL.) **47** E 6
Citrus Heights (CA.)
  111 D 3
City Point (FL.) **44** C 2
Civdad Acuña (Mex.)
  73 G 4
Civdad Juares (Mex.)
  72 B 2
Civdad Rio Bravo (Mex.)
  70 D 5
Claflin (KS.) **78** E 3
Claiborne (AL.) **47** E 5
Clair Engle Lake **110** B 4
Clairemont (TX.) **76** C 4
Clairette (TX.) **74** C 2
Clairton (PA.) **34** A 3
Clallam Bay (WA.) **114** A 1
Clam Lake (WI.) **58** C 5
Clan Alpine Mountains
  104 D 3
Clanton (AL.) **46** D 4
Clara (MS.) **49** E 2
Clara City (MN.) **61** F 5
Clare (MI.) **55** E 3
Claremont (CA.) **110** C 2
Claremont (N.H.) **29** E 7
Claremont (S.D.) **83** H 2
Claremore (OK.) **77** H 1
Clarence (IA.) **63** GH 4
Clarence (LA.) **68** C 2
Clarence (PA.) **34** D 2
Clarence Strait (AL.)
  117 E 2
Clarendon (AR.) **67** E 3
Clarendon (TX.) **76** C 3
Clareton (WY.) **93** H 2
Clarinda (IA.) **62** CD 5
Clarion (IA.) **63** E 3
Clarion (PA.) **34** B 2
Clarita (OK.) **77** G 3
Clark (S.D.) **83** H 3
Clark (WY.) **92** C 1
Clark Canyon Reservoir
  91 G 2
Clark Fork **88** E 2
Clark Fork (ID.) **88** D 1
Clark Hill Lake **42** C 3
Clark, Lake **119** E 1
Clark Mountain **107** G 2
Clarkdale (AZ.) **100** D 2
Clarkesville (GA.) **42** B 4
Clarkfield (MN.) **61** F 5
Clarkia (ID.) **88** D 2
Clarks (LA.) **68** C 1
Clarks (NE.) **81** G 3
Clarks Hill (IN.) **52** C 2
Clarks Point **119** D 2
Clarksburg (W.V.) **36** D 2

Clarksdale (MS.) **48** B 4
Clarkston (WA.) **115** H 3
Clarksville (AR.) **66** C 2
Clarksville (TN.) **50** C 4
Clarksville (TX.) **75** F 1
Clarksville (VA.) **37** F 5
Clatskanie (OR.) **114** B 3
Claude (TX.) **76** B 2
Clauene (TX.) **99** H 3
Claunch (N.M.) **96** E 4
Claxton (GA.) **43** D 2
Clay (W.V.) **36** C 3
Clay Center (KS.) **79** F 2
Clay Center (NE.) **81** FG 4
Clay City (IN.) **52** B 3
Clay Springs (AZ.) **101** F 2
Clayton (AL.) **47** E 3
Clayton (DE.) **37** J 2
Clayton (GA.) **42** B 4
Clayton (ID.) **91** E 2
Clayton (LA.) **68** D 2
Clayton (MO.) **65** G 3
Clayton (N.M.) **97** G 2
Clayton (N.Y.) **32** D 1
Clayton (OK.) **77** H 3
Clayton Lake (ME.) **28** B 4
Claytor Lake **36** D 4
Cle Elum (WA.) **114** E 2
Clear Creek (CA.) **110** A 5
Clear Lake (CA.) **110** C 4
Clear Lake (IA.) **63** E 2
Clear Lake (LA.) **68** B 2
Clear Lake (S.D.) **83** J 3
Clear Lake (UT.) **102** C 4
Clear Lake (UT.) **102** C 4
Clear Lake (WI.) **59** D 6
Clear Lake Reservoir
  110 A 3
Clear Site **121** F 3
Clearbrook (MN.) **60** C 5
Clearcreek (UT.) **102** C 3
Clearfield (IA.) **62** D 5
Clearfield (PA.) **34** C 2
Clearfield (UT.) **102** A 4
Clearlake Highlands (CA.)
  110 D 4
Clearlake Oaks (CA.)
  110 C 4
Clearmont (WY.) **93** F 1
Clearwater (FL.) **44** D 5
Clearwater (KS.) **79** F 4
Clearwater (NE.) **81** F 2
Clearwater Lake (MO.)
  65 G 4
Clearwater Mountains
  88 EF 3
Clearwater River **88** D 3
Cleator (AZ.) **100** D 2
Clebit (OK.) **77** J 3
Cleburne (TX.) **74** D 2
Clemson (S.C.) **40** C 2
Clendening Reservoir
  53 H 2
Cleo (TX.) **74** B 4
Cleveland (AL.) **46** B 4
Cleveland (GA.) **79** E 4
Cleveland (MS.) **48** C 4
Cleveland (OH.) **53** G 1
Cleveland (OK.) **77** G 1
Cleveland (TN.) **51** F 5
Cleveland (TX.) **75** F 4
Cleveland, Mount **89** G 1
Clewiston (FL.) **45** E 3
Clifford (N.D.) **85** J 3
Clifton (AZ.) **101** G 3
Clifton (KS.) **79** F 2

Clifton (LA.) **59** E 3
Clifton (TX.) **74** D 3
Clifton Forge (VA.) **36** D 4
Clinch River **51** G 4
Cline (TX.) **70** B 1
Clines Corners (N.M.)
  96 E 3
Clingmans Dome **51** G 5
Clinton (AL.) **46** D 5
Clinton (AR.) **66** D 2
Clinton (CT.) **35** J 2
Clinton (IA.) **63** H 4
Clinton (IL.) **56** C 3
Clinton (KY.) **50** B 4
Clinton (LA.) **69** E 3
Clinton (MA.) **30** E 3
Clinton (ME.) **28** D 4
Clinton (MI.) **55** F 2
Clinton (MO.) **64** D 3
Clinton (MS.) **48** D 4
Clinton (MT.) **89** G 3
Clinton (N.C.) **39** F 3
Clinton (OK.) **76** D 2
Clinton (TN.) **51** F 4
Clintonville (WI.) **59** E 2
Clintwood (KY.) **51** H 3
Clio (AL.) **47** E 3
Clio (S.C.) **41** F 2
Clive (UT.) **102** B 5
Cloquet (MN.) **60** D 2
Cloud Peak **93** E 1
Cloudcroft (N.M.) **99** E 3–4
Clover (S.C.) **40** D 1
Cloverdale (AL.) **46** B 5
Cloverdale (CA.) **111** D 5
Cloverdale (IN.) **52** C 3
Clovis (CA.) **111** F 1
Clovis (N.M.) **97** G 4
Clute (TX.) **71** G 1
Clyattville (GA.) **43** F 4
Clyde (KS.) **79** F 2
Clyde (ND.) **85** GH 2
Clyde (TX.) **74** D 2
Clyde Park (MT.) **86** C 4
Clymer (PA.) **34** B 3
Co-Operative (KY.) **51** F 4
Coachella (CA.) **107** F 4
Coachella Canal **107** G 4
Coahoma (TX.) **73** G 1
Coal City (IL.) **56** C 3
Coal City (IN.) **52** BC 3
Coal Creek **121** G 2
Coal Hill (AR.) **66** C 2
Coal River **117** F 1
Coal Valley **109** G 2
Coaldale (CO.) **94** E 3
Coalgate (OK.) **77** G 3
Coalinga (CA.) **111** F 2
Coalmont (CO.) **94** D 1
Coalville (UT.) **102** B 3
Coamo (P.R.) **124** B 2
Coarsegold (CA.) **111** E 1
Coast Mountains (AL.)
  117 D 1–2
Coast Ranges **114** B 3–4
Coatesville (PA.) **35** F 4
Cobalt (ID.) **89** F 4
Cobleskill (N.Y.) **33** F 3
Cobre (NV.) **105** G 1
Cochise (AZ.) **101** FG 4
Cochiti Pueblo (N.M.)
  96 D 3
Cochran (GA.) **43** D 4
Cochrane (WI.) **59** E 5
Cocoa (FL.) **44** C 2

Cocoa Beach (FL.) **44** C 2
Cocodrie (LA.) **69** E 4
Cocolalla (ID.) **88** D 1
Coconino (AZ.) **103** F 4
Coconino Plateau **103** G 4
Cocopah Indian
  Reservation (Mex.)
  107 H 5
Cod, Cape **31** G 4
Codman (TX.) **76** C 2
Cody (NE.) **80** C 2
Cody (WY.) **92** C 1
Coeur d'Alene (ID.) **88** D 2
Coeur d'Alene Indian
  Reservation **88** D 2
Coeur d'Alene Lake **88** D 2
Coffee Creek (MT.) **86** CD 2
Coffee Lake **57** D 4
Coffeeville (MS.) **48** C 3
Coffeyville (KS.) **79** H 4
Coggon (IA.) **63** G 3
Cohagen (MT.) **87** G 2
Cohoe **119** E 1
Cokeville (WY.) **92** B 3
Colbert (OK.) **77** G 4
Colbert (WA.) **115** H 2
Colby (KS.) **78** B 2
Colcord (W.V.) **36** C 4
Cold Bay (AL.) **118** C 2
Cold Mountain **51** H 5
Coldspring (TX.) **75** F 4
Coldwater (KS.) **95** D 4
Coldwater (MI.) **55** G 3
Coldwater (MO.) **65** G 4
Coldwater (MS.) **48** B 3
Coldwater (OH.) **52** E 2
Cole Camp (MO.) **64** D 3
Colebrook (N.H.) **28** D 6
Coleen River **121** G 2
Coleman (FL.) **44** C 4
Coleman (MI.) **55** E 3
Coleman (TX.) **74** B 3
Coleville (CA.) **111** D 1
Colfax (CA.) **110** C 2
Colfax (IL.) **56** C 3
Colfax (LA.) **68** C 2
Colfax (N.D.) **85** J 4
Colfax (WA.) **97** F 2
Colfax (WI.) **59** D 5
Collbran (CO.) **94** C 2
College (AL.) **121** F 3
College Grove (TN.) **50** D 5
College Heights (AR.)
  67 E 4
College Station (TX.) **75** E 4
Collierville (TN.) **67** G 2
Collins (MS.) **49** E 3
Collinston (LA.) **68** D 1
Collinsville (MS.) **48** D 2
Collinwood (TN.) **50** C 5
Collison (IL.) **56** C 2
Collyer (KS.) **78** C 2
Colmor (N.M.) **97** F 2
Coloma (WI.) **59** E 3
Colome (SD.) **83** F 4
Colona (CO.) **94** C 3
Colonial Heights (VA.)
  37 G 4
Colonias (N.M.) **97** F 3
Colony (KS.) **79** H 3
Colorado **94** B 4
Colorado (AK.) **121** F 3
Colorado (AL.) **118** F 5
Colorado City (AZ.) **103** F 5
Colorado City (TX.) **73** G 1
Colorado Desert **107** GH 4

Colorado National
  Monument **94** B 2
Colorado River **107** H 4–5
Colorado River (TX.) **71** F 1
Colorado River Indian
  Reservation **100** B 3
Colorado Springs (CO.)
  95 F 3
Colquitt (GA.) **43** E 5
Colstrip (MT.) **87** G 4
Colt (AR.) **67** F 2
Coltax (WA.) **115** H 3
Colter Peak **92** B 1
Colton (N.Y.) **33** F 1
Colton (UT.) **102** C 2
Coluille (AL.) **121** E 2
Columbia (AL.) **47** E 3
Columbia (IL.) **57** E 5
Columbia (KY.) **51** E 3
Columbia (LA.) **68** C 1
Columbia (MO.) **64–65** E 3
Columbia (MS.) **49** E 3
Columbia (N.C.) **39** H 3
Columbia (PA.) **34** E 3
Columbia (S.C.) **40** D 2
Columbia (S.D.) **83** G 2
Columbia (TN.) **50** D 5
Columbia (TN.) **50** D 5
Columbia (UT.) **102** C 2
Columbia City (IN.) **52** D 1
Columbia Falls (MT.) **89** F 1
Columbia Plateau
  113 G 1–4
Columbia River **113** F 1–2
Columbia Road Reservoir
  83 G 2
Columbiana (AL.) **46** C 4
Columbine (CO.) **94** C 1
Columbus (GA.) **43** D 5
Columbus (IN.) **52** D 3
Columbus (KS.) **79** J 4
Columbus (MS.) **48** C 2
Columbus (MT.) **86** D 4
Columbus (N.C.) **51** H 5
Columbus (ND.) **84** D 2
Columbus (NE.) **81** G 3
Columbus (N.M.) **98** C 5
Columbus (OH.) **53** F 3
Columbus (TX.) **71** F 1
Columbus (WI.) **59** F 3
Columbus Junction (IA.)
  63 G 4
Columbus Salt Marsh
  108 DE 1
Colusa (CA.) **110** C 4
Colville (WA.) **115** GH 1
Colville Indian Reservation
  115 FG 1
Comal (TX.) **70** D 1
Comanche (MT.) **86** E 3
Comanche (OK.) **77** E 3
Comanche (TX.) **74** C 3
Comanche Reservoir
  111 D 3
Combes (TX.) **71** F 4
Comerío (P.R.) **124** B 2
Comfort (TX.) **74** C 5
Comfrey (MN.) **61** F 4
Commerce (GA.) **42** B 4
Commerceo (MO.) **65** H 4
Como (MS.) **48** B 3
Comptche (CA.) **110** C 5
Comstock (NE.) **81** E 3
Comstock (TX.) **73** G 4
Concan (TX.) **70** C 1
Conception, Point **106** B 3

Conchas Dam (N.M.) **97** F 3
Conchas Lake **97** F 3
Concho (AZ.) **101** G 2
Concho River **74** A 3
Conconully (WA.) **115** EF 1
Concord (CA.) **111** E 3–4
Concord (MO.) **65** G 3
Concord (N.C.) **38** D 3
Concord (N.H.) **29** E 6
Concord (TN.) **51** F 5
Concordia (KS.) **79** F 2
Concrete (WA.) **114** D 1
Conda (ID.) **91** H 4
Conde (S.D.) **83** G 2
Condon (MT.) **89** G 2
Condon (OR.) **113** E 1
Cone (TX.) **76** B 4
Cone Mountain **120** D 2
Conecuh River **47** E 4
Conejos (CO.) **94** D 4
Confluence (PA.) **34** B 4
Congaree River **41** E 3
Congress (AZ.) **100** D 2
Conifer (CO.) **95** E 2
Conlen (TX.) **97** H 2
Conneaut (OH.) **53** J 1
Conneauville (PA.) **34** A 2
Connecticut **35**
Connecticut River **29** DE 7
Connell (WA.) **115** G 3
Connellsville (PA.) **34** B 3
Conner (MT.) **89** F 4
Connersville (IN.) **52** D 3
Conover (WI.) **58** C 3
Conrad (IA.) **63** F 3
Conrad (MT.) **86** B 1
Conroe (TX.) **75** F 4
Constance, Mount **114** B 2
Constellation (AZ.) **100** D 2
Contact (NV.) **105** G 1
Continental (OH.) **52** E 1
Continental Divide (N.M.)
  96 B 3
Continental Lake **104** C 1
Continental Peak **92** D 3
Controller Bay **116** BC 1–2
Convent (LA.) **69** E 3
Conway (AR.) **66** D 2
Conway (MO.) **64** E 4
Conway (N.H.) **29** E 6
Conway (S.C.) **41** FG 3
Conway (TX.) **76** B 2
Conway Springs (KS.)
  79 F 4
Conyers (GA.) **42** C 4
Cook (MN.) **60** C 2
Cook (NE.) **81** H 4
Cook Inlet (AL.) **119** E 1–2
Cooke City (MT.) **86** CD 4
Cookes Peak **98** C 4
Cookeville (TN.) **50** E 4
Coolidge (AZ.) **101** E 3
Coolidge (GA.) **43** E 4
Coolidge (KS.) **78** B 3
Coolidge Dam **101** F 3
Coon Rapids (MN.) **61** E 3
Cooper (AL.) **46** D 4
Cooper (TX.) **75** F 1
Cooperstown (N.D.) **85** H 3
Cooperstown (N.Y.) **33** F 3
Coopersville (MI.) **55** E 4
Coos Bay (OR.) **112** A 3
Coos Bay (OR.) **112** A 3
Coosa River **46** C 4
Copan (OK.) **77** G 1
Copano Bay **71** E 2

Cope (CO.) **95** H 2
Copeland (FL.) **45** F 3
Copeland (ID.) **88** D 1
Copeland (KS.) **78** C 4
Copeville (TX.) **75** E 1
Copper Butte **115** G 1
Copper Center (AL.)
  116 B 1
Copper Harbor (MI.) **58** B 1
Copper R. (AL.) **116** C 1
Copperas Cove (TX.) **74** C 3
Copperfield (NV.) **104** B 3
Coquille (OR.) **112** A 3
Cora (WY.) **92** C 3
Coralville (IA.) **63** G 4
Coralville Lake **63** G 4
Coram (MT.) **89** FG 1
Corazon (N.M.) **97** F 3
Corbin (KY.) **51** F 4
Corbin (MT.) **86** A 3
Corcoran (CA.) **111** F 1
Cordele (GA.) **43** E 4
Cordell (OK.) **76** D 2
Cordell (WA.) **115** F 1
Cordova (AL.) **116** B 1
Cordova (AL.) **46** C 5
Cordova (IL.) **56** B 5
Core Banks **39** H 4
Corinne (UT.) **102** A 4
Corinth (MS.) **48** B 2
Cornelia (GA.) **42** B 4
Cornell (WI.) **59** D 5
Corning (AR.) **67** F 1
Corning (CA.) **110** C 4
Corning (IA.) **62** D 5
Corning (NE.) **79** G 2
Corning (N.Y.) **32** C 3
Cornish (CO.) **95** F 1
Cornudas (TX.) **72** C 2
Cornville (AZ.) **100** E 2
Cornwall (Can.) **33** F 1
Cornwell (FL.) **45** D 3
Corona (CA.) **107** E 4
Corona (N.M.) **96** E 4
Coronado (CA.) **107** E 5
Corpus Christi (TX.) **71** E 3
Corpus Christi Bay **71** E 3
Corpus Christi, Lake
  70 DE 2
Corral (ID.) **90** E 3
Correo (N.M.) **96** C 4
Corrigan (TX.) **75** G 3
Corry (PA.) **34** B 2
Corsica (S.D.) **83** G 4
Corsicana (TX.) **75** E 2
Cortez (CO.) **94** B 4
Cortez Mountains **105** E 2
Cortland (NE.) **81** H 4
Cortland (N.Y.) **32** D 3
Cortland (OH.) **53** J 1
Corvallis (MT.) **89** F 3
Corvallis (OR.) **112** B 2
Corwin Springs (MT.)
  86 C 4
Corydon (IA.) **63** E 5
Corydon (IN.) **52** C 4
Coshocton (OH.) **53** GH 2
Costa Mesa (CA.) **107** E 4
Costilla (N.M.) **96** E 2
Cotati (CA.) **111** D 4
Coteau (ND.) **84** D 2
Coteau des Prairies **83** HJ 2
Coteau du Missouri
  85 F 3–5
Cottage Grove (OR.)
  112 B 3

Cottage Grove Lake 112 B 3
Cotton (MN.) 60 C 2
Cotton Plant (AR.) 67 E 2
Cottondale (AL.) 46 C 5
Cottondale (FL.) 47 F 3
Cottonwood (AZ.) 100 D 2
Cottonwood (CA.) 110 B 4
Cottonwood (ID.) 88 D 3
Cottonwood (MN.) 61 F 5
Cottonwood (SD.) 82 D 4
Cottonwood Falls (KS.) 79 G 3
Cottonwood Pass 106 B 2
Cottonwood River 61 F 5
Cotulla (TX.) 70 C 2
Coudersport (PA.) 34 C 2
Cougar (WA.) 114 C 3
Cougar Reservoir 112 C 2
Coulee (ND.) 84 D 2
Coulee City (WA.) 115 F 2
Coulee Dam (WA.) 115 G 2
Coulee Dam National Recreation Area 115 G 1
Coulterville (CA.) 111 E 2
Coulterville (IL.) 57 E 5
Council (AL.) 120 C 3
Council (ID.) 90 C 2
Council Bluffs (IA.) 62 C 4
Council Grove (KS.) 79 G 3
Council Grove Lake 79 G 3
Country Homes (WA.) 115 H 2
Coupeville (WA.) 114 C 1
Courtenay (FL.) 44 C 2
Courtland (AL.) 46 B 5
Courtland (VA.) 37 GH 5
Courtney (TX.) 75 E 4
Coushatta (LA.) 68 B 1
Cove (OR.) 113 H 1
Covelo (CA.) 110 C 5
Covert (KS.) 78 E 2
Covington (GA.) 42 C 4
Covington (IN.) 52 B 2
Covington (KY.) 51 F 1
Covington (LA.) 69 E 3
Covington (MI.) 58 C 2
Covington (OK.) 77 F 1
Covington (TN.) 67 G 2
Cow Head Lake 110 A 1–2
Cowan (TN.) 50 E 5
Coward (S.C.) 41 F 3
Cowdrey (CO.) 94 D 1
Cowen (W.V.) 36 D 3
Cowen, Mount 86 C 4
Coweta (OK.) 77 H 2
Cowles (N.M.) 96 E 3
Cowley (WY.) 92 D 1
Coyame (Mex.) 72 C 4
Coyote (N.M.) 98 E 3
Coyote Lake 107 F 2
Coyote Wells (CA.) 107 G 5
Cozad (NE.) 80 E 4
Crab Orchard (TN.) 51 E 5
Crab Orchard Lake 57 F 4
Crabtree (OR.) 112 C 2
Craig (AL.) 117 E 2
Craig (CO.) 94 C 1
Craig (MO.) 64 B 1
Craig (MT.) 86 B 2
Craig Pass 92 B 1
Craigmont (ID.) 88 D 3
Cranberry Lake 33 F 1
Crandon (WI.) 58 D 3
Crane (MO.) 64 D 5
Crane (MT.) 87 J 2
Crane (OR.) 113 G 3
Crane (TX.) 73 F 2
Crane Mountain 113 E 4
Crane Prairie Reservoir 112 D 3
Cranston (R.I.) 30 E 4
Crater Lake (OR.) 112 C 4
Crater Lake (OR.) 112 C 4
Crater Lake National Park 112 C 4
Craters of the Moon National Monument 91 F 3
Crawford (CO.) 94 C 3
Crawford (NE.) 80 A 2
Crawford (TX.) 74 D 3
Crawfordsville (IN.) 52 B 2
Crawfordville (FL.) 47 F 2
Crawfordville (GA.) 42 C 3
Crazy Mountains 86 C 3–4
Creede (CO.) 94 C 4
Creedmoor (N.C.) 39 F 2
Creighton (NE.) 81 G 2
Creighton (SD.) 82 C 3
Creole (LA.) 68 B 4
Crescent (OK.) 77 F 1–2
Crescent (OR.) 112 D 3
Crescent City (CA.) 110 A 6
Crescent City (FL.) 44 B 3
Crescent Junction (UT.) 102 D 1
Crescent Lake 44 B 3
Crescent Lake (OR.) 112 D 3
Cresco (IA.) 63 F 2
Cresson (TX.) 74 D 2
Crested Butte (CO.) 94 D 3
Crestline (CA.) 107 E 3
Crestline (NV.) 109 H 2
Crestline (OH.) 53 G 2
Creston (IA.) 62 D 4
Creston (LA.) 68 BC 2
Creston (WA.) 115 G 2
Creston (WY.) 92 E 4
Crestview (FL.) 47 F 4
Creswell (N.C.) 39 H 3
Creswell (OR.) 112 B 3
Crete (NE.) 81 H 4
Crillon, Mount 117 D 2
Cripple Creek (CO.) 95 E 3
Crisfield (MD.) 37 J 4
Crisp Point 54 B 4
Crivitz (WI.) 59 D 1
Crocker (MO.) 65 E 4
Crocker (N.M.) 98 C 3
Crockett (TX.) 75 F 3
Crockston (MN.) 60 C 6
Crofton (KY.) 50 C 3
Crofton (NE.) 81 G 2
Croghan (N.Y.) 33 E 2
Croix, Lac la 60 B 1
Cromwell (AL.) 46 D 6
Cromwell (MN.) 60 D 2
Crook (CO.) 95 H 1
Crooked Creek (AL.) 119 D 1
Crooked Island 47 F 3
Crooked River 112 E 2
Crooksville (OH.) 53 G 3
Crosby (MN.) 60 D 4
Crosby (MS.) 49 E 5
Crosby (ND.) 84 C 2
Crosby, Mount 92 C 2
Crosbyton (TX.) 76 B 4
Cross City (FL.) 44 B 5
Cross Hill (S.C.) 40 D 2
Cross Lake (ME.) 28 A 3
Cross Plains (TX.) 74 B 2
Cross Sound (AL.) 117 D 2
Crossett (AR.) 67 E 4
Crossman Peak 100 B 2
Crossroads (N.M.) 99 G 3
Crossville (IL.) 57 E 3
Crossville (TN.) 51 E 5
Croswell (MI.) 55 E 1
Crow Agency (MT.) 87 F 4
Crow Creek Indian Reservation 83 F 3
Crow Indian Reservation 87 EF 4
Crow Lake (Can.) 60 A 3
Crowe Peak 86 B 3
Crowell (TX.) 76 D 3–4
Crowheart (WY.) 92 C 2
Crowheart (WY.) 92 D 2
Crowley (LA.) 68 C 3
Crowley, Lake 108 D 2
Crowley Ridge 67 F 2
Crown City (OH.) 53 G 4
Crown Point (IN.) 52 B 1
Crown Point (LA.) 69 E 4
Crownpoint (N.M.) 96 B 3
Crows Nest Peak 82 B 3
Cruger (MS.) 48 C 4
Crump Lake 113 F 4
Crystal (MN.) 61 E 3
Crystal (N.D.) 85 J 2
Crystal Bay (FL.) 44 C 4
Crystal Bay (NV.) 104 B 3
Crystal City (MO.) 65 G 3
Crystal City (TX.) 70 B 2
Crystal Lake (IL.) 56 A 3
Crystal River (FL.) 44 C 4
Crystal Springs (MS.) 49 D 4
Cuba (AL.) 46 D 6
Cuba (IL.) 56 C 5
Cuba (KS.) 79 F 2
Cuba (MO.) 65 F 3
Cuba (N.Y.) 32 B 3
Cuchara (CO.) 95 E 4
Cudahy (WI.) 59 G 1–2
Cuddeback Lake 107 E 2
Cuddy Mountain 90 C 2
Cuero (TX.) 71 E 1
Cuervo (N.M.) 97 F 3
Cuesta Pass 106 B 2
Culbertson (MT.) 87 J 1
Culbertson (NE.) 80 D 4
Culebra, Isla de 124 C 2
Cullison (KS.) 78 DE 4
Cullman (AL.) 46 B 4
Culloden (GA.) 42 D 5
Culp Creek (OR.) 112 C 3
Culpeper (VA.) 37 G 3
Culver (OR.) 112 D 2
Cumberland (IA.) 62 D 4
Cumberland (KY.) 51 G 3–4
Cumberland (MD.) 37 F 2
Cumberland (OH.) 53 H 3
Cumberland (VA.) 37 F 4
Cumberland (WI.) 59 D 6
Cumberland City (TN.) 50 C 4
Cumberland Island 43 F 2
Cumberland Island National Seashore 43 F 2
Cumberland, Lake 51 F 4
Cumberland Plateau 51 EG 4–5
Cumberland Point 58 B 3
Cumberland River 50 C 4
Cumming (GA.) 42 B 5
Cundiff (TX.) 74 C 1
Cunningham (KS.) 78 E 4
Cunningham (WA.) 115 G 3
Cuprum (ID.) 88 D 4
Curecanti National Recreation Area 94 C 3
Currant Creek Peak 102 B 3
Currant Mountain 105 F 4
Currie (MN.) 61 F 5
Currie (NV.) 105 G 2
Currituck (N.C.) 39 J 2
Curry 116 B 1
Curtin (OR.) 112 B 3
Curtis (NE.) 80 D 4
Curwood, Mount 58 C 2
Cushenbury (CA.) 107 F 3
Cushing (OK.) 77 G 2
Cushman (OR.) 112 B 2
Cusick (WA.) 115 H 1
Cusseta (GA.) 43 D 5
Custer (MT.) 87 F 3
Custer (SD.) 82 B 4
Custer Battefiled National Monument 87 F 4
Custer City (OK.) 76 E 2
Cut Bank (MT.) 86 A 1
Cuthbert (GA.) 43 E 5
Cutler (CA.) 111 F 1
Cutter (AZ.) 101 F 3
Cutter (N.M.) 98 C 3
Cuyahoga Falls (OH.) 53 H 1
Cuyapaipe Indian Reservation 107 F 5
Cygnes River 79 HJ 3
Cynthiana (KY.) 51 F 2
Cypress (LA.) 68 BC 2

D

Dabney (TX.) 70 B 1
Dade City (FL.) 44 C 4
Dagett (CA.) 107 F 3
Dagger Mountain 73 E 4
Dahlgren (IL.) 57 E 3
Dahlia (N.M.) 96 E 3
Dahlonega (GA.) 42 B 4
Dailey (W.V.) 36 E 3
Daingerfield (TX.) 75 G 1
Dakota City (IA.) 62 D 3
Dakota City (NE.) 81 H 2
Dale (OR.) 113 G 2
Dale City (VA.) 37 G 3
Dale Hollow Lake 51 E 4
Dale Lake 107 G 3
Dalhart (TX.) 97 H 2
Dall I. (AL.) 117 E 3
Dall Lake (AL.) 119 C 1
Dallas (GA.) 42 C 5
Dallas (OR.) 112 B 2
Dallas (TX.) 75 E 2
Dallas Center (IA.) 62 D 4
Dalton (GA.) 42 B 5
Dalton (MA.) 30 C 3
Dalton (NE.) 80 B 3
Daly City (CA.) 111 E 4

Damascus (AR.) **66** D 2
Danbury (CT.) **35** H 2
Danbury (N.C.) **38** D 2
Danbury (NE.) **80** D 4
Danbury (WI.) **58** D 6
Danby Lake **107** G 3
Dandridge (TN.) **51** G 4
Danforth (ME.) **28** C 3
Danforth Hills **94** BC 1
Daniel (WY.) **92** B 3
Danielsville (GA.) **42** B 4
Dannebrog (NE.) **81** F 3
Dannemora (N.Y.) **33** G 1
Dansville (N.Y.) **32** C 3
Danville (AR.) **66** C 2
Danville (IL.) **56** C 2
Danville (IN.) **52** C 3
Danville (KY.) **51** F 3
Danville (PA.) **34** E 2–3
Danville (VA.) **36** E 5
Danville (VT.) **30** D 1
Danville (WA.) **115** G 1
Darby (MT.) **89** F 3
Darby, Cape **120** C 3
Dardanelle (AR.) **66** C 2
Dardanelle (CA.) **111** D 1
Dardanelle Lake **66** C 2
Darling, Lake **84** DE 2
Darlington (FL.) **47** F 3–4
Darlington (ID.) **91** F 3
Darlington (S.C.) **41** F 2
Darlington (WI.) **59** G 4
Darrington (WA.) **114** D 1
Darrouzett (TX.) **76** C 1
Darwin (IL.) **57** D 2
Dassel (MN.) **61** E 4
Dateland (AZ.) **100** C 4
Datil (N.M.) **96** C 4
Dauphin Island **47** F 6
Davant (LA.) **69** F 4
Davenport (CA.) **111** E 4
Davenport (IA.) **63** H 4
Davenport (N.D.) **85** JK 4
Davenport (OK.) **77** G 2
Davenport (WA.) **115** G 2
David (KY.) **51** G 3
David City (NE.) **81** G 3
Davidson (OK.) **76** D 3
Davidson Mountains (AL.) **121** G 2
Davis (CA.) **111** D 3
Davis (OK.) **77** F 3
Davis City (IA.) **62–63** E 5
Davis Dam **100** B 1
Davis, Lake **110** C 2
Davis Lake **112** D 3
Davis, Mount **34** B 4
Davis Mountains **72** DE 3
Davisson Lake **114** C 3
Dawson (GA.) **43** E 5
Dawson (MN.) **61** F 6
Dawson (ND.) **85** G 4
Dawson (OR.) **112** B 2
Dawson Range (AL.) **117** D 1
Dawson Springs (KY.) **50** C 3
Dawsonville (GA.) **42** B 5
Day (FL.) **44** A 5
Dayton (MT.) **89** F 2
Dayton (N.M.) **99** F 4
Dayton (OH.) **52** E 3
Dayton (TN.) **51** E 5
Dayton (TX.) **75** G 4
Dayton (WA.) **115** H 3
Dayton (WY.) **93** E 1
Daytona Beach (FL.) **44** B 2
Dayville (OR.) **113** F 2
De Beque (CO.) **94** B 2
De Funiak Springs (FL.) **47** F 4
De Gray Lake **66** C 3
De Kalb (IL.) **56** B 3
De Land (FL.) **44** B 3
De Leon (TX.) **74** C 2
De Leon Springs (FL.) **44** B 3
De Long Mountains (AL.) **120** C 2
De Pere (WI.) **59** E 2
De Queen (AR.) **66** B 3
De Quincy (LA.) **68** B 3
De Ridder (LA.) **68** B 3
De Sart (ND.) **84** D 4
De Smet (MT.) **89** F 3
De Smet (S.D.) **83** H 3
De Smet, Lake **93** F 1
De Soto (MO.) **65** G 3
De Tour Village (MI.) **54** B 3
De Valls Bluff (AR.) **67** E 3
De Witt (AR.) **67** E 3
De Witt (IA.) **63** H 4
De Witt (MI.) **55** F 3
De Witt (NE.) **81** H 4
Dead Knoll **92** B 3
Dead Lake **47** F 3
Deadhorse (AL.) **121** F 1
Deadman Bay **44** B 5
Deadman Lake **107** F 3
Deadmans Basin Reservoir **86** D 3
Deadwood (SD.) **82** B 3
Deadwood Reservoir **90** D 2
Dean (MT.) **86** D 4
Dearborn (MI.) **55** F 2
Deary (ID.) **88** D 3
Dease R. (AL.) **117** F 2
Death Valley (CA.) **109** EF 3
Death Valley (CA.) **109** EF 3
Death Valley National Monument **109** EF 3
Deatsville (AL.) **46** D 4
Deaver (WY.) **92** D 1
Debauch Mountain **120** D 3
Decatur (AL.) **46** B 5
Decatur (GA.) **42** C 5
Decatur (IL.) **56** D 3
Decatur (MS.) **48** D 3
Decatur (NE.) **81** H 3
Decatur (TX.) **74** D 1
Decaturville (TN.) **50** B 5
Decker (MT.) **87** G 4
Deckerville (MI.) **55** E 1
Decorah (IA.) **63** G 2
Deep Creek Lake **37** E 2
Deep Springs (CA.) **109** E 2
Deep Springs Lake **109** E 2
Deepwater (MO.) **64** D 3
Deer Creek (MN.) **60** D 5
Deer Creek Indian Reservation **60** C 3
Deer Creek Reservoir **102** B 3
Deer Isle **29** D 3
Deer Lodge (MT.) **86** A 3
Deer Park (AL.) **47** E 6
Deer Park (WA.) **115** H 2
Deer River (MN.) **60** C 3
Deer Trail (CO.) **95** F 2
Deerfield (KS.) **78** B 4
Deering (AL.) **120** C 2
Deering (ND.) **84** EF 2
Deerwood (MN.) **60** D 3
Deeth (NV.) **105** F 1
Defiance (IA.) **62** C 4
Defiance (OH.) **52** E 1
Defiance Plateau **103** FG 1
Dekalb (MS.) **48** D 2
Dekle Beach (FL.) **44** B 5
Del City (OK.) **77** F 2
Del Mar (CA.) **107** E 5
Del Norte (CO.) **94** D 4
Del Rio (TX.) **73** H 4
Del Valle (TX.) **74** D 4
Delacroix (LA.) **69** F 4
Delano (CA.) **106** C 2
Delano Peak **103** D 4
Delaplaine (AR.) **67** F 1
Delarof Islands (AL.) **116** J 1
Delavan (IL.) **56** C 4
Delaware **37** J 2–3
Delaware (KS.) **77** H 1
Delaware (OH.) **53** F 2
Delaware Bay **37** J 2–3
Delaware City (DE.) **37** J 2
Delaware Mountains **72** D 2
Delco (ID.) **91** F 4
Delco (N.C.) **39** F 4
Delevan (CA.) **110** C 4
Delgada, Point **110** B 6
Delhi (CO.) **95** G 4
Delhi (LA.) **68** D 1
Delhi (N.Y.) **33** F 3
Delhi (TX.) **74** D 5
Delia (KS.) **79** H 2
Dell (MT.) **91** G 2
Dellenbaugh, Mount **103** F 5
Delmar (DE.) **37** J 3
Delmarva Peninsula **37** J 3
Delmont (S.D.) **83** G 4
Delphi (IN.) **52** C 2
Delphia (MT.) **87** E 3
Delphos (KS.) **79** F 2
Delphos (N.M.) **97** G 4
Delphos (OH.) **52** E 2
Delray Beach (FL.) **45** E 2
Delta (CO.) **94** B 3
Delta (LA.) **69** D 1
Delta (UT.) **102** C 4
Delta Junction (AL.) **121** FG 3
Delta Peak **117** F 2
Delta Peak (AL.) **117** F 2
Delta River **121** F 3
Demarcation Point **121** G 2
Deming (N.M.) **98** C 4
Deming (WA.) **114** C 1
Demopolis (AL.) **46** D 5
Demotte (IN.) **52** B 1
Denali **121** F 3
Denali Nat. Park and Pres. (AL.) **121** E 3
Denhoff (ND.) **85** F 3
Denio (NV.) **104** C 1
Denison (IA.) **62** C 3
Denison (TX.) **77** G 4
Denmark (S.C.) **40** D 3
Denmark (WI.) **59** E 1
Dennehotso (AZ.) **103** F 1
Denton (TX.) **74** D 1
Denver (CO.) **95** F 2
Denver City (TX.) **99** H 3–4
Deoatur (IN.) **52** E 2
Deora (CO.) **95** H 4
Depew (OK.) **77** G 2
Depoe Bay (OR.) **112** A 2
Deposit (N.Y.) **33** E 3
Derby (KS.) **79** F 4
Derby (N.Y.) **32** A 3
Derby (TX.) **70** C 2
Dermott (AR.) **67** E 4
Dernieres, Isles **69** E 4
Derry (N.H.) **29** F 6
Des Allemands (LA.) **69** E 4
des Allemands, Lac **69** E 4
Des Arc (AR.) **67** E 3
Des Moines (IA.) **63** E 4
Des Moines (N.M.) **97** G 2
Des Moines River **63** F 4–5
Des Plaines (IL.) **56** AB 3
Descanso (CA.) **107** F 5
Deschutes River **112** E 1
Deschutes-Umatilla Plateau **113** F 1
Desecheo, Isla **124** A 2
Deseret (UT.) **102** C 4
Desert (CA.) **109** G 4
Desert (N.M.) **98** D 4
Desert Center (CA.) **107** G 4
Desert Hot Springs (CA.) **107** F 4
Desert Peak (UT.) **102** A 5
Desert Peak (UT.) **102** B 4
Desert Ranch Reservoir **105** E 1
Desert Valley **104** C 1
Deshler (NE.) **81** G 4
Deshler (OH.) **53** F 1
Desloge (MO.) **65** G 4
Destin (FL.) **47** F 4
Destruction Bay **117** D 1
Detroit (MI.) **55** F 1
Detroit (OR.) **112** C 2
Detroit Lake (OR.) **112** C 2
Detroit Lakes (MN.) **60** D 5
Devils Den (CA.) **106** C 2
Devils Lake (N.D.) **85** G 2
Devils Lake (ND.) **85** G 2
Devils Lake (TX.) **73** H 4
Devils Postpile National Monument **111** E 1
Devils Tower National Monument **93** H 1
Devine (TX.) **70** D 1
Dewey (OK.) **77** GH 1
Dewey (SD.) **82** B 4
Dewey Lake **51** H 3
Deweyville (TX.) **75** H 4
Dexter (KS.) **79** G 4
Dexter (ME.) **28** C 4
Dexter (MO.) **65** H 5
Dexter (N.M.) **99** F 3
Dexter (OR.) **112** C 3
Dezadeash Lake **117** D 1
D'Hanis (TX.) **70** C 1
Diablo (WA.) **114** D 1
Diablo Plateau **72** C 2
Diablo Range **111** EF 3
Diamond Dam **99** F 3
Diamond Lake (OR.) **112** C 3
Diamond Lake (OR.) **112** C 3
Diamond Peak (ID.) **91** F 2
Diamond Peak (NV.) **105** F 3
Diamond Peak (OR.) **112** C 3
Diamond Peak (WA.) **115** H 3

Diamond Springs (CA.) **111** D 2
Diamondville (WY.) **92** B 4
Diboll (TX.) **75** G 3
Dickens (TX.) **76** C 4
Dickinson (ND.) **84** D 4
Dickinson (TX.) **71** G 1
Dickson (TN.) **50** C 4
Dietrich (ID.) **91** E 4
Dighton (KS.) **78** C 3
Dilia (N.M.) **97** EF 3
Dilley (TX.) **70** C 2
Dillingham (AL.) **119** D 2
Dillon (CO.) **94** D 2
Dillon (MT.) **86** A 4
Dillon (S.C.) **41** F 2
Dillon Beach (CA.) **111** D 4
Dillon Lake **53** F 2
Dillon Reservoir **94** DE 2
Dimmitt (TX.) **97** H 4
Dimock (S.D.) **83** G 4
Dinero (TX.) **70** D 2
Dinosaur (CO.) **94** B 1
Dinosaur National
  Monument **102** B 1
Dinwiddie (VA.) **37** G 4
Dirty Devil River **103** D 2
Disappointment, Cape
  114 A 3
Dishman (WA.) **115** H 2
Dismal Swamp **37** H 5
District of Columbia **37** G 3
Diversion Lake **76** D 4
Divide (CO.) **95** E 3
Divide (MT.) **86** A 4
Dix (NE.) **80** A 3
Dixie (AL.) **47** E 4
Dixie (ID.) **88** E 4
Dixie (WA.) **115** G 3
Dixon (CA.) **111** D 3
Dixon (IL.) **56** B 4
Dixon (KY.) **50** C 3
Dixon (MO.) **65** E 3
Dixon (MT.) **89** F 2
Dixon (N.M.) **96** E 2
Dixon (WY.) **92–93** E 4
Dixon Entrance (AL.)
  117 E 3
Dixons Mills (AL.) **47** D 6
Dobson (N.C.) **38** D 2
Dockton (WA.) **114** C 2
Dodge (NE.) **81** H 3
Dodge Center (MN.)
  61 F 2–3
Dodge City (KS.) **78** C 4
Dodgeville (WI.) **59** G 4
Dodson (LA.) **68** C 1
Dodson (MT.) **87** E 1
Dog Island **47** G 2
Doland (S.D.) **83** G 3
Dolgeville (N.Y.) **33** F 2
Dollar Bay (MI.) **58** B 2
Dolores (CO.) **94** B 4
Dolores River **94** B 3
Domingo (N.M.) **96** D 3
Don Pedro Reservoir
  111 E 2
Dona (N.M.) **98** C 4
Dona Ana (N.M.) **98** D 4
Donaldson (AR.) **66** D 3
Donaldson (MN.) **60** B 6
Donaldsonville (LA.)
  68–69 DE 3
Donalsonville (GA.) **43** E 5
Donie (TX.) **75** E 3
Doniphan (MO.) **65** F 5

Doniphan (NE.) **81** F 4
Donjek R. (AL.) **117** D 1
Donnelly **121** F 3
Donnelly (ID.) **90** C 2
Donner Pass **110** C 2
Doole (TX.) **74** B 3
Doon (IA.) **62** B 2
Door Peninsula **59** DE 1
Dora (AL.) **46** C 5
Dorchester (S.C.) **41** E 3
Dorchester (WI.) **59** D 4
Dore (ND.) **84** C 3
Dorena Lake **112** C 3
Dorrance (KS.) **78** E 3
Dorris (CA.) **110** A 3
Dos Cabezas (AZ.) **101** G 4
Dos Palos (CA.) **111** F 2
Dos Rios (CA.) **110** C 5
Dot Lake **121** G 3
Dothan (AL.) **47** E 3
Double Mountain Fork
  76 BC 4
Double Springs (AL.)
  46 B 5
Douglas (AL.) **117** E 2
Douglas (GA.) **43** E 3
Douglas (ND.) **84** E 3
Douglas (WA.) **115** F 2
Douglas (WY.) **93** G 2
Douglas City (CA.) **110** B 4
Douglas Lake **51** G 5
Douglass (KS.) **79** G 4
Douglass (TX.) **75** G 3
Douro (TX.) **73** F 2
Dove Creek (CO.) **94** B 4
Dover (AR.) **66** C 2
Dover (DE.) **37** J 2
Dover (ID.) **88** D 1
Dover (N.C.) **39** G 3
Dover (N.H.) **29** E 5
Dover (OH.) **53** H 2
Dover (OK.) **77** F 1
Dover (TN.) **50** C 4
Dover-Foxcroft (ME.)
  28 C 4
Dow City (IA.) **62** C 4
Dowagiac (MI.) **55** F 5
Downey (ID.) **91** G 4
Downieville (CA.) **110** C 2
Downs (KS.) **78** E 2
Downs Mountain **92** C 2
Downsville (N.Y.) **32** E 3
Dows (IA.) **63** E 3
Doyle (CA.) **110** B 2
Doylestown (PA.) **35** F 3
Doyleville (CO.) **94** D 3
Dragoon (AZ.) **101** FG 4
Drain (OR.) **112** B 3
Drake (AZ.) **100** D 1
Drake (MO.) **65** F 3
Drake (ND.) **85** F 3
Drake Peak **113** E 4
Draper (UT.) **102** B 3
Drayton (N.D.) **85** J 2
Drayton Plains (MI.) **55** F 2
Dresden (KS.) **78** C 2
Dresden (TN.) **50** B 4
Drews Reservoir **112** E 4
Drifton (FL.) **44** A 5
Driftwood (PA.) **34** C 2
Driggs (ID.) **91** HJ 3
Driscoll (TX.) **71** E 3
Driskill Mountain **68** C 1
Drummond (ID.) **91** H 2
Drummond (WI.) **58** C 5
Drummond Island **54** BC 2

Drummondville (Can.)
  28 C 7
Drumright (OK.) **77** G 1
Dry Creek Mountain
  105 E 1
Dry Falls Dam **115** F 2
Dry Lake (N.D.) **85** G 2
Dry Lake (NV.) **109** H 3
Dry Lake (NV.) **104** B 2
Dry Tortugas **45** G 4
Dryden (N.Y.) **32** D 3
Dryden (TX.) **73** F 3
Du Bois (NE.) **81** H 4
Du Bois (PA.) **34** C 2
Du Quoin (IL.) **57** E 5
Dubach (LA.) **68** C 1
Dublin (GA.) **43** D 3
Dublin (TX.) **74** C 2
Dublin (VA.) **36** D 4
Dubois (ID.) **91** G 2
Dubois (WY.) **92** C 2
Dubuque (IA.) **63** H 3
Dubuque Hills **56** A 5
Duchesne (UT.) **102** B 2
Duck River **50** C 5
Duck Valley Indian
  Reservation **90** C 4
Ducktown (TN.) **51** F 5
Duckwater (NV.) **105** F 4
Duckwater Indian
  Reservation **105** EF 4
Ducor (CA.) **106** D 2
Duette (FL.) **45** D 4
Duffer Peak **104** C 1
Dufur (OR.) **112** D 1
Duke (OK.) **76** D 3
Dukes (FL.) **44** B 4
Dulce (N.M.) **96** C 2
Duluth (MN.) **60** D 2
Dumas (AR.) **67** E 4
Dumas (TX.) **97** H 3
Duncan (AZ.) **101** G 4
Duncan (MS.) **48** B 4
Duncan (OK.) **77** E 3
Dundalk (M.D.) **37** H 2
Dundas Island **117** E 2
Dundas Island (AL.) **117** E 3
Dundee (MI.) **55** G 2
Dundee (N.Y.) **32** C 3
Dunedin (FL.) **44** C 4
Dunken (N.M.) **99** E 4
Dunkirk (N.Y.) **32** A 3
Dunkirk (OH.) **53** F 2
Dunlap (IA.) **62** C 4
Dunlap (TN.) **51** E 5
Dunlay (TX.) **70** C 1
Dunlop (TX.) **76** C 3
Dunmor (KY.) **50** D 3
Dunmore (PA.) **35** F 2
Dunn (N.C.) **39** F 3
Dunn (TX.) **73** H 1
Dunn Center (ND.) **84** D 3
Dunnellon (FL.) **44** B 4
Dunnigan (CA.) **111** D 4
Dunning (NE.) **80** D 3
Dunphy (NV.) **105** E 2
Dunseith (ND.) **85** F 2
Dunsmuir (CA.) **110** A 4
Dupree (SD.) **82** D 2
Dupuyer (MT.) **86** A 1
Duran (N.M.) **96** E 4
Durand (MI.) **55** F 2
Durand (WI.) **59** E 5
Durango (CO.) **94** C 4
Durant (IA.) **63** G 4
Durant (MS.) **48** C 3

Durant (OK.) **77** G 3
Durbin (W.V.) **36** E 3
Durham (CA.) **110** C 3
Durham (KS.) **79** F 3
Durham (N.C.) **39** F 3
Durham (OK.) **76** D 2
Durham (WY.) **93** H 4
Durkee (OR.) **113** H 2
Dushore (PA.) **34** E 2
Dustin (OK.) **77** G 2
Dusty (WA.) **115** H 3
Dutch Harbor (AL.) **118** B 3
Dutch John (UT.) **102** B 1
Dutton (MT.) **86** B 2
Duvall (WA.) **114** D 2
Dwight (IL.) **56** B 3
Dwight (N.D.) **85** K 4
Dworshak Reservoir **88** D 3
Dwyer (WY.) **93** H 3
Dyer (NV.) **108** C 2
Dyersburg (TN.) **67** G 1
Dyersville (IA.) **63** G 3

E

E. Dubuque (IL.) **56** A 5
Eads (CO.) **95** H 3
Eagar (AZ.) **101** G 2
Eagle (AL.) **121** G 3
Eagle (CO.) **94** D 2
Eagle (ID.) **90** C 3
Eagle Bend (MN.) **61** D 4–5
Eagle Butte (SD.) **82** D 3
Eagle City (OK.) **76** E 2
Eagle Flat (TX.) **72** C 2
Eagle Grove (IA.) **62** E 3
Eagle Lake (CA.) **110** B 2
Eagle Lake (ME.) **28** A 3
Eagle Lake (ME.) **28** A 3
Eagle Lake (ME.) **28** B 4
Eagle Lake (TX.) **71** F 1
Eagle Mountain **58** B 4
Eagle Mountain Lake
  74 D 2
Eagle Nest (N.M.)
  96–97 E 2
Eagle Nest Butte **82** D 4
Eagle Nest Lake **97** E 2
Eagle Pass (TX.) **70** B 2
Eagle Peak (CA.) **110** A 2
Eagle Peak (CA.) **111** E 1
Eagle River (AL.) **116** B 1
Eagle River (WI.) **58** B 2
Eagle River (WI.) **58** D 3
Eagle Rock (VA.) **36** D 4
Eagle Summit (AL.) **121** F 2
Eagle Village **121** G 3
Eagleton (MT.) **86** D 2
Eagleville (CA.) **110** A 2
Eakly (OK.) **76** E 2
Earl, Lake **110** A 6
Earlimart (CA.) **106** C 2
Earlville (N.Y.) **32** E 3
Earp (CA.) **107** H 3
Earth (TX.) **97** H 4
Easley (S.C.) **40** C 2
East Amana (IA.) **63** G 4
East Bay (FL.) **47** F 3

East Bay (LA.) **69** F 4–5
East Bay (TX.) **71** H 1
East Bernad (TX.) **71** F 1
East Brady (PA.) **34** B 3
East Brewton (AL.) **47** E 5
East Chicago (IN.) **52** B 1
East Ely (NV.) **105** G 3
East Fork **121** F 2
East Glacier Park (MT.) **89** G 1
East Grand Forks (MN.) **60** C 6
East Grand Rapids (MI.) **55** F 4
East Helena (MT.) **86** B 3
East Lake (MI.) **55** D 5
East Lake (OR.) **112** D 3
East Lansing (MI.) **55** F 4
East Las Vegas (NV.) **109** H 3
East Liverpool (OH.) **53** J 2
East Lynn (W.V.) **36** B 3
East Nishnabotna River **62** C 4–5
East Olympia (WA.) **114** C 3
East Pack Reservoir **110** C 4
East Palatka (FL.) **44** B 3
East Point (GA.) **42** C 5
East Point (P.R.) **124** D 2
East Point (P.R.) **124** D 3
East Prairie (MO.) **65** H 5
East Pryor Mountain **86–87** E 4
East Ridge (TN.) **51** E 5
East Stroudsburg (PA.) **35** F 2
East Troy (WI.) **59** G 2
East Wenatchee (WA.) **114** E 2
Eastgate (NV.) **104** D 3
Easthampton (MA.) **30** D 3
Eastland (TX.) **74** C 2
Eastman (GA.) **43** D 4
Easton (MD.) **37** J 3
Easton (PA.) **35** F 3
Eastover (S.C.) **41** E 3
Eastport (ME.) **28** D 2
Eastville (VA.) **37** J 4
Eaton (CO.) **95** F 1
Eaton (OH.) **52** E 3
Eaton Rapids (MI.) **55** F 3
Eatonton (GA.) **42** C 4
Eatonville (WA.) **114** C 3
Eau Claire (WI.) **59** E 5
Ebensburg (PA.) **34** C 3
Echeta (WY.) **93** G 1
Echo (MN.) **61** F 5
Echo (UT.) **102** B 3
Eckerman (MI.) **54** B 4
Eckley (CO.) **95** H 1
Ecru (MS.) **48** B 2
Eddyville (KY.) **50** B 2
Eddyville (NE.) **81** E 3
Eden (MS.) **48** D 4
Eden (N.C.) **38** E 2
Eden (TX.) **74** B 3
Eden (WY.) **92** C 3
Eden Valley (MN.) **61** E 4
Edenton (N.C.) **39** H 2
Edgar (NE.) **81** G 4
Edgard (LA.) **69** E 3
Edgartown (N.Y.) **31** F 4
Edgefield (S.C.) **40** D 3
Edgeley (N.D.) **85** H 4

Edgemont (SD.) **82** B 4
Edgerton (KS.) **79** J 3
Edgerton (MN.) **61** G 6
Edgerton (WI.) **59** G 3
Edgerton (WY.) **93** F 2
Edgewater (FL.) **44** C 2
Edgewood (IA.) **63** G 3
Edgewood (IL.) **57** E 3
Edgewood (MD.) **37** H 2
Edina (MN.) **61** F 3
Edina (MO.) **65** E 1
Edinburg (IN.) **52** C 3
Edinburg (N.D.) **85** H 2
Edinburg (TX.) **70** D 4
Edisto Island **41** E 4
Edisto River **41** E 3
Edith, Mount **86** B 3
Edler (CO.) **95** H 4
Edmond (KS.) **78** D 2
Edmond (OK.) **77** F 2
Edmonds (ID.) **91** GH 3
Edmonds (WA.) **114** C 2
Edmonton (KY.) **50** E 4
Edmore (MI.) **55** E 4
Edmore (N.D.) **85** H 2
Edna (TX.) **71** F 1
Edna Bay **117** E 2
Edson Butte **112** A 4
Edwall (WA.) **115** H 2
Edwards (MS.) **48** D 4
Edwards (N.Y.) **33** E 1
Edwards Plateau **73** G 2–3
Edwardsville (IL.) **57** E 5
Edziza Peak **117** E 2
Eek (AL.) **119** C 1
Eel River **110** B 5
Effingham (IL.) **57** D 3
Effingham (S.C.) **41** F 2
Egan (S.D.) **83** J 4
Egan Range **105** G 3
Egbert (WY.) **93** H 4
Egegik (AL.) **119** D 2
Egeland (ND.) **85** G 2
Egg Harbor City (N.J.) **35** G 4
Egnar (CO.) **94** B 4
Ehrenberg (AZ.) **100** B 3
Ehrhardt (S.C.) **41** E 3
Ehtridge (TN.) **50** C 5
Ekalaka (MT.) **87** J 4
Eklutna **116** B 1
Ekuk **119** D 2
Ekwok **119** D 2
El Buro (Mex.) **73** G 4
El Cajon (CA.) **107** F 5
El Campo (TX.) **71** F 1
El Capitan Reservoir **107** F 5
El Centro (CA.) **107** G 5
El Dorado (AR.) **66** D 4
El Dorado (KS.) **79** G 4
El Indio (TX.) **70** B 2
El Mirage (AZ.) **100** D 3
El Mirage Lake **107** E 3
El Morro National Monument **96** B 3
El Nido (CA.) **111** E 2
El Paso (IL.) **56** C 3
El Paso (TX.) **72** B 2
El Portal (CA.) **111** E 1
El Porvenir (N.M.) **96** E 3
El Reno (OK.) **77** F 2
El Rio (CA.) **106** C 3
El Rito (N.M.) **96** D 2
El Sauz (TX.) **70** D 4
El Savz (Mex.) **72** B 4

El Sueco (Mex.) **72** B 4
El Vado (N.M.) **96** D 2
El Vado Reservoir **96** D 2
Elaine (AR.) **67** F 3
Elba (AL.) **47** E 4
Elba (ID.) **91** F 4
Elba (NE.) **81** F 3
Elbert (CO.) **95** F 2
Elbert (TX.) **74** B 1
Elbert, Mount **94** D 2
Elberta (UT.) **102** C 3
Elberton (GA.) **42** B 3
Elbow Lake (MN.) **61** E 5
Elderwood (CA.) **111** F 1
Eldon (IA.) **63** F 5
Eldon (MO.) **64** E 3
Eldon (WA.) **114** B 2
Eldora (IA.) **63** E 3
Eldorado (IL.) **57** F 3
Eldorado (OH.) **52** E 3
Eldorado (OK.) **76** D 3
Eldorado (TX.) **73** H 3
Eldorado Springs (MO.) **64** D 4
Eldridge (AL.) **46** C 5
Eldridge (ND.) **85** GH 4
Eldridge, Mount **121** G 3
Electra (TX.) **76** D 3
Electra Lake **94** C 4
Elekton (VA.) **37** F 3
Elephant Butte (N.M.) **98** C 3
Elephant Butte Reservoir **98** C 3
Elevenmile Canyon Reservoir **95** E 3
Elfrida (AZ.) **101** F 5
Elgin (IL.) **56** A 3
Elgin (ND.) **84** E 4
Elgin (NE.) **81** F 3
Elgin (NV.) **109** H 2
Elgin (OR.) **113** H 1
Elgin (TX.) **74** D 4
Eliasville (TX.) **74** C 2
Elida (N.M.) **99** G 3
Elim (AL.) **120** C 3
Elizabeth (CO.) **95** F 2
Elizabeth (IL.) **56** A 5
Elizabeth (N.J.) **35** G 3
Elizabeth (W.V.) **36** C 2
Elizabeth, Cape **114** A 2
Elizabeth City (N.C.) **39** H 2
Elizabethton (TN.) **51** H 4
Elizabethtown (IL.) **57** F 3
Elizabethtown (KY.) **50** E 3
Elizabethtown (N.C.) **39** F 4
Elizabethtown (N.Y.) **33** G 1
Elk (CA.) **110** C 5
Elk (N.M.) **99** E 4
Elk (WY.) **92** B 2
Elk City (ID.) **88** E 4
Elk City (KS.) **79** H 4
Elk City (OK.) **76** D 2
Elk City Lake **79** GH 4
Elk Creek (CA.) **110** C 4
Elk Grove (CA.) **111** D 3
Elk Head Mountains **94** C 1
Elk Hill **35** F 2
Elk Horn (KY.) **51** E 3
Elk Lake **54** D 4
Elk Mountain (WY.) **93** F 4
Elk Mountain (WY.) **93** F 4
Elk Peak **86** C 3
Elk Point (S.D.) **83** B 3
Elk River (ID.) **88** D 3

Elk River (MN.) **61** E 3
Elk River (TN.) **50** D 5
Elk Springs (CO.) **94** B 1
Elk Valley (TN.) **51** F 4
Elkader (IA.) **63** G 3
Elkhart (IN.) **52** D 1
Elkhart (KS.) **78** B 4
Elkhart (TX.) **75** F 3
Elkhorn (OR.) **112** C 2
Elkhorn (WI.) **59** G 2
Elkhorn City (KY.) **51** H 3
Elkhorn River **81** G 2
Elkin (N.C.) **38** D 2
Elkins (N.M.) **99** F 3
Elkins (W.V.) **36** E 3
Elko (NV.) **105** F 2
Elkton (KY.) **50** C 4
Elkton (OR.) **112** B 3
Elkton (S.D.) **83** J 3
Ellaville (FL.) **44** A 5
Ellaville (GA.) **43** D 5
Ellenboro (W.V.) **36** C 2
Ellendale (MN.) **61** G 3
Ellendale (N.D.) **85** H 4
Ellensburg (WA.) **114** E 2–3
Ellenville (N.Y.) **33** F 4
Ellicott (CO.) **95** F 3
Ellicott City (MD.) **37** G 2
Ellijay (GA.) **42** B 5
Ellington (MO.) **65** G 4
Elliott (IA.) **62** C 4
Elliott Key **45** F 2
Elliott Knob **36–37** E 3
Elliotts Bluff (GA.) **43** F 2
Ellis (ID.) **91** EF 2
Ellis (KS.) **78** D 3
Ellisville (MS.) **49** E 3
Ellsinore (MO.) **65** G 5
Ellsworth (KS.) **79** E 3
Ellsworth (ME.) **28** D 3
Ellsworth (MI.) **54** C 4
Ellsworth (MN.) **61** G 6
Ellsworth (NE.) **80** B 2
Ellsworth (WI.) **59** E 6
Ellwood City (PA.) **34** A 3
Elm Creek (NE.) **81** E 4
Elm Lake **83** G 2
Elm Springs (SD.) **82** C 3
Elma (IA.) **63** F 2
Elmendorf (N.M.) **98** D 3
Elmer (N.J.) **35** F 4
Elmer City (WA.) **115** G 1
Elmhurst (IL.) **56** B 3
Elmira (ID.) **88** D 1
Elmira (MI.) **54** C 3
Elmira (N.Y.) **32** D 3
Elmo (MT.) **89** F 2
Elmo (UT.) **102** C 2
Elmore (MN.) **61** G 4
Elmwood (NE.) **81** H 4
Elmwood (OK.) **76** C 1
Elnora (IN.) **52** B 4
Elnora (IN.) **52** B 4
Elora (TN.) **50** D 5
Eloy (AZ.) **100** E 4
Elsa (TX.) **70** D 4
Elsberry (MO.) **85** P 3
Elsie (MI.) **55** E 3
Elsie (OR.) **112** B 1
Elsinore (CA.) **107** E 4
Elsinore (UT.) **103** D 4
Elsinore, Lake **107** E 4
Elsmere (NE.) **80** D 2
Elsworth, Lake **76** E 3
Elton (LA.) **68** C 3
Eltopia (WA.) **115** G 3

Elwood (IN.) **52** D 2
Elwood (KS.) **64** C 2
Elwood (NE.) **80** D 4
Ely (NV.) **105** G 3
Elyria (OH.) **53** G 1
Embarras River **57** D 3
Emblem (WY.) **92** D 1
Embudo (N.M.) **96** E 2
Emelle (AL.) **46** D 6
Emerado (N.D.) **85** J 3
Emerson (AR.) **66** C 4
Emerson (MN.) **85** J 1
Emerson (NE.) **81** H 2
Emerson Lake **107** F 3
Emery (UT.) **102** D 3
Emida (ID.) **88** D 2
Emigrant (MT.) **86** C 4
Emigrant Gap (CA.) **110** C 2
Emily (MN.) **60** D 3
Eminence (KY.) **51** E 2
Emlenton (PA.) **34** B 2
Emmaus (PA.) **35** F 3
Emmet (NE.) **81** F 2
Emmetsburg (IA.) **62** D 2
Emmett (ID.) **90** C 3
Emmett (KS.) **79** G 2
Emmitsburg (MD.) **37** G 2
Emory (TX.) **75** F 2
Emory (UT.) **102** A 3
Emory Peak **73** E 4
Empire (NV.) **104** B 2
Empire Reservoir **95** F 1
Emporia (KS.) **79** G 3
Emporia (VA.) **37** G 5
Emporium (PA.) **34** C 2
Emundston (ME.) **28** A 3
Encampment (WY.) **93** F 4
Encinal (TX.) **70** C 2
Encinitas (CA.) **107** E 4
Encino (N.M.) **96** E 4
Encino (TX.) **70** D 4
Endeavor (WI.) **59** F 3
Endee (N.M.) **97** G 3
Enderlin (N.D.) **85** J 4
Enders (NE.) **80** C 4
Enders (NE.) **80** C 4
Enders Reservoir **80** C 4
Endicott (N.Y.) **32** D 3
Endicott (WA.) **115** H 3
Endicott Mountains (AL.) **121** EF 2
Endwell (N.Y.) **32** D 3
Enfield (N.C.) **39** G 2
Engelhard (N.C.) **39** J 3
England (AR.) **66** D 3
Engle (N.M.) **98** CD 3
Englewood (CO.) **95** F 2
Englewood (KS.) **78** C 4
Englewood (TN.) **51** F 5
English (IN.) **52** C 4
Enid (MT.) **87** J 2
Enid (OK.) **77** F 1
Enid Lake **48** B 3
Enning (SD.) **82** C 3
Ennis (MT.) **86** B 4
Ennis (TX.) **75** E 2
Ennis Lake **86** B 4
Enoch (UT.) **103** E 5
Enochs (TX.) **99** H 3
Enosburg Falls (VT.) **30** D 1
Enosville (IN.) **52** B 4
Ensign (KS.) **78** C 4
Enterprise (AL.) **47** E 3
Enterprise (CA.) **110** B 4
Enterprise (KS.) **79** F 3
Enterprise (MS.) **48** D 2

Enterprise (OR.) **113** H 1
Enterprise (UT.) **103** E 5
Entiat (WA.) **115** E 2
Entrance Island **117** E 2
Enumclaw (WA.) **114** D 2
Enurmino (AL.) **120** A 2
Eolia (MO.) **65** F 2
Epes (AL.) **46** D 6
Ephraim (UT.) **102** C 3
Ephrata (PA.) **35** E 3
Ephrata (WA.) **115** F 2
Epping (ND.) **84** C 2
Epping (N.H.) **29** E 6
Epps (LA.) **68** D 1
Epsie (MT.) **87** H 4
Erick (OK.) **76** D 2
Ericson (NE.) **81** F 3
Erie (CO.) **95** EF 1
Erie (KS.) **79** H 4
Erie (PA.) **34** AB 1
Erie Canal **32** B 2
Erin (TN.) **50** C 4
Errol (N.H.) **28** D 6
Erskine (MN.) **60** C 6
Erwin (TN.) **51** H 4
Escalante Desert **103** E 5
Escalante River **103** E 3
Escalon (CA.) **111** E 3
Escanaba (MI.) **54** C 6
Escanaba River **54** B 6
Escobas (TX.) **70** C 3
Escondido (CA.) **107** E 4
Eskota (TX.) **73** H 1
Eskridge (KS.) **79** G 3
Esmond (ND.) **85** G 2
Espanola (N.M.) **96** DE 2
Esparto (CA.) **111** D 3–4
Esperanza (P.R.) **124** C 2
Essex (CA.) **107** G 3
Essex (MT.) **89** G 1
Essex Junction (VT.) **30** C 1
Essexville (MI.) **55** E 2
Estacada (OR.) **112** C 1
Estancia (N.M.) **96** DE 4
Este, Punta **124** C 2
Estelline (S.D.) **83** J 3
Estelline (TX.) **76** C 3
Estero Bay **106** A 2
Estero, Point **106** A 2
Estes Park (CO.) **95** E 1
Estevan (ND.) **84** D 1
Estherville (IA.) **62** D 2
Estill (S.C.) **40** D 4
Ethan (S.D.) **83** G 4
Ethel (MS.) **48** C 3
Ethete (WY.) **92** D 2
Ethridge (MT.) **86** A 1
Etna (CA.) **110** A 4
Etna (UT.) **102** A 5–6
Etna (WY.) **92** B 2
Etolin (AL.) **117** E 2
Etolin strait (AL.) **118** B 1
Etowah (TN.) **51** F 5
Etter (TX.) **97** H 2
Eubank (KY.) **51** F 3
Euclid (OH.) **53** H 1
Eudora (AR.) **67** E 4
Eufaula (AL.) **47** E 3
Eufaula (OK.) **77** H 2
Eufaula Dam **77** H 2
Eufaula Lake **77** H 2
Eugene (OR.) **112** B 2
Eunice (LA.) **68** C 3
Eunice (N.M.) **99** G 4
Eupora (MS.) **48** C 3
Eureka (AK.) **116** B 1

Eureka (CA.) **110** B 6
Eureka (IL.) **56** C 4
Eureka (KS.) **79** G 4
Eureka (MT.) **88** EF 1
Eureka (NV.) **105** E 3
Eureka (SD.) **83** F 2
Eureka (UT.) **102** C 4
Eureka (WA.) **115** G 3
Eureka Springs (AR.) **66** C 1
Eustis (MT.) **86** B 3–4
Eustis (NE.) **80** D 4
Eutaw (AL.) **46** D 5
Eva (LA.) **68** D 2
Eva (OK.) **76** B 1
Evadale (TX.) **75** G 4
Evans (CO.) **95** F 1
Evans, Mount **94** E 2
Evanston (IL.) **56** A 2
Evanston (WY.) **92** AB 4
Evansville (IL.) **57** E 5
Evansville (IN.) **52** B 4–5
Evansville (WI.) **59** G 3
Evansville (WY.) **93** F 3
Evant (TX.) **74** C 3
Evart (MI.) **55** E 4
Eveleth (MN.) **60** C 2
Evening Shade (AR.) **67** E 1
Everest (KS.) **79** H 2
Everett (GA.) **43** E 2
Everett (WA.) **114** C 2
Everglades City (FL.) **45** F 3
Everglades National Park **45** F 2–3
Evergreen (AL.) **47** E 4
Ewa Beach (HI.) **122** C 2
Ewan (WA.) **115** H 2
Ewell (MD.) **37** J 3
Ewing (NE.) **81** F 2
Excelsior Mountain (CA.) **111** D 1
Excelsior Mountains (NV.) **104** C 2
Excelsior Springs (MO.) **64** C 2
Excursion Inlet **117** DE 2
Exeland (WI.) **58** D 5
Exeter (CA.) **111** F 1
Exeter (NE.) **81** G 4
Exeter (NH.) **29** E 5
Exira (IA.) **62** D 4
Exmore (VA.) **37** J 4
Exum (TX.) **97** H 2
Ezzell (TX.) **71** F 1

F

Fabens (TX.) **72** B 2
Faceville (GA.) **43** F 5
Fair Haven (VT.) **30** C 2
Fair Oaks (AR.) **67** F 2
Fair Plain (MI.) **55** F 5
Fairbank (AZ.) **101** F 5
Fairbanks (AL.) **121** F 3
Fairborn (OH.) **53** F 3
Fairburn (SD.) **82** B 4
Fairbury (NE.) **81** G 4
Fairchild (WI.) **59** E 4

Fairfax (AL.) **46** D 3
Fairfax (MN.) **61** F 4
Fairfax (S.C.) **40** D 4
Fairfax (SD.) **83** F 4
Fairfax (VA.) **37** G 3
Fairfield (AL.) **46** C 4
Fairfield (CA.) **111** D 4
Fairfield (CT.) **35** H 2
Fairfield (IA.) **63** G 4
Fairfield (ID.) **90** E 3
Fairfield (IL.) **57** E 3
Fairfield (MT.) **86** A 2
Fairfield (ND.) **84** C 3
Fairfield (NE.) **81** F 4
Fairfield (TX.) **75** E 3
Fairfield (UT.) **102** B 4
Fairfield (WA.) **115** H 2
Fairhope (AL.) **47** F 5
Fairland (TX.) **74** C 4
Fairmont (MN.) **61** G 4
Fairmont (W.V.) **36** D 2
Fairmount (GA.) **42** B 5
Fairmount (N.D.) **85** K 4
Fairmount (N.Y.) **32** D 2
Fairplay (CO.) **94** E 2
Fairpoint (SD.) **82** C 3
Fairport (KS.) **78** D 2
Fairport (MI.) **54** C 5
Fairvalley (OK.) **76** D 1
Fairview (IL.) **56** C 5
Fairview (KS.) **79** H 2
Fairview (MI.) **54** D 2
Fairview (MT.) **87** J 2
Fairview (OK.) **76** E 1
Fairview (TX.) **73** G 1
Fairview (UT.) **102** C 3
Fairview Peak **112** C 3
Faison (N.C.) **39** F 3
Faith (SD.) **82** C 2
Fajardo (P.R.) **124** C 2
Falcon (CO.) **95** F 3
Falcon (TX.) **70** C 4
Falcon, Cape **112** A 1
Falcon Reservoir **70** C 4
Falfurrias (TX.) **70** D 3
Falkirk (ND.) **84** E 3
Falkville (AL.) **46** B 4
Fall Creek (IL.) **56** D 6
Fall River (KS.) **79** G 4
Fall River (MA.) **31** E 4
Fall River Lake **79** G 4
Fall River Mills (CA.) **110** A 3
Fallbrook (CA.) **107** E 4
Fallon (MT.) **87** H 3
Fallon (NV.) **104** C 3
Fallon Indian Reservation **104** C 3
Falls City (NE.) **81** J 4
Falls City (OR.) **112** B 2
Falls City (TX.) **70** D 1–2
Falls Creek (PA.) **34** C 2
Falmouth (KY.) **51** F 2
Falmouth (MA.) **31** F 4
Falmouth (ME.) **29** E 5
Falmouth (MI.) **55** D 4
Falmouth (VA.) **37** G 3
False Pass (AL.) **118** C 3
Fanshaw **117** E 2
Farallon Islands **111** E 5
Farewell (AL.) **119** E 1
Fargo (GA.) **43** F 3
Fargo (N.D.) **85** K 4
Fargo (OK.) **76** D 1
Faribault (MN.) **61** F 3
Farmer (WA.) **115** F 2

Farmer City (IL.) **56** C 3
Farmersburg (IN.) **52** B 3
Farmersville (TX.) **75** E 1
Farmerville (LA.) **68** C 1
Farmington (CA.) **111** E 2
Farmington (IA.) **63** G 5
Farmington (IL.) **56** C 4
Farmington (ME.) **28** D 5
Farmington (MN.) **61** F 3
Farmington (MO.) **65** G 4
Farmington (N.H.) **29** E 6
Farmington (N.M.) **96** B 2
Farmington (UT.) **102** B 3
Farmington Reservoir **111** E 2
Farmville (N.C.) **39** G 3
Farmville (VA.) **37** F 4
Farnam (NE.) **80** D 4
Farner (TN.) **51** F 5
Farson (WY.) **92** C 3
Farthing (WY.) **93** G 4
Farwell (MI.) **55** E 3
Farwell (TX.) **97** H 4
Faulkton (SD.) **83** F 2
Faust (UT.) **102** B 4
Fay (OK.) **76** E 2
Fayette (AL.) **46** C 5
Fayette (IA.) **63** G 3
Fayette (MO.) **64** E 2
Fayette (MS.) **49** E 5
Fayette (OH.) **52** E 1
Fayetteville (AR.) **66** B 1
Fayetteville (GA.) **42** C 5
Fayetteville (N.C.) **39** F 3
Fayetteville (N.Y.) **32** E 2
Fayetteville (TN.) **50** D 5
Fayetteville (TX.) **75** E 5
Fayetteville (W.V.) **36** C 3
Faysville (TX.) **70** D 4
Faywood (N.M.) **98** B 4
Fear, Cape **39** G 5
Feather Falls (CA.) **110** C 3
Featherville (ID.) **90** D 3
Federal (WY.) **93** G 4
Federalsburg (MD.) **37** H 3
Felch (MI.) **54** C 6
Felda (FL.) **45** E 3
Fellsburg (KS.) **78** D 4
Fellsmere (FL.) **44** D 2
Felt (ID.) **91** H 3
Felt (OK.) **97** G 2
Fence Lake (N.M.) **96** B 4
Fenner (CA.) **107** G 3
Fennimore (WI.) **59** E 4
Fennville (MI.) **55** F 5
Fenton (MI.) **55** F 2
Fentress (TX.) **71** F 1
Feodora (TX.) **73** F 3
Fergus (MT.) **86** D 2
Fergus Falls (MN.) **61** D 6
Fern Ridge Lake **112** B 2
Fernandina Beach (FL.) **44** A 3
Ferndale (CA.) **110** B 6
Ferndale (WA.) **114** C 1
Ferney (S.D.) **83** G 2
Fernley (NV.) **104** B 3
Fernwood (ID.) **88** D 2
Ferrelo, Cape **112** A 4
Ferriday (LA.) **68** D 2
Ferris (TX.) **75** E 2
Ferron (UT.) **102** C 3
Ferrysburg (MI.) **55** E 5
Fertile (MN.) **60** C 6
Fessenden (ND.) **85** G 3
Festus (MO.) **65** G 3

Field (KY.) **51** G 4
Fields Landing (CA.) **110** B 6
Fife Lake (MI.) **55** D 4
Fifield (WI.) **58** D 4
Filer (ID.) **90** E 4
Fillmore (CA.) **106** D 3
Fillmore (ND.) **85** G 2
Fillmore (UT.) **102** D 4
Findlay (IL.) **57** D 3
Findlay (OH.) **53** F 1
Fine (N.Y.) **33** E 1
Fingal (N.D.) **85** J 4
Finley (OK.) **77** H 3
Finn Mountain **119** D 1
Fire Island **35** J 3
Firebaugh (CA.) **111** F 2
Firesteel (SD.) **82** D 2
Firth River **121** G 2
Fish Lake **103** D 3
Fish Lake Reservoir **60** D 2
Fishers Island **30** E 4
Fishers Peak **95** F 4
Fishing Creek (MD.) **37** H 3
Fitchburg (MA.) **30** E 3
Fith (ID.) **91** G 3
Fitzgerald (GA.) **43** E 4
Flagler (CO.) **95** G 2
Flagler Beach (FL.) **44** B 3
Flagstaff (AZ.) **100** E 1
Flagstaff Lake **28** C 5
Flambeau River **58** D 4
Flaming Gorge Dam **102** B 1
Flaming Gorge Reservoir **92** C 4
Flamingo (FL.) **45** F 2
Flandreau (S.D.) **83** J 3
Flanigan (NV.) **104** B 2
Flasher (ND.) **84** E 4
Flat (AL.) **119** D 1
Flat River (MO.) **65** G 4
Flat Rock (MI.) **55** F 2
Flat Top Mountain **102** B 4
Flat Tops **94** C 1–2
Flat Woods (TN.) **50** C 5
Flathead Indian Reservation **89** F 2
Flathead Lake **89** G 2
Flathead River **89** F 1
Flatonia (TX.) **71** E 1
Flats (NE.) **80** C 3
Flattery, Cape **114** A 1
Flatwillow (MT.) **87** E 3
Flaxton (ND.) **84** D 2
Flaxville (MT.) **87** H 1
Fleming (CO.) **96** H 1
Flemingsburg (KY.) **51** G 2
Fletcher (N.C.) **51** H 5
Fletcher (OK.) **77** E 3
Flint (MI.) **55** E 2
Flint Creek Range **89** G 3
Flint Hills **79** G 3–4
Flint River **43** E 5
Flippin (AR.) **66** D 1
Flomaton (AL.) **47** E 5
Flomot (TX.) **76** C 3
Floodwood (MN.) **60** D 3
Flora (IL.) **57** E 3
Flora (OH.) **113** H 1
Flora Vista (N.M.) **96** B 2
Floral City (FL.) **44** C 4
Florala (AL.) **47** E 4
Florence (AL.) **46** B 5
Florence (AZ.) **101** E 3
Florence (CO.) **95** E 3

Florence (KS.) **79** F 3
Florence (KY.) **51** F 1
Florence (MS.) **48** D 4
Florence (MT.) **89** F 3
Florence (OR.) **112** A 3
Florence (S.C.) **41** F 2
Florence (S.D.) **83** H 2
Florence (TX.) **74** D 4
Florence (WI.) **58** D 2
Florence Junction (AZ.) **101** E 3
Flores (AZ.) **100** D 2
Floresville (TX.) **70** D 1
Florey (TX.) **73** F 1
Florida **44–45**
Florida (N.M.) **98** C 4
Florida City (FL.) **45** F 2
Florida Keys **45** G 2–3
Florien (LA.) **68** B 2
Florissant (MO.) **65** G 3
Florissant National Monument **94–95** E 3
Florissant Fossil Beds National Monument (CO.) **95** E 3
Flowell (UT.) **102** D 4
Floyd (N.M.) **97** G 4
Floyd (VA.) **36** D 5
Floyd River **62** B 3
Floydada (TX.) **76** B 3
Flying H (N.M.) **99** E 3
Foard City (TX.) **76** CD 4
Foggy Island Bay **121** F 1
Foley (AL.) **47** F 5
Foley (MN.) **61** E 3
Folkston (GA.) **43** F 3
Follett (TX.) **76** C 1
Folly Beach (S.C.) **41** F 4
Folsom (LA.) **69** E 3
Folsom (N.M.) **97** G 2
Folsom Lake **111** D 3
Fond du Lac (WI.) **59** F 2
Fonda (IA.) **62** D 3
Fonda (N.Y.) **33** F 3
Fontana Lake **51** G 5
Fontana Village (NC.) **51** G 5
Fontenelle (WY.) **92** C 4
Fontenelle Reservoir **92** B 3
Foraker (OK.) **77** G 1
Forbes (ND.) **83** G 2
Forbestown (CA.) **110** C 3
Ford (KS.) **78** D 4
Ford (WA.) **115** H 2
Ford City (CA.) **106** C 2
Ford City (PA.) **34** B 3
Ford Dry Lake **107** H 4
Fords Prairie (WA.) **114** B 3
Fordville (N.D.) **85** HJ 2
Fordyce (AR.) **66** D 4
Forest (MS.) **48** D 3
Forest Center (MN.) **58** B 5
Forest City (IA.) **63** E 2
Forest City (N.C.) **38** C 3
Forest City (PA.) **35** F 2
Forest Grove (OR.) **112** B 1
Forest Hill (LA.) **68** C 2
Forest Lake (MN.) **61** E 3
Forest Park (GA.) **42** C 5
Forest Ranch (CA.) **110** C 3
Forest River (N.D.) **85** J 2
Foresthill (CA.) **110** C 2
Forestville (WI.) **59** E 1
Forgan (OK.) **76** C 1
Fork Mountain (TN.) **51** F 4

Forks (WA.) **114** A 2
Forman (N.D.) **85** J 4
Forrest (IL.) **56** C 3
Forrest City (AR.) **67** F 2–3
Forsyth (GA.) **42** C 4
Forsyth (MO.) **64** D 5
Forsyth (MT.) **87** G 3
Fort Adams (MS.) **49** E 5
Fort Apache Indian Reservation **101** FG 3
Fort Atkinson (WI.) **59** G 2
Fort Basinger (FL.) **45** D 3
Fort Belknap Agency (MT.) **86** DE 1
Fort Belknap Indian Reservation **86** E 1
Fort Belvoir (VA.) **37** G 3
Fort Benjamin Harrison (IN.) **52** C 3
Fort Benning (GA.) **43** D 5
Fort Benton (MT.) **86** C 2
Fort Berthold Indian eservation **84** D 3
Fort Bidwell Indian Reservation **110** A 2
Fort Bliss (TX.) **72** B 2
Fort Bragg (CA.) **110** C 5
Fort Bragg (N.C.) **39** E 3
Fort Branch (IN.) **52** B 4
Fort Bridger (WY.) **92** B 4
Fort Chadnourne (TX.) **74** C 3
Fort Clark (ND.) **84** E 3
Fort Cobb (OK.) **76** E 2
Fort Cobb Reservoir **76** E 2
Fort Collins (CO.) **95** E 1
Fort Covington (N.Y.) **33** F 1
Fort Davis (TX.) **72** E 3
Fort Dodge (IA.) **62** D 3
Fort Douglas (AR.) **66** C 2
Fort Drum (FL.) **45** D 2
Fort Duchesne (UT.) **102** B 1
Fort Eustis (VA.) **37** H 4
Fort Frances (Can.) **60** B 3
Fort Fredericia National Monument **43** E 2
Fort Gaines (GA.) **43** E 5–6
Fort Garland (CO.) **95** E 4
Fort Gay (W.V.) **36** B 3
Fort Gibson (OK.) **77** H 2
Fort Gibson Dam **77** H 2
Fort Gibson Lake **77** H 2
Fort Gordon (GA.) **42** C 3
Fort Griffin (TX.) **74** B 2
Fort Hall Indian Reservation **91** G 3–4
Fort Hancock (TX.) **72** C 2
Fort Hood (TX.) **74** D 3
Fort Jackson (S.C.) **41** E 2
Fort Jefferson National Monument **45** G 4
Fort Jones (CA.) **110** A 4
Fort Kent (ME.) **28** B 3
Fort Klamath (OR.) **112** C 4
Fort Knox (KY.) **50** E 3
Fort Laramie (WY.) **93** H 3
Fort Lauderdale (FL.) **45** E 2
Fort Leavenworth (KS.) **79** H 2
Fort Lee (VA.) **37** G 4
Fort Leonard Wood (MO.) **65** E 4
Fort Loudon Lake **51** F 5

Fort Lupton (CO.) **95** F 1
Fort Madison (IA.) **63** G 5
Fort Matanzas National
Monument **44** B 3
Fort McClellan (AL.) **46** C 3
Fort McDermitt Indian
Reservation **104** C 1
Fort McDowell Indian
Reservation **100–101** E 3
Fort McPherson (GA.)
42 C 5
Fort Meade (FL.) **44** D 3
Fort Meade (MD.) **37** H 2
Fort Mohave Indian
Reservation **100** B 2
Fort Monmouth (N.J.)
35 G 3
Fort Morgan (AL.) **47** F 5
Fort Morgan (CO.) **95** G 1
Fort Myers (FL.) **45** E 3
Fort Myers Beach (FL.)
45 E 3
Fort Ogden (FL.) **45** D 3
Fort Ord (CA.) **111** F 3
Fort Payne (AL.) **46** B 3
Fort Peck Dam **87** G 2
Fort Peck Indian
Reservation **87** H 1
Fort Peck Lake **87** G 2
Fort Phantom Hill, Lake
110 C 3
Fort Pierce (FL.) **45** D 2
Fort Pierre (SD.) **82** E 3
Fort Plain (N.Y.) **33** F 3
Fort Polk (LA.) **68** B 2
Fort Pulaski National
Monument **41** E 5
Fort Randall Dam **83** G 4
Fort Ransom (N.D.) **85** J 4
Fort Ripley (MN.) **61** D 4
Fort Ritchie (MD.) **37** G 2
Fort Robinson (NE.) **80** A 2
Fort Rucker (AL.) **47** E 3
Fort Scott (KS.) **79** J 4
Fort Sheridan (IL.) **56** A 2
Fort Smith (AR.) **66** B 2
Fort Stewart (GA.) **43** E 2
Fort Still (OK.) **76** E 3
Fort Stockton (TX.) **73** EF 3
Fort Sumner (N.M.) **97** F 4
Fort Supply (OK.) **76** D 1
Fort Supply Lake **76** D 1
Fort Thompson (SD.)
83 F 3
Fort Totten (ND.) **85** G 3
Fort Totten Indian
Reservation **85** GH 3
Fort Union National
Monument **96–97** E 3
Fort Valley (GA.) **43** D 4
Fort Walton Beach (FL.)
47 F 4
Fort Washakie (WY.) **92** C 2
Fort Wayne (IN.) **52** D 1
Fort White (FL.) **44** B 4
Fort Wolters (TX.) **74** C 2
Fort Worth (TX.) **74** D 2
Fort Yates (ND.) **84** F 4
Fort Yukon (AL.) **121** F 2
Fort Yuma Indian
Reservation **107** H 5
Fortification Hill **103** F 6
Fortine (MT.) **88** F 1
Fortress Mountain **92** C 1
Fortuna (ND.) **84** C 2
Foss Reservoir **76** D 2

Fossil (OR.) **113** E 1
Fossil Butte National
Monument **92** B 4
Fossil Lake **112** E 3
Fosston (MN.) **60** C 5
Foster (MT.) **87** F 4
Foster Lake **113** F 4
Fosters (AL.) **46** C 5
Fostoria (OH.) **53** F 1
Found du Lac Indian
Reservation **60** D 2
Fountain (CO.) **95** F 3
Fountain (FL.) **47** F 3
Fountain (MI.) **55** D 5
Fountain City (WI.) **59** E 5
Fountain Green (UT.)
102 C 3
Fountain Peak **107** G 3
Four Buttes (MT.) **87** H 1
Four Corners (WY.) **93** H 1
Four Peaks **101** E 3
Four Town (MN.) **60** B 5
Fourteen Mile Point
58 BC 3
Fourway (TX.) **97** H 3
Fowler (CA.) **111** F 1
Fowler (CO.) **95** F 3
Fowler (IN.) **52** B 2
Fowler (KS.) **78** C 4
Fowlerton (TX.) **70** D 2
Fowlerville (MI.) **55** F 2
Fowlkes (TN.) **67** G 2
Fowlstown (GA.) **43** F 5
Fox (OR.) **113** F 2
Fox Islands (AL.) **118** B 3
Fox Lake (IL.) **56** A 3
Fox Mountain **117** E 1
Fox River **56** B 3
Foxpark (WY.) **93** F 4
Foxworth (MS.) **49** E 3
Frances (AL.) **117** F 1
Frances, Lake **86** A 1
Francis (UT.) **102** B 3
Francis Case, Lake **83** F 4
Frankewing (TN.) **50** D 5
Frankfort (IN.) **52** C 2
Frankfort (KY.) **51** F 2
Frankfort (MI.) **55** D 5
Frankfort (NE.) **79** G 2
Frankfort (S.D.) **83** G 3
Franklin (AZ.) **101** G 4
Franklin (GA.) **42** C 6
Franklin (ID.) **91** H 4
Franklin (IN.) **52** C 3
Franklin (KY.) **50** D 4
Franklin (LA.) **68** D 4
Franklin (MT.) **86** D 3
Franklin (NE.) **81** F 4
Franklin (N.H.) **29** E 6
Franklin (N.J.) **35** G 2
Franklin (OH.) **52** E 3
Franklin (PA.) **34** B 2
Franklin (TN.) **50** D 5
Franklin (TX.) **75** E 3
Franklin (VA.) **37** H 5
Franklin (WI.) **59** G 2
Franklin (W.V.) **36** E 3
Franklin Delano Roosevelt
Lake **115** G 1
Franklin Lake (NV.) **105** F 2
Franklinton (LA.) **69** E 3
Franklinville (N.Y.) **32** B 3
Franks Peak **92** C 2
Frankston (TX.) **75** F 2
Frannie (WY.) **92** D 1
Frazee (MN.) **60** D 5

Frazer (MT.) **87** G 1
Frederic (MI.) **54** D 3
Frederic (WI.) **58** D 6
Frederick (MD.) **37** G 2
Frederick (OK.) **76** D 3
Frederick (S.D.) **83** G 2
Fredericksburg (TX.) **74** C 4
Fredericksburg (VA.)
37 G 3
Fredericktown (MO.)
65 G 4
Fredericktown (OH.) **53** G 2
Frederiksted **124** CD 3
Fredonia (AZ.) **103** F 4
Fredonia (KY.) **50** B 2
Fredonia (ND.) **85** G 4
Fredonia (N.Y.) **32** A 3
Freeburg (IL.) **57** E 5
Freeburg (MO.) **65** F 3
Freedom (WY.) **92** B 3
Freehold (N.J.) **35** G 3
Freel Peak **111** D 1
Freeland (MI.) **55** E 3
Freeman (S.D.) **83** H 4
Freeman (WA.) **115** H 2
Freemont (MI.) **55** E 5
Freeport (FL.) **47** F 4
Freeport (IL.) **56** A 4
Freeport (TX.) **71** G 2
Freer (TX.) **70** D 3
Freezeout Lake **86** A 2
Fremont (CA.) **111** F 3
Fremont (IA.) **63** F 4
Fremont (N.C.) **39** G 3
Fremont (NE.) **81** H 3
Fremont (OH.) **53** F 1
Fremont (WI.) **59** E 3
Fremount Island **102** A 4
French Broad River **51** G 5
French Camp (MS.) **48** C 3
French Lick (IN.) **52** C 4
Frenchburg (KY.) **51** G 3
Frenchglen (OR.) **113** FG 4
Frenchman (NV.) **104** C 3
Frenchman Creek (MT.)
87 F 1
Frenchman Creek (NE.)
80 C 4
Frenchman Flat **109** FG 3
Frenchman Lake (CA.)
110 C 2
Frenchman Lake (NV.)
109 G 3
Frenchtown (MT.) **89** F 2
Frenier (LA.) **69** E 3
Fresno (CA.) **111** F 1
Fresno (MT.) **86** D 1
Fresno Reservoir **86** D 1
Frewen (WY.) **92** D 4
Frewsburg (N.Y.) **32** A 3
Friant (CA.) **111** F 1
Friday Harbor (WA.)
114 BC 1
Friend (KS.) **78** B 3
Friendship (WI.) **59** F 3
Fries (VA.) **36** C 5
Frio River **70** C 1–2
Friona (TX.) **97** H 4
Frisco (CO.) **94** D 2
Frisco City (AL.) **47** E 5
Frisco Peak **103** D 5
Fritch (TX.) **76** B 2
Froid (MT.) **87** J 1
Fromberg (MT.) **86** E 4
Front Range **94** E 1–2
Front Royal (VA.) **37** F 3

Frontier (WY.) **92** B 4
Frostburg (MD.) **37** E 2
Fruita (CO.) **94** B 2
Fruita (UT.) **103** D 3
Fruitdale (AL.) **47** E 6
Fruitdale (OR.) **112** B 4
Fruitland (ID.) **90** C 2
Fruitland (MD.) **37** J 3
Fruitland (UT.) **102** B 2
Fruitland (WA.) **115** G 1
Fruitvale (ID.) **90** C 2
Fryeburg (LA.) **68** B 1
Fryeburg (ME.) **29** D 5
Fuguay-Varina (N.C.)
39 F 3
Fulda (MN.) **61** G 5
Fullerton (NE.) **81** F 3
Fullerville (TX.) **73** G 1
Fulton (IL.) **56** B 5
Fulton (KY.) **50** B 4
Fulton (MO.) **65** F 3
Fulton (MS.) **48** B 2
Fulton (N.Y.) **32** D 2
Fulton (TX.) **71** F 2

G

Gackle (ND.) **85** G 4
Gadsden (AL.) **46** BC 4
Gadsden (AZ.) **100** B 4
Gaffney (S.C.) **40** D 1
Gage (N.M.) **98** B 4
Gage (OK.) **76** D 1
Gail (TX.) **73** G 1
Gainesboro (TN.)
50–51 E 4
Gainesville (FL.) **44** B 4
Gainesville (GA.) **42** B 4
Gainesville (MO.) **64** E 5
Gainesville (TX.) **74** D 1
Gakona (AL.) **116** C 1
Galata (MT.) **86** B 1
Galatia (KS.) **78** E 3
Galax (VA.) **36** D 5
Galconda (IL.) **57** F 3
Galena (AL.) **120** C 3
Galena (IL.) **56** A 5
Galena (KS.) **79** J 4
Galena (MO.) **64** D 5
Galesburg (IL.) **56** C 5
Galesville (WI.) **59** E 5
Galeton (PA.) **34** D 2
Galion (OH.) **53** G 2
Galiuro Mountains **101** F 4
Gallatin (MO.) **64** D 2
Gallatin (TN.) **50** D 4
Gallatin River **86** B 4
Gallatin Tange **86** B 4
Gallinas (N.M.) **96** E 4
Gallipolis (OH.) **53** G 4
Gallo Mountains **96** B 4
Galloo Island **32** D 2
Gallup (N.M.) **96** B 3
Galt (CA.) **111** D 3
Galva (IL.) **62** C 3
Galva (IL.) **56** B 4
Galveston (IN.) **52** C 2
Galveston (TX.) **71** H 1

Galveston Bay **71** H 1
Galveston Island **71** H 1
Gambell (AL.) **120** A 3
Ganado (AZ.) **101** F 1
Ganado (TX.) **71** F 1
Gannett (ID.) **91** E 3
Gannett Peak **92** C 2
Gannvalley (SD.) **83** F 4
Gantt (AL.) **47** E 4
Garaldine (MT.) **86** C 2
Garber (OK.) **77** F 1
Garberville (CA.) **110** B 5
Garcia (CO.) **95** E 4
Garden (MI.) **54** C 5
Garden City (GA.) **43** D 2
Garden City (KS.) **78** C 4
Garden City (MO.) **64** C 3
Garden City (S.D.) **83** H 3
Garden City (TX.) **73** G 2
Garden City (UT.) **102** A 3
Garden Island Bay **69** FG 4
Garden Plain (KS.) **79** F 4
Garden Valley (ID.) **90** D 2
Gardena (ID.) **90** C 2–3
Gardendale (AL.) **46** C 4
Gardendale (MI.) **55** E 1
Gardendale (TX.) **70** C 2
Gardine (ME.) **29** D 4
Gardiner (MT.) **86** C 4
Gardiner (OR.) **112** AB 3
Gardiners Island **35** JK 2
Gardner (CO.) **95** E 4
Gardner (MA.) **30** D 3
Gardnerville (NV.) **104** B 4
Gareloi (AL.) **116** J 1
Garfield (KS.) **78** D 3
Garfield (N.M.) **98** C 4
Garfield (WA.) **115** H 2
Garfield Mountain **91** G 2
Garibaldi (OR.) **112** B 1
Garita (N.M.) **97** F 3
Garland (AL.) **47** E 4
Garland (MT.) **87** H 3
Garland (N.C.) **39** F 4
Garland (TX.) **75** E 2
Garland (UT.) **102** A 4
Garland (WY.) **92** D 1
Garner (IA.) **63** E 2
Garner (N.C.) **39** F 3
Garnet Range **89** G 3
Garnett (KS.) **79** H 3
Garrett (TX.) **75** E 2
Garrett (WY.) **93** G 3
Garrison (MN.) **61** D 4
Garrison (MT.) **86** A 3
Garrison (ND.) **84** E 3
Garrison (TX.) **75** G 3
Garrison (UT.) **102** D 5
Garrison Dam **84** E 3
Garryowen (MT.) **87** F 4
Garwood (TX.) **71** F 1
Gary (IN.) **52** B 1
Gary (S.D.) **83** J 3
Garza-Little Elm Reservoir **75** E 1
Gas City (IN.) **52** D 2
Gasconade River **64** E 4
Gasparilla Island **45** E 4
Gasquet (CA.) **110** A 5
Gassaway (W.V.) **36** C 3
Gaston, Lake **37** F 5
Gastonia (N.C.) **38** C 3
Gate (OK.) **76** C 1
Gate City (VA.) **36** B 2
Gates (CA.) **106** B 3
Gates (N.Y.) **32** C 2
Gates of the Arctic N.P. and pres. (AL.) **121** E 2
Gatesville (N.C.) **39** H 2
Gatesville (TX.) **74** D 3
Gateway (CO.) **94** B 3
Gatlinburg (TN.) **51** G 5
Gato (CO.) **94** C 4
Gauley Bridge (W.V.) **36** C 3
Gavins Point Dam **81** G 2
Gaviota (CA.) **106** B 3
Gaylord (KS.) **78** E 2
Gaylord (MI.) **54** C 3
Gaylord (MN.) **61** F 4
Gays Mills (WI.) **59** F 4
Gazelle (CA.) **110** A 4
Gearhart Mountain **112** E 4
Geary (OK.) **76–77** E 2
Gebo (WY.) **92** D 2
Geddes (S.D.) **83** G 4
Gehee (AR.) **67** E 4
General Treviñe (Mex.) **70** C 4
Genesee (ID.) **88** D 3
Geneseo (KS.) **79** E 3
Geneseo (N.Y.) **32** C 3
Geneso (IL.) **56** B 5
Geneva (AL.) **47** E 3
Geneva (ID.) **91** HJ 4
Geneva (NE.) **81** G 4
Geneva (N.Y.) **32** D 3
Geneva (OH.) **53** H 1
Genkanyy, Khrebet **120** A 2
Genoa (IL.) **56** A 3
Genoa (NE.) **81** G 3
Gentryville (MO.) **64** E 5
George (WA.) **115** EF 2
George ,Lake (FL.) **44** B 3
George, Lake (N.D.) **85** G 4
George, Lake (N.Y.) **33** G 2
George Washington Birthplace National Monument (VA.) **37** GH 3
George Washington Carver National Monument **64** C 4–5
George West (TX.) **70** D 2
Georgetown (CA.) **110** D 2
Georgetown (CO.) **94** E 2
Georgetown (DE.) **37** J 3
Georgetown (GA.) **43** E 6
Georgetown (ID.) **91** H 4
Georgetown (KY.) **51** F 2
Georgetown (LA.) **68** C 2
Georgetown (MS.) **49** E 4
Georgetown (OH.) **53** F 4
Georgetown (S.C.) **41** F 3
Georgetown (TX.) **74** D 4
Georgia (North) **53** F 3
Georgia (South) **42–43**
Georgiana (AL.) **47** E 4
Gerber (CA.) **110** B 4
Gerber Reservoir **112** D 4
Gering (NE.) **80** A 3
Gerlach (NV.) **104** B 2
Germann (AZ.) **100** E 3
Germfask (MI.) **54** B 5
Geronimo (AZ.) **101** F 3
Geronimo (OK.) **76** E 3
Gettysburg (PA.) **34** D 4
Gettysburg (SD.) **83** F 2
Gettysburg National Military Park (PA.) **34** D 4
Geyser (MT.) **86** C 2
Geyserville (CA.) **111** D 5
Gibbon (NE.) **81** F 4
Gibbon (OR.) **113** G 1
Gibson (GA.) **42** C 3
Gibson City (IL.) **56** C 3
Giddings (TX.) **74** D 4
Gifford (AR.) **66** D 3
Gifford (FL.) **45** D 2
Gila (N.M.) **98** B 4
Gila Bend (AZ.) **100** D 4
Gila Bend Indian Reservation **100** D 3
Gila Bend Mountains **100** CD 3
Gila Cliff Dwellings National Monument **98** B 3
Gila Desert **100** C 3–4
Gila Mountains (AZ.) **100** B 4
Gila Mountains (AZ.) **101** G 3
Gila River **100** C 4
Gila River Indian Reservation **100** DE 3
Gilbert (LA.) **68** D 1
Gilbert Peak **114** D 3
Gilbertown (AL.) **47** E 6
Gildford (MT.) **86** C 1
Gilett (AR.) **67** E 3
Gill (CO.) **95** F 1
Gillespie (IL.) **57** D 4
Gillett (WI.) **59** E 2
Gillette (WY.) **93** G 1
Gills Rock (WI.) **54** C 5
Gilluly (UT.) **102** C 3
Gilman (IL.) **56** C 2
Gilman (MT.) **86** A 2
Gilman (WI.) **59** D 4
Gilmer (TX.) **75** G 2
Gilmore City (IA.) **62** D 3
Gilroy (CA.) **111** F 3
Giltner (NE.) **81** F 4
Girard (IL.) **57** D 4
Girard (KS.) **79** J 4
Girard (PA.) **34** A 1
Girard (TX.) **76** C 4
Glacier (WA.) **114** D 1
Glacier Bay (AL.) **117** D 2
Glacier Bay N.P. and Pres. (AL.) **117** D 2
Glacier National Park **89** FG 1
Glacier Peak **114** D 1
Glad Valley (SD.) **82** CD 2
Glade (KS.) **78** D 2
Gladewater (TX.) **75** G 2
Gladstone (MI.) **54** C 6
Gladstone (MO.) **64** C 2
Gladstone (ND.) **84** D 4
Gladstone (N.M.) **97** F 2
Gladwin (MI.) **55** E 3
Gladys Lake **117** E 2
Glamis (CA.) **107** G 4
Glasco (KS.) **79** F 2
Glasgow (KY.) **50** E 3
Glasgow (MT.) **87** G 1
Glasgow (VA.) **36** E 4
Glass Mountains **73** E 3
Glassboro (N.J.) **35** F 4
Glazier (TX.) **76** C 1–2
Glen (MT.) **86** A 4
Glen (N.H.) **29** D 6
Glen Arbor (MI.) **54** D 4
Glen Canyon (UT.) **103** E 2
Glen Canyon (UT.) **103** E 3
Glen Canyon Dam **103** F 3
Glen Canyon National Recreation Area **103** E 2–3
Glen Elder (KS.) **79** E 2
Glen Rose (TX.) **74** D 2
Glen Ullin (ND.) **84** E 4
Glenbar (AZ.) **101** G 4
Glenburn (ND.) **84** E 2
Glencoe (KY.) **51** F 2
Glencoe (MN.) **61** F 4
Glencoe (N.M.) **99** E 3
Glendale (AZ.) **100** D 3
Glendale (CA.) **106** D 3
Glendale (KS.) **79** E 3
Glendale (NV.) **109** H 3
Glendale (OR.) **112** B 4
Glendale (UT.) **103** E 4
Glendevey (CO.) **94** D 1
Glendive (MT.) **87** J 2
Glendo (WY.) **93** G 3
Glendo Reservoir **93** H 3
Glenfield (N.Y.) **33** E 2
Glenham (SD.) **82** E 2
Glenmora (LA.) **68** C 3
Glenn (TX.) **76** C 4
Glennallen (AL.) **116** B 1
Glenns Ferry (ID.) **90** D 4
Glennville (GA.) **43** E 3
Glenoma (WA.) **114** CD 3
Glenrock (WY.) **93** G 3
Glens Falls (N.Y.) **33** G 2
Glenshaw (PA.) **34** A 3
Glenville (MN.) **61** G 3
Glenville (W.V.) **36** D 3
Glenwood (AR.) **66** C 3
Glenwood (MN.) **61** E 5
Glenwood (N.M.) **98** B 3
Glenwood (OR.) **112** B 1
Glenwood City (WI.) **59** D 6
Glenwood Springs (CO.) **94** C 2
Glidden (IA.) **62** D 3
Glidden (WI.) **58** C 4
Glide (OR.) **112** B 3
Globe (AZ.) **101** F 3
Glorieta (N.M.) **96** E 3
Gloucester (MA.) **31** F 3
Gloucester (VA.) **37** H 4
Glover (MO.) **65** G 4
Gloversville (N.Y.) **33** F 2
Goff (KS.) **79** H 2
Goffs (CA.) **107** G 3
Gogebic, Lake **58** C 3
Gogebic Range **58** C 3–4
Golconda (NV.) **104** D 2
Gold Beach (OR.) **112** A 4
Gold Creek **116** B 1
Gold Point (NV.) **109** E 2
Gold Rock (Can.) **60** A 2
Golden (CO.) **95** E 2
Golden City (MO.) **64** C 4
Golden Meadow (LA.) **69** E 4
Golden Valley (ND.) **84** D 3
Goldendale (WA.) **114** E 4
Goldfield (IA.) **62** E 3
Goldfield (NV.) **109** E 2
Goldsboro (N.C.) **39** F 3
Goldsmith (TX.) **73** F 1
Goldston (N.C.) **39** E 3
Goldthwaite (TX.) **74** C 3
Goleta (CA.) **106** C 3
Goliad (TX.) **71** E 2
Golovin (AL.) **120** C 3
Golva (ND.) **84** C 4
Gonzales (CA.) **111** F 3

Gonzales (TX.) **71** E 1
Goochland (VA.) **37** G 4
Gooding (ID.) **90** E 4
Goodland (KS.) **78** B 2
Goodlettsville (TN.) **50** D 4
Goodnews Bay (AL.)
  119 C 2
Goodnight (TX.) **76** B 2
Goodrich (CO.) **95** FG 1
Goodrich (TX.) **75** G 4
Goodsprings (NV.) **109** G 4
Goodwater (AL.) **46** C 3–4
Goodyear (AZ.) **100** D 3
Goose Lake **110** A 2
Goose River **85** J 3
Gorda, Punta **110** B 6
Gordon (NE.) **80** B 2
Gordon (WI.) **58** C 5
Gordonsville (VA.) **37** F 3
Gore (OK.) **77** H 2
Gore (VA.) **37** F 2
Gorgas (AL.) **46** C 5
Gorham (N.Y.) **32** C 3
Gorman (IA.) **106** D 3
Gorman (TX.) **74** C 2
Goshen (CA.) **111** F 1
Goshen (IN.) **52** D 1
Goshen (VA.) **36** E 4
Goshute (UT.) **102** C 5
Goshute Indian
  Reservation **105** G 3
Goshute Lake **105** G 2
Gosport (IN.) **52** C 3
Goss (MS.) **49** E 3
Gotebo (OK.) **76** E 2
Gothenburg (NE.) **80** D 4
Gould City (MI.) **54** B 4
Goulds (FL.) **45** F 2
Gouverneur (N.Y.) **32** E 1
Gove (KS.) **78** C 3
Government Peak **58** C 3
Gowanda (N.Y.) **32** B 3
Gowrie (IA.) **62** D 3
Grace (ID.) **91** H 4
Grace City (ND.) **85** GH 3
Graceville (MN.) **61** E 6
Grady (AR.) **67** E 3
Grady (N.M.) **97** G 4
Graford (TX.) **74** C 2
Grafton (IL.) **57** E 5
Grafton (N.D.) **85** J 2
Grafton (WI.) **59** F 2
Grafton (W.V.) **36** E 2
Graham (AL.) **117** E 3
Graham (N.C.) **39** E 2
Graham (TX.) **74** C 1
Graham Lake **28** D 3
Graham, Mount **101** G 4
Grainfield (KS.) **78** C 2
Gran Quivira (N.M.) **96** D 4
Gran Quivira National
  Monument **96** D 4
Granada (CO.) **95** H 3
Granbury (TX.) **74** D 2
Granbury, Lake **74** D 2
Granby (Can.) **28** C 7
Granby (CO.) **94** E 1
Granby, Lake **94** E 1
Grand Bay (AL.) **47** F 6
Grand Canyon **103** F 4
Grand Canyon National
  Park **103** F 4
Grand Chenier (LA.)
  68 C 4
Grand Coulee (WA.)
  115 G 2

Grand Coulee Dam
  115 FG 2
Grand Forks (N.D.) **85** J 3
Grand Glaise (AR.) **67** E 2
Grand Haven (MI.) **55** E 5
Grand Island (MI.) **54** B 5
Grand Island (NE.) **81** F 4
Grand Isle **69** F 4
Grand Junction (CO.)
  94 B 2
Grand Junction (IA.)
  62 D 3–4
Grand Lake (CO.) **94** E 1
Grand Lake (LA.) **68** C 4
Grand Lake (ME.) **28** C 2
Grand Lake (OH.) **52** E 2
Grand Ledge (MI.) **55** F 3
Grand Manan Channel
  28 D 1–2
Grand Marais (MI.) **54** B 4
Grand Meadow (MN.)
  61 G 2
Grand Mesa (CO.)
  94 BC 2–3
Grand Mesa (CO.) **94** C 2
Grand Portage Indian
  Reservation **58** B 3–4
Grand Prairie (TX.) **74** DE 2
Grand Rapids (MI.) **55** F 4
Grand Rapids (MN.) **60** C 3
Grand River (MO.) **64** D 2
Grand River (S.D.) **82** D 2
Grand Teton **92** B 2
Grand Teton National Park
  92 B 2
Grand Tower (IL.) **57** F 4
Grand Traverse Bay **54** C 4
Grand Valley (CO.) **94** B 2
Grand View (ID.) **90** C 3
Grand View (WI.) **58** C 5
Grand Wash Cliffs
  103 FG 6
Grande (N.M.) **97** G 2
Grande Ronde River
  113 H 1
Grandeeville (W.V.) **36** C 3
Grandfalls (TX.) **73** E 2
Grandfield (OK.) **76** E 3
Grandview (TX.) **74** D 2
Grandview (WA.) **115** F 3
Granger (TX.) **74** D 4
Granger (UT.) **102** B 3–4
Granger (WA.) **115** E 3
Granger (WY.) **92** BC 4
Grangeville (ID.) **88** D 4
Granite (CO.) **94** D 2
Granite (OR.) **113** G 2
Granite City (IL.) **57** E 5
Granite Falls (MN.) **61** F 5
Granite Mountain **120** C 2
Granite Mountains **92** E 3
Granite Pass **92** E 1
Granite Peak (MT.) **86** AB 4
Granite Peak (MT.) **86** D 4
Granite Peak (NV.) **104** D 1
Granite Range **104** B 1–2
Grant (MT.) **89** G 4
Grant (NE.) **80** C 4
Grant (NE.) **80** C 4
Grant City (MO.) **64** C 1
Grant, Mount **104** C 4
Grant Range **105** F 4
Grantham (N.H.) **29** E 7
Grants (N.M.) **96** C 3
Grants Pass (OR.) **112** B 4
Grantsburg (WI.) **58** D 6

Grantsdale (MT.) **89** F 3
Grantsville (UT.) **102** B 4
Grantsville (W.V.) **36** C 3
Granview (MO.) **64** C 3
Granville (AZ.) **101** G 3
Granville (ND.) **84** F 2
Grapeland (TX.) **75** F 3
Grapevine Lake **74** D 1
Grapevine Peak **109** E 3
Grasmere (ID.) **90** D 4
Grass Creek (WY.) **92** D 2
Grass Valley (CA.) **110** C 2
Grass Valley (OR.) **112** E 1
Grassrange (MT.) **86** E 2–3
Grassy Butte (ND.) **84** C 3
Grave Peak **88–89** F 3
Gravette (AR.) **66** B 1
Gravois Mills (MO.) **64** D 3
Gray (GA.) **42** C 4
Gray (OK.) **76** C 1
Gray Horse (OK.) **77** G 1
Gray Mountain (AZ.)
  103 G 3
Grayback, Mount **119** E 2
Grayland (WA.) **114** A 3
Grayling (AK.) **120** C 3
Grayling (MI.) **55** D 3
Grayling (MT.) **91** H 2
Grays Harbor **114** A 3
Grays Lake **91** H 3
Grays River (WA.) **114** B 3
Grayson (AL.) **46** B 5
Grayson (KY.) **51** H 2
Grayville (IL.) **57** E 3
Great Barrington (MA.)
  30 C 3
Great Basin **105** E 2–5
Great Basin National Park
  (NV.) **105** H 4
Great Bend (KS.) **78** E 3
Great Bend (N.D.) **85** K 4
Great Divide Basin
  92 DE 3–4
Great Falls (MT.) **86** B 2
Great Miami River **52** E 3
Great Plains Reservoirs
  95 H 3
Great Point **31** F 4
Great Salt Lake **102** A 4
Great Salt Lake Desert
  102 B 5
Great Salt Plains Lake
  77 E 1
Great Sand Dunes National
  Monument **94** E 4
Great Sandy Desert (OR.)
  112–113 E 3
Great Sitkin (AL.) **116** J 1
Great Smoky Mountains
  51 FG 5
Great Smoky Mountains
  National Park **51** G 5
Greathouse Peak **86** D 3
Greece (N.Y.) **32** C 2
Greeleyville (S.C.) **41** E 3
Greely (CO.) **95** F 1
Greely (NE.) **81** F 3
Green (OR.) **112** B 3
Green (WI.) **59** G 4
Green Bay (WI.) **59** E 1
Green Bay (WI./MI.)
  59 DE 1
Green City (MO.) **64** E 1
Green Cove Springs (FL.)
  44 AB 3
Green Forest (AR.) **66** C 1

Green Grass (SD.) **82** D 2
Green Lake (WI.) **59** F 2
Green Lake (WI.) **59** F 3
Green Mountain Reservoir
  94 D 2
Green Mountains **30** D 1
Green Peter Lake **112** C 2
Green Pond (S.C.) **41** E 4
Green River (KY.) **50** C 3
Green River (UT.) **102** C 2
Green River (UT.) **102** C 2
Green River (WY.) **92** C 4
Green River Lake **51** E 3
Green Swamp **39** F 4
Greenbank (WA.) **114** C 1
Greenbrier (AR.) **66** D 2
Greenbrier River **36** D 4
Greenbush (MN.) **60** B 6
Greencastle (IN.) **52** B 3
Greencastle (PA.) **34** D 4
Greene (N.Y.) **32** E 3
Greeneville (TN.) **51** H 4
Greenfield (CA.) **111** F 3
Greenfield (IA.) **62** D 4
Greenfield (IL.) **57** D 5
Greenfield (IN.) **52** D 3
Greenfield (IN.) **52** D 3
Greenfield (MA.) **30** D 3
Greenfield (MO.) **64** D 4
Greenfield (OH.) **53** F 3
Greenland (MI.) **58** C 2
Greenland (MI.) **58** C 2
Greenleaf (NE.) **79** G 2
Greenough (MT.) **89** G 3
Greenough, Mount **121** G 2
Greenport (N.Y.) **35** J 2
Greens Peak **101** G 2
Greensboro (AL.) **46** D 5
Greensboro (GA.) **42** C 4
Greensboro (N.C.) **38** E 2
Greensburg (IN.) **52** D 3
Greensburg (KY.) **50** E 3
Greensburg (LA.) **69** E 3
Greensburg (PA.) **34** B 3
Greenup (IL.) **57** D 3
Greenup (KY.) **51** H 2
Greenville (AL.) **47** E 4
Greenville (CA.) **110** B 2
Greenville (FL.) **44** A 5
Greenville (IL.) **57** E 5
Greenville (KY.) **50** C 3
Greenville (ME.) **28** C 4
Greenville (MI.) **55** E 4
Greenville (MO.) **65** G 4
Greenville (MS.) **48** C 5
Greenville (N.C.) **39** G 3
Greenville (N.H.) **29** F 6
Greenville (OH.) **52** E 2
Greenville (PA.) **34** A 2
Greenville (S.C.) **40** C 2
Greenville (TX.) **75** E 1
Greenway (SD.) **83** F 2
Greenwich (CT.) **35** H 2–3
Greenwich (OH.) **53** G 1
Greenwood (AR.) **66** B 2
Greenwood (FL.) **47** F 3
Greenwood (IN.) **52** C 3
Greenwood (KY.) **51** F 4
Greenwood (MS.) **48** C 4
Greenwood (S.C.) **40** C 2
Greenwood (WI.) **59** E 4
Greenwood, Lake **40** D 3
Greer (ID.) **88** D 3
Greer (S.C.) **40** C 2
Greers Ferry Lake **66** D 2

Gregory (SD.) **83** F 4
Gregory (TX.) **71** E 3
Grenada (CA.) **110** A 4
Grenada (MS.) **48** C 3
Grenada Lake **48** C 3
Grenola (KS.) **79** G 4
Grenora (ND.) **84** C 2
Gresham (OR.) **112** C 1
Gretna (NE.) **81** H 3
Gretna (VA.) **36** E 5
Grey Eagle (MN.) **61** E 4
Greybull (WY.) **92** DE 1
Greybull River **92** D 1
Greycliff (MT.) **86** D 4
Greylock, Mount **30** C 3
Greystone (CO.) **94** B 1
Gridley (CA.) **110** C 3
Gridley (KS.) **79** H 3
Griffin (GA.) **42** C 5
Griffith (AZ.) **100** B 1
Grifton (N.C.) **39** G 3
Grigston (KS.) **78** C 3
Grimsley (TN.) **51** F 4
Grinnell (IA.) **63** F 4
Grit (TX.) **74** B 4
Grizzly (OR.) **112** E 2
Grizzly Mountain **115** G 1
Groesbeck (TX.) **75** E 3
Groom (TX.) **76** B 2
Gros Ventre Range **92** B 2
Groton (S.D.) **83** G 2
Grotto (WA.) **114** D 2
Grottoes (VA.) **37** F 3
Grouse (ID.) **91** F 3
Grouse Creek (UT.) **102** A 5
Grouse Creek Mountain
91 F 2
Grove (OK.) **77** J 1
Grove City (MN.) **61** E 4
Grove City (OH.) **53** F 3
Grove City (PA.) **34** A 2
Grove Hill (AL.) **47** E 5
Grover (CO.) **95** F 1
Grover (UT.) **103** D 3
Grover City (CA.) **106** B 2
Groves (TX.) **75** H 5
Groveton (N.H.) **28** D 6
Groveton (TX.) **75** F 3
Growler (AZ.) **100** C 4
Growler Peak **100** C 4
Grundy (VA.) **36** B 4
Grundy Center (IA.) **63** F 3
Gruver (TX.) **76** B 1
Grygla (MN.) **60** B 5
Gu Achi (AZ.) **100** DE 4
Gu Komelik (AZ.) **100** F 4
Gu Oidak (AZ.) **100** D 5
Guadalupe (AZ.) **100** E 3
Guadalupe (CA.) **106** B 2–3
Guadalupe Bravos (Mex.)
72 B 2
Guadalupe Mountains
99 F 4–5
Guadalupe Mountains
National Park **72** D 2
Guadalupe Peak **72** D 2
Guadalupe River **71** E 1–2
Guadalupita (N.M.) **96** E 2
Gualala (CA.) **111** D 5
Guanajibo, Punta **124** A 2
Guánica (P.R.) **124** B 3
Guano Island **124** D 2
Guano Lake **113** F 4
Guayama (P.R.) **124** BC 2
Guayanilla (P.R.) **124** B 2
Guerneville (CA.) **111** D 5

Guernsey (WY.) **93** H 3
Guernsey Reservoir **93** H 3
Guerra (TX.) **70** D 2
Guerrero (Mex.) **70** C 4
Gueydan (LA.) **68** C 3
Guffey (CO.) **94** E 3
Guffy Peak **92** E 2
Guide Rock (NE.) **81** F 4
Guildhall (VT.) **30** E 1
Guilford (ME.) **28** C 4
Guin (AL.) **46** C 5
Gulf Breeze (FL.) **47** F 5
Gulf Islands National
Seashore **47** F 4–5
Gulf of Alaska (AL.)
116 BC 2
Gulf of Maine **31** GJ 3
Gulf of Santa Catalina
106–107 E 4
Gulf Shores (AL.) **47** F 5
Gulfport (FL.) **44** D 4
Gulfport (MS.) **49** F 3
Gulkana (AL.) **116** B 1
Gull Lake (MN.) **60** D 4
Gullivan Bay **45** F 3
Gulnare (CO.) **95** F 4
Gunnison (CO.) **94** D 3
Gunnison (UT.) **102** C 3
Gunnison, Mount **94** C 3
Gunnison River **94** BC 3
Guntersville (AL.) **46** B 4
Guntersville Lake **46** B 4
Gurdon (AR.) **66** C 4
Gurley (NE.) **80** B 3
Gustavus (AL.) **117** D 2
Gustine (CA.) **111** E 3
Gustine (TX.) **74** C 3
Guthrie (KY.) **50** C 4
Guthrie (OK.) **77** F 2
Guthrie (TX.) **76** C 4
Guthrie Center (IA.) **62** D 4
Guttenberg (IA.) **63** G 3
Guymon (OK.) **76** B 1
Gwinn (MI.) **54** B 6
Gwinner (N.D.) **85** J 4
Gypsum (CO.) **94** C 2
Gypsum (KS.) **79** E 3
Gypsum Hills **76** D 1

Hachita (N.M.) **98** B 5
Hackamore (CA.) **110** A 3
Hackberry (LA.) **68** B 3–4
Hackbery (AZ.) **100** C 1
Hackleburg (AL.) **46** B 5
Hackney (KS.) **79** F 4
Haddam (KS.) **79** F 2
Hadlock (WA.) **114** C 1
Haena (HI.) **88** B 2
Hagemeister (AL.) **119** C 2
Hagerhill (KY.) **51** H 3
Hagerman (ID.) **90** D 4
Hagerman (N.M.) **99** F 3
Hagerman Fossil Beds
National Monument (ID.)
90 DE 4
Hagerstown (MD.) **37** G 2

Hagewood (LA.) **68** B 2
Haggin, Mount **89** G 3
Hague (ND.) **85** G 4
Hagues Peak **94** E 1
Hahira (GA.) **43** E 4
Haig (NE.) **80** A 3
Haigler (NE.) **78** B 2
Haigler (NE.) **78** B 2
Hailey (ID.) **91** E 3
Haines (AL.) **117** D 2
Haines (OR.) **113** H 2
Haines City (FL.) **44** C 3
Haines Junction (AL.)
117 D 1
Haiwee Reservoir **109** E 3
Halawa (HI.) **123** E 2
Halawa, Cape **123** E 2
Hale (MO.) **64** D 2
Hale Center (TX.) **76** B 3
Haleakala National Park
123 E 3
Haletown (TN.) **50** E 5
Haley (ND.) **82** B 2
Haleyville (AL.) **46** B 5
Halifax (N.C.) **39** G 2
Halifax (VA.) **37** E 5
Hall (AL.) **118** A 1
Hall (MT.) **89** G 3
Hall Summit (LA.) **68** B 1
Halleck (NV.) **105** F 2
Hallettsville (TX.) **71** E 1
Halliday (ND.) **84** D 3
Halligan Reservoir
94–95 E 1
Hallock (MN.) **60** B 6
Hallstead (PA.) **35** F 2
Halsey (NE.) **80** D 3
Halsey (OR.) **112** B 2
Halstad (MN.) **60** C 6
Halton City (TX.) **74** D 2
Hamberg (ND.) **85** G 3
Hamburg (AR.) **67** E 4
Hamburg (CA.) **110** A 4
Hamburg (IA.) **62** C 5
Hamburg (N.Y.) **32** B 3
Hamburg (PA.) **35** F 3
Hamden (CT.) **35** J 2
Hamer (ID.) **91** G 3
Hamill (SD.) **83** F 4
Hamilton (AK.) **120** C 3
Hamilton (AL.) **46** B 5
Hamilton (CO.) **94** C 1
Hamilton (GA.) **42** D 5
Hamilton (IL.) **56** C 6
Hamilton (KS.) **79** G 4
Hamilton (MI.) **55** F 4
Hamilton (MO.) **64** C 2
Hamilton (MT.) **89** F 3
Hamilton (N.D.) **85** J 2
Hamilton (OH.) **52** E 3
Hamilton (TX.) **74** C 3
Hamilton Acres **121** F 3
Hamilton City (CA.) **110** C 3
Hamilton Dome (WY.)
92 D 2
Hamilton, Mount (AK.)
119 D 1
Hamilton, Mount (NV.)
105 F 3
Hamiltons Fort (UT.)
103 E 5
Hamlin (TX.) **73** H 1
Hamlin (W.V.) **36** B 3
Hammon (OK.) **76** D 2
Hammond (LA.) **69** E 3

Hammond (MT.) **87** J 4
Hammondsport (N.Y.)
32 C 3
Hammonton (N.J.) **35** G 4
Hampden (ND.) **85** H 2
Hampton (AR.) **66** D 4
Hampton (FL.) **44** B 4
Hampton (GA.) **42** C 5
Hampton (IA.) **63** E 3
Hampton (N.H.) **29** F 5
Hampton (OR.) **113** E 3
Hampton (S.C.) **40** D 4
Hampton (VA.) **37** H 4
Hampton Bays (N.Y.)
35 J 3
Hampton Butte
112–113 E 3
Hana (HI.) **123** E 3
Hanahan (S.C.) **41** F 4
Hanalei (HI.) **88** B 2
Hanapepe (HI.) **122** B 2
Hanceville (AL.) **46** B 4
Hancock (MD.) **37** F 2
Hancock (MI.) **58** B 2
Hancock (MN.) **61** E 5
Hancock (N.Y.) **33** A 4
Hancock, Mount **92** B 1
Haney (TX.) **76** B 2
Hanford (CA.) **111** F 1
Hanford (WA.) **115** F 3
Hankinson (N.D.) **85** K 4
Hanksville (UT.) **103** D 2
Hanna (UT.) **102** B 2
Hanna (WY.) **93** F 4
Hannaford (N.D.) **85** H 3
Hannah (N.D.) **85** H 2
Hannibal (MO.) **65** F 2
Hannibal (N.Y.) **32** D 2
Hannover (ND.) **84** E 3
Hanover (MT.) **86** D 2
Hanover (NE.) **79** G 2
Hanover (N.H.) **29** E 7
Hanover (Pa.) **34** E 4
Hanover (VA.) **37** G 4
Hansboro (ND.) **85** G 2
Hanska (MN.) **61** F 4
Hanston (KS.) **78** D 3
Happy (TX.) **76** B 3
Happy Camp (CA.) **110** A 5
Happy Jack (AZ.) **101** E 2
Harbor Beach (MI.) **55** E 1
Harbor Springs (MI.) **54** C 3
Harcuvar Mountains
100 C 2–3
Hardaway (FL.) **47** F 2
Hardeeville (S.C.)
40–41 DE 4
Hardesty (OK.) **76** B 1
Hardin (IL.) **57** D 5
Hardin (MT.) **87** F 4
Hardin (TX.) **75** G 4
Harding (SD.) **82** B 2
Harding, Lake **42** D 6
Hardinsburg (KY.) **50** D 3
Hardman (OR.) **113** F 1
Hardtner (KS.) **78** E 4
Hardwick (GA.) **42** C 4
Hardwick (VT.) **30** D 1
Hardy (IA.) **62** DE 3
Hardy (IA.) **62** DE 3
Hardy (MT.) **86** B 2
Hardy Dam Pond **55** E 4
Hargill (TX.) **70** D 4
Harlan (IA.) **62** C 4
Harlan County Lake **81** E 4

Harlem (MT.) **86** E 1
Harlingen (TX.) **71** E 4
Harlow (ND.) **85** G 2
Harlowton (MT.) **86** D 3
Harman (W.V.) **36** E 3
Harmony (MN.) **61** G 2
Harney (NV.) **105** E 2
Harney (OR.) **113** G 3
Harney Basin
  112–113 EG 3
Harney Lake **113** F 3
Harney Peak **82** B 4
Harper (KS.) **79** EF 4
Harper (OR.) **113** H 3
Harper (TX.) **74** B 4
Harper Lake **107** E 2
Harpers Ferry (MD.) **37** G 2
Harpster (ID.) **88** E 2
Harquahala Mountain
  100 C 3
Harriman (WY.) **93** G 4
Harrington (DE.) **37** J 3
Harrington (ME.) **28** D 2
Harrington (SD.) **82** D 4
Harrington (WA.) **115** G 2
Harris (MN.) **61** E 3
Harris, Lake **44** C 3
Harrisburg (AR.) **67** F 2
Harrisburg (IL.) **57** F 3
Harrisburg (NE.) **80** A 3
Harrisburg (OR.) **112** B 2
Harrisburg (PA.) **34** D 3
Harrison (AR.) **66** C 1
Harrison (ID.) **88** D 2
Harrison (MI.) **55** D 3
Harrison (NE.) **80** A 2
Harrison Bay (AL.) **121** E 1
Harrisonburg (LA.) **68** D 2
Harrisonburg (VA.) **37** E 3
Harrisonville (MO.) **64** C 3
Harriston (MS.) **49** E 4
Harrisville (N.Y.) **33** E 1
Harrisville (W.V.) **36** C 2
Harrodsburg (KY.) **51** E 3
Harrold (SD.) **83** F 3
Harrold (TX.) **76** D 3
Harry S. Truman Dam
  64 D 3
Harry S. Truman Reservoir
  64 D 3
Harry Strunk Lake **80** D 4
Hart (MI.) **55** E 5
Hart (TX.) **97** H 4
Hart Lake **113** F 4
Hartford (AL.) **47** E 3
Hartford (CT.) **35** J 2
Hartford (IA.) **63** E 4
Hartford (KY.) **50** D 3
Hartford (MI.) **55** F 5
Hartford (S.D.) **83** J 4
Hartford (WI.) **59** F 2
Hartford City (IN.) **52** D 2
Hartington (NE.) **81** G 2
Hartley (IA.) **62** C 2
Hartley (TX.) **97** H 3
Hartman (CO.) **95** H 3
Hartsel (CO.) **94** E 2
Hartselle (AL.) **46** B 4
Hartshorne (OK.) **77** H 3
Hartsville (S.C.) **41** E 2
Hartsville (TN.) **50** D 4
Hartville (MO.) **64** E 4
Hartville (WY.) **93** H 3
Hartwell (GA.) **42** B 3
Hartwell Lake **40** C 2
Harvard (ID.) **88** D 3

Harvard (IL.) **56** A 3
Harvard (NE.) **81** F 4
Harvard, Mount **94** D 3
Harvey (MI.) **54** B 6
Harvey (ND.) **85** G 3
Haskell (OK.) **77** H 2
Haskell (TX.) **74** B 1
Haslet (TX.) **74** D 1
Hassayampa River **100** D 3
Hassman (MN.) **60** D 3
Hastings (FL.) **44** B 3
Hastings (MI.) **55** F 4
Hastings (MN.) **61** F 2
Hastings (NE.) **81** F 4
Hasty (CO.) **95** G 3
Haswell (CO.) **95** G 3
Hat Creek (CA.) **110** B 3
Hatch (N.M.) **98** C 4
Hatch (UT.) **103** E 4
Hathaway (MT.) **87** G 3
Hatteras (N.C.) **39** J 3
Hatteras, Cape **39** J 3
Hatteras Island **39** J 3
Hattiesburg (MS.) **49** E 3
Hatton (AL.) **46** B 5
Hatton (N.D.) **85** J 3
Hauge (N.Y.) **33** G 2
Hauser (OR.) **112** A 3
Haut, Isle au **29** D 3
Hauula (HI.) **122** D 2
Havana (AR.) **66** C 2
Havana (FL.) **47** F 2
Havana (IL.) **56** C 4
Havasu, Lake **100** B 2
Havasupai Indian
  Reservation **103** F 4
Havelock (N.C.) **39** H 4
Havensville (NE.) **79** G 2
Haverhill (MA.) **31** E 3
Haviland (KS.) **78** D 4
Havre (MT.) **86** D 1
Havre de Grace (MD.)
  37 H 2
Haw Knob **51** FG 5
Hawaii **123** F 4
Hawaii Volcanoes National
  Park **123** F 4
Hawarden (IA.) **62** B 3
Hawesville (KY.) **50** D 3
Hawi (HI.) **123** F 3
Hawk Springs (WY.) **93** H 4
Hawkins (WI.) **59** D 4
Hawkinsville (GA.) **43** D 4
Hawksbill Mountain **38** C 3
Hawley (CO.) **95** G 4
Hawley (MN.) **60** D 6
Hawthorne (FL.) **44** B 4
Hawthorne (NV.) **104** C 4
Haxby (MT.) **87** G 2
Haxtun (CO.) **95** H 1
Hay Springs (NE.) **80** B 2
Hayden (AZ.) **101** F 3
Hayden (CO.) **94** C 1
Hayden Lake **88** D 2
Hayden Peak **90** C 4
Hayes (SD.) **82** DE 3
Hayes Center (NE.) **80** D 4
Hayesville (N.C.) **51** G 5
Hayfield (OR.) **112** C 2
Hayfield Lake **107** G 4
Hayford Peak **109** G 3
Hayfork Bally **110** B 5
Haynes (AR.) **67** F 3
Hayneville (AL.) **46** D 4
Hays (KS.) **78** D 3
Hays (MT.) **86** E 1

Haystack Mountain **105** F 1
Haystack Peak **102** C 5
Haysville (KS.) **79** F 4
Hayti (MO.) **65** H 5
Hayti (S.D.) **83** H 3
Hayward (CA.) **111** E 4
Hayward (WI.) **58** C 5
Hazard (KY.) **51** G 3
Hazard (NE.) **81** E 3
Hazel (WI.) **59** G 4
Hazelhurst (WI.) **58** D 3
Hazelton (ID.) **91** E 4
Hazelton (KS.) **78** E 4
Hazelton (ND.) **85** F 4
Hazelton Peak **93** E 1
Hazen (ND.) **84** E 3
Hazen (NV.) **104** BC 3
Hazen Bay **118** B 1
Hazlehurst (GA.) **43** E 3
Hazlehurst (MS.) **49** E 4
Hazleton (PA.) **35** F 3
Headland (AL.) **47** E 3
Headquarters (ID.) **88** E 2
Heafford Junction (WI.)
  58 D 3
Healdsburg (CA.) **111** D 5
Healdton (OK.) **77** F 3
Healy (KS.) **78** C 3
Healy Fork **121** F 3
Healy, Mount **121** EF 3
Hearne (TX.) **75** E 4
Heart Lake **92** B 1
Heart River **84** D 4
Heartwell (NE.) **81** F 4
Heath (MT.) **86** D 2
Heathsville (VA.) **37** H 4
Heavener (OK.) **77** J 3
Hebbronville (TX.) **70** D 3
Heber (AZ.) **101** F 2
Heber City (UT.) **102** B 3
Heber Springs (AR.) **66** D 2
Hebgen Lake **91** F 2
Hebo (OR.) **112** B 1
Hebron (IN.) **52** B 1
Hebron (ND.) **84** DE 4
Hebron (NE.) **81** G 4
Hebron (N.M.) **97** F 2
Hecla (S.D.) **83** G 2
Hector (MN.) **61** F 4
Hedgesville (MT.) **86** D 3
Hedley (TX.) **76** C 3
Hedwigs Hill (TX.) **74** B 4
Heflin (AL.) **46** C 3
Hefner, Lake **77** F 2
Heglar (ID.) **91** F 4
Heidelberg (MS.) **49** E 3
Heizer (KS.) **78** E 3
Helena (AR.) **67** F 3
Helena (CA.) **110** B 5
Helena (MT.) **86** A 3
Helena (OK.) **77** E 1
Helendale (CA.) **107** E 3
Heliotrope Mountain
  102 C 3
Hells Canyon **113** J 1
Hells Canyon Dam **88** D 4
Helm (CA.) **111** F 2
Helmville (MT.) **86** A 3
Helper (UT.) **102** C 2
Hemet (CA.) **107** F 4
Hemingford (NE.) **80** A 2
Hemingway (S.C.) **41** F 3
Hemlock (OR.) **112** B 1
Hempstead (TX.) **75** E 4
Henderson (IA.) **62** C 4
Henderson (KY.) **50** C 3

Henderson (MN.) **61** F 3
Henderson (N.C.) **39** F 2
Henderson (NV.) **109** G 3
Henderson (TN.) **50** B 5
Henderson (TX.) **75** G 2
Henefer (UT.) **102** A 3
Henlopen, Cape **37** JK 3
Henly (TX.) **74** C 4
Hennepin (IL.) **56** B 4
Hennessey (OK.) **77** F 1
Henniker (N.H.) **29** E 6
Henrietta (TX.) **77** E 4
Henry (ID.) **91** H 4
Henry (IL.) **56** B 4
Henry (NV.) **105** G 1
Henry (S.D.) **83** H 3
Henry, Cape **37** J 2
Henry Mountains **103** D 2
Henryetta (OK.) **77** G 2
Henrys Lake **91** H 2
Henshaw, Lake **107** F 4
Hephzibah (GA.) **42** C 3
Heppner (OR.) **113** F 1
Herber (CA.) **107** G 5
Herd (OK.) **77** G 1
Hereford (SD.) **82** C 3
Hereford (TX.) **97** H 4
Herington (KS.) **79** G 3
Herman (MN.) **61** E 6
Herman (NE.) **81** H 3
Hermanas (Mex.) **70** A 3
Hermann (MO.) **65** F 3
Hermansville (MI.) **54** C 6
Hermiston (OR.) **113** F 1
Hermitage (AR.) **66** D 4
Hermitage (MO.) **64** D 4
Hermleigh (TX.) **73** H 1
Hermosa (SD.) **82** B 4
Hermosa (TX.) **72** E 2
Hernandez (N.M.) **96** D 2
Hernando (MS.) **48** B 3
Herndon (KS.) **78** C 2
Herndon (PA.) **34** E 3
Heron (MT.) **88** E 1
Heron Bay (AL.) **47** F 6
Heron Lake (MN.) **61** G 5
Herreid (SD.) **83** EF 2
Herrin (IL.) **57** F 4
Herrington Lake **51** F 3
Hershey (NE.) **80** D 3
Hershey (PA.) **34** E 3
Hertford (N.C.) **39** H 2
Hesperia (CA.) **107** E 3
Hesperia (MI.) **55** E 5
Hesperus (CO.) **94** B 4
Hesperus Mountain **94** B 4
Hetch Hetchy Reservoir
  111 E 1
Hettinger (ND.) **82** C 2
Hewitt (MN.) **61** D 5
Hext (TX.) **74** B 4
Heyburn (ID.) **91** F 4
Heyburn, Lake **77** G 2
Heyworth (IL.) **56** C 3
Hiawassee (GA.) **42** B 4
Hiawatha (CA.) **94** B 1
Hiawatha (KS.) **79** H 2
Hiawatha (UT.) **102** C 2
Hibbing (MN.) **60** C 2
Hickman (KY.) **50** A 4
Hickman, Lake **81** H 4
Hickok (KS.) **78** B 4
Hickory (N.C.) **38** C 3
Hickory, Lake **38** C 3
Hickory Valley (TN.) **50** A 5
Hicksville (OH.) **52** E 1

Hico (TX.) **74** C 2–3
Hidalgo (TX.) **70** D 4
Higgins (TX.) **76** CD 1
Higgins Lake **55** D 3
Higginsville (MO.) **64** D 2
High Island **54** C 4
High Island (TX.) **75** G 5
High Point **35** G 2
High Point (N.C.) **38** D 3
High Rock (N.C.) **38** D 3
High Rock Lake (N.C.)
  38 D 3
High Rock Lake (NV.)
  104 B 1
High Springs (FL.) **44** B 4
Highland Home (AL.)
  47 E 4
Highland Park (IL.) **56** A 2
Highland Peak **111** D 1
Highlands (N.C.) **51** G 5
Highmore (SD.) **83** F 3
Highway (N.M.) **99** G 3
Highwood (MT.) **86** C 2
Highwood Baldy **86** C 2
Highwood Mountains
  86 C 2
Higüero, Punta **124** A 2
Hiko (NV.) **109** G 2
Hiland (WY.) **93** E 2
Hildreth (NE.) **81** EF 4
Hilger (MT.) **86** D 2
Hill (IL.) **57** D 5
Hill (MT.) **86** B 1
Hill City (ID.) **90** D 3
Hill City (MN.) **60** D 3
Hill City (SD.) **82** B 4
Hilland (SD.) **82** D 3
Hillcrest Center (CA.)
  106 D 2
Hilliard (FL.) **44** A 3
Hilliards (PA.) **34** B 2
Hillister (TX.) **75** G 4
Hillman (MI.) **54** C 3
Hillrose (CO.) **95** G 1
Hills (MN.) **61** G 6
Hills Creek Lake **112** C 3
Hillsboro (CA.) **42** C 4
Hillsboro (IL.) **57** D 4
Hillsboro (KS.) **79** F 3
Hillsboro (MO.) **65** G 3
Hillsboro (MT.) **87** E 4
Hillsboro (N.D.) **85** J 3
Hillsboro (N.H.) **29** E 6
Hillsboro (OH.) **53** F 3
Hillsboro (OR.) **112** C 1
Hillsboro (TX.) **74** D 2
Hillsboro (WI.) **59** F 4
Hillsboro Canal **45** E 2
Hillsborough (N.C.) **39** E 2
Hillsdale (MI.) **55** G 3
Hillsdale (WY.) **93** H 4
Hillside (AZ.) **100** C 2
Hillside (CO.) **94** E 3
Hillsville (VA.) **36** D 5
Hilo (FL.) **123** F 4
Hilo Bay **123** FG 4
Hilt (CA.) **110** A 4
Hilton Head Island **41** E 4
Himes (WY.) **92** D 1
Hinchin brook 1. (AL.)
  116 B 1
Hinckley (MN.) **61** D 2
Hinckley (UT.) **102** C 4
Hindman (KY.) **51** G 3
Hines (OR.) **113** F 3
Hinesville (GA.) **43** E 2

Hinkley (CA.) **107** E 3
Hinsdale (MT.) **87** F 1
Hinton (KY.) **51** F 2
Hinton (OK.) **77** E 2
Hinton (W.V.) **36** D 4
Hisle (SD.) **82** D 4
Hitchcock (OK.) **77** E 2
Hitchcock (S.D.) **83** G 3
Hitchland (OK.) **76** B 1
Hiwassee Lake **51** F 5
Hoban (TX.) **73** E 2
Hobart (OK.) **76** D 2
Hobbs (N.M.) **99** G 4
Hobbs Island (AL.) **46** B 4
Hobe Sound (FL.) **45** D 2
Hobergs (CA.) **111** D 4
Hobgood (N.C.) **39** G 2
Hobson (MT.) **86** D 2
Hochheim (TX.) **71** E 1
Hodge (CA.) **107** E 3
Hodgenville (KY.) **50** E 3
Hodges (MT.) **87** J 3
Hodzana River **121** F 2
Hoehne (CO.) **95** F 4
Hoffman (MN.) **61** E 5
Hog Island **37** J 4
Hogansville (GA.) **42** C 6
Hogback Mountain **91** G 2
Hogeland (MT.) **86** E 1
Hohenwald (TN.) **50** C 5
Hohokam Pima National
  Monument **100** E 3
Hoisington (KS.) **78** E 3
Hokah (MN.) **61** G 1
Holbrook (ID.) **91** G 4
Holbrook (NE.) **80** D 4
Holcomb (KS.) **78** C 3
Holcut (MS.) **48** B 2
Holdbrook (AZ.) **101** F 2
Holden (UT.) **102** C 4
Holdenville (OK.) **77** G 2
Holdrege (NE.) **81** E 4
Hole in the Mountain Peak
  105 F 2
Holgate (OH.) **53** E 1
Holitna (MN.) **119** D 1
Holladay (UT.) **102** B 3
Holland (MI.) **55** F 5
Holland (TX.) **74** D 4
Hollandale (MS.) **48** C 5
Holliday (TX.) **76** E 4
Hollidaysburg (PA.) **34** C 3
Hollis (AR.) **66** C 3
Hollis (OK.) **76** D 3
Hollister (CA.) **111** F 3
Hollister (ID.) **90** E 4
Holly (CO.) **95** H 3
Holly (MI.) **55** F 2
Holly Beach (LA.) **68** B 4
Holly Grove (AR.) **67** E 3
Holly Hill (S.C.) **41** E 3
Holly Springs (GA.) **42** B 5
Holly Springs (MS.) **48** B 3
Hollywood (FL.) **45** E 2
Hollywood (N.M.) **99** E 3
Holmes, Mount **92** D 1
Holopaw (FL.) **44** C 3
Holstein (IA.) **62** C 3
Holston River **51** H 4
Holt (MT.) **89** F 1
Holter Lake **86** B 3
Holton (KS.) **79** H 2
Holtville (CA.) **107** G 5
Holualoa (HI.) **123** F 4
Holy Cross (AL.) **119** D 1
Holyoke (CO.) **95** H 1

Holyoke (MA.) **30** D 3
Holyoke (MN.) **60** D 2
Holyrood (KS.) **78** E 3
Homedale (ID.) **113** HJ 3
Homer (AL.) **119** E 2
Homer (GA.) **42** B 4
Homer (LA.) **68** B 1
Homer (N.Y.) **32** D 3
Homer Youngs Peak **89** G 4
Homerville (GA.) **43** E 3
Homestead (FL.) **45** F 2
Homestead (MT.) **87** J 1
Homestead (OK.) **76** E 1
Homestead (OR.) **113** HJ 1
Homestead National
  Monument **81** H 4
Homewood (AL.) **46** C 4
Hominy (OK.) **77** G 1
Homosassa Springs (FL.)
  44 C 4
Honaker (VA.) **36** C 4
Honaunau (HI.) **123** EF 4
Hondo (N.M.) **99** E 3
Hondo (TX.) **70** C 1
Honea Path (S.C.) **40** C 2
Honea Reservoir **75** F 4
Honesdale (PA.) **35** F 2
Honey Lake **110** B 2
Honeydew (CA.) **110** B 6
Honeyville (UT.) **102** A 4
Honokaa (HI.) **123** F 3
Honokahua (HI.) **123** E 2–3
Honolulu (HI.) **122** D 2
Honomu (HI.) **123** FG 4
Honuapo (HI.) **123** F 4
Hood Canal **114** B 2
Hood, Mount **112** D 1
Hood River (OR.) **114** D 4
Hoodoo Peak **114–115** E 1
Hoodsport (WA.) **114** B 2
Hooker (OK.) **76** B 1
Hoolehua (HI.) **123** D 2
Hoonah (AL.) **117** DE 2
Hoopa (CA.) **110** A 5
Hoopa Valley Indian
  Reservation **110** A 5
Hooper (CO.) **94** DE 4
Hooper (NE.) **81** H 3
Hooper (WA.) **115** G 3
Hooper Bay (AL.) **118** B 1
Hoopeston (IL.) **56** C 2
Hoople (N.D.) **85** J 2
Hoosick Falls (N.Y.) **33** G 3
Hoosier Pass **94** DE 2
Hoover (SD.) **82** B 2
Hoover Dam **103** F 6
Hoover Reservoir **53** G 2
Hope (AK.) **116** B 1
Hope (AR.) **66** C 4
Hope (AZ.) **100** C 3
Hope (IN.) **52** D 2
Hope (N.D.) **85** J 3
Hope (N.M.) **99** F 4
Hopedale (LA.) **69** F 4
Hopewell (KS.) **78** E 4
Hopewell (VA.) **37** G 4
Hopi Buttes **101** F 1
Hopi Indian Reservation
  103 G 2
Hopkins (MO.) **64** C 1
Hopkinsville (KY.) **50** C 4
Hopland (CA.) **110** CD 5
Hoquiam (WA.) **114** AB 3
Horace Mountain **121** F 2
Horn Island **49** F 2
Hornbrock (CA.) **110** A 4

Horncut (CA.) **110** C 3
Hornell (N.Y.) **32** C 3
Horse Creek (WY.) **93** G 4
Horse Heaven Hills **115** F 3
Horse Lake **110** B 2
Horsehead Lake **85** G 3
Horseshoe Bend (ID.)
  90 C 3
Horseshoe Reservoir
  100 E 2
Horsetooth Reservoir
  95 E 1
Horton (MT.) **87** G 3
Hosford (FL.) **47** F 2
Hoskins (TX.) **71** G 1
Hosmer (SD.) **83** F 2
Hosta Butte **96** B 3
Hot Creek Range **105** E 4
Hot Spring (ID.) **90** D 4
Hot Springs (AR.) **66** D 3
Hot Springs (MT.)
  88–89 F 2
Hot Springs (SD.) **82** B 4
Hot Springs (VA.) **36** D 3
Hot Springs National Park
  (AR.) **66** CD 3
Hot Springs Peak (CA.)
  110 B 2
Hot Springs Peak (NV.)
  104 D 1
Hot Sulphur Springs (CO.)
  94 D 1
Hotchkiss (CO.) **94** C 3
Hotevilla (AZ.) **103** G 2
Hough (OK.) **76** B 1
Houghton (KS.) **78** B 4
Houghton (MI.) **58** B 2
Houghton (N.Y.) **32** B 3
Houghton Lake **55** D 3
Houghton Lake (MI.) **55** D 3
Houlka (MS.) **48** B 3
Houlton (ME.) **28** B 3
Houma (LA.) **69** E 4
House (N.M.) **97** G 4
Houston (MO.) **65** F 4
Houston (MS.) **48** C 2
Houston (TX.) **71** G 1
Houston, Lake **75** F 4–5
Hoven (SD.) **83** F 2
Hovenweep National
  Monument **103** E 1
Howard (CO.) **94** E 3
Howard (KS.) **79** G 4
Howard (OH.) **53** G 2
Howard (PA.) **34** D 2
Howard (S.D.) **83** H 3
Howard (WI.) **59** E 2
Howard City (MI.) **55** E 4
Howard Lake (MN.) **61** E 4
Howard Prairie Lake
  112 C 4
Howe (ID.) **91** G 3
Howe (OK.) **77** J 3
Howe (TX.) **75** E 1
Howell (MI.) **55** F 2
Howell (UT.) **102** A 4
Howes (SD.) **82** D 3
Hoxie (AR.) **67** E 1
Hoxie (KS.) **78** C 2
Hoyt (CO.) **95** FG 1
Hoyt (MT.) **87** J 3
Hualapai Indian
  Reservation **103** G 5
Hualapai Mountains
  100 C 2
Hualapai Peak **100** C 1

Hubbard (IA.) **63** E 3
Hubbard (TX.) **75** E 3
Hubbard Creek Lake **74** B 2
Hubbard Lake **54** D 2
Huckleberry Mountain **112** C 3
Hudson (FL.) **44** C 4
Hudson (IA.) **63** F 3
Hudson (KS.) **78** E 3
Hudson (MI.) **55** G 3
Hudson (N.Y.) **33** G 3
Hudson (WY.) **92** D 3
Hudson Falls (N.Y.) **33** G 2
Hudson River **33** G 3
Hueco Mountains **72** BC 2
Huelo Point **123** E 3
Huerfano River **95** F 4
Hugh Butler Lake **80** D 4
Hughes (AL.) **121** E 2
Hughes (AR.) **67** F 3
Hughson (CA.) **111** E 2
Hugo (CO.) **95** G 2
Hugo (OK.) **77** H 3
Hulah Lake **77** G 1
Hulahula River **121** G 2
Hulett (WY.) **93** H 1
Humacao (P.R.) **124** C 2
Humansville (MO.) **64** D 4
Humboldt (AZ.) **100** D 2
Humboldt (NE.) **81** J 4
Humboldt (NV.) **104** C 2
Humboldt (TN.) **50** B 5
Humboldt Bay **110** B 6
Humboldt Peak **94** E 4
Humboldt River **104** C 2
Humboldt Salt Marsh **104** D 3
Humboldt Sink **104** C 2–3
Humeston (IA.) **63** E 5
Humphrey (AR.) **67** E 3
Humphrey (ID.) **91** G 2
Humphrey (NE.) **81** G 3
Humphreys Peak **100** E 1
Hungerford (TX.) **71** F 1
Hungry Horse Reservoir **89** G 1
Hunt Mountain **92** E 1
Hunter (KS.) **78** E 2
Hunter (N.D.) **85** J 3
Hunterdon (OH.) **53** G 3
Huntingburg (IN.) **52** C 4
Huntingdon (PA.) **34** D 3
Huntingdon (TN.) **50** B 4–5
Huntington (IN.) **52** D 2
Huntington (OR.) **113** H 2
Huntington (TX.) **75** G 3
Huntington (UT.) **102** C 2
Huntington (W.V.) **36** B 3
Huntington Beach (CA.) **106** DE 4
Huntley (MT.) **87** E 4
Huntley (NE.) **81** E 4
Huntsville (AL.) **46** B 4
Huntsville (AR.) **66** C 1
Huntsville (MO.) **64** E 2
Huntsville (TN.) **51** F 4
Huntsville (TX.) **75** F 4
Huntsville (UT.) **102** A 3
Hurley (N.M.) **98** B 4
Hurley (S.D.) **83** HJ 4
Huron (CA.) **111** F 2
Huron (OH.) **53** G 1
Huron (S.D.) **83** G 3
Huron Beach (MI.) **54** C 3
Huron Mountains **58** C 1–2
Hurricane (AK.) **116** B 1
Hurricane (UT.) **103** E 5
Hurricane Cliffs **103** F 5
Hurtsboro (AL.) **46** D 3
Huslia (AL.) **121** D 2
Hustisford (WI.) **59** F 2
Hutch Mountain **101** E 2
Hutchinson (KS.) **79** F 3
Hutchinson (MN.) **61** F 4
Hutsonville (IL.) **57** D 2
Huttig (AR.) **66** D 4
Huttonsville (W.V.) **36** E 3
Huxford (AL.) **47** E 5
Hyampom (CA.) **110** B 5
Hyannis (MA.) **31** F 4
Hyannis (NE.) **80** C 3
Hyattville (WY.) **92** E 1
Hybart (AL.) **47** E 5
Hydaburg **117** E 2
Hyde Park (VT.) **30** D 1
Hyden (KY.) **51** G 3
Hyder (AZ.) **100** C 3
Hyder (Br. Col., Can.) **117** E 2
Hye (TX.) **74** C 4
Hyland River **117** F 1
Hyndman (PA.) **34** C 4
Hyndman Peak **91** E 3
Hyrum (UT.) **102** A 3
Hysham (MT.) **87** F 3

I

Iaeger (W.V.) **36** C 4
Ibapah (UT.) **102** B 5
Ice Harbor Dam **115** G 3
Iceberg Pass **94** E 1
Icy Bay **116** C 2
Icy Bay (AL.) **116** C 2
Icy cape (AL.) **120** C 1
Ida Grove (IA.) **62** C 3
Idabel (OK.) **77** J 4
Idaho City (ID.) **90** D 3
Idaho Falls (ID.) **91** G 3
Idalia (CO.) **95** H 2
Idalou (TX.) **76** B 4
Idanha (OR.) **112** CD 2
Idavada (ID.) **90** E 4
Ideal (SD.) **83** F 4
Iditarod River **119** D 1
Idleyld Park (OR.) **112** C 3
Idria (CA.) **111** F 2
Ignacio (CO.) **94** C 4
Iguigik (AL.) **119** D 2
Iivengood (AL.) **121** F 2
Ikatan **118** C 3
Ikuktlitlik Mountain **119** C 2
Iliad (MT.) **86** D 2
Iliamna (AL.) **119** E 2
Iliff (CO.) **95** G 1
Ilio Point **123** D 2
Illinois (North) **56–57**
Illinois (South) **56–57**
Illinois City (IL.) **56** B 5
Illinois River **56** D 5
Ilo, Lake **84** D 3
Ilwaco (WA.) **114** AB 3
Imbler (OR.) **113** H 1
Imlay (SD.) **82** C 4
Imman (NE.) **81** F 2
Immokalee (FL.) **45** E 3
Imnaha River **113** J 1
Imperial (CA.) **107** G 5
Imperial (NE.) **80** C 4
Imperial (NE.) **80** C 4
Imperial Beach (CA.) **107** E 5
Imperial, Point **103** F 3
Imperial Valley **107** G 5
Imuruk Lake **120** C 2
Inchoun **120** A 2
Independence (CA.) **108** D 3
Independence (IA.) **63** G 3
Independence (KS.) **79** H 4
Independence (KY.) **51** F 2
Independence (LA.) **69** E 3
Independence (MO.) **64** C 2
Independence (OR.) **112** B 2
Independence (VA.) **36** C 5
Independence Mountains **105** E 1–2
Independence Pass **94** D 2
Index (WA.) **114** D 2
Indialantic (FL.) **44** C 2
Indian Lake (MI.) **54** B 5
Indian Lake (N.Y.) **33** F 2
Indian Lake (N.Y.) **33** F 2
Indian Lake (OH.) **53** F 2
Indian Peak (UT.) **103** D 5
Indian Peak (WY.) **92** C 1
Indian River (MI.) **54** C 3
Indian River Inlet **37** JK 3
Indian Rocks Beach (FL.) **44** C 5
Indian Springs (NV.) **109** G 3
Indian Valley (ID.) **90** C 2
Indiana (North) **52**
Indiana (PA.) **34** B 3
Indiana (South) **53** F 3
Indiana Dunes National Lakeshore (IN.) **52** BC 1
Indianapolis (IN.) **52** C 3
Indianola (IA.) **63** E 4
Indianola (MS.) **48** C 4
Indianola (NE.) **80** D 4
Indianola (TX.) **71** F 2
Indianola (UT.) **102** C 3
Indiantown (FL.) **45** D 2
Indio (CA.) **107** F 4
Indus (MN.) **60** B 3
Industry (TX.) **75** E 4
Inez (KY.) **51** H 3
Inez (TX.) **71** F 2
Ingalls (KS.) **78** C 4
Inglewood (CA.) **106** D 4
Inglis (FL.) **44** B 4
Ingomar (MT.) **87** F 3
Ingot (CA.) **110** B 4
Ingram (TX.) **74** B 4
Inklin (AL.) **117** E 2
Inkster (N.D.) **85** J 2
Inlay City (MI.) **55** E 2
Inman (S.C.) **40** C 1
Innoko River **120** D 3
Inola (OK.) **77** H 1
Intake (MT.) **87** J 2
Interior (SD.) **82** D 4
International Falls (MN.) **60** B 3
Intracoastal City (LA.) **68** C 4
Inverness (CA.) **111** D 4–5
Inverness (FL.) **44** C 4
Inwood (IA.) **62** B 2
Inyan Kara Mountain **93** H 1
Inyo, Mount **109** E 3
Inyo Mountains **108** D 3
Inyokern (CA.) **107** E 2
Iola (CO.) **94** C 3
Iola (KS.) **79** H 4
Iona (SD.) **83** F 4
Ione (CA.) **111** D 2–3
Ione (OR.) **113** F 1
Ione (WA.) **115** H 1
Ionia (KS.) **78** E 2
Ionia (MI.) **55** F 4
Iowa **62–63**
Iowa City (IA.) **63** G 4
Iowa Falls (IA.) **63** E 3
Iowa Park (TX.) **76** E 4
Ipava (IL.) **56** C 5
Ipswich (SD.) **83** F 2
Ira (TX.) **73** G 1
Iraan (TX.) **73** G 3
Irene (S.D.) **83** H 4
Irish, Mount **109** G 2
Iron Belt (WI.) **58** C 4
Iron City (TN.) **50** C 5
Iron Mountain (AZ.) **101** E 3
Iron Mountain (MI.) **54** C 6
Iron Mountain (WA.) **114** D 1
Iron Mountains (N.C.) **36** C 5
Iron River (MI.) **58** C 2
Iron River (WI.) **58** C 5
Iron Springs (UT.) **103** E 5
Ironaton (AL.) **46** C 3
Irondequoit (N.Y.) **32** C 2
Ironside (OR.) **113** GH 2
Ironside (OR.) **113** GH 2
Ironton (MO.) **65** G 4
Ironton (OH.) **53** G 4
Ironwood (MI.) **58** C 4
Iroquois (S.D.) **83** H 3
Iroquois River **56** C 2
Irrigon (OR.) **113** F 1
Irvine (KY.) **51** G 3
Irving (TX.) **75** E 2
Irvington (KY.) **50** D 3
Irwinton (GA.) **42** D 4
Isabel (SD.) **82** D 2
Isabel Segunda **124** C 2
Isabela (P.R.) **124** AB 2
Isabella (MN.) **60** C 1
Isabella Lake **106** D 2
Isanti (MN.) **61** E 3
Ishpeming (MI.) **54** B 6
Iskut River (AL.) **117** E 2
Isla Caja de Muertos **124** B 3
Isla de Culebra **124** C 2
Isla de Vieques **124** C 2
Isla Desecheo **124** A 2
Isla Mona **124** A 2
Isla Monito **124** A 2
Isla Montague (Mex.) **100** B 5
Isla Vista (CA.) **106** B 3
Islamorada (FL.) **45** G 2
Island City (KY.) **51** G 3
Island Falls (ME.) **28** B 3
Island Lake Reservoir **60** C 2
Island Mountain (CA.) **110** B 5

Island Park (ID.) **91** H 2
Island Park Reservoir
91 H 2
Island Pond (VT.) **30** E 1
Islands of Four Mountains
(AL.) **117** K 1
Isle (MN.) **61** D 3
Isle au Haut **29** D 3
Isle Royale **58** B 2
Isle Royale National Park
58 A 2
Islen (NV.) **109** H 2
Isles Dernieres **69** E 4
Islesboro Island **29** D 3
Isleta (N.M.) **96** D 4
Isleta Indian Reservation
96 D 4
Isleton (CA.) **111** D 3
Ismay (MT.) **87** J 3
Isola (MS.) **48** C 4
Isto, Mount **121** G 2
Istokpoga, Lake **45** D 3
Italy (TX.) **75** E 2
Itasca (TX.) **74** D 2
Ithaca (N.Y.) **32** D 3
Ithaka (MI.) **55** E 3
Itkillik River **121** E 2
Itta Bena (MS.) **48** C 4
Iuka (KS.) **78** E 4
Iuka (MS.) **48** B 2
Iva (S.C.) **40** C 2
Ivan (TX.) **74** C 2
Ivan of Bay (AL.) **119** D 2
Ivanhoe (CA.) **111** F 1
Ivanhoe (MN.) **61** F 6
Ivanhoe (VA.) **36** C 5
Ivanpah (CA.) **107** G 2

J

J. Percy Priest Reservoir
50 D 4
Jack Mountain (MT.)
86 A 3
Jack Mountain (WA.)
114 E 1
Jackpot (NV.) **105** G 1
Jacksboro (TN.) **51** F 4
Jacksboro (TX.) **74** C 1
Jackson (AL.) **47** E 5
Jackson (CA.) **111** D 2
Jackson (GA.) **42** C 5
Jackson (KY.) **51** G 3
Jackson (MI.) **55** F 3
Jackson (MN.) **61** G 4
Jackson (MO.) **65** H 4
Jackson (MS.) **48** D 4
Jackson (MT.) **89** G 4
Jackson (N.C.) **39** G 2
Jackson (OH.) **53** G 3
Jackson (TN.) **50** B 5
Jackson (WY.) **92** B 2
Jackson Junction (IA.)
63 G 2
Jackson Lake (GA.) **42** C 4
Jackson Lake (WY.) **92** B 2
Jackson Reservoir **95** FG 1
Jacksonville (AR.) **66** D 3

Jacksonville (FL.) **44** A 4
Jacksonville (IL.) **56** D 5
Jacksonville (N.C.) **39** G 4
Jacksonville (OR.) **112** BC 4
Jacksonville (TX.) **75** F 3
Jacksonville Beach (FL.)
44 A 3
Jacob Lake (AZ.) **103** F 4
Jagged Mountain **119** C 2
Jake Creek Mountain
104–105 E 1
Jal (N.M.) **99** G 4
Jamaica (IA.) **62** D 4
Jamaica (VT.) **30** D 2
James, Lake **38** C 3
James River **37** GH 4
James River (S.D.) **83** H 4
Jamestown (CA.) **111** E 2
Jamestown (KS.) **79** E 2
Jamestown (KY.) **51** E 4
Jamestown (N.C.) **38** E 2–3
Jamestown (N.D.) **85** H 4
Jamestown (N.Y.) **32** A 3
Jamestown (PA.) **34** A 2
Jamestown (S.C.) **41** F 3
Jamestown (TN.) **51** F 4
Jamieson (OR.) **113** H 2
Jane Lew (W.V.) **36** D 2
Janesville (CA.) **110** B 2
Janesville (MN.) **61** F 3
Janesville (WI.) **59** G 3
Janney (MT.) **86** A 4
Jansen (CO.) **95** F 4
Jarbridge (NV.) **105** F 1
Jarratt (VA.) **37** G 5
Jarvisburg (N.C.) **39** J 2
Jasper (AL.) **46** C 5
Jasper (AR.) **66** C 1
Jasper (FL.) **44** A 4
Jasper (GA.) **42** B 5
Jasper (IN.) **52** C 4
Jasper (MN.) **61** G 6
Jasper (TN.) **50** E 5
Jasper (TX.) **75** H 4
Java (SD.) **83** F 2
Jay (FL.) **47** F 5
Jay (OK.) **77** J 1
Jay Em (WY.) **93** H 3
Jayton (TX.) **76** C 4
Jean (NV.) **109** G 4
Jean Lafitte National
Historic Park & Preserve
(LA.) **69** E 4
Jeanerette (LA.) **68** D 4
Jeffers (MN.) **61** F 5
Jefferson (GA.) **42** B 4
Jefferson (IA.) **62** D 3
Jefferson (N.C.) **38** C 2
Jefferson (OH.) **53** J 1
Jefferson (OR.) **112** B 2
Jefferson (TX.) **75** G 2
Jefferson (WI.) **59** FG 2
Jefferson City (MO.)
64–65 E 3
Jefferson City (MT.) **86** B 3
Jefferson City (TN.) **51** G 4
Jefferson, Mount (ID.)
91 H 2
Jefferson, Mount (NV.)
105 E 4
Jefferson, Mount (OR.)
112 D 2
Jefferson River **86** A 4
Jeffersonville (GA.) **42** D 4
Jeffersonville (IN.) **52** D 4
Jeffersonville (OH.) **53** F 3

Jeffrey City (WY.) **92** E 3
Jekyll Island **43** E 2
Jemez Indian Reservation
96 D 3
Jemez Mountains **96** D 3
Jemez Pueblo (N.M.)
96 D 3
Jemez Springs (N.M.)
96 D 3
Jena (FL.) **44** B 5
Jena (LA.) **68** C 2
Jenifer (AL.) **46** C 3
Jenison (MI.) **55** F 4
Jenner (CA.) **111** D 5
Jennings (FL.) **44** A 5
Jennings (KS.) **78** C 2
Jennings (LA.) **68** C 3
Jensen Beach (FL.) **45** D 2
Jenson (UT.) **102** B 1
Jericho (TX.) **76** C 2
Jericho (UT.) **102** C 4
Jerimoth Hill **35** K 2
Jerome (AZ.) **100** D 2
Jerome (ID.) **90** E 4
Jersey City (N.J.) **35** H 3
Jersey Mountain **88** E 4
Jerseyville (IL.) **57** D 5
Jesup (GA.) **43** E 2
Jesup (IA.) **63** F 3
Jet (OK.) **77** E 1
JetmoreĖ (KS.) **78** C 3
Jewell (AL.) **63** E 3
Jewell (KS.) **79** E 2
Jewell Cave National
Monument **82** B 4
Jewett (TX.) **75** E 3
Jicarilla Indian Reservation
96 C 2
Jim Thorpe (PA.) **35** F 3
Jim Woodruff Dam
47 F 2–3
Jimmy Carter National
Historic Site (GA.)
43 BC 4
Joaquin (TX.) **75** G 3
Job Peak **104** D 3
Jocassee, Lake **40** C 1–2
Joe Ward Camp **121** G 2
Joes (CO.) **95** H 2
Joffre (N.M.) **97** F 4
Johannesburg (CA.)
107 E 2
John Day (OR.) **113** G 2
John Day Fossil Buttes
National Monument
112–113 E 2
John Day River **112** E 1
John F. Kennedy Space
Center **44** C 2
John H. Kerr Reservoir
39 F 2
John Martin Reservoir
95 GH 3
John Redmond Reservoir
79 H 3
John W. Flannigan
Reservoir **36** B 4
Johnson (KS.) **78** B 4
Johnson City (N.Y.) **32** E 3
Johnson City (TN.) **51** H 4
Johnson City (TX.) **74** C 4
Johnsondale (CA.) **106** D 2
Johnsons Crossing (AL.)
117 E 1
Johnston (S.C.) **40** D 3
Johnstone (TX.) **70** B 1

Johnstown (NE.) **80** D 2
Johnstown (N.Y.) **33** F 2
Johnstown (PA.) **34** C 3
Joliet (IL.) **56** B 3
Joliet (MT.) **86** DE 4
Jolly (TX.) **77** E 4
Jones (OK.) **77** F 2
Jonesboro (AR.) **67** F 2
Jonesboro (GA.) **42** C 5
Jonesboro (IL.) **57** F 4
Jonesboro (LA.) **68** C 1
Jonesboro (TN.) **51** H 4
Jonesboro (TX.) **74** D 3
Jonestown (MS.) **48** B 4
Jonesville (MI.) **55** G 3
Jonesville (S.C.) **40** D 2
Jonesville (VA.) **36** A 2
Joplin (MO.) **64** C 4
Joplin (MT.) **86** C 1
Joppa (IL.) **57** F 3
Jordan (MN.) **61** F 3
Jordan (MT.) **87** G 2
Jordan Lake **46** D 4
Jordan Valley (OR.)
113 H 3
Jornado del Muerto
98 D 3–4
Joseph (OR.) **113** H 1
Joseph City (AZ.) **101** F 1–2
Joshua Tree (CA.) **107** F 3
Joshua Tree National
Monument **107** FG 4
Jost Van Dyke Island
124 D 2
Jourdanton (TX.) **70** D 2
Joy (IL.) **56** B 5
Juan de Fuca, Strait of
114 AB 1
Judith Gap (MT.) **86** D 3
Judith Mountains **86** DE 2
Judith River **86** D 2
Julesburg (CO.) **95** H 1
Julesburg Reservoir **95** H 1
Julian (CA.) **107** F 4
Juncos (P.R.) **124** C 2
Junction (TX.) **74** B 4
Junction (UT.) **103** D 4
Junction City (KS.) **79** G 2
Junction City (KY.) **51** F 3
Junction City (LA.)
66 D 4–5
Junction City (OR.) **112** B 2
June Lake (CA.) **111** E 1
Juneau (AL.) **117** C 2
Jungo (NV.) **104** C 2
Junipero Serra Peak
111 Γ 3
Juno (TX.) **73** G 3
Juno Beach (FL.) **45** E 2
Juntura (OR.) **113** G 3
Jupiter (FL.) **45** E 2

K

Ka Lae **123** F 5
Kaala **122** C 2
Kabetogama Lake **60** B 3
Kachess Lake **114** D 2

Kadoka (SD.) **82** D 4
Kaeleku (HI.) **123** EF 3
Kaena Point (HI.) **122** C 2
Kaena Point (HI.) **123** D 3
Kaffir (TX.) **76** B 3
Kagalaska (AL.) **117** J 1
Kahlotus (WA.) **115** G 3
Kahoka (MO.) **65** F 1
Kahoolawe **123** E 3
Kahuku Point **122** D 2
Kaibab Indian Reservation
  103 F 4
Kaibab Plateau **103** F 4
Kaibito Plateau **103** F 3
Kailua (HI.) **122** D 2
Kailua (HI.) **123** EF 4
Kaiparowits Plateau
  103 E 3
Kaiwi Channel **123** D 2
Kaiyuh Mountains (AL.)
  120 C 3
Kaka Point **123** E 3
Kakakulao (HI.) **123** E 3
Kake **117** E 2
Kakhonak (AL.) **119** E 2
Kaktovik (AL.) **121** G 1
Kalaheo (HI.) **122** B 2
Kalaloch (WA.) **114** A 2
Kalama (WA.) **114** C 3
Kalamazoo (MI.) **55** F 4
Kalaoa (HI.) **123** F 4
Kalapana (HI.) **123** G 4
Kalaupapa (HI.) **123** DE 2
Kalispel Indian Reservation
  115 H 1
Kalispell (MT.) **89** F 1
Kalkaska (MI.) **54** D 4
Kalohi Channel **123** D 3
Kalona (IA.) **63** G 4
Kalskag (AL.) **119** C 1
Kaltag (AL.) **120** C 3
Kalvesta (KS.) **78** C 3
Kamakou **123** DE 2
Kamalo (HI.) **123** E 2
Kamas (UT.) **102** B 3
Kamela (OR.) **113** G 1
Kamiah (ID.) **88** D 3
Kamiak Mountain **115** H 3
Kampsville (IL.) **57** D 5
Kanab (UT.) **103** E 4
Kanai Soldotna (AL.)
  119 E 1
Kanarraville (UT.) **103** E 5
Kanawha (IA.) **62–63** E 3
Kanawha River **36** C 3
Kane (PA.) **34** C 2
Kane (WY.) **92** D 1
Kaneohe (HI.) **122** D 2
Kankakee (IL.) **56** B 2
Kankakee River **56** B 2
Kannapolis (N.C.) **38** D 3
Kanopolis (KS.) **79** F 3
Kanopolis Lake **79** F 3
Kanorado (KS.) **78** B 2
Kanosh (UT.) **103** D 4
Kansas **78–79**
Kansas City (KS.) **79** J 2
Kansas City (MO.) **64** C 2
Kansas River **79** G 2
Kantishna (AL.) **121** E 3
Kantishna River **121** E 3
Kanuti River **121** E 2
Kapaa (HI.) **88** B 2
Kaplan (LA.) **68** C 3–4
Kapowsin (WA.) **114** C 2

Karlsruhe (ND.) **84** F 2
Karlstad (MN.) **60** B 6
Karluk (AL.) **119** E 2
Karnes City (TX.) **70** D 2
Karthaus (PA.) **34** C 2
Karval (CO.) **95** G 3
Kasaan **117** E 2
Kashanuk River
  118–119 C 1
Kashegelok **119** D 1
Kaskaskia River **57** E 5
Katahdin, Mount **28** C 3
Katalla **116** C 1
Katmai Nat. Park and Pres.
  (AL.) **119** E 2
Kauai **88** B 2
Kauai Channel **122** C 2
Kaufman (TX.) **75** E 2
Kauhola Point **89** F 3
Kaukauna (WI.) **59** E 2
Kaula Island **122** A 2
Kaulakahi Channel
  122 AB 1–2
Kaumalapau (HI.) **123** D 3
Kauna Point **123** EF 4
Kaunakakai (HI.) **123** D 2
Kaw City (OK.) **77** G 1
Kawaihae (HI.) **123** F 3
Kawaihae Bay **123** EF 4
Kawaihoa Point **122** A 2
Kaweah, Lake **108** D 3
Kawich Peak **109** F 1–2
Kawich Range **109** F 2
Kayak (AL.) **116** C 2
Kaycee (WY.) **93** F 2
Kayenta (AZ.) **103** F 2
Kaysvile (UT.) **102** A 3–4
Keaau (HI.) **123** G 4
Keahole Point **123** E 4
Kealaikahiki Channel
  123 E 3
Kealaikahiki Point **123** E 3
Kealakekua (HI.) **123** F 4
Kealia (HI.) **123** F 4
Keams Canyon (AZ.)
  103 G 2
Kearney (NE.) **81** E 4
Kearns (UT.) **102** B 3–4
Kearny (AZ.) **101** E 3
Keatchie (LA.) **68** B 1
Keating (OR.) **113** H 2
Keauhou (HI.) **123** EF 4
Keddie (CA.) **110** B 2
Keeler (CA.) **109** E 3
Keene (CA.) **106** D 2
Keene (ND.) **84** D 3
Keene (N.H.) **29** F 7
Keenesburg (CO.) **95** F 1
Keewatin (MN.) **60** C 3
Keithsburg (IL.) **56** B 5
Keizer (OR.) **112** B 1
Kekaha (HI.) **122** B 2
Keller (WA.) **115** F 2
Kellerville (TX.) **76** C 2
Kelleys Island **53** G 1
Kellogg (ID.) **88** D 2
Kellogg (MN.) **61** F 2
Kelly (WY.) **92** B 2
Kelso (CA.) **107** G 2
Kelso (WA.) **114** C 3
Kelvin (AZ.) **101** F 3
Kelvin (ND.) **85** G 2
Kemmerer (WY.) **92** B 4
Kemp (TX.) **75** E 2
Kemp, Lake **76** D 4
Kempner (TX.) **74** C 3

Kempton (IL.) **56** C 3
Kenai Fjords National Park
  (AK.) **116** B 2
Kenai Mts. (AL.)
  116 AB 1–2
Kenai Peninsula (AL.)
  119 E 2
Kenansville (FL.) **44** D 2
Kenansville (N.C.) **39** G 4
Kenbridge (VA.) **37** F 5
Kendall (FL.) **45** F 2
Kendall (KS.) **78** B 4
Kendall (N.Y.) **32** B 2
Kendrick (ID.) **88** D 3
Kenedy (TX.) **70–71** E 2
Kenel (SD.) **82** E 2
Kenesaw (NE.) **81** F 4
Kenly (N.C.) **39** F 3
Kenmare (ND.) **84** DE 2
Kenna (N.M.) **99** G 3
Kennaday Peak **93** F 4
Kennard (NE.) **81** H 3
Kennard (TX.) **75** F 3
Kennebec (SD.) **83** F 4
Kennebec River **28** CD 4
Kennebunk (ME.) **29** E 5
Kennebunkport (ME.)
  29 E 5
Kennedy (AL.) **46** C 5
Kennedy (NE.) **80** CD 2
Kennedy Entrance **119** E 2
Kennedy, Mount **117** D 1
Kenner (LA.) **69** E 3
Kennett (MO.) **65** G 5
Kennewick (WA.) **115** F 3
Kenosha (WI.) **59** G 1
Kensal (N.D.) **85** H 3
Kensington (KS.) **78** D 2
Kent (OR.) **112** E 1
Kent (TX.) **72** D 2
Kent (WA.) **114** C 2
Kent City (MI.) **55** E 4
Kentland (IN.) **52** B 2
Kenton (OH.) **53** F 2
Kenton (OK.) **97** G 2
Kenton (TN.) **50** B 4
Kentucky **53** F 3
Kentucky Lake **50** B 4
Kentucky River **51** F 2
Kenyon (MN.) **61** F 2
Keokea (HI.) **123** E 3
Keokuk (IA.) **63** H 5
Keosauqua (IA.) **63** G 5
Keota (CO.) **95** F 1
Keota (OK.) **77** J 2
Keowee, Lake **40** C 2
Kerick (TX.) **97** H 2
Kerkhoven (MN.) **61** E 5
Kerman (CA.) **111** F 2
Kermit (TX.) **73** E 2
Kermit (W.V.) **36** B 4
Kern River **106** D 2
Kernville (CA.) **106** D 2
Kerrick (MN.) **61** E 2
Kerrville (TX.) **74** B 4
Kersey (CO.) **95** F 1
Kershaw (S.C.) **41** E 2
Keshena (WI.) **59** E 2
Ketchikan (AL.) **117** E 2
Ketchum (ID.) **91** E 3
Ketchum Mountain **73** H 2
Kettering (OH.) **52** E 3
Kettle Falls (WA.) **115** G 1
Kettle River Range **115** G 1
Kettleman City (CA.)
  111 F 1

Keuka Lake **32** C 3
Kevin (MT.) **86** A 1
Kewa (WA.) **115** G 1
Kewanee (IL.) **56** B 4
Kewaunee (WI.) **59** E 1
Keweenaw Bay **58** BC 2
Keweenaw Peninsula
  58 B 2
Keweenaw Point **58** B 1
Key (TX.) **73** G 1
Key Colony Beach (FL.)
  45 G 3
Key Largo (FL.) **45** F 2
Key Largo (FL.) **45** F 2
Key West (FL.) **45** G 3
Keyapaha (SD.) **83** E 4
Keyes (OK.) **97** G 2
Keyhole Reservoir **93** H 1
Keystone (MN.) **63** F 4
Keystone (NE.) **80** C 3
Keystone (SD.) **82** B 4
Keystone Heights (FL.)
  44 B 3
Keystone Lake **77** G 1
Keystone Peak **101** E 5
Keysville (VA.) **37** F 4
Kgun Lake **119** C 1
Khrebet Genkanyy **120** A 2
Kiana (AL.) **120** C 2
Kickapoo Indian
  Reservation **79** H 2
Kickapoo, Lake **76** E 4
Kiel (WI.) **59** F 2
Kiholo Bay **123** EF 4
Kilauea (HI.) **88** B 2
Kilauea Crater **123** F 4
Kilbuck Mountains (AL.)
  119 CD 1
Kildare (GA.) **43** D 2
Kilgore (ID.) **91** GH 2
Kilgore (NE.) **80** C 2
Kilgore (TX.) **75** G 2
Kilkenny (N.C.) **39** H 3
Killdeer (ND.) **84** D 3
Killeen (TX.) **74** D 3
Killen (AL.) **46** B 5
Killik River **121** E 2
Killington Peak **30** D 2
Kilmarnock (VA.) **37** H 4
Kilmichael (MS.) **48** C 3
Kim (CO.) **95** G 4
Kimball (NE.) **80** A 3
Kimball (SD.) **83** G 4
Kimberly (ID.) **91** E 4
Kimberly (OR.) **113** F 2
Kimbrough (AL.) **47** D 5
Kincaid, Lake **57** D 4
Kinder (LA.) **68** C 3
Kindred (N.D.) **85** H 4
King and Queen Court
  House (VA.) **37** H 4
King City (CA.) **111** F 3
King City (MO.) **64** C 1
King Cove **119** C 2
King Cove (AL.) **118** C 3
King George (VA.) **37** G 3
King Hill (ID.) **90** D 3
King Island (AK.) **120** B 3
King Lear Peak **104** C 1
King Mountain (Br. Col.,
  Can.) **117** F 2
King Mountain (OR.)
  112 B 4
King Mountain (OR.)
  113 G 3
King Salmon **119** D 2

King William (VA.) **37** G 4
Kingdom City (MO.) **65** F 3
Kingfisher (OK.) **77** F 2
Kingman (AZ.) **100** B 1
Kingman (KS.) **79** E 4
Kings Beach (CA.) **110** C 2
Kings Canyon (CO.) **94** D 1
Kings Canyon National
  Park **108** D 3
Kings Peak (CA.) **110** B 6
Kings Peak (UT.) **102** B 2
Kings River **111** F 1
Kings Valley (OR.) **112** B 2
Kingsburg (CA.) **111** F 1
Kingsburg (S.D.) **83** G 5
Kingsbury Lake **86** C 2
Kingsford (WI.) **58** D 2
Kingsland (GA.) **43** F 2
Kingsland (TX.) **74** C 4
Kingsley (IA.) **62** C 3
Kingsley (MI.) **55** D 4
Kingsley Dam **80** C 3
Kingsport (TN.) **51** H 4
Kingston (Can.) **32** D 1
Kingston (MO.) **64** CD 2
Kingston (N.M.) **98** C 4
Kingston (N.Y.) **33** G 4
Kingston (OH.) **53** G 3
Kingston (OH.) **53** G 3
Kingston (OK.) **77** G 3
Kingston (PA.) **35** E 2
Kingstree (S.C.) **41** F 3
Kingsville (TX.) **71** E 3
Kingwood (W.V.) **36** E 2
Kinmundy (IL.) **57** E 3
Kinsale (VA.) **37** H 3
Kinsey (MT.) **87** H 3
Kinsley (KS.) **78** D 4
Kinston (N.C.) **39** G 3
Kinta (OK.) **77** H 2
Kinter (AZ.) **100** B 4
Kinzua (OR.) **113** EF 1
Kiowa (CO.) **95** F 2
Kiowa (KS.) **78** E 4
Kipahulu (HI.) **123** EF 3
Kipnuk (AL.) **118** C 2
Kirby (AR.) **66** C 3
Kirbyville (TX.) **75** G 4
Kirk (OR.) **112** D 4
Kirkby (MT.) **87** G 4
Kirkland (AZ.) **100** D 2
Kirkland (TX.) **76** CD 3
Kirkland (WA.) **114** C 2
Kirklin (IN.) **52** C 2
Kirkmansville (KY.) **50** C 3
Kirksville (MO.) **64** E 1
Kirkwood (MO.) **65** G 3
Kirley (SD.) **82** D 3
Kirwin (KS.) **78** D 2
Kirwin Reservoir **78** D 2
Kiska (AL.) **116** H 1
Kiska Volcano (AL.) **116** H 1
Kismet (KS.) **78** C 4
Kissimmee (FL.) **44** C 3
Kissimmee, Lake **44** D 3
Kissimmee River **45** D 3
Kit Carson (CO.) **95** H 3
Kittanning (PA.) **34** B 3
Kittery (ME.) **29** E 5
Kittitas (WA.) **115** E 2
Kitty Hawk (N.C.) **39** J 2
Kivalina (AL.) **120** BC 2
Kiwalik **120** C 2
Klamath (CA.) **110** A 5
Klamath Falls (OR.) **112** D 4
Klamath Marsh **112** D 3–4

Klamath Mountains
  110 A 5
Klamath River **110** A 5
Klatt Road **116** B 1
Klein (MT.) **86** E 3
Klickitat (WA.) **114** D 4
Kline (CO.) **94** B 4
Klondike Gold Rush
  National Historic Park
  (AK.) **117** D 2
Klondike River **117** D 1
Klowa (MT.) **89** G 1
Kluane Lake (AL.) **117** D 1
Kluane N.P. (AL.) **117** D 1
Klukwan (AL.) **117** D 2
Knife River **84** E 3
Knippa (TX.) **70** C 1
Knob Noster (MO.) **64** D 3
Knolls (UT.) **102** B 5
Knowles (OK.) **76** C 1
Knowlton (MT.) **87** H 3
Knox (IN.) **52** C 1
Knox City (MO.) **65** F 1
Knox City (TX.) **76** D 4
Knoxville (GA.) **43** D 4
Knoxville (IA.) **63** E 4
Knoxville (IL.) **56** C 5
Knoxville (TN.) **51** G 5
Kobuk (AL.) **120–121** D 2
Kobuk River (AL.) **120** C 2
Kobuk Valley N.P. (AL.)
  120 CD 2
Koch Peak **86** B 4
Kodiak (AL.) **119** E 2
Kodiak Island (AL.) **119** E 2
Koehler (N.M.) **97** F 2
Koehn Dry Lake **107** E 2
Kofa (AZ.) **100** C 4
Kofa Mountains **100** C 3
Koidern **116** CD 1
Kokadio (ME.) **28** C 4
Kokolik River **120** C 2
Kokomo (IN.) **52** C 2
Koliganek (AL.) **119** D 2
Kolin (MT.) **86** D 2
Koloa (HI.) **122** B 2
Konawa (OK.) **77** G 3
Konnarock (VA.) **36** C 5
Koocanusa, Lake **88** E 1
Koosharem (UT.) **103** D 4
Kooskia (ID.) **88** E 2
Kootenai River **88** E 1
Korbel (CA.) **110** B 5
Kornegay (N.M.) **99** G 4
Korovin Volcano (AL.)
  117 K 1
Kortes Dam (WY.) **93** F 3
Kosciusko (MS.) **48** C 3
Koshkonong (MO.) **65** F 5
Koshkonong, Lake **59** G 2
Kosse (TX.) **75** E 3
Kotik River **120** D 1–2
Kotzebue (AL.) **120** C 2
Kotzebue Sound (AL.)
  120 C 2
Kountze (TX.) **75** G 4
Kovgarok, Mount **120** B 2
Koyuk (AL.) **120** C 3
Koyuk River **120** C 2
Koyukuk (AL.) **120** C 3
Koyukuk R. (AL.)
  120 C 2
Koyukuk River (AL.)
  121 E 2
Kraemer (LA.) **69** E 4
Kramer (ND.) **84** F 2

Kramer Junction (CA.)
  107 E 2–3
Kranzburg (S.D.) **83** J 3
Krebs (OK.) **77** H 3
Kremmling (CO.) **94** D 1
Kress (TX.) **76** B 3
Krider (N.M.) **97** G 4
Krusenstern, Cape **120** C 2
Kruzof (AL.) **117** D 2
Kuee Ruins **123** F 4
Kuiu (AL.) **117** E 2
Kukalek Lake **119** DE 2
Kulm (ND.) **85** H 4
Kumukahi, Cape **123** G 4
Kuna (ID.) **90** C 3
Kuparuk River **121** EF 2
Kupreanof (AL.) **117** E 2
Kurten (TX.) **75** E 4
Kurtistown (HI.) **123** F 4
Kusawa Lake **117** D 1
Kuskokwim (AL.) **119** D 1
Kuskokwim Bay (AL.)
  118–119 C 2
Kuskokwim Mountains
  (AL.) **121** E 3
Kuzitrin River **120** C 2
Kvichak (AL.) **119** D 2
Kvichak Bay (AL.) **119** D 2
Kwethluk (AL.) **119** C 1
Kwigillingok (AL.)
  118–119 C 2
Kwiguk **120** BC 3
Kyburz (CA.) **111** D 2
Kyle (SD.) **82** C 4
Kyle (TX.) **74** D 5

La Barge (WY.) **92** B 3
La Belle (FL.) **45** E 3
La Canada (CA.) **106** D 3
La Cordillera **124** B 2
La Crescent (MN.) **61** G 1
La Crosse (KS.) **78** D 3
La Crosse (VA.) **37** F 5
La Crosse (WA.) **115** GH 3
La Crosse (WI.) **59** F 1
La Cueva (N.M.) **96** E 3
La Fayette (GA.) **42** B 6
La Feria (TX.) **71** E 4
La Follette (TN.) **51** F 4
La Garita (CO.) **94** D 4
La Grande (OR.) **113** G 1
La Grande (WA.) **114** C 3
La Grange (GA.) **42** C 5
La Grange (KY.) **51** E 2
La Grange (N.C.) **39** G 3
La Grange (TX.) **74** D 5
La Grange (WY.) **93** H 4
La Harpe (IL.) **56** C 5
La Jara (CO.) **94** E 4
La Jara (N.M.) **96** C 2
La Joya (N.M.) **96** D 4
La Junta (CO.) **95** G 4
La Marque (TX.) **71** G 1
La Mesa (CA.) **107** EF 5
La Mesa (N.M.) **98** D 4
La Moille (IL.) **56** B 4

La Moure (N.D.) **85** H 4
La Paloma (TX.) **71** E 4
La Pine (OR.) **112** D 3
La Plant (SD.) **82** E 2
La Plata (MD.) **37** H 3
La Plata (MO.) **64** E 1
La Plata (N.M.) **96** B 2
La Porte (IN.) **52** C 1
La Porte City (IA.) **63** F 3
La Pryor (TX.) **70** C 2
La Push (WA.) **114** A 2
La Sal (UT.) **103** D 1
La Sal Mountains **103** D 1
La Salle (CO.) **95** F 1
La Salle (IL.) **56** B 4
La Tuque (Can.) **28** A 7
La Verkin (UT.) **103** E 5
La Vernia (TX.) **70** D 1
La Veta (CO.) **95** F 4
Laau Point **123** D 2
Lac Aux Mortes **85** G 2
Lac Courte Oreilles Indian
  Reservation **58** D 5
Lac des Allemands **69** E 4
Lac du Flambeau Indian
  Reservation **58** CD 3
Lac la Croix **60** B 1
Lac Mégantic (Can.) **28** C 6
Lac qui Parle **61** E 6
Lacey (WA.) **114** C 2
Lachine (MI.) **54** C 2
Lackawanna (N.Y.) **32** B 3
Lacon (IL.) **56** C 4
Laconia (N.H.) **29** E 6
Lacoochee (FL.) **44** C 4
Laddonia (MO.) **65** F 2
Ladner (SD.) **82** B 2
Ladysmith (WI.) **59** D 5
Lafayette (AL.) **46** D 3
Lafayette (IN.) **52** C 2
Lafayette (LA.) **68** D 3
Lafayette (MN.) **61** F 4
Lafayette (TN.) **50** D 4
Lagrange (IN.) **52** D 1
Laguna (N.M.) **96** C 3
Laguna Beach (CA.)
  107 E 4
Laguna Beach (FL.) **47** F 4
Laguna de Janta Maria
  (Mex.) **98** C 5
Laguna del Perro **96** D 4
Laguna Indian Reservation
  96 C 3–4
Laguna Madre **71** E 4
Laguna Mountains
  107 F 4–5
Laguna Park (TX.) **74** D 3
Lahaina (HI.) **123** E 3
Lahontan Reservoir
  104 B 3
Laie (HI.) **122** D 2
Lajitas (TX.) **72** D 4
Lake (WY.) **92** B 1
Lake Albert (OR.)
  112–113 E 4
Lake Almanor **110** D 3
Lake Altus **76** D 3
Lake Andes (S.D.) **83** G 4
Lake Andes (S.D.) **83** G 4
Lake Anna **37** G 3
Lake Apopka **44** C 3
Lake Arbuckle **44–45** D 3
Lake Arrowhead **76** E 4
Lake Arthur (N.M.) **99** F 3
Lake Artur (LA.) **68** C 3
Lake Ashtabula **85** J 3

Lake Avalon **99** F 4
Lake Barkley **50** C 4
Lake Benton (MN.) **61** F 6
Lake Berryessa **111** D 4
Lake Billy Chinook **112** D 2
Lake Bistineau **68** B 1
Lake Blackshear **43** E 5
Lake Borgne **69** E 3
Lake Bowdoin **87** F 1
Lake Bridgeport **74** D 1
Lake Brownwood **74** B 3
Lake Burton **42** B 4
Lake Butler (FL.) **44** A 4
Lake Cachuma **106** C 3
Lake Carl Blackwell **77** F 1
Lake Champlain **30** C 1
Lake Charles (LA.) **68** B 3
Lake Chelan **115** E 1
Lake Chippewa **54** B 4
Lake City (AR.) **67** F 2
Lake City (CA.) **110** A 2
Lake City (CO.) **94** C 3
Lake City (FL.) **44** A 4
Lake City (KS.) **78** E 4
Lake City (MI.) **55** D 4
Lake City (MN.) **61** F 2
Lake City (S.C.) **41** F 3
Lake City (S.D.) **83** H 2
Lake City (TN.) **51** F 4
Lake Clark **119** E 1
Lake Clark National Park
  and Preserve **119** E 1
Lake Conway **66** D 2–3
Lake Cormorant (MS.)
  48 B 4
Lake Corpus Christi
  70 DE 2
Lake Creek (TX.) **75** F 1
Lake Crowley **108** D 2
Lake Crystal (MN.) **61** F 4
Lake Cumberland **51** F 4
Lake Darling **84** DE 2
Lake Davis **110** C 2
Lake De Smet **93** F 1
Lake Delton (WI.) **59** F 3
Lake Earl **110** A 6
Lake Elsinore **107** E 4
Lake Ellsworth **76** E 3
Lake Erie **53** HJ 1
Lake Erling **66** C 4
Lake Fort Phantom Hill
  110 C 3
Lake Frances **86** A 1
Lake Francis Case **83** F 4
Lake Gaston **37** F 5
Lake Geneva (WI.) **59** G 2
Lake George (CO.) **95** E 2
Lake George (FL.) **44** B 3
Lake George (N.D.) **85** G 4
Lake George (N.Y.) **33** G 2
Lake George (N.Y.) **33** G 2
Lake Gogebic **58** C 3
Lake Granbury **74** D 2
Lake Granby **94** E 1
Lake Greenwood **40** D 2
Lake Greeson **66** C 3
Lake Hamilton **66** C 3
Lake Harbor (FL.) **45** E 2
Lake Harding **42** D 6
Lake Harris **44** C 3
Lake Havasu **100** B 2
Lake Havasu City (AZ.)
  100 B 2
Lake Hefner **77** F 2
Lake Henshaw **107** F 4
Lake Heyburn **77** G 2

Lake Hickory **38** C 3
Lake Houston **75** F 4–5
Lake Hughes (CA.) **106** D 3
Lake Huron **54** C 1–2
Lake Ilo **84** D 3
Lake Isabella (CA.) **106** D 2
Lake Istokpoga **45** D 3
Lake Itasca (MN.) **60** C 5
Lake Jackson (TX.) **71** G 1
Lake James **38** C 3
Lake Jocassee **40** C 1–2
Lake Kaweah **108** D 3
Lake Kemp **76** D 4
Lake Keowee **40** C 2
Lake Kickapoo **76** E 4
Lake Kincaid **57** D 4
Lake Kissimmee **44** D 3
Lake Koocanusa **88** E 1
Lake Koshkonong **59** G 2
Lake Laberge (AL.) **117** D 1
Lake Lenore **115** F 2
Lake Linden (WI.) **58** B 2
Lake Livingston **75** F 4
Lake Louise **116** B 1
Lake Lowell **90** C 3
Lake Lucero **98** D 4
Lake Lyndon B. Johnson
  74 C 4
Lake Maloney **80** D 3
Lake Marion **41** E 3
Lake Mattamuskeet **39** H 3
Lake Maurepas **69** E 3
Lake Maxinkuckee **52** C 1
Lake McClure **111** E 2
Lake McConaughy **80** C 3
Lake McDonald **89** G 1
Lake McMillan **99** F 4
Lake Mead **109** H 3
Lake Mean National
  Recreation Area **109** H 3
Lake Mendocino **110** C 5
Lake Mendota **59** F 3
Lake Meredith (CO.) **95** G 3
Lake Meredith (TX.) **76** B 2
Lake Meredith National
  Recreation Area **76** B 2
Lake Merwin **114** C 3–4
Lake Michigamme **58** C 2
Lake Michigan
  54–55 DF 5–6
Lake Mills (IA.) **63** E 2
Lake Mitchell **46** D 4
Lake Mohave **100** B 1
Lake Moultrie **41** E 3
Lake Murray (OK.) **77** FG 3
Lake Murray (S.C.) **40** D 2
Lake Norden (S.D.) **83** H 3
Lake Norman **38** C 3
Lake O' The Cherokees
  77 J 1
Lake O' The Pines **75** G 2
Lake Oahe **82–83** E 2
Lake of the Ozarks **64** E 3
Lake of the Woods
  60 A 4–5
Lake Okeechobee **45** DE 2
Lake Ontario **32** BC 2
Lake Oroville **110** C 3
Lake Osakis **61** E 5
Lake Oswego (OR.) **112** C 1
Lake Ouachita **66** C 3
Lake Owyhee **113** H 3
Lake Park (FL.) **45** E 2
Lake Park (IA.) **62** C 2
Lake Park (MN.) **60** D 6
Lake Pend Oreille **88** D 1

Lake Pillsbury **110** C 4
Lake Placid (FL.) **45** D 3
Lake Placid (N.Y.) **33** G 1
Lake Pleasant (AZ.) **100** D 3
Lake Pleasant (N.Y.) **33** F 2
Lake Poinsett **83** HJ 3
Lake Pontchartrain **69** E 3
Lake Powell **103** E 3
Lake Poygan **59** E 2
Lake Providence (LA.)
  68 D 1
Lake Ray Hubbard **75** E 2
Lake Red Rock **63** E 4
Lake Sacajawea **115** G 3
Lake Saint Clair **55** F 1
Lake Sakakawea **84** D 2
Lake Salvador **69** E 4
Lake Sara **57** D 3
Lake Scugog (Can.) **32** B 1
Lake Seminole **43** F 5
Lake Shafer **52** C 2
Lake Shannon **114** D 1
Lake Sharpe **83** F 3
Lake Shelbyville **57** D 3
Lake Sidney Lanier **42** B 4
Lake Simcoe (Can.) **32** A 1
Lake Simtustus **112** D 2
Lake Sinclair **42** C 4
Lake Springfield **56** D 4
Lake Stamford **74** B 1
Lake Stevens (WA.)
  114 CD 1
Lake Success **106** D 1
Lake Sumner **97** F 4
Lake Superior **58** B 1–3
Lake Tahoe **110** CD 2
Lake Talquin **47** F 2
Lake Tawakoni **75** E 2
Lake Texarkana **75** G 1
Lake Texoma **77** G 4
Lake Thunderbird **77** F 2
Lake Tillery **38** D 3
Lake Tohopekaliga **44** C 3
Lake Traverse **61** E 6
Lake Travis **74** C 4
Lake Tschida **84** E 4
Lake Umatilla **115** F 4
Lake Verret **68–69** D 4
Lake Village (AR.) **67** E 4
Lake Waccamaw **39** F 4
Lake Walcott **91** F 4
Lake Walk **73** H 4
Lake Wallenpaupack **35** F 2
Lake Wallula **115** FG 3
Lake Wappapello **65** G 4–5
Lake Washington **114** C 2
Lake Wawasee **52** D 1
Lake Whatcom **114** C 1
Lake Whitney **74** D 2–3
Lake Wichita **76** E 4
Lake Wilson (MN.) **61** G 5
Lake Winnebago **59** EF 2
Lake Winnibigoshish
  60 C 3–4
Lake Winnipesaukee **29** E 6
Lake Wissota **59** E 5
Lake Worth (FL.) **45** E 2
Lake Wylie **40** D 1
Lakehurst (N.J.) **35** G 4
Lakeland (FL.) **44** C 3
Lakeland (GA.) **43** E 4
Lakeport (CA.) **110** C 5
Lakeport (MI.) **55** E 1
Lakeshore (CA.) **111** E 1
Lakeside (AZ.) **101** G 2
Lakeside (MT.) **89** F 1

Lakeside (OH.) **53** G 1
Lake Placid (FL.) **45** D 3
Lakeside (OR.) **112** A 3
Lakeside (UT.) **102** A 4
Laketon (TX.) **76** C 2
Laketown (UT.) **102** A 3
Lakeview (MI.) **55** E 4
Lakeview (MI.) **55** F 4
Lakeview (MT.) **91** H 2
Lakeview (OR.) **113** E 4
Lakeview (N.Y.) **76** C 3
Lakewood (CO.) **95** E 2
Lakewood (N.J.) **35** G 3
Lakewood (N.M.) **99** F 4
Lakewood (N.Y.) **32** A 3
Lakewood (N.Y.) **53** GH 1
Lakewood (WI.) **59** D 2
Lakewood Center **114** C 2
Lakin (KS.) **78** B 4
Lakota (IA.) **62** D 2
Lakota (N.D.) **85** H 2
Lamar (CO.) **95** H 3
Lamar (MO.) **64** C 4
Lamar (TX.) **71** F 2
Lambert (MT.) **87** J 2
Lame Deer (MT.) **87** G 4
Lamesa (TX.) **73** G 1
Lamoille (NV.) **105** F 2
Lamoine (CA.) **110** B 4
Lamoni (IA.) **62** D 5
Lamont (CA.) **106** D 2
Lamont (FL.) **44** A 5
Lamont (ID.) **91** H 3
Lamont (OK.) **77** F 1
Lamont (WA.) **115** GH 2
Lamont (WY.) **93** E 3
Lampasas (TX.) **74** C 3
Lampazos de Naranjo
  (Mex.) **70** B 3–4
Lamy (N.M.) **96** E 3
Lanagan (MO.) **64** C 5
Lanai **123** E 3
Lanai City (HI.) **123** DE 3
Lanaihale **123** E 3
Lanare (CA.) **111** F 2
Lanark (N.M.) **98** D 4–5
Lancaster (CA.) **106** D 3
Lancaster (KY.) **51** F 3
Lancaster (MN.) **60** B 6
Lancaster (MO.) **64** E 1
Lancaster (OH.) **53** G 3
Lancaster (PA.) **35** E 3
Lancaster (S.C.) **41** E 2
Lancaster (TX.) **75** E 2
Lancaster (VA.) **37** H 4
Lancaster (VT.) **30** E 1
Lancaster (WI.) **59** G 4
Lance Creek (WY.) **93** H 2
Land O'Lakes (WI.) **58** C 3
Landa (ND.) **84** F 2
Lander (WY.) **92** D 3
Landsdale (PA.) **35** F 3
Landusky (MT.) **86** E 2
Lane (OK.) **77** H 3
Lane (S.D.) **83** G 3
Lane City (TX.) **71** F 1
Langdon (N.D.) **85** H 2
Langford (S.D.) **83** H 2
Langley (WA.) **114** C 1
Langlois (OR.) **112** A 3
Langtry (TX.) **73** G 4
L'Anse (MI.) **58** C 2
L'Anse Indian Reservation
  58 C 2
Lansford (ND.) **84** E 2
Lansing (IA.) **63** G 2
Lansing (MI.) **55** F 3

Laona (WI.) **58** D 2
Lapeer (MI.) **55** E 2
Laporte (PA.) **34** E 2
Lapwai (ID.) **88** D 3
Laramie (WY.) **93** G 4
Laramie Mountains
  93 G 3–4
Laramie Peak **93** G 3
Laramie River **93** G 4
Laredo (MT.) **86** D 1
Laredo (TX.) **70** C 3
Larimore (N.D.) **85** J 3
Larkspur (CO.) **95** F 2
Larned (KS.) **78** D 3
Larose (LA.) **69** E 4
Larsen Bay **119** E 2
Larslan (MT.) **87** G 1
Las Animas (CO.) **95** G 3
Las Cruces (N.M.) **98** D 4
Las Cruces (NV.) **106** B 3
Las Vegas (N.M.) **97** E 3
Las Vegas (NV.) **109** G 3
Lassen Peak **110** B 3
Lassen Volcanic National
  Park **110** B 3
Last Chance (CO.) **95** G 2
Latham (KS.) **79** G 4
Lathrop (CA.) **111** E 3
Lathrop Wells (NV.) **109** F 2
Latimer (IA.) **63** E 3
Latimer (UT.) **103** D 5
Laton (CA.) **111** F 1
Latta (S.C.) **41** F 2
Lauderdale (MS.) **48** D 2
Laughlin Peak **97** F 2
Laurel (MS.) **49** E 3
Laurel (MT.) **86** E 4
Laurel (NE.) **81** G 2
Laurel Bay (S.C.) **41** E 4
Laurens (S.C.) **40** C 2
Laurier (WA.) **115** G 1
Laurinburg (N.C.) **39** E 4
Laurium (WI.) **58** B 2
Lautz (TX.) **97** HJ 2
Lava Beds National
  Monument **110** A 3
Lava Hot Springs (ID.)
  91 H 4
Lavaca River **71** F 1
Laveen (AZ.) **100** D 3
Laverne (OK.) **76** D 1
Lavic Lake **107** F 3
Lavina (MT.) **86** E 3
Lavon Lake **75** E 1
Lavonia (GA.) **42** B 4
Lavrentiya (AL.) **120** A 2
Lawn (TX.) **74** B 2
Lawndale (N.C.) **38** C 3
Lawrence (IN.) **52** D 3
Lawrence (KS.) **79** H 3
Lawrence (MA.) **31** E 3
Lawrence (NE.) **81** F 4
Lawrenceburg (IN.) **52** D 3
Lawrenceburg (KY.) **51** E 2
Lawrenceburg (TN.) **50** C 5
Lawrenceville (GA.) **42** C 4
Lawrenceville (IL.) **57** E 2
Lawrenceville (VA.) **37** G 5
Laws (CA.) **108** D 2
Lawson (MO.) **64** C 2
Lawtey (FL.) **44** A 4
Lawton (MI.) **55** F 4
Lawton (N.D.) **85** H 2
Lawton (OK.) **76** E 3
Lay (CO.) **94** C 1
Layton (FL.) **45** G 2

Layton (UT.) **102** A 3
Laytonville (CA.) **110** C 5
Lazare (TX.) **76** C 3
Le Center (MN.) **61** F 3
Le Grand (CA.) **111** E 2
Le Mars (IA.) **62** B 3
Le Roy (KS.) **79** H 3
Le Roy (MN.) **61** G 2
Le Sueur (MN.) **61** F 3
Leaburg (OR.) **112** C 2
Leachville (AR.) **67** F 2
Lead Hill (AR.) **66** C 1
Leadbetter Point **114** A 3
Leadore (ID.) **91** F 2
Leadville (CO.) **94** D 2
Leaf River **49** E 3
League City (TX.) **71** G 1
Leakesville (MS.) **49** E 2
Leakey (TX.) **70** C 1
Leary (GA.) **43** E 5
Leatherwood (KY.) **51** G 3
Leavenworth (KS.) **79** H 2
Leavenworth (WA.) **114** E 2
Lebam (WA.) **114** B 3
Lebanon (IN.) **52** C 2
Lebanon (KS.) **78** E 2
Lebanon (KY.) **51** E 3
Lebanon (MO.) **64** E 4
Lebanon (N.H.) **29** E 7
Lebanon (OH.) **53** E 3
Lebanon (OR.) **112** C 2
Lebanon (PA.) **34** E 3
Lebanon (SD.) **83** F 2
Lebanon (TN.) **50** D 4
Lebanon (VA.) **36** B 5
Lebeau (LA.) **68** D 3
Lebec (CA.) **106** D 3
Lecompte (LA.) **68** C 2
Ledger (MT.) **86** B 1
Ledger (N.C.) **51** H 5
Lee (NV.) **105** F 2
Lee Vining (CA.) **111** E 1
Leech Lake **60** C 4
Leech Lake Indian
  Reservation **60** C 4
Leedey (OK.) **76** D 2
Leeds (AL.) **46** C 4
Leeds (ND.) **85** G 2
Leeds (UT.) **103** E 5
Lees Summit (MO.) **64** C 3
Leesburg (FL.) **44** C 3
Leesburg (GA.) **43** E 5
Leesburg (VA.) **37** G 2
Leesville (LA.) **68** B 2
Leesville (TX.) **71** E 1
Leesville Lake **53** H 2
Leesville Lake **37** E 4
Lefor (ND.) **84** D 4
Lefors (TX.) **76** C 2
Leggett (CA.) **110** C 5
Lehi (UT.) **102** B 3
Lehr (ND.) **85** G 4
Lehua I. (AL.) **122** A 1
Lehua Island **107** H 3
Leidy, Mount **92** B 2
Leigh (NE.) **81** G 3
Leila Lake (TX.) **76** C 3
Leitchfield (KY.) **50** D 3
Leiter (WY.) **93** F 1
Lela (TX.) **76** C 2
Leland (MI.) **54** C 4
Leland (MS.) **48** C 4
Lemhi (ID.) **91** F 2
Lemhi Range **91** F 2
Lemhi River **91** F 2
Leming (TX.) **70** D 1

Lemitar (N.M.) **96** D 4
Lemmon (SD.) **82** C 2
Lemmon (SD.) **82** C 2
Lemmon, Mount **101** F 4
Lemoncove (CA.) **108** D 3
Lemoore (CA.) **111** F 1
Lena (WI.) **59** E 1
Lennep (MT.) **86** C 3
Lennox (S.D.) **83** J 4
Lenoir (N.C.) **38** C 3
Lenoir City (TN.) **51** F 5
Lenorah (TX.) **73** FG 1
Lenore (ID.) **88** D 3
Lenore, Lake **115** F 2
Lenox (GA.) **43** E 4
Lenox (MA.) **30** C 3
Leo (TX.) **74** D 1
Leo (TX.) **74** D 1
Leola (SD.) **83** G 2
Leon (IA.) **63** E 5
Leon (KS.) **79** G 4
Leon River **74** D 3
Leon Valley (TX.) **70** D 1
Leonard (N.D.) **85** J 4
Leonard (TX.) **75** E 1
Leonardstown (MD.)
  37 H 3
Leonardville (KS.) **79** G 2
Leonora (KS.) **78** C 2
Leoti (KS.) **78** B 3
Leroy (MT.) **86** D 2
Leslie (AR.) **66** D 2
Lester (WA.) **114** D 2
Letcher (S.D.) **83** G 4
Lettsworth (LA.) **68** D 3
Leucadia (CA.) **107** E 4
Levan (UT.) **102** C 3
Levelland (TX.) **99** H 3
Leveloch **119** D 2
Levis (Can.) **28** B 6
Levittown (PA.) **35** G 3
Levy (N.M.) **97** F 2
Lewellen (NE.) **80** B 3
Lewes (DE.) **37** J 3
Lewis (CO.) **94** B 4
Lewis (KS.) **78** D 4
Lewis and Clark Lake
  83 H 5
Lewis Lake **92** B 1
Lewis, Mount **105** E 2
Lewis Range **89** G 1
Lewis Smith Lake **46** BC 5
Lewisburg (KY.) **50** D 4
Lewisburg (PA.) **34** D 3
Lewisburg (TN.) **50** D 5
Lewisburg (W.V.) **36** D 4
Lewisetta (VA.) **37** H 3
Lewiston (ID.) **115** HJ 3
Lewiston (ME.) **29** D 5
Lewiston (MI.) **54** D 3
Lewiston (N.C.) **39** G 2
Lewiston (N.Y.) **32** B 2
Lewiston (UT.) **102** A 3
Lewistown (IL.) **56** C 5
Lewistown (MO.) **65** F 1
Lewistown (MT.) **86** D 2
Lewistown (PA.) **34** D 3
Lewisville (AR.) **66** C 4
Lewisville (ID.) **91** G 3
Lewisville (TX.) **74–75** E 1
Lexa (AR.) **67** F 3
Lexington (GA.) **42** C 4
Lexington (KY.) **51** F 2
Lexington (MO.) **64** D 2
Lexington (MS.) **48** C 4
Lexington (N.C.) **38** D 3

Lexington (NE.) **80–81** E 4
Lexington (OK.) **77** F 2
Lexington (OR.) **113** F 1
Lexington (S.C.) **40** D 3
Lexington (TN.) **50** B 5
Lexington (TX.) **74** D 4
Lexington (VA.) **36** E 4
Liamna L. (AL.) **119** D 1–2
Liard River **117** F 2
Libby Dam **88** E 1
Liberal (KS.) **78** C 4
Liberal (MO.) **64** C 4
Liberty (IL.) **56** D 6
Liberty (IN.) **52** D 3
Liberty (KY.) **51** E 3
Liberty (MO.) **64** C 2
Liberty (MS.) **49** E 4
Liberty (N.C.) **38** E 3
Liberty (NE.) **81** H 4
Liberty (N.Y.) **33** F 4
Liberty (TN.) **50** E 4
Liberty (TX.) **75** G 4
Liberty Center (OH.) **53** F 1
Liberty Hill (TX.) **74** D 4
Liberty Reservoir **37** G 2
Licking (MO.) **65** F 4
Licking River **51** G 2
Lida (NV.) **109** E 2
Lidgerwood (N.D.) **85** J 4
Liebenthal (KS.) **78** D 3
Lighthouse Point (FL.)
  45 E 2
Lignite (ND.) **84** D 2
Ligurta (AZ.) **100** B 4
Lihue (HI.) **122** B 2
Likely (CA.) **110** A 2
Lillington (N.C.) **39** F 3
Lima (MT.) **91** G 2
Lima (OH.) **53** E 2
Lima Reservoir **91** G 2
Lime (OR.) **113** H 2
Lime Village **119** E 1
Limeston (ME.) **28** B 3
Limestone (MT.) **86** D 4
Limon (CO.) **95** G 2
Linch (WY.) **93** F 2
Lincoln (AR.) **66** B 2
Lincoln (CA.) **111** D 3
Lincoln (ID.) **91** H 3
Lincoln (IL.) **56** C 4
Lincoln (KS.) **79** E 2
Lincoln (ME.) **28** C 3
Lincoln (MI.) **54** D 2
Lincoln (MO.) **64** D 3
Lincoln (MT.) **86** A 3
Lincoln (NE.) **81** H 4
Lincoln (N.M.) **99** E 3
Lincoln (TX.) **74** D 4
Lincoln City (IN.) **52** C 4
Lincoln Home National
  Historic Site (IL.) **56** C 4
Lincoln Park (MI.) **55** F 2
Lincoln Village (CA.)
  111 D 3
Lincolnton (GA.) **42** C 3
Lincolnton (N.C.) **38** C 3
Lind (WA.) **115** G 3
Linda (CA.) **110** C 3
Lindale (TX.) **75** F 2
Linden (AL.) **46** D 5
Linden (AZ.) **101** F 2
Linden (CA.) **111** D 3
Linden (TN.) **50** C 5
Linden (TX.) **75** G 1
Lindon (CO.) **95** G 2
Lindsay (CA.) **111** F 1

Lindsay (MT.) **87** H 2
Lindsay (NE.) **81** G 3
Lindsay (OK.) **77** F 3
Lindsborg (KS.) **79** F 3
Lineville (AL.) **46** C 3
Lineville (IA.) **63** E 5
Lingle (WY.) **93** H 3
Linn (KS.) **79** F 2
Linn (MO.) **65** F 3
Linn (TX.) **70** D 4
Linneus (MO.) **64** D 2
Linton (IN.) **52** B 3
Linton (KY.) **50** C 4
Linton (ND.) **85** F 4
Lipscomb (TX.) **76** C 1
Lisbon (N.D.) **85** J 4
Lisbon (N.M.) **98** B 4
Lisbon (OH.) **53** J 2
Lisco (NE.) **80** B 3
Lismore (MN.) **61** G 5
Litchfield (IL.) **57** D 4
Litchfield (MN.) **61** E 4
Litchfield (NE.) **81** E 3
Litchville (N.D.) **85** H 4
Little America (WY.) **92** C 4
Little Belt Mountains **86** C 3
Little Blue River **81** G 4
Little Colorado River **101** EF 1
Little Creek (TN.) **51** F 4
Little Eagle (SD.) **82** D 2
Little Falls (MN.) **61** DE 4
Little Goose Dam **115** H 3
Little Humboldt River **104** D 1
Little Lake (CA.) **107** E 2
Little Lake (MI.) **54** B 6
Little Missouri Badlands **84** C 3–4
Little Missouri River **84** C 3
Little Powder River **87** H 4–5
Little River (KS.) **79** E 3
Little River (OK./AR.) **77** J 3–4
Little Rock (AR.) **66** D 3
Little Rocky Mountains **86** DE 2
Little Sable Point **55** E 5
Little Salt Lake **103** E 4
Little Sioux River **62** C 3
Little Sitkin (AL.) **116** H 1
Little Tanaga (AL.) **117** J 1
Little Traverse Bay **54** C 4
Little Valley (N.Y.) **32** B 3
Littlefield (AZ.) **103** F 5
Littlefield (TX.) **99** H 3
Littlefork (MN.) **60** B 3
Littlestown (PA.) **34** D 4
Littleton (CO.) **95** F 2
Littleton (N.H.) **29** D 6
Littleton (W.V.) **36** D 2
Liva Oak (CA.) **110** C 4
Live Oak (CA.) **110** C 3
Live Oak (FL.) **44** A 4
Live Oak Springs (CA.) **107** F 5
Livermore (CA.) **111** E 3
Livermore (CO.) **95** E 1
Livermore (IA.) **62** D 3
Livermore (KY.) **50** C 3
Livermore Falls (ME.) **28** D 5
Livermore, Mount **72** D 3
Liverpool (TX.) **71** G 1
Livingston (AL.) **46** D 6
Livingston (CA.) **111** E 2
Livingston (KY.) **51** F 3
Livingston (LA.) **69** E 3
Livingston (MT.) **86** C 4
Livingston (TN.) **51** E 4
Livingston, Lake **75** F 4
Livington (TX.) **75** G 4
Livona (ND.) **84** F 4
Livonia (LA.) **68** D 3
Livonia (MI.) **55** F 2
Livonia (NY.) **32** C 3
Livornia (N.Y.) **32** C 3
Lizard Head Peak **92** C 3
Llano (TX.) **74** C 4
Llano Estacado **99** GH 3
Llano River **74** BC 4
Lloyd (MT.) **86** D 1
Loa (UT.) **103** D 3
Lobecks Pass **107** H 3
Lobo (TX.) **72** D 3
Locate (MT.) **87** H 3
Lochsa River **88** E 2
Lock Haven (PA.) **34** D 2
Locke (N.Y.) **32** D 3
Lockeford (CA.) **111** D 3
Lockhart (TX.) **74** D 5
Lockney (TX.) **76** B 3
Lockout (CA.) **110** A 3
Lockport (N.Y.) **32** B 2
Lockwood (CA.) **106** A 2
Lodge Grass (MT.) **87** F 4
Lodge pole (SD.) **82** C 2
Lodgepole (MT.) **86** E 1
Lodgepole (NE.) **80** B 3
Lodi (CA.) **111** D 3
Lodi (OH.) **53** GH 2
Lodi (WI.) **59** F 3
Lodoga (CA.) **110** C 4
Lofgreen (UT.) **102** B 4
Logan (IA.) **62** C 4
Logan (KS.) **78** D 2
Logan (MT.) **86** B 4
Logan (N.M.) **97** G 3
Logan (OH.) **53** G 3
Logan (OK.) **76** C 1
logan (UT.) **102** A 3
Logan (W.V.) **36** C 4
Logan Martin Reservoir **46** C 4
Logan, Mount (WA.) **114** E 1
Logan Mountains (AL.) **117** F 1
Logan Pass **89** G 1
Logandale (NV.) **109** H 3
Logansport (IN.) **52** C 2
Logansport (LA.) **68** B 1
Lohrville (IA.) **62** D 3
Loíza Aldea (P.R.) **124** C 2
Lola, Mount **110** C 2
Loleta (CA.) **110** B 6
Lolita (TX.) **71** F 2
Lolo (MT.) **123** F 3
Lolo Hot Springs (MT.) **88–89** F 3
Lolo Peak **89** F 3
Loma (CO.) **94** B 2
Loma (MT.) **86** C 2
Loma Alta (TX.) **73** H 4
Loma Prieta **111** E 3
Lomax (IL.) **56** C 6
Lometa (TX.) **74** C 3
Lompoc (CA.) **106** B 3
London (KY.) **51** F 3
London (OH.) **53** F 3
London (TX.) **74** B 4
Lone Mountain **82** B 2
Lone Mountains **109** E 1–2
Lone Pine (CA.) **108** D 3
Lone Wolf (OK.) **76** D 2
Long Bay **41** G 3
Long Beach (CA.) **106** D 4
Long Beach (MS.) **49** F 3
Long Beach (N.Y.) **35** H 3
Long Beach (WA.) **114** A 3
Long Branch (N.J.) **35** H 3
Long Creek (OR.) **113** F 2
Long Island (KS.) **78** D 2
Long Island (N.Y.) **35** HJ 3
Long Island Sound **35** J 2
Long Lake (ME.) **28** A 3
Long Lake (ME.) **28** B 4
Long Lake (MI.) **54** C 2
Long Lake (N.D.) **85** F 4
Long Lake (N.Y.) **33** F 2
Long Lake (WA.) **115** H 2
Long Lake (WA.) **115** H 2
Long Pine (NE.) **81** E 2
Long Prairie (MN.) **61** E 4
Long Tom Reservoir **90** D 3
Long Valley Wash **105** F 2–3
Longfellow (TX.) **73** F 3
Longford (KS.) **79** F 2
Longmont (CO.) **95** E 1
Longs Peak **94–95** E 1
Longton (KS.) **79** G 4
Longvalley (SD.) **82** D 4
Longview (TX.) **75** G 2
Longview (WA.) **114** BC 3
Lontree (WY.) **92** B 4
Lookout, Cape (N.C.) **39** H 4
Lookout, Cape (OR.) **112** A 1
Lookout Mountain **112–113** E 2
Lookout Point Lake **112** C 3
Lookout Ridge (AL.) **120** D 2
Loomis (NE.) **81** E 4
Loon Lake (WA.) **115** H 1
Loop (TX.) **73** F 1
Lopeno (TX.) **70** C 4
Lopez Point **111** F 3
Lorain (OH.) **53** G 1
Loraine (TX.) **73** H 1
Lordsburg (N.M.) **98** B 4
Lorenzo (ID.) **91** H 3
Lorenzo (NE.) **80** AB 3
Lorequville (LA.) **68** D 3
Loretta (WI.) **58** D 5
Loretto (TN.) **50** C 5
Lorida (FL.) **45** D 3
Loring (MT.) **87** F 1
Loris (S.C.) **41** G 2
Lorman (MS.) **49** E 5
Los Alamos (CA.) **106** B 3
Los Alamos (N.M.) **96** D 3
Los Angeles (CA.) **106** D 4
Los Banos (CA.) **111** E 2
Los Coyotes Indian Reservation **107** F 4
Los Fresnos (TX.) **71** E 4
Los Gatos (CA.) **111** E 4
Los Lunas (N.M.) **96** D 4
Los Molinos (CA.) **110** B 3–4
Lost Cabin (WY.) **92** E 2
Lost City (VA.) **37** F 3
Lost Hills (CA.) **106** C 2
Lost Peak **103** E 5
Lost Springs (WY.) **93** H 3
Lost Sprs (KS.) **79** F 3
Lost Trail Pass **89** G 4
Lostwood (ND.) **84** D 2
Lott (TX.) **74** D 3
Loudon (TN.) **51** F 5
Loudonville (OH.) **53** G 2
Louisa (KY.) **51** H 2
Louisa (VA.) **37** F 3
Louisburg (KS.) **79** J 3
Louisburg (N.C.) **39** F 2
Louise (MS.) **48** D 4
Louise (TX.) **71** F 1
Louise, Lake **116** B 1
Louisiana **68–69**
Louisiana (MO.) **65** F 2
Louisville (CO.) **95** E 2
Louisville (GA.) **42** C 3
Louisville (IL.) **57** E 3
Louisville (KY.) **50** D 2
Louisville (MS.) **48** C 2–3
Louisville (NE.) **81** H 4
Loup City (NE.) **81** E 3
Loup River **81** FG 3
Louviers (CO.) **95** F 2
Lovelady (TX.) **75** F 3
Loveland (CO.) **95** E 1
Loveland Pass **94** E 2
Lovell (WY.) **92** D 1
Lovelock (NV.) **104** C 2
Loves Park (IL.) **56** A 3–4
Lovewell Reservoir **78–79** E 2
Loving (N.M.) **99** F 4
Loving (TX.) **74** C 1
Lovingston (VA.) **37** F 4
Lovington (IL.) **56** D 3
Lovington (N.M.) **99** G 3–4
Low (UT.) **102** B 4
Lowell (MA.) **30** E 3
Lowell (OR.) **112** C 3
Lowell, Lake **90** C 3
Lowelltown (ME.) **28** C 5
Lowemont (KS.) **79** H 2
Lowemont (MO.) **85** H 3
Lower Brule (SD.) **83** F 3
Lower Brule Indian Reservation **83** EF 3
Lower Goose Creek Reservoir **91** F 4
Lower Kalskag **119** C 1
Lower Klamath Lake **110** A 3
Lower Lake (CA.) **110** D 4
Lower Lake (CA./NV.) **110** A 1–2
Lower Monumental Dam **115** G 3
Lower Post (AL.) **117** F 1
Lower Red Lake **60** C 5
Lower Ugashik Lake **119** D 2
Lowman (ID.) **90** D 2
Lowry City (MO.) **64** D 3
Lowville (N.Y.) **32** E 2
Loyal Valley (TX.) **74** B 4
Loyalton (CA.) **110** C 2
Loyalton (SD.) **83** F 2
Loyd (WI.) **59** F 4
Lozeau (MT.) **89** F 2
Lua Makiki **123** E 3
Lubbock (TX.) **76** B 4
Lubeck (ME.) **28** D 2
Lucas (KS.) **78** E 2
Lucas (KY.) **50** E 4

Lucas (SD.) **83** F 4
Lucasville (OH.) **53** F 4
Lucca (N.D.) **85** J 4
Lucedale (MS.) **49** F 2
Lucerne (CA.) **110** C 4
Lucerne (WA.) **114** E 1
Lucerne (WY.) **92** D 2
Lucerne Lake **107** F 3
Lucerne Valley (CA.)
   107 F 3
Lucero (Mex.) **72** B 3
Lucero (N.M.) **97** E 2
Lucero, Lake **98** D 4
Lucile (ID.) **88** D 4
Lucin (UT.) **102** A 5
Luck (WI.) **58** D 6
Lucky Peak Lake **90** D 3
Lucy (N.M.) **96** E 4
Ludden (N.D.) **83** G 2
Ludington (MI.) **55** E 5
Ludlow (CA.) **107** F 3
Ludlow (CO.) **95** F 4
Ludlow (MS.) **48** D 3
Ludlow (SD.) **82** B 2
Ludlowville (N.Y.) **32** D 3
Ludowici (GA.) **43** E 2
Lueders (TX.) **74** B 2
Lufkin (TX.) **75** G 3
Lukachukai (AZ.) **103** F 1
Lukeville (AZ.) **100** D 5
Lula (MS.) **48** B 4
Luling (TX.) **71** E 1
Lumberton (MS.) **49** E 3
Lumberton (N.C.) **39** F 4
Lummi Indian Reservation
   114 C 1
Lumpkin (GA.) **43** D 5
Luna Pier (MI.) **55** G 2
Lund (UT.) **103** D 5
Lunenburg (VA.) **37** F 5
Luning (NV.) **104** C 4
Lupton (AZ.) **101** F 1
Luquillo (P.R.) **124** C 2
Luquillo, Sierra de **124** C 2
Luray (KS.) **78** E 2
Luray (VA.) **37** F 3
Lushton (NE.) **81** G 4
Lusk (WY.) **93** H 3
Lustre (MT.) **87** G 1
Luther (IA.) **62–63** E 4
Luther (MI.) **55** D 4
Luther (MT.) **86** D 4
Luther (OK.) **77** F 2
Lutie (TX.) **76** C 2
Luverne (AL.) **47** E 4
Luverne (IA.) **62** D 3
Luverne (MN.) **61** G 6
Luxora (AR.) **67** G 2
Lyle (MN.) **61** G 2
Lyman (IA.) **62** D 4
Lyman (WY.) **92** B 4
Lyman Lake **101** G 2
Lynch (NE.) **81** F 2
Lynchburg (MO.) **65** E 4
Lynchburg (S.C.) **41** E 2
Lynchburg (TN.) **50** D 5
Lynchburg (VA.) **37** E 4
Lynches River **41** E 2
Lynden (WA.) **114** C 1
Lyndon (KS.) **79** H 3
Lyndon B. Johnson, Lake
   74 C 4
Lyndonville (VT.) **30** D 1
Lynn (AL.) **46** B 5
Lynn (IN.) **52** E 2
Lynn (MA.) **31** F 3

Lynn (UT.) **102** A 5
Lynn Canal (AL.) **117** D 2
Lynndyl (UT.) **102** C 4
Lynnwood (WA.) **114** C 2
Lyon Mountain (N.Y.)
   33 F 1
Lyons (GA.) **43** D 3
Lyons (KS.) **79** E 3
Lyons (NE.) **81** H 3
Lyons (TX.) **75** E 4
Lyons Falls (N.Y.)
   32–33 E 2
Lysite (WY.) **92** E 2
Lytle (TX.) **70** D 1

M

Maalaea (HI.) **123** E 3
Mabank (TX.) **75** E 2
Mabelle (TX.) **76** D 4
Mableton (GA.) **42** C 5
Mabton (WA.) **115** EF 3
Mac Grath (AL.) **119** D 1
Macclenny (FL.) **44** A 4
Macdoel (CA.) **110** A 3
MacDonald Pass **86** A 3
Machias (ME.) **28** D 2
Mack (CO.) **94** B 2
Mackay (ID.) **91** F 3
Mackay Reservoir **91** F 3
Mackinac Island (MI.)
   54 C 3
Mackinac, Stratis of **54** C 3
Mackinaw City (MI.) **54** C 3
Mackinaw River **56** C 3–4
Macksville (KS.) **78** E 4
Macomb (IL.) **56** C 5
Macon (GA.) **42** D 4
Macon (MO.) **64** E 2
Macon (MS.) **48** C 2
Macwahoc (ME.) **28** C 3
Mad Lake **91** G 3
Mad River **53** F 2
Madawaska (ME.) **28** A 3
Maddock (ND.) **85** G 3
Madelia (MN.) **61** F 4
Madeline (CA.) **110** A 2
Madeline Island **58** C 4
Madera (CA.) **111** F 2
Madill (OK.) **77** G 3
Madison (AL.) **46** D 4
Madison (FL.) **44** A 5
Madison (GA.) **42** C 4
Madison (IN.) **52** D 4
Madison (KS.) **79** G 3
Madison (ME.) **28** D 4
Madison (MN.) **61** E 6
Madison (MS.) **48** D 4
Madison (N.C.) **38** E 2
Madison (NE.) **81** G 3
Madison (S.D.) **83** H 4
Madison (VA.) **37** F 3
Madison (WI.) **59** F 3
Madison (W.V.) **36** C 3
Madison Range **86** B 4
Madison River **86** B 4
Madisonville (KY.) **50** C 3
Madisonville (TN.) **51** F 5

Madisonville (TX.) **75** E 4
Madras (OR.) **112** D 2
Madrid (AL.) **47** E 3
Madrid (IA.) **62–63** E 4
Madrid (NE.) **80** C 4
Madrid (NE.) **80** C 4
Magazine Mountain **66** C 2
Magdalena (N.M.) **96** C 4
Magee (MS.) **49** E 3
Magic Reservoir **91** E 3
Magma (AZ.) **101** E 3
Magnolia (AR.) **66** C 4
Magnolia (KY.) **50** E 3
Magnolia (MS.) **49** E 4
Magnolia (TX.) **75** F 4
Magruder Mountain
   109 E 2
Magwalt (TX.) **73** E 2
Mahaska (KS.) **81** G 4
Mahnomen (MN.) **60** C 5
Mahogany Mountain
   113 H 3
Maida (N.D.) **85** H 2
Maine **28–29**
Maine, Gulf of **31** GJ 3
Maitland (CO.) **95** F 4
Makah Indian Reservation
   114 A 1
Makahuena Point **122** B 2
Makapuu Point **123** D 2
Makushin Volcano (AL.)
   118 B 3
Malaga (N.M.) **99** F 4
Malakoff (TX.) **75** E 2
Malaspina Glacier (AL.)
   116–117 C 2
Malden (MO.) **65** G 5
Malheur Lake **113** G 3
Malheur Reservoir **113** H 2
Malheur River **113** H 3
Malin (OR.) **112** D 4
Maljamar (N.M.) **99** G 4
Malmo (MN.) **61** D 3
Malo (WA.) **115** G 1
Malone (FL.) **47** F 3
Malone (N.Y.) **33** F 1
Maloney, Lake **80** D 3
Malott (WA.) **115** F 1
Malta (ID.) **91** F 4
Malta (MT.) **87** F 1
Malvern (AR.) **66** D 3
Malvern (IA.) **62** C 4–5
Mammoth (AZ.) **101** F 4
Mammoth Cave (KY.)
   50 D 3
Mammoth Cave National
   Park **50** D 3
Mammoth Hot Springs
   (WY.) **92** B 1
Mammoth Lakes (CA.)
   108 D 2
Mammoth Pool Reservoir
   111 E 1
Mammoth Spring (AR.)
   67 E 1
Mamou (LA.) **68** C 3
Mana (HI.) **88** B 3
Manassas (VA.) **37** G 3
Manatí (P.R.) **124** B 2
Mancelona (MI.) **54** D 4
Manchester (AL.) **110** D 5
Manchester (CT.) **35** J 2
Manchester (GA.) **42** D 5
Manchester (KS.) **79** F 2
Manchester (KY.) **51** G 3

Manchester (MA.) **31** E 3
Manchester (N.H.) **29** F 6
Manchester (OH.) **53** F 4
Manchester (TN.) **50** D 5
Manchester (VT.) **30** C 2
Mancos (CO.) **94** B 4
Mandan (N.D.) **84** EF 4
Mandaree (ND.) **84** D 3
Manderson (WY.) **92** E 1
Mandeville (LA.) **69** E 3
Mangum (OK.) **76** D 3
Manhattan (KS.) **79** G 2
Manhattan (MT.) **86** B 4
Manila (AR.) **67** F 2
Manila (UT.) **102** B 1
Manilla (IA.) **62** C 4
Manistee (MI.) **55** D 5
Manistee River **55** D 4
Manistique (MI.) **54** C 5
Manistique Lake **54** B 4
Manito (IL.) **56** C 4
Manitou Island **58** B 1
Manitou Springs (CO.)
   95 F 3
Manitowish (WI.) **58** C 3
Manitowoc (WI.) **59** E 1
Mankato (KS.) **79** E 2
Mankato (MN.) **61** F 3
Mankins (TX.) **76** E 4
Manley Hot Springs (AL.)
   121 EF 2
Manly (IA.) **63** E 2
Manning (IA.) **62** C 4
Manning (ND.) **84** D 3
Manning (S.C.) **41** E 3
Mannington (W.V.) **36** D 2
Manns Harbor (N.C.) **39** J 3
Manokotek **119** D 2
Manor (TX.) **74** D 4
Mansfield (AR.) **66** B 2
Mansfield (GA.) **42** C 4
Mansfield (LA.) **68** B 1
Mansfield (MO.) **64** E 4
Mansfield (OH.) **53** G 2
Mansfield (PA.) **34** D 2
Mansfield (WA.) **115** F 2
Mansfield Lake **52** B 3
Mansfield, Mount **30** CD 1
Manson (IA.) **62** D 3
Manson (WA.) **115** E 2
Mansura (LA.) **68** CD 2
Manteca (CA.) **111** E 3
Manteo (N.C.) **39** J 3
Manti (UT.) **102** C 3
Manton (CA.) **110** B 3
Manton (MI.) **55** D 4
Mantorville (MN.) **61** F 2
Mantua (OH.) **53** H 1
Manuel Benavides (Mex.)
   72 D 4
Manuelito (N.M.) **101** G 1
Manvel (N.D.) **85** J 2
Manville (WY.) **93** H 3
Many (LA.) **68** B 2
Manzanita (OR.) **112** A 1
Manzano Mountains
   96 D 4
Manzano Peak **96** D 4
Manzanola (CO.) **95** G 3
Maple Peak **101** G 3
Maple River **85** J 4
Maplesville (AL.) **46** D 5
Mapleton (IA.) **62** C 3
Mapleton (MN.) **61** G 3
Mapleton (OR.) **112** B 2
Maquoketa (IA.) **63** H 3

Maquon (IL.) **56** C 5
Marana (AZ.) **101** E 4
Marathon (TX.) **73** E 3
Marble (CO.) **94** C 2
Marble (N.C.) **51** G 5
Marble (WA.) **115** GH 1
Marble Canyon **103** F 3
Marble City (OK.) **77** J 2
Marble Falls (TX.) **74** C 4
Marble Hill (MO.) **65** H 4
Marble Rock (IA.) **63** F 3
Marblemount (WA.)
  114 D 1
Marbleton (WY.) **92** B 3
Marcellus (WA.) **115** G 2
Marco (FL.) **45** F 3
Marcola (OR.) **112** BC 2
Marcus (IA.) **62** C 3
Marcy, Mount **33** F 1
Marell (AR.) **67** E 3
Marengo (IA.) **63** F 4
Marengo (WA.) **115** G 2
Marengo (WI.) **58** C 4
Marenisco (MI.) **58** C 3
Marfa (TX.) **72** D 3
Margaretville (N.Y.) **33** F 3
Marianna (AR.) **67** F 3
Marianna (FL.) **47** F 3
Marias Pass **89** G 1
Marias River **86** B 1
Maricao (P.R.) **124** B 2
Maricopa (AZ.) **100** DE 3
Maricopa (CA.) **106** C 2
Marienthal (KS.) **78** B 3
Marienville (PA.) **34** B 2
Marietta (GA.) **42** C 5
Marietta (OH.) **53** H 3
Marietta (OK.) **77** F 4
Marine City (MI.) **55** F 1
Marineland (FL.) **44** B 3
Marinette (WI.) **59** D 1
Marion (AL.) **46** D 5
Marion (AR.) **67** F 2
Marion (IA.) **63** G 3
Marion (ID.) **91** EF 4
Marion (IL.) **57** F 3
Marion (IN.) **52** D 2
Marion (KS.) **79** G 3
Marion (KY.) **50** B 2
Marion (LA.) **68** C 1
Marion (MT.) **89** F 1
Marion (N.C.) **38** C 3
Marion (N.D.) **85** H 4
Marion (OH.) **53** F 2
Marion (S.C.) **41** F 2
Marion (S.D.) **83** H 4
Marion (WI.) **59** E 3
Marion Junction (AL.)
  46 D 5
Marion, Lake **41** E 3
Marion Lake **79** F 3
Mariposa (CA.) **111** E 1
Markagunt Plateau **103** E 4
Marked Tree (AR.) **67** F 2
Markesan (WI.) **59** F 2
Markham (TX.) **71** F 2
Markham Ferry Reservoir
  77 HJ 1
Markleeville (CA.)
  111 D 1–2
Marks (MS.) **48** B 4
Marksville (LA.) **68** CD 2
Marland (OK.) **77** F 1
Marlette (MI.) **55** E 1–2
Marlin (TX.) **75** E 3
Marlin (WA.) **115** G 2

Marlinton (W.V.) **36** D 3
Marlow (OK.) **77** E 3
Marmarth (ND.) **84** C 4
Marmot Bay **119** E 2
Marmot Peak **88** E 2
Marquesas Keys **45** G 4
Marquette (KS.) **79** E 3
Marquette (MI.) **54** B 6
Marquette Island **54** C 3
Marquez (N.M.) **96** C 3
Marquez (TX.) **75** E 3
Marrero (LA.) **69** E 4
Mars Hill (ME.) **28** B 3
Mars Hill (N.C.) **51** H 5
Marseilles (IL.) **56** B 3
Marsh (TX.) **97** H 3
Marsh Island **68** D 4
Marsh Peak **102** B 1
Marshall (AL.) **119** C 1
Marshall (AR.) **66** D 2
Marshall (IL.) **57** D 2
Marshall (IN.) **52** B 3
Marshall (MI.) **55** F 3
Marshall (MN.) **61** F 5
Marshall (MO.) **64** D 2
Marshall (ND.) **84** D 3
Marshall (TX.) **75** G 2
Marshall (VA.) **37** G 3
Marshall (WA.) **115** H 2
Marshall (WY.) **93** G 3
Marshalltown (IA.) **63** F 3
Marshfield (MO.) **64** E 4
Marshfield (WI.) **59** E 4
Marsing (ID.) **90** C 3
Marsland (NE.) **80** A 2
Mart (TX.) **75** E 3
Martha's Vineyard **31** F 4
Marthasville (MO.) **65** FG 3
Martin (ND.) **85** F 3
Martin (SD.) **82** D 4
Martin (TN.) **50** B 4
Martin Dam **46** D 3
Martin Lake **46** D 3
Martin Luther King Jr.
  National Historic Site
  (GA.) **42** B 3
Martinez (CA.) **111** D 4
Martinez Lake **107** H 5
Martins Ferry (W.V.) **36** D 1
Martinsburg (PA.) **34** C 3
Martinsburg (W.V.) **37** F 2
Martinsdale (MT.) **86** C 3
Martinsville (IL.) **57** D 3
Martinsville (IN.) **52** C 3
Martinsville (VA.) **36** E 5
Marvine, Mount **103** D 3
Maryhill (WA.) **114** E 4
Maryland **37**
Maryneal (TX.) **73** H 1
Marys Igloo **120** C 2
Marys River **105** F 1
Marysvale (UT.) **103** D 4
Marysville (CA.) **110** C 3
Marysville (NE.) **79** G 2
Marysville (OH.) **53** F 2
Marysville (WA.) **114** C 1
Maryville (MI.) **55** F 1
Maryville (MO.) **64** B 1
Maryville (TN.) **51** G 5
Masardis (ME.) **28** B 3
Mason (TN.) **67** G 2
Mason (TX.) **74** B 4
Mason City (IA.) **63** E 2
Mason City (IL.) **56** C 4
Mason City (NE.) **81** E 3
Massachusetts **33**

Massachusetts Bay **31** F 3
Massacre Lake **104** B 1
Massadona (CO.) **94** B 1
Massena (N.Y.) **33** F 1
Masset (AL.) **117** E 3
Massillon (OH.) **53** H 2
Masters (CO.) **95** F 1
Masterson (TX.) **97** H 3
Matador (TX.) **76** C 3
Matagorda (TX.) **71** F 2
Matagorda Bay **71** F 2
Matagorda Island **71** F 2
Matagorda Peninsula
  71 F 2
Matamoros (Mex.) **71** E 5
Matanuska River **116** B 1
Matfield Green (KS.) **79** G 3
Mather (CA.) **111** E 1
Matheson (CO.) **95** G 2
Mathews (VA.) **37** H 4
Mathis (TX.) **71** E 2
Mathiston (MS.) **48** C 3
Matinicus Island **29** E 3
Mattamuskeet, Lake **39** H 3
Mattawamkeag (ME.)
  28 C 3
Matterhorn (NV.) **105** F 1
Matthews (N.C.) **38** D 3
Mattoon (IL.) **57** D 3
Mattydale (N.Y.) **32** D 2
Maud (OK.) **77** G 2
Maud (TX.) **75** G 1
Maudlow (MT.) **86** B 3
Maui **123** E 3
Maumee (OH.) **53** F 1
Maumee River **52** E 1
Mauna Kea **123** F 4
Mauna Loa **123** F 4
Maunaloa (HI.) **123** D 2
Maupin (OR.) **112** D 1
Maurepas, Lake **69** E 3
Mauriceville (TX.) **75** H 4
Maurine (SD.) **82** C 2
Mauston (WI.) **59** F 4
Max (ND.) **84** E 3
Maxbass (ND.) **84** E 2
Maxie (MS.) **49** EF 3
Maxinkuckee, Lake **52** C 1
Maxville (MT.) **89** G 3
Maxwell (NE.) **80** D 3
Maxwell (N.M.) **97** F 2
May (OK.) **76** D 1
May (TX.) **74** C 2–3
May, Cape **35** G 5
Mayagüez (P.R.) **124** A 2
Maybell (CO.) **94** B 1
Maybeury (W.V.) **36** C 4
Mayer (AZ.) **100** D 2
Mayfield (ID.) **90** D 3
Mayfield (KY.) **50** B 4
Mayfield (OK.) **76** D 2
Mayfield (UT.) **102** C 3
Mayfield Reservoir **114** C 3
Mayhill (N.M.) **99** E 4
Maynardville (TN.) **51** G 4
Mayo (FL.) **44** A 5
Mays Landing (N.J.)
  35 G 4
Maysville (MO.) **64** C 2
Maysville (N.C.) **39** G 4
Mayville (N.D.) **85** J 3
Mayville (N.Y.) **32** A 3
Mayville (WI.) **59** F 2
Maywood (NE.) **80** D 4
Mayworth (WY.) **93** F 2
Mazama (WA.) **115** E 1

Mazatzal Mountains
  100–101 E 2–3
Mazomanie (WI.) **59** F 3
Mc Arthur (OH.) **53** G 3
Mc Bain (MI.) **55** D 4
Mc Cabe (MT.) **87** J 1
Mc Cammon (ID.) **91** G 4
Mc Clave (CO.) **95** H 3
Mc Cloud (CA.) **110** A 4
Mc Clusky (N.D.) **85** F 3
Mc Cook (NE.) **80** D 4
Mc Coy (CO.) **94** D 2
Mc Cracken (KS.) **78** D 3
Mc Dermitt (NV.) **104** D 1
Mc Fadden (WY.) **93** F 4
Mc Faddin (TX.) **71** E 2
Mc Gill (NV.) **105** G 3
Mc Gregor (ND.) **84** D 2
Mc Gregor (TX.) **74** D 3
Mc Henry (N.D.) **85** H 3
Mc Intosh (SD.) **82** D 2
Mc Kee (KY.) **51** F 3
Mc Kinleyville (CA.)
  110 B 6
Mc Kinnon (WY.) **92** C 4
Mc Laughlin (SD.) **82** E 2
Mc Lean (IL.) **56** C 4
Mc Leod (N.D.) **85** J 4
Mc Roberts (KY.) **51** H 3
Mc Ville (N.D.) **85** H 3
McAlester (OK.) **77** H 3
McAlister (N.M.) **97** G 4
McAllen (TX.) **70** D 4
McAllister (MT.) **86** B 4
McBaine (MO.) **64** E 3
McBee (S.C.) **41** E 2
McCall (ID.) **90** C 2
McCamey (TX.) **73** F 2
McCarthy (AL.) **116** C 1
McCartys (N.M.) **96** C 3
McCleary (WA.) **114** B 2
McClellanville (S.C.) **41** F 3
McClure, Lake **111** E 2
McComb (MS.) **49** E 4
McConaughy, Lake **80** C 3
McConnellsburg (PA.)
  34 C 4
McConnelsville (OH.)
  53 H 3
McCormick (S.C.) **40** C 3
McCredie Springs (OR.)
  112 C 3
McCullough Mountain
  109 G 4
McCurtain (OK.) **77** HJ 2
McDade (TX.) **74** D 4
McDame (AL.) **117** F 2
McDavid (FL.) **47** F 5
McDonald (KS.) **78** B 2
McDonald (N.M.) **99** G 3
McDonald, Lake **89** G 1
McDonough (GA.) **42** C 5
McDougall, Mount **92** B 3
McFarland (CA.) **106** C 2
McGrath (MN.) **61** D 3
McGregor (MN.) **60** D 3
McGuire, Mount **89** F 4
McIntosh (AL.) **47** E 5
McKay Reservoir **113** G 1
McKeesport (PA.) **34** B 3
McKenzie (AL.) **47** E 4
McKenzie (TN.) **50** B 4
McKenzie Bridge (OR.)
  112 C 2
McKinley Park (AL.) **121** F 3
McKinney (TX.) **75** E 1

McKinney Mountain **72** E 4
McKittrick (CA.) **106** C 2
McKittrick Summit **106** C 2
McLain (MS.) **49** E 2
McLaurin (MS.) **49** E 3
McLean (TX.) **76** C 2
McLeansboro (IL.) **57** E 3
McLeod (MT.) **86** C 4
McLoughlin, Mount **112** C 4
McMillan (MS.) **48** C 3
McMillan, Lake **99** F 4
McMinnville (OR.) **112** B 1
McMinnville (TN.) **50** D 5
McNab (AR.) **66** C 4
McNary (AZ.) **101** G 2
McNary (TX.) **72** C 2
McNary Dam **115** F 4
McNeil (AR.) **66** C 4
McNeil (TX.) **74** D 4
McPherson (KS.) **79** F 3
McRae (GA.) **43** D 3
McVeigh (KY.) **51** H 3
Mead, Lake **109** H 3
Meade (KS.) **78** C 4
Meade Peak **91** H 4
Meade R. (AL.) **121** D 1–2
Meaden Peak **94** C 1
Meadow (SD.) **82** C 2
Meadow (TX.) **99** H 3
Meadow (UT.) **102** D 4
Meadow Valley Wash **109** H 2
Meadowdale (WY.) **93** H 3
Meadville (PA.) **34** A 2
Meath (AZ.) **100** D 1
Mecca (CA.) **107** F 4
Mechanicville (N.Y.) **33** G 3
Mechigmen **120** A 2
Mechigmenskiy Zaliv (AL.) **120** A 2
Medford (MA.) **30–31** E 3
Medford (OK.) **77** F 1
Medford (OR.) **112** C 4
Medford (WI.) **59** D 4
Mediapolis (IA.) **63** G 4–5
Medical Lake (WA.) **115** H 2
Medical Springs (OR.) **113** H 1
Medicine Bow (WY.) **93** F 4
Medicine Bow Mountains **93** F 4
Medicine Lake (MT.) **87** J 1
Medicine Lake (MT.) **87** J 1
Medicine Lodge (KS.) **78** E 4
Medicine Mound (TX.) **76** D 3
Medina (ND.) **85** G 4
Medina (N.Y.) **32** B 2
Medina (OH.) **53** GH 1
Medina (TX.) **70** C 1
Medina Lake **70** D 1
Medina River **70** C 1
Medira **121** DE 3
Medora (KS.) **79** F 3
Medora (ND.) **84** C 4
Meeker (CO.) **94** C 1
Meeker (OK.) **77** G 2
Meeks Bay (CA.) **110** C 2
Meeteetse (WY.) **92** D 1
Megargel (TX.) **74** B 1
Meggett (S.C.) **41** E 4
Meherrin River **37** G 5
Meigs (GA.) **43** E 5
Mekinock (N.D.) **85** J 3
Mekoryuk (AL.) **118** B 1
Melba (ID.) **90** C 3
Melbourne (AR.) **67** E 1
Melbourne (FL.) **44** C 2
Melbourne (IA.) **63** E 4
Melcher (IA.) **63** E 4
Mellen (WI.) **58** C 4
Mellette (S.D.) **83** G 2
Melrose (MT.) **86** A 4
Melrose (N.M.) **97** G 4
Melrose (WI.) **59** E 4
Melstone (MT.) **87** F 3
Melvern (KS.) **79** H 3
Melville (MT.) **86** D 3
Melvin (TX.) **74** B 3
Memphis (MO.) **65** E 1
Memphis (TN.) **67** G 2
Memphis (TX.) **76** C 3
Mena (AR.) **66** B 3
Menahga (MN.) **60** D 5
Menard (MT.) **86** B 3
Menard (TX.) **74** B 4
Menasha (WI.) **59** E 2
Mendenhall (MS.) **49** E 3
Mendocino (CA.) **110** C 5
Mendocino, Cape **110** B 6
Mendocino, Lake **110** C 5
Mendota (CA.) **111** F 2
Mendota (IL.) **56** B 4
Mendota (TX.) **76** C 2
Mendota (VA.) **36** B 5
Mendota, Lake **59** F 3
Mendoza (TX.) **74** D 4
Menentor (KY.) **51** F 2
Menno (S.D.) **83** H 4
Meno (OK.) **77** E 1
Menominee (MI.) **54** C 6
Menominee Indian Reservation **59** DE 2
Menominee River **54** C 6
Menomonee Falls (WI.) **59** F 2
Menomonie (WI.) **59** E 6
Mentasta (AL.) **116** C 1
Mentone (TX.) **73** E 2
Mentor (OH.) **53** H 1
Meramec River **65** F 3
Merced (CA.) **111** E 2
Mercedes (TX.) **70** D 4
Mercer (ND.) **84** F 3
Mercer (PA.) **34** A 2
Mercersburg (PA.) **34** D 4
Mercury (NV.) **109** G 3
Meredith (N.H.) **29** E 6
Meredith, Lake (CO.) **95** G 3
Meredith, Lake (TX.) **76** B 2
Meredosia (IL.) **56** D 5
Meriden (CT.) **35** J 2
Meriden (WY.) **93** H 4
Meridian (GA.) **43** E 2
Meridian (MS.) **48** D 2
Meridian (TX.) **74** D 3
Merkel (TX.) **73** H 1
Merlin (OR.) **112** B 4
Merna (NE.) **81** E 3
Merna (WY.) **92** B 3
Merriam (IN.) **52** D 1
Merrill (IA.) **62** B 3
Merrill (MI.) **55** E 3
Merrill (OR.) **112** D 4
Merrill (WI.) **59** D 3
Merrillan (WI.) **59** E 4
Merrimack River **29** E 6
Merriman (NE.) **80** C 2
Merritt Island (FL.) **44** C 2
Merritt Island (FL.) **44** C 2
Merritt Reservoir **80** D 2
Mertzon (TX.) **73** H 2
Merwin, Lake **114** C 3–4
Mesa (AZ.) **100** E 3
Mesa (CO.) **94** B 2
Mesa (ID.) **90** C 2
Mesa (WA.) **115** G 3
Mesa Peak **94** D 4
Mesa Verde **94** B 4
Mesa Verde National Park (CO.) **94** B 4
Mesabi Range **60** C 2–3
Mescalero (N.M.) **99** E 3
Mescalero Indian Reservation **99** E 3
Mesick (MI.) **55** D 4
Mesilla (N.M.) **98** D 4
Mesquite (N.M.) **98** D 4
Mesquite (TX.) **75** E 2
Mesquite Flat **109** F 3
Mesquite Lake **107** F 3
Mesquite Lake **107** G 2
Meszah Peak **117** E 2
Metairie (LA.) **69** E 4
Metaline (WA.) **115** H 1
Metaline Falls (WA.) **115** H 1
Metcalf (GA.) **43** F 4
Metcalf (KS.) **79** F 4
Metlakatla **117** E 2
Metropolis (IL.) **57** F 3
Metter (GA.) **43** D 3
Mexia (TX.) **75** E 3
Mexicali (Mex.) **107** G 5
Mexican Springs (N.M.) **96** B 3
Mexican Water (AZ.) **103** F 1
Mexico (ME.) **28** D 5
Mexico (MO.) **65** F 2
Mexico Beach (FL.) **47** G 3
Meyers Chuck **117** E 2
Meyersdale (PA.) **34** C 4
Miami (AZ.) **101** F 3
Miami (FL.) **45** F 2
Miami (OK.) **77** J 1
Miami (TX.) **76** C 2
Miami Beach (FL.) **45** F 2
Miami Canal **45** E 2
Miami Springs (FL.) **45** F 2
Michigamme, Lake **58** C 2
Michigan **54–55**
Michigan (N.D.) **85** H 2
Michigan Center (MI.) **55** F 3
Michigan City (IN.) **52** C 1
Michigan Island **58** C 4
Michipicoten Bay (Can.) **54** A 4
Michipicoten Island (Can.) **54** A 5
Midas (NV.) **105** E 1
Middle Alkali Lake **110** A 2
Middle Fork (AK.) **121** E 2
Middle Fork (AK.) **121** F 2
Middle Fork (ID.) **90** E 1–2
Middle Fork (KS.) **78** B 2
Middle Loup River **80–81** E 3
Middle River (MN.) **60** B 6
Middle Water (TX.) **97** H 3
Middlebourne (W.V.) **36** D 2
Middleburg (N.Y.) **33** F 3
Middleburg (PA.) **34** D 3
Middleburry (VT.) **30** C 2
Middleport (OH.) **53** G 3
Middlesboro (KY.) **51** G 4
Middleton (ID.) **90** C 3
Middleton (TN.) **50** B 5
Middleton Island **116** B 2
Middleton Island (AL.) **116** B 2
Middletown (CA.) **111** D 4
Middletown (CT.) **35** J 2
Middletown (DE.) **37** J 2
Middletown (IL.) **56** C 4
Middletown (N.Y.) **33** F 4
Middletown (OH.) **52** E 3
Middletown (W.V.) **37** F 2
Middleville (MI.) **55** F 4
Midfield (TX.) **71** F 2
Midford (N.J.) **35** G 4
Midland (CA.) **107** H 4
Midland (Can.) **32** A 1
Midland (MI.) **55** E 3
Midland (SD.) **82** D 3
Midland (TX.) **73** F 1
Midlothian (TX.) **74** D 2
Midpines (CA.) **111** E 1
Midvales (ID.) **90** C 2
Midville (GA.) **42** D 3
Midway (AL.) **47** D 3
Midway (AZ.) **100** D 4
Midway (GA.) **43** E 2
Midway (TX.) **75** F 3
Midway (UT.) **102** B 3
Midwest (WY.) **93** F 2
Midwest City (OK.) **77** F 2
Miffin (OH.) **53** G 2
Mikelumne Hill (CA.) **111** D 2
Milaca (MN.) **61** E 3
Milan (GA.) **43** DE 4
Milan (MI.) **55** F 2
Milan (MN.) **61** E 5
Milan (MO.) **64** D 1
Milan (N.M.) **96** C 3
Milan (TN.) **50** B 5
Milano (TX.) **75** E 4
Milbank (S.D.) **83** J 2
Milburn (OK.) **77** G 3
Mildred (MT.) **87** J 3
Miles (TX.) **73** H 2
Miles (WA.) **115** G 2
Miles City (MT.) **87** H 3
Milesville (SD.) **82** D 3
Milford (CA.) **110** B 2
Milford (CT.) **35** J 2
Milford (DE.) **37** J 3
Milford (IA.) **62** C 2
Milford (MA.) **30** E 3
Milford (NE.) **81** G 4
Milford (N.H.) **29** F 6
Milford (PA.) **35** G 2
Milford (UT.) **103** D 4
Milford (WY.) **92** D 3
Milford Center (OH.) **53** F 2
Milford Lake **79** G 2
Milk River **87** G 1
Mill City (NV.) **104** CD 2
Mill City (OR.) **112** C 2
Mill Hall (PA.) **34** D 2
Mill Iron (MT.) **87** J 4
Mille Lacs Lake **61** D 3
Milledgeville (GA.) **42** C 4
Millen (GA.) **42** D 2
Miller (AL.) **46** D 5
Miller (NE.) **81** E 4
Miller (SD.) **83** G 3
Miller House **121** F 2

Millers Ferry (AL.) **47** D 5
Millersburg (OH.) **53** G 2
Millersview (TX.) **74** B 3
Millerton Lake **111** E 1
Millington (TN.) **67** G 2
Millinocket (ME.) **28** C 3
Millinocket Lake **28** C 3
Millry (AL.) **47** E 6
Mills (NE.) **81** E 2
Mills (N.M.) **97** F 2
Mills (UT.) **102** C 4
Mills (WY.) **93** F 3
Millstone (W.V.) **36** C 3
Millville (N.J.) **35** G 4
Millwood Lake **66** C 4
Milner (CO.) **94** C 1
Milnesand (N.M.) **99** G 3
Milnor (N.D.) **85** J 4
Milolii (HI.) **123** F 4
Milroy (PA.) **34** D 3
Milton (FL.) **47** F 5
Milton (N.D.) **85** H 2
Milton (PA.) **34** E 2
Milton (VT.) **30** C 1
Milton (W.V.) **36** B 3
Milton Freewater (OR.) **113** G 1
Milton Reservoir **95** F 1
Miltonvale (KS.) **79** F 2
Milwaukee (WI.) **59** F 1
Milwaukie (OR.) **112** C 1
Mimbres Mountains **98** C 4
Mims (FL.) **44** C 2
Mina (NV.) **104** C 4
Mina (S.D.) **83** G 2
Minam (OR.) **113** H 1
Minatare (NE.) **80** A 3
Minchumina Lake (AL.) **121** E 3
Minco (OK.) **77** F 2
Minden (LA.) **68** B 1
Minden (NE.) **81** E 4
Minden (NV.) **104** B 4
Minden City (MI.) **55** E 2
Mindenmines (MO.) **64** C 4
Mineola (TX.) **75** F 2
Miner (MT.) **86** C 4
Mineral (CA.) **110** B 3
Mineral (VA.) **37** G 3
Mineral (WA.) **114** C 3
Mineral Point (WI.) **59** G 4
Mineral Springs (AR.) **66** B 4
Mineral Wells (TX.) **74** C 2
Minersville (UT.) **103** D 5
Minerva (OH.) **53** H 2
Minerva (TX.) **74** D 4
Minidoka (ID.) **91** F 4
Mink Creek (ID.) **91** H 4
Minneapolis (KS.) **79** F 2
Minneapolis (MN.) **61** EF 3
Minnehaha Sprs (W.V.) **36** E 3
Minneola (KS.) **78** C 4
Minnesota **60–61**
Minnesota City (MN.) **61** F 1–2
Minnesota River **61** F 4
Minnewaukan (ND.) **85** G 2
Minong (WI.) **58** C 5–6
Minonk (IL.) **56** C 3
Minot (N.D.) **84** E 2
Minster (OH.) **52** E 2
Minter (AL.) **46** D 4
Mintle (NE.) **80** A 3
Minto (N.D.) **85** J 2
Minturn (CO.) **94** D 2
Mio (MI.) **55** D 3
Miracle Hot Springs (CA.) **106** D 2
Miranda (CA.) **110** B 5
Misenheimer (N.C.) **38** D 3
Mishawaka (IN.) **52** C 1
Misheguk Mountains **120** CD 2
Mishicot (WI.) **59** E 1
Mission (SD.) **82** E 4
Mission (TX.) **70** D 4
Mission Range **89** G 2
Mission Ridge (SD.) **82** D 3
Mississinewa River **52** D 2
Mississippi (North) **48–49**
Mississippi (South) **48–49**
Mississippi River **68** D 2
Mississippi River Delta **69** FG 4
Mississippi Sound **49** F 2
Missoula (MT.) **89** G 3
Missouri **64–65**
Missouri Buttes **93** H 1
Missouri River **65** F 3
Missouri Valley (IA.) **62** B 4
Mist (OR.) **112** B 1
Misty Fjoros Nat. Mon. (AL.) **117** E 2
Mitchell (IN.) **52** C 4
Mitchell (NE.) **80** A 3
Mitchell (OR.) **113** E 2
Mitchell (S.D.) **83** G 4
Mitchell, Lake **46** D 4
Mitchell, Mount **51** H 5
Mize (MS.) **49** E 3
Mizpah (MT.) **87** H 3
Moab (UT.) **103** D 1
Moapa (NV.) **109** H 3
Mobeetie (TX.) **76** C 2
Moberly (MO.) **64** E 2
Mobile (AL.) **47** F 5–6
Mobile (AZ.) **100** D 3
Mobile Bay **47** F 6
Mobridge (SD.) **82** E 2
Moccasin (AZ.) **103** F 4
Moccasin (CA.) **111** E 2
Moccasin (MT.) **86** C 2
Moccasin Gap (VA.) **36** B 2
Mocksville (N.C.) **38** D 3
Moclips (WA.) **114** A 2
Moddersville (MI.) **55** D 3
Model (CO.) **95** F 4
Modena (UT.) **103** E 5
Modesto (CA.) **111** E 3
Modoc (S.C.) **40** C 3
Modoc Point (OR.) **112** D 4
Moenkopi (AZ.) **103** F 3
Moffat (CO.) **94** C 1
Moffat (CO.) **94** D 4
Moffit (ND.) **85** F 4
Mogollon Baldy Peck **98** B 3
Mogollon Range **98** B 3
Mogollon Rim **101** F 2
Mohall (ND.) **84** E 2
Mohave, Lake **100** B 1
Mohawk (AZ.) **100** C 4
Mohawk (N.Y.) **33** E 2
Mohawk (WI.) **58** B 2
Mohawk Valley **100** C 4
Mohon Peak **100** C 2
Mojave (CA.) **106** D 2
Mojave Desert **107** EG 3
Mojave River **107** F 3
Molalla (OR.) **112** C 1
Moline (IL.) **56** B 5
Moline (KS.) **79** G 4
Molino (FL.) **47** F 5
Molokai **123** E 2
Molt (MT.) **86** E 4
Molybdenite Mountain **115** H 1
Momence (IL.) **56** B 2
Mona (UT.) **102** C 3
Mona, Isla **124** A 2
Mona Reservoir **102** C 3
Monadnock Mountain **29** F 7
Monahans (TX.) **73** E 2
Monango (N.D.) **85** H 4
Monarch (MT.) **86** C 2
Monarch Pass **94** D 3
Moncks Corner (S.C.) **41** F 3
Monclova (Mex.) **70** A 4
Mondovi (WI.) **59** E 5
Monero (N.M.) **96** D 2
Monessen (PA.) **34** B 3
Moneta (WY.) **92** E 2
Monett (MO.) **64** D 5
Monhegan Island **29** E 4
Monida (MT.) **91** G 2
Monida Pass **91** G 2
Monito, Isla **124** A 2
Monitor Range **105** E 4
Monmouth (IL.) **56** C 5
Monmouth (OR.) **112** B 2
Mono Lake (CA.) **111** D 1
Mono Lake (CA.) **108** D 1
Monomoy Island **31** G 4
Monon (IN.) **52** B 2
Monona (WI.) **59** F 3
Monroe (GA.) **42** C 4
Monroe (IA.) **63** E 4
Monroe (LA.) **68** C 1
Monroe (MI.) **55** G 2
Monroe (N.C.) **38** D 3–4
Monroe (OR.) **112** B 2
Monroe (WA.) **114** C 2
Monroe (WI.) **59** G 3
Monroe City (MO.) **65** F 2
Monroe Lake **52** C 3
Monroeville (AL.) **47** E 5
Monse (WA.) **115** F 1
Mont Belvieu (TX.) **71** H 1
Mont Torbert (AL.) **119** E 1
Montague (CA.) **110** A 4
Montague (MI.) **55** E 5
Montague (MT.) **86** C 2
Montague (TX.) **74** D 1
Montague Island (AL.) **116** B 2
Montana (AK.) **116** B 1
Montana (East) **86–87**
Montana (West) **92** B 3
Montana City (MT.) **86** B 3
Montauk (N.Y.) **35** K 2
Monte Clare (S.C.) **41** F 2
Monte Vista (CO.) **94** D 4
Montello (NV.) **105** G 1
Montello (WI.) **59** F 3
Monterey (CA.) **111** F 3
Monterey (TN.) **51** E 4
Monterey (VA.) **36** E 3
Monterey Bay **111** F 3–4
Montesano (WA.) **114** B 2
Montevallo (AL.) **46** C 4
Montevideo (MN.) **61** F 5
Monteview (ID.) **91** G 3
Montezuma (IA.) **63** F 4
Montezuma (KS.) **78** C 4
Montezuma Castle National Monument **100** E 2
Montgomery (AL.) **46** D 4
Montgomery (MN.) **61** F 3
Montgomery (TX.) **75** F 4
Montgomery City (MO.) **65** F 2–3
Montgomery Creek (CA.) **110** B 3
Monticello (AR.) **67** E 4
Monticello (FL.) **44** A 5
Monticello (GA.) **42** C 4
Monticello (IA.) **63** G 3
Monticello (IL.) **56** C 3
Monticello (IN.) **52** C 2
Monticello (KY.) **51** F 4
Monticello (MO.) **65** F 1
Monticello (MS.) **49** E 4
Monticello (N.M.) **98** C 3
Monticello (N.Y.) **33** F 4
Monticello (UT.) **103** E 1
Monticello (WI.) **59** G 3
Montmagny (Can.) **28** B 5
Montour (ID.) **90** C 3
Montour Falls (N.Y.) **32** D 3
Montpelier (CA.) **111** E 2
Montpelier (ID.) **91** H 4
Montpelier (MS.) **48** C 2
Montpelier (VT.) **30** D 1
Montrose (AR.) **67** E 4
Montrose (CO.) **94** B 3
Montrose (MS.) **49** D 3
Montrose (PA.) **35** F 2
Montrose (S.D.) **83** H 4
Montross (VA.) **37** H 3
Monument (OR.) **113** F 2
Monument Peak (CO.) **94** C 2
Monument Peak (ID.) **90–91** E 4
Monument Valley **103** E 1
Moody (TX.) **74** D 3
Moon Lake **110** A 2
Moon Reservoir **113** F 3
Moorcroft (WY.) **93** H 1
Moore (ID.) **91** F 3
Moore (MT.) **86** D 3
Moore (OK.) **77** F 2
Moore (TX.) **70** D 1
Moore Haven (FL.) **45** E 3
Moorefield (W.V.) **37** F 2
Mooreland (OK.) **76** D 1
Mooresville (IN.) **52** C 3
Mooresville (N.C.) **38** D 3
Moorhead (MN.) **60** D 6
Moorhead (MT.) **87** H 4
Moose (WY.) **92** B 2
Moose Lake (MN.) **60** D 2
Moose Pass (AL.) **116** B 1
Moose River (ME.) **28** C 5
Moosehead Lake **28** C 4
Mooselookmeguntic Lake **28** D 5
Mora (MN.) **61** E 3
Mora (N.M.) **96** E 2–3
Morales (TX.) **71** F 1
Moran (KS.) **79** H 4
Moran (MI.) **54** B 3
Moran (TX.) **74** B 2
Moran (WY.) **92** B 2
Moravia (IA.) **63** F 5
Moravia (N.Y.) **32** D 3
Morden (N.D.) **85** H 1
Moreau River **82** C 2
Morehead (KY.) **51** G 2

Moreland (GA.) **42** C 5
Moreland (KY.) **51** E 3
Morenci (AZ.) **101** G 3
Morenci (MI.) **55** G 3
Morey Peak **105** E 4
Morgan (GA.) **43** E 5
Morgan (MN.) **61** F 4
Morgan (MT.) **87** F 1
Morgan (UT.) **102** A 3
Morgan City (AL.) **46** B 4
Morgan City (LA.) **68** D 4
Morgan Hill (CA.) **111** E 3
Morgan Lake **96** B 2
Morgan Mill (TX.) **74** C 2
Morgan, Mount **108** D 2
Morganfield (KY.) **50** C 3
Morganton (N.C.) **38** C 3
Morgantown (KY.) **50** D 3
Morgantown (W.V.) **36** E 2
Moriah, Mount **105** G 3
Moriarty (N.M.) **96** D 3
Morland (KS.) **78** C 2
Morley (MI.) **55** E 4
Morley (MO.) **65** H 4
Mormon Lake **100–101** E 2
Mormon Mountains
  109 H 2
Mormon Reservoir **90** E 3
Moro (OR.) **112** E 1
Morongo Indian
  Reservation **107** F 4
Moroni (CO.) **102** C 3
Morovis (P.R.) **124** B 2
Morrill (NE.) **80** A 3
Morrilton (AR.) **66** D 2
Morris (IL.) **56** B 3
Morris (MN.) **61** E 5
Morris (N.D.) **85** J 1
Morrison (IL.) **56** B 5
Morrisonville (IL.) **57** D 4
Morristown (AZ.) **100** D 3
Morristown (N.J.) **35** G 3
Morristown (N.Y.)
  32–33 E 1
Morristown (SD.) **82** D 2
Morristown (TN.) **51** G 4
Morro Bay (CA.) **106** B 2
Morrow (LA.) **68** C 3
Morse (TX.) **76** B 1
Morton (IL.) **56** C 4
Morton (MN.) **61** F 4
Morton (MS.) **48** D 3
Morton (TX.) **99** H 3
Morton (WA.) **114** C 3
Morven (GA.) **43** F 4
Morzhovel **118** C 3
Mosby (MT.) **87** F 3
Moscow (ID.) **115** HJ 3
Moscow (KS.) **78** B 4
Moselle (MS.) **49** E 3
Moses Lake (WA.) **115** F 2
Moses Lake (WA.) **115** F 2
Moses Point (AL.) **120** C 3
Mosher (SD.) **82** E 4
Mosinee (WI.) **59** E 3
Mosquero (N.M.) **97** F 3
Mosquito Creek Lake
  53 J 1
Moss Point (MS.) **49** F 2
Motley (MN.) **61** D 4
Motoursville (PA.) **34** E 2
Mott (ND.) **84** D 4
Moulton (AL.) **46** B 5
Moulton (IA.) **63** F 5
Moulton Heights (AL.)
  46 B 4

Moultrie (GA.) **43** E 4
Moultrie, Lake **41** E 3
Mound City (IL.) **57** F 4
Mound City (KS.) **79** J 3
Mound City (MO.) **64** B 1
Mound City (SD.) **83** EF 2
Mound City Group
  National Monument
  53 G 3
Moundridge (KS.) **79** F 3
Mounds (OK.) **77** G 2
Mounds (UT.) **102** C 2
Moundsville (W.V.) **36** D 2
Moundville (AL.) **46** CD 5
Mount Adal **117** DE 2
Mount Adams **114** D 3
Mount Airy (N.C.) **38** D 2
Mount Aix **114** D 3
Mount Antero **94** D 3
Mount Ascutney **30** D 2
Mount Ayr (IA.) **62** D 5
Mount Baker **114** D 1
Mount Bangs **103** F 5
Mount Bendeleben **120** C 2
Mount Blackburn (AL.)
  116 C 1
Mount Blackmore **86** BC 4
Mount Bona (AL.) **116** C 1
Mount Bonaparte **115** F 1
Mount Brown **86** B 1
Mount Cabot **28** D 6
Mount Callaghan **105** E 3
Mount Calm (TX.) **75** E 3
Mount Carmel (IL.) **57** E 2
Mount Carmel (UT.)
  103 E 4
Mount Carroll– (IL.) **56** A 4
Mount Chiginagak **119** D 2
Mount Churchill **116** C 1
Mount Clemens (MI.)
  55 F 1
Mount Cleveland **89** G 1
Mount Constance **114** B 2
Mount Cowen **86** C 4
Mount Crillon **117** D 2
Mount Crosby **92** C 2
Mount Curwood **58** C 2
Mount Davis **34** B 4
Mount Dellenbaugh
  103 F 5
Mount Denison (AL.)
  119 E 2
Mount Desert Island **29** D 3
Mount Devils Paw **117** E 2
Mount Doonerak (AL.)
  121 EF 2
Mount Dora (N.M.) **97** G 2
Mount Edith **86** B 3
Mount Elbert **94** D 2
Mount Eldridge **121** G 3
Mount Enterprise (TX.)
  75 G 3
Mount Evans **94** E 2
Mount Fairweather (AL.)
  117 D 2
Mount Foraker (AL.)
  116 A 1
Mount Foster (AL.) **117** D 2
Mount Gilead (OH.) **53** G 2
Mount Graham **101** G 4
Mount Grant **104** C 4
Mount Grayback **119** E 2
Mount Greenough **121** G 2
Mount Greylock **30** C 3
Mount Gunnison **94** C 3
Mount Haggin **89** G 3

Mount Hamilton (AK.)
  119 D 1
Mount Hamilton (NV.)
  105 F 3
Mount Hancock **92** B 1
Mount Harper (AL.)
  121 G 3
Mount Harvard **94** D 3
Mount Hayes (AL.) **121** F 3
Mount Healy **121** E 3
Mount Holly Springs (PA.)
  34 D 3
Mount Holmes **92** B 1
Mount Hood **112** D 1
Mount Hope (KS.) **79** F 4
Mount Hope (W.V.) **36** C 4
Mount Horeb (WI.) **59** FG 3
Mount Ida (AR.) **66** C 3
Mount Inyo **109** E 3
Mount Irish **109** G 2
Mount Isto **121** G 2
Mount Jefferson (ID.)
  91 H 2
Mount Jefferson (NV.)
  105 E 4
Mount Jefferson (OR.)
  112 D 2
Mount Jewett (PA.) **34** C 2
Mount Katahdin **28** C 3
Mount Katmai (AL.) **119** E 2
Mount Kennedy **117** D 1
Mount Kimball (AL.)
  121 G 3
Mount Kovgarok **120** B 2
Mount Leidy **92** B 2
Mount Lemmon **101** F 4
Mount Lewis **105** E 2
Mount Livermore **72** D 3
Mount Logan (AL.) **116** C 1
Mount Logan (WA.)
  114 E 1
Mount Lola **110** C 2
Mount Lucania (AL.)
  116–117 CD 1
Mount Mansfield **30** CD 1
Mount Marcus Baker (AL.)
  116 B 1
Mount Marcy **33** F 1
Mount Marvine **103** D 3
Mount McDougall **92** B 3
Mount McGuire **89** F 4
Mount McKinley (AL.)
  116 A 1
Mount McLoughlin **112** C 4
Mount Michelson (AL.)
  121 G 2
Mount Mitchell **51** H 5
Mount Montgomery (NV.)
  108 D 2
Mount Morgan **108** D 2
Mount Moriah **105** G 3
Mount Muir **116** B 1
Mount Murray **117** F 1
Mount Nebo **102** C 3
Mount Nesselrode **117** E 2
Mount Ogden **117** E 2
Mount Olive (MS.) **49** E 3
Mount Olivet (KY.) **51** G 2
Mount Olympus **114** B 2
Mount Orab (OH.) **53** F 3
Mount Ouray **94** D 3
Mount Pattullo (AL.)
  117 E 2
Mount Peale **103** D 1
Mount Pennell **103** E 2
Mount Perkins **100** B 1

Mount Pinos **106** C 3
Mount Pleasant (IA.) **63** G 5
Mount Pleasant (MI.)
  55 E 3
Mount Pleasant (PA.)
  34 B 3
Mount Pleasant (S.C.)
  41 F 4
Mount Pleasant (TN.)
  50 C 5
Mount Pleasant (TX.)
  75 G 1
Mount Pleasant (UT.)
  102 C 3
Mount Pleasant (WA.)
  114 B 1–2
Mount Pulaski (IL.) **56** C 4
Mount Rainier **114** D 3
Mount Rainier National
  Park **114** D 3
Mount Ratz (AL.) **117** E 2
Mount Ritter **111** E 1
Mount Rogers **36** C 5
Mount Rushmore **82** B 4
Mount Rushmore National
  Memorial (S.D.) **82** B 4
Mount Russel **119** E 1
Mount Saint Elias (AL.)
  116 C 1
Mount Saint Helens
  114 C 3
Mount Saint Nicholas
  89 G 1
Mount San Antonio
  107 E 3
Mount Sanford (AL.)
  116 C 1
Mount Scott (OK.) **76** E 3
Mount Scott (OR.)
  112 CD 4
Mount Sedgewick **96** B 3
Mount Shasta **110** A 4
Mount Shasta (CA.)
  110 A 4
Mount Spokane **115** H 2
Mount Steele **93** F 4
Mount Steller **115** F 2
Mount Sterling (IL.) **56** D 5
Mount Sterling (KY.)
  51 G 2
Mount Sterling (OH.)
  53 F 3
Mount Storm (W.V.) **37** E 2
Mount Storm Lake **37** E 2
Mount Sunflower **78** AB 2
Mount Taylor **96** C 3
Mount Tazi **121** E 2
Mount Tipton **100** B 1
Mount Tobin **104** D 2
Mount Trumbull **103** F 5
Mount Turnbull **101** F 3
Mount Union (PA.) **34** D 3
Mount Veniaminof (AL.)
  119 D 2
Mount Vernon (AL.) **47** E 5
Mount Vernon (GA.) **42** D 3
Mount Vernon (IL.) **57** E 3
Mount Vernon (KY.) **51** F 3
Mount Vernon (MO.)
  64 D 4
Mount Vernon (OH.) **53** G 2
Mount Vernon (OR.)
  113 F 2
Mount Vernon (TX.) **75** F 1
Mount Vernon (WA.)
  114 C 1

Mount Vsevidof (AL.)
118 B 3
Mount Warner 113 F 4
Mount Washington 29 D 6
Mount Whitney 108 D 3
Mount Will 117 F 2
Mount Wilson (AZ.)
103 G 6
Mount Wilson (CO.)
94 BC 4
Mount Wilson (NV.)
105 G 4
Mount Withington 98 C 3
Mount Wolf (PA.) 34 E 3
Mount Wood 86 D 4
Mount Wrightson 101 F 5
Mount Zirkel 94 D 1
Mountain (WI.) 59 D 2
Mountain Brook (AL.)
46 C 4
Mountain City (GA.) 42 B 4
Mountain City (NV.)
105 F 1
Mountain City (TN.) 38 C 2
Mountain Creek (AL.)
46 D 4
Mountain Grove (MO.)
64 E 4
Mountain Home (AR.)
66 D 1
Mountain Home (ID.)
90 D 3
Mountain Home (TX.)
74 B 4
Mountain Meadows
Reservoir 110 B 2
Mountain Pass 107 G 2
Mountain Pine (AR.) 66 C 3
Mountain Point 117 E 2
Mountain View (AR.)
66 D 2
Mountain View (CA.)
111 E 4
Mountain View (MO.)
65 F 4
Mountain Village (AL.)
118–119 C 1
Mountain Wiew (WY.)
93 F 3
Mountainair (N.M.) 96 D 4
Mountainview (WY.) 92 B 4
Moxee City (WA.) 115 E 3
Moyie Spring (ID.) 88 D 1
Mud Butte (SD.) 82 C 3
Mud Lake 109 EF 2
Mud Lake Reservoir 83 G 2
Muddy Creek (UT.) 103 D 3
Muddy Creek Reservoir
95 G 4
Muddy Gap (WY.) 93 E 3
Muddy River 109 H 3
Muir, Mount 116 B 1
Muir Woods National
Monument (CA.)
111 D 4–5
Mukilteo (WA.) 114 C 2
Mulberry (TN.) 50 D 5
Mulchatna (AL.) 119 D 1
Muldoon (TX.) 71 E 1
Mule Creek (N.M.)
101 GH 3
Muleshoe (TX.) 97 H 4
Mulgrave Hills 120 C 2
Mulhall (OK.) 77 F 1
Mullan (ID.) 88 E 2
Mullen (NE.) 80 C 2

Mullens (W.V.) 36 C 4
Mullett Lake 54 C 3
Mullin (TX.) 74 C 3
Mullinville (KS.) 78 D 4
Mulvane (KS.) 79 F 4
Mumford (TX.) 75 E 4
Muncie (IN.) 52 D 2
Muncy (PA.) 34 E 2
Munday (TX.) 76 D 4
Mundelein (IL.) 56 A 3
Munford (TN.) 67 G 2
Munfordville (KY.) 50 D 3
Munising (MI.) 54 B 5
Murdo (SD.) 82 E 4
Murdock (FL.) 45 D 4
Murfreesboro (AR.) 66 C 3
Murfreesboro (N.C.) 39 G 2
Murfreesboro (TN.) 50 D 5
Murphy (ID.) 90 C 3
Murphy (OR.) 112 B 4
Murphysboro (IL.) 57 F 4
Murray (KY.) 50 B 4
Murray (UT.) 102 B 3
Murray, Lake (OK.) 77 FG 3
Murray, Lake (S.C.) 40 D 2
Murray, Mount 117 F 1
Murrayville (IL.) 57 D 5
Murtaugh (ID.) 91 E 4
Murtaugh Lake 91 E 4
Muscatine (IA.) 63 G 4
Muscoda (WI.) 59 F 4
Muskegon (MI.) 55 E 5
Muskegon Heights (MI.)
55 E 5
Muskegon River 55 E 4
Muskogee (OK.) 77 H 2
Musselshell (MT.) 87 E 3
Musselshell River 87 F 2
Mustang Island 71 E 3
Mutual (UT.) 102 C 3
Myakka City (FL.) 45 D 4
Myrtle Beach (S.C.) 41 G 3
Myrtle Creek (OR.) 112 B 3
Myrtle Point (OR.) 112 A 3
Myton (UT.) 102 B 1–2

Naalehu (HI.) 123 F 4
Nabesna 116 C 1
Nabesna River 116 C 1
Naches (WA.) 114 E 3
Naches River 114 DE 3–4
Nacogdoches (TX.) 75 G 3
Nagai Islands (AL.) 119 D 3
Nageezi (N.M.) 96 C 2
Nahma (MI.) 54 C 5
Nahunta (GA.) 43 E 2
Nakalele Point 123 E 2
Naknek (AL.) 119 D 2
Naknek Lake 119 D 2
Namakan Lake 60 B 2
Nambe Indian Reservation
96 E 3
Namiquipa (Mex.) 72 A 4
Nampa (ID.) 90 C 3
Nanakuli (HI.) 122 C 2
Nancy (KY.) 51 F 3

Nanticoke (PA.) 35 E 2
Nantucket (N.Y.) 31 F 4
Nantucket Island 31 G 4
Nantucket Sound 31 FG 4
Naomi Peak 102 A 3
Napa (CA.) 111 D 4
Napamute 119 D 1
Napavine (WA.) 114 BC 3
Naper (NE.) 81 E 2
Naperville (IL.) 56 B 3
Naples (FL.) 45 E 3
Naples (ID.) 88 D 1
Naples (N.Y.) 32 C 3
Naples (TX.) 75 G 1
Naples Park (FL.) 45 E 3
Napoleon (ND.) 85 G 4
Napoleon (OH.) 53 E 1
Napoleonville (LA.)
68–69 D 4
Naquabo (P.R.) 124 C 2
Nara Visa (N.M.) 97 G 3
Narrowsburg (N.Y.) 33 F 4
Nash (OK.) 77 EF 1
Nashua (IA.) 63 F 3
Nashua (MN.) 61 D 6
Nashua (MT.) 87 G 1
Nashua (N.H.) 29 F 6
Nashville (AR.) 66 C 4
Nashville (GA.) 43 E 4
Nashville (IL.) 57 E 5
Nashville (IN.) 52 C 3
Nashville (KS.) 78 E 4
Nashville (N.C.) 39 F 3
Nashville (TN.) 50 C 4
Nasukoin Mountain
88–89 F 1
Natanes Plateau 101 F 3
Natchez (MS.) 49 E 5
Natchitoches (LA.) 68 B 2
Nathrop (CO.) 94 D 3
National City (CA.) 107 E 5
National Monument (AL.)
121 F 2
Natoma (KS.) 78 E 2
Natrona (WY.) 93 F 2
Natrona Heights (PA.)
34 B 3
Natural Bridge (AL.) 46 B 5
Natural Bridges National
Monument 103 E 2
Naturita (CO.) 94 B 3
Natwick (WY.) 93 G 4
Naugatuck (CT.) 35 H 2
Nava (Mex.) 70 B 2
Navajo (AZ.) 101 G 1
Navajo-Hopi Indian
Reservation 103 F 2
Navajo Indian Reservation
103 F 1–2
Navajo Mountain 103 E 2
Navajo National
Monument 103 F 2
Navajo Reservoir 96 C 2
Navarro Head 110 C 5
Navarro Mills Lake 75 E 3
Navasota (TX.) 75 E 4
Navasota River 75 E 3–4
Navidad River 71 F 1
Near Islands (AL.) 116 G 1
Nebo, Mount 102 C 3
Nebraska (North) 80–81
Nebraska (South) 80–81
Nebraska City (NE.) 81 J 4
Necedah (WI.) 59 E 4
Neche (N.D.) 85 J 2
Neches (TX.) 75 F 3

Nederland (TX.) 75 G 5
Neebish Island 54 B 3
Needle Mountain 92 C 1
Needle Range 103 D 5
Needles (CA.) 107 H 3
Needmore (PA.) 34 C 4
Needmore (TX.) 97 H 4
Needmore (TX.) 99 H 3
Neely Henry Lake 46 C 4
Neelyville (MO.) 65 G 5
Neenah (WI.) 59 E 2
Negaunee (MI.) 54 B 6
Negra (N.M.) 96 E 4
Nehalem River 112 B 1
Neihart (MT.) 86 C 3
Neillsville (WI.) 59 E 4
Neilton (WA.) 114 B 2
Nekoma (N.D.) 85 H 2
Nekoosa (WI.) 59 E 4
Neligh (NE.) 81 F 2
Nelson (AZ.) 100 C 1
Nelson (NE.) 81 F 4
Nelson (NV.) 109 H 4
Nelson Island (AL.)
118 BC 1
Nelson Reservoir 87 F 1
Nemah (WA.) 114 B 3
Neodesha (KS.) 79 H 4
Neola (IA.) 62 C 4
Neola (UT.) 102 B 1–2
Neopit (WI.) 59 E 2
Neosho (MO.) 64 C 5
Neosho River 79 H 4
Nephi (UT.) 102 B 3
Neptune (N.J.) 35 G 3
Neshkan 120 A 2
Nesika Beach (OR.) 112 A 4
Nespelem (WA.) 115 G 1
Ness City (KS.) 78 C 3
Nesselrode, Mount 117 E 2
Nestoria (MI.) 58 C 2
Net Lake Indian
Reservation 60 B 3
Netcong (N.J.) 35 G 3
Nett Lake (MN.) 60 B 3
Nettleton (MS.) 48 B 2
Neuces Plains 70 C 2
Neuse River 39 G 3
Nevada 104
Nevada (IA.) 63 F 3
Nevada (MO.) 64 C 4
Nevada City (CA.) 110 C 3
New Albany (IN.) 52 C 4
New Albany (MS.) 48 B 2
New Athens (IL.) 57 E 5
New Bedford (MA.)
30–31 E 4
New Berlin (N.Y.) 33 E 3
New Bern (N.C.) 39 GH 3
New Bloomfield (PA.)
34 D 3
New Braunfels (TX.) 70 D 1
New Britain (CT.) 35 J 2
New Brunswick (N.J.)
35 G 3
New Buffalo (MI.) 55 G 5
New Canton (VA.) 37 F 4
New Castle (CO.) 94 C 2
New Castle (IN.) 52 D 3
New Castle (KY.) 51 E 2
New Castle (PA.) 34 A 2
New Castle (VA.) 36 D 4
New City (N.Y.) 33 F 4
New Creek (W.V.) 37 E 2
New Edinburg (AR.)
66 D 4

New Effington (S.D.)
83 HJ 2
New England (ND.) 84 D 4
New Florence (MO.) 65 F 3
New Franklin (MO.) 64 E 2
New Glarus (WI.) 59 G 3
New Hampshire 30–31
New Hampton (IA.) 63 F 2
New Haven (CT.) 35 J 2
New Haven (IN.) 52 E 1
New Haven (W.V.) 36 C 3
New Haven (WY.) 93 H 1
New Hogan Lake 111 D 2
New Hradec (ND.) 84 D 3
New Iberia (LA.) 68 D 3
New Jersey 35 H 7
New Kensington (PA.)
34 B 3
New Kent (VA.) 37 G 4
New Leipzig (ND.) 84 E 4
New Lexington (OH.)
53 G 3
New Lisbon (WI.) 59 F 4
New London (CT.) 35 J 2
New London (IA.) 63 G 5
New London (MN.) 61 E 5
New London (OK.) 77 F 3
New London (MO.) 65 F 2
New London (WI.) 59 E 3
New Madrid (MO.) 65 H 5
New Market (AL.) 46 B 4
New Market (VA.) 37 F 3
New Martinsville (W.V.)
36 D 2
New Meadows (ID.)
90 C 1–2
New Melones Lake 111 E 2
New Orleans (LA.) 69 F 3–4
New Paris (OH.) 52 E 3
New Philadelphia (OH.)
53 H 2
New Pine Creek (OR.)
112 E 4
New Plymouth (ID.)
90 C 2–3
New Port Richey (FL.)
44 C 5
New Prague (MN.) 61 F 3
New Raymer (CO.) 95 G 1
New Richmond (OH.)
52–53 E 4
New River 36 C 3–4
New Roads (LA.) 68 D 3
New Rochelle 35 H 3
New Rockford (ND.) 85 G 3
New Salem (ND.) 84 E 4
New Sharon (IA.) 63 F 4
New Smyrna Beach (FL.)
44 B 2
New Stuvahok (AL.)
119 D 2
New Taiton (TX.) 71 F 1
New Town (ND.) 84 D 2
New Ulm (MN.) 61 F 4
New Vienna (OH.) 53 F 3
New Waverly (TX)
75 F 4
New York (City) 35 H 3
New York (State) 33
New York Mills (MN.)
60 D 5
Newark (AR.) 67 E 2
Newark (DE.) 37 J 2
Newark (N.J.) 35 G 3
Newark (N.Y.) 32 C 2
Newark (OH.) 53 G 2
Newark Lake 105 F 3

Newark Valley (N.Y.)
32 D 3
Newaygo (MI.) 55 E 4
Newberg (OR.) 112 C 1
Newberry (FL.) 44 B 4
Newberry (MI.) 54 B 4
Newberry (S.C.) 40 D 2
Newberry Springs (CA.)
107 F 3
Newburgh (N.Y.) 33 F 4
Newburyport (MA.) 31 F 3
Newcastle (CA.) 111 D 3
Newcastle (TX.) 74 C 1
Newcastle (UT.) 103 E 5
Newcastle (WY.) 93 H 2
Newcomb (N.M.) 96 B 2
Newcomerstown (OH.)
53 H 2
Newell (SD.) 82 B 3
Newellton (LA.) 68 D 1
Newfane (VT.) 30 D 2–3
Newfoundland Mountains
102 A 5
Newhalen (WA.) 114 D 1
Newhall (CA.) 106 D 3
Newkirk (N.M.) 97 F 3
Newkirk (OK.) 77 FG 1
Newland (N.C.) 38 C 2
Newlin (TX.) 76 C 3
Newman (CA.) 111 E 3
Newman (N.M.) 98 D 4
Newman Gr (NE.) 81 G 3
Newnan (GA.) 42 C 5
Newport (AR.) 67 E 2
Newport (IN.) 52 B 3
Newport (ME.) 28 D 4
Newport (NE.) 81 E 2
Newport (N.H.) 29 E 7
Newport (OR.) 112 B 2
Newport (PA.) 34 D 3
Newport (R.I.) 30 E 4
Newport (TN.) 51 G 5
Newport (TX.) 74 C 1
Newport (VT.) 30 D 1
Newport (WA.) 115 H 1
Newport Beach (CA.)
106 DE 4
Newport News (VA.) 37 H 4
Newtok 118 C 1
Newton (GA.) 43 E 5
Newton (IA.) 63 E 4
Newton (IL.) 57 E 3
Newton (KS.) 79 E 3
Newton (MA.) 30 E 3
Newton (MS.) 48 D 3
Newton (N.C.) 38 C 3
Newton (N.J.) 35 G 2
Newton (TX.) 75 H 4
Newton (UT.) 102 A 4
Newton Falls (N.Y.) 33 E 1
Newton Grove (N.C.) 39 F 3
Newville (LA.) 110 C 4
Newville (PA.) 34 D 3
Nez Perce Indian
Reservation 88 D 3
Nezperce (ID.) 88 D 3
Niagara Falls (N.Y.)
32 AB 2
Niarada (MT.) 89 F 2
Nicatous Lake 28 C 3
Niceville (FL.) 47 F 4
Nicholasville (KY.) 51 F 3
Nichols (S.C.) 41 F 2
Nicholson (MS.) 49 F 3
Nickel Creek (TX.) 72 D 2
Nickerson (KS.) 79 E 3

Nicodemus (KS.) 78 D 2
Niihau 122 AB 2
Nikolski (AL.) 118 B 3
Niland (CA.) 107 G 4
Niles (MI.) 55 G 5
Nimrod Lake 66 C 3
Ninaview (CO.) 95 G 4
Niobrara (NE.) 81 F 2
Niobrara River 81 E 2
Niordenskiold River
117 D 1
Nipton (CA.) 107 G 2
Nisland (SD.) 82 B 3
Nisling River 117 D 1
Nisswa (MN.) 60 D 4
Nisutlin River 117 E 1
Nixon (TX.) 71 E 1
Noatak (AL.) 120 C 2
Noatak National Preserve
(AL.) 120 D 2
Noatak R. (AL.) 120 D 2
Noblesville (IN.) 52 C 2
Nocona (TX.) 77 F 4
Node (WY.) 93 H 3
Noelke (TX.) 73 H 2
Nohili Point 88 B 2
Nohly (MT.) 87 J 2
Nolan 121 E 2
Nolanville (TX.) 74 D 3
Nolin Lake 50 D 3
Noma (FL.) 47 F 3
Nomans Land 31 F 4
Nome (AL.) 120 B 3
Nondalton 119 D 1–2
Nonuianuk Lake 119 D 2
Noonan (ND.) 84 C 2
Noorvik (AL.) 120 C 2
Nora Springs (IA.) 63 F 2
Norcatur (KS.) 78 C 2
Norden (NE.) 80 D 2
Nordman (WA.) 115 H 1
Norfolk (CO.) 95 E 1
Norfolk (NE.) 81 G 2
Norfolk (VA.) 37 H 5
Norfork (AR.) 66 D 1
Norfork Lake 66 D 1
Norias (TX.) 71 E 4
Norlina (N.C.) 39 F 2
Normal (AL.) 46 B 4
Normal (IL.) 56 C 3
Norman (AR.) 66 C 3
Norman (NE.) 81 F 4
Norman (OK.) 77 F 2
Norman Island 124 D 2
Norman, Lake 38 C 3
Normangee (TX.) 75 E 3
Norris (MT.) 86 B 4
Norris City (IL.) 57 F 3
Norris Lake 51 G 4
Norristown (PA.) 35 F 3
Norsho Junction (MN.)
60 C 1
North (S.C.) 40 D 3
North Adams (MA.) 30 C 3
North Augusta (S.C.)
40 D 3
North Battle Mountain
(NV.) 105 E 2
North Beach Peninsula
114 A 3
North Bend (NE.) 81 H 3
North Bend (OR.) 112 A 3
North Bonneville (WA.)
114 C 4
North Branch (MN.)
61 E 2

North Branch (MO/W.V.)
37 E 2
North Canadian River
76–77 E 2
North Canton (OH.) 53 H 2
North Carolina 38–39
North Cascades National
Park 114 D 1
North Channel (Can.)
54 B 2
North Charleston (S.C.)
41 F 4
North Chicago (IL.) 56 A 2
North College Hill (OH.)
52 E 3
North Creek (N.Y.) 33 G 2
North Dakota 84–85
North Dam 115 FG 2
North East (MD.) 37 J 2
North East (PA.) 34 A 1
North English (IA.) 63 FG 4
North Fork (AK.) 121 E 3
North Fork (ID.) 89 F 4
North Fork (KS.) 78 D 2
North Fork (NV.) 105 F 1
North Fork (OK./TX.)
76 D 2
North Fork (S.C.) 40 D 3
North Fort (CO.) 94–95 E 2
North Fort Myers (FL.)
45 E 3
North Fox Island 54 C 4
North Hero (VT.) 30 C 1
North Highlands (CA.)
111 D 3
North Island (S.C.) 41 F 3
North Judson (IN.) 52 C 1
North La Veta Pass 95 E 4
North Las Vegas (NV.)
109 G 3
North Little Rock (AR.)
66 D 3
North Loon Mountain
88 E 4
North Loup River 80–81 E 3
North Mamm Peak 94 C 2
North Manchester (IN.)
52 D 2
North Manitou Island
54 C 5
North Miami Beach (FL.)
45 F 2
North Pack (IL.) 56 A 4
North Peak 101 E 2
North Platte (NE.) 80 D 3
North Platte River 80 B 3
North Point 54 C 2
North Pole (AK.) 121 F 3
North Powder (OR.)
113 GH 1
North Richland Hills (TX.)
74 D 2
North Rim (AZ.) 103 F 4
North Roby (TX.) 73 H 1
North Salt Lake (UT.)
102 B 3
North Schell Peak 105 G 3
North Shoshone Peak
104 D 3
North Slope (AL.)
120–121 DE 1
North Stratford (VT.) 30 E 1
North Syracuse (N.Y.)
32 D 2
North Umpqua River
112 C 3

North Zulch (TX.) **75** E 4
Northampton (MA.) **30** D 3
Northeast Cape (AL.)
  120 B 3
Northern Cheyenne Indian
  Reservation **87** G 4
Northern Light Lake **58** A 4
Northfield (MA.) **30** D 3
Northfield (MN.) **61** F 3
Northfield (TX.) **76** C 3
Northfield (VT.) **30** D 1
Northgate (ND.) **84** D 2
Northland (MI.) **54** B 6
Northome (MN.) **60** C 4
Northport (AL.) **46** C 5
Northport (MI.) **54** C 4
Northport (WA.) **115** H 1
Northville (N.Y.) **33** F 2
Northville (S.D.) **83** G 2
Northway Junction (AL.)
  121 G 3
Northwood (IA.) **63** E 2
Northwood (N.D.) **85** J 3
Northwood (N.H.) **29** E 6
Norton (KS.) **78** D 2
Norton (W.V.) **36** D 3
Norton Bay (AL.) **120** C 3
Norton Reservoir **78** D 2
Norton Sound (AL.)
  120 C 3
Nortonville (KS.) **79** H 2
Nortonville (KY.) **50** C 3
Nortonville (N.D.) **85** H 4
Nortport (NE.) **80** A 3
Norwalk (CT.) **35** H 2
Norwalk (OH.) **53** G 1
Norway (KS.) **79** F 2
Norway (MI.) **54** C 6
Norwich (CT.) **35** J 2
Norwich (KS.) **79** F 4
Norwich (N.Y.) **32** E 3
Norwood (CO.) **94** B 3
Norwood (N.C.) **38** D 3
Norwood (N.Y.) **33** F 1
Norwood (OH.) **52** E 3
Notch Peak **102** C 5
Notrees (TX.) **73** F 2
Nottoway River **37** G 5
Novato (CA.) **111** D 4
Novice (TX.) **74** B 2
Nowata (KS.) **77** H 1
Nowitna (AL.) **121** D 3
Nowlin (SD.) **82** D 3
Nowood River **93** E 1–2
Noxapater (MS.) **48** C 2–3
Noxon Reservoir **88** E 2
Nubieber (CA.) **110** A 3
Nucla (CO.) **94** B 3
Nueces River **70** D 2
Nueva Rosita (Mex.) **70** A 3
Nuevo Año, Point **111** E 4
Nuevo Laredo (Mex.)
  70 C 3
Nuiqsut (AL.) **121** E 1
Nulato (AL.) **120** C 3
Nunda (S.D.) **83** J 3
Nunivak Island (AL.)
  118 B 2
Nunn (CO.) **95** F 1
Nunnelly (TN.) **50** C 5
Nunyamo (AL.) **120** A 2
Nursery (TX.) **71** E 2
Nushagak (AL.) **119** D 2
Nushagak Bay **119** D 2
Nushagak Peninsula
  119 D 2

Nutrioso (AZ.) **101** G 2
Nutt (N.M.) **98** C 4
Nyac **118–119** CD 1
Nyassa (OR.) **113** H 3
Nys Dezhneva (AL.)
  120 B 2

O

O' The Cherokees, Lake
  77 J 1
O' The Pines, Lake **75** G 2
Oahe Dam **82** E 3
Oahe, Lake **82–83** E 2
Oahu **122** CD 2
Oak City (UT.) **102** C 4
Oak Creek (CO.) **94** D 1
Oak Creek Reservoir **73** H 1
Oak Grove (LA.) **68** D 1
Oak Harbor (WA.) **114** C 1
Oak Hill (FL.) **44** C 2
Oak Hill (OH.) **53** G 4
Oak Hill (TN.) **50** D 4
Oak Hill (TX.) **74** D 4
Oak Hill (W.V.) **36** C 3–4
Oak Lawn (IL.) **56** B 2–3
Oak Park Reservoir **102** B 1
Oak Ridge (TN.) **51** F 4
Oakdale (CA.) **111** E 2
Oakdale (LA.) **68** C 3
Oakdale (NE.) **81** F 2
Oakes (N.D.) **85** H 4
Oakesdale (WA.) **115** H 2
Oakhurst (CA.) **111** E 1
Oakland (CA.) **111** E 4
Oakland (IA.) **62** C 4
Oakland (IL.) **56** D 2
Oakland (MD.) **36–37** E 2
Oakland (ME.) **28** D 4
Oakland (MS.) **48** B 3
Oakland (NE.) **81** H 3
Oakland (OR.) **112** B 3
Oakland City (IN.) **52** B 4
Oakland Park (FL.) **45** E 2
Oakley (ID.) **91** F 4
Oakley (KS.) **78** BC 2
Oakley (MI.) **55** E 3
Oakridge (OR.) **112** C 3
Oaktown (IN.) **52** B 4
Oakville (Can.) **32** A 2
Oakwood (TX.) **75** E 3
Oasis (CA.) **109** E 2
Oasis (NV.) **105** G 1
Obar (N.M.) **97** G 3
Oberlin (KS.) **78** C 2
Oberlin (LA.) **68** C 3
Oberlin (OH.) **53** G 1
Oberon (ND.) **85** G 3
Obion (TN.) **50** A 4
O'Brien (OR.) **112** B 4
O'Brien (TX.) **76** D 4
Observation Peak **110** B 2
Ocala (FL.) **44** C 2
Ocate (N.M.) **97** EF 2
Ocean City (MD.) **37** J 3
Ocean City (N.J.) **35** G 4
Ocean Lake **92** D 2
Ocean Park (WA.) **114** A 3

Ocean Springs (MS.) **49** F 2
Oceana (W.V.) **36** C 4
Oceano (CA.) **106** B 2
Oceanside (CA.) **107** E 4
Ochlockonee River **43** F 5
Ochoa (TX.) **72** D 4
Ocilla (GA.) **43** E 4
Ocmulgee River **42** CD 4
Oconee River **42–43** D 3
Oconto (NE.) **80** E 3
Oconto (WI.) **59** E 1
Ocracoke (N.C.) **39** J 3
Ocracoke Island **39** J 3
Odell (NE.) **81** H 4
Odell (TX.) **76** D 3
Odell Lake **112** D 3
Odem (TX.) **71** E 3
Odessa (TX.) **73** F 2
Odessa (WA.) **115** G 2
Odgers Ranch Indian
  Reservation **105** FG 2
O'Donnell (TX.) **73** G 1
Oelrichs (SD.) **82** B 4
Oelwein (IA.) **63** G 3
Offerle (KS.) **78** D 4
Ogala (SD.) **82** C 4
Ogallah (KS.) **78** D 3
Ogallala (NE.) **80** C 3
Ogden (KS.) **79** G 2
Ogden (UT.) **102** A 3
Ogden, Mount **117** E 2
Ogdensburg (N.Y.) **33** E 1
Ogeechee River **43** D 2
Ogg (TX.) **76** B 3
Ogilby (CA.) **107** H 5
Ogilvie (MN.) **61** E 3
Oglethorpe (GA.) **43** D 5
Oguossoc (ME.) **28** D 5
Ohio (North) **52–53**
Ohio (South) **52–53**
Ohio City (OH.) **52** E 2
Ohio River **50** B 2
Oil City (LA.) **68** B 1
Oil City (PA.) **34** B 2
Oil City (TX.) **76** B 2
Oildale (CA.) **106** CD 2
Oilmont (MT.) **86** B 1
Oilton (OK.) **77** G 1
Ojai (CA.) **106** C 3
Ojibwa (WI.) **58** D 5
Ojinaga (Mex.) **72** D 4
Okahumpka (FL.) **44** C 3
Okanogan (WA.) **115** F 1
Okanogan River **115** F 1
Okarche (OK.) **77** F 2
Okeechobee (FL.) **45** D 2
Okeechobee, Lake **45** DE 2
Okeene (OK.) **77** E 1
Okefenokee Swamp **43** F 3
Okemah (OK.) **77** G 2
Oklahoma **76–77**
Oklahoma City (OK.) **77** F 2
Oklee (MN.) **60** C 5
Okmulgee (OK.) **77** G 2
Okolona (KY.) **50** E 2
Okolona (MS.) **48** BC 2
Ola (ID.) **90** C 2
Ola Grande, Punta
  124 BC 3
Olancha (CA.) **109** E 3
Olancha Peak **108** D 3
Olathe (CO.) **94** C 3
Olathe (KS.) **79** J 3
Old Crow (AL.) **121** G 2
Old Dominion Mountain
  115 H 1

Old Forge (N.Y.) **33** F 2
Old Fort (N.C.) **51** H 5
Old Glory (TX.) **76** CD 4
Old Harbar (AL.) **119** E 2
Old Hickory Lake **50** D 4
Old Mines (MO.) **65** G 3
Old Orchard Beach (ME.)
  29 E 5
Old Speck Mountain **28** D 5
Old Town (FL.) **44** B 5
Oldham (S.D.) **83** H 3
Olean (N.Y.) **32** B 3
Olene (OR.) **112** D 4
Olex (OR.) **113** E 1
Olive (MT.) **87** H 4
Olive Branch (MS.) **48** B 3
Olive Hill (KY.) **51** G 2
Olivehurst (CA.) **110** C 3
Oliver Springs (TN.) **51** F 4
Olivet (S.D.) **83** H 4
Olivia (MN.) **61** F 4
Olney (IL.) **57** E 3
Olney (MT.) **89** F 1
Olney (TX.) **74** C 1
Olowalu (HI.) **123** E 3
Olpe (KS.) **79** G 3
Olsonville (SD.) **82** E 4
Olton (TX.) **97** H 4
Olustee (FL.) **44** A 4
Olustee (OK.) **76** D 3
Olympia (WA.) **114** BC 2
Olympic Mountains
  114 B 2
Olympic National Park
  114 B 2
Olympus, Mount **114** B 2
Omaha (NE.) **81** H 3
Omaha Indian Reservation
  81 H 2
Omak (WA.) **115** F 1
Omak Lake **115** F 1
Omak Mountain **115** F 1
Omemee (ND.) **85** F 2
Omo Ranch (CA.) **111** D 2
Omro (WI.) **59** E 2
Onaga (NE.) **79** G 2
Onaka (SD.) **83** F 2
Onamia (MN.) **61** D 3
Onancock (VA.) **37** J 4
Onarga (IL.) **56** C 2
Onava (N.M.) **97** E 3
Onawa (IA.) **62** B 3
Onaway (MI.) **54** C 3
O'Neals (CA.) **111** E 1
Oneida (IL.) **56** B 5
Oneida (N.Y.) **32** E 2
Oneida (TN.) **51** F 4
Oneida Indian Reservation
  59 E 2
Oneida Lake **32** DE 2
O'Neill (NE.) **81** F 2
Oneill (MT.) **87** H 3
Oneonta (AL.) **46** C 4
Oneonta (N.Y.) **33** E 3
Onida (SD.) **83** EF 3
Ono (CA.) **110** B 4
Onondaga Indian
  Reservation **32** D 3
Onslow Bay **39** G 4
Ontario (CA.) **107** E 3
Ontario (OR.) **113** H 2
Ontario, Lake **32** BC 2
Ontonagon (MI.) **58** C 3
Onyx (CA.) **106** D 2
Oologah Lake **77** H 1
Oostburg (WI.) **59** F 1

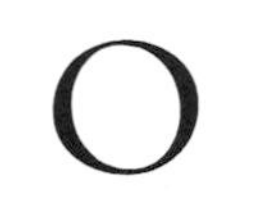

Opal (SD.) **82** C 3
Opelika (AL.) **47** D 3
Opelousas (LA.) **68** C 3
Opheim (MT.) **87** G 1
Ophir (AL.) **120** C 3
Ophir (OR.) **112** A 4
Opihikao (HI.) **123** G 4
Opp (AL.) **47** E 4
Opportunity (MT.) **86** A 3
Opportunity (WA.) **115** H 2
Optima (OK.) **76** B 1
Optimo (N.M.) **97** F 3
Oracle (AZ.) **101** F 4
Oracle Junction (AZ.)
　101 EF 4
Oraibi (AZ.) **103** G 2
Orange (TX.) **75** H 4
Orange (VA.) **37** F 3
Orange City (FL.) **44** C 3
Orange City (IA.) **62** B 2
Orange Grove (TX.) **70** D 3
Orange Lake (FL.) **44** B 4
Orange Love (CA.) **111** F 1
Orange Park (FL.) **44** A 3
Orangeburg (S.C.) **41** E 3
Orangville (UT.) **102** C 3
Orbisonia (PA.) **34** D 3
Orcas Island **114** C 1
Orchard (ID.) **90** C 3
Orchard (NE.) **81** F 2
Orchard City (CO.) **94** B 3
Orchard Homes (MT.)
　89 F 3
Orchard Valley (WY.)
　93 H 4
Orcutt (CA.) **106** B 3
Ord (NE.) **81** EF 3
Ord Mountain **107** F 3
Ordway (CO.) **95** G 3
Ore City (TX.) **75** G 2
Oreana (IL.) **56** D 4
Oreana (NV.) **104** C 2
Oregon **113**
Oregon (IL.) **56** A 4
Oregon (MO.) **64** B 1–2
Oregon (OH.) **53** F 1
Oregon Butte **115** H 3
Oregon Caves National
　Monument **112** B 4
Oregon City (OR.) **112** C 1
Orem (UT.) **102** B 3
Organ (TX.) **98** D 4
Organ Peak **98** D 4
Organ Pipe Cactus
　National Monument
　100 D 4
Orick (CA.) **110** A 6
Orient (IA.) **62** D 4
Orient (SD.) **83** F 3
Orient (WA.) **115** G 1
Orienta (OK.) **76** E 1
Oriental (N.C.) **39** H 3
Orillia (Can.) **32** A 1
Orin (WY.) **93** G 3
Orion (IL.) **56** B 5
Oriskany (N.Y.) **33** E 2
Orla (TX.) **72** E 2
Orland (CA.) **110** C 4
Orlando (FL.) **44** C 3
Orlando (OK.) **77** F 1
Orleans (CA.) **110** A 5
Orleans (MA.) **31** G 4
Orleans (NE.) **81** E 4
Orleans (VT.) **30** D 1
Ormond Beach (FL.)
　44 B 2–3

Ormond-by-the-Sea (FL.)
　44 B 2–3
Oro Grande (CA.) **107** E 3
Orofino (ID.) **88** D 3
Orogrande (N.M.) **98** D 4
Orono (ME.) **28** D 3
Orovada (NV.) **104** D 1
Oroville (CA.) **110** C 3
Oroville (WA.) **115** F 1
Oroville Dam **110** C 3
Oroville, Lake **110** C 3
Orpha (WY.) **93** G 3
Orrin (ND.) **85** F 2
Orting (WA.) **114** C 2
Ortonville (MN.) **61** E 6
Orwell (OH.) **53** J 1
Osage (IA.) **63** F 2
Osage (WY.) **93** H 2
Osage City (KS.) **79** H 3
Osage Indian Reservation
　77 G 1
Osage River **64** E 3
Osakis (MN.) **61** E 5
Osakis, Lake **61** E 5
Osawatomie (KS.) **79** H 3
Osborne (KS.) **78** E 2
Oscarville **119** C 1
Osceola (AR.) **67** F 2
Osceola (IA.) **62** E 4
Osceola (MO.) **64** D 3
Osceola (NE.) **81** G 3
Osceola (S.D.) **83** H 3
Oscoda (MI.) **55** D 2
Oscura (N.M.) **98** DE 3
Osgood (IN.) **52** D 3
Oshawa (Can.) **32** A 2
Oshkosh (NE.) **80** B 3
Oshkosh (WI.) **59** E 2
Oshoto (WY.) **93** G 1
Oskaloosa (IA.) **63** F 4
Oskaloosa (MO.) **79** H 2
Osmond (NE.) **81** G 2
Osoyoos (Can.) **115** F 1
Ossabaw Island **43** E 1–2
Osseo (WI.) **59** E 5
Ossineke (MI.) **54** D 2
Ossining (N.Y.) **33** G 4
Ossipee (N.H.) **29** E 6
Ostrova Diomida (AL.)
　120 B 2
O'Sullivan Dam **115** F 3
Oswego (KS.) **79** H 4
Oswego (MT.) **87** H 1
Oswego (N.Y.) **32** D 2
Osyka (MS.) **49** E 4
Othello (WA.) **115** F 3
Otis (CO.) **95** H 1
Otis (KS.) **78** E 3
Otoe (NE.) **81** H 4
Otsego (MI.) **55** F 4
Otsego Lake **33** F 3
Ottawa (IL.) **56** B 3
Ottawa (KS.) **79** H 3
Ottawa (OH.) **53** EF 1
Otter (MT.) **87** G 4
Otter Creek (FL.) **44** B 4
Otter Creek Reservoir
　103 D 3
Otter Lake (MI.) **55** E 2
Otter Tail Lake **60–61** D 5
Ottertail (MN.) **60** D 5
Ottumwa (IA.) **63** F 4
Ottumwa (SD.) **82** D 3
Ouachita Mountains
　66 AB 3
Ouachita River **68** C 1

Ouinhagak (AL.) **119** C 2
Ouray (CO.) **94** C 3
Ouray (UT.) **102** B 1
Ouray, Mount **94** D 3
Outer Island **58** B 4
Outer Santa Barbara
　Passage **106** D 4–5
Outlook (MT.) **87** J 1
Outpost Mountain **121** E 2
Ovando (MT.) **89** G 2
Overton (NE.) **81** E 4
Overton (NV.) **109** H 3
Overton (TX.) **75** F 2
Ovett (MS.) **49** E 3
Ovid (MI.) **55** E 3
Owanka (SD.) **82** C 3
Owasco Lake **32** D 3
Owasso (OK.) **77** H 1
Owatonna (MN.) **61** F 3
Owego (N.Y.) **32** D 3
Owego (TX.) **73** F 2
Owen (WI.) **59** E 4
Owens Lake **109** E 3
Owens River **108** D 2
Owensboro (KY.) **50** C 3
Owensville (MO.) **65** F 3
Owenton (KY.) **51** F 2
Owingsville (KY.) **51** G 2
Owl Creek Mountains
　92 CD 2
Owosso (MI.) **55** E 3
Owyhee (NV.) **105** E 1
Owyhee, Lake **113** H 3
Owyhee Mountains
　90 C 3–4
Owyhee River **113** H 3
Oxbow (ME.) **28** B 3
Oxbow Dam **113** HJ 2
Oxford (KS.) **79** F 4
Oxford (MI.) **55** F 2
Oxford (MS.) **48** B 3
Oxford (N.C.) **39** F 2
Oxford (NE.) **81** E 4
Oxford (OH.) **52** E 3
Oxford (TX.) **74** C 4
Oxford (WI.) **59** F 3
Oxford Junction (IA.)
　63 H 4
Oxford Peak **91** G 4
Oxnard (CA.) **106** C 3
Oysterville (WA.) **114** A 3
Ozark (AL.) **47** E 3
Ozark (AR.) **66** F 2
Ozark (MO.) **64** D 4–5
Ozark Plateau **64** DE 4–5
Ozark Reservoir **66** BC 2
Ozarks, Lake of the **64** E 3
Ozette Lake **114** A 1
Ozona (TX.) **73** G 3

P

Paauilo (HI.) **123** F 3
Pablo (MT.) **89** F 2
Pacheco Pass **111** E 3
Pachuta (MS.) **49** D 2
Pacific (MO.) **65** G 3
Pacific City (OR.) **112** A 1

Pacific Grove (CA.)
　111 F 3–4
Pacifica (CA.) **111** E 4
Packaway Lake **59** F 3
Packwood (WA.) **114** D 3
Padre Island **71** E 3
Padre Island National
　Seashore **71** E 4
Padroni (CO.) **95** G 1
Paducah (KY.) **50** B 2
Paducah (TX.) **76** C 3
Page (AZ.) **103** F 3
Page (N.D.) **85** J 3
Page (NE.) **81** F 2
Page City (KS.) **78** B 2
Pageland (S.C.) **41** E 2
Pagoda Peak **94** C 1
Pagosa Springs (CO.)
　94 D 4
Pahala (HI.) **123** F 4
Pahoa (HI.) **123** FG 4
Pahute Mesa **109** F 2
Pahute Peak **104** B 1
Paicines (CA.) **111** F 3
Paige (TX.) **74** D 4
Pailolo Channel **123** E 2
Painesdale (MI.) **58** B 2
Painesville (OH.) **53** H 1
Paint Rock (TX.) **74** A 3
Painted Desert **103** FG 3
Painted Rock Dam **100** C 3
Paintsville (KY.) **51** H 3
Paisano (TX.) **72** E 3
Paisley (OR.) **112** E 4
Pájaros Point **124** D 2
Pala (CA.) **107** E 4
Pala Indian Reservation
　107 E 4
Palacios (TX.) **71** F 2
Palaoa Point **123** D 3
Palatka (FL.) **44** B 3
Palco (KS.) **78** D 2
Palen Dry Lake **107** G 4
Palestine (TX.) **75** F 3
Palisade (CO.) **94** B 2
Palisade (NE.) **80** C 4
Palisade (NV.) **105** E 2
Palisades (ID.) **91** H 3
Palisades (WA.) **115** F 2
Palisades Reservoir **91** H 3
Palm Bay (FL.) **44** C 2
Palm Springs (CA.) **107** F 4
Palmdale (CA.) **106** D 3
Palmdale (FL.) **45** E 3
Palmer (AK, U.S.A.)
　116 B 1
Palmer (NE.) **81** F 3
Palmer (TN.) **50** E 5
Palmer Lake (CO.) **95** F 2
Palmers (MN.) **60** D 1
Palmerton (PA.) **35** F 3
Palmyra (MO.) **65** F 2
Palmyra (PA.) **34** E 3
Palmyra (WI.) **37** F 4
Palo Flechado Pass
　96–97 E 2
Palo Pinto (TX.) **74** C 2
Palo Pinto Creek Reservoir
　74 C 2
Palo Verde (AZ.) **100** D 3
Palo Verde (CA.) **107** H 4
Palomar Mountain **107** F 4
Palomas (N.M.) **97** G 3
Palouse (WA.) **115** H 3
Pamlico Sound **39** HJ 3
Pampa (TX.) **76** C 2

Pamplin (VA.) **37** F 4
Pana (IL.) **57** D 4
Panaca (NV.) **109** H 2
Panacea (FL.) **47** F 2
Panama (OK.) **77** J 2
Panama City (FL.) **47** F 3
Panama City Beach (FL.)
  47 F 3
Panamint Range **109** E 3
Pancake Range **105** EF 4
Panguitch (UT.) **103** E 4
Panguitch Lake **103** E 4
Panhandle (TX.) **76** B 2
Paniau **122** A 2
Panola (AL.) **46** D 6
Panora (IA.) **62** D 4
Pantano (AZ.) **101** F 4
Pantego (N.C.) **39** H 3
Paola (KS.) **79** J 3
Paoli (IN.) **52** C 4
Paonia (CO.) **94** C 3
Papa (HI.) **123** F 4
Papaaloa (HI.) **123** F 4
Papago Indian Reservation
  100 DE 4
Papaikou (HI.) **123** F 4
Papalote (TX.) **71** E 2
Papillon (NE.) **81** H 3
Parade (SD.) **82** D 2
Paradise (CA.) **110** C 3
Paradise (KS.) **78** D 2
Paradise (MI.) **54** B 4
Paradise (MT.) **88** EF 2
Paradise (TX.) **74** D 1
Paradise Beach (FL.) **47** F 5
Paradise Valley (AZ.)
  100 E 3
Paradise Valley (NV.)
  104 D 1
Paragonah (UT.) **103** E 4
Paragould (AR.) **67** F 1
Paramore Island **37** J 4
Parguera (P.R.) **124** AB 3
Paria Plateau **103** F 3–4
Paris (AR.) **66** C 2
Paris (ID.) **91** H 4
Paris (IL.) **56** D 2
Paris (KY.) **51** F 2
Paris (MO.) **65** F 2
Paris (TN.) **50** B 4
Paris (TX.) **75** F 1
Park City (KS.) **79** F 4
Park City (KY.) **50** E 3
Park City (MT.) **86** E 4
Park Falls (WI.) **58** D 4
Park Grove (MT.) **87** G 1
Park Range **94** D 1–2
Park Rapids (MN.) **60** D 4–5
Park River (N.D.) **85** J 2
Park Valley (UT.) **102** A 5
Park View (N.M.) **96** D 2
Parkdale (CO.) **95** E 3
Parkdale (OR.) **112** D 1
Parker (AZ.) **100** B 2
Parker (WA.) **114** E 3
Parker Dam **100** B 2
Parkers Prairie (MN.)
  61 D 5
Parkersburg (IA.) **63** F 3
Parkersburg (IL.) **57** E 3
Parkersburg (W.V.) **36** C 2
Parkin (AR.) **67** F 2
Parkland (WA.) **114** C 2
Parkman (WY.) **93** E 1
Parks (AZ.) **100** D 1
Parkston (S.D.) **83** H 4

Parle, Lac qui **61** E 6
Parma (ID.) **90** C 3
Parma (MO.) **65** H 5
Parma (OH.) **53** H 1
Parmelee (SD.) **82** E 4
Parnell (TX.) **76** C 3
Parowan (UT.) **103** E 4
Parran (NV.) **104** C 3
Parris Island **41** E 4
Parrish (AL.) **46** C 5
Parrish (FL.) **45** D 4
Parshall (CO.) **94** D 1
Parshall (ND.) **84** D 3
Parsons (KS.) **79** H 4
Parsons (TN.) **50** B 5
Parsons (W.V.) **36** E 2
Partridge (KS.) **79** EF 4
Pasadena (CA.) **106** D 3
Pasadena (TX.) **71** G 1
Pascagoula (MS.) **49** F 2
Pascagoula River **49** F 2
Pasco (WA.) **115** F 3
Paskenta (CA.) **110** C 4
Paso Robles (CA.) **106** B 2
Passage Keys **45** D 4
Passaic (N.J.) **35** G 3
Pastol Bay **120** C 3
Pastora Peak **103** F 1
Pastura (N.M.) **97** E 4
Pat Mayse Lake **77** H 4
Pataha City (WA.) **115** H 3
Paterson (N.J.) **35** G 3
Pathfinder Reservoir **93** F 3
Pathrump (NV.) **109** G 3
Patricia (TX.) **73** F 1
Patroon (TX.) **75** H 3
Patsville (NV.) **105** F 1
Patten (ME.) **28** C 3
Patterson (CA.) **111** E 3
Patterson (ID.) **91** F 2
Patterson (N.Y.) **33** G 4
Patterson, Mount **117** E 1
Pattison (MS.) **49** E 4
Patton (MO.) **65** G 4
Patton (PA.) **34** C 3
Pattonsburg (MO.) **64** C 1
Paul (ID.) **91** F 4
Paulden (AZ.) **100** D 2
Paulding (MS.) **49** D 3
Paulding (OH.) **52** E 1
Paulina (OR.) **113** EF 2
Paulina Marsh **112** DE 3
Paulina Peak **112** D 3
Pauloff Harbour **118** C 3
Pauls Valley (OK.) **77** F 3
Paunsaugunt Plateau
  103 E 4
Pauwela (HI.) **123** E 3
Pavant Range **102** CD 4
Pavlof Bay **118–119** C 2
Pavlof Island (AL.)
  118–119 C 2–3
Pavlof Volcano (AL.)
  118 C 2
Pavo (GA.) **43** F 4
Paw Paw (MI.) **55** F 4
Paw Paw (W.V.) **37** F 2
Paw Paw Lake (MI.) **55** F 5
Pawhuska (OK.) **77** G 1
Pawnee (OK.) **77** G 1
Pawnee City (NE.) **81** H 4
Pawnee River **78** CD 3
Pawnee Rock (KS.) **78** D 3
Pawtucket (R.I.) **30** E 4
Paxson (AL.) **116** BC 1
Paxton (IL.) **56** C 3

Paxton (NE.) **80** C 3
Payette (ID.) **90** C 2
Payette Lake **90** C 1–2
Payette River **90** C 3
Paynesville (MN.) **61** E 4
Payson (AZ.) **101** E 2
Payson (UT.) **102** B 3
Pe Ell (WA.) **114** B 3
Pea River **47** E 4
Peabody (KS.) **79** F 3
Peach Springs (AZ.)
  100 C 1
Peacock (TX.) **76** C 4
Peaked Mountain **28** B 4
Peale, Mount **103** D 1
Pearce (AZ.) **101** F 5
Pearisburg (VA.) **36** D 4
Pearl (IL.) **57** D 5
Pearl Harbor **122** CD 2
Pearl Peak **105** F 2
Pearl River (LA.) **69** E 3
Pearland (TX.) **71** G 1
Pearsall (TX.) **70** C 2
Pearsoll Peak **112** B 4
Pearson (GA.) **43** E 3
Pease River **76** D 3
Pebble Beach (CA.) **111** F 3
Peckerwood Lake **67** E 3
Pecos (N.M.) **96** E 3
Pecos (TX.) **73** E 2
Pecos National Monument
  96 E 3
Pecos Plains **99** F 3
Pecos River **73** G 3
Pedro (SD.) **82** C 3
Pee Dee River **38** E 3–4
Peebles (OH.) **53** F 4
Peekskill (N.Y.) **33** F 4
Peerless (MT.) **87** GH 1
Peetz (CO.) **95** G 1
Peever (S.D.) **83** J 2
Pehastin (WA.) **114** E 2
Pekin (IL.) **56** C 4
Pekin (IN.) **52** D 4
Pekin (N.D.) **85** H 3
Pelican (AL.) **117** D 2
Pelican Lake (MN.) **60** B 2
Pelican Lake (WI.) **59** D 3
Pelican Rapids (MN.)
  60 D 6
Pelion (S.C.) **40** D 3
Pella (IA.) **63** F 4
Pellston (MI.) **54** C 3
Pelly Mountains (AL.)
  117 E 1
Peloncillo Mountains
  98 B 4
Pemadumcook Lake **28** C 3
Pembina (N.D.) **85** J 2
Pembina Mountains
  85 H 1–2
Pembina River **85** HJ 2
Pembine (WI.) **58** D 2
Pembroke (GA.) **43** D 2
Penasco (N.M.) **96** E 2
Pend Oreille, Lake **88** D 1
Pend Oreille River **115** HJ 1
Pender (NE.) **81** H 2
Pendleton (IN.) **52** D 2
Pendleton (OR.) **113** G 1
Pendroy (MT.) **86** A 1
Penfield (PA.) **34** C 2
Pengilly (MN.) **60** C 3
Penn Yan (N.Y.) **32** C 3
Pennell, Mount **103** E 2
Pennsylvania (East) **34–35**

Pennsylvania, West **34–35**
Penobscot Bay **29** D 3
Penobscot River **28** C 3
Penrose (CO.) **95** F 3
Penrose (UT.) **102** A 4
Pensacola (FL.) **47** F 5
Pensacola Bay **47** F 5
Pentwater (MI.) **55** E 5
Penwell (TX.) **73** F 2
Penzance (AZ.) **101** F 2
Peoa (UT.) **102** B 3
Peoria (IL.) **56** C 4
Peoria Heights (IL.) **56** C 4
Peotone (IL.) **56** B 2
Pepacton Reservoir **33** F 3
Pequop (NV.) **105** G 1
Pequop Mountains **105** G 2
Pequot Lakes (MN.) **60** D 4
Peralta (N.M.) **96** D 4
Perdido (AL.) **47** E 5
Perdido River **47** F 5
Perdiz (TX.) **72** D 4
Perez (CA.) **110** A 3
Perham (MN.) **60** D 5
Peridot (AZ.) **101** F 3
Perkins (OK.) **77** F 2
Perkins, Mount **100** B 1
Perma (MT.) **89** F 2
Pernell (OK.) **77** F 3
Perrin (TX.) **74** C 1
Perrine (FL.) **45** F 2
Perris (CA.) **107** E 4
Perro, Laguna del **96** D 4
Perry (FL.) **44** A 5
Perry (GA.) **43** D 4
Perry (IA.) **62** D 4
Perry (LA.) **68** C 4
Perry (MI.) **55** F 3
Perry (MO.) **65** F 2
Perry (N.Y.) **32** C 3
Perry (OK.) **77** F 1
Perry (UT.) **102** A 3–4
Perry Lake **79** H 2
Perryton (TX.) **76** C 1
Perryville (AL.) **119** D 2
Perryville (AR.) **66** D 2
Perryville (MO.) **65** H 4
Persia (IA.) **62** C 4
Perth Amboy (N.J.) **35** G 3
Perth-Andover (Can.)
  28 B 2
Peru (IL.) **56** B 4
Peru (IN.) **52** C 2
Peru (WY.) **92** C 4
Pescadero (CA.) **111** E 4
Peshawbestown (MI.)
  54 D 4
Peshtigo (WI.) **59** D 1
Petal (MS.) **49** E 3
Petaluma (CA.) **111** D 4
Petenwell Lake **59** E 3
Peter Island **124** D 2
Peterborough (Can.) **32** B 1
Petersburg (AL.) **117** E 2
Petersburg (IL.) **56** C 4
Petersburg (IN.) **52** B 4
Petersburg (NE.) **81** F 1
Petersburg (TN.) **50** D 5
Petersburg (TX.) **76** B 3
Petersburg (VA.) **37** G 4
Petersburg (W.V.) **37** E 3
Peterstown (W.V.) **36** D 4
Petoskey (MI.) **54** C 3
Petrified Forest National
  Park **101** G 2
Petrolia (CA.) **110** B 6

Petrolia (TX.) **77** E 3
Pettibore (ND.) **85** G 3
Pettus (TX.) **71** E 2
Peyton (CO.) **95** F 2
Pfeifer (KS.) **78** D 3
Pharr (TX.) **70** D 4
Pheba (MS.) **48** C 2
Phelps (WI.) **58** C 3
Phelps Lake **39** H 3
Phenix City (AL.) **47** D 3
Phil Campbell (AL.) **46** B 5
Philadelphia (MS.) **48** D 3
Philadelphia (N.Y.) **32** E 1
Philadelphia (PA.) **35** G 3
Philip (SD.) **82** D 3
Philip Smith Mountains
  (AL.) **121** F 2
Philipp (MS.) **48** C 4
Philippi (W.V.) **36** E 2
Philipsburg (MT.) **89** G 3
Philipsburg (PA.) **34** C 3
Phillips (ME.) **28** D 5
Phillips (TX.) **76** B 2
Phillips (WI.) **58** D 4
Phillipsburg (KS.) **78** D 2
Phillipsburg (N.J.) **35** F 3
Philo (CA.) **110** C 5
Philomath (OR.) **112** B 2
Phippsburg (CO.) **94** D 1
Phoenix (AZ.) **100** D 3
Phoenixville (PA.) **35** F 3
Pica (AZ.) **100** C 1
Picabo (ID.) **91** E 3
Picacho (AZ.) **101** E 4
Picacho (N.M.) **99** E 3
Picacho del Centinela
  (Mex.) **73** F 4–5
Picayune (MS.) **49** F 3
Pick City (ND.) **84** E 3
Pickens (MS.) **48** D 3
Pickens (S.C.) **40** C 2
Pickens (W.V.) **36** D 3
Pickford (MI.) **54** B 3
Pickstown (S.D.) **83** G 4
Pickwick Lake **46** B 5
Pico Atalaya **124** A 2
Pictured Rocks National
  Lakeshore **54** B 5
Picuris Indian Reservation
  96 E 2
Pie Town (N.M.) **96** B 4
Piedmont (AL.) **46** C 3
Piedmont (MO.) **65** G 4
Piedmont (OH.) **53** H 2
Piedmont (SD.) **82** B 3
Piedra (AZ.) **100** D 4
Piedras Blancas, Point
  106 A 2
Piedras Negras (Mex.)
  70 B 2
Pierce (CO.) **95** F 1
Pierce (NE.) **81** G 2
Pierce City (MO.) **64** C 5
Pierceville (KS.) **78** C 4
Pierpont (S.D.) **83** H 2
Pierre (S.D.) **82** E 3
Pierz (MN.) **61** E 4
Pigeon (MI.) **55** E 2
Piggott (AR.) **67** F 1
Pikes Peak **95** EF 3
Pikesville (MD.) **37** H 2
Pikeville (KY.) **51** H 3
Pikeville (TN.) **51** E 5
Pilger (NE.) **81** G 2
Pillar Point **111** E 4

Pillsbury (N.D.) **85** J 3
Pillsbury, Lake **110** C 4
Pilot Grove (MO.) **64** D 3
Pilot Hill (CA.) **111** D 2
Pilot Knob (MT.) **88** E 4
Pilot Knob (TN.) **50** D 4
Pilot Mountain (N.C.)
  38 D 2
Pilot Peak (NV.) **104** D 4
Pilot Peak (NV.) **105** G 1–2
Pilot Point (AK.) **119** D 2
Pilot Point (TX.) **74** DE 1
Pilot Rock (OR.) **113** G 1
Pilot Station **119** C 1
Pilottown (LA.) **69** F 4
Pinckneyville (IL.) **57** E 5
Pinconning (MI.) **55** E 3
Pine (AZ.) **101** E 2
Pine (ID.) **90** D 3
Pine Apple (AL.) **47** E 4
Pine Bluff (AR.) **66** D 3
Pine Bluffs (WY.) **93** HJ 4
Pine Bush (N.Y.) **33** F 4
Pine City (WA.) **115** H 2
Pine Creek (NV.) **105** E 2
Pine Creek (PA.) **34** D 2
Pine Creek Lake **77** H 3
Pine Flat Dam **111** F 4
Pine Flat Lake **111** F 1
Pine Grove (CA.) **111** D 2
Pine Grove (OR.) **112** D 1
Pine Grove (W.V.) **36** D 2
Pine Island **45** E 4
Pine Mountain **106** A 2
Pine Mountain (OR.)
  112 E 3
Pine Mountain (WY.)
  92 C 4
Pine Peak **100** C 2
Pine Ridge (SD.) **82** C 4
Pine Ridge Indian
  Reservation **82** CD 4
Pine River (MN.) **60** D 4
Pine Springs (TX.) **72** D 2
Pinedale (N.M.) **96** B 3
Pinedale (WY.) **92** C 3
Pinehurst (ID.) **88** D 2
Pineland (TX.) **75** H 3
Pinellas Park (FL.) **44** D 4
Pinetop (AZ.) **101** G 2
Pineville (KY.) **51** G 4
Pineville (MO.) **64** C 5
Pineville (N.C.) **38** D 3
Pineville (W.V.) **36** C 4
Piney Buttes **87** G 2
Piney Point **44** B 5
Pingree (ND.) **85** G 3
Pinnacle Buttes **92** C 3
Pinnacle Peak **92** B 2
Pinnacles National
  Monument **111** F 3
Pinola (MS.) **49** E 3
Pinon (AZ.) **103** F 2
Pinos Altos Range **98** B 3
Pinos, Mount **106** C 3
Pinta (AZ.) **101** G 1
Pintura (UT.) **103** E 5
Pioche (NV.) **109** H 2
Pioneer (OH.) **52** E 1
Pioneer Mountains
  89 GH 4
Pipe Creek (TX.) **70** D 1
Pipe Spring National
  Monument **103** F 4
Pipestone (MN.) **61** F 6
Piqua (OH.) **52** E 2

Pisinimo (AZ.) **100** D 4
Pismo Beach (CA.) **106** B 2
Pistol River (OR.) **112** A 4
Pit River **110** B 3
Pitkin (CO.) **94** D 3
Pittsboro (MS.) **48** C 3
Pittsboro (N.C.) **39** E 3
Pittsburg (KS.) **79** J 4
Pittsburg (TX.) **75** G 1–2
Pittsburgh (PA.) **34** A 3
Pittsfield (MA.) **30** C 3
Pittsfield (ME.) **28** D 4
Pittston (PA.) **35** F 2
Pittsview (AL.) **47** D 3
Pittsville (WI.) **59** E 4
Piute Peak **106** D 2
Piute Reservoir **103** D 4
Pixley (CA.) **106** C 2
Placerville (CA.) **111** D 2
Placerville (CO.) **94** BC 3
Placidia (FL.) **45** E 4
Placitas (N.M.) **96** D 3
Plaguemine (LA.) **68** B 1
Plain City (UT.) **102** A 4
Plain Dealing (LA.) **68** B 1
Plainfield (IN.) **52** C 3
Plainfield (N.J.) **35** G 3
Plainfield (N.J.) **59** E 3
Plains (KS.) **78** C 4
Plains (MT.) **88** EF 2
Plains (TX.) **99** H 3
Plains of San Agustin
  98 BC 3
Plainview (MN.) **61** F 2
Plainview (NE.) **81** G 2
Plainview (TX.) **76** B 3
Plainville (KS.) **78** D 2
Plainwell (MI.) **55** F 4
Planada (CA.) **111** E 2
Plankinton (S.D.) **83** G 4
Plano (TX.) **75** E 1
Plant City (FL.) **44** C 4
Plantation (FL.) **41** E 3
Plantersville (AL.) **46** D 5
Plaster City (CA.) **107** G 5
Plata (TX.) **72** D 4
Plateau (TX.) **72** D 2
Platina (CA.) **110** B 4
Platinum **119** C 2
Platt National Park **77** G 3
Platte (SD.) **83** G 4
Platte Center (NE.) **81** G 3
Platte City (MO.) **64** C 2
Platte River **81** GH 3
Platte River (MO.) **64** C 2
Platteville (CO.) **95** E 1
Platteville (WI.) **59** G 4
Plattsburg (MO.) **64** C 2
Plattsburgh (N.Y.) **33** G 1
Plattsmouth (NE.) **81** J 4
Playas Lake **98** B 5
Plaza (ND.) **84** D 2
Plaza (WA.) **115** H 2
Pleasant Grove (UT.)
  102 B 3
Pleasant Hill (LA.) **68** B 2
Pleasant Hill (MO.) **64** C 3
Pleasant Hill (N.M.) **97** G 4
Pleasant, Lake **100** D 3
Pleasant, Mount **114** B 1–2
Pleasant View (CO.) **94** B 4
Pleasant View (UT.)
  102 A 3
Pleasanton (KS.) **79** J 3
Pleasanton (TX.) **70** D 2
Pleasantville (N.J.) **35** G 4

Plentywood (MT.) **87** J 1
Plevna (MT.) **87** J 3
Plum Island **35** J 2
Plummer (ID.) **115** HJ 2
Plush (OR.) **113** F 4
Plymouth (CA.) **111** D 2
Plymouth (IL.) **56** C 5
Plymouth (IN.) **52** C 1
Plymouth (MA.) **31** F 4
Plymouth (N.C.) **39** H 3
Plymouth (NE.) **81** G 4
Plymouth (N.H.) **29** E 6
Plymouth (WA.) **115** F 4
Plymouth (WI.) **59** F 2
Pocahontas (AR.) **67** F 1
Pocahontas (IA.) **62** D 3
Pocasset (OK.) **77** E 2
Pocatello (ID.) **91** G 4
Pocomoke City (MD.)
  37 J 3
Pocono Mountains **35** F 2
Poinsett, Lake **83** HJ 3
Point Año Nuevo **111** E 4
Point Arena (CA.) **110** D 5
Point Arguello **106** B 2
Point au Fer Island **68** D 4
Point aux Barques **55** D 1
Point Brown **114** A 3
Point Buchon **106** B 2
Point Cabrillo **110** C 5
Point Carmel **111** F 3–4
Point Conception **106** B 3
Point Delgada **110** B 4
Point Estero **106** A 2
Point Harbor (N.C.) **39** J 2
Point Hope (AL.) **120** B 2
Point Imperial **103** F 3
Point Lay (AL.) **120** C 2
Point Marion (PA.) **34** B 4
Point of Rocks (WY.) **92** D 4
Point Piedras Blancas
  106 A 2
Point Pleasant (N.J.)
  35 GH 3
Point Pleasant (W.V.)
  36 B 3
Point Reyes **111** E 5
Point Reyes National
  Seashore **111** D 4–5
Point Saint George **110** A 6
Point Sal **106** B 3
Point Sur **111** F 3
Pointblank (TX.) **75** F 4
Pointe a la Hache (LA.)
  69 F 4
Pointe aux Pins (MI.) **54** C 3
Points of Rocks (MD.)
  37 G 2
Pojoaque (N.M.) **96** D 3
Pokegama Lake **60** C 3
Polacca (AZ.) **103** G 2
Poland (N.Y.) **33** EF 2
Polaris (MT.) **89** GH 4
Pole Mountain **93** G 4
Polk (NE.) **81** G 3
Polk City (FL.) **44** C 3
Pollock (ID.) **88** D 4
Pollock (SD.) **82** E 2
Polo (IL.) **56** B 4
Polo (MO.) **64** CD 2
Polson (MT.) **89** F 2
Pomeroy (OH.) **53** H 3
Pomeroy (TX.) **76** B 2
Pomeroy (WA.) **115** H 3
Pomme de Terre Lake
  64 D 4

Pomme de Terre River **64** D 4
Pomona (CA.) **107** E 3
Pomona (KS.) **79** H 3
Pomona (MO.) **65** F 5
Pompano Beach (FL.) **45** E 2
Pompeys Pillar (MT.) **87** F 4
Pompton Lakes (N.J.) **35** G 2
Ponca (NE.) **81** H 2
Ponca City (OK.) **77** FG 1
Ponce (P.R.) **124** B 2
Ponce de Leon (FL.) **47** F 3
Ponce de Leon Bay (FL.) **94** D 3
Poncha Springs (CO.) **94** D 3
Ponchatoula (LA.) **69** E 3
Pond (CA.) **106** C 2
Pond Creek (OK.) **77** F 1
Pondosa (CA.) **110** A 3
Pontchartrain, Lake **69** E 3
Pontiac (IL.) **56** C 3
Pontiac (MI.) **55** F 2
Pontotoc (MS.) **48** B 2
Pontotoc (TX.) **74** B 4
Pony (MT.) **86** B 4
Poorman (AL.) **120** C 3
Pope (MS.) **48** B 4
Pope Valley (CA.) **111** D 4
Popes Creek (MD.) **37** H 3
Poplar (MT.) **87** H 1
Poplar (WI.) **58** C 5
Poplar Bluff (MO.) **65** G 5
Poplar River **87** H 1
Poplarville (MS.) **49** F 3
Porcupine (AL.) **121** G 2
Porcupine (SD.) **82** C 4
Porphyry Peak **86** D 2
Port Allegany (PA.) **34** C 2
Port Allen (LA.) **68** D 3
Port Angeles (WA.) **114** B 1
Port Arthur (TX.) **75** H 5
Port Austin (MI.) **55** D 2
Port Bolivar (TX.) **71** H 1
Port Charlotte (FL.) **45** DE 4
Port Chilkoot **117** DE 2
Port Clarence **120** B 2
Port Clements **117** F 2
Port Clements (AL.) **117** E 3
Port Clinton (OH.) **53** F 1
Port Edwards (WI.) **59** E 3
Port Gamble (WA.) **114** C 2
Port Gibson (MS.) **49** E 5
Port Graham (AL.) **119** E 2
Port Heiden (AL.) **119** D 2
Port Henry (N.Y.) **33** G 1
Port Hope (MI.) **55** E 1
Port Hueneme (CA.) **106** C 3
Port Huron (MI.) **55** EF 1
Port Isabel (TX.) **71** E 4
Port Jefferson (N.Y.) **35** H 3
Port Jervis (N.Y.) **33** F 4
Port Lavaca (TX.) **71** F 2
Port Mansfield (TX.) **71** E 4
Port Matilda (PA.) **34** C 3
Port Mayaca (FL.) **45** E 2
Port Moller (AL.) **119** C 2
Port Neches (TX.) **75** H 4
Port Norris (N.J.) **35** G 4
Port O'Connor (TX.) **71** F 2
Port Orange (FL.) **44** B 2
Port Orchard (WA.) **114** C 2
Port Orford (OR.) **112** A 4

Port Royal (PA.) **34** D 3
Port Royal (VA.) **37** G 3
Port Royal Sound **41** E 4
Port Saint Joe (FL.) **47** G 3
Port Sanilac (MI.) **55** E 1
Port Sulphur (LA.) **69** F 4
Port Townsend (WA.) **114** C 1
Port Wakefield **119** E 2
Port Wakefield (AL.) **119** E 2
Port Washinton (WI.) **59** F 1
Port Wing (WI.) **58** C 5
Portage (IN.) **55** F 4
Portage (MT.) **86** B 2
Portage (UT.) **102** A 4
Portage (WI.) **59** F 3
Portageville (MO.) **65** H 5
Portageville (N.Y.) **32** B 3
Portal (AZ.) **101** F 5
Portal (ND.) **84** D 1
Portales (N.M.) **97** G 4
Porter (WA.) **114** B 3
Porterville (CA.) **111** F 1
Porterville (MS.) **48** D 2
Porthill (ID.) **88** D 1
Portis (KS.) **78** E 2
Portland (IN.) **52** E 2
Portland (ME.) **29** E 5
Portland (MI.) **55** F 3
Portland (N.D.) **85** J 3
Portland (OR.) **112** C 1
Portland (TN.) **50** D 4
Portland (TX.) **71** E 3
Portneuf Range **91** GH 4
Portneuf Reservoir **91** H 4
Portola (CA.) **110** C 2
Portsmouth (N.H.) **29** E 5
Portsmouth (OH.) **53** F 4
Portsmouth (VA.) **37** H 5
Portsmouth Island **39** H 3
Portville (N.Y.) **32** B 3
Porum (OK.) **77** H 2
Posen (MI.) **54** C 2
Possum Kingdom Lake **74** C 2
Post (OR.) **112** E 2
Post (TX.) **76** B 4
Post Creek (MT.) **89** F 2
Post Falls (ID.) **88** D 2
Postor. (S.C.) **41** F 3
Postville (IA.) **63** G 2
Pot Mountain **88** E 2
Potato Creek (SD.) **82** D 4
Potawatomi Indian Reservation **79** G 2
Poteau (OK.) **77** J 2
Poteet (TX.) **70** D 1
Poth (TX.) **70** D 1
Potholes Reservoir **115** F 2
Potlatch (ID.) **88** D 3
Potomac (IL.) **56** C 2
Potomac River **37** H 3
Potosi (MO.) **65** G 4
Potsdam (N.Y.) **33** F 1
Potter (NE.) **80** A 3
Potter Valley (CA.) **110** C 5
Potts Camp (MS.) **48** B 3
Pottstown (PA.) **35** F 3
Pottsville (PA.) **35** E 3
Poughkeepsie (N.Y.) **33** G 4
Poulsbo (WA.) **114** C 2
Pound (WI.) **59** D 2
Poverty Mountain **103** F 5
Poway (CA.) **107** E 5
Powder River (MT.) **87** H 3

Powder River (OR.) **113** H 2
Powder River (WY.) **93** F 2
Powder River Pass **92–93** E 1
Powder Wash (CO.) **94** B 1
Powderhorn (CO.) **94** C 3
Powderly (TX.) **77** H 4
Powderville (MT.) **87** H 4
Powell (WY.) **92** D 1
Powell Butte (OR.) **112** D 2
Powell, Lake **103** E 3
Power (MT.) **86** B 2
Powers (MI.) **54** C 6
Powers (OR.) **112** AB 4
Powers Lake (ND.) **84** D 2
Powhatan (LA.) **68** B 2
Powhatan (VA.) **37** G 4
Powhatan Pt (OH.) **53** H 3
Poygan, Lake **59** E 2
Prague (NE.) **81** H 3
Prague (OK.) **77** G 2
Praire (ID.) **90** D 3
Prairie City (OR.) **113** G 2
Prairie City (SD.) **82** C 2
Prairie Dog Creek **78** C 2
Prairie du Chien (WI.) **59** F 5
Prairie View (KS.) **78** D 2
Prairie View (TX.) **75** F 4
Prairie Village (KS.) **79** J 3
Pratt (KS.) **78** E 4
Prattville (AL.) **46** D 4
Premont (TX.) **70** D 3
Prentice (WI.) **58** D 4
Prentiss (MS.) **49** E 3
Prescott (AR.) **66** C 4
Prescott (AZ.) **100** D 2
Presho (SD.) **83** E 4
Presque Isle (ME.) **28** B 3
Presque Isle (MI.) **54** C 2
Presque Isle (WI.) **58** C 3
Preston (GA.) **43** D 5
Preston (ID.) **91** H 4
Preston (KS.) **78** E 4
Preston (MN.) **61** G 2
Preston (NV.) **105** FG 4
Prestonsburg (KY.) **51** G 3
Pretty Prairie (KS.) **79** E 4
Prettyboy Reservoir **37** H 2
Prewitt (N.M.) **96** C 3
Prewitt Reservoir **95** G 1
Pribilof Islands (AL.) **118** AB 2
Price (UT.) **102** C 2
Prichard (AL.) **47** F 6
Priddy (TX.) **74** C 3
Priest Lake **88** D 1
Priest Rapids Dam **115** F 3
Priest River (ID.) **88** D 1
Primghar (IA.) **62** C 2
Prince (NV.) **109** H 2
Prince Frederick (MD.) **37** H 3
Prince George (VA.) **37** G 4
Prince William Sound (AL.) **116** B 1
Princess Anne (MD.) **37** J 3
Princeton (AR.) **66** D 3
Princeton (CA.) **110** C 3
Princeton (IL.) **56** B 4
Princeton (IN.) **52** B 4
Princeton (KY.) **50** C 3
Princeton (ME.) **28** C 2
Princeton (MN.) **61** E 3
Princeton (MO.) **64** D 1

Princeton (N.J.) **35** G 3
Princeton (OR.) **113** G 3
Prineville (OR.) **112** E 2
Prineville Reservoir **112** E 2
Pringle (SD.) **82** B 4
Pringle (TX.) **76** B 2
Prins of Wales Island (AL.) **117** E 2
Pritchett (CO.) **95** G 4
Proberta (CA.) **110** B 4
Proctor (NV.) **105** G 2
Proctor (TX.) **74** C 3
Proctor Lake **74** C 2
Progreso (TX.) **71** E 4
Promontory Mountains **102** A 4
Promontory Point (UT.) **102** A 4
Pronto (NV.) **104** C 2
Prophetstown (IL.) **56** B 4
Prospect (OR.) **112** C 4
Prosper (TX.) **75** E 1
Prosser (WA.) **115** F 3
Protection (KS.) **78** D 4
Providence (KY.) **50** C 3
Providence (R.I.) **30–31** E 4
Provincetown (MA.) **31** F 3
Provo (SD.) **82** B 4
Provo (UT.) **102** B 3
Prudgoe Bay (AL.) **121** F 1
Pruess Lake **102** D 5
Pryor (MT.) **86** E 4
Pryor (OK.) **77** H 1
Puako (HI.) **123** F 4
Puckett (MS.) **49** D 3
Pueblo (CO.) **95** F 3
Pueblo Mountain **113** G 4
Pueo Point **122** AB 2
Puerca, Punta **124** C 2
Puerto Rico **124** B 2
Puerto Rico **124** B 2
Puertocito Indian Reservation **96** C 4
Puget Sound **114** C 2
Pulaski (N.Y.) **32** D 2
Pulaski (TN.) **50** C 5
Pulaski (VA.) **36** D 4
Pulaski (WI.) **59** E 2
Pullman (WA.) **115** H 3
Pumpkin Buttes **93** G 2
Pumpville (TX.) **73** GH 4
Punaluu (HI.) **123** F 4
Pungo Lake **39** H 3
Punta Arenas **124** C 2
Punta Borinquen **124** A 2
Punta Brea **124** B 3
Punta Este **124** C 2
Punta Gorda (CA.) **110** B 6
Punta Gorda (FL.) **45** E 3
Punta Guanajibo **124** A 2
Punta Guayanés **124** C 2
Punta Higüero **124** A 2
Punta Ola Grande **124** BC 3
Punta Puerca **124** C 2
Punto, Cerro de **124** B 2
Punxsutawney (PA.) **34** B 2–3
Puolo Point **122** B 2
Purcell (OK.) **77** F 2
Purcell Mountains (MT.) **88** E 1
Purdum (NE.) **80** D 2
Purdy (OK.) **77** F 2
Purgatoire Peak **95** E 4
Purgatoire River **95** G 4
Purisima Point **106** B 3

Purvis (MS.) **49** E 3
Put-in-Bay (OH.) **53** F 1
Putnam (CT.) **35** J 2
Putnam (OK.) **76** D 2
Putnam (TX.) **74** B 2
Putney (S.D.) **83** G 2
Puu o Keokeo **123** F 4
Puuanahulu (HI.) **123** F 4
Puukolii (HI.) **123** E 3
Puuwai (HI.) **122** A 2
Puxico (MO.) **65** G 5
Puyallup (WA.) **114** C 2
Pymatuning Reservoir **34** A 2
Pyramid Head **106** D 5
Pyramid Lake **104** B 2–3
Pyramid Lake Indian Reservation **104** B 2

Q

Quaboin Reservoir **30** D 3
Quakertown (PA.) **35** F 3
Quanah (TX.) **76** D 3
Quantico (VA.) **37** G 3
Quarryville (PA.) **35** E 4
Quartz Hill (CA.) **106** D 3
Quartz Mountain **112** C 3
Quartzsite (AZ.) **100** B 3
Quay (N.M.) **97** G 4
Québec (Can.) **28** B 6
Quebec (TX.) **72** D 3
Quebeck (TN.) **51** E 5
Quebradillas (P.R.) **124** B 2
Queen Anne (MD.) **37** J 3
Queen City (MO.) **64** E 1
Queets (WA.) **114** A 2
Quemado (N.M.) **96** B 4
Quemado (TX.) **70** B 2
Questa (N.M.) **96** E 2
Quietus (MT.) **87** G 4
Quijotoa (AZ.) **100** D 4
Quimby (IA.) **62** C 3
Quinault Indian Reservation **114** A 2
Quincy (CA.) **110** C 3
Quincy (FL.) **47** F 2
Quincy (IL.) **56** D 6
Quincy (MA.) **31** E 3
Quincy (WA.) **115** F 2
Quinlan (OK.) **76** DE 1
Quinn River **104** D 1
Quinter (KS.) **78** C 2
Quinton (OK.) **77** H 2
Quitaque (TX.) **76** B 3
Quitman (GA.) **43** F 4
Quitman (MS.) **49** D 2
Quitman (TX.) **75** F 2
Quitman Mountains **72** C 2–3
Quivero (AZ.) **100** D 1
Qulin (MO.) **65** G 5

R

Rabbit Ears Pass **94** D 1
Race Point **31** F 3
Raceland (LA.) **69** E 4
Racepond (GA.) **43** E 3
Rachal (TX.) **70** D 4
Racine (WI.) **59** G 1
Raco (MI.) **54** B 3
Radersburg (MT.) **86** B 3
Radford (VA.) **36** D 4
Radium Springs (N.M.) **98** D 4
Raeford (N.C.) **39** E 4
Raft River Mountains **102** A 5
Ragan (WY.) **92** B 4
Ragged Top Mountain **93** G 4
Ragland (N.M.) **97** G 4
Rago (KS.) **79** EF 4
Rainbow Bridge National Monument **103** E 2
Rainbow Plateau **103** F 2–3
Rainelle (W.V.) **36** D 4
Rainier, Mount **114** D 3
Rains (S.C.) **41** F 2
Rainy Lake (MN.) **60** B 3
Rainy River **60** B 3–4
Raleigh (MS.) **49** D 3
Raleigh (N.C.) **39** F 3
Raleigh (ND.) **84** E 4
Raleigh Bay **39** HJ 4
Ralls (TX.) **76** B 4
Ralph (SD.) **82** BC 2
Ralston (PA.) **34** E 2
Ralston (WA.) **115** G 3
Ralston (WY.) **92** CD 1
Ramah Indian Reservation **96** B 4
Ramer (AL.) **47** D 4
Ramirez (TX.) **70** D 3
Ramona (CA.) **107** F 4
Ramona (S.D.) **83** H 3
Rampart (AL.) **121** F 2
Ramsay (MT.) **86** A 3
Ramsey (Can.) **54** A 1
Ramsey (IL.) **57** D 4
Rancheria **117** E 1
Rancherie Rock **113** E 2
Ranchester (WY.) **93** E 1
Ranchos de Taos (N.M.) **96** E 2
Rand (CO.) **94** D 1
Randado (TX.) **70** C 3
Randleman (N.C.) **38** E 3
Randlett (OK.) **76** E 3
Randolph (AZ.) **100–101** E 4
Randolph (IA.) **62** C 5
Randolph (NE.) **79** G 2
Randolph (UT.) **102** A 3
Randolph (VT.) **30** D 2
Random Lake (WI.) **59** F 1
Rangeley (ME.) **28** C 5
Ranger (TX.) **74** C 2
Rangley (CO.) **94** B 1
Rankin (TX.) **73** F 2
Ransom (KS.) **78** D 3
Rantoul (IL.) **56** C 3
Rapelje (MT.) **86** D 4
Rapid City (MI.) **54** D 4
Rapid City (S.D.) **82** B 3
Rapid River (MI.) **54** C 5
Rappahannock River **37** H 3–4
Rat (AL.) **116** H 1
Rat Islands (AL.) **116** H 1
Rathbun Lake **63** EF 5
Ratliff City (OK.) **77** F 3
Raton (N.M.) **97** F 2
Raub (ND.) **84** D 3
Raupelyan (AL.) **120** A 2
Ravalli (MT.) **89** F 2
Ravena (N.Y.) **33** G 3
Ravendale (CA.) **110** B 2
Ravenna (MT.) **89** G 3
Ravenna (NE.) **81** E 3
Ravenna (OH.) **53** H 1
Ravenwood (MO.) **64** C 1
Ravia (OK.) **77** G 3
Ravinia (S.D.) **83** G 4
Rawlins (WY.) **93** E 4
Ray (MN.) **60** B 3
Ray (ND.) **84** C 2
Ray City (GA.) **43** E 4
Ray Hubbard, Lake **75** E 2
Ray Mountains **121** E 2
Raymond (CA.) **111** E 1
Raymond (IL.) **57** D 4
Raymond (KS.) **78** E 3
Raymond (MN.) **61** E 5
Raymond (MS.) **48** D 4
Raymond (MT.) **87** J 1
Raymond (WA.) **114** B 3
Raymondville (TX.) **71** E 4
Raynesford (MT.) **86** C 2
Raytown (MO.) **64** C 2–3
Rayville (LA.) **68** D 1
Reading (KS.) **79** H 3
Reading (MI.) **55** G 3
Reading (OH.) **52** E 3
Reading (PA.) **35** F 3
Readlyn (IA.) **63** F 3
Readstown (WI.) **59** F 4
Reagan (TN.) **50** B 5
Realitos (TX.) **70** D 3
Reardan (WA.) **115** H 2
Reata (Mex.) **70** A 4
Rector (AR.) **67** F 1
Red Bank (N.J.) **35** G 3
Red Bank (TN.) **51** E 5
Red Bank (TN.) **51** E 5
Red Bluff (CA.) **110** B 4
Red Bluff Lake **72–73** E 2
Red Boiling Spring (TN.) **50** E 4
Red Bud (IL.) **57** E 5
Red Buttes (WY.) **93** G 4
Red Ciff (CO.) **94** D 2
Red Cliff (WI.) **58** C 4
Red Cliff Indian Reservation **58** C 4
Red Cloud (NE.) **81** F 4
Red Devil (AL.) **119** D 1
Red Elm (SD.) **82** D 2
Red Feather Lakes (CO.) **94–95** E 1
Red Hill **123** E 3
Red Hills **78** DE 4
Red House (NV.) **104** D 1–2
Red Lake (AZ.) **100** C 1
Red Lake (S.D.) **83** F 4
Red Lake Falls (MN.) **60** C 6
Red Lake Indian Reservation **60** B 4–5
Red Lake River **60** C 6
Red Level (AL.) **47** E 4
Red Lodge (MT.) **86** D 4
Red Mountain (CA.) **107** E 2
Red Mountain (MT.) **86** A 2
Red Mountain Pass **94** C 4
Red Oak (IA.) **62** C 4
Red Oak (OK.) **77** HJ 3
Red River (LA.) **68** CD 2
Red River (MN/N.D.) **85** J 2
Red River Hot Springs (ID.) **88** EF 4
Red River Valley **60** BC 6
Red Rock (AZ.) **103** F 1
Red Rock (MT.) **91** G 2
Red Rock (TX.) **74** D 4–5
Red Rock, Lake **63** E 4
Red Rock Lakes **91** H 2
Red Shirt (SD.) **82** C 4
Red Springs (N.C.) **39** E 4
Red Wing (MN.) **61** F 2
Redbird (WY.) **93** H 2
Redding (CA.) **110** B 4
Redfield (S.D.) **83** G 3
Redford (TX.) **72** D 4
Redig (SD.) **82** B 2
Redington (NE.) **80** A 3
Redkey (IN.) **52** D 2
Redlake (MN.) **60** C 5
Redlands (CA.) **107** E 3
Redmesa (CO.) **94** B 4
Redmond (OR.) **112** D 2
Redmond (UT.) **102** C 3
Redoubt Volcano (AL.) **119** E 1
Redowl (SD.) **82** C 3
Redrock (N.M.) **98** B 4
Redstar (AR.) **66** C 2
Redstone (CO.) **94** C 2
Redstone (MT.) **87** J 1
Redstone Arsenal (AL.) **46** B 4
Redwater River **87** H 2
Redwood (MS.) **48** D 4
Redwood City (CA.) **111** E 4
Redwood Falls (MN.) **61** F 5
Redwood National Park **110** A 6
Redwood Valley (CA.) **110** C 5
Reece (KS.) **79** G 4
Reed City (MI.) **55** E 4
Reed Point (MT.) **86** D 4
Reedley (CA.) **111** F 1
Reeds Peak **98** C 3
Reedsburg (WI.) **59** F 4
Reedsport (OR.) **112** AB 3
Reedville (VA.) **37** H 4
Reelfoot Lake **65** H 5
Reese (MI.) **55** E 2
Reese River **104** D 2

Reform (AL.) **46** C 5
Refugio (TX.) **71** E 2
Regent (ND.) **84** D 4
Rehoboth Beach (DE.)
   37 J 3
Reidsville (GA.) **43** D 3
Reidsville (N.C.) **38** E 2
Reisterstown (MD.) **37** G 2
Reliance (WY.) **92** C 4
Remer (MN.) **60** C 3
Remington (VA.) **37** G 3
Remus (MI.) **55** E 4
Rend Lake **57** E 5
Renick (W.V.) **36** D 3
Reno (NV.) **104** B 3
Renovo (PA.) **34** D 2
Rensselaer (IN.) **52** B 2
Rensselaer (N.Y.) **33** G 3
Renton (WA.) **114** C 2
Repton (AL.) **47** E 5
Republic (KS.) **79** F 2
Republic (MO.) **64** D 4
Republican City (NE.)
   81 E 4
Republican River **81** F 4
Requina (CA.) **110** A 6
Reserve (MT.) **87** J 1
Reserve (N.M.) **98** B 3
Reva (SD.) **82** B 2
Revilla Gigedo I. (AL.)
   117 E 2
Revillo (S.D.) **83** J 2
Rexburg (ID.) **91** H 3
Rexford (KS.) **78** C 2
Rexford (MT.) **88** E 1
Rexton (MI.) **54** B 4
Reyes, Point **111** E 5
Reynolds (N.D.) **85** J 3
Reynosa (Mex.) **70** D 4
Rhame (ND.) **84** C 4
Rhinelander (WI.) **58** D 3
Rhode Island **30−31** EF 4
Rhode Island Sound **30** E 4
Rhodhiss Lake **38** C 3
Rib Lake (WI.) **59** D 4
Ricardo (N.M.) **97** F 4
Ricardo (TX.) **71** E 3
Rice (CA.) **107** H 3
Rice (WA.) **115** G 1
Rice Lake (WI.) **59** D 5
Riceville (IA.) **63** F 2
Rich Bar (CA.) **110** B 3
Rich Hill (MO.) **64** C 3
Rich Square (N.C.) **39** G 2
Richards Mountain **88** E 1
Richardson (TX.) **74−75** E 2
Richardson Lakes **28** D 5
Richardton (ND.) **84** D 4
Richey (MT.) **87** H 2
Richfield (ID.) **91** E 3
Richfield (KS.) **78** B 4
Richfield (PA.) **34** D 3
Richfield (UT.) **103** D 4
Richfield Springs (N.Y.)
   33 F 3
Richford (VT.) **30** D 1
Richland (GA.) **43** D 5
Richland (MI.) **55** F 4
Richland (MO.) **64** E 4
Richland (MT.) **87** GH 1
Richland (OR.) **113** H 2
Richland (TX.) **75** E 3
Richland (WA.) **115** F 3
Richland Center (WI.)
   59 F 4

Richlands (N.C.) **39** G 4
Richlands (VA.) **36** C 4
Richlands Springs (TX.)
   74 C 3
Richmond (CA.) **111** E 4
Richmond (IN.) **52** E 3
Richmond (KS.) **79** H 3
Richmond (KY.) **51** F 3
Richmond (ME.) **29** D 4
Richmond (MO.) **64** D 2
Richmond (TX.) **71** G 1
Richmond (UT.) **102** A 3−4
Richmond (VA.) **37** G 4
Richmond Hill (Can.)
   32 A 2
Richmond Hill (GA.) **43** E 2
Richton (MS.) **49** E 2
Richwood (W.V.) **36** D 3
Rico (CO.) **94** C 4
Riddle (ID.) **90** C 4
Riddle (OR.) **112** B 4
Riddle Mountain **113** G 3
Ridge (MT.) **87** J 4
Ridgecrest (CA.) **107** E 2
Ridgeland (S.C.) **41** E 4
Ridgely (TN.) **67** G 1
Ridgeview (SD.) **82** E 2
Ridgeway (CO.) **94** C 3
Ridgeway (MO.) **64** C 1
Ridgeway (S.C.) **41** E 2
Ridgway (PA.) **34** C 2
Rienzi (MS.) **48** B 2
Rieth (OR.) **113** G 1
Rifle (CO.) **94** C 2
Rifstangi **110** B 5
Rigby (ID.) **91** H 3
Riggins (ID.) **88** D 4
Riley (KS.) **79** G 2
Riley (OR.) **113** F 3
Rillito (AZ.) **101** E 4
Rincon (AL.) **124** A 2
Rincon Indian Reservation
   107 F 4
Ringgold (GA.) **42** B 6
Ringgold (LA.) **68** B 1
Ringgold (NE.) **80** D 3
Ringling (MT.) **86** C 3
Ringling (OK.) **77** F 3
Ringsted (IA.) **62** D 2
Ringwood (OK.) **77** E 1
Rio Blanco (CO.) **94** B 2
Rio Conchos (Mex.) **72** D 4
Rio Dell (CA.) **110** B 6
Río Grande (P.R.) **124** C 2
Rio Grande (TX./Mexico)
   70 D 4
Rio Grande City (TX.)
   70 D 4
Rio Grande Wild and
   Scenic River (TX.) **73** F 4
Rio Hondo (TX.) **71** E 4
Rio Pecos (TX.) **73** F 2
Río Pedras (P.R.) **124** BC 2
Rio Vista (CA.) **111** D 3
Rio Vista (TX.) **74** D 2
Riomedina (TX.) **70** D 1
Rios (TX.) **70** D 3
Ripley (CA.) **107** H 4
Ripley (MS.) **48** B 2
Ripley (OH.) **53** F 4
Ripley (TN.) **67** G 2
Ripley (W.V.) **36** C 3
Ripon (CA.) **111** E 3
Ripon (WI.) **59** F 2
Ririe (ID.) **91** H 3
Risco (MO.) **65** H 5

Rising Star (TX.) **74** C 2
Rising Sun (IN.) **52** D 4
Rison (AR.) **66** D 4
Ritter, Mount **111** E 1
Ritzville (WA.) **115** G 2
River Falls (WI.) **59** E 6
River, Niordenskiold
   117 D 1
Riverbank (CA.) **111** E 2
Riverdale (CA.) **111** F 1
Riverdale (ND.) **84** E 3
Riverhead (N.Y.) **35** J 3
Riverside (CA.) **107** E 4
Riverside (OR.) **113** G 3
Riverside (TX.) **75** F 4
Riverside (WA.) **115** F 1
Riverside Reservoir **95** F 1
Riverton (WY.) **92** D 2
Riverview (WY.) **93** H 2
Rives (TN.) **50** A 4
Rives Junction (MI.) **55** F 3
Riviera (TX.) **71** E 3
Riviera Beach (FL.) **45** E 2
Roach (NV.) **109** G 4
Roach Lake **109** G 4
Roachdale (IN.) **52** B 3
Road Town **124** D 2
Roads End (CA.) **106** D 2
Roan Plateau **102** C 1
Roanoke (AL.) **46** C 3
Roanoke (VA.) **36** E 4
Roanoke Rapids (N.C.)
   39 G 2
Roanoke Rapids Lake
   39 G 2
Roanoke River **39** G 2
Roaring Springs (TX.)
   76 C 4
Robbins (CA.) **111** D 3
Robert Lee (TX.) **73** H 2
Robert Lee Reservoir
   73 H 2
Robert S. Kerr Reservoir
   77 HJ 2
Roberts (ID.) **91** G 3
Roberts (MT.) **86** D 4
Roberts Creek Mountain
   105 E 3
Roberts Mountain **118** B 1
Robertsdale (AL.) **47** F 5
Robinson (IL.) **57** D 2
Robinson (TX.) **74** D 3
Robinson Mountain **88** E 1
Robles Junction (AZ.)
   101 E 4
Robstown (TX.) **71** E 3
Roby (TX.) **73** H 1
Rochelle (IL.) **56** B 4
Rochelle (TX.) **74** B 3
Rochester (IN.) **52** C 1
Rochester (MN.) **61** F 2
Rochester (N.H.) **29** E 6
Rochester (N.Y.) **32** C 2
Rochester (TX.) **76** CD 4
Rochester (WA.) **114** B 3
Rochford (SD.) **82** B 3
Rock (MI.) **54** B 6
Rock Candy Mountain
   88 E 1
Rock Cave (W.V.) **36** D 3
Rock Creek (NV.) **105** E 1−2
Rock Creek (OR.) **113** E 1
Rock Creek Butte **113** G 2
Rock Falls (IL.) **56** B 4
Rock Hall (MD.) **37** H 2
Rock Hill (S.C.) **40** D 2

Rock Lake **115** H 2
Rock Rapids (IA.) **62** B 2
Rock River (IL.) **56** B 4
Rock River (WY.) **93** G 4
Rock Springs (AZ.) **100** D 2
Rock Springs (MT.) **87** G 3
Rock Springs (WY.) **92** C 4
Rock Valley (IA.) **62** B 2
Rockdale (TX.) **74** D 4
Rockford (AL.) **46** D 4
Rockford (ID.) **91** G 3
Rockford (IL.) **56** A 4
Rockham (SD.) **83** G 3
Rockingham (N.C.) **38** E 4
Rockinstraw Mountain
   101 F 3
Rocklake (ND.) **85** G 2
Rockland (ID.) **91** FG 4
Rockland (ME.) **29** D 4
Rockland (MI.) **58** C 3
Rockledge (FL.) **44** C 2
Rockmart (GA.) **42** B 5−6
Rockport (CA.) **110** C 5
Rockport (IN.) **52** B 5
Rockport (MA.) **31** F 3
Rockport (MO.) **64** B 1
Rockport (TX.) **71** E 2
Rocksprings (TX.) **74** A 4
Rockton (IL.) **56** A 4
Rockville (IN.) **52** B 3
Rockville (MD.) **37** G 2
Rockville (UT.) **103** E 4−5
Rockwell (IA.) **63** E 2
Rockwell City (IA.) **62** D 3
Rockwood (ME.) **28** C 4
Rockwood (MI.) **55** F 2
Rockwood (PA.) **34** B 4
Rockwood (TX.) **74** B 3
Rocky (OK.) **76** DE 2
Rocky Boy (MT.) **86** D 1
Rocky Boys Indian
   Reservation **86** D 1
Rocky Dam **99** G 3
Rocky Island Dam
   114−115 E 2
Rocky Mount (N.C.) **39** G 3
Rocky Mount (VA.)
   36 E 4−5
Rocky Mountain (MT.)
   86 A 2
Rocky Mountain National
   Park **94−95** E 1
Rocky Point (AK.) **120** C 3
Rocky Point (CA.) **110** A 6
Rocky Reach Dam **115** E 2
Rocky Top **112** C 2
Rockypoint (WY.) **93** GH 1
Rodanthe (N.C.) **39** J 3
Rodeo (N.M.) **98** B 5
Roe (N.C.) **39** H 4
Roff (OK.) **77** G 3
Rogers (N.D.) **85** H 3
Rogers (TX.) **74** D 4
Rogers City (MI.) **54** C 2
Rogers Lake (AK.) **107** E 3
Rogers Lake (AZ.) **100** E 1
Rogers, Mount **36** C 5
Rogerson (ID.) **90** E 4
Rogersville (AL.) **46** B 5
Rogersville (MO.) **64** D 4
Rogersville (TN.) **51** G 4
Rogue River **112** B 4
Rogue River (OR.) **112** B 4
Rojo, Cabo **124** A 3
Roland (IA.) **63** E 3
Rolette (ND.) **85** G 2

Rolfe (IA.) **62** D 3
Roll (AZ.) **100** B 4
Roll (OK.) **76** D 2
Rolla (KS.) **78** B 4
Rolla (MO.) **65** F 4
Rolla (ND.) **85** G 2
Rolling Fork (MS.) **48** D 4
Rollins (MT.) **89** F 2
Roma - Los Saenz (TX.)
   70 D 4
Romain, Cape **41** F 4
Roman Nose Mountain
   112 B 3
Romano, Cape **45** F 3
Romanzof Mountains (AL.)
   121 G 2
Rome (GA.) **42** B 6
Rome (N.Y.) **32** E 2
Rome (TN.) **50** D 4
Romeo (CO.) **94** D 4
Romeo (MI.) **55** F 1
Romero (TX.) **97** H 3
Romeroville (N.M.) **97** E 3
Romney (TX.) **74** B 2
Romney (W.V.) **37** F 2
Romoland (CA.) **107** E 4
Ronan (MT.) **89** F 2
Roof Butte **103** F 1
Roosevelt (AZ.) **101** E 3
Roosevelt (MN.) **60** B 5
Roosevelt (OK.) **76** D 3
Roosevelt (UT.) **102** B 1
Roosville (MT.) **88** EF 1
Ropesville (TX.) **99** H 3
Rosalia (WA.) **115** H 2
Rosamond (CA.) **106** D 3
Rosamond Lake **106** D 3
Rosanky (TX.) **74** D 5
Roscoe (SD.) **83** F 2
Roscoe (TX.) **73** H 1
Roscommon (MI.) **55** D 3
Rose (NE.) **81** E 2
Rose City (MI.) **55** D 3
Rose Hill (N.C.) **39** G 4
Rose Hill (VA.) **36** A 2
Rose Peak **101** G 3
Roseau (MN.) **60** B 5
Roseau River **60** B 6
Roseboro (N.C.) **39** F 4
Rosebud (MT.) **87** G 3
Rosebud (SD.) **82** DE 4
Rosebud (TX.) **74** D 3
Rosebud Indian
   Reservation **82–83** E 4
Roseburg (OR.) **112** B 3
Rosedale (MS.) **48** C 4–5
Roseglen (ND.) **84** E 3
Rosette (UT.) **102** A 5
Roseville (CA.) **111** D 3
Roseville (IL.) **56** C 5
Roseville (MI.) **55** F 1
Roseworth (ID.) **90** D 4
Rosholt (S.D.) **83** J 2
Rosholt (WI.) **59** E 3
Rosita (TX.) **70** D 3
Roslyn (S.D.) **83** H 2
Roslyn (WA.) **114** E 2
Rosman (N.C.) **51** H 5
Ross (ND.) **84** D 2
Ross Lake **114** DE 1
Ross R. Barnett Reservoir
   48 D 3
Rosston (OK.) **76** C 1
Roswell (GA.) **42** B 5
Roswell (N.M.) **99** G 3
Rotan (TX.) **73** H 1

Rothiemay (MT.) **86** D 3
Rothsay (MN.) **60** D 6
Rougemont (N.C.) **39** E 2
Rough River Lake **50** D 3
Round Mound **78** D 3
Round Mountain (NV.)
   104 D 4
Round Mountain (TX.)
   74 C 4
Round Rock (AZ.) **103** F 1
Round Rock (TX.) **74** D 4
Round Valley Indian
   Reservation **110** C 5
Roundup (MT.) **86** E 3
Rowe (N.M.) **96** E 3
Rowena (TX.) **73** H 2
Rowland (N.C.) **39** E 4
Rowland (NV.) **105** F 1
Roxboro (N.C.) **39** F 2
Roxboro Lake **39** EF 2
Roxie (MS.) **49** E 5
Roy (ID.) **91** G 4
Roy (MT.) **86** E 2
Roy (N.M.) **97** F 3
Roy (UT.) **102** A 4
Roy (WA.) **114** C 2
Royal City (WA.) **115** F 3
Royale, Isle **58** B 2
Royalton (MN.) **61** E 4
Royalty (TX.) **73** EF 2
Royse City (TX.) **75** E 1–2
Royston (GA.) **42** B 4
Rozel (KS.) **78** D 3
Rozet (WY.) **93** G 1
Rubonia (FL.) **45** D 4
Ruby (AL.) **121** D 3
Ruby (WA.) **115** H 1
Ruby Lake **105** F 2
Ruby Mountains **105** F 2–3
Ruby Range **86** A 4
Ruby Valley (NV.) **105** F 2
Rubys Inn (UT.) **103** E 4
Ruch (OR.) **112** BC 4
Rudolph (TX.) **71** E 4
Rudy Dome **105** F 2
Rudyard (MI.) **54** B 3
Rudyard (MT.) **86** C 1
Ruff (WA.) **115** G 2
Ruffin (S.C.) **41** E 3
Ruffling Point **124** D 2
Rufus (OR.) **112** E 1
Rugby (ND.) **85** G 2
Ruidosa (TX.) **72** D 3
Ruidoso (N.M.) **98–99** E 3
Rule (TX.) **76** D 4
Ruleville (MS.) **48** C 4
Rulo (NE.) **81** J 4
Runge (TX.) **71** E 2
Rupert (GA.) **43** D 5
Rupert (ID.) **91** F 4
Rupert (W.V.) **36** D 4
Rural Hall (N.C.) **38** D 2
Rush (CO.) **95** F 3
Rush Center (KS.) **78** D 3
Rush City (MN.) **61** E 2
Rush Springs (OK.) **77** E 3
Rushford (MN.) **61** G 1
Rushmore, Mount **82** B 4
Rushville (IL.) **56** C 5
Rushville (IN.) **52** D 3
Rushville (NE.) **80** B 2
Rusk (TX.) **75** F 3
Ruskin (FL.) **45** D 4
Ruso (ND.) **84** F 3
Russel (KS.) **78** DE 3
Russel, Mount **119** E 1

Russel Springs (KS.) **78** B 3
Russel Springs (KY.) **51** E 3
Russell (MN.) **61** F 5
Russell Cave National
   Monument **46** B 3–4
Russellville (AL.) **46** B 5
Russellville (AR.) **66** C 2
Russellville (KY.) **50** C 4
Russian Mission **119** C 1
Russian River **111** D 4
Rustburg (VA.) **37** E 4
Ruston (LA.) **68** C 1
Ruth (MS.) **49** E 4
Ruth (NV.) **105** F 3
Ruther Glen (VA.) **37** G 4
Rutherfordton (N.C.) **51** H 5
Ruthton (MN.) **61** F 6
Ruthven (IA.) **62** D 2
Rutland (N.D.) **85** J 4
Rutland (VT.) **30** C 2
Rutledge (TN.) **51** G 4
Ryan (OK.) **77** E 3
Ryan (TX.) **72** D 3
Ryan Park (WY.) **93** F 4
Ryan Peak **90–91** E 3
Ryder (ND.) **84** E 3
Ryderwood (WA.) **114** BC 3
Rye (CO.) **95** F 4
Rye Patch Reservoir
   104 C 2
Ryegate (MT.) **86** D 3

Sa-Nos-tee (N.M.) **96** B 2
Sabetha (KS.) **79** H 2
Sabinal (N.M.) **96** D 4
Sabinal (TX.) **70** C 1
Sabinas (Mex.) **70** A 3
Sabinas Hidalgo (Mex.)
   70 B 4
Sabine (TX.) **75** H 5
Sabine Lake **75** H 5
Sabine Pass (TX.) **75** H 5
Sabine River **75** H 4
Sable, Cape (FL.) **45** F 3
Sac and Fox Indian
   Reservation **79** H 2
Sac City (IA.) **62** D 3
Sacagawea Peak **86** BC 4
Sacajawea, Lake **115** G 3
Sacajawea Peak **113** H 1
Sacandaga Reservoir
   33 F 2
Saco (ME.) **29** E 5
Saco (MT.) **87** F 1
Sacramento (CA.) **111** D 3
Sacramento (N.M.) **99** E 4
Sacramento Mountains
   98–99 E 3–4
Sacramento River
   110 C 3
Sacramento Valley
   110 C 3–4
Saddle Mountain (WA.)
   112 B 1
Saddle Mountain (WY.)
   92 C 1

Saddle Mountains (WA.)
   115 EF 3
Saddle Peak **115** E 1
Saddlestring (WY.) **93** F 1
Safford (AL.) **46** D 5
Safford (AZ.) **101** G 4
Sagavanirktou (AL.)
   121 F 2
Sage (WY.) **92** B 4
Sagerton (TX.) **76** C 4
Sagerton (TX.) **76** C 4
Saginaw (MI.) **55** E 2
Saginaw Bay **55** E 2
Saguache (CO.) **94** D 3
Saguaro National
   Monument **100–101** EF 4
Sagwon (AL.) **121** F 2
Sahuarita (AZ.) **101** F 5
Saint Albans (W.V.) **36** C 3
Saint Andrew Sound
   43 EF 2
Saint Augustine (FL.)
   44 B 3
Saint Catherines Island
   43 E 2
Saint Charles (MN.)
   61 G 1–2
Saint Charles (MO.) **65** G 3
Saint Charles (SD.) **83** F 4
Saint Clair (MN.) **61** F 3
Saint Clair (MO.) **65** G 3
Saint Clair, Lake **55** F 1
Saint Clair River **55** F 1
Saint Clair Shores (MI.)
   55 F 1
Saint Cloud (FL.) **44** C 3
Saint Cloud (MN.) **61** E 4
Saint Croix **124** D 3
Saint Croix Island Int'l
   Historic Site (ME.) **28** F 3
Saint Croix River (ME.)
   28 C 2
Saint Croix River (MN./WI.)
   61 E 2
Saint David (AZ.) **101** F 5
Saint Francis (SD.) **82** E 4
Saint Francisville (LA.)
   68 D 3
Saint Francois Mountains
   65 G 4
Saint Froid Lake **28** B 3
Saint George (GA.) **43** F 3
Saint George (S.C.) **41** E 3
Saint George Island **47** G 2
Saint George, Point
   110 A 6
Saint-Georges (Can.)
   28 B 6
Saint Helena Sound **41** E 4
Saint Helens, Mount
   114 C 3
Saint Ignatius (MT.) **89** F 2
Saint James (MN.) **61** G 4
Saint James (MO.) **65** F 3
Saint Jo (TX.) **74** D 1
Saint Joe River **88** D 2
Saint John (ND.) **85** G 2
Saint John (P.R.) **124** D 2
Saint John (WA.) **115** H 2
Saint Johns (AZ.) **101** G 2
Saint Johns River **44** AB 3
Saint Joseph (LA.) **68** D 2
Saint Joseph (MI.) **55** F 5
Saint Joseph (MO.) **64** C 2
Saint Joseph Island
   71 F 2–3

Saint Joseph Point **47** G 3
Saint Joseph River **52** D 1
Saint Landry (LA.) **68** C 3
Saint Léonard (Can.) **28** A 2
Saint Louis (MO.) **65** G 3
Saint Louis River **60** C 2
Saint Marks (FL.) **47** F 2
Saint Martin, Cape **109** H 3
Saint Martin Island **54** C 5
Saint Martinville (LA.) **68** D 3
Saint Mary (MT.) **89** G 1
Saint Mary Lake **89** G 1
Saint Marys (GA.) **43** F 2
Saint Marys River **43** F 2
Saint Matthews (S.C.) **41** E 3
Saint Maurice River (Can.) **28** B 7
Saint Michael (AL.) **120** C 3
Saint Michaels (AZ.) **101** G 1
Saint Nicholas, Mount **89** G 1
Saint Onge (SD.) **82** B 3
Saint Patrick Peak **89** F 3
Saint Paul (MN.) **61** F 2
Saint Pauls (N.C.) **39** E 4
Saint Peter (KS.) **78** C 2
Saint Peter (MN.) **61** F 4
Saint Petersburg (FL.) **45** D 5
Saint Petersburg Beach (FL.) **44** D 4
Saint Regis (MT.) **88** E 2
Saint Regis Indian Reservation **33** F 1
Saint Simons Island **43** E 2
Sàint Stephen (Can.) **28** C 2
Saint Stephen (S.C.) **41** F 3
Saint Teresa Beach (FL.) **47** G 2
Saint Thomas (P.R.) **124** CD 2
Saint Vincent Island **47** G 3
St Clair (MI.) **55** F 1
St Clairsville (OH.) **53** H 2
St Francis (KS.) **78** B 2
St Francis (KS.) **78** B 2
St Francis (ME.) **28** A 4
St Charles (ID.) **91** H 4
St Charles (MI.) **55** E 3
St. Marys (AL.) **119** C 1
St. Mattheu (AL.) **118** A 1
St. Paul (KY.) **51** G 2
St. Paul (NE.) **81** F 3
St. Paul (VA.) **36** B 5
St. Paul Islands (AL.) **118** AB 2
St. Xavier (MT.) **87** F 4
St. Lawrence Island (AL.) **120** B 3
St. Lawrence River (Can.) **28** A 5
St Albans (VT.) **30** C 1
St Michales (MD.) **37** H 3
St Joe (ID.) **88** D 2
Sainte Genevieve (MO.) **65** G 3
St. Regis Falls (N.Y.) **33** F 1
St. George Island (AL.) **118** B 2
St. Phillip (MT.) **87** J 3
St John (KS.) **78** E 3
St Johns (MI.) **55** E 3
St Johnsbury (VT.) **30** E 1
St. Vincent (MN.) **85** J 2
St Helena (CA.) **111** D 4
St. Elias Mts. (AL.) **117** CD 1
St James (MI.) **54** C 4
St Elmo (IL.) **57** D 3
St Ignace (MI.) **54** C 3
St Anne (IL.) **56** B 2
St. John River (Can.) **28** B 2
St Croix falls (WI.) **59** D 6
St. Tomas (N.D.) **85** J 2
St George (UT.) **103** E 5
St Maries (ID.) **88** D 2
St Marys (KS.) **79** G 2
St Marys (OH.) **52** E 2
St Marys (PA.) **34** C 2
St Marys (W.V) **36** C 2
St Anthony (ID.) **91** H 3
St Anthony (ND.) **84** F 4
St Edward (NE.) **81** G 3
Sakakawea, Lake **84** D 2
Sal, Point **106** B 3
Salduro (UT.) **102** B 5
Sale Creek (TN.) **51** E 5
Salem (AR.) **67** E 1
Salem (FL.) **44** B 5
Salem (IA.) **63** G 5
Salem (IL.) **57** E 3
Salem (IN.) **52** C 4
Salem (MA.) **31** F 3
Salem (MO.) **65** F 4
Salem (N.Y.) **33** G 2
Salem (OR.) **112** BC 2
Salem (PA.) **35** F 4
Salem (S.D.) **83** H 4
Salem (VA.) **36** D 4
Salem (W.V.) **36** D 2
Salesville (TX.) **74** C 2
Salida (CO.) **94** E 3
Salina (AZ.) **103** F 1
Salina (KS.) **79** F 3
Salina (UT.) **102** D 3
Salinas (CA.) **111** F 3
Salinas (P.R.) **124** B 2
Salinas Peak **98** D 3
Salinas River **111** F 3
Saline (LA.) **68** C 1
Saline Lake **68** C 2
Saline River (AR.) **66** D 4
Saline River (KS.) **78** D 2
Salineno (TX.) **70** C 4
Salisbury (MD.) **37** J 3
Salisbury (N.C.) **38** D 3
Salisbury (PA.) **34** B 4
Salkum (WA.) **114** C 3
Sallisaw (OK.) **77** J 2
Salmon (ID.) **89** FG 4
Salmon Creek Reservoir **90** E 4
Salmon Mountains **110** AB 5
Salmon River **88** D 4
Salmon River Mountains **88** E 4
Salome (AZ.) **100** C 3
Salon Springs (WI.) **58** C 6
Salt Flat (TX.) **72** C 2
Salt Fork (OK.) **76** D 3
Salt Fork (OK.) **77** EF 1
Salt Fork (TX.) **76** C 4
Salt Gap (TX.) **74** B 3
Salt Lake (N.M.) **99** G 4
Salt Lake City (UT.) **102** B 3
Salt Marsh Lake **102** C 5
Salt River **101** F 3
Salt River Indian Reservation **100** E 3
Salt Springs (FL.) **44** B 3
Salt Wells (NV.) **104** C 3
Saltdale (CA.) **107** E 2
Saltillo (MS.) **48** B 2
Saltillo (TN.) **50** B 5
Salton Sea **107** G 4
Saltville (VA.) **36** C 5
Saluda (S.C.) **40** D 2–3
Saluda (VA.) **37** H 4
Saluda River **40** D 2
Salvador, Lake **69** E 4
Salyer (CA.) **110** B 5
Salyersville (KY.) **51** H 3
Sam Rayburn Dam **75** G 3
Sam Rayburn Reservoir **75** G 3
Samalga Pass (AL.) **118** B 3
Samaria (ID.) **91** G 4
Samoa (CA.) **110** B 6
Samson (AL.) **47** E 4
San Acacia (N.M.) **96** D 4
San Agustin, Plains of **98** BC 3
San Andreas (CA.) **111** D 2
San Andres Mountains **98** D 3–4
San Andres Peak **98** D 4
San Angelo (TX.) **73** H 2
San Angelo Lake **73** H 2
San Anselmo (CA.) **111** D 4
San Antonio (CO.) **94** E 4
San Antonio (N.M.) **98** D 3
San Antonio (TX.) **70** D 1
San Antonio Bay **71** F 2
San Antonio, Mount **107** E 3
San Antonio Mountain **96** D 2
San Antonio Reservoir **106** A 2
San Antonio River **71** E 2
San Ardo (CA.) **111** F 2
San Augustin Pass **98** D 4
San Augustin Pass (TX.) **71** E 4
San Augustine (TX.) **75** G 3
San Barnardino (CA.) **107** E 3
San Benito (CA.) **111** F 3
San Benito Mountain **111** F 2
San Bernardino Mountains **107** F 3–4
San Blas (Mex.) **70** A 3
San Blas, Cape **47** G 3
San Carlos (AZ.) **101** F 3
San Carlos Indian Reservation **101** FG 3
San Carlos Lake **101** F 3
San Clemente (CA.) **107** E 4
San Clemente Island **106** D 5
San Diego (CA.) **107** E 5
San Diego (TX.) **70** D 3
San Fernando (CA.) **106** D 3
San Francisco (CA.) **111** E 4
San Francisco Bay **111** E 4
San Francisco Mountains (AZ.) **100** DE 1
San Francisco Mountains (N.M.) **98** B 2–3
San Gabriel Mountains **106–107** DE 3
San Germán (P.R.) **124** AB 2
San Gorgonio Mountain **107** F 3
San Isidro (TX.) **70** D 4
San Jacinto (NV.) **105** G 1
San Jacinto Mountains **107** F 4
San Jacinto Peak **107** F 4
San Joaquin (CA.) **111** F 2
San Joaquin River **111** EF 2
San Joaquin Valley **111** E 2–3
San Jon (N.M.) **97** G 3
San Jose (CA.) **111** E 3
San Jose (N.M.) **96** E 3
San Juan (P.R.) **124** BC 2
San Juan Basin **96** BC 2
San Juan Indian Reservation **96** D 2
San Juan Island **114** B 1
San Juan Mountains **94** CD 4
San Juan River **103** E 2
San Leandro (CA.) **111** E 4
San Lucas (CA.) **111** F 2
San Luis (AZ.) **100** B 4
San Luis (CO.) **95** E 4
San Luis Obispo (CA.) **106** B 2
San Luis Obispo Bay **106** B 2
San Luis Peak **94** D 4
San Luis Reservoir **111** E 3
San Manuel (AZ.) **101** F 4
San Marcial (N.M.) **98** D 3
San Marcos (TX.) **74** D 5
San Mateo (CA.) **111** E 4
San Mateo (N.M.) **96** C 3
San Miguel (CA.) **106** B 2
San Miguel (N.M.) **96** D 2
San Miguel Island **106** B 3
San Nicolas Island **106** C 4
San Pablo (CO.) **95** E 4
San Pablo Bay **111** D 4
San Pedro (CO.) **94–95** E 4
San Pedro (TX.) **71** E 3
San Pedro Chammel **106** D 4
San Pedro River **101** F 4
San Rafael (CA.) **111** E 4
San Rafael (N.M.) **96** C 3
San Rafael Mountains **106** BC 3
San Rafael River **102–103** D 2
San Rafael Swell **103** D 2
San Saba (TX.) **74** C 3
San Saba River **74** B 3–4
San Sebastián (P.R.) **124** B 2
San Simeon (CA.) **106** B 2
San Simon (AZ.) **101** G 4
San Simon Valley **101** G 4
San Xavier Indian Reservation **101** EF 4
San Ygnacio (TX.) **70** C 3
Sanak Islands (AL.) **118** C 3
Sanborn (MN.) **61** F 5
Sanborn (N.D.) **85** H 4
Sanchez (N.M.) **97** F 3
Sand Creek **93** G 2
Sand Draw (WY.) **92** D 3
Sand Hills **80** C 3
Sand Island **58** C 5
Sand Pass (NV.) **104** B 2

Sand Point (AL.) **119** CD 2
Sand Springs (MT.) **87** F 2
Sand Springs (OK.) **77** G 1
Sanders (AZ.) **101** G 1
Sanders (MT.) **87** F 3
Sanderson (TX.) **73** F 3
Sandersville (GA.) **42** D 4
Sandersville (MS.) **49** E 2
Sandia Crest **96** D 3
Sandia Pueblo (N.M.)
   96 D 3
Sandow (TX.) **74** D 4
Sands Key **45** F 2
Sandstone (MN.) **61** D 2
Sandusky (MI.) **55** E 1
Sandusky (OH.) **53** G 1
Sandwich (MA.) **31** F 4
Sandy (OR.) **112** C 1
Sandy (TX.) **74** C 4
Sandy Hook (KY.) **51** G 2
Sandy Hook (MS.) **49** E 3
Sandy Springs (GA.) **42** C 5
Sanford (FL.) **44** C 3
Sanford (KS.) **78** D 3
Sanford (ME.) **29** E 5
Sanford (MI.) **55** E 3
Sanford (N.C.) **39** E 3
Sangamon River **56** D 4
Sanger (CA.) **111** F 1
Sanger (TX.) **74** D 1
Sangerfield (N.Y.) **33** E 3
Sangre de Cristo
   Mountains **94–95** E 3–4
Sanibel Island **45** E 4
Sanpoil River **115** G 1
Santa (ID.) **88** D 2
Santa Ana (CA.) **107** E 4
Santa Ana Mountains
   107 E 4
Santa Ana Pueblo (N.M.)
   96 D 3
Santa Anna (TX.) **74** B 3
Santa Barbara (CA.)
   106 C 3
Santa Barbara Channel
   106 BC 3
Santa Barbara Island
   106 C 4
Santa Catalina, Gulf of
   106–107 E 4
Santa Catalina Island
   106 D 4
Santa Clara (CA.) **111** E 4
Santa Clara (Mex.) **72** B 4
Santa Clara (UT.) **103** E 5
Santa Clara Indian
   Reservation **96** D 3
Santa Clara Valley **111** EF 3
Santa Cruz (CA.) **111** EF 4
Santa Cruz Island
   106 C 3–4
Santa Cruz River
   100–101 E 4
Santa Cruz Wash **100** D 3
Santa Fe (N.M.) **96** D 3
Santa Fe Baldy **96** E 3
Santa Fe River **44** B 4
Santa Isabel (P.R.) **124** B 3
Santa Lucia Range **111** F 3
Santa Margarita (CA.)
   106 B 2
Santa Margarita Lake
   106 B 2
Santa Maria (CA.) **106** B 3
Santa Maria River **100** C 2
Santa Monica (CA.) **106** D 3

Santa Monica Bay **106** D 4
Santa Paula (CA.) **106** C 3
Santa Rita (N.M.) **98** BC 4
Santa Rosa (CA.) **111** D 4
Santa Rosa (N.M.) **97** F 4
Santa Rosa (TX.) **71** E 4
Santa Rosa Beach (FL.)
   47 F 4
Santa Rosa Island (CA.)
   106 B 4
Santa Rosa Island (FL.)
   47 F 4
Santa Rosa Mountains
   107 FG 4
Santa Rosa Range **104** D 1
Santa Ynez (CA.) **106** B 3
Santa Ynez Mountains
   106 BC 3
Santa Ysabel (CA.) **107** F 4
Santa Ysabel Indian
   Reservation **107** F 4
Santaquin (UT.) **102** C 3
Santee Indian Reservation
   81 G 2
Santee River **41** F 3
Santiago Mountains
   73 EF 4
Santiam Pass **112** D 2
Santo (TX.) **74** C 2
Santo Domingo Pueblo
   (N.M.) **96** D 3
Santo Felipe Pueblo (N.M.)
   96 D 3
Sapelo Island **43** E 2
Sappa Creek **78** C 2
Sapphire Mountains
   89 G 3
Sappho (WA.) **114** A 1
Sappington (MT.) **86** B 4
Sapulpa (OK.) **77** G 1
Sara, Lake **57** D 3
Saragosa (TX.) **72–73** E 2
Saraland (AL.) **47** F 6
Saranac Lake (N.Y.) **33** F 1
Sarasota (FL.) **45** D 4
Saratoga (CA.) **111** E 4
Saratoga (TX.) **75** G 4
Saratoga (WY.) **93** F 4
Saratoga Springs (N.Y.)
   33 G 2
Sarcoxie (MO.) **64** C 4
Sardis (AL.) **46** D 4
Sardis (GA.) **42** CD 2
Sardis (MS.) **48** B 3
Sardis Lake **48** B 3
Sarepta (LA.) **68** B 1
Sargent (NE.) **81** E 3
Sargents (CO.) **94** D 3
Sarita (TX.) **71** E 3
Sarles (ND.) **85** H 2
Sassafras Mountain **40** C 1
Satanta (KS.) **78** B 4
Satellite Beach (FL.) **44** C 2
Satilla River **43** E 3
Satolah (GA.) **42** B 4
Sauceda Mountains
   100–101 E 4
Saucier (MS.) **49** F 3
Saugatuck (MI.) **55** F 5
Saugerties (N.Y.) **33** F 3
Saugus (CA.) **106** D 3
Sauk Centre (MN.) **61** E 4
Sauk City (WI.) **59** F 3
Sauk Rapids (MN.) **61** E 4
Sault Sainte Marie (MI.)
   54 B 3

Saunders (KS.) **78** B 4
Savage (MT.) **87** J 2
Savageton (WY.) **93** G 2
Savanna (WI.) **56** A 5
Savannah (GA.) **43** D 2
Savannah (MO.) **64** C 2
Savannah (TN.) **50** B 5
Savannah Beach (GA.)
   41 E 4
Savannah River **40** D 4
Savoonga (AL.) **120** A 3
Savoy (MT.) **86** E 1
Sawatch Range **94** D 2–3
Saweyrs Bar (CA.) **110** A 5
Sawtooth Mountains
   58 B 4–5
Sawtooth Range **90** DE 2–3
Sawyer (KS.) **78** E 4
Sawyer (ND.) **84** E 2
Saxton (PA.) **34** C 3
Sayre (OK.) **76** D 2
Sayreville (N.J.) **35** G 3
Scammon Bay (AL.)
   118 BC 1
Scandia (KS.) **79** F 2
Scappoose (OR.) **112** BC 1
Scar Hill **111** B 3
Scarface Peak **89** G 2
Scenic (WA.) **114** D 2
Schell City (MO.) **64** C 3–4
Schell Creek Range
   105 G 3–4
Schenectady (N.Y.) **33** G 3
Schleswig (IA.) **62** C 3
Schoenchen (KS.) **78** D 3
Scholle (N.M.) **96** D 4
Schrag (WA.) **115** G 2
Schriever (LA.) **69** E 4
Schroon Lake **33** G 2
Schuchk (AZ.) **100** E 4
Schulenburg (TX.) **71** F 1
Schurz (NV.) **104** C 4
Schuyler (NE.) **81** G 3
Schwatka Mountains (AL.)
   121 D 2
Scio (OR.) **112** C 2
Scioto River **53** F 2
Scipio (UT.) **102** C 4
Scobey (MT.) **87** H 1
Scofield Reservoir **102** C 3
Scooba (MS.) **48** D 2
Scotia (NE.) **81** F 3
Scotland (MD.) **37** H 3
Scotland (S.D.) **83** H 4
Scotland (TX.) **76** E 4
Scotlandville (LA.)
   68–69 D 3
Scott (MS.) **48** C 5
Scott City (KS.) **78** B 3
Scott, Mount **112** CD 4
Scott Mountain **90** D 2
Scott Peak **91** G 2
Scotts Bluff National
   Monument **80** A 3
Scottsbluff (NE.) **80** A 3
Scottsboro (AL.) **46** B 4
Scottsburg (IN.) **52** D 4
Scottsdale (AZ.) **100** DE 3
Scottsville (KY.) **50** D 4
Scottville (MI.) **55** E 5
Scranton (ND.) **84** C 4
Scranton (PA.) **35** F 2
Screven (GA.) **43** E 2
Scribner (NE.) **81** H 3
Sea Island (GA.) **43** E 2
Sea Isle City (N.J.) **35** G 4

Sea Pines (S.C.) **41** E 4
Seadrift (TX.) **71** F 2
Seaford (DE.) **37** J 3
Seagraves (TX.) **73** F 1
Seagrove (N.C.) **38** E 3
Seal Island **29** E 3
Sealy (TX.) **75** E 5
Searchlight (NV.) **109** G 4
Searcy (AR.) **67** E 2
Searles (CA.) **107** E 2
Searles Lake **107** E 2
Seaside (CA.) **111** F 3
Seaside (OR.) **112** AB 1
Seaside Park (N.J.) **35** G 4
Seattle (WA.) **114** C 2
Sebago Lake **29** E 5
Sebastian (TX.) **71** E 4
Sebastopol (CA.) **111** D 4–5
Sebec Lake **28** C 4
Sebeka (MN.) **60** D 5
Sebewaing (MI.) **55** E 2
Seboeis Lake **28** C 3
Seboomook Lake **28** C 4
Seboyeta (N.M.) **96** C 3
Sebree (KY.) **50** C 3
Sebring (FL.) **45** D 3
Sedalia (MO.) **64** D 3
Sedgewick, Mount **96** B 3
Sedgwick (CO.) **95** H 1
Sedgwick (KS.) **79** F 4
Sedona (AZ.) **100** E 2
Seeley Lake (MT.) **89** G 2
Seguam (AL.) **117** K 1
Seguin (KS.) **78** C 2
Seguin (TX.) **70** D 1
Segula (AL.) **116** H 1
Seibert (CO.) **95** H 2
Seiling (OK.) **76** E 1
Selawik (AL.) **120** C 2
Selawik Lake (AL.)
   120 CD 2
Selby (SD.) **83** EF 2
Selbyville (DE.) **37** J 3
Selden (KS.) **78** C 2
Seldovia (AL.) **119** E 2
Selfridge (ND.) **84** F 4
Seligman (AZ.) **100** D 1
Seligman (MO.) **64** C 5
Selkirk (KS.) **78** B 3
Selkirk Mountains (ID.)
   88 D 1
Sellersburg (IN.) **52** CD 4
Sells (AZ.) **100** E 5
Selma (AL.) **46** D 4
Selma (CA.) **111** F 1
Selma (OR.) **112** B 4
Selmer (TN.) **50** B 5
Selway River **88** E 2
Selz (ND.) **85** G 3
Semichi Islands (AL.)
   116 G 1
Semidi Islands **119** D 2
Seminoe Dam (WY.) **93** E 3
Seminoe Reservoir **93** F 3
Seminole (FL.) **44** D 4
Seminole (OK.) **77** G 2
Seminole (TX.) **73** F 1
Seminole, Lake **43** F 5
Semisopochnoi (AL.)
   116 HJ 1
Semmes (AL.) **47** F 6
Senatobia (MS.) **48** B 4
Seneca (MO.) **64** C 5
Seneca (NE.) **79** G 2
Seneca (NE.) **80** D 2
Seneca (N.Y.) **32** B 3

Seneca (NY.) **32** D 3
Seneca (OR.) **113** FG 2
Seneca (SD.) **83** F 2
Senecaville Lake **53** H 3
Seney (MI.) **54** B 4
Senoia (GA.) **42** C 5
Sentinel (AZ.) **100** C 4
Sentinel (OK.) **76** D 2
Sentinel Butte (N.D.) **84** C 4
Sentinel Plain **100** C 4
Separ (N.M.) **98** B 4
Sequim (WA.) **114** B 1
Sequoia National Park
108 D 3
Sergant Bluff (IA.) **62** B 3
Seshan **120** A 2
Seth Ward (TX.) **76** B 3
Seul Choix Point **54** C 4
Seven Devils Mountains
88 D 4
Seven Sisters (TX.) **70** D 2
Severy (KS.) **79** G 4
Sevier (UT.) **103** D 4
Sevier Bridge Reservoir
102 C 3
Sevier Desert **102** C 4
Sevier Lake **102** D 5
Sevier Plateau **103** D 4
Sevier River **103** D 4
Sevierville (TN.) **51** G 5
Seville (FL.) **44** B 3
Seward (AL.) **116** B 1
Seward (KS.) **78** E 3
Seward (NE.) **81** G 4
Seward Peninsula (AL.)
120 C 2–3
Seymour (IN.) **52** C 4
Seymour (MO.) **64** E 4
Seymour (TX.) **76** D 4
Shadehill (SD.) **82** C 2
Shadehill (SD.) **82** C 2
Shadehill Reservoir **82** C 2
Shady Cove (OR.) **112** C 4
Shady Dale (GA.) **42** C 4
Shady Grove (FL.) **44** A 5
Shafer Butte **90** C 3
Shafer, Lake **52** C 2
Shafter (CA.) **106** C 2
Shafter (TX.) **72** D 4
Shageluk (AL.) **119** D 1
Shaker Heights (OH.)
53 H 1
Shaktoolik (AL.) **120** C 3
Shallotte (N.C.) **39** F 5
Shallow Water (KS.) **78** C 3
Shallowater (TX.) **99** H 3
Shamokin (PA.) **34** E 3
Shamrock (TX.) **76** C 2
Shaniko (OR.) **112** E 1
Shannon (GA.) **42** B 6
Shannon (MS.) **48** B 2
Shannon, Lake **114** D 1
Sharon (N.D.) **85** J 3
Sharon (PA.) **34** A 2
Sharon Springs (KS.)
78 B 3
Sharonville (OH.) **52** E 3
Sharpe, Lake **83** F 3
Sharpsburg (N.C.) **39** G 3
Sharpsville (PA.) **34** A 2
Shasta (CA.) **110** B 4
Shasta Dam **110** B 4
Shasta Lake **110** B 4
Shasta, Mount **110** A 4
Shattuck (OK.) **76** D 1
Shaw (MS.) **48** C 4

Shawano (WI.) **59** E 2
Shawmut (MT.) **86** D 3
Shawnee (OH.) **53** G 3
Shawnee (OK.) **77** G 2
Shawneetown (IL.) **57** F 3
Sheboygan (WI.) **59** F 1
Sheckler Reservoir **104** C 3
Sheenjek (AL.) **121** G 2
Sheep Mountain **100** B 4
Sheep Peak **72** D 2
Sheep Range **109** G 3
Sheep Springs (N.M.)
96 B 2
Sheffield (AL.) **46** B 5
Sheffield (IA.) **63** E 3
Sheffield (PA.) **34** B 2
Sheffield (TX.) **73** G 3
Shelbina (MO.) **65** EF 2
Shelby (MI.) **55** E 5
Shelby (MS.) **48** C 4
Shelby (MT.) **86** B 1
Shelby (N.C.) **38** C 3
Shelby (NE.) **81** G 3
Shelby (OH.) **53** G 2
Shelbyville (IL.) **57** D 3
Shelbyville (IN.) **52** D 3
Shelbyville (KY.) **51** E 2
Shelbyville (MO.) **65** E 2
Shelbyville (TN.) **50** D 5
Shelbyville (TN.) **50** D 5
Shelbyville, Lake **57** D 3
Sheldon (IA.) **62** C 2
Sheldon (MO.) **64** C 4
Sheldon Point (AL.) **120** B 3
Shelikof Strait (AL.) **119** E 2
Shelikof Strait (AL.) **119** E 2
Shell (WY.) **92** E 1
Shell Beach (LA.) **69** F 4
Shell Island **47** F 3
Shell Keys **68** D 4
Shell Lake (N.D.) **84** D 2
Shell Lake (WI.) **58** D 5
Shelley (ID.) **91** G 3
Shelton (WA.) **114** B 2
Shenandoah (IA.) **62** C 5
Shenandoah (PA.) **35** E 3
Shenandoah (VA.) **37** F 3
Shenandoah Mountain
36–37 E 3
Shenandoah National Park
37 F 3
Shenandoah River **37** G 2
Shepherd (MI.) **55** E 3
Shepherd (MT.) **86–87** E 4
Shepherd (TX.) **75** G 4
Shepherdsville (KY.) **50** E 3
Sherbrooke (Can.) **28** C 6
Sherburn (MN.) **61** G 4
Sherburne (N.Y.) **33** E 3
Sheridan (AR.) **66** D 3
Sheridan (MT.) **86** A 4
Sheridan (OR.) **112** B 1
Sheridan (TX.) **71** F 1
Sheridan (WY.) **93** F 1
Sheridan Lake (CO.) **95** H 3
Sherman (N.M.) **98** C 4
Sherman (N.Y.) **32** A 3
Sherman (TX.) **75** E 1
Sherman Reservoir **81** EF 3
Sherman Station (ME.)
28 C 3
Sherwood (AR.) **66** D 3
Sherwood (ND.) **84** E 2
Sherwood (OH.) **52** E 1
Sheyenne (ND.) **85** G 3
Sheyenne River **85** J 4

Shickley (NE.) **81** G 4
Shidler (OK.) **77** G 1
Shields (KS.) **78** C 3
Shields (ND.) **84** E 4
Shiner (TX.) **71** E 1
Shingleton (MI.) **54** B 5
Shingletown (CA.) **110** B 4
Shinnston (W.V.) **36** D 2
Shiocton (WI.) **59** E 2
Ship Bottom (N.J.) **35** G 4
Ship Rock (CO.) **96** B 2
Shippensburg (PA.) **34** D 3
Shippenville (PA.) **34** B 2
Shiprock (N.M.) **96** B 2
Shirley Mountain **93** F 3
Shishaldin Volcano **118** C 3
Shishmaref (AL.) **120** B 2
Shively (CA.) **110** B 5
Shively (KY.) **50** E 2
Shivwits (UT.) **103** E 5
Shivwits Plateau **103** F 5
Shoals (IN.) **52** C 4
Shonkin (MT.) **86** C 2
Shoshone (CA.) **107** F 1–2
Shoshone (ID.) **90** E 4
Shoshone Basin **92** DE 3
Shoshone Lake **92** B 1
Shoshone Mountains
104 D 3–4
Shoshone Peak **109** F 2
Shoshone River **92** D 1
Shoshoni (WY.) **92** D 2
Shoup (ID.) **89** F 4
Show Low (AZ.) **101** F 2
Show Low Lake **101** FG 2
Shreveport (LA.) **68** B 1
Shublik Mountains **121** F 2
Shubuta (MS.) **49** E 2
Shugualak (MS.) **48** CD 2
Shumagin Islands (AL.)
119 D 2
Shuman House **121** G 2
Shungnak (AL.) **120** C 2
Shuyak (AL.) **119** E 2
Siasconsett (N.Y.) **31** G 4
Sibley (IA.) **62** C 2
Sibley (LA.) **68** B 1
Sibley (MS.) **49** E 5
Sicily Island (LA.) **68** D 2
Sidnaw (MI.) **58** C 2
Sidney (IA.) **62** C 5
Sidney (IL.) **56** C 3
Sidney (MT.) **87** J 2
Sidney (NE.) **80** B 3
Sidney (N.Y.) **33** E 3
Sidney (OH.) **53** E 2
Sidney Lanier, Lake **42** B 4
Sierra Blanca **72** C 2
Sierra Blanca Peak **98** E 3
Sierra City (CA.) **110** C 2
Sierra de la Tasajera (Mex.)
72 BC 4
Sierra de las Tunas (Mex.)
72 A 4
Sierra de Luquillo **124** C 2
Sierra del Nido (Mex.)
72 B 4
Sierra Grande (Mex.)
72 D 3–4
Sierra Madre (WY.) **93** EF 4
Sierra Nevada
110–111 CE 1–2
Sierra Vieja **72** D 3
Signal Peak (AZ.) **100** B 3
Signal Peak (UT.) **103** E 5
Sigourney (IA.) **63** F 4

Sigurd (UT.) **103** D 3
Sikes (LA.) **68** C 1
Sikeston (MO.) **65** H 5
Sil Nakya (AZ.) **100** E 4
Silas (AL.) **47** E 6
Siler City (N.C.) **39** E 3
Silesia (MT.) **86** E 4
Siletz (OR.) **112** B 2
Silicon Valley **111** E 3
Silio (N.M.) **96** E 4
Siloam Springs (AR.)
66 B 1
Silsbee (TX.) **75** G 4
Siltcoos (OR.) **112** AB 3
Silver (TX.) **73** H 1
Silver Bow Park (MT.)
86 A 4
Silver City (ID.) **90** C 3
Silver City (MI.) **58** C 3
Silver City (N.M.) **98** B 4
Silver City (SD.) **82** B 3
Silver City (UT.) **102** C 4
Silver Cliff (CO.) **95** E 3
Silver Creek (MS.) **49** E 3
Silver Creek (NE.) **81** G 3
Silver Creek (N.Y.) **32** A 3
Silver Island Mountains
102 AB 5
Silver Lake (CA.) **107** F 2
Silver Lake (OR.) **112** D 3
Silver Lake (OR.) **112** E 3
Silver Lake (OR.) **113** F 3
Silver Lake (WA.) **114** C 3
Silver Peak Range **109** E 2
Silver Spring **37** H 3
Silver Springs (NV.)
104 B 3
Silver Star Mountain
114–115 E 1
Silver Valley (TX.) **74** B 3
Silvertip Mountain **89** G 2
Silverton (CO.) **94** C 4
Silverton (OR.) **112** C 1
Silverton (TX.) **76** B 3
Silverton (WA.) **114** D 1
Silvies (OR.) **113** G 2
Silvies River **113** F 3
Simi Valley (CA.) **106** D 3
Simla (CO.) **95** F 2
Simms (MT.) **86** AB 2
Simmesport (OR.) **112** D 2
Simpson (LA.) **68** C 2
Simpson (MN.) **61** G 2
Simpson (MT.) **86** C 1
Simpson Peak **117** E 2
Sims (IL.) **57** E 3
Simtustus, Lake **112** D 2
Sinclair (WY.) **93** E 4
Sinclair, Lake **42** C 4
Singer (LA.) **68** B 3
Singleton (TX.) **75** E 4
Sinton (TX.) **71** E 2
Sioux Center (IA.) **62** B 2
Sioux City (IA.) **62** B 3
Sioux Falls (S.D.) **83** HJ 4
Sioux Pass (MT.) **87** J 2
Sioux Rapids (IA.) **62** C 3
Sipsey River **46** C 5
Siren (WI.) **58** D 6
Siskiyou (OR.) **112** C 4
Siskiyou Mountains
110 A 5
Sisselton (S.D.) **83** H 2
Sisseton Indian
Reservation **83** HJ 2
Sissonville (W.V.) **36** C 3

Sister Bay (WI.) **54** C 6
Sisters (OR.) **112** D 2
Sitka (AL.) **117** D 2
Sitkinak Strait **119** E 2
Sixes (OR.) **112** A 4
Sixteen (MT.) **86** C 3
Skagit River **114** D 1
Skagway (AL.) **117** DE 2
Skamokawa (WA.) **114** B 3
Skaneateles Lake **32** D 3
Skeena Mountains (AL.)
  117 F 2
Skellytown (TX.) **76** B 2
Skiatook (OK.) **77** G 1
Skidmore (TX.) **71** E 2
Skime (MN.) **60** B 5
Skokie (IL.) **56** AB 2
Skokomish Indian
  Reservation **114** B 2
Skowhegan (ME.) **28** D 4
Skull Valley (AZ.) **100** D 2
Skull Valley Indian
  Reservation **102** B 4
Skunk River **63** G 4
Skwentna **119** E 1
Skwentna River **119** E 1
Slapout (OK.) **76** C 1
Slater (MO.) **64** D 2
Slater (WY.) **93** H 4
Slaton (TX.) **76** B 4
Slaty Fork (W.V.) **36** D 3
Slaughter (LA.) **68** D 3
Slayton (MN.) **61** F 5
Sledge (MS.) **48** B 4
Sleeping Bear Dunes
  National Lakeshore
  54 D 5
Sleepy Eye (MN.) **61** F 4
Sleetmute **119** D 1
Slick Rock (CO.) **94** B 3
Slide Mountain **33** F 4
Slidell (LA.) **69** E 3
Sliderock Mountain **89** G 3
Sligo (PA.) **34** B 2
Slim Buttes **82** B 2
Sloan (IA.) **62** B 3
Sloan (NV.) **107** G 2
Sloat (CA.) **110** C 2
Small (TX.) **72** C 2
Small, Cape **29** E 4
Smethport (PA.) **34** C 2
Smiley (TX.) **71** E 1
Smith (NV.) **104** B 4
Smith Bay (AL.) **121** E 1
Smith Center (KS.) **78** E 2
Smith Falls (Can.) **32** D 1
Smith Island (N.C.) **39** G 5
Smith Island (VA.) **37** J 4
Smith Mountain Lake
  36 E 4
Smith Peak **88** D 1
Smith River (CA.) **110** A 6
Smith River (MT.) **86** B 2
Smithfield (N.C.) **39** F 3
Smithfield (UT.) **102** A 3
Smithfield (VA.) **37** H 5
Smiths Ferry (ID.) **90** C 2
Smithville (GA.) **43** E 5
Smithville (OK.) **77** J 3
Smithville (TN.) **50** E 5
Smithville (TX.) **74** D 4
Smithwick (SD.) **82** B 4
Smoke Creek (NV.)
  104 B 2
Smoke Creek Desert
  104 B 2

Smoke Creek Reservoir
  104 B 2
Smoky Dome **90** E 3
Smoky Hill River **78** E 3
Smoky Hills **78** DE 2
Smoot (WY.) **92** B 3
Smyrna (DE.) **37** J 2
Smyrna (TN.) **50** D 5
Smyrna Mills (ME.) **28** B 3
Snag (AL.) **116** CD 1
Snake Range **105** G 3–4
Snake River (NE,) **80** C 2
Snake River (WA.) **115** H 3
Sneedville (TN.) **51** G 4
Snelling (CA.) **111** E 2
Snohomish (WA.) **114** CD 2
Snoqualmie (WA.) **114** D 2
Snoqualmie Pass **114** D 2
Snover (MI.) **55** E 2
Snow Hill (MD.) **37** J 3
Snow Hill (N.C.) **39** G 3
Snow Mountain (NV.)
  110 C 4
Snow Peak **115** G 1
Snow Water Lake **105** G 2
Snowdoun (AL.) **46** D 4
Snowflake (AZ.) **101** F 2
Snowmass Mountain
  94 C 2
Snowshoe Peak **88** E 1
Snowside Peak **90** E 3
Snowville (ID.) **91** G 4
Snyder (CO.) **95** G 1
Snyder (OK.) **76** D 3
Snyder (TX.) **73** H 1
Soap Lake (WA.) **115** F 2
Society Hill (S.C.) **41** E 2
Socorro (N.M.) **96** D 4
Socorro (TX.) **72** B 2
Soda Lake (CA.) **107** F 2
Soda Springs (CA.) **110** C 2
Soda Springs (ID.) **91** H 4
Soddy - Daisy (TN.) **51** E 5
Sodus Pt (N.Y.) **32** C 2
Sofia (N.M.) **97** G 2
Solano (N.M.) **97** F 3
Soldier Pond (ME.) **28** A 3
Soledad (CA.) **111** F 3
Solen (ND.) **84** F 4
Solomon (AZ.) **101** G 4
Solomon (KS.) **79** F 3
Solomon River **79** EF 2
Solon (IA.) **63** G 4
Solon (ME.) **28** D 4
Solvang (CA.) **106** B 3
Sombrero Peak **101** F 3
Somers (IA.) **62** D 3
Somers (MT.) **89** F 1
Somerset (CO.) **94** C 3
Somerset (KY.) **51** F 3
Somerset (OH.) **53** G 3
Somerset (PA.) **34** B 3
Somerset (TX.) **70** D 1
Somerton (AZ.) **100** B 4
Somerville (N.J.) **35** G 3
Somerville (TN.) **50** A 5
Somerville (TX.) **75** E 4
Somerville Lake **75** E 4
Somes Bar (CA.) **110** A 5
Sonda de Vieques **124** C 2
Sonestown (PA.) **34** E 2
Sonnette (MT.) **87** H 4
Sonoita (AZ.) **101** F 5
Sonoma (CA.) **111** D 4
Sonoma Peak **104** D 2

Sonora (AZ.) **101** EF 3
Sonora (CA.) **111** E 2
Sonora (TX.) **73** H 3
Sonora Desert **100** AC 3
Sopchoppy (FL.) **47** F 2
Soperton (GA.) **43** D 3
Sorum (SD.) **82** C 2
Sour Lake (TX.) **75** G 4
Souris Plain **85** FG 2
Souris River (N.D.) **84** F 2
Soutbeach (OR.) **112** A 2
South Baldy **96** C 4–5
South Bay (FL.) **45** E 2
South Bend (IN.) **52** C 1
South Bend (WA.) **114** B 3
South Boston (VA.) **37** E 5
South Branch **37** F 2
South Burlington (VT.)
  30 C 1
South Carolina **40–41**
South Dakota **82–83**
South Fork (AK.) **121** E 2
South Fork (AK.) **119** E 1
South Fork (CO.) **94** D 4
South Fork (CO./KS.)
  95 H 2
South Fork (KS.) **78** C 2
South Fork (KS.) **78** D 2
South Fork (MT.) **88** E 4
South Fork (S.C.) **40** D 3
South Fork Indian
  Reservation **105** F 2
South Fox Island **54** C 4
South Garcia (N.M.) **96** C 4
South Haven (KS.) **79** F 4
South Haven (MI.) **55** F 5
South Holston Lake **51** J 4
South Island (S.C.) **41** F 3
South Lake Tahoe (CA.)
  110–111 D 2
South Loup River
  80–81 B 3
South Manitou Island
  54 C 5
South Milwaukee (WI.)
  59 G 1
South Mountain **90** C 4
South Paris (ME.) **29** D 5
South Pass (CA.) **107** H 3
South Pass (WY.) **92** D 3
South Pass City (WY.)
  92 D 3
South Patrick Shores (FL.)
  44 C 2
South Plains (TX.) **76** B 3
South Platte River **95** GH 1
South Ponte Vedra Beach
  (FL.) **44** A 3
South Portland (ME.)
  29 E 5
South Punta Gorda Heights
  (FL.) **45** E 3
South Saint Paul (MN.)
  61 F 2–3
South Shore (S.D.) **83** J 2
South Sioux City (IA.)
  62 B 3
South Torrington (WY.)
  93 H 3
South Umpqua River
  112 B 3
South Ventana Cone
  111 F 3
Southampton (N.Y.) **35** J 3
Southern Ute Indian
  Reservation **94** C 4

Southland (TX.) **76** B 4
Southport (FL.) **47** F 3
Southport (N.C.) **39** G 5
Southwest Cape (P.R.)
  124 CD 3
Southwest Harbor (ME.)
  29 D 3
Spade (TX.) **73** G 1
Spalding (ID.) **88** D 3
Spalding (NE.) **81** F 3
Spanish Fork (UT.) **102** B 3
Spanish Fork Peak **102** B 3
Spanish Peak **113** F 2
Spanish Town **124** D 2
Sparks (NE.) **80** D 2
Sparks (NV.) **104** B 3
Sparta (GA.) **42** C 3
Sparta (IL.) **57** E 5
Sparta (N.C.) **38** C 2
Sparta (TN.) **51** E 5
Sparta (WI.) **59** F 4
Spartanburg (S.C.) **40** D 2
Spearfish (SD.) **82** B 3
Spearman (TX.) **76** B 1
Spearville (KS.) **78** D 4
Speedway (IN.) **52** C 3
Speight (KY.) **51** H 3
Spenard (AL.) **116** A 1
Spencer (IA.) **62** C 2
Spencer (ID.) **91** G 2
Spencer (IN.) **52** C 3
Spencer (NE.) **81** F 2
Spencer (N.Y.) **32** D 3
Spencer (S.D.) **83** H 4
Spencer (TN.) **51** E 5
Spencer (W.V.) **36** C 3
Sperryville (VA.) **37** F 3
Spickard (MO.) **64** D 1
Spirit Lake (IA.) **62** C 2
Spirit Lake (IA.) **61** G 5
Spirit Lake (ID.) **88** D 1–2
Spirit Lake (WA.) **114** CD 3
Spofford (TX.) **70** B 1
Spokane (WA.) **115** H 2
Spokane Indian
  Reservation **115** GH 2
Spokane, Mount **115** H 2
Spokane River **115** GH 2
Spoon River **56** C 5
Spooner (WI.) **58** D 6
Sportsmans Lake **79** F 2
Spotsylvania (VA.) **37** G 3
Spotted Horse (WY.)
  93 G 1
Spraberry (TX.) **73** G 2
Sprague (AL.) **47** D 4
Sprague (WA.) **115** GH 2
Sprague River (OR.)
  112 D 4
Spray (OR.) **113** F 2
Spring (TX.) **75** F 4
Spring Branch (TX.) **74** C 5
Spring Butte **92** D 4
Spring City (TN.) **51** F 5
Spring City (UT.) **102** C 3
Spring Green (WI.) **59** F 4
Spring Grove (MN.) **61** G 1
Spring Lake (N.C.) **39** F 3
Spring Mountains
  109 G 3–4
Spring Valley (MN.) **61** G 2
Spring Valley (NV.)
  105 G 3–4
Springdale (AR.) **66** B 1
Springdale (MT.) **86** C 4
Springdale (WA.) **115** GH 1

Springer (N.M.) **97** F 2
Springerville (AZ.) **101** G 2
Springfield (CO.) **95** H 4
Springfield (FL.) **47** F 3
Springfield (GA.) **43** D 2
Springfield (ID.) **91** G 3
Springfield (IL.) **56** D 4
Springfield (KY.) **51** E 3
Springfield (MA.) **30** D 3
Springfield (MN.) **61** F 4
Springfield (MO.) **64** D 4
Springfield (OH.) **53** E 3
Springfield (OR.) **112** C 2
Springfield (S.C.) **40** D 3
Springfield (S.D.) **83** G 5
Springfield (TN.) **50** D 4
Springfield, Lake **56** D 4
Springhill (LA.) **66** C 4
Springlake (TX.) **97** H 4
Springview (NE.) **80–81** E 2
Springville (CA.) **106** D 1
Springville (N.Y.) **32** B 3
Spruce Mountain (AZ.)
100 D 2
Spruce Mountain (NV.)
105 G 2
Spud Rock **101** F 4
Spur (TX.) **76** C 4
Squa Pan Lake **28** B 3
Square Butte (MT.) **86** C 2
Squaw Hill **93** G 4
Squaw Lake (MN.) **60** C 4
Squaw Peak **89** F 2
Squaw Valley (CA.) **111** F 1
Stafford (KS.) **78** E 3–4
Stafford (VA.) **37** G 3
Stallo (MS.) **48** D 3
Stamford (CT.) **35** H 2
Stamford (NE.) **81** E 4
Stamford (N.Y.) **33** F 3
Stamford (TX.) **74** B 2
Stamford, Lake **74** B 1
Stampede Reservoir
110 C 2
Stamps (AR.) **66** C 4
Stanardsville (VA.) **37** F 3
Standing Rock (N.M.)
96 B 3
Standing Rock Indian
Reservation **82** DE 2
Standish (CA.) **110** B 2
Standish (MI.) **55** E 2
Stanfield (AZ.) **100** E 4
Stanfield (OR.) **113** F 1
Stanford (KY.) **51** F 3
Stanford (MT.) **86** C 2
Stanley (ID.) **90** E 2
Stanley (ND.) **84** D 2
Stanley (N.M.) **96** E 3
Stansberry (MO.) **64** C 1
Stanton (KY.) **51** G 3
Stanton (MI.) **55** E 4
Stanton (ND.) **84** E 3
Stanton (NE.) **81** G 3
Stanton (TN.) **67** G 2
Stanton (TX.) **73** G 1
Stanwood (WA.) **114** C 1
Staples (MN.) **60** D 4
Stapleton (AL.) **47** F 5
Stapleton (NE.) **80** D 3
Star (N.C.) **38** E 3
Star City (AR.) **67** E 4
Star City (IN.) **52** C 2
Star Peak **104** C 2
Starbuck (MN.) **61** E 5
Starbuck (WA.) **115** G 3

Starke (FL.) **44** B 4
Starkville (MS.) **48** C 2
Starkweather (ND.) **85** G 2
Starvation Reservoir
102 B 2
State Bridge (CO.) **94** D 2
State College (MS.) **48** C 2
State College (PA.) **34** D 3
State Line (MS.) **49** E 2
Staten Island **35** G 3
Statenville (GA.) **43** F 3
Statesboro (GA.) **43** D 2
Statesville (N.C.) **38** D 3
Statue of Liberty National
Monument (N.Y.)
35 GH 3
Staunton (IL.) **57** D 4
Staunton (VA.) **37** E 3
Stayton (OR.) **112** C 2
Stead (N.M.) **97** G 2
Steamboat Canyon (AZ.)
103 G 2
Steamboat Springs (CO.)
94 D 1
Stearns (KY.) **51** F 4
Stebbins **120** C 3
Steele (MO.) **65** H 5
Steele (ND.) **85** G 4
Steele City (NE.) **81** H 4
Steele, Mount **93** F 4
Steelville (IL.) **57** EF 4
Steelville (MO.) **65** F 4
Steens Mountain **113** G 4
Stehekin (WA.) **114** E 1
Steinaker Reservoir
102 B 1
Steinauer (NE.) **81** H 4
Steinhatchee (FL.) **44** B 5
Steins (N.M.) **101** G 4
Steller, Mount **116** C 1
Stephan (SD.) **83** F 3
Stephen (MN.) **60** B 6
Stephens City (VA.) **37** F 2
Stephens Knob **51** F 4
Stephens Passage (AL.)
117 E 2
Stephenson (MI.) **54** C 6
Stephenville (TX.) **74** C 2
Steptoe (WA.) **115** H 2
Steptoe Valley **105** G 2
Sterling (AK.) **119** E 1
Sterling (CO.) **95** G 1
Sterling (IL.) **56** B 4
Sterling (MI.) **55** D 3
Sterling (ND.) **85** F 4
Sterling (NE.) **81** H 4
Sterling City (TX.) **73** H 2
Sterling Reservoir **95** G 1
Sterlington (LA.) **68** C 1
Steuben (MI.) **54** B 5
Steubenville (OH.) **53** J 2
Stevens Pass **114** DE 2
Stevens Peak **88** E 2
Stevens Point (WI.) **59** E 3
Stevens Village **121** F 2
Stevenson (WA.) **114** CD 4
Stevenson Entrance (AL.)
119 E 2
Stevensville (MT.) **89** F 3
Stewardson (IL.) **57** D 3
Stewart (AL.) **117** E 2
Stewarts Point (CA.)
111 D 5
Stewartstown (PA.) **34** E 4
Stewartsville (MO.) **64** C 2

Stewartville (MN.) **61** G 2
Stickney (S.D.) **83** G 4
Stigler (OK.) **77** H 2
Stikine Ranges (AL.)
117 E 2
Stikine River **117** E 2
Stiles (TX.) **73** G 2
Stillhouse Hollow
Reservoir **74** D 3
Stillwater (MN.) **61** E 2
Stillwater (NV.) **104** C 3
Stillwater (OK.) **77** FG 1
Stillwater (WI.) **59** D 6
Stillwater Range **104** C 3
Stillwater Reservoir **33** E 2
Stilwell (OK.) **77** J 2
Stine Mountain **89** G 4
Stinnett (TX.) **76** B 2
Stirling City (CA.) **110** C 3
Stirrat (W.V.) **36** C 4
Stockbridge (MI.) **55** F 3
Stockbridge Indian
Reservation **59** E 2
Stockdale (TX.) **70** D 1
Stockett (MT.) **86** B 2
Stockholm (ME.) **28** A 3
Stockport (IA.) **63** G 5
Stockton (AL.) **47** E 5
Stockton (CA.) **111** E 3
Stockton (GA.) **43** F 3
Stockton (IL.) **56** A 4
Stockton (KS.) **78** D 2
Stockton (MO.) **64** D 4
Stockton Island **58** C 4
Stockton Lake **64** D 4
Stockton Plateau **73** F 3
Stockville (NE.) **80** D 4
Stone City (CO.) **95** F 3
Stone Harbor (N.J.) **35** G 4
Stoneham (CO.) **95** G 1
Stoner (CO.) **94** B 4
Stonewall (OK.) **77** G 3
Stonington (CO.) **95** H 4
Stonington (ME.) **29** D 3
Stony (AL.) **119** D 1
Stony Gorge Reservoir
110 C 4
Stony Point **32** D 2
Stony Point (N.C.) **38** C 3
Stony River (AL.) **119** D 1
Stonyford (CA.) **110** C 4
Storla (S.D.) **83** G 4
Storm King Mountain
114 C 3
Storm Lake (IA.) **62** C 3
Storm Mountain **119** E 2
Stormy Mountain
114–115 E 2
Story (WY.) **93** EF 1
Story City (IA.) **62–63** E 3
Stoughton (WI.) **59** G 3
Stoun Lake (WI.) **58** D 5
Strait of Juan de Fuca
114 AB 1
Straits of Mackinac **54** C 3
Strasburg (CO.) **95** F 2
Strasburg (ND.) **85** F 4
Stratford (CA.) **111** F 1
Stratford (IA.) **62** E 3
Stratford (OK.) **77** F 3
Stratford (TX.) **97** HJ 2
Stratford (WA.) **115** F 2
Stratford (WI.) **59** E 4
Strathmore (CA.) **111** F 1
Stratton (CO.) **95** H 2
Stratton (ME.) **28** C 5

Stratton (NE.) **80** C 4
Strauss (N.M.) **98** D 5
Strawberry Daniels Pass
102 B 3
Strawberry Mountain
113 G 2
Strawberry Point (IA.)
63 G 3
Strawberry Reservoir
102 B 3
Strawn (TX.) **74** C 2
Streator (IL.) **56** B 3
Streeter (ND.) **85** G 4
Strogonof Point **119** D 2
Stromsburg (NE.) **81** G 3
Strong (AR.) **66** D 4
Strong City (KS.) **79** G 3
Strong City (OK.) **76** D 2
Strongsville (OH.) **53** H 1
Stryker (MT.) **89** F 1
Stuart (FL.) **45** D 2
Stuart (IA.) **62** D 4
Stuart (NE.) **81** E 2
Stuart (VA.) **36** D 5
Stuart I. (AL.) **120** C 3
Stuarts Draft (VA.) **37** F 3
Stump Lake **85** H 3
Sturgeon (MO.) **64** E 2
Sturgeon Bay (WI.) **59** E 1
Sturgis (KY.) **50** C 3
Sturgis (OK.) **97** G 2
Sturgis (SD.) **82** B 3
Stuttgart (AR.) **67** E 3
Sublett Range **91** G 4
Sublette (KS.) **78** B 4
Success, Lake **106** D 1
Sudden (CA.) **106** D 1
Suffolk (VA.) **37** H 5
Sugar City (CO.) **95** G 3
Sugar City (ID.) **91** H 3
Sugar Island **54** B 3
Sugarville (UT.) **102** C 4
Suisun Bay **111** D 3
Sula (MT.) **89** G 4
Sulligent (AL.) **46** C 6
Sullivan (IL.) **57** D 3
Sullivan (IN.) **52** B 3
Sullivan (MO.) **65** F 3
Sulphur (LA.) **68** B 3
Sulphur (NV.) **104** C 2
Sulphur (OK.) **77** G 3
Sulphur Springs (TX.)
75 F 1
Sulphurdale (UT.) **103** D 4
Sultan (WA.) **114** D 2
Sumas (WA.) **114** C 1
Sumatra (FL.) **47** F 2
Sumatra (MT.) **87** F 3
Summer Island **54** C 5
Summer Lake (OR.) **112** E 4
Summer Strait **117** E 2
Summerfield (N.C.) **38** E 2
Summerhaven (AZ.)
101 F 4
Summerland Key (FL.)
45 G 3
Summersville (MO.) **65** F 4
Summersville (W.V.)
36 D 3
Summersville Lake **36** D 3
Summertone (S.C.) **41** E 3
Summertown (TN.) **50** C 5
Summerville (GA.) **42** B 6
Summerville (S.C.) **41** E 3
Summit (AK.) **121** F 3
Summit (MS.) **49** E 4

Summit (N.M.) **98** B 4
Summit (S.D.) **83** H 2
Summit Lake **104** B 1
Summit Lake (WI.) **59** D 3
Summit Lake Indian
  Reservation **104** C 1
Summit Mountain **105** E 3
Summit Peak **94** D 4
Sumner (IA.) **63** F 3
Sumner (MO.) **64** D 2
Sumner (MS.) **48** C 4
Sumner (OK.) **77** F 1
Sumner, Lake **97** F 4
Sumrall (MS.) **49** E 3
Sumter (S.C.) **41** E 3
Sun City (AZ.) **100** D 3
Sun Prairie (MT.) **87** F 2
Sun Prairie (WI.) **59** F 3
Sun River **86** A 2
Sun River (MT.) **86** B 2
Sun Valley (ID.) **91** E 3
Sun Valley (NV.) **104** B 3
Sunbeam (ID.) **90** E 2
Sunburst (MT.) **86** B 1
Sunbury (N.C.) **39** H 2
Sunbury (PA.) **34** E 3
Suncock (N.H.) **29** E 6
Sundance (WY.) **93** H 1
Sunflower (AZ.) **100** E 3
Sunflower (MS.) **48** C 4
Sunflower, Mount **78** AB 2
Sunnyside (NV.) **105** G 4
Sunnyside (TX.) **97** H 4
Sunnyside (UT.) **102** C 2
Sunnyside (WA.) **115** F 3
Sunnyvale (CA.) **111** E 3–4
Sunray (TX.) **76** B 1
Sunset (LA.) **68** C 3
Sunset (TX.) **74** D 1
Sunset Crater National
  Monument **101** E 1
Suntrana **121** F 3
Superior (AZ.) **101** EF 3
Superior (MT.) **88** E 2
Superior (NE.) **81** FG 4
Superior (WI.) **58** C 6
Superior (WY.) **92** D 4
Sur, Point **111** F 3
Surf City (N.C.) **39** G 4
Suring (WI.) **59** E 2
Surrency (GA.) **43** E 3
Surrey (ND.) **84** E 2
Surry (VA.) **37** H 4
Survey Pass (AL.) **121** E 2
Susan (VA.) **37** H 4
Susanville (CA.) **110** B 2
Susitna **119** E 1
Susitna R. (AL.) **116** A 1
Susitna R. (AL.) **116** B 1
Susquehanna (PA.) **35** F 4
Susquehanna River **35** E 2
Sussex (VA.) **37** G 5
Sussex (WY.) **93** F 2
Sutcliffe (NV.) **104** B 3
Sutherland (IA.) **62** C 3
Sutherland (NE.) **80** C 3
Sutherland Reservoir
  80 C 3
Sutherlin (OR.) **112** B 3
Sutter (CA.) **110** C 3
Sutter Buttes **110** C 3
Sutton (AK.) **116** B 1
Sutton (N.D.) **85** H 3
Sutton (NE.) **81** G 4
Sutton (W.V.) **36** D 3
Sutton Lake **36** D 3

Sutwik Island (AL.) **119** D 2
Suwannee (FL.) **44** B 5
Suwannee River **44** B 4
Suwannee Sound **44** B 5
Swainsboro (GA.) **43** D 3
Swan Lake (MO.) **64** D 2
Swan Lake (MT.) **89** G 2
Swan Lake (S.D.) **83** F 2
Swan Peak **89** G 2
Swan Range **89** G 2
Swan River (MN.) **60** C 3
Swan Valley (ID.) **91** H 3
Swanquarter (N.C.) **39** H 3
Swans Island **29** D 3
Swansboro (NC.) **39** G 4
Swansea (S.C.) **40** D 3
Swanson Lake **80** C 4
Swanton (VT.) **30** C 1
Swasey Peak **102** C 5
Swatara (MN.) **60** D 3
Swea City (IA.) **62** D 2
Swearingen (TX.) **76** C 3
Sweeny (TX.) **71** G 1
Sweet Home (OR.) **112** C 2
Sweet Springs (MO.)
  64 D 3
Sweet Springs (W.V.)
  36 D 4
Sweetgrass (MT.) **86** A 1
Sweetgrass Hills **86** B 1
Sweetwater (OK.) **76** D 2
Sweetwater (TN.) **51** F 5
Sweetwater (TX.) **73** H 1
Sweetwater Lake **85** H 2
Sweetwater River **92** D 3
Swenson (TX.) **76** C 4
Swift Reservoir **114** CD 3
Swift River (AL.) **117** E 2
Swinomish Indian
  Reservation **114** C 1
Sycamore (GA.) **43** E 4
Sycan Marsh **112** D 4
Sydney (N.D.) **85** H 4
Sylacauga (AL.) **46** C 4
Sylva (NC.) **51** G 5
Sylvan Grove (KS.) **78** E 2
Sylvan Hills (AR.) **66** D 3
Sylvan Pass **92** B 1
Sylvania (GA.) **42** D 2
Sylvania (OH.) **53** F 1
Sylvester (GA.) **43** E 4
Sylvester (TX.) **73** H 1
Sylvia (KS.) **78** E 3–4
Syracuse (KS.) **78** B 3
Syracuse (MO.) **64** E 3
Syracuse (NE.) **81** H 4
Syracuse (N.Y.) **32** D 2

T

Table Mountain **101** F 4
Table Rock (WY.) **92** D 4
Table Rock Lake **64** D 5
Table Top **100** D 4
Tabor (S.D.) **83** H 5
Tabor City (N.C.) **39** F 4
Tacna (AZ.) **100** B 4
Tacoma (CO.) **94** C 4

Tacoma (WA.) **114** C 2
Taconite Harbor (MN.)
  58 B 4
Tad Park (UT.) **102** B 4
Taft (CA.) **106** C 2
Taft (OK.) **77** H 2
Tagish L. (AL.) **117** D 1
Tagus (ND.) **84** E 2
Tahlequah (OK.) **77** J 2
Tahoe City (CA.) **110** C 2
Tahoe, Lake **110** CD 2
Tahoka (TX.) **76** B 4
Taiban (N.M.) **97** F 4
Takotra **120** D 3
Takslesluk Lake **119** C 1
Taku Arm (AL.) **117** E 1–2
Talbotton (GA.) **42** D 5
Talco (TX.) **75** F 1
Talihina (OK.) **77** J 3
Talkeetna (AL.) **116** B 1
Talkeetna Mts. (AL.)
  116 B 1
Talladega (AL.) **46** C 4
Tallahassee (FL.) **47** F 2
Tallapoosa River **47** D 3–4
Tallmadge (OH.) **53** H 1
Tallulah (LA.) **68** D 1
Taloga (OK.) **76** D 1
Talpa (TX.) **74** B 3
Talquin, Lake **47** F 2
Tama (IA.) **63** F 4
Tamaqua (PA.) **35** F 3
Tamaroa (IL.) **57** E 5
Tampa (FL.) **44** C 4
Tampa Bay **44–45** D 4
Tampico (MT.) **87** FG 1
Tanacross (AL.) **121** G 3
Tanaga (AL.) **116** J 1
Tanana (AL.) **121** E 2
Tanana River **116** C 1
Tanana River (AL.)
  121 E 2–3
Tangier Island **37** H 4
Tankersley (TX.) **73** H 2
Tanque (AZ.) **101** G 4
Tanque Verde (AZ.) **101** F 4
Taos Indian Reservations
  96 E 2
Taos Pueblo (N.M.) **96** E 2
Tappahannock (VA.) **37** G 4
Tappan Lake **53** H 2
Tappen (ND.) **85** G 4
Tar River **39** G 3
Tarboro (N.C.) **39** G 3
Targhee Pass **91** H 2
Tarkio (MO.) **64** B 1
Tarkio (MT.) **89** F 2
Tarpon Springs (FL.) **44** C 5
Tarryall (CO.) **95** E 2
Tarzan (TX.) **73** F 1
Tasco (KS.) **78** C 2
Tascosa (TX.) **97** H 3
Tatum (N.M.) **99** G 3
Tatum (TX.) **75** G 2
Taum Sauk Mountain
  65 G 4
Taunton (MA.) **31** E 4
Tavaputs Plateau
  102 C 1–2
Tavernier (FL.) **45** F 2
Tawakoni, Lake **75** E 2
Tawas City (MI.) **55** D 2
Taylor (AL.) **120** C 2
Taylor (AR.) **66** C 4
Taylor (AZ.) **101** F 2
Taylor (NE.) **81** E 3

Taylor (TX.) **74** D 4
Taylor, Mount **96** C 3
Taylor Mountain **91** E 2
Taylor Mountains **119** D 1
Taylor Park Reservoir
  94 D 3
Taylorsville (CA.) **110** B 2
Taylorsville (KY.) **50–51** E 2
Taylorsville (MS.) **49** E 3
Taylorsville (N.C.) **38** C 3
Taylorville (IL.) **57** D 4
Tazewell (TN.) **51** G 4
Tazewell (VA.) **36** C 4
Tazi,Mount **121** E 2
Tchula (MS.) **48** C 4
Tea (S.D.) **83** J 4
Teague (N.M.) **99** G 4
Teague (TX.) **75** E 3
Teahwhit Head **114** A 2
Teasdale (UT.) **103** D 3
Tecate (CA.) **107** F 5
Tecolote (Mex.) **107** G 5
Tecopa (CA.) **107** F 2
Tecumseh (NE.) **81** H 4
Tecumseh (OK.) **77** F 2
Teec Nos Pas (AZ.) **103** F 1
Tegarden (OK.) **76** E 1
Tehachapi (CA.) **106** D 2
Tehachapi Mountains
  106 D 2–3
Teigen (MT.) **86** E 2
Tejon Pass **106** D 3
Tekamah (NE.) **81** H 3
Tekoa (WA.) **115** H 2
Tekonsha (MI.) **55** F 3
Telegraph (TX.) **74** A 4
Telegraph Creek **117** E 2
Telescope Peak **109** E 3
Telida **121** E 3
Tell City (IN.) **52** C 4–5
Teller (AL.) **120** B 2
Teller Mission **120** B 2
Telluride (CO.) **94** C 4
Telma (WA.) **114** E 2
Telocaset (OR.) **113** H 1
Telton (ID.) **91** H 3
Temblor Range **106** BC 2
Temecula (CA.) **107** E 4
Tempe (AZ.) **100** DE 3
Temperanceville (VA.)
  37 J 4
Tempiute (NV.) **109** G 2
Temple (OK.) **77** E 3
Temple (TX.) **74** D 3
Temvik (ND.) **85** F 4
Ten Thousand Islands
  45 F 3
Tenaha (TX.) **75** G 3
Tendoy (ID.) **91** F 2
Tenino (WA.) **114** C 3
Tenkiller Ferry Lake **77** J 2
Tenmile (OR.) **112** B 3
Tennessee **53** F 3
Tennessee Pass **94** D 2
Tennessee River **50** C 5
Tennyson (TX.) **73** H 2
Tensas River **68** D 1
Tensed (ID.) **88** D 2
Tensleep (WY.) **92–93** E 1
Terlingua (TX.) **73** E 4
Termo (CA.) **110** B 2
Terra Bella (CA.) **106** CD 2
Terral (OK.) **77** F 4
Terre Haute (IN.) **52** B 3
Terrebonne (OR.) **112** D 2
Terrebonne Bay **69** E 4

Terrell (TX.) **75** E 2
Terreton (ID.) **91** G 3
Terry (MT.) **87** H 3
Terry Peak **82** B 3
Teshekpuk Lak (AL.) **121** E 1
Teslin (AL.) **117** E 1
Teslin Lake (AL.) **117** E 1
Teslin River **117** E 2
Teslin River (AL.) **117** E 1
Tesuque (N.M.) **96** D 3
Teton Pass **92** B 2
Teton Range **92** B 1–2
Teton River **86** B 2
Tetonia (ID.) **91** H 3
Texarkana (AR.) **66** BC 4
Texarkana (TX.) **75** G 1
Texarkana, Lake **75** G 1
Texas (East) **70–71**
Texas (West) **96**
Texas City (TX.) **71** H 1
Texas Creek (CO.) **94–95** E 3
Texhoma (TX.) **76** B 1
Texico (N.M.) **97** G 4
Texline (TX.) **97** GH 2
Texoma, Lake **77** G 4
Texon (TX.) **73** G 2
Thackerville (OK.) **77** F 4
Thalia (TX.) **76** D 3
Thaneta Pass **116** B 1
Thatcher (AZ.) **101** G 4
Thatcher (CO.) **95** F 4
Thatcher (ID.) **91** H 4
Thayer (MO.) **65** F 5
Thayer Junction (WY.) **92** CD 4
Thayne (WY.) **92** B 3
The Dalles (OR.) **112** D 1
The Everglades **45** EF 2
The Grove (TX.) **74** D 3
The Heads **112** A 4
The Village (OK.) **77** F 2
Thedford (NE.) **80** D 3
Theodore (AL.) **47** F 6
Theodore Roosevelt Lake **101** E 3
Theresa (N.Y.) **32** E 1
Theriot (LA.) **69** E 4
Thermalito (CA.) **110** C 3
Thermopolis (WY.) **92** D 2
Thetford Mines (Can.) **28** B 6
Thibodaux (LA.) **69** E 4
Thief Lake **60** B 5
Thief River Falls (MN.) **60** B 6
Thistle (UT.) **102** C 3
Thomas (OK.) **76** E 2
Thomas (W.V.) **36** E 2
Thomas Hill Reservation **64** E 2
Thomaston (GA.) **42** D 5
Thomasville (AL.) **47** E 5
Thomasville (GA.) **43** F 4
Thomasville (N.C.) **38** D 3
Thompson (N.D.) **85** J 3
Thompson (UT.) **102** D 1
Thompson Falls (MT.) **88** E 2
Thompson Peak **110** A 4–5
Thompson Reservoir **112** D 4
Thompson River **64** D 1
Thompsons Station (TN.) **50** D 5

Thompsonville (MI.) **55** D 4
Thomson (GA.) **42** C 3
Thomson (IL.) **56** B 5
Thoreau (N.M.) **96** B 3
Thorne (NV.) **104** C 4
Thornton (CO.) **95** F 2
Thornton (TX.) **75** E 3
Thorp (WA.) **114** E 2
Thorsby (AL.) **46** D 4
Thousand Lake Mountain **103** D 3
Thousand Oaks (CA.) **106** D 3
Three Forks (MT.) **86** B 4
Three Lakes (WI.) **58** D 3
Three Rivers (CA.) **108** D 3
Three Rivers (MI.) **55** G 4
Three Rivers (N.M.) **98** D 3
Three Rivers (TX.) **70** D 2
Three Sisters **112** D 2
Throckmorton (TX.) **74** B 1
Thunder Bay (Can.) **58** A 3
Thunder Bay (MI.) **54** CD 2
Thunder Butte (SD.) **82** CD 2
Thunderbird, Lake **77** F 2
Tibbie (AL.) **47** E 6
Tiber Reservoir **86** B 1
Ticonderoga (N.Y.) **33** G 2
Tidioute (PA.) **34** B 2
Tie Plant (MS.) **48** C 3
Tie Siding (WY.) **93** G 4
Tierra Amarilla (N.M.) **96** D 2
Tieton (WA.) **114** E 3
Tiffany (CO.) **94** C 4
Tiffany Mountain **115** F 1
Tiffin (OH.) **53** F 1
Tifton (GA.) **43** E 4
Tiftona (TN.) **51** E 5
Tigalda (AL.) **118** C 3
Tignall (GA.) **42** C 3
Tijeras (N.M.) **96** D 3
Tijuana (Mex.) **107** E 5
Tikchik Lakes (AL.) **119** D 1
Tilden (NE.) **81** G 2
Tilden (TX.) **70** D 2
Tillamook (OR.) **112** B 1
Tillamook Bay **112** A 1
Tillamook Head **112** A 1
Tillery, Lake **38** D 3
Tilton (N.H.) **29** E 6
Timbalier Island **69** E 4
Timber Lake (SD.) **82** DE 2
Timber Peak **106** BC 2
Timms Hill **59** D 4
Timpanogos Cave National Monument **102** B 3
Timpas (CO.) **95** G 4
Timpson (TX.) **75** G 3
Tims Ford Lake **50** D 5
Tin City (AL.) **120** B 2
Tinaja (TX.) **72** E 3
Tingmerkpuk Mountains **120** C 2
Tinsley (MS.) **48** D 4
Tioga (ND.) **84** C 2
Tioga (PA.) **34** D 2
Tioga Pass **111** E 1
Tionesta (CA.) **110** A 3
Tionesta (PA.) **34** B 2
Tipler (WI.) **58** D 2
Tippett (NV.) **105** G 3
Tipton (CA.) **111** F 1
Tipton (IA.) **63** G 4
Tipton (IN.) **52** D 2

Tipton (KS.) **78** E 2
Tipton (OK.) **76** D 3
Tipton, Mount **100** B 1
Tiptonville (TN.) **67** G 1
Tishomingo (MS.) **48** B 2
Tishomingo (OK.) **77** G 3
Titley (TX.) **73** E 3
Titonka (IA.) **62** DE 2
Titusville (FL.) **44** C 2
Titusville (PA.) **34** B 2
Tivoli (TX.) **71** F 2
Toana Range **105** G 1–2
Tobacco Root Mountains **86** A 4
Tobias (NE.) **81** G 4
Tobin, Mount **104** D 2
Tobyhanna (PA.) **35** F 2
Toccoa (GA.) **42** B 4
Tocito (N.M.) **96** B 2
Toddville (MD.) **37** H 3
Togiak (AL.) **119** C 2
Togiak Bay **119** C 2
Togo (MN.) **60** C 3
Togwotee Pass **92** B 2
Tohakum Peak **104** B 2
Tohatchi (N.M.) **96** B 3
Tohopekaliga, Lake **44** C 3
Toiyabe Range **104** DE 3
Tok (AL.) **121** G 3
Tokeland (WA.) **114** B 3
Tokio (TX.) **99** H 3
Toledo (IA.) **63** F 3
Toledo (IL.) **57** D 3
Toledo (OH.) **53** F 1
Toledo (OR.) **112** B 2
Toledo Bend Dam **68** B 2
Toledo Bend Reservoir **68** B 2
Tolley (ND.) **84** E 2
Tollhouse (CA.) **111** F 1
Tolono (IL.) **56** D 3
Tom (OK.) **77** J 4
Tomahawk (WI.) **59** D 3
Tomales Bay **111** D 4
Tomales Point **111** D 5
Tombigbee River **47** DE 6
Tombstone (AZ.) **101** F 5
Tompkinsville (KY.) **50** E 4
Toms Place (CA.) **108** D 2
Toms River (N.J.) **35** G 4
Tonalea (AZ.) **103** F 2
Tonasket (WA.) **115** F 1
Tonawanda (N.Y.) **32** B 2
Tongue River (MT.) **87** G 4
Tongue River (N.D.) **85** J 2
Tongue River Reservoir **87** G 4
Tonkawa (OK.) **77** F 1
Tonopah (AZ.) **100** D 3
Tonopah (NV.) **109** E 1
Tonto National Monument **101** EF 3
Tooele (UT.) **102** B 4
Toolik River **121** F 2
Toonerville (CO.) **95** G 4
Topano (VA.) **37** H 4
Topawa (AZ.) **100** E 5
Topaz Lake **104** B 4
Topeka (KS.) **79** H 2
Topock (AZ.) **100** B 2
Toponas (CO.) **94** D 1
Toppenish (WA.) **114–115** E 3
Topsail Beach (N.C.) **39** G 4
Topsfield (ME.) **28** C 2
Topton (N.C.) **51** G 5

Torch Lake **54** C 4
Tornillo (TX.) **72** B 2
Toro (LA.) **68** B 2
Toro Peak **107** F 4
Toronto (Can.) **32** A 2
Toronto (KS.) **79** H 4
Toronto (S.D.) **83** J 3
Toronto (W.V.) **36** D 1
Toronto Lake **79** GH 4
Torrance (CA.) **106** D 4
Torres Martinez Indian Reservation **107** F 4
Torrington (CT.) **35** H 2
Torrington (WY.) **93** H 3
Tortilla Flat (AZ.) **100–101** E 3
Tortola **124** D 2
Toston (MT.) **86** B 3
Totson Mountain **120** D 3
Toulon (IL.) **56** B 4
Toulon Lake **104** C 2
Towanda (PA.) **34** E 2
Towaoc (CO.) **94** B 4
Tower (WY.) **92** B 1
Tower City (N.D.) **85** J 4
Tower City (PA.) **34** E 3
Towne Pass **109** E 3
Towner (CO.) **95** H 3
Towner (ND.) **85** F 2
Townsend (MT.) **86** B 3
Towson (MD.) **37** H 2
Toy (NV.) **104** C 2
Toyah (TX.) **72** E 2
Toyahvale (TX.) **72** E 3
Toygunen (AL.) **120** A 2
Tracy (CA.) **111** E 3
Tracy (MN.) **61** F 5
Tracy (MT.) **86** B 2
Trail (Can.) **115** H 1
Trail City (SD.) **82** E 2
Trapper Peak **89** F 4
Trask Mountain **112** B 1
Traverse City (MI.) **54** D 4
Traverse, Lake **61** E 6
Traverse Peak **120** D 2
Travis, Lake **74** C 4
Trego (NV.) **104** B 2
Trego (WI.) **58** D 5
Trementina (N.M.) **97** F 3
Tremont (PA.) **34** E 3
Tremonton (UT.) **102** A 4
Trenary (MI.) **54** B 5
Trenton (FL.) **44** B 4
Trenton (GA.) **42** B 6
Trenton (MO.) **64** D 1
Trenton (N.C.) **39** G 3
Trenton (ND.) **84** C 2
Trenton (NE.) **80** C 4
Trenton (NE.) **80** C 4
Trenton (N.J.) **35** G 3
Trenton (TN.) **50** B 5
Trenton (TX.) **75** E 1
Tres Montosas **96** C 4
Tres Piedras (N.M.) **96** E 2
Tribune (KS.) **78** B 3
Trident Peak **104** C 1
Trigo Mountains **100** B 3
Trimble (CO.) **94** C 4
Trimmer (CA.) **111** F 1
Trimont (MN.) **61** G 4
Trinchera (CO.) **95** F 4
Trinidad (CA.) **110** A 6
Trinidad (CO.) **95** F 4
Trinidad (TX.) **75** E 2
Trinity (TX.) **75** F 4
Trinity Center (CA.) **110** B 4

Trinity Dam **110** B 4
Trinity Islands (AL.) **119** E 2
Trinity Islands (AL.) **119** E 2
Trinity Mountain **90** D 3
Trinity Mountains **110** B 4
Trinity Peak **104** C 2
Trinity Range **104** C 2
Trinity River **110** B 5
Trinity River **75** G 4
Trinway (OH.) **53** H 2
Tripp (S.D.) **83** G 4
Trois Rivières (Can.) **28** B 7
Trotters (ND.) **84** C 3
Troup (TX.) **75** F 2
Trout Creek (MI.) **58** C 2
Trout Creek (MT.) **88** E 2
Trout Creek (UT.) **102** C 5
Trout Creek Pass **94** D 3
Trout Lake (MI.) **54** B 4
Trout Lake (WA.) **114** D 3
Trout Peak **92** C 1
Trout Run (PA.) **34** D 2
Troy (AL.) **47** E 3
Troy (ID.) **88** D 3
Troy (KS.) **79** H 2
Troy (MT.) **88** E 1
Troy (N.C.) **38** E 3
Troy (N.Y.) **33** G 3
Troy (OH.) **52** E 2
Troy (OR.) **113** H 1
Troy (PA.) **34** E 2
Troy (TX.) **74** D 3
Troy Lake **107** F 3
Troy Peak **105** F 4
Truchas (N.M.) **96** E 2
Truckee (CA.) **110** C 2
Trujillo (N.M.) **97** F 3
Truman (MN.) **61** G 4
Trumann (AR.) **67** F 2
Trumbull, Mount **103** F 5
Truscott (TX.) **76** D 4
Trussville (AL.) **46** C 4
Truth or Consequences
(N.M.) **98** C 3
Truxton (AZ.) **100** C 1
Tryon (NE.) **80** C 3
Tsala Apopka Lake **44** C 4
Tschida, Lake **84** E 4
Tuba City (AZ.) **103** F 3
Tucker (GA.) **42** C 5
Tucson (AZ.) **101** E 4
Tucumari (N.M.) **97** G 3
Tulalip Indian Reservation
114 C 1
Tulare (CA.) **111** F 1
Tulare (S.D.) **83** G 3
Tulare Lake Bed **111** F 1
Tularosa (N.M.) **98** D 3
Tularosa Valley **98** D 4
Tule Lake **110** A 3
Tule River Indian
Reservation **106** D 1–2
Tule Valley **102** C 5
Tulelake (CA.) **110** A 3
Tulia (TX.) **76** B 3
Tullahoma (TN.) **50** D 5
Tulloch Reservoir **111** E 2
Tulsa (OK.) **77** G 1
Tuluksak **119** C 1
Tumalo (OR.) **112** D 2
Tumble Mountain **86** C 4
Tumtum Lake **113** G 4
Tumwater (WA.) **114** BC 3
Tunica (MS.) **48** B 4
Tunkhannock (PA.) **35** E 2
Tununak (AL.) **118** B 1

Tuolumne (CA.) **111** E 2
Tupelo (MS.) **48** B 2
Tupelo (OK.) **77** G 3
Tupper Lake (N.Y.) **33** F 1
Turbeville (S.C.) **41** E 3
Turell (AR.) **67** F 2
Turkey (TX.) **76** C 3
Turkey Mountain **70** B 1
Turkey Ridge **83** H 4
Turkey River **63** G 2–3
Turley (N.M.) **96** C 2
Turley (OK.) **77** G 1
Turlock (CA.) **111** E 2
Turlock Lake **111** E 2
Turnbull, Mount **101** F 3
Turner (MT.) **87** E 1
Turner (WA.) **115** H 3
Turon (KS.) **78** E 4
Turpin (OK.) **76** C 1
Turret Peak **100** E 2
Turtle Flambeau Flowage
58 C 4
Turtle Lake (ND.) **84** F 3
Turtle Lake (WI.) **59** D 6
Turtle Mountain Indian
Reservation **85** G 2
Turtle Mountains **84–85** F 2
Tusayan (AZ.) **103** FG 4
Tuscaloosa (AL.) **46** C 5
Tuscarawas River **53** H 2
Tuscarora (NV.) **105** E 1
Tuscarora Mountain (PA.)
34 D 3
Tuscarora Mountains (NV.)
105 E 1–2
Tuscola (IL.) **56** D 3
Tuscola (TX.) **74** B 2
Tuscumbia (AL.) **46** B 5
Tuscumbia (MO.)
64–65 E 3
Tuskegee (AL.) **47** D 3
Tustumena Lake **119** E 1
Tuttle (ND.) **85** G 3
Tuttle Creek Lake **79** G 2
Tututalak Mountains
120 C 2
Tutwiler (MS.) **48** B 4
Tuxedo (TX.) **74** A 2
Tuzigoot National
Monument **100** E 2
Twain (CA.) **110** B 3
Twain Harte (CA.) **111** D 2
Tweedy Mountain **86** A 4
Twentynine Palms (CA.)
107 F 3
Twichell (TX.) **76** C 1
Twin Bridges (MT.) **86** A 4
Twin Buttes **112** C 2
Twin Buttes Reservoir
73 H 2
Twin City (GA.) **43** D 3
Twin Falls (ID.) **90** E 4
Twin Hills **119** C 2
Twin Lake (MI.) **55** E 5
Twin Lakes (CO.) **94** D 2
Twin Peaks **90–91** E 2
Twin Valley (MN.)
60 C 6
Twitchell Reservoir
106 B 2–3
Twitty (TX.) **76** C 2
Two Buttes (CO.) **95** H 4
Two Buttes Reservoir
95 H 4
Two Guns (AZ.) **101** E 2
Two Rivers (WI.) **59** E 1

Two Rivers Reservoir
99 G 3
Twodot (MT.) **86** C 3
Tygart Lake **36** E 2
Tygh Valley (OR.)
112 D 1
Tyler (MN.) **61** F 6
Tyler (TX.) **75** F 2
Tyler (WA.) **115** H 2
Tylertown (MS.) **49** E 4
Tyndall (S.D.) **83** H 4
Tyonek **119** E 1
Tyrone (CO.) **95** F 4
Tyrone (OK.) **76** B 1
Tyrone (PA.) **34** C 3

Union (N.J.) **35** G 3
Union (OR.) **113** H 1
Union (S.C.) **40** D 2
Union (TX.) **73** G 1
Union (WA.) **114** B 2
Union (W.V.) **36** D 4
Union Center (SD.)
82 C 3
Union Church (MS.)
49 E 4
Union City (GA.) **42** C 5
Union City (OH.) **52** E 2
Union City (PA.) **34** B 2
Union City (TN.) **67** G 1
Union Creek (OR.) **112** C 4
Union Gap (WA.) **115** E 3
Union Point (GA.) **42** C 4
Union Springs (AL.)
47 D 3
Union Valley Reservoir
111 D 2
Uniontown (AL.) **46** D 5
Uniontown (KY.) **50** C 3
Uniontown (PA.) **34** B 4
Uniontown (WA.) **115** H 3
Unionville (MI.) **55** E 2
Unionville (MO.) **64** E 1
Unionville (NV.) **104** C 2
Unity (ME.) **28** D 4
Unity (OR.) **113** G 2
Universal City (TX.)
70 D 1
University City (MO.)
65 G 3
Upalco (UT.) **102** B 2
Upham (ND.) **84** F 2
Upham (N.M.) **98** CD 4
Upolu Point **123** EF 3
Upper Arlington (OH.)
53 F 2
Upper Klamath Lake
112 D 4
Upper Lake **110** A 2
Upper Lake (CA.)
110 C 4
Upper Liard **117** F 1
Upper Marlboro (MD.)
37 H 3
Upper Red Lake **60** B 4
Upper Ugashik Lake
119 D 2
Upton (WY.) **93** H 1
Uravan (CO.) **94** B 3
Urbana (IL.) **56** C 3
Urbana (OH.) **53** F 2
Urbandale (IA.) **62** E 4
Urich (MO.) **64** D 3
Ursa (IL.) **56** C 6
Ursine (NV.) **109** H 2
Usibelli **121** F 3
Usk (WA.) **115** H 1
USS Arizona Memorial
(HI.) **88** CD 2

U

Ucolo (UT.) **103** E 1
Ucross (WY.) **93** F 1
Uelen (AL.) **120** B 2
Ugashik (AL.) **119** D 2
Uinta and Ouray Indian
Reservation **102** B 2
Uinta Mountains
102 B 1–2
Ukiah (CA.) **110** C 5
Ukiah (OR.) **113** G 1
Ullen (MN.) **60** C 6
Ullin (IL.) **57** F 5
Ulm (MT.) **86** B 2
Ulm (WY.) **93** F 1
Ulmer (S.C.) **40** D 3
Ulupalakua (HI.)
123 E 3
Ulysses (KS.) **78** B 4
Ulysses (NE.) **81** G 3
Umatilla (OR.) **113** F 1
Umatilla Indian
Reservation **113** G 1
Umatilla, Lake **115** F 4
Umbagog Lake **28** D 6
Umbarger (TX.) **97** H 4
Umiat (AL.) **121** E 2
Umikoa (HI.) **123** F 4
Umnak **118** B 3
Umnak Passage **118** B 3
Umpqua (OR.) **112** B 3
Umpqua River **112** B 3
Unadilla (GA.) **43** D 4
Unalakleet (AL.) **120** C 3
Unalakleet River
120 CD 3
Unalaska **118** B 3
Unalaska (AL.) **118** B 3
Uncompahgre Peak **94** C 3
Uncompahgre Plateau
94 BC 3
Underwood (ND.) **84** E 3
Underwood (TX.)
76 B 3–4
Unga **119** C 2
Unimak (AL.) **118** C 3
Unimak Pass (AL.)
118 BC 3
Union (LA.) **69** E 3
Union (MO.) **65** F 3
Union (MS.) **48** D 3

Utah **62**
Utah Lake **102** B 3
Ute (IA.) **62** C 3
Ute Mountain Indian
Reservation **94** B 4
Ute Reservoir **97** G 3
Utica (KS.) **78** C 3
Utica (MS.) **49** D 4
Utica (MT.) **86** C 3
Utica (N.Y.) **33** F 2
Utica (OH.) **53** G 2
Utleyville (CO.) **95** G 4
Utopia (TX.) **70** C 1

Utuado **124** B 2
Utukok River (AL.)
  120 C 2
Uvada (MN.) **109** H 2
Uvak **119** E 2
Uvalda (GA.) **43** D 3
Uvalde (TX.) **70** C 1

Vacaville (CA.) **111** D 4
Vaiden (MS.) **48** C 3
Vail (AZ.) **101** F 4
Vail (IA.) **62** C 3
Valdez (AL.) **116** B 1
Valdez (N.M.) **96** E 2
Valdosta (GA.) **43** F 4
Vale (OR.) **113** H 3
Vale (SD.) **82** B 3
Valentine (AZ.) **100** C 1
Valentine (MT.) **87** E 2
Valentine (NE.) **80** D 2
Valentine (TX.) **72** D 3
Valier (MT.) **86** A 1
Vallecito (CO.) **94** C 4
Vallecito Reservoir **94** C 4
Vallejo (CA.) **111** D 4
Valley (NE.) **81** H 3
Valley (WA.) **115** H 1
Valley (WY.) **92** C 1
Valley Center (CA.)
  107 EF 4
Valley Center (KS.) **79** F 4
Valley City (N.D.) **85** H 4
Valley Falls (KS.) **79** H 2
Valley Falls (OR.) **113** E 4
Valley Farm (TX.)
  72–73 E 2
Valley Forge National
  Historic Park (PA.) **35** F 3
Valley Head (W.V.) **36** D 3
Valley Mills (TX.) **74** D 3
Valley Springs (CA.)
  111 D 2
Valley Springs (S.D.) **83** J 4
Valley Station (KY.) **50** D 2
Valley View (TX.) **74** D 1
Valmont (N.M.) **98** E 4
Valmy (NV.) **104** D 2
Valparaiso (FL.) **47** F 4
Valparaiso (IN.) **52** BC 1
Valparaiso (NE.) **81** H 3
Valsetz (OR.) **112** B 2
Van Buren (AR.) **66** B 2
Van Buren (MO.) **65** G 4–5
Van Horn (TX.) **72** D 2
Van Meter (IA.) **62** E 4
Van Metre (SD.) **82** DE 3
Van Norman (MT.) **87** G 2
Van Tassell (WY.) **93** H 3
Van Wert (OH.) **52** E 2
Vananda (MT.) **87** G 3
Vance (TX.) **70** C 1
Vanceboro (ME.) **28** C 2
Vanceboro (N.C.) **39** G 3
Vanceburg (KY.) **51** G 2
Vancleave (MS.) **49** F 2
Vancorum (CO.) **94** B 3

Vancourt (TX.) **73** H 2
Vancouver (Can.) **114** B 1
Vancouver (WA.) **114** C 4
Vandalia (IL.) **57** E 5
Vandalia (MO.) **65** F 2
Vandalia (MT.) **87** G 1
Vandalia (OH.) **53** E 3
Vanderbilt (TX.) **71** F 2
Vanderpool (TX.) **70** C 1
Vandervoort (AR.) **66** B 3
Vansant (VA.) **36** B 4
Vantage (WA.) **115** E 3
Vass (N.C.) **39** E 3
Vassar (MI.) **55** E 2
Vaughn (MT.) **86** B 2
Vaughn (N.M.) **96** E 4
Veblen (S.D.) **83** H 2
Vega (TX.) **97** H 3
Vega Baja (P.R.) **124** B 2
Veguita (N.M.) **96** D 4
Velva (ND.) **84** F 2
Venango (NE.) **80** C 4
Veneta (OR.) **112** B 2
Venetie (AL.) **121** F 2
Venice (FL.) **45** D 4
Venice (LA.) **69** F 4
Ventura (CA.) **106** C 3
Venturia (ND.) **83** F 2
Venus (FL.) **45** D 3
Veon (ID.) **91** H 3
Vera (IL.) **57** D 4
Vera (TX.) **76** D 4
Verde River **100** E 2
Verdigre (NE.) **81** F 2
Verdon (NE.) **81** J 4
Vergennes (VT.) **30** C 1
Verhalen (TX.) **73** E 2
Vermilion Bay **68** CD 4
Vermilion Lake **60** C 2
Vermillion (OH.) **53** G 1
Vermillion (S.D.) **83** B 3
Vermont **30**
Vernal (UT.) **102** B 1
Vernon (AL.) **46** C 6
Vernon (CO.) **95** H 2
Vernon (FL.) **47** F 3
Vernon (IN.) **52** D 4
Vernon (TX.) **76** D 3
Vernon (UT.) **102** B 4
Vernonia (OR.) **112** B 1
Vero Beach (FL.) **45** D 2
Verona (N.D.) **85** H 4
Verona (WI.) **59** G 3
Verret, Lake **68–69** D 4
Versailles (IN.) **52** D 3
Versailles (KY.) **51** F 2
Versailles (MO.) **64** E 3
Verse (WY.) **93** G 2
Vetal (SD.) **82** D 4
Veteran (WY.) **93** H 4
Vevay (IN.) **52** D 4
Veyo (UT.) **103** E 5
Vian (OK.) **77** J 2
Viboras (TX.) **70** D 4
Viborg (S.D.) **83** HJ 4
Vici (OK.) **76** D 1
Vick (TX.) **74** A 3
Vicksburg (AZ.) **100** C 3
Vicksburg (MI.) **55** F 4
Vicksburg (MS.) **48** D 4
Victor (CO.) **94** E 3
Victor (ID.) **91** H 3
Victor (MT.) **89** F 3
Victoria (KS.) **78** D 3
Victoria (TX.) **71** E 2
Victoriaville (Can.) **28** B 6

Victorville (CA.) **107** E 3
Vida (MT.) **87** H 2
Vidal (CA.) **107** H 3
Vidal Junction (CA.)
  107 H 3
Vidalia (GA.) **43** D 3
Vidauri (TX.) **71** E 2
Vienna (GA.) **43** D 4
Vienna (IL.) **57** F 3
Vienna (MD.) **37** J 3
Vienna (MO.) **65** F 3
Vienna (S.D.) **83** H 3
Vienna (W.V.) **36** C 2
Vieques, Isla de **124** C 2
Viewfield (SD.) **82** C 3
Vigo Park (TX.) **76** B 3
Vilas (CO.) **95** H 4
Villa Ahumada (Mex.)
  72 B 3
Villa Frontera (Mex.)
  70 A 3–4
Villa Grove (CO.) **94** E 3
Villa Grove (IL.) **56** D 3
Villaldama (Mex.) **70** B 4
Villanueva (N.M.) **96** E 3
Ville Platte (LA.) **68** C 3
Villegreen (CO.) **95** G 4
Vina (CA.) **110** C 3
Vinalhaven (ME.) **29** D 3
Vinalhaven Island **29** D 3
Vincennes (IN.) **52** B 4
Vincent (AL.) **46** C 4
Vincent (TX.) **73** G 1
Vinegar Hill **113** G 2
Vineland (N.J.) **35** F 4
Vinemont (AL.) **46** B 4
Vineyard Sound **31** EF 4
Vineyards Haven (MA.)
  31 F 4
Vinita (OK.) **77** H 1
Vinson (OK.) **76** D 3
Vinton (CA.) **110** C 2
Vinton (IA.) **63** F 3
Viola (CA.) **110** B 3
Viola (IL.) **56** B 5
Virden (N.M.) **98** B 4
Virgelle (MT.) **86** C 1
Virgil (KS.) **79** G 3
Virgil (S.D.) **83** G 3
Virgin Gorda **124** D 2
Virgin Islands **124** CD 2–3
Virgin River **109** H 3
Virginia **36–37**
Virginia (ID.) **91** G 4
Virginia (IL.) **56** D 5
Virginia (MN.) **60** C 2
Virginia Beach (VA.) **37** J 2
Virginia City (MT.) **86** B 4
Virginia City (NV.) **104** B 3
Virginia Peak **104** B 3
Viroqua (WI.) **59** F 5
Visalia (CA.) **111** F 1
Vista (CA.) **107** E 4
Vivian (LA.) **68** B 1
Vivian (SD.) **82** E 4
Vizcaino, Cape **110** C 5
Voca (TX.) **74** B 3
Volborg (MT.) **87** H 4
Volcano House (HI.)
  123 F 4
Volin (S.D.) **83** H 5
Vollmar (CO.) **95** EF 1
Volt (MT.) **87** H 1
Volta (CA.) **111** E 2
Von Frank Mountain
  120 DE 3

Von Frank Mountain (AL.)
  121 E 3
Voodbine (IA.) **62** C 4
Voyageors National Park
  60 B 2
Vya (NV.) **104** B 1

W

Wabash (IN.) **52** D 2
Wabash River **52** B 4
Wabasha (MN.) **61** F 2
Wabasso (FL.) **44** D 2
Wabeno (WI.) **59** D 2
Wabuska (NV.) **104** B 3
Waccamaw, Lake **39** F 4
Waccasassa Bay **44** B 4
Waco (TX.) **74** D 3
Waco Lake **74** D 3
Waconda Reservoir
  78–79 E 2
Waddington (N.Y.) **33** E 1
Wadena (MN.) **60** D 5
Wadesboro (N.C.) **38** D 4
Wadley (AL.) **46** C 3
Wadley (GA.) **42** D 3
Wadsworth (NV.) **104** B 3
Wadsworth (OH.) **53** H 1–2
Wadsworth (TX.) **71** F 2
Waelder (TX.) **71** E 1
Wagarville (AL.) **47** E 6
Wagner (S.D.) **83** G 4
Wagon Mound (N.M.)
  97 F 2
Wagon Wheel Gap (CO.)
  94 D 4
Wagoner (OK.) **77** H 2
Wagontire (OR.) **113** F 3
Wagontire Mountain
  113 F 3
Wah Wah Mountains
  103 D 5
Wahiawa (HI.) **122** D 2
Wahoo (NE.) **81** H 3
Wahpeton (N.D.) **85** K 4
Waialeale **88** B 2
Waialee (HI.) **122** C 2
Waialua (HI.) **122** C 2
Waianae (HI.) **122** C 2
Wailua (HI.) **123** E 3
Wailuku (HI.) **123** F 3
Waimea (HI.) **123** F 3
Wainwright (AL.) **120** C 1
Waite Park (MN.) **61** E 4
Waitsburg (WA.) **115** G 3
Waka (TX.) **76** BC 1
Wake Forest (N.C.)
  39 F 2–3
Wakeeney (KS.) **78** D 2
Wakefield (KS.) **79** F 2
Wakefield (MI.) **58** C 3
Wakefield (R.I.) **30** E 4
Wakita (OK.) **77** F 1
Wakpala (SD.) **82** E 2
Wakulla (FL.) **47** G 4
Walapai (AZ.) **100** C 1
Walcott (N.D.) **85** K 4
Walcott (WY.) **93** F 4

Walcott, Lake **91** F 4
Walden (CO.) **94** D 1
Walden Reservoir **94** D 1
Waldenburg (AR.) **67** E 2
Waldo (FL.) **44** B 4
Waldo Lake **112** C 3
Waldorf (MD.) **37** H 3
Waldport (OR.) **112** A 2
Waldron (AR.) **66** B 3
Waldron (MI.) **55** G 3
Wales (AL.) **120** B 2
Wales (MN.) **60** C 1
Walhalla (N.D.) **85** H 2
Walhalla (S.C.) **40** B 2
Walk, Lake **73** H 4
Walker (IA.) **63** G 3
Walker (MN.) **60** C 4
Walker (SD.) **82** D 2
Walker Lake **104** C 4
Walker River Indian
  Reservation **104** C 3–4
Walkers Point **29** E 5
Walkersville (W.V.) **36** D 3
Walkerton (IN.) **52** C 1
Wall (SD.) **82** C 3
Wall Lake (IA.) **62** C 3
Walla Walla (WA.) **115** G 3
Wallace (ID.) **88** E 2
Wallace (KS.) **78** B 3
Wallace (N.C.) **39** G 4
Wallace (NE.) **80** C 4
Wallenpaupack, Lake
  35 F 3
Wallinford (VT.) **30** C 2
Wallis (TX.) **71** F 1
Wallisville Lake **75** G 5
Wallowa (OR.) **113** H 1
Wallowa Mountains
  113 H 1
Walls (MS.) **48** AB 4
Wallula (WA.) **115** G 3
Wallula, Lake **115** FG 3
Walnut (IL.) **56** B 4
Walnut (KS.) **79** HJ 4
Walnut (MS.) **48** B 2
Walnut (N.C.) **51** H 5
Walnut Canyon National
  Monument **101** E 1
Walnut Grove (CA.)
  111 D 3
Walnut Grove (MS.) **48** D 3
Walnut Ridge (AR.) **67** F 1
Walnut Springs (TX.)
  74 D 2
Walpole (N.H.) **29** E 7
Walrus I (AL.) **119** C 2
Walsenburg (CO.) **95** F 4
Walsh (CO.) **95** H 4
Walt Disney World **44** C 3
Walter F. George Dam
  43 E 5–6
Walter F. George Reservoir
  47 E 3
Walterboro (S.C.) **41** E 4
Walters (LA.) **68** D 2
Walters (OK.) **77** E 3
Waltersville (MS.) **48** D 4
Walthall (MS.) **48** C 3
Walthill (NE.) **81** H 2
Waltman (WY.) **93** E 2
Walton (KY.) **51** F 2
Walton (N.Y.) **33** E 3
Wamego (KS.) **79** G 2
Wamsutter (WY.) **92** E 4
Wanapum Dam **115** F 3
Wanblee (SD.) **82** D 4

Wanilla (MS.) **49** E 4
Wannaska (MN.) **60** B 5
Wanship (UT.) **102** B 3
Wapakoneta (OH.) **53** E 2
Wapanucka (OK.) **77** G 3
Wapato (WA.) **114** E 3
Wapello (IL.) **63** G 4
Wapinitia Pass **112** CD 1
Wapiti (WY.) **92** C 1
Wappapello, Lake **65** G 4–5
Wapsipinicon River **63** F 3
War (W.V.) **36** C 4
War Eagle (AR.) **66** C 1
Ward Mountain **89** F 3
Warden (WA.) **115** FG 3
Wardensville (W.V.) **37** F 2
Ware (TX.) **97** H 2
Wareham (MA.) **31** F 4
Warm Springs (NV.)
  105 G 3
Warm Springs (OR.)
  112 D 2
Warm Springs (VA.) **36** E 3
Warm Springs Indian
  Reservation **112** D 1–2
Warm Springs Reservoir
  113 G 3
Warner (OK.) **77** H 2
Warner (S.D.) **83** G 2
Warner Lakes **113** F 4
Warner, Mount **113** F 4
Warner Mountains **110** A 2
Warner Robins (GA.)
  43 D 4
Warner Springs (CA.)
  107 F 4
Warren (AR.) **66** D 4
Warren (ID.) **88** E 4
Warren (IL.) **56** A 4
Warren (IN.) **52** D 2
Warren (MI.) **55** F 2
Warren (MT.) **86** E 4
Warren (OH.) **53** J 1
Warren (PA.) **34** B 2
Warren Peaks **93** H 1
Warrens (WI.) **59** E 4
Warrensburg (MO.) **64** D 3
Warrensburg (N.Y.) **33** F 2
Warrenton (GA.) **42** C 3
Warrenton (MO.) **65** F 3
Warrenton (N.C.) **39** F 2
Warrenton (OR.) **114** AB 3
Warrenton (VA.) **37** G 3
Warrington (FL.) **47** F 5
Warrior (AL.) **46** C 4
Warroad (MN.) **60** B 5
Warsaw (IN.) **52** C 1
Warsaw (MO.) **64** D 3
Warsaw (N.C.) **39** FG 3
Warsaw (N.Y.) **32** B 3
Warsaw (VA.) **37** H 4
Wartburg (TN.) **51** F 4
Warthen (GA.) **42** C 3
Wartrace (TN.) **50** D 5
Warwick (N.D.) **85** H 3
Warwick (R.I.) **30** E 4
Wasatch Range **102** AC 3
Wasco (CA.) **106** C 2
Wasco (OR.) **112** E 1
Waseca (MN.) **61** F 3
Washburn (N.D.) **84** F 3
Washburn (TX.) **76** B 2
Washburn (WI.) **58** C 5
Washington (D.C.) **37** H 3
Washington (GA.) **42** C 3
Washington (IA.) **63** G 4

Washington (IN.) **52** B 4
Washington (KS.) **79** F 2
Washington (MO.) **65** F 3
Washington (N.C.) **39** G 3
Washington (PA.) **34** A 3
Washington (State) **115**
Washington (VA.) **37** F 3
Washington 1 (WI.) **54** C 5
Washington Court House
  (OH.) **53** F 3
Washington Island **54** C 5
Washington, Lake **114** C 2
Washington, Mount **29** D 6
Washington Terrace (UT.)
  102 A 3
Washita River **77** F 3
Washoe City (NV.) **104** B 3
Washoe Lake **104** B 3
Washtucna (WA.) **115** G 3
Waskish (MN.) **60** B 4
Wassaw Island **43** E 1
Wassuk Range **104** C 4
Wasta (SD.) **82** C 3
Watauga (SD.) **82** D 2
Watauga Lake **51** J 4
Water Valley (MS.) **48** B 3
Water Valley (TX.) **73** H 2
Waterbury (CT.) **35** H 2
Waterbury (VT.) **30** D 1
Wateree (S.C.) **41** E 3
Wateree Lake **41** E 2
Wateree River **41** E 2–3
Waterflow (N.M.) **96** B 2
Waterford (CA.) **111** E 2
Waterford (WI.) **59** G 2
Waterloo (AR.) **66** C 4
Waterloo (IA.) **63** F 3
Waterloo (IL.) **57** E 5
Waterman (IL.) **56** B 3
Watersmeet (MI.) **58** C 3
Watertown (FL.) **44** A 4
Watertown (N.Y.) **32** E 2
Watertown (S.D.) **83** H 3
Watertown (WI.) **59** F 2
Waterville (ME.) **28** D 4
Waterville (MN.) **61** F 3
Waterville (NE.) **79** G 2
Waterville (WA.) **115** E 2
Watford City (ND.) **84** C 3
Watkins Glen (N.Y.) **32** D 3
Watkinsville (GA.) **42** C 4
Watonga (OK.) **76–77** E 2
Watrous (N.M.) **97** E 3
Watseka (IL.) **56** C 2
Watson (TX.) **74** D 4
Watson Lake (AL.) **117** F 1
Watsonville (CA.) **111** F 3
Watts Bar Lake **51** F 5
Wattsville (AL.) **46** C 4
Waubay (S.D.) **83** H 2
Waubay Lake **83** H 2
Wauchula (FL.) **45** D 3
Waucoba Mountain
  108 D 2
Waugh Mountain
  88–89 F 4
Waukegan (IL.) **56** A 2
Waukesha (WI.) **59** F 2
Waukon (IA.) **63** G 2
Wauneta (NE.) **80** C 4
Waupaca (WI.) **59** E 3
Waupun (WI.) **59** F 2
Waurika (OK.) **77** E 3
Wausa (NE.) **81** G 2
Wausau (WI.) **59** E 3
Wausaukee (WI.) **59** D 2

Wauseon (OH.) **53** E 1
Wautoma (WI.) **59** E 3
Wauwatosa (WI.) **59** F 2
Waveland (AR.) **66** C 2
Waveland (MS.) **49** F 3
Waverley (N.Y.) **32** D 3
Waverly (IA.) **63** F 3
Waverly (IL.) **57** D 5
Waverly (KS.) **79** H 3
Waverly (MO.) **64** D 2
Waverly (TN.) **50** C 4
Waverly (VA.) **37** G 4
Wawasee, Lake **52** D 1
Wawawai (WA.) **115** H 3
Wawina (MN.) **60** C 3
Wawona (CA.) **111** E 1
Waxahachie (TX.) **75** E 2
Waycross (GA.) **43** E 3
Wayland (MI.) **55** F 4
Wayland (N.Y.) **32** C 3
Wayne (KS.) **79** F 2
Wayne (NE.) **81** GH 2
Wayne (OK.) **77** F 3
Wayne (W.V.) **36** B 3
Waynesboro (GA.) **42** C 2
Waynesboro (MS.) **49** E 2
Waynesboro (PA.) **34** D 4
Waynesboro (TN.) **50** C 5
Waynesboro (VA.) **37** F 3
Waynesburg (PA.) **34** A 4
Waynesville (MO.) **65** E 4
Waynesville (N.C.) **51** H 5
Waynoka (OK.) **76** DE 1
Weatherford (OK.) **76** E 2
Weatherford (TX.) **74** C 2
Weaubleau (MO.) **64** D 4
Weaverville (N.C.) **51** H 5
Webb (TX.) **70** C 3
Webb City (MO.) **64** C 4
Weber City (N.M.) **97** G 4
Webster (MA.) **30** E 3
Webster (MT.) **87** J 3
Webster (ND.) **85** G 2
Webster (S.D.) **83** H 2
Webster (WI.) **58** D 6
Webster City (IA.) **62** E 3
Webster Reservoir **78** D 2
Webster Springs (TX.)
  71 G 1
Webster Sprs (W.V.) **36** D 3
Wedowee (AL.) **46** C 3
Weed (CA.) **110** A 4
Weed (N.M.) **99** E 4
Weed Heights (NV.)
  104 B 3
Weeks (LA.) **68** D 4
Weimar (CA.) **110** C 3
Weimar (TX.) **71** F 1
Weippe (ID.) **88** E 2
Weir (KS.) **79** J 4
Weirsdale (FL.) **44** C 3
Weirton (W.V.) **36** D 1
Weiser (OR.) **90** BC 2
Weiser River **90** C 2
Weiss Lake **46** B 3
Welch (KS.) **77** H 1
Welch (TX.) **73** F 1
Welch (W.V.) **36** C 4
Weldon (MT.) **87** H 2
Weldon (N.C.) **39** G 2
Wellborn (TX.) **75** E 4
Wellfleet (MA.) **31** G 4
Wellfleet (NE.) **80** D 4
Wellington (KS.) **79** F 4
Wellington (NV.) **104** B 4

Wellington (OH.) **53** G 1
Wellington (TX.) **76** C 3
Wellington (UT.) **102** C 2
Wellman (TX.) **99** H 3
Wells (MN.) **61** G 3
Wells (NV.) **105** FG 1
Wells (N.Y.) **33** F 2
Wells Dam **115** EF 2
Wellsboro (PA.) **34** D 2
Wellston (OH.) **53** G 3
Wellsville (MO.) **65** F 2
Wellsville (UT.) **102** A 3
Wellton (AZ.) **100** B 4
Welty (OK.) **77** G 2
Wenatchee (WA.)
114–115 E 2
Wenatchee Mountains
114–115 E 2
Wendel (CA.) **110** B 2
Wendell (ID.) **90** E 4
Wenden (AZ.) **100** C 3
Wendover (NV.) **105** G 2
Wendte (SD.) **82** E 3
Wenona (IL.) **56** B 3
Wentworth (S.D.) **83** J 3
Weott (CA.) **110** B 6
Weskan (KS.) **95** H 3
Weslaco (TX.) **70** D 4
Wesley (IA.) **62** E 2
Wesley (ME.) **28** D 2
Wessington (S.D.) **83** G 3
Wessington Springs (S.D.)
83 G 3
West (MS.) **48** C 3
West (TX.) **74** D 3
West Allis (WI.) **59** FG 1
West Bay (LA.) **69** F 4
West Bay (TX.) **71** GH 1
West Bend (IA.) **62** D 3
West Bend (WI.) **59** F 2
West Branch (IA.) **63** G 4
West Branch (MI.) **55** D 3
West Des Moines (IA.)
62 DE 4
West Elk Mountains **94** C 3
West Fork **87** H 1
West Frankfort (IL.) **57** F 3
West Glacier (MT.) **89** F 1
West Grand Lake **28** C 2
West Helena (AR.) **67** F 3
West Lafayette (IN.) **52** B 2
West Lake Wales (FL.)
44 D 3
West Liberty (IA.) **63** G 4
West Liberty (KY.) **51** G 3
West Memphis (AR.) **67** F 2
West Monroe (LA.) **68** C 1
West Nishnabotna River
62 C 4
West Palm Beach (FL.)
45 E 2
West Panama City Beach
(FL.) **47** F 4
West Pensacola (FL.) **47** F 5
West Plains (MO.) **65** F 5
West Point (GA.) **42** D 6
West Point (KY.) **50** E 3
West Point (MS.) **48** C 2
West Point (NE.) **81** H 3
West Point (VA.) **37** H 4
West Richland (WA.)
115 F 3
West Salem (WI.) **59** F 5
West Spanish Peak **95** F 4
West Thumb (WY.) **92** B 1
West Union (IA.) **63** G 3

West Union (OH.) **53** F 4
West Union (W.V.) **36** D 2
West Unity (OH.) **52** E 1
West Virginia **36–37**
West Warwick (R.I.) **30** E 4
West Yellowstone (MT.)
91 HJ 2
Westbay (FL.) **47** F 3
Westboro (MO.) **64** B 1
Westbrook (ME.) **29** E 5
Westbrook (TX.) **73** H 1
Westby (MT.) **87** JK 1
Westby (WI.) **59** F 4
Westcliffe (CO.) **94** E 3
Westend (CA.) **107** E 2
Westerly (R.I.) **30** E 4
Western (NE.) **81** G 4
Western Grove (AR.)
66 D 1
Westernport (MD.) **37** F 2
Westerville (NE.) **81** E 3
Westerville (OH.) **53** F 2
Westfall (OR.) **113** H 3
Westfield (MA.) **30** D 3
Westfield (ND.) **85** F 4
Westfield (N.Y.) **32** A 3
Westfield (PA.) **34** D 2
Westfield (TX.) **75** F 4
Westhoff (TX.) **71** E 1
Westhope (ND.) **84** E 2
Westley (CA.) **111** E 3
Westminster (CO.) **95** E 2
Westminster (MD.) **37** H 2
Westminster (S.C.) **40** B 2
Westmoreland (KS.) **79** G 2
Westmoreland (TN.) **50** D 4
Westmorland (CA.) **107** G 4
Weston (CO.) **95** F 4
Weston (ID.) **91** G 4
Weston (OR.) **113** G 1
Weston (W.V.) **36** D 2
Weston (WY.) **93** G 1
Westover (SD.) **82** E 4
Westport (CA.) **110** C 5
Westport (IN.) **52** D 3
Westport (OR.) **114** B 3
Westport (WA.) **114** A 3
Westvaco (WY.) **92** C 4
Westville (IL.) **56** C 2
Westville (OK.) **77** J 1
Westwater (UT.) **102** C 1
Westwego (LA.) **69** E 4
Westwood (CA.) **110** B 3
Westwood Lakes (FL.)
45 F 2
Wet Mountains **95** E 3–4
Wetmore (CO.) **95** E 3
Wetonka (S.D.) **83** G 2
Wetumka (OK.) **77** G 2
Wetumpka (AL.) **46** D 4
Wewahitchka (FL.) **47** F 3
Wewela (SD.) **83** F 4
Wewoka (OK.) **77** G 2
Weymouth (MA.) **31** F 3
Wharton (TX.) **71** F 1
Whatcom, Lake **114** C 1
Whatley (AL.) **47** E 5
Wheat Ridge (CO.) **95** E 2
Wheatland (CA.) **110** C 3
Wheatland (N.M.) **97** G 4
Wheatland (WY.) **93** H 3
Wheatland Reservoir No 2
93 G 4
Wheaton (MD.) **37** GH 2
Wheaton (MN.) **61** E 6
Wheelbarrow Peak **109** F 2

Wheeler (KS.) **78** B 2
Wheeler (MS.) **48** B 2
Wheeler (OR.) **112** A 1
Wheeler (TX.) **76** C 2
Wheeler (WA.) **115** F 2
Wheeler Lake **46** B 5
Wheeler Peak (CA.) **111** D 1
Wheeler Peak (N.M.) **96** E 2
Wheeler Peak (NV.)
105 G 4
Wheeler Ridge (CA.)
106 D 2–3
Wheeler Springs (CA.)
106 C 3
Wheeless (OK.) **97** FG 2
Wheeling (W.V.) **36** D 1
Whidbey Island **114** C 1
Whiskeytown Lake **110** B 4
Whiskeytown–Shasta–
Trinity National
Recreation Area **110** B 4
Whitakers (N.C.) **39** G 2
White Bear Lake (MN.)
61 E 3
White Bird (ID.) **88** D 4
White Butte (N.D.) **84** C 4
White Butte (SD.) **82** C 2
White Canyon (UT.)
103 E 2
White City (KS.) **79** G 3
White City (OR.) **112** C 4
White Deer (TX.) **76** B 2
White Earth (ND.) **84** D 2
White Earth Indian
Reservation **60** C 5
White Hall (AL.) **46** D 4
White Hall (IL.) **57** D 5
White Heath (IL.) **56** C 3
White Lake (LA.) **68** C 4
White Lake (WI.) **59** D 2
White Mountain (AL.)
120 C 3
White Mountain Peak
108 D 2
White Mountains (AL.)
121 F 2
White Mountains (CA.)
108 D 2
White Mountains (N.H.)
29 D 6
White Oak Late **66** CD 4
White Owl (SD.) **82** C 3
White Pass (AL.) **117** E 2
White Pass (WA.) **114** D 3
White Pigeon (MI.) **55** G 4
White Pine (MI.) **58** C 3
White Pine (TN.) **51** G 4
White Pines (CA.) **111** D 2
White Plains (N.Y.) **33** F 4
White River (AR.) **67** E 3
White River (IN.) **52** B 4
White River (NV.) **109** G 2
White River (S.D.) **82** E 4
White River (SD.) **82** E 4
White River Reservoir
76 B 4
White Salmon (WA.)
114 D 4
White Sands (N.M.) **98** D 4
White Sands National
Monument **98** D 4
White Settlement (TX.)
74 D 2
White Stone (VA.) **37** H 4
White Sulphur Springs
(MT.) **86** BC 3

White Swan (WA.) **114** E 3
Whitebead (OK.) **77** F 3
Whiteclay (NE.) **80** B 2
Whiteface (TX.) **99** H 3
Whiteface Reservoir **60** C 2
Whitefall (MT.) **87** H 1
Whitefield (N.H.) **28** D 6
Whitefish Bay (MI.) **54** B 3
Whitefish Bay (WI.) **59** F 1
Whitefish Lake (AK.)
119 D 1
Whitefish Lake (MT.) **89** F 1
Whitefish Point **54** B 3
Whitefish Range **89** F 1
Whitehall (MI.) **55** E 5
Whitehall (MT.) **86** AB 4
Whitehall (N.Y.) **33** G 2
Whitehall (OH.) **53** G 3
Whitehall (WI.) **59** E 5
Whitehorse (AL.) **117** E 1
Whites City (N.M.) **99** F 4
Whitesboro (TX.) **75** E 1
Whitesburg (KY.) **51** G 3
Whitesville (KY.) **50** D 3
Whitethorn (CA.) **110** B 5
Whiteville (N.C.) **39** F 4
Whiteville (TN.) **50** A 5
Whitewater (CO.) **94** B 2
Whitewater (KS.) **79** F 4
Whitewater (MT.) **87** F 1
Whitewater (N.M.) **98** B 4
Whitewater (WI.) **59** G 2
Whitewater Bay **45** F 2–3
Whitharral (TX.) **99** H 3
Whiting (WI.) **59** E 3
Whitlash (MT.) **86** B 1
Whitley City (KY.) **51** F 4
Whitman (NE.) **80** C 2
Whitmire (S.C.) **40** D 2
Whitney (NE.) **80** A 2
Whitney, Lake **74** D 2–3
Whitney, Mount **108** D 2
Whitney Point (N.Y.) **32** D 3
Whitsett (TX.) **70** D 2
Whittemore (IA.) **62** D 2
Whittemore (MI.) **55** D 2
Whittier (AL.) **116** B 1
Whitwell (TN.) **51** F 3
Whtiterocks (UT.) **102** B 1
Wibaux (MT.) **87** J 2
Wichita (KS.) **79** F 4
Wichita Falls **76–77** E 4
Wichita, Lake **76** E 4
Wichita Mountains **76** E 3
Wickenburg (AZ.) **100** D 2
Wickersham (WA.) **114** C 1
Wickiup Reservoir **112** D 3
Wickliffe (KY.) **50** B 4
Wide Bay **119** D 2
Wiggins (CO.) **95** F 1
Wiggins (MS.) **49** F 3
Wigwam (CO.) **95** F 3
Wilber (NE.) **81** G 4
Wilbur (OR.) **112** B 3
Wilbur (WA.) **115** G 2
Wilburn Dam **46** C 5
Wilburton (OK.) **77** H 3
Wilcox (PA.) **34** C 2
Wilcox (WY.) **93** G 2
Wild Horse (CO.) **95** H 3
Wild Horse (TX.) **72** D 2
Wild Horse Lake **86** C 1
Wild Horse Reservoir
105 F 1
Wild Rose (WI.) **59** E 3
Wildcat (WY.) **93** G 1

Wilder (ID.) **90** C 3
Wildersville (TN.) **50** B 5
Wildrose (ND.) **84** C 2
Wildwood (N.J.) **35** G 4–5
Wiley City (WA.) **114** E 3
Wilkerson Pass **95** E 2
Wilkes-Barre (PA.) **35** F 2
Wilkesboro (N.C.) **38** C 2
Wilkins (NV.) **105** G 1
Wilkinsburg (PA.) **34** B 3
Will, Mount **117** F 2
Willaha (AZ.) **103** G 4
Willamette River **112** B 2
Willamina (OR.) **112** B 1
Willapa Bay **114** A 3
Willapa Hills **114** B 3
Willara (UT.) **102** A 4
Willard (MT.) **87** J 3
Willard (N.M.) **96** D 4
Willcox (AZ.) **101** G 4
Willcox Playa **101** G 4
William "Bill" Dannelly Reservoir **47** D 4–5
Williams (AZ.) **100** D 1
Williams (CA.) **110** C 4
Williams (MN.) **60** B 5
Williams Bay (WI.) **59** G 2
Williams Fork Reservoir **94** D 1–2
Williamsburg (IA.) **63** F 4
Williamsburg (KY.) **51** F 4
Williamsburg (VA.) **37** H 4
Williamson (W.V.) **36** B 4
Williamsport (IN.) **52** B 2
Williamsport (PA.) **34** D 2
Williamston (N.C.) **39** G 3
Williamstown (KS.) **79** H 2
Williamstown (KY.) **51** F 2
Williamstown (W.V.) **36** C 2
Williamsville (IL.) **56** D 4
Williamsville (MO.) **65** G 4–5
Willimantic (CT.) **35** J 2
Williston (FL.) **44** B 4–5
Williston (N.D.) **84** C 2
Williston Basin **84** BD 3
Willits (CA.) **110** C 5
Willmar (MN.) **61** E 4–5
Willoughby (OH.) **53** H 1
Willow (AL.) **116** B 1
Willow (OK.) **76** D 2
Willow City (ND.) **85** F 2
Willow Creek (CA.) **110** B 5
Willow Creek (MT.) **86** B 4
Willow Creek Reservoir **105** E 1
Willow Lake (S.D.) **83** H 3
Willow Lake (WY.) **92** C 2
Willow Ranch (CA.) **110** A 2
Willow Springs (MO.) **65** F 5
Willowdale (OR.) **112** E 2
Willowick (OH.) **53** H 1
Willows (CA.) **110** C 4
Wills Point (TX.) **75** E 2
Wilma (FL.) **47** F 2
Wilmington (DE.) **37** J 2
Wilmington (IL.) **56** B 3
Wilmington (N.C.) **39** F 4
Wilmington (OH.) **53** F 3
Wilmore (KS.) **78** D 4
Wilmot (AR.) **67** E 4
Wilmot (S.D.) **83** H 2
Wilsall (MT.) **86** C 4
Wilson (AR.) **67** F 2
Wilson (KS.) **78** E 3
Wilson (N.C.) **39** G 3
Wilson (N.Y.) **32** B 2
Wilson (OK.) **77** F 3
Wilson (TX.) **76** C 4
Wilson Lake (AL.) **46** B 5
Wilson Lake (KS.) **78** E 3
Wilson Lake Reservoir **91** E 4
Wilson, Mount (AZ.) **100** B 1
Wilson, Mount (CO.) **94** BC 4
Wilson, Mount (NV.) **105** G 4
Wilsonia (CA.) **108** D 3
Wilsonville (NE.) **80** D 4
Wilton (ME.) **28** D 5
Wilton (ND.) **84** F 3
Wilton (WI.) **59** F 4
Wimbledon (N.D.) **85** H 3
Winamac (IN.) **52** C 1
Winchell (TX.) **74** B 3
Winchendon (MA.) **30** E 3
Winchester (ID.) **88** D 3
Winchester (IL.) **57** D 5
Winchester (IN.) **52** E 2
Winchester (KY.) **51** F 3
Winchester (NV.) **109** G 3
Winchester (TN.) **50** D 5
Winchester (VA.) **37** F 2
Winchester (WY.) **92** D 2
Winchester Bay (OR.) **112** A 3
Wind Cave National Park **82** B 4
Wind Mountain **99** E 4–5
Wind River (WY.) **92** C 2
Wind River Indian Reservation **92** CD 2
Wind River Peak **92** C 3
Wind River Range **92** C 2–3
Winder (GA.) **42** B 4
Windham (ME.) **29** E 5
Windham (MT.) **86** C 2
Windom (MN.) **61** G 5
Windom Mountain **94** C 4
Windsor (Can.) **55** F 2
Windsor (CT.) **35** J 2
Windsor (IL.) **57** D 3
Windsor (MO.) **64** D 3
Windsor (N.C.) **39** H 3
Windsor Forest (GA.) **43** D 2
Windsor Locks (CT.) **35** J 2
Windthorst (TX.) **74** C 1
Windy Peak **115** F 1
Winfield (AL.) **46** C 5
Winfield (KS.) **79** G 4
Winfield (W.V.) **36** C 3
Wing (ND.) **85** F 3
Winifred (MT.) **86** D 2
Wink (TX.) **73** E 2
Winkelman (AZ.) **101** F 3–4
Winlock (WA.) **114** C 3
Winnebago (MN.) **61** G 4
Winnebago (NE.) **81** H 2
Winnebago Indian Reservation **81** H 2
Winnebago, Lake **59** EF 2
Winnemucca (NV.) **104** D 2
Winnemucca Lake **104** B 2
Winner (SD.) **83** F 4
Winnett (MT.) **87** E 2
Winnfield (LA.) **68** C 2
Winnibigoshish, Lake **60** C 3–4
Winnie (TX.) **75** G 5
Winnipesaukee, Lake **29** E 6
Winnsboro (LA.) **68** D 1
Winnsboro (S.C.) **40** D 2
Winnsboro (TX.) **75** F 2
Winona (AZ.) **101** E 1
Winona (KS.) **78** B 2
Winona (MI.) **58** C 2
Winona (MN.) **61** F 1
Winona (MO.) **65** F 4
Winona (MS.) **48** C 3
Winona (TX.) **75** F 2
Winona (WA.) **115** H 3
Winooski (VT.) **30** C 1
Winooski River **30** CD 1
Winside (NE.) **81** G 2
Winslow (AZ.) **101** F 1
Winsted (CT.) **35** H 2
Winsted (MN.) **61** F 4
Winston (MT.) **86** B 3
Winston (N.M.) **98** C 3
Winston-Salem (N.C.) **38** D 2
Winter (WI.) **58** D 4
Winter Beach (FL.) **44** D 2
Winter Garden (FL.) **44** C 3
Winter Haven (FL.) **44** C 3
Winter Park (CO.) **94** E 2
Winter Park (FL.) **44** C 3
Winters (CA.) **111** D 4
Winters (TX.) **73** H 2
Wintersburg (AZ.) **100** D 3
Winterset (IA.) **62** D 4
Winthrop (AR.) **66** B 4
Winthrop (ME.) **29** D 5
Winthrop (MN.) **61** F 4
Winton (N.C.) **39** H 2
Winton (WA.) **114** E 2
Winton (WY.) **92** C 4
Wiscassel (ME.) **29** D 4
Wisconsin **58** G 8
Wisconsin Dells (WI.) **59** F 3
Wisconsin Rapids (WI.) **59** E 3
Wisconsin River **59** F 3–4
Wisdom (MT.) **89** G 4
Wise (VA.) **36** B 1
Wise River (MT.) **86** A 4
Wiseman (AL.) **121** F 2
Wishek (ND.) **85** G 4
Wishram (WA.) **114** D 4
Wisner (NE.) **81** G 3
Wissota, Lake **59** E 5
Wister (OK.) **77** J 2–3
Withington, Mount **98** C 3
Withrow (WA.) **115** F 2
Witten (SD.) **83** E 4
Wittenberg (WI.) **59** E 3
Wittmann (AZ.) **100** D 3
Wolbach (NE.) **81** F 3
Wolcott (CO.) **94** D 2
Wolcott (IN.) **52** B 2
Wolcott (N.Y.) **32** D 2
Wolcottville (IN.) **52** D 1
Wolf (KS.) **78** B 3
Wolf Creek (MT.) **86** A 2
Wolf Creek (OR.) **112** B 4
Wolf Creek Pass **94** D 4
Wolf Island **43** E 2
Wolf Lake (MI.) **55** E 5
Wolf Lake (Yukon, Can.) **117** E 1
Wolf Mountain **121** E 2
Wolf Point (MT.) **87** H 1
Wolf River **49** F 3
Wolfe City (TX.) **75** E 1
Wolfeboro (N.H.) **29** E 6
Wolfforth (TX.) **99** H 3
Wolford (ND.) **85** G 2
Wolsey (S.D.) **83** G 3
Wolverine (MI.) **54** C 3
Wolverine Mountain **121** E 2
Wolverine Peak **92** C 3
Wood (SD.) **82** E 4
Wood Lake (NE.) **80** D 2
Wood, Mount **86** D 4
Wood Mountain **101** G 4
Wood River (AK.) **119** D 2
Wood River (NE.) **81** F 4
Wood River Lakes (AL.) **119** D 2
Wood River Mountains **119** D 2
Woodall Mountain **48** B 2
Woodbine (GA.) **43** F 2
Woodbridge (VA.) **37** G 3
Woodburn (OR.) **112** C 1
Woodbury (GA.) **42** D 5
Woodbury (MI.) **55** F 4
Woodbury (N.J.) **35** F 4
Woodbury (TN.) **50** D 5
Woodchopper **121** G 2
Woodfords (CA.) **111** D 1
Woodlake (CA.) **111** F 1
Woodland (CA.) **111** D 3
Woodland (WA.) **114** C 4
Woodland Park (CO.) **95** F 3
Woodland Park (MI.) **55** E 5
Woodrow (CO.) **95** G 2
Woodruff (S.C.) **40** D 2
Woodruff (UT.) **102** A 3
Woodruff (WI.) **58** D 3
Woodruff Norrows Reservoir **92** B 4
Woods Hole (MA.) **31** F 4
Woods Landing (WY.) **93** G 4
Woods Reservoir **50** DE 5
Woodsboro (TX.) **71** E 2
Woodsfield (OH.) **53** H 3
Woodside (UT.) **102** C 2
Woodson (TX.) **74** BC 1
Woodstock (AL.) **46** C 5
Woodstock (Can.) **28** B 2
Woodstock (IL.) **56** A 3
Woodstock (VA.) **37** F 3
Woodstock (VT.) **30** D 2
Woodsville (N.H.) **29** D 6
Woodville (MS.) **49** E 5
Woodville (OH.) **53** F 1
Woodville (TX.) **75** G 4
Woodward (OK.) **76** D 1
Woody Creek (CO.) **94** C 2
Woolsey (NV.) **104** C 2
Woolsey Peak **100** D 3
Woonsocket (R.I.) **30** E 3–4
Woonsocket (S.D.) **83** G 3
Wooster (OH.) **53** G 2
Worcester (MA.) **30** E 3
Worden (MT.) **87** E 3
Worden (OR.) **112** CD 4
Worland (WY.) **92** E 1
Worthington (IN.) **52** B 3
Worthington (MN.) **61** G 5
Worthington (OH.) **53** F 2
Worthington Peak **109** G 2
Wounded Knee (SD.) **82** C 4

Wrangell (AL.)
117 E 2
Wrangell Mountains
(AL.) **116** C 1
Wrangell Saint
Elias N.P. and Pres.
(AL.) **116** C 1
Wray (CO.) **95** H 1
Wright (KS.) **78** D 4
Wright Brothers
National Monument
(N.C.) **39** J 2–3
Wright City (OK.)
77 J 3
Wright Peak **110** D 4
Wrightson, Mount
101 F 5
Wrightsville (GA.)
42 D 3
Wrightsville Beach
(N.C.) **39** G 4
Wrightwood (CA.)
107 E 3
Wrigley (TN.)
50 C 5
Wupatki National
Monument **100–101** E 1
Wyalusing (PA.)
34 E 2
Wyandotte (MI.)
55 F 2
Wyarno (WY.) **93** F 1
Wyatt (MO.) **65** H 5
Wyeville (WI.)
59 F 4
Wylie (TX.) **75** E 1
Wylie, Lake **40** D 1
Wylliesburg (VA.)
37 F 5
Wymer (WA.) **115** E 3
Wymore (NE.) **81** H 4
Wyndmere (N.D.)
85 J 4
Wynnburg (TN.)
67 G 1
Wynne (AR.) **67** F 2
Wynnewood (OK.)
77 F 3
Wynona (OK.) **77** G 1
Wynot (NE.) **81** G 2
Wyocena (WI.)
59 F 3
Wyola (MT.) **87** F 4
Wyoming (East)
92–93
Wyoming (IA.) **63** H 3
Wyoming (MI.) **55** F 4
Wyoming (West)
92 B 3
Wyoming (WY.) **93** G 4
Wyoming Peak **92** B 3

Wyoming Range
92 B 2–3
Wyoming Ranges
92 B 4
Wytheville (VA.)
36 C 5

Xenia (OH.) **53** F 3
XL Ranch Indian
Reservation **110** A 2

Yaak (MT.) **88** E 1
Yabucoa (P.R.) **124** BC 2
Yachts (OR.) **112** A 2
Yadkin River **38** C 2
Yadkinville (N.C.) **38** D 2
Yainax Butte **112** D 4
Yakima (WA.) **114** E 3
Yakima Indian Reservation
114 DE 3
Yakima River **114** E 3
Yakt (MT.) **88** E 1
Yakutat (AL.) **117** CD 2
Yakutat Bay (AL.)
117 CD 2
Yale Lake **114** C 3–4
Yale Point **103** F 1
Yampa (CO.) **94** D 1
Yampa River **94** C 1
Yamsay Mountain **112** D 4
Yancey (TX.) **70** C 1
Yanceyville (N.C.) **39** E 2
Yankton (S.D.) **83** H 5
Yankton Indian
Reservation **83** G 4
Yaquina Bay **112** A 2
Yaquina Head **112** A 2
Yarmouth (ME.) **29** E 5
Yarnell (AZ.) **100** D 2
Yates (N.M.) **97** G 2
Yates Center (KS.) **79** H 4

Yates City (IL.) **56** C 4
Yauco (P.R.) **124** B 2
Yavapai Indian Reservation
100 D 2
Yazoo City (MS.) **48** D 4
Yazoo River **48** D 4
Yellow Dam **87** F 4
Yellow Pine (ID.) **90** D 2
Yellow River (FL.) **47** F 4
Yellowstone Lake **92** B 1
Yellowstone National Park
92 B 1
Yellowstone River **87** J 2
Yellowtail Reservoir
86–87 E 4
Yellville (AR.) **66** D 1
Yemassee (S.C.) **41** E 4
Yentna River **119** E 1
Yerington (NV.) **104** B 3–4
Yerington Indian
Reservation **104** B 3
Yermo (CA.) **107** F 3
Yeso (N.M.) **97** F 4
Yoakum (TX.) **71** E 1
Yoder (WY.) **93** H 4
Yogo Peak **86** C 3
Yomba Indian Reservation
104 D 3
Yoncalla (OR.) **112** B 3
Yonkers **35** H 3
York (AL.) **46** D 6
York (ND.) **85** G 2
York (NE.) **81** G 4
York (PA.) **34** E 4
York (S.C.) **40** D 1
York River **37** H 4
Yorktown (TX.) **71** E 1
Yorkville (IL.) **56** B 3
Yosemite National Park
111 E 1
Yosemite Village (CA.)
111 E 1
Yost (UT.) **102** A 5
Youghiogheny River Lake
36 E 2
Youngstown (FL.) **47** F 3
Youngstown (N.Y.) **32** B 2
Youngstown (OH.) **53** J 1
Youngsville (LA.) **68** C 3
Youngsville (N.M.) **96** D 2
Youngsville (PA.) **34** B 2
Yountville (CA.) **111** D 4
Ypsilanti (MI.) **55** F 2
Yreka (CA.) **110** A 4
Yuba City (CA.) **110** C 3
Yucca (AZ.) **100** B 2
Yucca House National
Monument **94** B 4
Yucca Lake **109** F 3
Yucca Valley (CA.) **107** F 3
Yukon (AL.) **120** C 3

Yukon (AL.) **121** G 2
Yukon (MO.) **65** F 4
Yukon-Charley River
Nat.Pres. (AL.)
121 FG 2–3
Yukon Flats (AL.) **121** F 2
Yukon Plateau (AL.)
117 D 1
Yulee (FL.) **44** A 3
Yuma (AZ.) **100** B 4
Yuma (CO.) **95** H 1
Yuma Desert **100** B 4
Yunaska (AL.) **118** A 3

Zahl (ND.) **84** C 2
Zama (MS.) **48** D 3
Zane Hills **121** D 2
Zanesville (OH.) **53** H 3
Zap (ND.) **84** E 3
Zapata (TX.) **70** C 4
Zaragoza (Mex.) **70** B 2
Zavalla (TX.) **75** G 3
Zebulon (GA.) **42** C 5
Zebulon (N.C.) **39** F 3
Zeeland (MI.) **55** F 4
Zeeland (SD.) **83** EF 2
Zenia (CA.) **110** B 5
Zeona (SD.) **82** C 2
Zephyr (TX.) **74** C 3
Zephyrhills (FL.)
44 C 4
Zia Indian Reservation
96 D 3
Zillah (WA.) **115** E 3
Zion (IL.) **56** A 2
Zion National Park
103 E 4–5
Zion Reservoir **101** G 2
Zionsville (IN.)
52 C 3
Zirkel, Mount **94** D 1
Zolfo Springs (FL.)
45 D 3
Zumbrota (MN.) **61** F 2
Zuni (N.M.) **96** B 3
Zuni Indian Reservation
96 B 3
Zuni Mountains
96 B 3
Zurich (MT.) **86** DE 1
Zwolle (LA.) **68** B 2

Legend

New York More than 5,000,000 inhabitants

Houston 1,000,000–5,000,000 inhabitants

■ **New Orleans** 250,000–1,000,000 inhabitants

● **Shreveport** 100,000–250,000 inhabitants

● Pine Bluff 50,000–100,000 inhabitants

• Charlesbourg Less than 50,000 inhabitants

▫ Memorial Small cities

WASHINGTON National capital

Baton Rouge State capital

───────── Limited access highway

───────── Toll road

┄┄┄┄┄┄┄ Access highway under construction

───────── Principal through highway

───────── Other through highway

– – – – – Other highway

– – – – – Ferry

┼┼┼┼┼┼┼ Railway

International boundary

State boundary

National park, National monument, National recreation area

I.R. Indian reservation

11316 ft
3449 m   Height above sea level in feet and meters

33ft
10m   Depth in feet and meters

✈ Airport

🛡15 Interstate highway

Pass

Dam

Waterfall

Canal

Intermittent stream

Intercoastal waterway

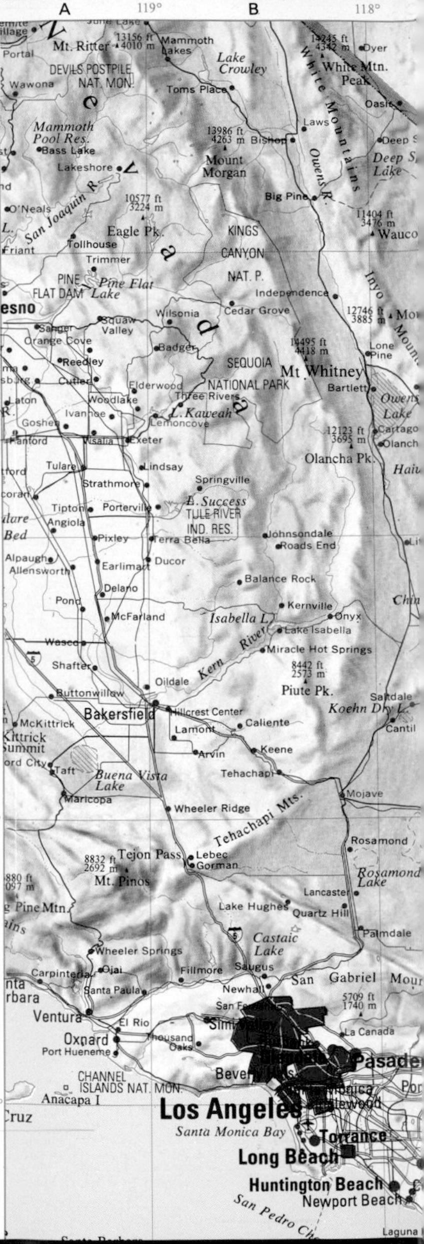